The
INVENTION
OF CANADA

Readings in Pre-Confederation History

The

INVENTION
OF CANADA

Readings in Pre-Confederation History

Edited by

Chad Gaffield

University of Ottawa

Copp Clark Longman Ltd.
Toronto

ISBN: 0-7730-5252-6

Editor: Pamela Erlichman
Executive editor: Jeff Miller
Design: Kyle Gell
Cover illustration: Rocco Baviera
Maps and illustrations: Martyn Lengden, Michael Dixon
Typesetting: B.J. Weckerle
Printing and binding: Best Gagné Book Manufacturers

Canadian Cataloguing in Publication Data

Main entry under title:

The Invention of Canada: readings in pre-Confederation history

Includes bibliographical references.

ISBN 0-7730-5252-6
1. Canada–History.   I. Gaffield, Chad, 1951–   .

FC161.I58 1994   971   C94-930218-X
F1026.I58 1994

Copp Clark Longman Ltd.
2775 Matheson Blvd. East
Mississauga, Ontario
L4W 4P7

Associated companies:
Longman Group Ltd., London
Longman Inc., New York
Longman Cheshire Pty., Melbourne
Longman Paul Pty., Auckland

Printed and bound in Canada

1 2 3 4 5   5252-6   98 97 96 95 94

*This book is dedicated to all the students in
Canadian history courses who have inspired me
to continue seeking an understanding of our past.*

C O N T E N T S

• Part IV: Industrializing Canada

ACKNOWLEDGMENTS

I am indebted to Jeff Miller and Pamela Erlichman for all their support, encouragement, and hard work on this book. Valuable suggestions and helpful comments were generously provided by John Bonnett, Marg Conrad, Alvin Finkel, Johanna Gaffield, Pam Gaffield, Jan Grabowski, Lorne Hammond, Cornelius Jaenen, Peter MacLeod, Nikki Strong-Boag, and the members of this year's doctoral seminar at the University of Ottawa.

INTRODUCTION

THE REWRITING OF PRE-CONFEDERATION HISTORY

Not too long ago, the study of pre-Confederation history was left to a small number of scholars who usually studied the ways in which certain powerful and influential men transformed Canada from a colony to a nation. In history departments in Canadian universities as recently as the early 1960s, only a minority of professors (perhaps one-fifth) taught and researched about Canada. Although there were some important exceptions, their interest was generally limited to the thoughts and actions of famous political, economic, and cultural leaders. As a result, few Canadians knew much about their history, especially before Confederation. The most that could be expected was the proper ordering of certain dates and events beginning with Jacques Cartier's voyages and ending with the passing of the British North America Act in 1867.

In recent years, however, a significant number of scholars have begun rewriting the history of pre-Confederation Canada. Historians of Canada now form a large part, if not the majority, of most university history departments. Using new concepts, examining new sources, and developing innovative research strategies, these scholars have dramatically changed the ways in which we think about the origins of Canada.[1] The readings in this volume illustrate some of the exciting research projects now being undertaken to explore these origins.

• Rethinking the Historical Process in Canada

The title of this book, *The Invention of Canada*, might well seem quite odd since the word *invention* is usually associated with scientific or technological discoveries. However, scholars now use the concept of invention to emphasize that all aspects of history are created over long periods of time. From this perspective, cultures are invented, economies are invented, governments are invented, and so on.[2] In this sense, this book examines the invention of a new country in 1867 by focussing on historical processes that spanned centuries and centuries.

In addition to extending the concept of invention to include history as a whole, scholars have also redefined the usual understanding of inventors as well as the actual process of invention. Rather than being a single person or perhaps a small group, the inventors of history are now considered to be all members of the population, the anonymous as well as the famous, women as well as men, minorities as well as the majority, and residents of all parts of Canada. Similarly, historians now emphasize that the thoughts and actions, dreams and ambitions, of all these individuals were exceedingly diverse; rather than collectively engaging in a single process of invention, individuals and groups pursued different goals in keeping with their different situations and values. While scholars have found evidence of co-operation and consensus in these pursuits, recent work emphasizes the extent of conflict and contradiction, often leading to violence as distinct individuals and groups came into contact in the same space. The resulting inventions were thus not the products of orderly, linear progressions, but rather reflected complex and often competing forces that were not within any individual's or group's full control.

The concept of invention also emphasizes that nothing about the origins of Canada was inevitable or predetermined. Although it might be hard to imagine that our history could have unfolded very differently, recent research shows the importance of understanding how the ideas and behaviour of individuals and groups, both famous and anonymous, could have led to different outcomes. In inventing Canada, decisions were made, sometimes within great constraints, sometimes with significant freedom. This process was very complex. Indeed, historians now emphasize that, just as no one succeeded in fully controlling their own destiny, no one was a complete victim no matter how much they were victimized. Canadian historians are now just as likely to emphasize failure or unintended consequences as fulfilled ambitions, and to discover hope and integrity despite oppression and abuse. It is in this sense that more and more historians agree that everyone in Canada's past deserves to be studied as part of the historical process. The sum total of all decisions, great and small, led to the invention of Canada.

In abandoning an exclusive focus on the leaders of the dominant society, scholars are being increasingly forced to come to grips with a diversity that reaches to the foundations of history as a discipline, even including a "problematizing" of the concept of time. Until recently, historians viewed time as an absolute; at least in theory, everyone's clock was considered to tick at the same speed. However, historians are realizing that "time" depends upon whose clock is being used. For example, they know now that the European-origin concept of time must not be used to understand the ideas and behaviour of Natives in Canada. Clearly, different groups use different clocks in setting the pace of everyday life. Similarly, historians also now use expressions such as *family time* to indicate how humans determine time according to context; an excellent illustration of this approach is Louise A. Tilly and Joan W. Scott's chapter in this book on the family economy.[3]

Historians also apply the concept of invention to the ways in which descriptions and understandings of the past are created in the present.[4] Just as common usage of the word *invention* includes the possibility of fabricating something in the mind (such as "inventing an excuse"), historians have come to admit that the past is not really knowable in a definitive sense. Indeed, as will be discussed, fewer and fewer historians believe in the possibility of establishing "facts" that reflect everyone's experience, and some doubt the existence of an objective reality that exists outside the perceptions and comprehension of each individual. Describing what happened is no longer considered to be a straightforward process involving the examination of as much evidence as possible. Some years ago, historians assumed that each additional piece of evidence would bring them closer and closer to a historical truth that included everyone. Instead, they have found that additional evidence sometimes clarifies the topic under study, and sometimes reveals further complexity in keeping with the diverse experiences of individuals and groups. While Canadian historians agree on a great number of facts (such as the dates of wars and the identities of political leaders), they are increasingly reluctant to offer a one-dimensional version of Canada's past. It is still very important to know the facts that are currently agreed upon by historians, but gone are the days when the memorization of a single chronology of events was the central strategy for learning Canadian history. Now, historians seek to establish many chronologies, and to understand how they intersect at various moments in time. Not too long ago, for example, everyone learned that Christopher Columbus discovered America in 1492; now, no one would be taught this "fact."[5]

Since scholars increasingly agree that the historical process is "many-centred," the decision by researchers to focus on any one individual or group becomes very important. Historians stress that the "centre" of the historical process depends upon the particular point of view of the person looking back at the past. While the goal of "total history" remains elusive, historians have been striving to do justice to the perspectives and experiences—the stories—of all members of past societies. Rather than aiming to present a single narrative of Canadian history, scholars seek to understand and explain many narratives and their convergences in specific contexts. In so doing, historians invent Canada's past.

In keeping with the current rewriting of Canada's past, the following readings offer new ways to think about Canadian history, to understand the historical process, and to view the background of contemporary life. It is hoped that these readings will have an impact that endures long after the specific details are forgotten.

•Identities and Relationships

One way of characterizing current research on modern Canada is in terms of the study of identities and relationships. At any particular time and place, how did individuals and groups see themselves? How did others see them? How did they interact with others? What was the nature of these relationships, and how can they be explained? These questions emphasize the importance of context. They suggest that everyone in Canada's past must be situated with respect to others and that their history reflects the identities and relationships of this situation.

The study of identities and relationships, however, poses serious challenges that reflect the complexity of Canada's past. How can individuals and groups be categorized for analysis? Recent research has shown that even very familiar labels must be used with great caution. For example, a number of scholars have shown that concepts of childhood and definitions of children have hardly been static. Rather, the process of growing-up has varied enormously in keeping with social, economic, and cultural differences. Similarly, historians have rethought their use of words like *family* or *relative*. Not only have official definitions of such words changed over time, but they have also had very different meanings within different social and cultural settings as well-illustrated in the following reading of Kenneth Donovan's study of Louisbourg.[6]

In the same way, recent work has begun to call into question the value and meaning of many racial and ethnic terms such as *white* or *indian* or *eskimo*. Whose perspectives are represented by such names? In what sense can the ambiguities of identity be boiled down to a single label? Should we think in terms of multiple identities in which individuals see themselves, and are seen, in different ways depending on the historical context? The authors of the readings in this book do not all agree on the answers to such questions but, taken together, their studies provide a firm foundation for going beyond the destructive stereotypes sometimes associated with Canadian history.

In current research on Canada's past, the central aspects of identities and relationships include those of social class, gender, ethnicity, and region. The importance of social class in pre-Confederation Canada was first actively pursued by historians in the 1970s who looked at the vast majority of anonymous men who laboured as farmers, artisans, fishermen, fur traders, and many other occupations in the colonies of New France and British North America. Previous historians had left these men, along with almost all women and children, out of their analysis in the belief that they did not really count; their places in society meant that they were not considered to be among the makers, or inventors, of Canadian history. In contrast, scholars began to publish findings that showed how men without material advantage or formal authority had their own stories that deserved telling. Moreover, these men did affect the ideas and actions of elites; they were not simply passive victims of those in apparent control. Historians showed how poor and disadvantaged men did all they could, within the limits that enclosed them, to pursue their lives with dignity and self-respect. In certain cases, they clearly affected the course of history, perhaps most visibly in events such as the Rebellions of 1837–38 as described in this book by Allan Greer.[7]

In studying the identities and relationships of the previously ignored men of Canadian history, scholars began addressing wide-ranging questions of thought and behaviour. In different times and places, did men see themselves or act as part of a social class? Was there a peasantry in pre-Confederation Canada as in Europe? Did the "frontier" of North America prevent the transplanting of European social relations to the New World? What were the identities and relationships among artisans, unskilled workers, farmers, fishermen, and the many other groups of labouring men?[8] And what were their relationships with the privileged and powerful? The importance of addressing such questions is vividly illustrated in the following readings by the work of Louise Dechêne on Montreal, and by Kenneth Donovan on Louisbourg, as well as by Allan Greer's study of the Rebellions of 1837–38.

Within a few years, scholars of women's history began redirecting the study of the anonymous of Canadian history by turning their attention to the "neglected majority." They pointed out that, along with the conventional study of elites, the study of class structure and relations was substantially, though not exclusively, based on men. Historians showed that much of the newer research on the popular classes, as well as the older research on official leaders, ignored the history of women in Canada. Initially, scholars aimed to add women to the established accounts of male experience but, soon, feminist theory began transforming how everything—ranging from the operation of government to daily life in households—was viewed. New questions were posed that probed to the heart of all established versions of Canadian history. For example, to what extent were the dates of the familiar chronology of Canadian history appropriate for women? Are the key dates of our past the same for men and women? Or are there many chronologies depending upon the individuals, groups, and processes under study?[9]

Feminist scholarship also helped move the study of Canadian history beyond social, economic, and political themes to include the study of feelings, emotions, and the metaphysical dimensions of everyday human experience. Beyond knowing information about the type of work being done, for example, historians began pointing to the importance of learning about how individuals felt about their work. Furthermore, scholars challenged existing definitions of words such as *work*, which had previously been used to mean remunerated labour. Because so many women worked at home, their labour was usually not acknowledged in official records (characteristically written by men). Historians began revealing the gender-specific definition of many words commonly assumed to apply to both sexes, and they began to show the extent to which such definitions slighted or ignored the history of women in Canada. The contribution of Louise A. Tilly and Joan W. Scott to this book illustrates the new ways in which historians have been analysing the economic roles of both men and women.[10]

Research on the history of women in Canada has led quite recently to studies of gender, and thus, to the history of masculinity. While historical research has traditionally focussed on men, they have usually been presented as gender-neutral representatives of all humanity. Only during the past few years have questions been raised about the construction of masculinity. How have boys learned to be men? What values and characteristics have been associated with manliness? What pressures, conflicts, and contradictions have been associated with growing up male in Canada? How can we understand the violence and rage, the wife-battering and child abuse, now found in Canadian history? Consideration of such questions is adding considerably to our understanding of the meaning of gender in our past as illustrated in this book by Katherine M.J. McKenna's study of men and women in leading families of Upper Canada.

Especially since the 1970s, historians have also been coming to grips with the ethnic diversity of Canada's past.[11] Rather than viewing ethnicity as a label or category, historians have been examining it as a dynamic process. Particular attention has been devoted to understanding Canada as an immigrant society that is far more complex than the common emphasis on "two founding peoples." For example, historians rarely use the expression *English Canada* anymore; not only are significant components of non-francophone Canada excluded by the adjective *English*, but even the "English" population is quite diverse, as illustrated by studies of the Irish and Scots.[12] Moreover, scholars have studied religious differences as illustrated in the following readings by Nancy Christie's examination of two evangelical groups in the Maritimes and Upper Canada, Phillip McCann's study of Newfoundland, and William Westfall's analysis of Protestants in Ontario. Similarly, scholars have produced excellent studies (as illustrated by Sylvia Van Kirk's chapter in this book) of the complexities of identity that resulted from contact between Amerindians and those people of European origin.[13]

Non-Native historians have also begun to analyse the history of Native groups in Canada.[14] While Native groups have always had a strong sense of their past (communicated through oral tradition), their history has usually been neglected or misrepresented in cultures based on print. Only recently have both non-Natives and Natives begun to use these oral traditions as well as to adapt the research methods of the dominant society in writing Native history.[15] In this collection, D. Peter MacLeod uses oral tradition as historical evidence to show how one group of Amerindians see themselves as having "discovered Europe" rather than as having been passively discovered. Similarly, Georges E. Sioui, a Huron, calls for an Amerindian "auto-history" in his re-examination of the first half of the seventeenth century.

Beyond looking at previously neglected "makers" of Canada, one of the most distinguishing features of current work is a greater preference for regional history, often involving research at the level of individuals, families, and communities. The concept of region varies a great deal, with some historians studying a small geographic area, perhaps a town and the surrounding countryside, while other researchers examine the collective experience of a province or group of provinces. These researchers show that a central theme of Canadian history concerns the complex relationships among different parts of the country. Their approach, as well as that centring on smaller geographic areas, reflects a new sensitivity to the diversity of Canadian history across the vast lands from ocean to ocean. Scholars are now convinced that the history of Canada is not simply a larger version of the history of any one area.[16] This conclusion is well illustrated by W.J. Eccles' examination of imperial attitudes toward the western land of New France. His work shows the importance of not viewing the colony simply in terms of the St Lawrence Valley. Similarly, Phillip Buckner reassesses the last stages of the invention of Canada by taking the point of view of the Maritimes toward Confederation.

Beyond attention to the relationships among individuals and groups, historians are now studying the interactions of humans and the environment, including both flora and fauna and the land that sustains them. Environmental historians emphasize the interconnectedness of all components of the biosphere. In this view, humans are just one of many species on history's stage, and while it may be tempting to focus on divisions of class, gender, ethnicity, and region, such divisions need to be situated within the larger relationships of humans to animals and plants, the land and the sea. Environmental history raises new questions about familiar topics as well as suggesting completely new topics for study. Among the authors in this book, for example, Lorne Hammond reinterprets aspects of the fur trade by studying the animals as much as on the hunters, and E.C. Pielou examines the early history of North America in terms of the changing mammals and birds that made the continent a dynamic environment long before the arrival of humans. Although this approach is only recently being taken by Canadian historians, environmental history will undoubtedly continue its rapid growth as an emerging research area involving many disciplines from history to the natural sciences.[17]

• Rethinking the Selection and Use of Historical Evidence

In order to pursue questions of social class, gender, ethnicity, and region, historians have begun finding new ways to study familiar documents as well as to examine evidence that had previously been ignored. In terms of documents, historians have learned to read between the lines or decode and deconstruct written evidence. In the case of Native history, for example, historical documents generally reflect the views of "others" about Natives rather than expressing the views of Natives themselves. If taken at face value, such evidence tells us about the ambitions and actions of European-origin society rather than Native experience. Scholars have shown, however, that when analysed with sensitivity, documents created by the dominant society can indeed provide insight into the actual history of Native groups, as demonstrated in this book by Cornelius J. Jaenen.

Similar approaches to documentary sources have been taken to learn about the economically disadvantaged, women and children, ethnic minorities, and related groups for whom much of the written evidence was created by others. Historians of the nineteenth century have particularly taken advantage of the newspapers that became more and more important with each passing decade. Historians have found that although newspapers were created by a small minority, they usually include valuable information on the activities of many different groups. In this book, for example, Jane Errington uses newspapers to examine political ideology in Upper Canada as it developed between influences from Britain and the United States.

The most novel evidence used to study the "anonymous" of Canadian history has come from *routinely generated sources*, an expression used to describe manuscript census returns, tax rolls, land records, parish registers of birth, marriage, and death, employment lists, and similar documents created by governments, churches, businesses, and other institutions in the course of everyday life. Such sources allow historians to learn about the lives of whole populations. Who held which occupations? Who controlled how much land? Who migrated to new communities? When did couples marry and how many children did they have? Louise Dechêne's reading is an excellent example of how historians are transforming our knowledge of the past by piecing together evidence from routinely generated sources. Dechêne was one of the pioneers in the use of the rich notarial records that have documented so many aspects of life in New France and Quebec. Similarly, Fernand Ouellet uses information on commercial transactions to examine the extent to which the actual performance of the colonial economy was consistent with the hopes of imperial policy.

Routinely generated sources usually do not provide direct information about why individuals had certain experiences, but they do indicate something about the details of their lives. For example, an employment record will not tell why a particular person ended up working in a particular factory, but it may well provide valuable information about the terms and conditions of the actual work. When many such employment records are systematically examined (and perhaps linked to other sources), a great deal can be learned about the history of work in Canada. Another approach is to link together the disparate information of routinely generated sources to learn about a specific individual; a convincing example from the following readings is Brian Young's re-evaluation of the personal life of George-Étienne Cartier.

Greater interest in the history of emotions, feelings, and personal experience, and some dissatisfaction with the limitations of routinely generated sources and documents such as newspapers, encouraged historians to look for direct expressions of ideas, perceptions, and activity. Two important sources found in this search are personal papers such as diaries and letters. The value of personal papers has long been recognized by historians of famous individuals such as prime ministers. Such evidence was rarely used, however, to probe emotional and personal issues. In addition, scholars have now shown that evidence like the correspondence among family members or friends, or the entries made in private diaries can also tell a great deal about the lives of quite "ordinary" men and women. Researchers have been surprised by how many of these documents were created (even by those with little formal education), and how many that can still be found both within repositories and in private attics.[18]

The difficulties of using documents to study cultures or groups who have not left the usual types of historical evidence have encouraged historians to expand their definition of what constitutes a historical source. One important example of this expansion is the recent examination of oral traditions among Native groups. Once dismissed by non-Natives as simply fiction, such traditions are now being taken seriously as a key feature of the Native historical record.[19] Similarly, scholars are increasing studying material culture as a way of probing into past societies. All the objects of daily life, ranging from tools and dwellings to costumes and art, are now being examined in order to understand values and behaviour. Among the following readings, Kenneth Donovan effectively uses this approach to study the social history of Louisbourg, especially the question of social class.[20]

•New Ways of Doing Historical Research

In addition to posing new questions and using new sources, historians have developed innovative research strategies in recent years. Perhaps the most important trend has been the emergence of *micro-history*, which involves the detailed study of individuals within specific settings such as in households, workplaces, neighbourhoods, or communities. For some scholars, such settings serve as a laboratory within which general processes can be studied in detail. In this approach, the ambition of the research is not primarily to learn about the specific setting under study; rather, the goal is to contribute to a better understanding of a historical process common to many similar settings. Scholars choose their laboratories according to the historical questions under examination. For example, Michael Katz's chapter reports on his detailed study of the city of Hamilton, Ontario, that served as a focus for questions about the social structure of commercial cities in mid-nineteenth-century Canada.

Micro-history also offers the opportunity to analyse the ways in which large-scale historical change is articulated at the level of individual experience.[21] By looking at specific populations in specific settings, historians can examine the constellation of relationships that has shaped the lives of Canadians in different parts of the country at various times in history. This approach allows the study of abstract concepts such as imperialism, mercantilism, seigneurialism, assimilation, gendered space, and many others in terms of personal experience. John Robert McNeill's chapter in this book illustrates the value of this approach by comparing Cape Breton and Havana.

Similarly, historians use a micro-historical approach as a way of analysing the interplay of the larger forces of class, gender, ethnicity, and region. Some years ago, historians assumed that this interplay was quite similar across various communities. However, it soon became apparent that no two contexts were really identical, and the hope of general explanations gave way to the more modest ambition of understanding the range of diversity associated with specific aspects of the historical process. With each new study, historians have gained a greater appreciation of the complexity of Canadian history and the inappropriateness of reducing this history to a single narrative description based on one setting. In this book, Elizabeth Mancke's study of Nova Scotia and Maine is an excellent example of how historians are seeking to understand the interplay of policy and place.

Canadian historians are also increasingly joining forces with other scholars in recognition that new perspectives and research strategies are needed to analyse our complex history. Among the following readings, Olive Patricia Dickason's discussion of the human occupation of North America thousands of years ago illustrates the value of integrating research findings from archaeology, anthropology, and linguistics. My own work on the origins of mass schooling relies on both demographic and economic evidence. Such interdisciplinary research has certainly been more talked about than actually undertaken up to this point, but increasing collaboration among different scholars can be expected in future years. Perhaps the most promising area for such collaboration is in the emerging field of environmental history, which could benefit from scholars in both the arts and sciences. Thus far, most collaborators in historical research have come from the social sciences such as sociology, anthropology, archaeology, and geography.[22] Scholars from these disciplines have contributed different concepts and methods to historical research; in turn, historians have challenged the generalizations of their collaborators' disciplines by insisting on contextual specificity and change over time. Historians constantly remind social scientists that the historical process is often unpredictable and exceedingly complex, in keeping with the infinite possibilities of human existence. Despite the common saying, history never really does repeat itself.[23]

Another new approach to historical research has been the mounting of major projects involving several professors along with graduate students and research assistants. This approach departs dramatically from the traditional method in which individual historians worked on their own topics, doing their own research, and coming to their own conclusions; a metaphor for this method might be the making of a jigsaw puzzle in which each researcher's goal was to contribute a piece. The launching of major research projects is generally based on quite different assumptions. Rather than aiming to add a piece to a puzzle, these projects view history as a complex and multidimensional process that can be best grasped by collective conceptual and methodological effort. This approach is still not common among Canadian historians (as reflected in the absence of multi-authored readings in this collection) with the exception of historians in Quebec who, in many cases, are members of research teams that receive collective funding for their work. A fine example in the following readings is the study by Serge Courville, Jean-Claude Robert, and Normand Séguin of economic change along the axis of the St Lawrence River.

As a result of posing new questions and developing new research strategies, historians have also come to see computers as helpful tools. While the image of a solitary historian carefully taking notes on index cards has not been fully replaced by the picture of research teams entering data on lap-tops or optically scanning documents, there is no doubt that historians have entered the Information Age. All aspects of the research process have been affected. Bibliographies are being compiled automatically by using key words to search vast databases, historical evidence is being transformed into machine-readable files, analyses are being word processed, and references are being checked by modem connection to remote locations. Research collaborators keep in constant touch and, indeed, are beginning to co-author, as they drive the new electronic highways now connecting distant points around the world.

But computerization has raised new questions that promise to demand increasing attention in the coming years. To what extent can human experience be captured by the quantitative examination of empirical data? Can a document be usefully examined by computer-based textual analysis? Can the ambiguities and "grey zones" of the historical process be done justice in the creation of databases? Clearly, the answers to such questions are not simply negative or positive. Although computers are undoubtedly here to stay as part of research activity in Canada, historians will increasingly be forced to grapple with unprecedented issues as they strive to benefit from the new technological possibilities for probing the past.[24]

• Conclusion

Recent changes in the discipline of history are part of a larger rethinking of research throughout the arts and sciences. In fact, the ways in which historians are now conceptualizing and researching Canadian history can be compared to the new directions of the scientific disciplines. Unlike earlier years when scientific models based on empiricism and objectivity influenced the work of historians, the sciences now seem increasingly humanistic. For example, the research of physicists lends full support to the rejection of history as the linear unfolding of a chain of causes and effects. Like historians, scientists are also emphasizing the unexpected, the indeterminate, and the unpredictable. Indeed, discussions among scientists about chaos are not completely dissimilar to the debates among historians about contingency and context. Overall, researchers across the arts and sciences are gaining a new appreciation of complexity, and they are far more humble about their ability to fully understand or explain what they observe. While scientists now agree that the "laws of physics" are not one set of rules obeyed in all situations, few historians hope to achieve a general theory of change that could explain human thought and behaviour in all times and places.[25]

If recent years are any indication, the study of Canada's past will continue to take unexpected directions and to lead to unanticipated ways of thinking about the background of contemporary society. New questions, re-discovered evidence, and innovative research strategies should make the re-writing of pre-Confederation Canadian history an ongoing process that constantly adds to the richness of our own lives. The following readings illustrate some of the exciting ways in which this process is now underway.

• Notes

[1] The changing perspectives of Canadian historians are discussed in Carl Berger, *The Writing of Canadian History*, 2nd ed. (Toronto: University of Toronto Press, 1986); M. Brook Taylor, *Promoters, Patriots and Partisans: Historiography in Nineteenth-Century English Canada* (Toronto: University of Toronto Press, 1990); Serge Gagnon, *Quebec and Its Historians, 1840–1920* (Montreal: Harvest House, 1982); and M. Brook Taylor, ed., *Beginnings to Confederation* (Toronto: University of Toronto Press, 1994).

[2] For a recent example, see Pierre Lanthier and Guildo Rousseau, eds., *La culture inventée: Les stratégies culturelles aux 19ᵉ et 20ᵉ siècles* (Québec: Institut québécois de recherche sur la culture, 1992). My use of the concept of invention includes, but is much more inclusive than, the fascinating interpretation (based on scientific thought) presented by Suzanne Zeller in *Inventing Canada*.

[3] For a general discussion of recent debate that places historians within a larger context, see Pauline Marie Rosenau, *Post-Modernism and the Social Sciences: Insights, Inroads, and Intrusions* (Princeton, NJ: Princeton University Press, 1992).

[4] In addition to the article by Phillip McCann in this book, recent work by

other scholars of Atlantic Canada who explicitly use the concept of invention includes Ian McKay, "Among the Fisherfolk: J.F.B. Livesay and the Invention of Peggy's Cove," *Journal of Canadian Studies* 23 (Spring/Summer 1988): 23–45; and John G. Reid, "The Excellence Debate and the Invention of Tradition at Mount Allison: A Case Study in the Generation of Mythology at a Canadian University," *Dalhousie Review* 69 (Summer 1989): 190–210.

[5] For a Canadian view, see Ramsay Cook, *1492 and All That: Making a Garden out of a Wilderness* (North York, ON: Robarts Centre for Canadian Studies, 1993).

[6] The changing views of childhood and family are reflected in Neil Sutherland, *Children in English-Canadian Society: Framing the Twentieth-Century Consensus* (Toronto: University of Toronto Press, 1976); Joy Parr, ed., *Childhood and Family in Canadian History* (Toronto: McClelland and Stewart, 1982); Bettina Bradbury, ed., *Canadian Family History* (Toronto: Copp Clark Pitman, 1992); and Joy Parr, *Labouring Children: British Immigrant Apprentices to Canada, 1869–1924* (Toronto: University of Toronto Press, 1993).

[7] Allan Greer, *The Patriots and the People: The Rebellion of 1837 in Rural Lower Canada* (Toronto: University of Toronto Press, 1993).

8 One of the best examples of this approach is Eric Sager, *Seafaring Labour: The Merchant Marine in Atlantic Canada* (Montreal: McGill-Queen's University Press, 1989).

9 The now classic contribution is Susan Mann Trofimenkoff and Alison Prentice, eds., *The Neglected Majority: Essays in Canadian Women's History* (Toronto: McClelland and Stewart, 1977). The results of research undertaken in the 1970s and early 1980s are synthesized in Alison Prentice et al., *Canadian Women: A History* (Toronto: Harcourt Brace Jovanovich, 1988) and Clio Collective, *Quebec Women: A History* (Toronto: Women's Press, 1987). More recent work is presented in Veronica Strong-Boag and Anita Clair Fellman, eds., *Rethinking Canada: The Promise of Women's History*, 2nd ed. (Toronto: Copp Clark Pitman, 1991). Important new studies include Wendy Mitchinson, *The Nature of their Bodies: Women and their Doctors in Victorian Canada* (Toronto: University of Toronto Press, 1992).

10 An excellent example is Bettina Bradbury, *Working Families: Age, Gender, and Daily Survival in Industrializing Montreal* (Toronto: McClelland and Stewart, 1993).

11 The initial research undertaken in the 1970s and early 1980s is reviewed in Roberto Perrin, "Clio as an Ethnic: The Third Force in Canadian Historiography," *Canadian Historical Review* 64, 4 (1983): 441–67.

12 Recent research includes J.I. Little, *Crofters and Habitants: Settler Society, Economy and Culture in a Quebec Township, 1848–1881* (Montreal: McGill-Queen's University Press, 1991); Marianne McLean, *The People of Glengarry: Highlanders in Transition, 1745–1820* (Montreal: McGill-Queen's University Press, 1991); and Bruce Elliott, *Irish Migrants in the Canadas: A New Approach* (Montreal: McGill-Queen's University Press, 1988). Pauline Greenhill argues for the usefulness of the concept of English Canada in *Ethnicity in the Mainstream: Three Studies of English Canadian Culture in Ontario* (Montreal: McGill-Queen's University Press, 1993).

13 The two classic studies are Jennifer Brown, *Strangers in Blood: Fur Trade Company Families in the Indian Country* (Vancouver: University of British Columbia Press, 1980); and Sylvia Van Kirk, *"Many Tender Ties": Women in Fur Trade Society in Western Canada, 1670-1870* (Winnipeg: Watson and Dwyer, 1980).

14 The results of recent research are presented in Bruce G. Trigger, *Natives and Newcomers: Canada's "Heroic Age" Reconsidered* (Montreal: McGill-Queen's University Press, 1986); Denys Delage, *Bitter Feast: Amerindians and Europeans in Northeastern North America, 1600–1664* (Vancouver: University of British Columbia Press, 1993); Robin Fisher and Kenneth Coates, eds., *Out of the Background: Readings on Canadian Native History* (Toronto: Copp Clark Pitman, 1988); J.R. Miller, *Skyscrapers Hide the Heavens: A History of Indian-White Relations in Canada* (Toronto: University of Toronto Press, 1989); and Olive Patricia Dickason, *Canada's First Nations: A History of Founding Peoples from Earliest Times* (Toronto: McClelland and Stewart, 1992).

15 Georges E. Sioui, *For an Amerindian Autohistory: An Essay on the Foundations of a Social Ethic* (Montreal: McGill-Queen's University Press, 1992).

16 The study of "subprovincial" regions is illustrated by David Gagan, *Hopeful Travellers: Families, Land and Social Change in Mid-Victorian Peel County, Canada West* (Toronto: University of Toronto Press, 1981); Allan Greer, *Peasant, Lord and Merchant: Rural Society in Three Quebec Parishes* (Toronto: University of Toronto Press, 1985); and Françoise Noel, *The Christie Seigneuries: Estate Management and Settlement in the Upper Richelieu Valley, 1764–1854* (Montreal: McGill-Queen's University Press, 1992), while province-level analyses are presented in Douglas McCalla, *Planting the Province: The Economic History of Upper Canada, 1784–1870*

(Toronto: University of Toronto Press, 1993); Fernand Ouellet, *Economy, Class and Nation in Quebec: Interpretive Essays* (Toronto: Copp Clark Pitman, 1991); and Graeme Wynn, *Timber Colony: A Historical Geography of Early Nineteenth-Century New Brunswick* (Toronto: University of Toronto Press, 1981).

[17] Michel Girard, "The New History of the Environment," Canadian Historical Association *Newsletter* 16, 3 (Summer 1990): 1–3.

[18] See, for example, Margaret Conrad, Toni Laidlaw, and Donna Smyth, eds., *No Place Like Home: Diaries and Letters of Nova Scotia Women 1771–1938* (Halifax: Formac, 1988), and Peter Ward, *Courtship, Love and Marriage in Nineteenth-Century English Canada* (Montreal: McGill-Queen's University Press, 1990).

[19] For another example, see Joan M. Vastokas, "Native Art as Art History: Meaning and Time From Unwritten Sources," *Journal of Canadian Studies*, 21, 4 (1987): 7–36.

[20] For a discussion of this methodology, see Thomas Schlereth, "Towards a Material History Methodology," *Material History Bulletin* 22 (1985): 31–40.

[21] Recent examples of this approach include Jacalyn Duffin, *Langstaff: A Nineteenth-Century Medical Life* (Toronto: University of Toronto Press, 1993); and Katherine M.J. McKenna, *A Life of Propriety: Anne Murray Powell and Her Family, 1755–1849* (Montreal: McGill-Queen's University Press, 1993).

[22] Stephen R. Grossbart, "Quantitative and Social Science Methods for Historians: An Annotated Bibliography of Selected Books and Articles," *Historical Methods* 25, 3 (Summer 1992): 100–20.

[23] The wide range of possibilities for interdisciplinary work is suggested by the joining of history and genetics as discussed in Gerard Bouchard, "Population Studies and Genetic Epidemiology in Northeast Quebec," *Canadian Studies in Population* 16, 1 (1989): 61-86; of history and law as illustrated by Constance Backhouse, *Petticoats and Prejudice: Women and the Law in Nineteenth-Century Canada* (Toronto: Women's Press, 1991); of history and geography as shown in Graeme Wynn, ed., *People, Places, Patterns, Processes: Geographical Perspectives on the Canadian Past* (Toronto: Copp Clark Pitman, 1990); and of history and literature as evident in Carl Ballstadt, Elizabeth Hopkins, and Michael Peterman, eds., *Letters of Love and Duty: The Correspondence of Susanna and John Moodie* (Toronto: University of Toronto Press, 1993).

[24] Some of these complex issues are addressed in Chad Gaffield, "Machines and Minds: Historians and the Emerging Collaboration," *Histoire sociale/Social History* 21, 42 (Nov. 1988): 312–17.

[25] It should be remembered that significant differences (especially concerning the concept of order) still separate many humanists, social scientists, and scientists. Stephen H. Kellert analyses recent developments in the sciences in *In the Wake of Chaos: Unpredictable Order in Dynamical Systems* (Chicago: University of Chicago Press, 1993).

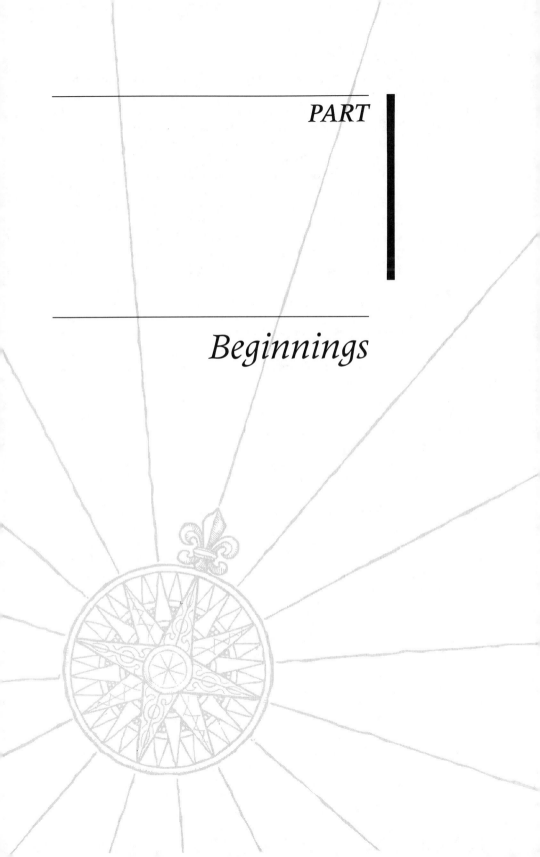

PART I

Beginnings

Until quite recently, scholars defined the starting point of Canadian history in terms of the European "discovery" of North America. This definition, however, is now recognized to reflect an ethnocultural bias that does not do justice to the complex processes that eventually led to Confederation in 1867. As the articles in this section emphasize, Canadian history must be understood as the interplay of place and people beginning thousands and thousands of years before significant European immigration.

One key feature of recent research on the origins of human activity in North America is the debate about the timing of first settlement. In this debate, the traditional importance attributed to Christopher Columbus's voyage in 1492 appears quite unjustified. As Olive Patricia Dickason discusses in the first article of this section, scholars have now shown that human occupation dates back at least 12 000 to 17 000 years, and perhaps as long as 50 000 years. Dickason's article deserves careful reading because it shows the extent to which the study of history has come to involve the research findings of other disciplines such as archeology, anthropology, and linguistics. This development results from a recognition that, by limiting its attention to the study of written evidence, historical research has often ignored many human processes and events. In this sense, the notion of "prehistoric" has loss substantive meaning, and is seen to reflect an unacceptable cultural bias against societies that have not left their own written legacy.

The nature of human activity in North America before the arrival of Europeans is still not well understood partly because the available evidence is fragmentary and not easily interpreted. However, there is no doubt that the various societies were hardly inactive or unchanging. The historical picture that emerges from the work of researchers such as E.C. Pielou is dynamic and diverse. For example, scholars are now debating the nature of the changing relationship between hunter and hunted across the centuries and territory of the continent. As Pielou describes, theories related to the environment, climate, and ferocity of the hunters have all attracted supporters who seek to explain the extinctions of certain mammals and birds. These theories all undermine the static image of a tranquil paradise in which humans and nature lived in perfect harmony. Rather, the continent underwent constant change throughout the thousands of years before the arrival of those like Jacques Cartier.

In addition to understanding the background of North America, Canadian historians have also increasingly emphasized the importance of knowledge about Europeans in the years leading up to their activity in the "new world." The work of Louise A. Tilly and Joan W. Scott focusses on the ways in which the European economy was the sum of family economies composed of men and women in productive roles. There was no separation between the household and the place of work; the modern expression, "going to work," would have had no meaning in these European societies. Since women played such constant and diverse roles in ensuring the livelihood of their families, Tilly and Scott define women as the "cornerstone of the family and economy." As will be seen in later articles, this European background relates directly to questions of both the ideology and experience of men and women throughout Canadian history.

The final two articles of this section provide examples of the ways in which different groups may view the same process or event in quite different ways according to their own values and experience. D. Peter MacLeod reverses the words of the usual expression "the discovery of America" to emphasize that Amerindians were not passive objects of European initiative. In the case of the Anishinabeg, for example, the Amerindians actively chose to "discover" Europe. MacLeod's article is also noteworthy for its use of oral tradition as evidence for historical research. For his part, Georges E. Sioui offers a new analysis of the destruction of Huronia in his call for an "Amerindian autohistory." Sioui re-interprets well-known French documents to propose a different understanding of the cultural and spiritual battle waged between Europeans and Amerindians during the first half of the seventeenth century.

Taken together, the articles of this section illustrate the increasing interdisciplinarity of historical research as scholars call upon a vast array of concepts and methods to study Canadian history. These articles challenge familiar ideas and assumptions by focussing on the first human occupants, the changing birds and animals, the economic roles of both women and men, and the perspectives of different cultural groups. This research indicates some of the ways in which Canadian scholars are providing a better understanding of the beginnings of Canada.

AND THE
PEOPLE CAME*

OLIVE PATRICIA DICKASON

That people were living in the Americas during the later Ice Ages is no longer debated; what is not agreed on is when the movement from the Old World to the New began. When modern humans (*Homo sapiens sapiens,* "man doubly wise") appeared on the world scene early during the Wisconsin glaciation, 50 000–10 000 B.P., their cultural development was comparatively rapid, blossoming in an ever-increasing variety through Europe and across Asia.[1] Their appearance in the New World is more problematic, as bones have not preserved well in its soils, and identifying early campsites and tools can be difficult. The two Americas are the world's only continents where the evidence of early human presence has been based on artifacts, not skeletal remains.[2] As matters stand at present, the oldest dates for human habitation have come out of unglaciated South America, and the most recent ones for pre-contact migration have come from the ice-bound Arctic. When Europeans stumbled on the Caribbean islands in the late fifteenth century, they found Amerindians in what they considered to be their cultural infancy and assumed they were a young people who could have been here only for a few hundred years. An observant few, among them the Dominican Bartolomé de Las Casas (1484–1566), recognized traces of early habitation that had become grown over, and realized that this could only have happened over long periods of time.[3] Majority first impressions, however, proved to be persistent, and only comparatively

*From *Canada's First Nations* by O. Dickason. Used by permission of the Canadian Publishers, McClelland & Stewart, Toronto.

recently has a long occupation time depth been accepted for the Americas. This raises the question of the place of origin for *Homo sapiens sapiens*. Impassioned attempts to prove an American genesis for modern Indians have not made a convincing case.[4] The identification by archeologist Louis Leakey (1903–1972) of fractured pebbles found at Calico Hills, California, as 100 000- to 200 000-year-old tools would establish the presence of pre-modern humans—possibly even of *Homo erectus*—if he could have substantiated his argument, which neither he nor others have been able to do.

Many Indians believe this is the land of their origin, and their myths, with their metaphoric descriptions of the genesis of humans and the present world, are many and varied; their different perceptions of time and nature place these tales at another level of reality than that of this work.[5] The myths emphasize and confirm the peoples' fundamental attachment to the land. The Gitksan of northern British Columbia maintain that the Upper Skeena River valley is their Garden of Eden; several groups, such as the Salish Thompson River people and the Ojibwa, believe that their first ancestors were born of the earth[6]; the Athapaskan Beaver hold that humans crawled through a hollow log in order to reach earth, an obvious birth analogy[7]; the Iroquoians (including the Huron), that the mother of mankind, Aataentsic, fell through a hole in the sky and landed on a tortoise with earth piled on its back.[8] On another plane, the Tsimshian have legends in which migration is a theme.[9]

The most generally held anthropological theory, based on observable data, that *Homo sapiens sapiens* came from Asia via the Bering Strait, was first proposed by Jesuit José de Acosta (c. 1539–1600) in *Historia Natural y Moral de las Indias,* published in 1590.[10] Today it is widely accepted by anthropologists and archeologists that Indians made the crossing on foot during periods when intensification of the Ice Ages lowered the sea level, transforming Bering Strait into a grassy and often boggy steppe called Beringia. Geologists inform us that there were several periods during the late Pleistocene geological age (the Wisconsin stage) when the land bridge called Beringia emerged, the first identifiable one dating back to about 75 000 B.P., and the last one ending about 14 000 years ago.[11] This expanse of open grassland and tundra at one point was more than 2000 kilometres wide, more like a continent than a bridge. It provided forage for such animals as mammoth, mastodon, giant bison, saiga antelope, and the predators that preyed on them. That human hunters followed the herds is a reasonable assumption supported by archeological evidence from both sides of the Bering Strait, including 11 000-year-old bifacially flaked stone points and knives, and, on occasion, microblades—small, thin, very sharp stone flakes that were being made 15 000 to 4500 years ago. Their production required considerable skill. If this was the route, then Siberia must have been inhabited first. Soviet archeologists have reported evidence for the peopling of Yakuktia in central Siberia some 300 000 years ago, long before the appearance of *Homo sapiens sapiens*[12]; Chukotka, on the northeastern tip of Siberia, has yielded a date of 35 000 B.P., which is within the range of modern humans.[13]

Since game abounded, should we then assume that the first *Homo sapiens sapiens* in the Americas were principally big-game hunters? Yes, as far as Canada is concerned; but for the New World as a whole, that may not have been the case. As archaeological techniques become more sophisticated and research expands, evidence is turning up in South America to suggest that the first humans in those regions may have been primarily foragers (fishing being a form of gathering) and hunters of small game.[14] What is more, the indications are that they were inclined to stay where their food resources were, usually by the shores of sea, lake, or river. They exploited those resources on water as well as on land, which suggests that they used watercraft.[15] Archeologist Peter Schledermann, working in the eastern Arctic, has concluded that sea mammals were the principal source of food for the people of the Arctic Small Tool Tradition (3000 B.C.–1200 B.C.).[16] Even the later, more mobile hunters who pursued big game inland preferred to camp by water, and probably for at least one of the same reasons—the facility of water travel.

• Option of the Sea

To return to the means by which people arrived in the Americas: there is no reason to conclude that because Beringia offered a convenient pedestrian route, it was therefore the only one available or used. Nor is there any reason to believe that Beringia's inhabitants were land-bound, ignoring the rich marine life on and off its coasts. The sea also offered options; in the Pacific, the Japanese current sweeping from the Asiatic coast eastward to the Americas provided a natural aquatic highway that would not have presented insuperable challenges. The argument that humans at this early stage had not yet developed the skills to undertake travel by water under dangerous Arctic conditions is tenuous at best, particularly in view of the sea voyages that occurred at other latitudes. One could even argue that deep-sea sailing in some respects is not as hazardous as coasting, and that both are easier than walking. That travel by water could have been more practical than travelling by land has long been maintained by archeologist Knut Fladmark.[17] As he has pointed out, humans have been capable of traversing stretches of water at least as wide as Bering Strait for 30 000 years or more; there is also the fact that the west coast was largely unglaciated during a temperate period about 60 000 to 25 000 years ago in the late Pleistocene. This may have been the case in southwestern Alberta as well.[18] Australia was peopled about 50 000 B.P., and that could only have been by boat, although admittedly not under Arctic conditions, and involving no enormous distances, as at that period sea levels would have been lower than they are today. Island hopping from the Malaysian archipelago to Australia would have faced reduced—but still formidable—sea barriers.[19]

In North America, the coastal route may have been a factor in producing the abundance of languages along the Pacific coasts of the two Americas, one of the most complex linguistic regions in the world. (In the sixteenth century, the New World had an estimated 2200 languages.) Recent studies by anthropologist Richard A. Rogers have shown that in North America, unglaciated areas contained by far the greatest number of languages, 93 percent, along with a higher degree of differentiation from those that had been glaciated. It is an accepted principle in linguistics that language diversification proceeds very slowly and is proportional to the length of human occupation; where diversification has reached the point of obscuring original linguistic relationships, then substantial time depth is indicated. Archaeologist Ruth Gruhn has called attention to the fact that North America's greatest diversification of language stocks is in California and on the Gulf coast, while in South America more than 1500 languages were spoken, differing widely in their grammatical constructions and vocabularies. In Gruhn's view all of these languages from both continents are ultimately related in three major stocks. She believes their proliferation to be too great to be explained solely by a series of migrations, but rather that the languages evolved locally over a very long span of time, perhaps close to 50 000 years.[20] She is in accord with anthropologist Joseph H. Greenberg, who sees a possibility that all Indian languages, except for Na-Dene (Athapaskan) and Eskimo-Aleut, developed from a single prototype called Amerind. This highly controversial theory postulates a minimum of three founding migrations, the first of which brought Amerind, by far the largest, most widespread, and most diversified of the three proposed basic groups.[21]

Linguistic evidence suggesting that South America was settled early has been supported by recent archaeological discoveries at Monte Verde in Chile and at Tocado Boqueirão do Pedra Furada in Brazil, which indicate that people may have been present in the Americas as early as 32 000 years ago.[22] There are also tantalizing suggestions of extreme antiquity for humans in North America, perhaps as early as 22 000 B.C.[23] Sites in Pennsylvania, California, Texas, and Mexico have all hinted at a presence that is dated earlier as one proceeds south; finds in southcentral New Mexico, announced by archaeologist Richard MacNeish, are of campsites that have been radiocarbon-dated to 36 000 years ago.[24] The one possible exception to this is the unglaciated Yukon, where human occupation dating back to 40 000 years has been argued by archeologist William N. Irving. If established, this would support the primacy of the Beringia route.[25] The best evidence so far for early humans in the Yukon has come from Bluefish Caves, south of Old Crow. There, debris has been found that was left behind by hunters of about 24 000 to 12 000 years ago. Most of the butchered bones are of land mammals. However, no hearths or human remains have been found on the location.[26] That famous caribou-bone flesher discovered by Loucheux Peter Lord near Old Crow in 1966, and once dated to 27 000 B.P., is now believed to be only 1000 years old.[27] Even if the more secure dates of 18 000 to 15 000 years ago are preferred for the arrival of humans in North America, there was still plenty of time for the plenitude of languages to have developed on the Pacific coast. That pattern of settlement can best be explained by coastal travel.

• Ice-free Corridor

Such a route could also provide an explanation why the ice-free corridor along the eastern slopes of the Rockies that has been hypothesized as the most likely migration path has not yielded the expected archeological sites, or even artifacts, unlike the well-documented route between the Andes and the Pacific in South America.[28] Geological data indicate the Canadian corridor was a forbidding region of loose rock, shifting shorelines of glacial lakes, and rugged slopes: no significant faunal remains dating to the period of the late Wisconsin glaciation have been found in the central and northern portions. It is possible that the interior plateau was used, but there is no evidence there either. As far as interior land travel is concerned, most movements seem to have been from south to north; for example, the Algonquian speakers who occupy so much of Canada's subarctic forest, the taiga, fanned northward from the Great Lakes, and the buffalo hunters of the northwestern Plains came from two directions, south and east. Exceptions are the Athapaskans, who, after living in the Far North since about 9000 years ago, began to move south following a volcanic eruption near White River,[29] and the Inuit, who spread eastward across the Arctic from Siberia. For the rest, as our information stands at present, people somehow looped south of the glaciers, then headed north again as the ice retreated.

The lack of visible archeological sites on the Pacific northwest coast is easier to explain: they were drowned as the ocean rose with the melting of the glaciers. Whether on foot or on water, or a combination of both, Indians reached the southern tip of South America by at least 11 000 B.P. Canada's High Arctic was the last region to be populated, after 2000 B.C., following some movement into lower Arctic regions a little earlier. Human entry into the Americas seems to have been in the form of a filtering action, perhaps in waves—three, perhaps four, main ones are currently being hypothesized—stretching over long periods of time. While such movements are nearly always considered in connection with Beringia and the Pacific, at certain epochs they would also have been possible along the discontinuous glacial front across the Atlantic into eastern North America. However, the biological evidence indicating Asiatic origins for Indians appears to be secure.[30]

• Population Densities

As with languages, the greatest density of pre-contact populations was on the Pacific coast, thought to be about 10 percent of the total for the two continents. Estimates for the hemispheric population have been going steadily upward in recent years, and have reached a very high 112.5 million for the fifteenth century on the eve of European arrival.[31] For North America north of the Rio Grande in the early sixteenth century, estimates range up to an unlikely 18 million and even higher.[32] They have increased with better understanding of Native subsistence bases and with greater awareness of the effect of imported diseases in the sixteenth century; in some cases these spread far ahead of the actual presence of Europeans, decimating up to 93 percent of Native populations. The earliest European accounts of the New World all spoke of the "great multitudes" of people; it was later, when colonization was gaining momentum, that large stretches of territory were found unoccupied, and the notion of an "empty continent" gained currency.[33] Archaeological evidence is mounting to the point where it can now be argued with growing conviction, if not absolute proof, that the pre-Columbian Americas were inhabited in large part to the carrying capacities of the land for the ways of life that were being followed and the types of food preferred.

Original migrations probably involved very small groups. Recent genetic studies suggest that Indians have all descended from four primary maternal lineages, although this is vigorously disputed by advocates of a multiplicity of migrations.[34] Research techniques have now developed to the point where it is considered possible to reconstruct migrations by means of genetic evidence, particularly when it can be related to dental traits and linguistic affiliations.[35] It has been calculated that twenty-five individuals could have increased in 500 years to a population of 10 million, if it had doubled every generation (about thirty years). That was the rate of growth in European colonies during their early years in North America (the colonists, however, had far more children than their contemporary tribal peoples, and were reinforced by a steady stream of immigration from Europe). In any event, that rate would have been even faster if a generation is reckoned at twenty years, in which case the saturation point for hunting and gathering populations could have been reached in less than 1000 years, but this did not likely actually happen.[36]

By 11 000 years ago, about the time of the last known mammoth and mastodon kills, campsites of peoples with different economic adaptations and cultural traditions were scattered the length and breadth of the two continents. In that period, and during the next 3000 years or so, some 200 species representing sixty or more genera of major animals disappeared from the Americas. We do not know what caused these extinctions any more than we know what caused that of the dinosaurs; however, there is speculation that in the former case big-game hunters could have tipped the balance as their population expanded in consequence of the plentifulness of game. Recent work by Schledermann has demonstrated the ease with which a small group of hunters could reduce musk-ox and caribou to near extinction in the Arctic.[37] Paleontologist Paul S. Martin has pointed to the analogy of the Polynesian arrival in New Zealand and the consequent extinction of the moa bird.[38] In North America, the great auk and the passenger pigeon suffered similar fates when Europeans arrived. On the other hand, there are those who hold that mammoth kills were probably rare[39]; archeological evidence so far has revealed only about a dozen known kill sites, all west of the Mississippi. About 8000–5000 years ago, when climate, sea levels, and land stabilized into configurations that approximate those of today, humans crossed a population and cultural threshold, if one is to judge by the increase in numbers and complexity of archaeological sites.

The megafaunal disappearances do not appear to have involved a radical change in hunting patterns, as such game as bison and caribou was always important. If there was a population drop, as the scarcity of sites from this period has led some archeologists to believe, it did not last long. People survived for the same reason then as later: by being adaptable. The way of life that developed, based on the exploitation of a wide variety of food sources, called Archaic, was destined to last in some parts of Canada until long after the arrival of Europeans. Around 9200 to 8500 B.C., the making of fluted points displaced earlier forms of manufacture and spread across Canada with extraordinary speed, a phenomenon that remains without parallel in the country's early history. This may have been part of a continent-wide development, as fluted points have been found from Alaska to northern Mexico.[40] In Canada, these points have been found at Debert, Nova Scotia, Charlie Lake Cave, in British Columbia, and at the Vermilion Lakes in Alberta. The hunters who made these implements concentrated on bison or caribou, depending on the region; later, from about 8000 to 6000 B.C., their descendants on the western Plains, who had abandoned the fluted point for the Plano with its distinctive rippled flaking, were hunting bison by means of drives. That practice became common in Canada around 3000 B.C. Contemporary with Plano, Early Archaic developed in the eastern woodlands, characterized by distinctive side-notching of points for hafting. Archaeologist James V. Wright says that about 6000 B.C. eastern Early Archaic peoples migrated to the western Plains, where they came in contact with Plano peoples. Out of this interaction the Plains culture developed.[41] Still another lifestyle had already appeared on the Northwest Coast (beginning about 7000 B.C.), centred on salmon fishing and sea hunting, also with its distinctive lithic tradition of leaf-shaped projectile points. Receptivity to new ideas and willingness to experiment characterized these Stone Age craftsmen. When Europeans arrived, the whole of the New World was populated not only in all its different landscapes and with

varying degrees of density, but also with a rich cultural kaleidoscope of something like 2000 or more different societies.[42]

• Physical Characteristics

Even as they widely share certain physical characteristics, such as having little or no body hair (and what they have is usually black), Amerindians are biologically diverse. For example, some groups, particularly on the Pacific coast or in the Great Basin, have facial hair, sometimes heavy. Like the Filipinos, Amerindians are almost universally lacking in A and B blood types, but there are some striking exceptions. A is found among the peoples of the Northwest Coast (in similar frequences to Hawaiians), as well as among the Beaver, Slavey, and Assiniboine in the interior; most striking of all is the fact that the Blackfoot, Blood, and Peigan of the northwestern Plains have the highest known percentages of A in the world. Inuit have a high incidence of B; early reports of a concentration of B among the Yahgan of Tierra del Fuego, however, have not been confirmed.[43] In Central and South America, the preponderance of Amerindians belong to the O class, with the proportion being somewhat less in North America. This concentration exceeds anything known in the Old World, including the peoples of northern Siberia who are believed to be the source for the Beringian migrations, and indeed genetic studies have indicated that Amerindians are not as closely connected to modern Mongoloids as has been generally believed.[44] These biological data have led to speculation that Indians might be of ancient racial stocks predating contemporary Siberian peoples.[45] Dental studies, which indicate an original stock living 20 000 years ago, support such a hypothesis.[46] On the basis of this evidence, anthropologist Christy G. Turner II theorizes that most Indians are descended from the mammoth hunters of the Clovis culture. Inuit, on the other hand, are genetically distinct from most Indians, except for the Athapaskan speakers of the Northwest.[47]

• Technological Developments[48]

Stone Age technology reached its highest point of development in the Americas, in delicately crafted projectile points and later in the massive constructions of the Maya, Mexica, and Inca; the Inca created the largest Stone Age empire in the world,[49] the "realm of the Four Quarters" that incorporated more than 200 ethnic groups. Archeologist Alan Bryan maintains that several different early lithic traditions developed in various parts of the Americas, a range that includes 11 000-year-old "fish-tail" points near the Straits of Magellan, 13 000-year-old willow-leaf-shaped El Jobo points in northern Venezuela, and the 11 000-year-old Clovis fluted points that spread throughout unglaciated North America.[50] The tools used in making these elegant points have been identified; a modern attempt to make one using such tools succeeded in about two hours, and subsequent stone-knappers have shortened that time to forty minutes. The rate of spoilage was high, about 10 percent; one of the reasons we have been able to rediscover so much about Stone Age technology is because it left so much debris.

Development of stone and bone tools represented one of humanity's great strides forward into technological sophistication; and while such technology can in a way be regarded as "simple," it was viable only because of acute and careful observation of nature—still a basic requirement today. Stone Age technology was effective insofar as it was based on detailed and accurate observation, on the one hand, and supported by a workable social organization, on the other. Technology, Stone Age or otherwise, is the product of an accumulated fund of knowledge and is an indicator of peoples' approach to the world and to their own societies. Symbolic logic appears to have influenced tool design from very early; for instance, some speculate that the biface hand axe was based on the human hand as model.[51] The intelligent manipulation of nature backed by supportive social structures made survival possible under extremely difficult conditions. The process is a dynamic one; although rates of change can and do vary, even between the different components of a given society, no living culture is static. Technologies, including that of the Stone Age, change more readily than ideologies. A successful Stone Age technician had to know his materials, where they could be found, how they could be worked, how they would behave under different conditions, and to what uses they could be put. Many of the construction and sculpture achievements of the pre-contact Americas, once thought to be impossible with a Stone Age technology and therefore attributed to vanished races and even to creatures from outer space, are now known to have been within its capabilities. For example, how could jade, the hardest of stone, be carved with Stone Age tools? The answer has been found in the use of abrasives and water. Such a process, of course, was laborious and slow; Stone Age technology was labour- and time-intensive. It could also be material-intensive: its huge structures yielded comparatively little usable space, a result, however, more attributable to ideology than technology.

• Archaic Efficiency

In some aspects, this early technology was very efficient indeed. Cutting edges, for example, could be sharper than those achievable with metal. The war club of the Mexica, with its serrated edges made with a row of obsidian blades inserted into a wooden base, was a deadly weapon capable of decapitating a man with one blow. A latter-day stone-knapper, Don E. Crabtree, when faced with the necessity for heart surgery, insisted on making the required tools from obsidian. The result was faster healing and less scarring than would have been the case with steel instruments. Even simple stone fleshing blades were very suitable for the job. Metal's big advantage was durability; stone was easily broken, so that early tool and weapon makers were perpetually busy keeping themselves equipped. One of the results of this incessant activity was the great variety of artifacts and styles that proliferated; in some cases, even the work of individuals can be ascertained. "Style," however, can simply be the result of resharpening and consequent reshaping, which could and did result in such modifications as shortening a blade or transforming it from one form into another, such as a spear point into a knife. Not all peoples everywhere had the same type of tool kit, even when following similar ways of life; for example, artifacts associated with seed grinding have restricted distribution in South America but are widespread in southern and western North America. Similarly, the hafting of stone points to bone or wooden bases was not universally adopted. The bow and arrow, which is associated with the intensified use of land mammals, appeared comparatively late in the Americas; earliest evidence for their use in North America has come from Aishihik sites in the Yukon, dating around A.D. 250.[52] On the other hand, ropemaking, netting, and basketmaking appeared very early, during the late Pleistocene.[53]

Questions are now being raised as to the uses to which early tools were put. Archeologists have concentrated on the hunting aspect; but what about gathering and processing? Geographer Carl Sauer (1889–1975) noted that the Stone Age tool kit was as useful for cutting and preparing wood, bark, and bast, as well as for gathering and preparing foods such as roots and fruit, as it was for dressing meat and hides. If little is known about these early tools used for collecting and grinding, it is largely because their products were perishable and tended to disappear without a trace, causing them to be overlooked as attention focussed on hunting, which left recognizable debris. The development of grinding tools made a wider variety of seeds available for food, such as the small seeds of grasses and amaranths. Peoples who depended on such resources tended to remain in one place, where their supplies were readily at hand. In other words, the mobile lifestyle in pursuit of different food resources cannot be assumed to have been universal at any period; and even when it was practised, it followed a seasonal pattern within a known area. The vision of early humans as aimless wanderers in search of food does not equate with the evidence at hand; in fact, the contrary is strongly indicated, that they have always lived in communities that were as stable as food resources permitted.[54]

In conclusion, there is now general agreement that humans were present in the Americas between 15 000 and 10 000 B.C., a date that some would push back to 50 000 B.C.; environmentally, this would have been possible at an even earlier date.[55] That at least part of the earlier migrations were on land via Beringia seems reasonably clear[56]; more controversial is the question of migration by sea. As evidence slowly accumulates about the earliest patterns of human residence on the two continents, it appears more and more likely that water was at least as important as land for getting about, and perhaps even more so. By about 11 000 B.P. humans were inhabiting the length and breadth of the Americas, with the greatest concentration of population being along the Pacific coast of the two continents. A thousand or so years later many animal species had disappeared from the American scene, a phenomenon that has not been satisfactorily explained. If an analogy were to be drawn with the faunal exterminations that occurred in the wake of the arrival of Europeans in the Americas, then humans were a factor. In any event, people were firmly established throughout the hemisphere, and in some parts of Central and South America they began experimenting with domesticating plants perhaps as early as 9000 years ago.

• Notes

1 Cultures have been described as symbolic structures that provide the means for human satisfaction once survival has been assured. See David Rindos, "The Evolution of the Capacity for Culture: Sociobiology, Structuralism, and Cultural Evolution," *Current Anthropology* 27, 4 (1986): 326.

2 Tom D. Dillehay, "The Great Debate on the First Americans," *Anthropology Today* 7, 4 (1991): 13.

3 Brian M. Fagan, *The Great Journey* (London: Thames and Hudson, 1987), 26.

4 See, for example, Jeffrey Goodman, *American Genesis* (New York: Summit Books, 1981). Some of the various approaches to the study of early man in the Americas are found in *The First Americans: Origins, Affinities and Adaptation*, ed. William S. Laughlin and Albert B. Harper (New York and Stuttgart: Gustav Fischer, 1979).

5 Knut R. Fladmark demonstrates the complementarity of myth and scientific discourse by using legends to amplify his text in *British Columbia Prehistory* (Ottawa: National Museums of Canada, 1986).

6 Norval Morrisseau, *Legends of My People the Great Ojibway* (Toronto: Ryerson, 1965), 15; Mircea Eliade, *Gods, Goddesses, and Myths of Creation* (New York: Harper and Row, 1974), 135–36.

7 A variation of this myth is found among the Athapaskan Carrier of the Cordilleran plateau. See A.G. Morice, *Au pays de l'ours noir* (Paris: Delhomme et Briguet, 1897), 76–78.

8 A survey of types of creation myths and their distribution in North America is that of Anna Birgitta Rooth, "The Creation Myths of the North American Indians," *Anthropos* 52 (1957): 497–508.

9 For one, "The Origin of Gitxawn Group at Kitsumkalem" in *Tsimshian Narratives* 2, coll. Marius Barbeau and William Beynon (Ottawa: Canadian Museum of Civilization Mercury Series Paper No. 3, 1987), 1–4. Others are in Marius Barbeau, *Tsimshian Myths* (Ottawa: National Museum of Canada Bulletin No. 174, 1961).

10 Joseph de Acosta, *The Natural and Morall History of the East and West Indies,* tr. E.G., 2 vols. (London: Hakluyt Society, 1880; rprt. of 1604 edition), vol. 1, 57–61; first published in Latin in 1589. A current joke among Indians illustrative of their attitude toward the Bering Strait migration route has it that the reason why their people wound up in the Americas instead of staying in Asia was that "they couldn't get their bearings straight."

11 Steven B. Young, "Beringia: An Ice-Age View," in *Crossroads of Continents: Cultures of Siberia and Alaska,* ed.

William W. Fitzhugh and Aron Crowell (Washington, DC: Smithsonian Institution, 1988), 106–10.

12 Robert E. Ackerman, "A Siberian Journey: Research Travel in the USSR, July 20–August 20, 1990," (report to the National Endowment for the Humanities and Washington State University, 25 Sept. 1990).

13 Anthropologist Alan L. Bryan, personal communication. The view that Siberia was not peopled before 20 000 years ago is maintained by Nikolai N. Dikov, "On the Road to America," *Natural History* 97, 1 (1988): 14.

14 Virginia Morell, "Confusion in Earliest America," *Science* 248 (1990): 441.

15 Carl Ortwin Sauer in *Land and Life*, ed. John Leighly (Berkeley: University of California Press, 1969), 300–312.

16 Peter Schledermann, *Crossroads to Greenland: 3000 Years of Prehistory in the Eastern High Arctic* (Calgary: The Arctic Institute of North America, 1990), 314–15. Four possible ways by which the Arctic could have been peopled are presented in schematized form by Robert McGhee in *Canadian Arctic Prehistory* (Scarborough, ON: Van Nostrand Reinhold, 1978), 18–21.

17 Knut R. Fladmark, "The Feasibility of the Northwest Coast as a Migration Route for Early Man" in *Early Man in America From a Circum-Pacific Perspective,* ed. Alan Lyle Bryan (Edmonton: Archaeological Researches International, 1978), 119–28.

18 Knut R. Fladmark, "Times and Places: Environmental Correlates of Mid-to-Late Wisconsinan Human Population Expansion in North America" in *Early Man in the New World,* ed. Richard Shutler, Jr (Beverly Hills: Sage, 1983), 27.

19 See Richard Shutler, Jr, "The Australian Parallel to the Peopling of the New World" in *Early Man in the New World,* ed. Shutler, 43–45.

20 Ruth Gruhn, "Linguistic Evidence in Support of the Coastal Route of Earliest Entry into the New World," *Man,* new series, 23, 2 (1988): 77–100.

21 Joseph H. Greenberg, *Language in the Americas* (Stanford, CA: Stanford University Press, 1987), 331–37. Greenberg espouses the classification of all the languages of the world into fifteen basic stocks, to which a number of isolated languages would have to be added. His ultimate goal is to relate them all in a single language family. Some of the pros and cons of Greenberg's theories are discussed by Jared M. Diamond, "The Talk of the Americas," *Nature* 344 (1990): 589–90.

22 N. Guidon and G. Delibrias, "Carbon-14 Dates Point to Man in the Americas 32 000 Years Ago," *Nature* 321 (1986): 769–71. Also, "American Visitors 32 000 Years Ago," *The Times* (London), 8 Aug. 1986.

23 Niède Guidon, "Cliff Notes," *Natural History* 96, 8 (1987): 8. Carbonized hearth remains from Santa Rosa Island off the southern California coast have yielded 30 000-year-old dates, but these are vigorously disputed. See L.S. Cressman, *Prehistory of the Far West: Homes of Vanquished Peoples* (Salt Lake City: University of Utah Press, 1977), 69–70; William J. Wallace, "Post-Pleistocene Archaeology, 9000 to 2000 B.C." in *Handbook of North American Indians,* vol. 8, *California,* ed. Robert F. Heizer (Washington, DC: Smithsonian Institution, 1978), 30.

24 "Relics Suggest That Humans Came to New World 36 000 Years Ago," *Edmonton Journal,* 2 May 1991.

25 William N. Irving, "The First Americans: New Dates for Old Bones," *Natural History* 96, 2 (1987): 8–13. Irving and paleobiologist Richard Harrington claim that a campsite at Old Crow River dates back 150 000 years. See Barry Estabrook, "Bone Age Man," *Equinox* 1, 2 (1982): 84–96.

26 Jacques Cinq-Mars, "La place des grottes du Poisson-Bleu dans la

préhistoire beringienne," *Revista de Arqueología Americana* 1 (1990): 9–32. See also Catharine McClellan, *Part of the Land, Part of the Water: A History of the Yukon Indians* (Vancouver: Douglas & McIntyre, 1987), 50–51. On the debate about pre-Clovis sites, see Eliot Marshall, "Clovis Counterrevolution," *Science* 249 (1990): 738–41.

27 McClellan, *Part of the Land,* 49–50.

28 Knut R. Fladmark, "The First Americans: Getting One's Berings," *Natural History* (Nov. 1986): 8–19. For the view that the corridor could have been used for migrations, see N.W. Rutter, "Late Pleistocene History of the Western Canadian Ice-Free Corridor," *Canadian Journal of Anthropology* 1, 1 (1980): 1–8. The entire issue of the *Journal* is devoted to studies of the corridor.

29 D. Wayne Moodie, Kerry Abel, and Alan Catchpole, "Northern Athapaskan Oral Traditions and the White River Volcanic Eruption" (paper presented at Aboriginal Resource Use in Canada: Historical and Legal Aspects Conference, University of Manitoba, 1988). See also McClellan, *Part of the Land,* 54–55.

30 See, for example, Douglas C. Wallace, Katherine Garrison, and William Knowles, "Dramatic Founder Effects in Amerindian Mitochondrial DNAs," *American Journal of Physical Anthropology* 68 (1985): 149–55.

31 Russell Thornton, *American Indian Holocaust and Survival: A Population History Since 1492* (Norman: University of Oklahoma Press, 1987), 15–41; Henry F. Dobyns, *Their Number Become Thinned: Native American Population Dynamics in Eastern North America* (Knoxville: University of Tennessee Press, 1983), 34–45. See also Pierre Chaunu, *L'Amérique et les Amériques* (Paris: Armand Colin, 1964), 21.

32 Dobyns, *Their Number Become Thinned,* 42; Thornton, *American Indian Holocaust,* 25–33.

33 Pre-Columbian population estimates were beginning to be revised early in this century. In 1913, for instance, the U.S. Bureau of Ethnology calculated that the Amerindian population of the United States had declined 65 percent since the arrival of Europeans. Joseph K. Dixon, *The Vanishing Race: The Last Great Indian Council* (Garden City, NY: Doubleday, 1913), 6.

A recent study points to the danger of assuming that early epidemics alone caused the catastrophic population drops. In northern Manitoba, despite heavy death rates during the influenza epidemic following the First World War, population recovery could be swift if other factors did not intervene. Ann Herring, "The 1918 Flu Epidemic in Manitoba Aboriginal Communities: Implications for Depopulation Theory in the Americas" (paper presented to the American Society for Ethnohistory, Toronto, 1990).

34 Theodore G. Schurr et al., "Amerindian Mitochondrial DNA Have Rare Asian Mutations at High Frequencies, Suggesting They Derived from Four Primary Maternal Lineages," *American Journal of Human Genetics* 46 (1990): 613–23. For a different interpretation of the evidence, see Milford H. Wolpoff's article in *Emergence of Modern Humans: Biocultural Adaptations in the Late Pleistocene,* ed. Erik Trinkaus (Cambridge: Cambridge University Press, 1989).

35 J.H. Greenberg, C.G. Turner II, and S.L. Zegura, "The Settlement of the Americas: A Comparison of the Linguistic, Dental, and Genetic Evidence," *Current Anthropology* 27, 4 (1986): 477–97.

36 One population estimate for the entire neolithic world of 10 000 years ago sets it at 75 million, organized into something like 150 000 tribal nations. John H. Bodley, ed., *Tribal Peoples and Development Issues: A Global Overview* (Mountain View, CA:

Mayfield Publishers, 1988), 1. Today, the number of tribal peoples still in existence may be as many as 200 000 000 (ibid., iii).

37 Schledermann, *Crossroads to Greenland,* 319.

38 Paul S. Martin, "Prehistoric Overkill" in *Pleistocene Extinctions: The Search for a Cause,* ed. P.S. Martin and H.E. Wright, Jr. (New Haven: Yale University Press, 1967), 75–105. Also P.S. Martin, "The Pattern and Meaning of Holarctic Mammoth Extinctions" in *Paleoecology of Beringia,* ed. David M. Hopkins et al. (New York: Academic Press, 1982), 399–408.

39 William H. Hodge, *The First Americans Then and Now* (New York: Holt, Rinehart and Winston, 1981), 15–16.

40 R. Cole Harris, ed., *Historical Atlas of Canada,* vol. 1 (Toronto: University of Toronto Press, 1987), plate 2.

41 Ibid., plates 5 and 6.

42 Fagan, *The Great Journey,* 8.

43 Sauer, *Land and Life,* 237–40; W.C. Boyd, *Genetics and the Races of Man: An Introduction to Modern Physical Anthropology* (Boston: Little, Brown, 1950), 227.

44 Michael Brown, *The Search for Eve* (New York: Harper and Row, 1990), 315.

45 Sauer, *Land and Life,* 239.

46 Christy G. Turner II, "Ancient Peoples of the North Pacific Rim" in *Crossroads of Continents,* ed. Fitzhugh and Crowell, 113–15. Amerindians share with Asiatics the conformity of their incisors, which are scooped out at the back, "shovel-shaped." Turner believes that this feature, combined with genetic evidence, suggests three basic groups for original Amerindians: Amerind, Na-Dene, and Aleut-Inuit.

47 Emöke J.E. Szathmary, "Human Biology of the Arctic" in *Handbook of North American Indians,* vol. 5, *Arctic,* ed. David Damas (Washington, DC: Smithsonian Institution, 1984), 70–71.

48 This section has been drawn, in part, from my article, "A Historical Reconstruction for the Northwestern Plains," *Prairie Forum* 5, 1 (1980): 19–27.

49 Although the Inca were skilled metallurgists, they used it largely, although not entirely, for ceremonial purposes. However, recent studies have revealed that copper alloy metallurgy was more important than previously thought, and was used for mundane purposes. See Izumi Shamada and John F. Merkel, "Copper Alloy Metallurgy in Ancient Peru," *Scientific American* 265, 1 (1991): 80–86. Inca architecture, roads, and engineering projects were based on Stone Age technology. This technology, of course, was no more confined to stone than that of the Bronze Age was to bronze, or the Iron Age to iron. It may well be that bone and wood were just as important as stone, or even more so; their perishability, however, particularly that of wood, has made it highly unlikely that this can ever be determined with any precision. As stone and bone technology gave way to that of metals, some tribal peoples came to regard stone tools as thunderbolts. See C.J.M.R. Gullick, *Myths of a Minority* (Assen: Van Gorcum, 1985), 25.

50 Alan L. Bryan, "An Overview of Paleo-American Prehistory from a Circum-Pacific Perspective" in *Early Man in America,* ed. Bryan, 306–27.

51 J.Z. Young et al., *The Emergence of Man* (London: The Royal Society and The British Academy, 1981), 207–8. Similarly, red, the colour of life, was very early attributed high symbolic significance. Red ochre was thus prized by tribal peoples around the world.

52 Archery was practised at least 10 000 years ago in Japan. See Fumiko Ikawa-Smith, "Late Pleistocene and Early Holocene Technologies" in *Windows on the Japanese: Studies in Archaeology and Prehistory,* ed. Richard Pearson (Ann Arbor: Center for Japanese Studies, University of Michigan, 1986), 212.

53 Sauer, *Land and Life,* 284.

54 Ibid., 175. The recent discovery of a 6000-year-old wooden walkway buried in a peat bog in England has pointed to the existence of very early stable communities. See John M. Coles, "The World's Oldest Road," *Scientific American* 201, 5 (1989): 100–106. On the difficulties of interpreting archaeological data, see Ian Hodder, *Reading the Past* (Cambridge: Cambridge University Press, 1986).

55 Fladmark, "Times and Places," 41.

56 A map of historic trade systems between Siberia and North America probably also indicates earlier routes. See *Crossroads of Continents,* ed. Fitzhugh and Crowell, 236–37.

THE GREAT WAVE
OF EXTINCTIONS*

E.C. PIELOU

The most striking ecological change marking the end of the Pleistocene epoch in North America was, sad to say, a great loss. In the space of three millennia at most, in the interval from 12 k B.P. to 9 k B.P., between thirty-five and forty species of large mammals became extinct.[1] This wave of extinctions is one of the most noteworthy, and most puzzling, events in ecological history. The reasons for it have been debated for decades, and none of the many explanations put forward is entirely satisfactory.

It is interesting to look at this tremendous extinction episode in its context in time and space. There are several questions to consider: Were there earlier extinction "waves," and what happened between waves? What happened in the rest of the world, outside North America? What kinds of animals became extinct? And if large mammals vanished, what about small ones? Were they involved too?

To take the last question first: the term *large mammal* is unscientifically vague and needs to be defined. Paleontologists use a variety of definitions. Taking weight as the criterion, some[2] put the dividing line between "large" and "small" at 44 kilograms; others,[3] at 5 kilograms.

The different definitions do not create as much confusion as might be thought; an intuitive classification puts the great majority into the right slot whichever criterion is used. Thus mastodons, mammoths, sabretooths, bison, shrub-oxen, muskoxen, camels, horses, bears, giant ground sloths, wolves, and the like are undeniably large. Mice, rats, squirrels, weasels, and the like are small. Surprisingly few are borderline.

*From *After the Ice Age: The Return of Life to Glaciated North America* (Chicago and London: University of Chicago Press, 1991), 251–66. Reprinted with permission of the publisher.

In the wave of extinctions we are considering, in the last three millennia of the Pleistocene, most of the victims were large; only about five small victims are known.[4]

• Extinction Waves: When, Where, and What

Extinction waves, or extinction episodes as they are often called, have happened many times in this continent's history. For example, at least six are believed to have occurred in the past ten million years, and they seem to have happened at the end of glaciations.[5] "Our" wave, the most recent of them, ranked second in the six, being exceeded only by one that occurred 5 million years ago. Indeed, considering only large mammals, ours was probably the worst. Although the total number of extinctions was slightly greater in the earlier episode, a much larger proportion of the victims were small species. (It is well to avoid giving precise numbers; new discoveries mean that the numbers change continually.)

There have been other extinctions in addition to those occurring in waves. A few large mammal species (perhaps nine or ten) became extinct at various times during the 60 000 to 80 000 years of the Wisconsin glaciation before the final 3000 years. Indeed, in the long run, extinctions of species are as inevitable as the deaths of individual animals, and it may be that the causes of extinctions are as varied as the causes of individual deaths.

A wave of extinctions—a sudden diminution in the number of species—is analogous to a sudden big drop in the size of a human population, an event that deserves to be explained even though the individual people would inevitably have died sooner or later anyway. Catastrophes in human populations have many causes: war, famine, and pestilence are the possibilities that first spring to mind. There may be equally many causes for evolutionary catastrophes, as waves of extinctions could well be called. Another possibility, however, is that extinctions come in waves that are part of a recurring cycle. It would then be the cycle itself, rather than each individual wave in the cycle, that would need to be explained. If there is such a cycle, it presumably follows a cycle in the inorganic world, such as cyclical climatic changes.

Besides considering other times, we must also consider other places. Was the late Pleistocene extinction episode worldwide in scope, or was it confined to North America? Paleontological research shows that there were similar sudden waves of extinctions in South America and Australia. The South American wave came at the same time as the North American, but the Australian was 10 000 years earlier.[6] There were extinctions, too, in Eurasia and Africa, but in these two continents the losses were much less severe and they were spread over a longer period of time.

Thus the extinction wave seems to have involved the whole world. Even so, the differences in timing and duration in different parts of the world make it unlikely that the extinctions were caused astronomically. An astronomical cause has indeed been suggested, at least for the demise of the mammoths.[7] According to this theory, the earth picked up, temporarily, a diffuse, reflective shell of cometary particles above the atmosphere; as a result, sunlight was reflected, temperature dropped, and mammoths died out. But if this theory were correct, the extinctions would have been synchronous everywhere, and they were not.

Regardless of whether all the extinction waves of the past ten million years had the same cause or whether each was unique, it seems reasonable to suppose that all the extinctions *within* a wave had the same cause. The disappearance of thirty-five to forty large mammal species in the most recent wave can hardly be coincidence. It is worth inquiring whether the victims, as a group, simultaneously resembled one another and differed from extant large mammals. The answer seems to be no. The mammals that became extinct range from species almost indistinguishable from extant species to the totally unfamiliar.

To take some North American examples: the extinct dire wolf was a heavily built version of the extant timber wolf and had much bigger teeth.[8]

FIGURE 1 *Dire Wolf*

The two species shared large parts of the continent, with dire wolves being much the more numerous until about 10 k B.P. Then dire wolves became extinct, and timber wolf populations grew; thereafter, timber wolves were abundant until they were all but exterminated by modern humans. Other extinct species that closely resembled their living relatives were five species of Pleistocene horses and the western camel, all of which became extinct in North America between 12 k and 10 k B.P. They must have looked very like their extant counterparts (though modern camels differ enough to be assigned to a different genus), which do not live in North America.

Many of the species that became extinct differed strikingly from any animal now alive; they would be totally unfamiliar to us if it were not for museum restorations. Many have been mentioned on earlier pages. Among the most bizarre of the others were the giant beaver, as big as a black bear and with enormous incisors, and the Shasta ground sloth. It would be easy to extend the list.

FIGURE 2   *Giant Beaver and Shasta Ground Sloth*

All these now extinct animals either migrated into recently glaciated areas before extinction overtook them, or (presumably) would have done so if they had survived. The extinctions occurred throughout the ice-free part of the continent, and a variety of theories have been put forward to account for them. Indeed, the wave of extinctions is the subject of one of the great debates of Ice Age paleoecology.

There are two chief theories, each containing variant subtheories. According to one theory, the species that vanished were exterminated by human hunters; according to the other, the species that vanished were those unable to adapt to the rapidly changing environment. Let us look at the theories in turn.

• The Prehistoric Overkill Hypothesis

The hypothesis that numerous species, in all continents, were driven to extinction by human hunting has become known as the prehistoric overkill hypothesis. Its chief proponent is Paul S. Martin of the University of Arizona.[9]

Considering the world as a whole, the supporting arguments are strong. Extinctions were most numerous, and most sudden, in those continents (North and South America, Australia) that were invaded by humans who had evolved and developed their hunting skills elsewhere. Extinctions were fewer and took place more gradually in Africa and Eurasia, the continents of human origin, where the earliest members of our species slowly evolved in lands they shared with herds of large mammals. It is reasonable to suppose that African and Eurasian mammals, living for generation after generation in an environment where human predators were one of the risks to be faced regularly, grew wary; the prey mammals adapted their behaviour as fast (almost) as the hunters improved their skills. American and Australian mammals, by contrast, were unprepared for the onslaught when newly arrived, weapon-bearing humans began to hunt them; they succumbed without ever having time to develop evasive tactics.

It is believed that the numerous North American extinctions at the very end of the Pleistocene were the work of Clovis people, who, judging from archaeological discoveries, came suddenly into prominence at 11.5 k B.P.[10] Their ancestors presumably invaded from Beringia and penetrated to the lands south of the ice sheets as soon as the ice-free corridor became passable. Compared with the humans already living in midlatitude North America—if, indeed, there were any—the immigrant Clovis people were more numerous and more advanced in their hunting methods. They hunted many large mammals to extinction: in a word, their hunting amounted to overkill. According to this theory, the end of the Wisconsin glaciation was only indirectly responsible for the extinctions; it caused the opening of the ice-free corridor, the portal through which the hunters came.

There is further support for the overkill hypothesis. It was noted previously that the Australian extinctions were earlier than the North American. Correspondingly, humans arrived in Australia earlier than in midlatitude North America. However, there is not a perfect match between the two continents in the way effect (extinctions) followed cause (the arrival of human hunters). In North America, the extinctions seem to have started as soon as Clovis people arrived. In Australia, there was a gap[11]: the human population dates from about 40 k B.P., whereas the wave of extinctions (which occupied 11 000 years) did not begin until 26 k B.P.

Yet another argument in favour of overkill comes from comparing the mammals that did and did not go extinct in midlatitude North America.[12] Twelve genera of grazers and browsers that no doubt served as human food disappeared between 11.5 k B.P. and the end of the Pleistocene. They were camels, llamas, two genera of deer, two genera of pronghorn, stag-moose, shrub-oxen, woodland muskoxen, mastodons, mammoths, and also horses, which became extinct in North America though not elsewhere. All these animals were descended from ancestors that had lived in North America for more than one million years in an environment devoid of ruthless, expert human hunters (perhaps devoid of humans altogether). They never evolved the art of co-existing with so relentless a predator.

Now compare them with the nine genera of large grazers and browsers that were present in the Pleistocene and survive to the present day. They are bison, moose, wapiti or elk, caribou, deer, pronghorn, muskox, bighorn sheep, and mountain goat. All except pronghorn were immigrants from Asia; no doubt they were adapted to the presence of human hunters and able to survive in spite of being hunted.

FIGURE 3 *Four-horned Pronghorn*

It seems, indeed, entirely plausible that the two groups of animals—the native American victims and the immigrant survivors—differed in their capacity to withstand armed hunters. But notice that this argument is not equivalent to saying, simply, that immigrant species were wary and native American species too trusting. As present-day hunters know, existing game animals (all belonging to the nine genera just listed) may be wary or trusting, depending on whether they live in an area where hunting is permitted or excluded. The valuable adaptation possessed only by the immigrant species is the ability to learn from experience. This adaptation was the outcome of natural selection: animals that did not learn to be wary of human hunters have left no descendants.

There is no reason to believe that mammoths and mastodons, to take only the largest victims, were too big for human hunters to kill. They were probably as vulnerable to primitive hunting methods as African elephants are today. There are many ways of killing large prey.[13] They could have been captured in pitfalls, or with footsnares, and then been speared when they had become exhausted, using Clovis points as spear tips. (A footsnare is a device, weighted with a log, that clings to the leg of an animal that puts its foot into it.) They could have been caught in noose-type snares. They could have been killed by weighted spears suspended from tree branches. They could have been stampeded over cliffs, as was done in historic times with bison, which were driven over so-called buffalo jumps. It has even been suggested that they may have been hunted with poison-dipped spears, although this seems unlikely in North America, where few, if any, suitable plant poisons are available.

All in all, the arguments for human overkill as the cause of the extinctions seem, at first, very persuasive. But there are equally persuasive arguments against it.

• The Arguments Against Overkill

The chief objection to the overkill hypothesis is that, in Clovis times, the human population was small and human hunters few, too few in the opinion of many archaeologists to have had any significant effect on other animal species.

Another obvious objection is this. A species on its way to extinction is bound to become increasingly rare and hard to find as its numbers dwindle. Why, then, did human hunters not switch their efforts to more abundant animals, such as bison, whenever an earlier quarry became scarce? (Perhaps this objection can be overruled by arguing that when a particular quarry became so scarce as to be not worth hunting, it was doomed to dwindle to extinction anyway.)[14]

The same objection applies to nonhuman predators, both extant (such as the timber wolf) and extinct (such as the sabretooth). It seems at first thought reasonable to suppose that the extinct carnivores died out because their food supply vanished. But why did they not, like surviving predators, switch to surviving prey? A possible explanation is suggested at the end of the following section.

It is worth comparing the origins of extant and extinct carnivores in the same way as we compared the origins of extant and extinct herbivores in the preceding section, even though the comparison does not suggest any conclusions. The facts, so far as they are known, are these.

Five species of carnivorous mammals disappeared at the end of the Pleistocene (enough is known for us to consider species rather than genera). They were the giant short-faced bear and the American cheetah, which may both have become extinct before 11.5 k B.P., when Clovis people became numerous; the American lion; the sabretooth; and the dire wolf. The lion is believed to have been a fairly recent immigrant from Asia; the origin of the dire wolf is unknown; and the other three descended from North American ancestors.

FIGURE 4 *American Lion*

Only four species of large, "menacing" carnivores have survived. They are the timber wolf, the grizzly bear, the cougar, and the wolverine. (Because they are rarely a threat to large herbivores, we exclude coyotes, black bears, badgers, red and grey foxes, lynxes and bobcats, even though all are extant large carnivores if the division between large and small is put at 5 kilograms. Polar bears are excluded, too, because they are marine.) Grizzly bears are quite recent immigrants to middle latitudes; they arrived (as did moose) from Beringia after the ice sheets melted. Timber wolves and wolverines have North American ancestors. And cougars have been here at least 200 000 years.

Still another compelling argument against the overkill hypothesis is that fossils of extinct mammals are hardly ever found in association with human remains at archaeological "kill sites." The exceptions to this generalization are mammoths and extinct species of bison. However, the genus *Bison* still survives; it was not killed off during the late Pleistocene extinctions; rather, the species of bison living then have been replaced by modern descendants. As for mammoths, their bones have been found at about one-third of the known archaeological sites representing the Clovis culture,[15] and they often show signs of butchering. The majority of these places are in the southern United States. The map in figure 5 shows most of the known Clovis sites in land within or near the southernmost margins of the last ice sheets; sites with mammoth fossils are marked, as are sites with remains of other extinct species. These last are clearly rare. One might infer that human hunters were selective and for an unknown reason concentrated nearly all their efforts on bison, mammoth, and animals that happen to be still extant, such as caribou and elk.

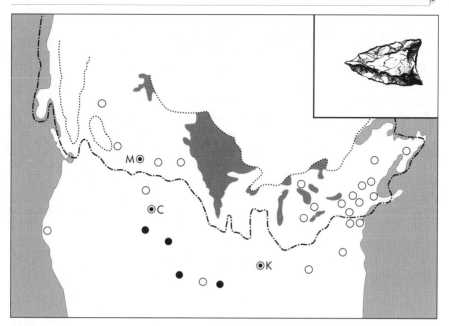

FIGURE 5 *Midlatitude (35° to 60° north) North America, showing ice sheets, lakes, and coastline at 10 k B.P., and archaeological sites dating from the Clovis period (11.5 k to 10 k B.P.). O, sites with signs of human occupancy only. ●, sites with human and mammoth remains. ◉, sites with remains of humans and other extinct mammals: M, Medicine Hat, Alberta (mammoth, Mexican wild ass, camel?); C, Colby, Wyoming (mammoth, camel); K, Kimmswick, Missouri (mastodon). The ice front at 18 k B.P. is also shown. Inset, a Clovis point.*

There is another possibility, however. The proponents of the overkill theory have a counterargument to explain why evidence of human life and the fossils of extinct mammals are so seldom found together. It is as follows.[16] It assumes that an invading horde of human hunters, of unprecedented ferocity, entered midlatitude North America through the bottleneck formed by the ice-free corridor and spread in all directions, occupying an ever expanding, more or less circular area. The periphery of this area formed a narrow front, along which the hunters encountered defenceless North American game animals for the first time. They annihilated them. As the area occupied by the ever growing human population expanded, the front moved continuously outward. Therefore, hunters and hunted were simultaneously present only in a narrow, moving zone, which crossed any given spot of ground in a very short time (a few decades or centuries).

The theory seems farfetched, but it gives a possible explanation of why fossils of the extinct animals (other than mammoths) are so seldom found at archaeological sites. Fossils of any kind are rare, and those that have been found represent the accumulated deaths of tens of thousands of years. If the hypothesis is correct, only deaths occurring in the final decades of a species' existence would have been caused by human hunting, and these deaths amounted to only a tiny fraction of the accumulated total. All earlier deaths would have been natural, leaving fossils in "natural" deposits (that is, deposits devoid of human artifacts). The theory does not explain why mammoth remains are comparatively common at archaeological sites, whereas mastodons, horses, camels, and the like are so rare.

Although the first version of the theory assumed that the geographical starting point of the invading hunters was in the ice-free corridor, according to a later version[17] the invasion came from northeastern Siberia and was responsible for the Beringian extinctions as well as those south of the ice. This cannot be reconciled with the arguments[18] of prehistorians who maintain that Clovis culture, and with it the skills and tools needed to hunt large animals efficiently, developed south of the great ice sheets among primitive people already living there.

This brings us back to the unsolved problem of when people first reached the lands south of the ice. If overkill could only be perpetrated by people of Clovis culture, and the ancient Beringians were too primitive, the extinctions in Beringia are left unexplained. It is even possible that human invaders were for a time prevented from crossing the Beringian land bridge by the larger, fiercer carnivores already there. Human hunters pursued their prey in a dangerous environment. They, as well as the animals they hunted, were prey themselves, and no doubt many people were killed and eaten by American lions and the terrifyingly big, swift, agile, and ferocious short-faced bears.

FIGURE 6 *Giant Short-faced Bear*

• Changing Environment Theories

Most paleoecologists who disbelieve the overkill theory invoke environmental change, resulting from the climatic change that brought an end to the Wisconsin glaciation, as the only possible cause of the great wave of extinctions. There are a number of such theories. Some fail because they apply to only one or two animal species, others because they apply only in small regions. It strains credibility to suppose that different species, in different places, all went extinct for different causes at roughly the same time.

General theories, designed to explain all the late Pleistocene extinctions everywhere in North America, face a very serious objection even before they are propounded. Surely the climatic amelioration and the tremendous expansion of habitable land area that came with the disappearance of the ice sheets should have caused animal populations to grow bigger rather than dwindle to extinction. The phenomenon to be explained is the direct opposite of what common sense would suggest. We must therefore inquire: How can seemingly better conditions kill whole populations of many large mammal species?

Here are some of the suggestions that have been made. Most lead only to "particular" theories, that is theories explaining the extinction of a single species or several extinctions in a single locality.

The extinctions in Beringia seem easy to explain for those who believe that at the height of the Wisconsin glaciation the area was covered by so-called arctic steppe, which provided copious forage for herds of grazing animals. Disappearance of the steppe must have caused disappearance of the herds. The steppe began to shrink soon after Bering Strait broke through the land bridge at 15.5 k B.P.; as the sea flooded the extensive Beringian lowlands, the climate became milder and moister, and the grassy arctic steppe (if it ever existed) gave way to shrub tundra and later to forests of poplar, willow, alders, and spruce. The major vegetation change seems to have happened long in advance of the extinctions, but if one accepts that the disappearance of suitable fodder caused mammoths, camels, horses, long-horned bison, and the rest to go extinct, then one can easily argue that a few small patches of steppe lasted long enough to accommodate a few shrinking herds of game for as long as the fossil evidence requires. However, the theory is unconvincing to disbelievers in the arctic steppe, and it does not apply to extinctions south of the ice sheets.

Several other particular theories are based on environmental change, or habitat destruction, as it could equally well be called. For example, it may have been habitat destruction that drove mastodons to extinction.[19] Between 12 k and 10 k B.P., their favourite browse—spruce—disappeared from the big region south of the Great Lakes where mastodons were most numerous. Spruce forest was replaced by pine forest, which was acceptable if not optimal for them. But then pine, too, became scarce, because of the northward advance of deciduous forests. The pine forests became fragmented into isolated patches that became smaller and smaller. Deprived of a habitat that had been at least tolerable, the mastodons died out, probably by 10 k B.P.

Similarly in the west, the changing climate in the rain shadow of the Rocky Mountains caused a change in the available fodder. The increasing aridity of the plains caused short grasses to replace taller grasses. This, it is argued,[20] put grazers adapted to comparatively tall grasses, such as horses, camels, and mammoths, which can digest grass stems, at a competitive disadvantage vis à vis bison, which graze on the leafier short grasses. Consequently horses, camels, and mammoths disappeared, and bison flourished in their stead.

Loss of habitat has also been blamed[21] for the extinction of the giant beaver, which, like modern beavers, inhabited ponds and swamps. Competition with modern beavers for the shrinking supply of suitable habitat may have contributed to their extinction, but it seems impossible to judge why *Castor* should have defeated *Castoroides* in the struggle for living space rather than the other way around.

Likewise, competition has been blamed for the extinction of the huge stag-moose, which was probably a muskeg dweller. It is argued that when the melting ice allowed the similar but smaller modern moose to migrate into midlatitude North America from Beringia, stag-moose was the loser in the competition for habitat. It is not clear, however, why the invader should have succeeded in crowding out the established species.

However, to say that a species became extinct because of loss of habitat entails a circular argument. With the disappearance of the ice sheets, *all* habitats changed; and when a habitat changes, the old habitat can be described either as "changed" or "destroyed." It is a matter of semantics. It is easy to say that the habitat of an extinct species was destroyed, whereas that of a still extant species was merely changed. But if the reason for saying so is simply that the extinct species is extinct, and the extant one extant, then the statement is not an explanation at all, but a play on words.

Many animals—all the survivors—managed to adapt to the changes that accompanied disappearance of the ice sheets. Some responded by altering their geographical ranges. A good example[22] is provided by four small mammals that currently inhabit markedly different habitats: the smoky shrew of mature, eastern deciduous forests; the thirteen-lined ground squirrel of the prairies; the heather vole of the boreal forest; and the Ungava lemming of the tundra. Nowadays their ranges do not overlap (figure 7), but fossils of all four species, dating from 11 k B.P., have been found together in a cave in Pennsylvania. There is no way of knowing how extensive their shared range was then.

The ancient environment at the fossil site was probably an open parkland in which spruces, pines, and birch grew amidst ground vegetation having some of the attributes of tundra and some of prairie. Such a mixed environment, which has no modern counterpart, may have covered a large area, and it would have met the requirements of all four species. For the

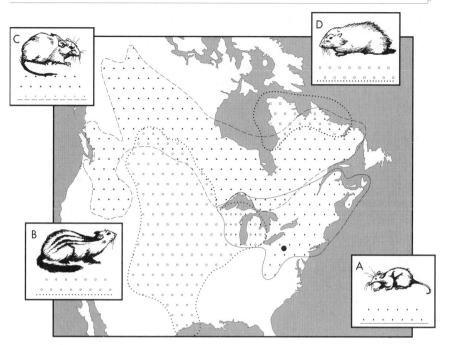

FIGURE 7 *The present-day ranges of (A) the smoky shrew, (B) the thirteen-lined ground squirrel, (C) the heather vole, and (D) the Ungava lemming. ●, site in Pennsylvania where 11 000-year-old fossils of all four species have been found together.*

thirteen-lined ground squirrel, for instance, it would have served as an eastern extension of the western grasslands. When the mixed environment was destroyed, instead of going extinct the animals fanned out into the four separate regions where their different requirements could be met. One wonders why all animals whose habitats were changed did not do likewise. Some paleoecologists argue that environmental change is much less damaging to small mammals than to large; presumably the reason for saying so is that very few small mammals went extinct!

Some theories assert that the changed climate itself caused the extinctions directly, independently of changes in the vegetation. According to one of these theories,[23] the opening of the ice-free corridor between the Laurentide and Cordilleran ice sheets created a funnel for bitterly cold winds out of the arctic; the result is believed to have been a catastrophic fall in temperature that killed off the horses, camels, and bison living at the southern end of the corridor.

Another "climatic" theory[24] argues that at the end of the Pleistocene, the climate became much more seasonal than it had been; summers were hotter, winters colder, and the seasons were more strongly contrasted in their precipitation as well. Hence, according to the argument, the period during each year in which conditions were mild enough for the survival of newborn young would have become shorter. Large herbivores may have had a reproductive cycle (the interval from one birth to the next) that failed to synchronize with the seasonal cycle. Many births would have taken place in unfavourable times of the year, and extinctions were the result.

The numerous "environmental" theories put forward to account for the extinctions—the ones described are only a sample—all fail (in my opinion) in being too farfetched or too "particular" (in the sense previously defined). Moreover, they all seem to overlook the fact that tremendous environmental changes occurred during the Wisconsin glaciation as well as at the end of it. The overkill theory has fatal objections, too.

Could it be that some short-lived catastrophe killed off vast numbers of all large mammals (or all large herbivores) and that species now extant are those few that managed to build up their numbers again after the catastrophe was over? If so, what *was* the catastrophe? It would have had to have been one that left no evidence of its occurrence and was short-lived enough to leave no perceptible gap in the fossil record. All that can now be said is that the cause of the great mammal extinctions is still an unsolved puzzle.

• Extinct Birds

The great wave of late Pleistocene extinctions affected birds as well as mammals.[25] The casualties were mostly flesh eaters, especially carrion feeders: extinct species of eagles, vultures and condors, and teratorns.

These birds probably relied on the dead bodies of large herbivorous mammals for a constant supply of carrion. They were as dependent on them as were the mammalian carnivores—sabretooths, American lions,

FIGURE 8 *Teratorn*

dire wolves, and the like. It therefore seems reasonable, at first thought, to blame the extinctions of all the flesh eaters, birds as well as mammals, on the disappearance of the herbivores.

Against this theory it could be argued that even when mammoths, mastodons, camels, horses, and all the other now extinct herbivores vanished, the flesh eaters had only to switch to bison, elk, caribou, deer, and all the other living herbivores to survive. But, perhaps, as already suggested, some undiscovered catastrophe caused all species of herbivores to be scarce for a short period. Then all flesh eaters—mammals and birds alike—would have been at risk of starvation. Though many species died out, a few of the tough ones survived, and their descendants are with us still.

If there was indeed a catastrophe, its nature has not even been surmised. It is worth repeating that the great wave of extinctions at the end of the Pleistocene has yet to be convincingly explained.

• Notes

1 B. Kurtén and E. Anderson, *Pleistocene Mammals of North America* (New York: Columbia University Press, 1980). Also S.D. Webb, "Ten Million Years of Mammal Extinctions in North America" in *Quaternary Extinctions*, ed. P.S. Martin and R.G. Klein (Tucson: University of Arizona Press, 1984), 189–210.

2 P.S. Martin, "Refuting Late Pleistocene Extinction Models" in *Dynamics of Extinction*, ed. D.K. Elliott (New York: Wiley-Interscience, 1986), 107–30.

3 Webb, "Ten Million Years."

4 Ibid.

5 Ibid.

6 D.R. Horton, "Red Kangaroos: Last of the Australian Megafauna" in *Quaternary Extinctions*, ed. Martin and Klein, 639–80.

7 E.J. Butler and F. Hoyle, "On the Effects of a Sudden Change in the Albedo of the Earth," *Astrophysics and Space Sciences* 60 (1979): 505–11.

8 Kurtén and Anderson, *Pleistocene Mammals.*

9 P.S. Martin, "Prehistoric Overkill: The Global Model" in *Quaternary Extinctions*, ed. Martin and Klein, 354–403. Also Martin, "Refuting."

10 F.H. West, "The Antiquity of Man" in *Late Quaternary Environments of the United States*, vol. 1, *The Late Pleistocene*, ed. S.C. Porter (Minneapolis: University of Minnesota Press, 1983), 364–82.

11 Horton, "Red Kangaroos."

12 Martin, "Prehistoric Overkill."

13 D.L. Johnson, P. Kawano, and E. Ekker, "Clovis Strategies of Hunting Mammoth *(Mammuthus columbi),*" *Canadian Journal of Anthropology* 1 (1980): 107–14.

14 S.L. Whittington and B. Dyke, "Simulating Overkill: Experiments with the Mosimann and Martin Model" in *Quaternary Extinctions*, ed. Martin and Klein, 451–65.

15 West, "Antiquity of Man."

16 J.E. Mosimann and P.S. Martin, "Simulating Overkill by PaleoIndians," *American Scientist* 63 (1975): 304–13.

17 P.S. Martin, "The Pattern and Meaning of Holarctic Mammoth Extinction" in *Paleoecology of Beringia*, ed. D.M. Hopkins, J.V. Matthews, Jr., C.E. Schweger, and S.B. Young (New York: Academic Press, 1982), 399–408.

18 D.E. Dumond, "The Archaeology of Alaska and the Peopling of America" *Science* 209 (1980): 984–91.

[19] J.E. King and J.J. Saunders, "Environmental Insularity and the Extinction of the American Mastodont" in *Quaternary Extinctions*, ed. Martin and Klein, 315–39.

[20] R.D. Guthrie, "Bison and Man in North America," *Canadian Journal of Anthropology* 1 (1980): 55–73.

[21] Kurtén and Anderson, *Pleistocene Mammals*.

[22] R.W. Graham, "Plant-Animal Interactions and Pleistocene Extinctions" in *Dynamics of Extinction*, ed. Elliott, 131–54. Also J.E. Guilday, "Pleistocene Extinction and Environmental Change: Case Study of the Appa-lachians" in *Quaternary Extinctions*, ed. Martin and Klein, 250–58.

[23] R.A. Bryson and W.M. Wendland, "Radiocarbon Isochrones of the Retreat of the Laurentide Ice Sheet" (Technical Report No. 35, University of Wisconsin, Department of Meteorology, 1967).

[24] R.A. Kiltie, "Seasonality, Gestation Time, and Large Mammal Extinctions" in *Quaternary Extinctions*, ed. Martin and Klein, 299–314.

[25] D.W. Steadman and P.S. Martin, "Extinction of Birds in the Late Pleistocene of North America" in *Quaternary Extinctions*, ed. Martin and Klein, 466–77.

MARRIED WOMEN IN THE FAMILY ECONOMY*

LOUISE A. TILLY AND JOAN W. SCOTT

The married couple was the "simple community of work, the elementary unit" in the preindustrial household.[1] The contribution of each spouse was vital for the creation and survival of the family. From its outset, marriage was an economic partnership. Each partner brought to the union either material resources, or the ability to help support each other. Peasant sons brought land, craftsmen brought their tools and skill. Daughters brought a dowry and sometimes a marketable skill as well. The dowry of a peasant or artisan daughter was usually a contribution to the establishment of the couple's household. These might include "a bit of cash, furniture, linen, tools. Sometimes a loom, one or two skeins of wool, several pounds of wool and silk, a boat, a thousand eels for a fish merchant, sometimes a house or part of a house in the city, a meadow and some plots of land in the country."[2]

In Bayeux, a marriage contract from 1700 shows that the wife brought to her new household: "a bed, a half dozen sheep, an oak chest, a cow, a year old heifer, a dozen sheep, 20 pounds of linen, two dresses and a half dozen table napkins."[3]

Among the propertyless there was only the promise of work and wages. In Amiens in 1687, Francois Pariès, a mason, and Marie Hugues declared in their contract that they had no material possessions and that "they are mutually satisfied with their well-being and with one another."[4] The point was that the wife as well as the husband made an economic contribution (or a promise of one) which helped set up the new household. In addition, however, it represented a commitment to help support the new

*From *Women, Work, and Family* (New York: Holt, Rinehart and Winston, 1978), 43-60.

family. The resources brought to the marriage were only a beginning. The continuing labour of each partner was required to maintain the couple and, later, its children. In the course of a lifetime, the work of husband and wife was the major source of the family's support. Families were productive and reproductive units, centres of economic activity and creators of new life. Married women contributed to all aspects of family life and thus fulfilled several roles within their households. They engaged in production for exchange and production for household consumption, both of which contributed to the family's economic well-being. And they performed the reproductive role of bearing and raising children.

• Married Women's Work

A married woman's work depended on the family's economic position, on whether it was involved in agriculture or manufacturing, whether it owned property or was propertyless. But whether labour or cash were needed, married women were expected to contribute it. The fact that a woman bore children influenced the kind of work she did, but it did not confine her to a single set of tasks, nor exclude her from participation in productive activity. The organization of production in this period demanded that women be contributing members of the family economy. It also permitted women to control the time and pace of their work, and to integrate their various domestic activities.

Within the preindustrial household, whether on the farm or in the craftshop, among property holders and wage earners, there was a division of labour by age and by sex. The levels of skill expected of children advanced with age, with young children performing the simplest and crudest chores. Certain kinds of heavy work were reserved for men, but women also did many heavy tasks which today are considered too arduous for females. Hauling and carrying were often women's tasks. Rural and urban wives sometimes had occupations of their own, or they shared their husbands' occupations performing specified tasks within the productive process. Indeed, the jobs women did reflected the fact that they performed several functions for the family. The normative family division of labour tended to give men jobs away from the household or jobs which required long and uninterrupted commitments of time or extensive travel, while women's work was performed more often at home and permitted flexible time arrangements.

• Rural Women

On farms, men worked in the fields, while women ran the household, made the family's clothes, raised and cared for cows, pigs, and poultry, tended a garden, and marketed surplus milk, vegetables, chickens, and eggs. A French peasant saying went: "No wife, no cow, hence no milk, no cheese, neither hens, nor chicks, nor eggs."[5] The sale of these items often brought in the only cash a family received. Women's participation in local markets reflected their several family roles. They earned money as an outgrowth of activities concerned with family subsistence; and they might use the money to purchase food and supplies for their families. Their domestic and market activities overlapped, and both served important economic functions for the family. Moderately prosperous farm families owed their success to a variety of resources, not the least of which was the wife's activity. Rétif de la Bretonne, the eighteenth-century French writer, describing the peasant Covin and his wife Marguerite in mid-eighteenth-century Burgundy, attributed their good fortune to a combination of factors. In addition to the fact that they owned a house, "their two hectares of field furnish some wheat for their bread; their half hectare of vineyard gives Covin his pocket money and his wine; . . . The weaving the couple does puts a bit of butter on the spinach. . . . Marguerite makes some money from her spinning, from the eggs of her six hens, from the wool of her seven sheep, from the milk, butter and cheese of her cow and from the vegetables in her garden."[6]

Wives of propertyless labourers also contributed to the family economy. They themselves became hired hands, "working in the fields and doing all kinds of hard jobs." Others became domestic textile workers. Still others alternated these activities. When Vauban, justifying his fiscal recommendations under Louis XIV, described the family of an agricultural labourer, he emphasized the importance of the wife's ability to earn money: "by the work of her distaff, by sewing, knitting some stockings, or by a bit of lace-making, according to the region."[7] Without this and her cultivation of a garden and some animals, "it would be difficult to subsist." Home work most commonly involved spinning or sewing. Lacemaking, straw plaiting, glovemaking, knitting, and needlework were the major areas of domestic manufacture. Pinchbeck estimates that lacemaking alone employed as many as 100 000 women and children in seventeenth-century England. About a million women and children worked in the clothing trades as a whole in England in that period.[8] And in France, as rural industry took hold in some areas, the numbers of women employed in spinning rose. Women earned low wages spinning, perhaps five sous a day in Picardy at the end of the seventeenth century.[9] Male weavers earned double that amount. Yet the individual wage a married woman could earn was less important than was her contribution to a joint effort. Spinning and weaving together were the complementary bases of the family economy.

When no home work was available, a wife marketed her household activities, shopping for others at the market, hawking some wares: extra pieces of linen she had woven or lengths of thread she had spun and not used. Rural women also became wet nurses, nursing and raising the children of middle-class women and of urban artisans who could afford to pay them. In the countryside around Paris and around the silk-weaving centre of Lyons, for example, wet nursing was a common way for a rural woman to earn some additional money while caring for her own child. In areas around big cities in France particularly, this might be an organized enterprise. In Paris, for example, men or women (called *meneurs* or *messagères*) located rural nurses, recruited urban babies, then transported the infants in carts to the country, where they often remained until they were three or four years old, if they survived infancy. One late-eighteenth-century estimate places at about 10 000 the number of Parisian infants sent out to nurse. Maurice Garden suggests that close to a third of all babies born in Lyons (some 2000 of 5000–6000) were carted off to the countryside. Until the late eighteenth century these included the children of the upper classes as well as of artisan and shopkeeping families.[10] Most often, however, the more prosperous families hired wet nurses who lived in the household. The wet-nurse "business" was most developed, it appears, in large preindustrial urban centres where married women played an active role in artisan and commercial enterprise. There was little supervision of the nurses in this period. The job could be fairly lucrative and demand was high, so some women "nursed" babies long after their own children had grown and their milk dried up.

Married women, then, would often alternate different kinds of work, putting together a series of jobs in order to increase their earnings or to earn enough to help their families survive. Indeed the absence of employment for the wives of wage earners was often given as the reason for a family's destitution.

Although women tended to work at or near home, they did not do so exclusively. On farms, the rhythm of the seasons with their periods of intensive labour brought women into the fields to sow and harvest, as well as glean. Here is an account from mid-seventeenth-century Yorkshire which describes women and men together harvesting grain and peas. Jobs were allocated according to physical strength:

> Wee allways have one man, or else one of the ablest of the women to abide on the meow, besides those that goe with the waines. . . . It is usual in some places (wheare the furres of landes are deepe worne with raines) to imploy women, with wain-rakes, to gather the corne. . . . Wee use meanes allwayes to gett eyther 18 or else 24 pease pullers, which wee sette allways sixxe on a lande, viz, a woman and a man, . . . a woman or boy and a man, etc., the wakest couple in the fore furre. . . . It is usuall in most places after they gette all pease pulled, or the last graine downe, to invite all the workefolkes and wives (that helped them harvest) to supper.[11]

The situation might also be reversed, with men joining women as extra hands for the harvest, while the women carried on all the farm work in the fields and the house during most of the year. In areas where small property holders worked as agricultural labourers or as tradesmen, women tended the family plot and men worked away from home "except for about a week in hay harvest, and for a few days at other times, when the gathering of manure or some work which the women cannot perform" required the men's assistance.[12] In the vineyards of the Marne "the wife [was] really the working partner of her husband: she share[d] all of his burdens," cultivating the grapes.[13]

On the other hand, there was household work which included the entire family. In villages in France, for example, the kneading and preparation of bread (which was baked in a communal oven) "mobilized the energies of everyone in the house every other week in summer and once a month in winter."[14] And the winter slaughter of a pig took all family members and sometimes some additional help. When the farm or the household needed labour, it incorporated all hands, regardless of sex, in periods of intensive activity. At other times, though work roles were different, they were complementary. The family economy depended upon the labour of both husband and wife.

• Urban Women

Wives of skilled craftsmen who worked at home usually assisted their husbands, sharing the same room, if not the same bench or table. The wife sometimes prepared or finished materials on which the husband worked. Thus wives spun for their weaver husbands, polished metal for cutlers, sewed buttonholes for tailors, and waxed shoes for shoemakers. Sometimes a wife's work was identical to her husband's, as this romanticized portrait of two broadloom weavers makes clear:

> Or if the broader mantle be the task
> He chooses some companion to his toil
> from side to side, with amicable aim
> Each to the other darts the nimble bolt.[15]

If the wife was not her husband's constant companion at the loom, however, or if spinning was her customary job, she still must be able to take his place when he had other tasks, when he was ill, or when he died. Pinchbeck cites a long poem from eighteenth-century England, which included a discussion between a clothier, departing to buy wool, and his wife, who protests at the additional work she will have when he is gone. She calms down, however, when he reminds her of the importance of the trade.

> Bessie and thee mun get up soon
> And stir about and get all done
> For all things mun be aside laid
> When we want help about our trade.[16]

The fact that all family members worked together and benefited jointly from the enterprise meant that some jobs were learned by both sexes and could be interchangeable. It meant, too, as the verse suggests, that the family's joint economic activity was the first priority for everyone.

If the products made at home were sold there, then a craftsman's wife was usually also a shopkeeper. She handled transactions, kept accounts, and helped supervise the workers in the shop. Many of these women hired servants to free them from "the routine of domestic drudgery." When work pressed, as it did in the Lyonnais silk trade (where the typical female occupation was silk spinning or assistance with weaving), mothers sent their infants off to nurses rather than break the rhythm of work in the shop.[17]

Yet, if a wife was her husband's indispensable partner in many a trade, and even if her skill equaled his, she remained his assistant while he lived. Married women were granted full membership in certain guilds only after their husbands had died and then so long as they did not remarry. Occupational designations in all but the food and clothing trades usually were male. Women were referred to as the wives of the craftsmen, even when they were widows and practising the trade on their own. Hence, Mrs Baskerville, a widow of a printer and letter founder, "begs leave to inform the Public, . . . that she continues the business of letter-founding, in all its parts, with the same care and accuracy that was formerly observed by Mr Baskerville."[18] The practice reflected a family division of labour which undoubtedly took into account a woman's domestic tasks: her other activities might claim her time while the husband could be a full-time craftsman. In addition, in the most skilled trades, an investment in long years of training might be unwise for a woman in the light of the lost time, the illnesses, and the higher mortality of women usually associated with childbirth.[19] The exclusion of women also represented a means of controlling the size of a craft. Only when labour was scarce were women permitted to practise certain trades. The press of numbers, however, led to their exclusion from goldsmithing, for example, in England by 1700. (Women were employed, however, as unskilled assistants—often called servants—in large shops. But these were usually young, single women.) By and large, in the home-based skilled trades, married women were part of the family labour force.

Some women did have crafts or trades of their own in the cities of England and France in 1700. Most of these were associated with the production and distribution of food and clothing. The all-female corporations in seventeenth-century France include seamstresses, dressmakers, combers of hemp and flax, embroiders, and hosiers. In addition, there were fan and wig makers, milliners, and cloak makers.[20] Lists from English cities are similar.

In many of these trades women regularly took on apprentices. In millinery, for example, an apprenticeship lasted from five to seven years and required a substantial fee. The women ran their enterprises independently of their husbands, whose work often took them away from home. The Customs of London provided in the seventeenth century that:

Married women who practise certain crafts in the city alone and without their husbands, may take girls as apprentices to serve them and learn their trade, and these apprentices shall be bound by their indentures of apprenticeship to both husband and wife, to learn the wife's trade as is aforesaid, and such indentures shall be enrolled as well for women as for men.[21]

Women were represented, too, in the retail trades, assisting their husbands and running their own businesses as well. In England, brewing once was a female monopoly. It was no longer by the eighteenth century, but women still practised the trade. Women were also bakers, grocers, innkeepers, and butchers. At least one woman butcher in eighteenth-century London "lived by killing beasts in which . . . she was very expert."[22]

By far the most numerous group of married women working independently were the wives of unskilled labourers and journeymen. They were women in precarious economic situations, since their husbands never earned enough money to cover household needs. These women had no skills, nor did they have capital for goods or a shop. No family productive enterprise claimed their time. So they became petty traders, and itinerant peddlers selling such things as bits of cloth or "perishable articles of food from door to door" accompanied by their children.[23] The street was their shop; their homes were their workplaces; and their work required no investment in tools or equipment. On the list of nonguild members in Paris there were 1263 women and only 486 men. The women were lodging-house keepers and retailers or "repairers of old clothes and hats, of rags and old ironware, buckles and hardware."[24] When they did not sell items they had scavenged or repaired, they sold their labour, carting goods, water, or sewage, doing laundry, and performing a host of other unskilled services which were always in demand in the city and usually outside the control of the guilds. Their work was an aspect of "the economy of makeshift" which characterized their entire lives. As such, the time spent earning wages was sporadic and discontinuous: "a poor woman . . . goes three dayes a week to wash or scoure abroad, or one that is employed in Nurse keeping three or four Months in a Year, or a poor Market woman, who attends 3 or 4 mornings in a Week with her Basket."[25]

The writer advocated spinning as a means of continuously employing these women at home and of making them "much more happy and cheerful." His description nonetheless captures the variety of jobs that might be done by a poor woman as she sought ways of contributing to the family fund.

The time required of women differed greatly in different situations. During harvesting and planting, wives worked day and night in the fields. Wives of urban butchers and bakers spent many hours in the family shop. Lyons' silk spinners paid others to nurse their babies. Women doing casual labour had to spend long hours earning a few pence or sous. Yet the work of most married women permitted a certain flexibility, some control over the time and pace of work. Some studies estimated that in the course of a year, a woman probably spent fewer days at cash-earning activities than did her husband. While a man worked about 250 days a year, a woman worked about 125 to 180 days. The studies, based on contemporaries' analyses of family budgets of French weavers in 1700 and agricultural labourers in 1750, assumed that a married woman worked less "because of the supplementary demands of her sex: housekeeping, childbirth, etc."[26] In the fields, women could stop work to nurse a baby or feed a young child. In craft and retail shops, they could allocate some time for domestic responsibilities. In addition, they could include young children in certain aspects of their work, teaching them to wind thread or clean wool. Those who walked the street, selling their wares, were invariably accompanied by their children. Yet rather than "working less," as contemporaries described it, it seems more accurate to say that demands on women's time were more complex. In this period, the type of work women did meant that even if home and workplace were not the same, a woman could balance her productive and domestic activities.

• Widows

We have described so far a "normal" situation, in which both husband and wife were alive. Yet mortality statistics indicate that quite frequently death changed this picture. The death of a husband disrupted the family division of labour and left the wife solely responsible for maintaining the family. Sometimes, of course, there were children to assist her, to run the farm or earn some wages. But often they were too young or too inexperienced to contribute much.

In the best of circumstances, a widow gained the right to practise her husband's craft. She became the legal representative of the family, and her mastery and autonomy were publicly recognized. Advertisements from eighteenth-century English newspapers capture a certain sense of the strength and competence a widow could have:

> M. Hawthorn, Widow of the late John Hawthorn, Watchmaker of this town, tenders her grateful thanks to the friends of her late husband; and begs to acquaint them and the public, that she will carry on the said Business (having engaged able workmen therein) and hope for the continuance of their favours, which she will at all times studiously endeavour to merit.[27]

Widowhood, however, was usually a more difficult situation. Deprived of a husband's assistance, many women could not continue a family enterprise and instead sought new kinds of work. In the French town of Châteaudun, for example, wives of vineyard owners, who had managed the household side of the family enterprise while their husbands lived, took in sewing and spinning when they died. The wife could not do the heavy work of harvesting the grapes herself. And she could rarely afford to pay hired help. The few opportunities for her to earn money—usually as a seamstress—were poorly paid and were insufficient to keep up the activities of the vineyard.[28] In cities, women who did the most onerous jobs were often widows whose need led them to take any work they could find. Many of these women were unable to support themselves despite their work, for wages were so low. The jobs available to these women—as seamstresses, or unskilled workers—were notoriously poorly paid. Hence it was impossible for women and their families to live on earnings alone. So they often sent their children off to charitable institutions, or to fend for themselves. Widows and orphans made up the bulk of names on charity lists in the seventeenth and eighteenth centuries. In Châteaudun most of the women on the lists of those with no resources were widows. In Le Puy, "17 widows, 12 of them lacemakers, had dependent upon them 49 people. . . . There were a further 32 households of 93 people who were given over to cadging a livelihood: 21 of these were headed by widows (62 people)."[29]

Remarriage was clearly the happiest solution for a widow, since an economic partnership was the best means of survival. Widows and widowers did remarry if they could. One study of the Parisian region found that in the sixteenth, seventeenth, and eighteenth centuries men remarried within a few months or even weeks of their wives' deaths.[30] Among the lower classes, the rates of remarriage were much higher than among the upper classes, who were protected from penury by the money or property specifically designated for widowhood in marriage contracts. Prosperous widows were sometimes prevented from remarrying by children who did not want their inheritance threatened. If she could find a husband, a second marriage for a widow of the popular classes meant a restoration of the household division of labour. If she had a craftshop or some land, a widow might attract a younger man eager to become a master craftsman or a farmer. (As the husband of a master's widow a man was legally entitled to take over the mastership.) But if she had no claim to property or if she had to relinquish those claims because of the difficulty of maintaining the enterprise alone, she would marry a man whose economic situation was considerably worse than her first husband's. In these instances, farm wives, for example, would become agricultural field labourers or, perhaps, spinners.[31]

In most cases, however, widows failed to find new spouses and they had to manage on their own. Widowers more often chose younger, single women as their second wives. A widow's advanced age or the fact that she had children lessened her chances of finding a husband. (Sometimes the price of remarriage was the abandonment of her children, since a prospective husband might be unwilling or unable to contribute to their support. But even this alternative might be preferable to the precarious existence of a widow on her own who might have to abandon her children anyway.) The charity rolls and hospital records of the seventeenth and eighteenth centuries starkly illustrate the plight of a widow with young children or of an elderly widow, desperately struggling and usually failing to earn her own bread. "Small wonder," comments Hufton, "the widow and her brood were common beggars. What other resource had they?"[32]

Although there were fewer of them (they either remarried or simply abandoned their children), widowers too were on the charity lists. Like the widows, these men had great difficulty supporting themselves and their dependent children. Such men and women were eloquent testimony to the fact that the line between survival and starvation, between poverty and destitution, was an extremely thin one. They clearly demonstrate as well that two partners were vital to family survival. The family division of labour reflected an economy based on the contributions of husband and wife. The loss of one partner usually meant the destruction of the family economy. Although the jobs they performed may have differed, the work of husband and wife were equally necessary to the household. It was this partnership of labour that struck one observer in eighteenth-century France:

> In the lowest ranks [of society], in the country and in the cities, men and women together cultivate the earth, raise animals, manufacture cloth and clothing. Together they use their strength and their talents to nourish and serve children, old people, the infirm, the lazy and the weak. . . . No distinction is made between them about who is the boss; both are.[33]

It is not entirely clear that a partnership of labour meant there existed a "rough equality" between husband and wife in all areas of family life.[34] It is clear, however, that the survival of the family depended on the work of both partners. The household division of labour reflected the biological differences between husband and wife. But tasks performed were complementary. The differentiation of work roles was based in part on the fact that women also had to bear children and manage the household, activities which were necessary, too, to the family economy. The family economy reproduced itself as the basic economic unit of production. Children were important as well for the sustenance of aged and dependent parents.

• Married Women's Domestic Activity

The wife's major domestic responsibility was the provision of food for the family. The work of all family members contributed directly or indirectly to subsistence, but wives had a particular responsibility for procuring and preparing food. In a peasant family, "the duties of the mother of the family were overwhelming; they were summed up in one word: food."[35] In the unskilled labourer's home, too, the wife raised chickens, a cow, a pig, or a goat. Her garden supplemented the miserable wages she earned sewing and those her husband made in the fields. Urban wives frequented markets, where they haggled and bargained over the prices of food and other goods. Some also kept small gardens and a few animals at home. Whether she grew food or purchased it— whether, in other words, she was a producer or consumer—the wife's role in providing food served her family. A wife's ability to garden and tend animals, or to bargain and to judge the quality of items for sale, could mean the difference between eating decently and not eating at all. In more desperate circumstances, women earned the family's food by begging for it or by organizing their children to appeal for charity. They supervised the "economy of makeshift," improvising ways of earning money or finding food, and going without food in order to feed their children. One curé in Tours compared such women to "the pious pelican of the *Adoro Te,* who gave her blood to feed her young." Hufton's careful study of the poor in eighteenth-century France has led her to conclude that "the importance of the mother within the family economy was immense; her death or incapacity could cause a family to cross the narrow but extremely meaningful barrier between poverty and destitution."[36]

Food was the most important item in the budgets of most families. Few families had any surplus funds to save or to spend on anything other than basic necessities. A French artisan's family, for example, whose members earned 43 *sols* a day, spent in 1701 approximately 36 *sols* on food: bread, herring, cheese, and cider. Poorer families ate less varied fare. Rural and urban wage earners in eighteenth-century France could spend more than half of their income on bread alone.[37]

The fact that she managed the provision of food gave the wife a certain power within the family. She decided how to spend money, how to allocate most of the family's few resources. She was the acknowledged manager of much of the monetary exchange of the family and her authority in this sphere was unquestioned. Legally, women were subordinate to their husbands. And some were clearly subject to physical mistreatment as well. Recent studies of criminality, violence, and divorce among the lower classes during the seventeenth and eighteenth centuries indicate that wife beating occurred and that women were at a disadvantage in seeking redress in court.

The law tolerated male adultery and punished it in females; and it also tolerated violence by men against their wives.[38] The studies, of course, focus on examples of family breakdown and disharmony which reached the criminal courts. They do not, therefore, adequately describe the day-to-day dealings of husband and wife, nor do they detail *distribution* of power within the household. Yet it is precisely the distribution that is important. Men had the physical and legal power, but women managed the poor family's financial resources. Within the households of the popular classes there seem to have been not just one, but several sources of power. Men did not monopolize all of them. Wives' power in the household stemmed from the fact that they managed household expenditures for food. Among families which spent most of their money on food this meant that the wife decided how to spend most of the family's money.

• Women in Popular Politics

The wife's role in providing food could lead to her involvement in public, political actions. Household concerns and economic issues overlapped in this period; the family was a public as well as a private institution. The politics of the disenfranchised popular classes was a politics of protest. Groups of people gathered to complain about what they considered unjust prices or taxes. And, lacking any other means of influencing the elites who governed them, they often took matters into their own hands, refusing to pay high prices or taxes, and burning tolls and fiscal records. Women and men engaged in these disturbances, the most typical of which was the bread or grain riot.

The bread riot was usually a protest against the adulteration of flour by millers, the hoarding of wheat and bread, or what the crowd considered unjust prices. These demonstrations were often led by women, and women formed a large proportion of their participants. George Rudé and E. P. Thompson have analysed bread-and-grain riots at length. They have shown that the demonstrations were a means used by the popular classes to protest the introduction of laissez-faire capitalist practices. When local authorities reduced their customary attempts to control the price of grain and bread, as was done in England and France in the eighteenth and early nineteenth centuries, prices soared, especially in time of shortage. People rioted in the name of traditional justice, demanding that prices once again be fixed so that the poor, too, might eat. The rioters were not the abject poor but representatives of the industrious classes, peasants and artisans, tradesmen and their wives. Women frequently began the protests as they waited outside a bakery to buy their families' bread or as they arrived at the market and learned that the price of grain had increased, or that no grain was available. Crowds of women and their children, joined by men, then descended on the miller or the baker, seizing his supplies and selling them at a "just price," punishing him by damaging machinery or simply distributing available flour or bread. Thompson cites a number of examples in England.

> In 1693 we learn of a great number of women going to Northampton market, "with knives stuck in their girdles to force corn at their own rates." . . . The mob was raised in Stockton (Durham) in 1740 by a "Lady with a stick and a horn." At Haverfordwest (Pembroke) in 1795 an old-fashioned J. P. who attempted, with the help of his curate, to do battle with the colliers, complained that "the women were putting the Men on, and were perfect furies. . . . " A Birmingham paper described the Snow Hill riots as the work of "a rabble urged on by furious women."[39]

And, in 1800, in protest against an act which forced millers to make only whole meal flour, in Sussex,

A number of women . . . proceeded to Gosden wind-mill, where, abusing the miller for serving them with brown flour, they seized on the cloth which he was then dressing . . . and cut it into a thousand pieces, threatening at the same time to serve all similar utensils he might in future attempt to use in the same manner. The Amazonian leader of this petticoated cavalcade afterwards regaled her associates with a guinea's worth of liquor at the Crab-Tree public house.[40]

Natalie Davis has argued that in the sixteenth century women's preponderant role in these and other disturbances reflected popular views which saw women as inclined to passion and disorder. They were also legally exempt from punishment, hence not responsible to the authorities for their behaviour. She suggests, too, that women, particularly if they were mothers, were understood to have a moral right to speak the truth and denounce injustice.[41] In addition, of course, the bread riots flowed from the concrete and collective experiences of women as they carried out their family role of consumer and food provider. These women were responsible for marketing, and they best knew the consequences for their families of higher prices, of products of inferior quality, and of deprivation. Englishwomen protesting the Brown Bread Act of 1800 said the bread was "disagreeable to the taste . . . utterly incompetent to support them under their daily labour, and . . . productive of bowelly complaints to them and to their children in particular." Yet though the specific issue was particularly compelling for women, the form of protest was the same as that employed by men.[42] The market riot, and the tax riot, grew out of routine assemblies of people going about their everyday business and pursuing their household and community concerns.

• Childbirth and Nurture

The role of food provider was an important aspect of a married woman's productive economic activity and it was also tied to her reproductive role. For it was she who bore and nurtured children, she who clothed and cared for them. Children were the inevitable consequence of marriage; childbearing was an exclusively female activity. Married women expected to spend much of their married lives pregnant or caring for young children. High infant mortality rates and ensuing high fertility meant that at least two-thirds of a wife's married years involved reproductive activity. For women the risks and pain of childbirth, the need to spend some time nursing an infant, the supervision and feeding of children were all part of the definition of marriage.

The activities surrounding childbirth were almost exclusively performed by females. Midwives sometimes assisted at the birth of a child.

These were usually local women who had "inherited" the few skills they had from their own mothers or from another woman in the community. But a midwife's services cost money and often women simply helped one another, with no previous training or experience. Their lack of knowledge contributed to maternal and infant disability and death. An eighteenth-century account details what could occur:

> If we consider their technique . . . we see that they do not hesitate to lop off with a kitchen knife an arm—should the arm appear first in the passage. They . . . attach the mother to a ladder, feet in the air in order to push the child back should the presentation be irregular. If the child emerges buttocks first they use a hook, and they do not hesitate to cut the mother barbarously to facilitate the exit of the child.[43]

The presence of another woman was helpful to a mother for a practical and legal reason also. If the baby died, she could serve as a witness that it had not been deliberately murdered by its mother. In the seventeenth century, in both England and France, male doctors began to take an interest in childbirth. They developed new methods of assistance and regulated the practice of midwifery. Books of instruction were prepared, and investigations of local practices were made. In France, regulation of midwives was partly a consequence of a drive by church officials to increase the custom of baptism. One clergyman, Mgr Rochefoucauld, visited every parish in the diocese of Bourges early in the eighteenth century. He found many women helping one another in childbirth and urged all women to get together and elect one or two "official" midwives, who would be trained and certified by the state and church. In the villages and towns he visited, some women apparently followed his instructions. But the reforms did not change the practice in most regions.[44] Well into the nineteenth century babies were delivered by untrained women. As Hufton has put it, "The actual birth of the child was surrounded by a 'complicity' of females."[45] Childbirth created a bond among women. They not only shared the experience, but also assisted and nursed one another as best they could.

Yet after the birth of a baby, in the list of household priorities the care of children ranked quite low. Work and the provision of food for the family had first claim on a married woman's time. In the craftshop or on the farm, skilled or unskilled, most labour was time-intensive. Men and women spent the day at work, and what little leisure they had was often work-related. Hence in the rural *veillée* people would gather in barns on winter evenings to keep warm, to talk, but also to repair farm tools, to sew, to sort and clean fruit and vegetables. In cities when women were not formally employed or when their paid work was through, they put in long hours spinning, buying and preparing food, or doing laundry. Household tasks were tedious and no labour-saving technology lightened the chores of a working woman. She simply did not have time to spare to devote specifically to children. The demands of the family enterprise or the need to earn wages for the unskilled could not be postponed or put aside to care for children who, in their earliest years, represented only a drain on family resources. Busy mothers in French cities sent their babies out to be nursed by wet nurses if they could afford it. Silk spinners in Lyons, as well as the wives of butchers and bakers, entrusted newborn infants to strangers rather than interrupt their work to care for them, even when this increased the likelihood that the infant would die.[46] Indeed, death rates among children put out to nurse were almost twice as high as among infants nursed by their own mothers. Even infants who remained at home, however, did not receive a great deal of care. The need for special attention for young children simply was not recognized. As Pinchbeck and Hewitt have put it, "Infancy was but a biologically necessary prelude to the sociologically all important business of the adult world."[47]

Philippe Ariès' pathbreaking book on family life demonstrated that ideas about children and the experience of childhood have had an important history. Before about the eighteenth century, children were not central to family life. They were dressed as miniature adults almost as soon as they could walk, and they were included in all aspects of adult activity, work as well as games. While childhood was understood as a stage of dependency, there nonetheless was no special treatment prescribed for children, no notion that their physical and emotional needs might differ from those of adults. New ideas about childhood began to spread among the upper classes by the latter half of the seventeenth century, but Ariès indicates that these did not reach the popular classes until late in the nineteenth century. So in seventeenth- and eighteenth-century working-class and peasant families, children from infancy to about age seven were dependent beings, but their presence in no way altered family priorities. Children were incorporated into ongoing activities, and had only a minimal claim on material resources and parental time.

The position of children in a family was the result of several factors: high infant and child mortality rates and a relative scarcity of both time and material resources. The likelihood was great that a child would die before it reached maturity. Parents' treatment of their children clearly took these odds into account. They often gave successive children the same name, anticipating the fact that only one would survive. Since the life of any child was so fragile, there was no reason to try to limit or prevent pregnancy. Moreover, as two historians have put it:

> The high rates of mortality prevailing amongst children inevitably militated against the individual child being the focus and principal object of parental interest and affection. . . . The precariousness of child life also detracted from the importance of childhood as an age-status. In a society where few lived to grow old, age was of less significance than survival.[48]

The needs of the family economy and not children's individual needs or the needs of "childhood" determined whether or not children remained at home from infancy onward. If they were not put out to a wet nurse, children might be sent into service or apprenticeship at age seven or eight. They were expected to work hard and were sometimes subjected to harsh treatment by their masters and mistresses. (Court records are full of accounts of young servants and apprentices fleeing from cruel employers.) On the other hand, if the family needed their labour, children worked at home.

Children were a family resource only if their labour could be used. In propertied families, of course, one child was also important as an heir. As soon as they were able, young children began to assist their parents in the work of the household. In time of scarcity, those not working might be abandoned or sent away, for they were of limited usefulness to the household as it attempted to balance labour and food.

As family labourers, children were accorded no special treatment. They simply worked as members of the family "team." Their interest and their needs were not differentiated from the family interest. The mother's services to the family were therefore services to them as well. Although she spent time as a childbearer, a mother allocated little time to activities specifically connected with child-rearing. Children were fed and trained to work in the course of the performance of her other responsibilities. Married women allocated their time among three major activities. The organization of production in this period permitted them to integrate their activity, to merge wage work, production for household consumption, and reproduction.

Production was most often located in the household, and individuals for the most part controlled the time and pacing of their work. Production for the market was often an outgrowth of production for household consumption. Although household chores were time-consuming, they did not demand a broad range of skill or expertise. Childbirth interrupted a woman's routine and claimed some of her time, but after a few days, a woman was usually back to work, taking time out only to nurse the infant. Views of children and standards of child care were such that children were either sent away at a young age or were incorporated into adult routines and adult work. Hence it was possible for a married woman to earn wages or to produce for the market, to manage her household, and to bear children. Each activity influenced the others, but no single activity defined her place nor claimed all of her time. In the course of her lifetime, indeed in the course of a year or a day, a married woman balanced several types of activity and performed them all. She was the cornerstone of the family economy.

• Notes

1 Jean-Marie Gouesse, "Parenté, famille et mariage en Normandie aux XVIIᵉ et XVIIIᵉ siècles," *Annales: Économies, Sociétés, Civilisations* 27 (1972): 1146–47.

2 Pierre Deyon, *Amiens, capitale provinciale: Étude sur la société urbaine au 17ᵉ siècle* (Paris and The Hague: Mouton, 1967), 341.

3 Mohammed El Kordi, *Bayeux au XVIIᵉ et XVIIIᵉ siècles* (Paris and The Hague: Mouton, 1970), 257.

4 Deyon, *Amiens*, 254.

5 André Armengaud, *La Famille et l'enfant en France et en Angleterre du XVIᵉ au XVIIIᵉ siècle: Aspects démographiques* (Paris: Société d'édition d'enseignement supérieur, 1975), 75.

6 Emmanuel Le Roy Ladurie, "De la crise ultime à la vraie croissance, 1660–1789" in *L'Age classique des Paysans, 1340–1789* (Paris: Seuil, 1975), 447.

7 Sebastien Le Prestre de Vauban, cited in Michel Morineau, "Budgets populaires en France au XVIIIᵉ siècle," *Revue d'histoire économique et sociale* 50 (1972): 236; see also Jean-Louis Flandrin, *Familles: Parenté, maison, sexualité dans l'ancienne société* (Paris: Hachette, 1976), 113.

8 Ivy Pinchbeck, *Women Workers and the Industrial Revolution, 1750–1850* (New York: G. Routledge, 1930), 203; Alice Clark, *The Working Life of Women in the Seventeenth Century* (London: G. Routledge, 1919), 97; rprt. (London: Frank Cass, 1968).

9 Madeleine Guilbert, *Les Fonctions des femmes dans l'industrie* (Paris and The Hague: Mouton, 1966), 30–31.

10 Maurice Garden, *Lyon et les lyonnais au XVIIIᵉ siècle* (Paris: Les Belles-Lettres, 1970), 324.

11 Clark, *The Working Life of Women*, 61.

12 Pinchbeck, *Women Workers*, 20.

13 Flandrin, *Familles*, 113.

14 R.-J. Bernard, "Peasant Diet in Eighteenth-Century Gevaudan" in *European Diet from Pre-Industrial to Modern Times*, ed. Elborg Forster and Robert Forster (New York: Harper and Row), 30.

15 Pinchbeck, *Women Workers*, 157.

16 Ibid., 127.

17 Clark, *The Working Life of Women*, 156; see also Olwen Hufton, "Women and the Family Economy in Eighteenth Century France," *French Historical Studies* 9 (Spring 1975): 12.

18 Pinchbeck, *Women Workers*, 284–85.

19 Deyon, *Amiens*, 39.

20 Guilbert, *Les Fonctions*, 21–22.

21 Clark, *The Working Life of Women*, 194.

22 Pinchbeck, *Women Workers*, 295.

23 Clark, *The Working Life of Women*, 150, 290; Olwen Hufton, *The Poor of Eighteenth Century France, 1750–1789* (Oxford: Clarenden Press, 1974).

24 Jeffry Kaplow, *The Names of Kings: The Parisian Laboring Poor in the Eighteenth Century* (New York: Basic Books, 1972), 45.

25 Clark, *The Working Life of Women*, 135.

26 Michel Morineau, "Budgets populaires en France au XVIIIᵉ siècle," *Revue d'histoire économique et sociale* 50 (1972): 210, 221.

27 Pinchbeck, *Women Workers*, 284–85.

28 Micheline Baulant, "The Scattered Family: Another Aspect of Seventeenth Century Demography" in *Family and Society*, ed. Robert Forster and Orest Ranum (Baltimore, MD: Johns Hopkins University Press, 1976), 106.

29 Hufton, *The Poor of Eighteenth Century France*, 116.

30 Baulant, "The Scattered Family," 104.

31 Marcel Couturier, *Recherches sur les structures sociales de Châteaudun, 1525–1789* (Paris: S.E.V.P.E.N., 1969), 139.

32 Hufton, *The Poor of Eighteenth Century France*, 117.

33 Cited in ibid., 38.

34 This is the position of Eileen Power, *Medieval Women* (Cambridge: Cambridge University Press, 1975), 34.

35 Le Roy Ladurie, "De la crise ultime," 481.

36 Olwen Hufton, "Women in Revolution, 1789–1796," *Past and Present* 53 (1971): 92.

37 Le Pelletier cited in Morineau, "Budgets populaires en France," 210; Georges Lefebvre, *Études Orléannaises*, vol. 1 (Paris: CNRS, 1962), 218; Hufton, *The Poor of Eighteenth Century France*, 46–48.

38 Roderick Phillips, "Women and Family Breakdown in Eighteenth Century France: Rouen 1780–1800," *Social History* 2 (May 1976): 197–218; Nicole Castan, "La Criminalité familiale dans le ressort du Parlement de Toulouse, 1690–1730" in *Crimes et criminalité en France, XVIIe–XVIIIe siècles*, ed. André Abbiateci et al. (Paris: Colin, 1971); Yves Castan, *Honnêteté et relations sociales en Languedoc (1715–1780)* (Paris: Plon, 1974).

39 E.P. Thompson, "The Moral Economy of the English Crowd in the Eighteenth Century," *Past and Present* 50 (1971): 115. Other work on bread riots can be found cited in "The Food Riot as a Form of Political Conflict in France," ed. Louise A. Tilly, *Journal of Interdisciplinary History* 2 (1971): 23–57.

40 Thompson, "The Moral Economy," 82.

41 Natalie Zemon Davis, "Women on Top" in *Culture and Society in Early Modern Europe*, ed. Natalie Zemon Davis (Stanford, CA: Stanford University Press, 1975).

42 Thompson, "The Moral Economy," 82.

43 Olwen Hufton, "Women and Marriage in Pre-Revolutionary France" (paper, University of Reading, England, 1974), 16.

44 Archives Departementales, Cher, Cote 1, MI 23. This reference was given to us by Nancy Fitch of UCLA. We are grateful for her help.

45 Hufton, "Women and Marriage," 14.

46 Garden, *Lyon*, 324; Hufton, *The Poor of Eighteenth Century France*, 318; George Sussman, "The Wet-Nursing Business in Nineteenth Century France," *French Historical Studies* 9 (Fall 1975): 304–23.

47 Ivy Pinchbeck and Margaret Hewitt, *Children in English Society*, vol. 1 (London: Routledge and Kegan Paul, 1969), 8.

48 Ibid., 7.

THE AMERINDIAN DISCOVERY OF EUROPE: Accounts of First Contact in Anishinabeg Oral Tradition*

D. PETER MacLEOD

This paper deals with one account of first contact between Amerindians and French during the seventeenth century, when a small group of people made a voyage of exploration and discovery, then returned home bearing new and exotic goods and strange tales of their encounter with a new and profoundly alien civilization. It examines how this first contact expanded into a permanent relationship between two peoples.

Narratives of first contact in the seventeenth century are of course very common. Yet, most, in fact almost all, of our narrative sources from this time are found in European documents. They naturally express the perceptions and prejudices of their writers, and thus portray the contact period as a time when Europeans discovered America. In these narratives, Europeans are the actors, and Amerindians the passive objects of discovery.

In this paper, on the other hand, we will be examining an account of the contact period which is based entirely upon Amerindian sources. This version of the history of first contact is of particular interest because the "explorers" and "discoverers" are Amerindians.

*From *Arch Notes* (July/Aug. 1992): 11–15. Reprinted with permission of the publisher. This paper was read at the 11th Annual Ottawa Valley Archaeological Symposium, "'The Mythical Kingdom of the Saguenay': Archaeology of the Contact Period in Eastern Ontario," Ontario Archaeological Society, Ottawa Chapter, 28 March 1992.

More specifically, they were Anishinabeg. The Anishinabeg, or Ojibwa, belong to the Algonquian family nations and, although this is something of a simplification, during the contact period they lived in the upper Great Lakes region, roughly the area east and west of what is now Sault Ste Marie.

We know of their impressions of the contact period through their oral traditions. Those Anishinabeg who first encountered Europeans in the seventeenth century passed on their memories of events to their children. These recollections were subsequently transmitted by tribal elders, from generation to generation, until the mid-nineteenth century. Then, they were preserved in print by a group of Anishinabeg authors. These writers, who had received European-style educations, used the oral tradition as the basis for a series of histories of the Great Lakes region from the perspective of the Anishinabeg.[1] One version of the Anishinabeg traditions of the contact period was obtained by a missionary in the Lake Superior region who interviewed Peter Jones, an Anishinabeg who had become a Methodist minister.[2]

We examine here an account of first contact that tells how one group of Amerindians remembered their nation's first contact with Europeans.

In the oral traditions of the Anishinabeg first contact with Europeans occurred soon after the arrival of the French in the St Lawrence valley. At this time word reached the Anishinabeg of the existence of "some strange persons living on this continent."[3] In some versions these were supernatural "spirits in the form of men,"[4] in others they were just "extraordinary people."[5] The Anishinabeg met in council to decide how to respond to this information and eventually decided to prepare an expedition to travel eastward to seek out the strangers.[6]

This expedition, organized and led by a shaman, departed early in the spring soon after the breakup. The Anishinabeg explorers travelled down the Great Lakes, along the French River, then down the Ottawa. Towards the mouth of the Ottawa River they discovered the first physical evidence of the existence of the newcomers—a hut standing in a clearing, surrounded by the stumps of large trees that had not been cut with stone axes.[7] The trees appeared, in fact, "to have been cut through by the teeth of a colossal beaver."[8] The shaman and his party deduced that this was a campsite of the strange people and were pleased to have found this tangible indication of their reality.

Further down the river the intrepid explorers were further encouraged when they found another clearing and a cabin that had apparently been occupied by the strangers during the previous winter.[9]

Finally, the party reached the St Lawrence River. There they found a settlement occupied by the strangers who greeted them cordially. These people were indeed very odd and, in fact, rather resembled squirrels. This was because, according to the oral tradition, they kept: "their goods and provisions in hollow places, but instead of digging holes in the ground like squirrels, they took the trouble to put several pieces of wood together, in the shape of a hollow tree sometimes, fastened with hoops, where they kept their provisions."[10]

From these strangers the Anishinabeg travellers acquired, either as gifts or through trade, a variety of items, including cloth, metal axes and knives, flint and steel, beads, blankets, and firearms.[11] Then they set out for home.

Immediately following their return a second council was called. The travellers provided a complete account of their successful voyage and displayed the interesting items that they had obtained. These goods aroused considerable interest among the Anishinabeg. Hunters came in from the forest to obtain shavings or chunks of wood that had been cut with an ax. Bolts of cloth were cut into small pieces so that everyone could have one. Splinters of wood and shreds of cloth were attached to poles and sent from village to village spreading the word of the arrival of the strangers.[12]

Now this account of first contact between the Anishinabeg and the French is most notable for the fact that rather than waiting passively to be "discovered" by European "explorers," it is the Anishinabeg who discovered the French and took the initiative in opening commercial relations. Although they were impressed by some aspects of European technology and intrigued by unusual French customs it was the Anishinabeg who remained firmly in control of the situation and the Europeans who responded graciously to Anishinabeg overtures. According to these oral traditions the Anishinabeg remained in control when the first French traders travelled to the Anishinabeg country.

Some of these traders produced accounts which suggest that the Amerindians were most impressed with these heroes. Pierre Radisson, in particular, appears to have believed himself to be rather charismatic and left his readers with little doubt that the mere presence of a pair of Europeans and their goods was enough to dominate the nations of Lake Superior. In his own words:

> We weare Caesars, being nobody to contradict us. We went away free from any burden, whilst those poore miserable [Amerindians] thought themselves happy to carry our Equipage, for the hope that they had that we should give them a brasse ring, or an awle, or a needle. . . . Wee . . . weare lodged in ye cabban of the chiefest captayne. . . . We like not the company of that blind, therefore left him. He wondered at this, but durst not speake, because we were demi-gods.[13]

The Amerindians who compiled the oral traditions were apparently less impressed. Their accounts of this visit is rather different. According to the oral tradition:

> Early the next morning . . . the young men once more noticed the smoke arising from the eastern end of the unfrequented island, and led on by curiosity, they ran thither and found a small log cabin in which they discovered two white men in the last stages of starvation.

The young Ojibways filled with compassion, carefully conveyed them to their village, where, being nourished with great kindness, their lives were preserved.[14]

So in this phase of the contact period the oral traditions contrast the resourceful, confident, and compassionate Native community with rather pathetic commercial travellers who need indigenous help to keep from starving to death in the midst of one of the richest fishing grounds in the Great Lakes region. Inspiring neither respect nor fear the two Europeans were wholly dependent upon the tolerance and charity of the peoples through whose homelands they travel. They were welcomed but valued only for the products that they sold. For they could contribute nothing else to the lives of their Anishinabeg rescuers and hosts except perhaps the entertainment afforded by the presence of such unusual individuals.

Yet these goods were valued and trade between the Anishinabeg and the French flourished. As the trade continued the two groups decided to formalize their relationship with an alliance. The terms of the alliance were amicably negotiated at a meeting near the site of Sault Ste Marie in 1671.

The reports that delegates brought home from this conference reflected widely varying interpretations of the nature of the relationship. Simon Francois Daumont de St Lusson, representing the French crown, produced an account for his superiors that depicted the Anishinabeg as completely subordinate to the French:

> IN THE NAME OF THE MOST HIGH, MOST MIGHTY AND MOST REDOUBTABLE MONARCH LOUIS, THE XIVTH OF THE CHRISTIAN NAME, KING OF FRANCE AND NAVARRE, we take possession of the said place of St Mary of the Falls as well as of Lakes Huron and Superior, the Island of Caientolon [Manitoulin] and of all other Countries, rivers, lakes and tributaries, contiguous and adjacent thereunto, . . . declaring to the aforesaid Nations that henceforward as from this moment they were dependent on his Majesty, subject to be controlled by his laws and to follow his customs.[15]

Yet St Lusson was evidently a good deal more circumspect when negotiating with the Anishinabeg for a less baroque but more convincing account of the same meeting was preserved by the descendants of the member of the Crane Clan that represented the Anishinabeg: "Sieur de Lusson . . . the envoy of the French king, asked, in the name of his nation, for permission to trade in the country, and for free passage to and from their villages all times thereafter. He asked that the fires of the French and Ojibway nations might be made one, and everlasting."[16]

The alliance thus established was remembered by the Anishinabeg as characterized by the close adherence of the French to Anishinabeg customs and forms.[17] This alliance entailed only the granting of access to Anishinabeg villages to French traders and certainly no surrender of Anishinabeg sovereignty or freedom of action.

Yet if the impact of the Europeans themselves was something less than overwhelming their technology was nonetheless very much appreciated for both its novelty and its utility. Of all European products it was firearms that received the most attention in the oral traditions of the contact period. In these traditions, the Anishinabeg portrayed themselves as quickly mastering a new technology and using it to further their goals.

In one narrative the acquisition of firearms by the party that first set forth in search of Europeans makes their return rather more dramatic than they might have intended. For as the returning adventurers came in sight of their homes they used one of their new muskets to fire a shot into the air. According to the oral tradition:

> they arrived at their village on an exceedingly calm day, and the water was in perfect stillness. . . . The Indians saw the canoe coming towards the shore of the village, when suddenly a puff of smoke was seen and a terrific clash of sound followed immediately. All the inhabitants were panic stricken, and thought it was something supernatural approaching the shore.[18]

This confusion was resolved when the explorers landed and the Anishinabeg began to consider the strategic implications of this new military technology. One account of this process is rather charming:

> Intercourse had been opened between the French and the Ottawas and Chippewas on the straits of Mackinac and being supplied with fire arme [sic] and axes by the French people, it occurred to the Ottawas that these implements would be effective in battle.[19]

According to Anishinabeg sources some unsuspecting enemies "thought that they [firearms] were nought but clubs" but were then taken by surprise and suffered a "crushing defeat."[20] In fact, the oral traditions relate a series of victories by the Anishinabeg over enemies who were not equipped with firearms. This continues until these enemies themselves gain access to European weapons.[21] So European weapons, if not Europeans themselves, are portrayed in the oral traditions as quickly becoming a key element in the military balance in the Great Lakes region. A nation possessed of firearms was in a position to dominate its neighbours. Enemies with equal access to European military technology on the other hand met on equal terms.

Yet apart from supplying military technology the French are not portrayed as exercising any great influence on the course of events in the Great Lakes region during the contact period. At the end of the contact period the Anishinabeg remain as firmly in control of their lives as they had been when they first became aware of the existence of Europeans.

This is, on the face of it, a rather ordinary story of how the Anishinabeg hear of a new and mysterious people, of unknown potential, and then follow up and investigate, establish commercial relations and an alliance, and acquire new technology. It is most important for what it reveals of Anishinabeg attitudes regarding first contact. Some historians have successfully used Anishinabeg oral traditions as a guide to actual events.[22] Here we are concerned less with what happened than with how it was perceived and remembered by Amerindians.

The Anishinabeg remembered the contact period as a time when their lives were enhanced and their power increased through contact with Europeans and access to European technology. The French appear in Anishinabeg histories of the contact period, not so much as intrusive aliens, but as a new people who are at first discovered then accepted and incorporated into the world of the Anishinabeg. They are remarkable only for a number of rather peculiar but harmless habits and for their technology. In the beginning this technology had been impressive, even frightening, but it was quickly mastered and exploited by the Anishinabeg. According to Anishinabeg oral traditions Europeans, in the contact period, posed no threat to the Anishinabeg who remained very much in control of their lives and destinies.

First contact had occurred as the result of the actions of the Anishinabeg. Their oral traditions demonstrate very clearly that the Anishinabeg did not remember their ancestors as the passive objects of discovery by Europeans. Instead, they remembered these ancestors as actors who had themselves taken the decision to seek out and contact the Europeans. So for the Anishinabeg the history of the contact period is not the story of the European discovery of America, but of the Amerindian discovery of Europe.

• Notes

[1] D. Peter MacLeod, "The Anishinabeg Point of View: The History of North America to 1800 in Nineteenth-Century Mississauga, Odawa and Ojibwa Historiography," *Canadian Historical Review* 72, 2 (June 1992): 70–75.

[2] J. G. Kohl, *Kitchi-Gami: Wanderings Round Lake Superior* (London: Chapman and Hall, 1860), 244.

[3] Andrew J. Blackbird, *History of the Ottawa and Chippewa Indians of Michigan: A Grammar of their Language, and Personal and Family History of the Author* (Ypsilanti, MI: The Ypsilantian Job Printing House, 1887), 92.

[4] William Whipple Warren, *History of the Ojibways, Based Upon Traditions and Oral Statements* (St Paul, MN: Minnesota Historical Society, 1885), 118; rprt. *History of the Ojibway People* (St Paul, MN: Minnesota Historical Society Press, 1984).

[5] Francis Assikinack, "Social and Warlike Customs of the Odahwah Indians," *The Canadian Journal of Industry, Science, and Art* 3, 16 (July 1858): 307.

[6] Kohl, *Kitchi-Gami*, 245.

[7] Warren, *History of the Ojibways*, 119.

[8] Kohl, *Kitchi-Gami*, 246.

[9] Warren, *History of the Ojibways*, 119.

[10] Assikinack, "Social and Warlike Customs," 307.

[11] Ibid.; Blackbird, *History of the Ottawa and Chippewa Indians*, 93; Warren, *History of the Ojibways*, 119.

12 Blackbird, *History of the Ottawa and Chippewa Indians*, 93; Kohl, *Kitchi-Gami*, 247; Warren, *History of the Ojibways*, 119–20.

13 Pierre Esprit Radisson, *Voyages of Peter Esprit Radisson, Being an Account of his Travels and Experiences Among the North American Indians, from 1652 to 1684*, ed. Gideon D. Scull (Boston: Prince Society Publications, 1885), 200–201; rprt. (New York: Peter Smith, 1943).

14 Warren, *History of the Ojibways*, 122; Grace Lee Nute, *Caesars of the Wilderness: Medard Chouart, Sieur des Groseilliers and Pierre Esprit Radisson, 1618–1710* (New York: D. Appleton-Century, 1943), 62n; rprt. (St Paul, MN: Minnesota Historical Society Press, 1978).

15 E.B. O'Callaghan, *Documents Relative to the Colonial History of the State of New York: Procured in Holland, England, and France, by John Romeym Brodhead, esq., Agent Under and by Virtue of an Act of the Legislature Entitled "An Act to Appoint an Agent to Procure and Transcribe Documents in Europe Relative to the Colonial History of the State,"* vol. 9 (Albany, NY: Weed, Parson, and Company, 1855), 803–4.

16 Warren, *History of the Ojibways*, 131.

17 Ibid., 132, 135.

18 Blackbird, *History of the Ottawa and Chippewa Indians*, 93.

19 Ibid.

20 Ibid.

21 Warren, *History of the Ojibways*, 120, 124, 126, 148, 223.

22 W.J. Eccles, "Sovereignty Association, 1500–1783," *Canadian Historical Review* 65, 4 (Dec. 1984): 475–510; Leroy V. Eid, "The Ojibwa-Iroquois War: The War the Five Nations Did Not Win," *Ethnohistory* 26, 4 (Fall 1979): 297–324; Peter S. Schmalz, "The Role of the Ojibwa in the Conquest of Southern Ontario, 1650–1701," *Ontario History* 76, 4 (Dec. 1984): 327–28.

THE DESTRUCTION
OF HURONIA*

GEORGES E. SIOUI

In recent decades, a certain number of researchers have been critically examining George T. Hunt's theory that the Iroquois waged war for economic reasons. For Bruce G. Trigger, there is both a cultural and an economic dimension to the matter: he maintains that because the Five Nations did not possess the entrepreneurial tradition of the Wendat, they tried to increase their trading power by acquiring new hunting territories rather than trade routes.

Most recent studies, however, are closer to the older, so-called "cultural" theory advanced in the writings of Francis Parkman, which attributed the wars waged by the Iroquois on so many other Amerindians to an enmity that, under certain favourable conditions (for example, the European invasion), would lead to the annihilation of one party.

In addition, revision of the earliest Amerindian demographic data has led other investigators to explain the nature of these conflicts differently. One of these, Wichita University historian Karl H. Schlesier, in a discussion of the "legend" of Amerindian middlemen, says that "the Iroquois never attempted to become middlemen in the fur trade: neither did other Indian tribes, including the Huron or Ottawa. They all were touched by far more powerful forces than European trade goods."[1] He explains that "smallpox (the main epidemic disease brought from the Old World) emerges as the most significant among those forces. Much of the historical and ethnological literature before and after Hunt propounds biases which not only do injustice to the Iroquois, but prevent a deeper understanding

*From *For an Amerindian Autohistory*, trans. Sheila Fischman (Montreal: McGill-Queen's University Press, 1992), 39–60. Reprinted with permission of the publisher.

of the historical truth."[2] Most authors still present what we call "the myth of economic war," attributing to Native peoples on the brink of disaster the motives, interests, and intentions of people leading a normal existence. In fact, all Amerindians were waging desperate cultural war on an invader whose pathogenic allies made his very presence a disaster.

• Interpreting the Facts According to Autohistory

Louis Hall Karaniaktajeh, a Mohawk artist and philosopher from Kahnawake, sums up the Amerindian's feelings about history with bittersweet humour: "Twistory," he says, "is written in such a way that you think that they [the colonizers] are heroes. They're out there plundering Indian land and looting, but it's their right, their God-given right . . . and the Indians are not supposed to do anything about it, they're supposed to like it; they're supposed to even help the writers of these history books to plunder them."[3]

Of all Amerindians, the Iroquois are those who have least wanted "to help" the Europeans to "plunder" them, and for that very reason they spread terror and animosity among the first generations of Europeans to establish themselves in northeastern North America.

"The good Hurons were destroyed by the wicked Iroquois," we were led to believe from the time we were old enough to absorb prejudices, in order to distract an entire society from the real story of the grabbing of Amerindian land.

Always bearing in mind that microbes, not men, determined this continent's history, we shall use data provided by our Amerindian autohistorical analysis to try to elucidate the circumstances that enabled Europeans to destroy the order Amerindians had established for countless generations.

In 1492, the Wendat were situated geopolitically at the centre of a very important society of Amerindian nations. Wendake (the Wendat country) was the heartland that was the origin and focus of the main trade networks linking this vast extended family of societies, whose spirit perfectly reflected the Amerindian's social ideal: interdependence and redistribution around the common circle.

We may assume that communications networks in the original Amerindian world, free of national boundaries, while they were far less rapid than today's, were functional and reliable, and that news about the Spanish military and epidemiological devastations reached the northern peoples after a few years at most.

In 1498, the Italian John Cabot reported having visited Nova Scotia and Labrador, while in 1501 the Portuguese Gaspar Corte-Real captured fifty-seven Amerindians, probably Beothuks. When Jacques Cartier arrived in 1534, the Amerindians had already suffered from epidemic diseases brought by Europeans.

Some recent opinions, even when well-supported, do not sufficiently recognize the terrifying consequences for Amerindians of the Europeans' arrival. In "European Contact and Indian Depopulation in the Northeast: The Timing of the First Epidemics," Dean Snow and Kim M. Lanphear attempt to invalidate the hypothesis put forward by Henry F. Dobyns in *Their Number Become Thinned,* where he postulates on pandemics in the northeast during the sixteenth century. Moreover, they also appear to dismiss three fundamental considerations:

- First, while inland peoples such as the Mohawk—living in what is now the state of New York—could defend themselves against epidemics, coastal nations such as the St Lawrence Wendat-Iroquois, the Mi'kmaq, and the Montagnais, who inevitably came into contact with European crews, could not. In fact, while no ship went up the St Lawrence to Stadacona (now Quebec) before Jacques Cartier, a good number certainly did so during the rest of the sixteenth century.

- Secondly, the epidemic that ravaged Stadacona during the winter of 1535–36 (and that may well have had more than the fifty victims, Cartier reports) was undoubtedly not the only one that occurred over the 115 years between the arrival of the first ships in the Gulf of St Lawrence around 1500 and the first "official" epidemic of 1616.

- Thirdly, both the very nature of the culture and way of life of these Amerindian societies, that is, their close union and the uniformity of their cosmo-political conception, encouraged the spread of contagious diseases.

Once these elements are considered, it is likely that the St Lawrence Wendat-Iroquois disappeared in the sixteenth century because of the epidemics that raged in the St Lawrence valley before the beginning of the seventeenth century.

In other words, depopulation of the northern part of North America had already begun in the sixteenth century, probably spreading panic through Amerindian society at large. Taioagny and Domagaya, the two sons of Donnacona, the "seigneur of Canada," made a forced journey to France in 1534, returning in 1535. Cartier thought that he could use them to disorganize the Amerindian country, but as it turned out they bore him a barely concealed suspicion. Better than anyone, these chief's sons were aware of the danger. Cartier left after having defied the Amerindian order, spurned their advice (which cost the lives of twenty-five members of his crew who, unprepared for the Canadian climate, died of scurvy at the beginning of winter), and captured the father of the two young men along with nine other members of their family, including at least one young girl.

While it is certain that the bulk of pre-contact Amerindian society did not live in perfect, constant harmony, archaeology informs us that those Amerindians did not experience significant conflicts, likely because they had the ideological and social means to maintain relative peace among themselves. "In every case," writes archaeologist James A. Tuck, "village and tribal movements A.D. 1000–1500 are devoid of drastic population shifts, conquests and the annihilation of whole prehistoric populations."[4]

It is very likely that the Wendat-Iroquois migrated north from southern countries, taking root fairly recently at the heart of the Algonquian world. Their way of life—they were farmers and traders with a remarkable gift for political organization—had enabled them, long before the Europeans arrived, to establish particularly harmonious relations with other nations. History and even prehistory prove beyond a doubt that the vast majority of the Algonquian nations had long since assigned the Wendat confederation a key role in the political, commercial, cultural, and religious sectors of a vast and strategically located territory.

It appears that at the time of European contact, the confederacy of the Five Nations Iroquois was the only one not yet integrated into this extensive trading system. Ironically, the people who originally were probably the least numerous and geopolitically the most marginal were the only ones able to resist the invader and provide a refuge for the survivors of previously stronger nations. In that way, the ideology common to all aboriginal nations was able to survive.

There is every reason to believe that the decimated residents of Stadacona, led to Wendake by Donnacona's descendants, as revealed by archaeology[5]—tried once they were resettled there to persuade the Wendats to form a great league of nations. It is conceivable that the central idea was open resistance to the pale and dangerous visitors and that, frustrated at having been ignored, a certain "prophet" named Deganawidah, a member of that ideological clan, had taken his message to the Iroquois nations. The latter, located outside the great Wendat trading network and thus spared the task of facing the Europeans head-on, were more receptive to the message.

According to Iroquois tradition, it was a Wendat—one "whose people had not wanted to listen to him"—who disclosed the prophetic message about the need to form the Iroquois league.

Most of the speculations by Elizabeth Tooker as to when the Iroquois confederacy was founded place it around 1540 to 1590, a period that corresponds fairly closely to the Wendat-Iroquoian exodus to Huronia.

In any case, the Wendat were traditionally considered as standard-bearers for the Amerindian ideology which claims that, if the world is to be and to remain what it is, it must be founded on communication and exchange between humans of all origins. The vision of a prophet of the resistance, no matter how enlightened, can never take ascendancy over the ideology of a society of nations that groups together hundreds of thousands of individuals, one that has always been nurtured at the inspiring, appeasing sources of the great circle.

In 1894, the historian J.N.B. Hewitt pointed out that "no league or confederation of peoples was perhaps ever formed without a sufficient motive in the nature of outside pressure."[6] We may assume that the Wendat, because of the refugees they took in by virtue of a clear cultural kinship (for example, the Stadaconans), or adopted, apparently by force (as seems to have been the case for at least part of the Hochelagans[7]), felt the need to reform their confederacy before the Five Nations Iroquois did, and this led to the consolidation of the Iroquois confederacy. As the Wendat were chiefs of the great Amerindian society of the northeast, they inevitably devised a union that was centred on trade. Naturally there was a place in it for the French and other Europeans, despite the disastrous consequences of their coming: it lasted about half a century, if we bear in mind that a pandemic in 1520 to 1524 had "almost certainly reached the Seneca"[8] and other neighbours of the Wendat long before its European carriers arrived, and that yet another, between 1564 and 1570, had made them abandon some of their villages.

The Iroquois, realizing the extent of the disaster, opted for defence. By allying themselves against the French-Amerindian force, they now declared their dissidence from prehistoric political and trading organization. The Iroquois made the difficult but inevitable decision to embark upon a war they knew would be very long and destructive, and whose logic was utterly foreign to Amerindian thinking.

According to Amerindian cultural logic, the Iroquois were the northeastern nations best situated to resist the invasion, although they had virtually no chance of succeeding. Consequently, the Iroquois nations were no longer "the worst of all savages" or "the Indians of Indians" as they have so often been called. Instead, they were an extremely valorous people who, to enable the Amerindian race to survive, had to fight against the European powers, forcibly adopting nations that were already gravely decimated. For the Iroquois, the goal of this war was to extinguish the power of strangers in the way one extinguishes a raging fire. With extraordinary strength of character, they had to eliminate part of their own race so as to save it.

To explain the Iroquois' political offensive in relation to the French, historian John A. Dickinson quotes ethnohistorian Bruce G. Trigger: "The majority of Huron were killed or captured as a result of the general warfare that was going on between the Mohawk and the French; however, the emphasis that the Mohawk placed on capturing Huron prisoners reflected their long-term ambition to incorporate all of the Huron who had come to Quebec into their own society or, failing this, to kill them." "Thus," Dickinson observes, "the French would be deprived of allies."[9] He concludes by stating that when the Iroquois attacked Long Sault, they did not intend to destroy the colony by massacring the settlers, but to paralyze it by abducting most of the remaining Huron warriors—mercenaries in the service of New France. "If the [Iroquois] army went up the Ottawa River," Dickinson explains,

> it is because their goal was to take Annaotaha [the chief of the Hurons] and his companions; Dollard's band was completely out-

side the Iroquois' preoccupations. For seven years, the Iroquois had been trying by every means possible to destroy [that is, to take away from the French] the whole Huron colony and here, at long last, was the chance to do it. Marie de l'Incarnation was amazed that the enemy's army was content with "so few people," but the reason is that this small group was the quarry the Iroquois had been looking for. For the Iroquois, the meaning of Long Sault was not the defeat of the seventeen Frenchmen, but the annihilation of the remaining Huron warriors. For them, it was a great victory.[10]

In the final analysis, both the Wendat and the Iroquois realized that they could not unite, because of the age-old order of the country. The Wendat noted impassively that the end was rapidly approaching. They would never accept the numerous peace overtures by their Iroquois cousins, nor would they make the choice—which seemed to the Jesuits so logical—of eliminating those priests who "established themselves in the heart of the Country [Wendake] to better bring about its ruin."[11] The Wendat, like any people, were ineluctably caught in the logic of their civilization. They had to trade until the end, like beavers who will get caught in traps until they are extinct: they were victims of their own nature.

The historiographic concept of "the destruction of Huronia by the Iroquois" is an axiom in the traditional history of the northeast that justifies North American sociopolitical attitudes. In the light of Amerindian autohistory, this cliché becomes an example of the manipulation of history, absolving Europe (particularly France) of the destruction of the most politically significant aboriginal people north of Mexico, a people who best represented the Amerindian interethnic fabric in northeastern North America. This is a spectacular historic fraud: responsibility for the sociodemographic calamity in the northeast is assigned not to microbes, but to the Iroquois.

Karl H. Schlesier refers us to the Jesuits' pitiful descriptions of the Wendat and other nations in 1640, after several successive epidemics:

> Disease, war and famine are the three scourges with which God has been pleased to smite our Neophytes since they have commenced to adore him, and to submit to his Laws. . . . All these events have so greatly thinned the number of our Savages that, where eight years ago one could see eighty or a hundred cabins, barely five or six now can be seen; a Captain, who then had eight hundred warriors under his command, now has not more than thirty or forty; instead of fleets of three or four hundred canoes, we see now but twenty or thirty. And the Pitiful part of it is, that these remnants of Nations consist almost entirely of Women. [12]

Later, Schlesier asks, "Where after these tremendous losses, are the men supposed to have come from to fight continuous wars during this period? . . . These wars sprung only from the imagination of scholars."[13]

• Traditional Amerindian Values of the Wendat-Iroquois in Lafitau's Time

Our twofold aim here is an historical rehabilitation of the Iroquois, and a demonstration of their profound adherence to the Amerindian value system. Even if the defensive action of the Five Nations towards the Europeans—particularly the French—was basically a fight to the finish between two civilizations, the Iroquois continued to live according to essential Amerindian values. From what we know of the present vitality of Amerindian social consciousness, we can study a particularly revealing description of Iroquois (and, in secondary fashion, Wendat) cultural consciousness at the beginning of the eighteenth century, left by the Jesuit Joseph-François Lafitau.

This missionary, who lived among the Wendat and then among the Iroquois, knew these peoples intimately. His *Customs of the American Indians* is an unusually valuable account of their philosophy and spirituality.

Lafitau, whose church was facing a rise in religious skepticism, drew from the Amerindian peoples a series of arguments to support a thesis of many contemporary theologians concerning the innate existence of a religious sense in man. For thinkers of the time, the "sauvages amériquains" were "the humans who show themselves in the most simple form in which they can be conceived to exist."

To an informed modern reader, Lafitau's work may seem to go beyond his original objective. In reality, he contributed to alleviating the Amerindians' crushing historical burden and was one of the rare individuals who conceded them any right to survival. Moreover, Lafitau's work provides a solid mass of arguments and evidence that help restore dignity to the people descended from the "savage" nations Lafitau describes. Even more, he enables modern men and women to acquire or rediscover respect and a salutary admiration for human nature.

"Deganawidah [founder of the league of the Iroquois] brought a message of peace, say the contemporary Iroquois. . . . He devised the means of lifting up men's minds with the condolence ritual [addressing the emotions in order to attain reason], which provided for paying presents to the aggrieved. The same ceremony on a broader scale took former enemies into a network of alliances."[14]

The contemporary Seneca historian John Mohawk helps us penetrate deeper inside Iroquois thinking about their confederacy. He stresses the importance in Iroquois society of the development of oratorical art, since for them as for all Amerindians, no one has arbitrary power over any other person. Hence the importance of the art of persuasion. For John Mohawk, the "greatness" of the confederacy of the Five Nations comes from its high development of this art. He adds:

This greatness [of the oratorical art] is the very idea of the Hodenosaunee: all human beings possess the power of rational thought; all human beings can think; all human beings have the same kinds of needs; all human beings want what is good for society; all human beings want Peace. . . . Out of that idea will come the power . . . that will make the people of the Five Nations among the most influential thinkers in the history of human thought. . . . The basic fundamental truth contained in that idea is that so long as we believe that everybody in the world has the power to think rationally, we can negotiate with them to a position of Peace.[15]

Almost three centuries ago, Lafitau, like all contemporary observers of Amerindian society, emphasized how the Wendat and the Iroquois kept order in their councils. He was impressed by their confidence (which they still possess today) in the human's capacity for rational thought, provided that society respected individuality. "In general, we may say that they are more patient than we in examining all the consequences and results of a matter. They listen to one another more quietly, show more deference and courtesy towards people who express opinions opposed to theirs, not knowing what it is to cut a speaker off short, still less to dispute heatedly: they have more coolness, less passion, at least to all appearances, and bear themselves with more zeal for the public welfare."[16]

Faced with the Amerindians' choice of gentle persuasion in their relations with their fellows, as opposed to the coercive modes of European societies, Lafitau experienced the same sense of wonder as European chroniclers of all times:

While the petty chiefs of the monarchical states have themselves borne on their subjects' shoulders and have many duties paid them, they have neither distinctive mark, nor crown nor sceptre nor consular axes to differentiate them from the common people. Their power does not appear to have any trace of absolutism. It seems that they have no means of coercion to command obedience in case of resistance. They are obeyed, however, and command with authority; their commands, given as requests, and the obedience paid them, appear entirely free. . . . Good order is kept by this means; and in the execution of things, there is found a mutual adaptation of chiefs and members of society and a hierarchy such as could be desired in the best regulated state.[17]

By observing some of the social traits noted by Lafitau, we can better understand how the integrity of the human person, as well as the quality of relations between humans, are at the heart of Amerindian social ideology. He frequently contrasts Amerindian solidarity with the European competitive spirit:

They should . . . be done this justice, that among themselves, they spare each other more than Europeans do. They regard, with reason, as something barbarous and ferocious, the brutality of duels and the ease of mutual destruction introduced by a point of honour badly misunderstood. . . . They are no less astonished by the indifference of the Europeans for their fellow countrymen, by the slight attention paid by them to the death of their compatriots killed by their enemies.[18]

Lafitau openly admires the strength of the Amerindian social fabric, source of the individual's keen respect for the private life of others. This helps explain the gift-giving mechanisms for preventing and settling conflicts.

• The Amerindian Conflict

In Lafitau's day, Amerindian societies, especially the Iroquois and Wendat, were in profound political disarray because of the European presence. In this stormy climate, the missionary was much better able to portray the Amerindian character than if the time had been peaceful. Much has been said about Amerindian cruelty and torture. As the Iroquois of that period were the prototype of the "cruel American savage," they contributed, in spite of themselves, to the elaboration of that image, one that was later applied to all Amerindians. Using Lafitau's descriptions and observations, we will now present a brief analysis of this historiographical "knot."

In the Amerindian ideological universe, "war for the sake of war," to use Lafitau's expression, does not exist. War—if the term can even be used with reference to Amerindian societies—is always the result of disruption of the political order, provoked by an enemy agent. The Iroquois, like all Amerindians, resigned themselves to war while being fully aware of its gravity: "The Council," Lafitau reports, "decides on war only after considering the plan for a long time and weighing with mature consideration all the factors pro and con."[19]

Because Amerindians saw their compatriots as the ultimate wealth, war assumed a meaning for them that compels admiration. In the conflict between Amerindians and Euroamericans, the Iroquois, as the most engaged Native people, were the ones who most often went to war, and consequently they lost the largest number of members. It was logical, then, for these nations to try to capture replacements for those who had been killed or seized; thus they did not simply indulge in murderous expeditions, as we are often led to believe. "The loss of *a single person*," Lafitau writes, "is a great one, but one which must necessarily be repaired by replacing the person missing with one or many others, according to the importance of him who is to be replaced."[20]

On this matter, Lafitau shows us how, in a natural and matriarchal society, the women recognized as sages (matriarchs) have supreme control over even the nation's military affairs. When there is a loss of one or many persons, it is not up to the members of the same household [the longhouse, which among the Wendat and Iroquois could contain as many as two hundred people] to repair this loss, but to all those men who have marriage links with that house, or their *Athonni,* as they say; and in that fact, resides the advantage of having many men born in it. For these men, although isolated at home and limited to themselves, marry into different lodges. The children born of these different marriages become obligated to their fathers' lodge, to which they are strangers, and contract the obligation of replacing them; in this way the "matron" (matriarch) who has the principal authority in this household, can force these children to go to war if it seems best to her, or keep them at home if they have undertaken a war displeasing to her.

When, then, this "matron" judges it time to raise up the tree again, or to lay again on the mat someone of her family whom death has taken away from her, she addresses herself to some one of those who have their *Athonni* at her home and who she believes is most capable of executing her commission. She speaks to him by a wampum belt, explaining her intention of engaging him to form a war party. This is soon done.[21]

When it is time to set out and capture replacements, the leader of the expedition (still according to Lafitau) makes a public prayer, accompanied by all his relatives, who have dressed and adorned themselves in their best attire, as is done at the farewell feast for one who is about to die—for going to war is going towards death. All those who remain in the village hasten to obtain a relic from those who are leaving, and to give them some present. "Together," Lafitau tells us, "they exchange robes, coverings, or whatever other goods they may have. A typical warrior, before leaving the village, is despoiled more than twenty or thirty times."[22]

For Amerindians, no success or victory is great enough to make them forget, even for a moment, the value of one lost human life. In their society, the cult of the human, or of being (as opposed to the cult of having), assumes its full force and meaning. Lafitau is astonished at their respect for the dead:

> They have such respect for each other that, however complete may be their victory, and whatever advantage they may have gained from it, the first sentiment which they show is that of grief for those of their people whom they have lost. All the village has to participate in it. The good news of the success is told only after the dead have been given the first regrets which are their due. . . . The women do the same thing in regard to the men who have gone hunting or to war. For, at the moment of their return, they go to wait for them on the shore. And in place of showing (them) the joy which they must feel at seeing them arrive in good health, they begin by weeping for those of their relatives who died in the village during their absence.[23]

• The Treatment of Captives

Of all the Amerindians, the Iroquois are known for the intensity of their defence against the crushing European invasion. For two centuries, from 1500 to 1700, they had to concentrate their strength in order to maintain the existence of a union of Amerindian nations. In response to the formidable onslaught of the epidemics, to say nothing of the European ideological assault, they developed a policy of adoption: as stated earlier, their "wars against the Wendat and their allies aimed above all at restoring their own numbers.

In Native societies in general, war, "established by the need to protect oneself from injustice, to repulse force by force and to right the injuries which the tribes might have received from each other, [is] also sanctified by religion."[24] Yet for the Amerindians, war, as made known to them by the white man, never became the exercise of destruction and extermination it represents for other cultures. In 1609, Champlain was indignant at the behaviour of the Wendat and Montagnais, who cried victory when the Mohawk fled after a French musket-shot cost them three of their chiefs. Champlain did not comprehend why his Amerindian allies did not set out in pursuit of the Iroquois, to exterminate them to the last man; he claimed that the Wendat and Montagnais were "cowards" who "know nothing about making war."

But it is the Amerindians, not the Europeans, who have been given the title of champions of cruelty in the history books. This view is wrong. Amerindians never inflicted torture on anyone because of religious or political ideas. During the two hundred years of the crusades, millions of people were killed because they did not share the crusaders' beliefs. To establish a point of comparison with America, the Dominican bishop Bartolomé de Las Casas wrote in 1552: "We furnish as a very sure and true number, that during the said forty years (1492–1532), have died because of the said tyranny and infernal works of the Christians, unjustly and in a tyrannical manner, more than 12 million persons, men, women, and children, and I believe, trusting that I do not err that it was, in reality, more than 15 million."[25]

As for the Amerindians, if one of their warriors took a human life he did so only to gain respect for his nation, following a process always marked by the same humanity that characterizes his social vision of the great circle. Lafitau, in fact, recognized the rationality of the Amerindians' behaviour: "If they did not return the same treatment to those who treat them inhumanly, they would become their dupes, and their moderation would only serve to harden their enemies. The gentlest people are forced to put aside their natural gentleness when they see that it becomes a pretext for barbarous neighbours to become prouder and more intractable."[26]

The Iroquois themselves—and Lafitau supports them—deny being crueler than any other nation, white or Amerindian. Lafitau wrote: "The Iroquois, so fearsome to the French on account of the great number[27] of those they caused to perish in these frightful tortures, have gained an even worse reputation with us than all the other tribes. . . . To hear the Iroquois speak, however, they claim to be less cruel than the others and treat the captives thus only by reprisal."[28]

Their treatment of captives shows the very humane nature of the Iroquois people, even in the midst of the catastrophe represented by European interference in Amerindian society.

Returning from a capture expedition, those who had captives to offer clans who needed them gave them away ceremonially. "The warriors who give a slave [more correctly, a captive]," Lafitau recounts, "award him with their belt which has served as a symbol of his engagement in their enterprise, or serves them as parole, to say that they have fulfilled their obligation."[29]

Among the Iroquois in particular, it was very unusual for prisoners—who had been captured with such difficulty, and whose lives were eminently precious to a nation so frequently decimated—to be condemned to torture by fire. Indeed, their fate would have stirred the envy of more than one hostage of a "civilized" country. Lafitau tells us that, after being handed over, "the captives are led to the lodges to which they have been given and introduced. . . . There, they are immediately given something to eat. The people of this household, however, their relatives and friends, are still weeping for the dead whom these captives replace, as if they were losing them entirely, and in this ceremony shed genuine tears to honour the memory of those persons, to whom the sight of these captives recalls a bitter recollection, renewing their grief in their loss."[30]

The adoption was then formally carried out, in a way that shows that the Amerindian social ideal is based and focussed on maintaining and developing relations between humans, as well as on faith in the capacity for reasoning of all humans, so long as their dignity is recognized. Lafitau observes:

> Among the Iroquois and Huron, it [the condition of "slave"] is gentler in proportion as that of those thrown into the fire is more cruel. The moment that he enters the lodge to which he is given and where he is to be kept, his bonds are untied. . . . He is washed with warm water to erase the colours with which his face was painted and he is dressed properly. Then he receives visits from relatives and friends of the family into which he is entering. A short time afterwards a feast is made for all the village to give him the name of the person whom he is resurrecting. The friends and allies of the dead man also give a feast to do him honour: and from that moment, he enters upon all his rights. If the captive is a girl, given to a household where there is nobody of her sex in a position to sustain the lineage, it is good fortune for this household and for her. All the hope of the family is placed in this captive who becomes the mistress of this family and the branches dependent on it. If the captive is a man who requickens an Ancient, a man of consequence, he becomes important himself and has authority in the village if he can sustain by his own personal merit the name which he takes.[31]

• Cruelty

The severity of Amerindian punishment should not be seen as cruelty, madness, or blindness. On the contrary, it was compassionate, logical, and rational, and was dictated by the Amerindian's unshakeable morality, modelled on nature herself.

If we avoid sentimentality, cruelty can be evoked only in the context of aggression and domination, and not self-defence. It is therefore absurd—and unfair—to talk about the cruelty of persons who are only defending themselves, for such cruelty is a legitimate and noble act of physical self-protection, as well as an equally noble effort to safeguard the honour which has been imperilled by the assailant's deed. Cruelty is therefore an argument to justify aggression, which is itself linked to a desire for domination or, in other words, destruction, partial or total.

Among Amerindians, human sacrifice did not have the character of social diversion it had for the Romans. Even less did it represent a punitive act that was religious or political in nature. Torture was, indeed, intended to be a way of killing the war itself; to achieve this, harshness was the best guarantee of success. By aiming violently at the actual enemy, it imposed respect and restraint, and so can be considered a more humane response to violence than are the conventional means used by so-called civilized societies.

In 1626, in view of the difficulties presented by the conversion of Natives, Father Joseph Le Caron warned the young priests whose ambition was to die as martyrs in Canada: "The general opinion [of Amerindians] is that one must not contradict any one, but leave each one have his own thinking. There is, here, no hope of suffering martyrdom: the Savages do not put Christians to death for matters of religion; they leave every one to his belief."[32]

The cruelty of the Amerindian was simply political. Once again, Lafitau helps us penetrate to the core of Amerindian philosophy through a description of the scene preceding the torture of an enemy by the Iroquois. "From the appearance of everyone assembled around a wretch who is going to end his days in the most horrible torment, we should guess that there is no question of such a bloody tragedy as is about to take place before their eyes. All exhibit the greatest calm in the world. They are seated or lying on mats as they are in the councils. Each one talks loudly with his neighbour, lights his pipe and smokes with the most marvellous tranquillity."[33]

Among Amerindians, the sacrifice for political reasons of a human being was devoid of hatred or sadism. It was a considered, rational, and necessary act. The person to be tortured was fully aware of this and did not try to elude his fate. "In the intervals in which they are left in repose," reports Lafitau, "they talk coldly of different matters, of news, of what is happening in their country, or they inform themselves calmly of the customs of those who are busy burning them."[34]

The Amerindians' well-known heroic steadfastness under torture results from an unshakeable faith in their moral and spiritual values. Lafitau, like all missionaries, admires them for that: "This heroism is real and the result of great and noble courage. What we have admired in the martyrs of the primitive church which was, in them, the result of grace and a miracle, is natural to these people and the result of the strength of their spirit. The Savages, as I have already shown, seem to prepare for this event from the tenderest age."[35]

Just as victims showed great dignity and courage, so did those who had to sacrifice them show their compassion, proving once more the centrality of the human being in the Amerindian social vision: "When a captive is burned among the Iroquois," Lafitau notes, "there are few who do not pity him and say that he is worthy of compassion. Many . . . have not the courage to be present at his execution. . . . Some . . . give him relief when he asks for something."[36]

• Cannibalism

The French philosopher Michel de Montaigne claimed that "there is nothing barbarous or savage in that nation [Amerindians], from what I have been told, except that each man calls barbarism, whatever is not his own practice; for indeed it seems we have no other test of truth and reason than the example and pattern of opinions and customs of the country we live in."[37]

The notion of cannibalism as practised by "primitive" cultures is a product of the racist thinking of so-called civilized societies. In a society where the human being was at the centre, how did one dispose of the body of the individual who had to be tortured? How was the dignity of the human race to be preserved?

We know that evoking the Amerindians' bloody cruelty was a powerful means used by the colonial (mainly religious) authorities to attract the favour, sympathy, and financial support of their country's upper classes. Aside from this self-seeking attitude, some sources, particularly oral accounts, indicate that torture and its corollary, cannibalism, never had the importance attributed to them. Besides, our autohistorical study of Amerindian philosophy has provided ample evidence to destroy this fable.

One fact is certain, however, and it deserves the greatest respect: Amerindians did sometimes consume one or several parts (for example, the heart) of the body of a prisoner who died a particularly courageous death. The Amerindian gesture of consuming human flesh was as consistent with their conception of the great circle as was their proverbial generosity. When they had to defend themselves against their fellow humans, they did not like to kill instantaneously or massively as is done with mechanical weapons. They preferred to glorify their captive enemies in death by giving them the chance to die courageously. The remains of a life thus ennobled until death and in death could not be simply thrown away as garbage; they deserved to be eaten. Amerindians had to treat with honour the flesh of those whose lives they had to take. They consumed it because they thought they must: they had been required to destroy persons who, deep down, they admired and loved because they were brothers whose hearts were filled with love, trust, and veneration for their Creator, and thus for their fellow human beings.

• Morality

In his *Customs of the American Indians,* Lafitau compares Amerindian morality favourably with European. He maintains that Amerindian moral force invariably diminished upon contact with whites. He talks about the northern nomads as being "more distant peoples, who are fortunate enough not to know us [Europeans]."[38]

Amerindians practised to a high degree those individual and social virtues known as Christian. According to Lafitau, they were charitable: "If a household of famished people meets another whose provisions are not entirely exhausted yet, the latter share with the newly-arrived the little food which they have left, without waiting to be asked, although in so doing, they are left exposed to the same danger of perishing as those whom they are helping at their expense, with such humanity and nobility of soul. In Europe under similar circumstances, we would find little disposition to such noble and magnanimous generosity."[39]

Similarly, their courtesy to visitors should be edifying to people of any culture: "Whoever enters their homes is well received" Lafitau observes. "The one who arrives or comes to visit has scarcely entered than food is put before him, without saying anything: and he himself eats without ceremony, before opening his mouth to declare the subject which brings him."[40]

• Respect Between the Sexes

The Amerindians' modesty and their discretion in matters of sex are well documented. Lafitau recounts customs that fell into disuse because of the example of the French. One such custom, according to Lafitau, was "to pass the first year after the marriage without consummating it. Any advance made before that time would be insulting to the wife and would make her think that the alliance was sought less because of esteem for her than out of brutality."[41]

Another Amerindian custom, still practised among the Iroquois and others, does not allow an individual to marry another member of the same clan. This is true even if the person has been adopted by the clan, "for," as Lafitau explains, "since by giving them life the name of a particular person of this family is revived in them, they are given all the rights of adoption and represent those being resurrected as if they were those people themselves."[42]

The Amerindian of Lafitau's time would break off his intimate life with his wife as soon as a pregnancy occurred; "the general rule for all Savages is to stop living with their wives from the moment they declare themselves pregnant."[43]

• Being Faithful to One's Word

Lafitau cites an "old Huron" who told him that "it was a law from time immemorial in their country that a village had a right to put to death anyone who . . . did not fulfil the obligations of his pledge."[44] Friendship is sacred among Amerindians. The ties that bind friends together are stronger than the ties of blood. An individual cannot marry a friend's relative, since the bonds of their friendship make them kin. Usually, Lafitau tells us, "friends follow each other to the stake."[45]

• Respect for Ancestors' Souls

Finally, Amerindians were admired by the first Euroamericans, especially the priests, because of their remarkable devotion to the souls of their dead. To the missionaries and perhaps more particularly to Lafitau because of the thesis he was defending, this natural disposition of the Amerindian was proof of the immortality of the soul, and so of the existence of God. Echoing numerous European observers, Lafitau wrote:

> It could be said that all their work, all their sweating and all their trade comes back almost solely to doing honour to the dead. They have nothing precious enough for this. And so they sacrifice their beaver robes, maize, axes, and wampum, in such quantity that it could be believed they attach no importance to them, although they constitute all the wealth of the country. They can be seen almost naked in the winter cold, while they have, in their chests, good fur or woolen robes destined for the funeral duties. On these occasions, each person makes it a point of honour or religion to appear liberal to the point of magnificence or prodigality.[46]

• Conclusion

Despite historians' tendency to produce an image of the Amerindian that serves the interests of colonialist societies, Amerindian ideology has lost nothing of its essence. To cite historian Robert E. Berkhofer, "The remarkable persistence of cultural and personality traits and ethnic identity in Indian societies in the face of white conquest and efforts at elimination or assimilation"[47] is proof that America has never had and will never have any lasting spiritual culture other than its Native one. White America has lost the cultural battle it waged against the Amerindian people. Most ironically, the Iroquois nation, which has most often served as a pretext for whites to denigrate the aboriginal population, is now recognized even internationally as one of the most vibrant Amerindian cultures in the Americas. According to Mohawk historian and journalist Doug George, the Iroquois possess "an innate gift for organization." "You can find innumerable references in the historical documents that demonstrate the ability of the Iroquois people to pull it out of the fire, when things look their darkest, to create something out of that."[48] He points out that the Iroquois periodical *Akwesasne Notes*, founded in 1968, is "a device created [by the Iroquois] that has given stimulus to Indian movements across the hemisphere."[49]

Historically, the Iroquois' vision of peace was not limited to the Native people of North America, but has always been universal. To cite George again: "In 1656, a Mohawk delegation . . . went to Quebec City and asked the French [who had the technology to do it] to take this message of Peace throughout the world . . . to bring all the Nations together at Onondaga, under the Great Tree of Peace. . . . These were people who were gifted with world vision 300 years before the Europeans finally, after two world wars, stumbled across it."[50]

Today, the Iroquois still acknowledge "the duty of trying to reach the non-Native world as well." George adds that "even on the other side of the [Atlantic] Ocean . . . we can see the influence of the Confederacy in movements like the Green Party that's taking hold among the young people of Europe, transcending national boundaries, an expression of the concern [in] those nations that they have 'a responsibility for their generations up until the seventh generation' [following the Amerindian maxim]."[51]

This triumph of Iroquois traditionalism, despite the fact that Amerindian culture has been severely undermined by the shock of contact, is proof enough in our opinion of the solid strength of America's original philosophy.

• Notes

[1] Karl H. Schlesier, "Epidemics and Indian Middlemen: Rethinking the Wars of the Iroquois," *Ethnohistory* 23, 2 (1976): 131.

[2] Ibid., 29.

[3] Interview with Louis Hall Karaniaktajeh (aged sixty-eight), painter and writer of the Mohawk nation of Kahnawake, at Kahnawake, 5 July 1985, author's personal files.

[4] James A. Tuck, "Northern Iroquoian Prehistory" in *Handbook of North American Indians*, vol. 15, *Northeast*, ed. Bruce G. Trigger (Washington, DC: Smithsonian Institution, 1978), 324.

[5] Elizabeth Tooker, "The League of the Iroquois: Its History, Politics and Ritual" in *Handbook of North American Indians*, vol. 15, ed. Trigger, 419–22.

[6] John Napoleon Brinton Hewitt, cited in ibid., 421–22.

[7] William Douw Lightall, *Hochelagans and Mohawks* (Ottawa: J. Hope and Sons, 1899), 208–9.

8 Henry F. Dobyns, *Their Number Become Thinned: Native American Population Dynamics in Eastern North America* (Knoxville: University of Tennessee Press, 1983), 314–21.

9 Bruce G. Trigger, *The Children of Aataentsic: A History of the Huron People to 1660*, cited in "Annaotaha et Dollard vus de l'autre côté de la palissade," ed. John A. Dickinson, *Revue d'histoire de l'Amérique française* 35, 2 (1981): 171.

10 Ibid., 177–78.

11 Reuben Gold Thwaites, ed., *The Jesuits' Relations and Allied Documents, 1610–1791*, vol. 15 (New York: Pageant Books, 1959), 171.

12 Schlesier, cited in ibid., vol. 25, 105, 109.

13 Ibid., 141.

14 William N. Fenton, "Northern Iroquoian Culture Patterns," in *Handbook of North American Indians*, vol. 15, ed. Trigger, 315.

15 Remarks by John Mohawk, Seneca historian and professor at the University of Buffalo, New York, during a conference on Iroquois communications, 11–12 April 1985, at the Native American Center for the Living Arts, Niagara Falls, New York, author's personal files.

16 Joseph-François Lafitau, *Moeurs des Sauvages américains comparées aux moeurs des premiers temps*, ed. Edna Hindie Lemay, vol. 2 (Paris: Maspéro, 1983), 88.

17 Ibid., 83.

18 Ibid., vol. 1, 99.

19 Ibid., vol. 2, 12.

20 Ibid., 6 (my emphasis).

21 Ibid., 6–7.

22 Ibid., 27.

23 Ibid., vol. 1, 80.

24 Ibid., vol. 2, 13.

25 Bartolomé de las Casas, *Brevisima Relacion de la Destruccion de las Indias*, trans. Georges Sioui (Santiago de Chili: Editorial Nascimiento, 1972), 30.

26 Lafitau, *Moeurs des Sauvages américains*, vol. 2.

27 Université de Montréal historian John A. Dickinson has carried out a critical study of the "great number" of French victims of the Iroquois during this period. See Dickinson, "La guerre iroquoise et la mortalité en Nouvelle-France, 1608–1666," *Revue d'histoire de l'Amérique française* 36, 1 (June 1982): 31–47.

28 Lafitau, *Moeurs des Sauvages américains*, vol. 2.

29 Ibid.

30 Ibid.

31 Ibid., 111.

32 Joseph Le Caron, "Plainte de la Nouvelle-France dite Canada à la France sa germaine" (factum) (Paris, 1626).

33 Lafitau, *Moeurs des Sauvages américains*, vol. 2, 88.

34 Ibid., 95.

35 Ibid., 91.

36 Ibid., 98.

37 Donald H. Frame, ed., *Montaigne's Essays and Selected Writings*, cited in *Friend and Foe*, ed. Cornelius J. Jaenen (Toronto: McClelland and Stewart, 1973), 122.

38 Lafitau, *Moeurs des Sauvages américains*, vol. 2, 31.

39 Ibid., vol. 1, 234.

40 Ibid., 232.

41 Ibid., 157.

42 Ibid., 145.

43 Ibid., 146.

44 Ibid., 23.

45 Ibid., 182.

46 Ibid., vol. 2, 151–52.

47 Robert E. Berkhofer, Jr, "The Political Context of a New Indian History," *Pacific Historical Review* 40, 3 (1971): 358.

48 Remarks by Doug George, historian and journalist of the Mohawk nation of Akwesasane (Quebec, Ontario, and New York), during a conference on Iroquois communications, 11–12 April 1985, at the Native American Center for the Living Arts, Niagara Falls, New York, author's personal files.

49 Ibid.

50 Ibid.

51 Ibid.

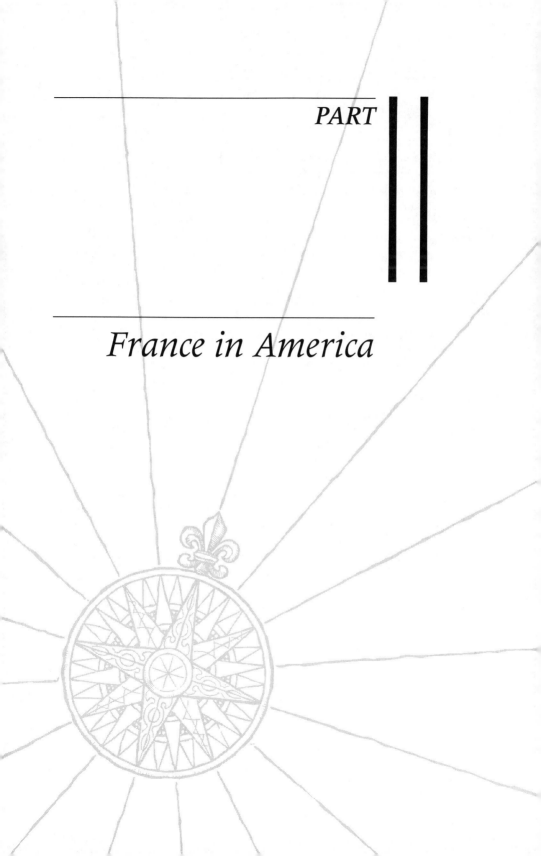

PART

II

France in America

The expression "France in America" suggests that the "Old World" society of the *ancien régime* was recreated in the "New World." As described in the following articles, this expression should not be taken literally since scholars have discovered elements of both change and continuity in the establishment of the French empire in North America. Moreover, recent research has revealed considerable diversity within and among the various colonial communities. Rather than generalizing about life in New France, historians now insist on the need to consider differences as well as similarities across time and place.

The increasing recognition of the complexity of the French colonial period has resulted in part from the posing of new questions and the study of previously neglected sources. Louise Dechêne's contribution to the readings of this section is an example of her effort to study all the individuals who comprised the early population of Montreal. In this case, Dechêne has pieced together information from census enumerations, tax rolls, seigneurial documents, and notarial records. Any one of these sources provides only very fragmentary evidence, perhaps indicating, for example, the occupations of certain individuals. But by combining this evidence with information from other sources (perhaps, for example, on the individual's family background), Dechêne is able to present a quite full picture of those living in early Montreal.

Louise Dechêne undertook her analysis of society in Montreal in order to address questions related to the "transplanting" of France's social system to North America. Her examination of documents created in the course of everyday transactions and events leads to the conclusion that a hierarchical social structure was indeed established in Montreal. Kenneth Donovan pursues similar questions but does so by studying material culture. Donovan uses sources such as the inventories produced at the time of death to learn about everyday life in Louisbourg. What kinds of clothes were worn by different individuals? Who sat where in church? What kind of parental care did children receive? By addressing such questions, Donovan is able to compare systematically the lifestyles of both the poor and well-to-do. Like Dechêne, his approach allows us to go beyond the familiar historical documents that reflect only the perceptions and observations of elites.

In addition to analysing the nature of communities such as Montreal and Louisbourg, scholars have also focussed on the international context within which such communities developed during the seventeenth and eighteenth centuries. John Robert McNeill has undertaken a direct comparison of Louisbourg and Havana in order to better understand the Atlantic empires of France and Spain. His work is a forceful reminder that no country's history can be studied in isolation. Not only is it important to understand the relationships among different societies, but it is also necessary to analyse any one place within a comparative framework. Cape Breton's economic resources and strategic advantages, for example, can only be evaluated by comparing them to those of other places, such as Havana.

The final two articles in this section view developments in North America from two very different perspectives, that of the Amerindians, and that of the French imperial authorities. Cornelius J. Jaenen argues that, although the nonliterate Amerindians did not leave their own documents, their attitudes and perceptions can be studied through an informed reading of French writings. He concludes that the Amerindians were hardly in awe of the French colonists; in fact, they were not impressed by many aspects of French culture including the Europeans' religious and medical practices. Jaenen's work also illustrates how two groups can mutually differentiate themselves from "the other." As will be shown in other articles in this collection, this process is a central theme of Canadian history since so many different groups have come face-to-face across the land.

In a similar way, W.J. Eccles describes the quite distinct viewpoint of the French authorities who were less and less committed to New France as anything more than a "mere instrument of French imperial policy." In order to make this argument, Eccles focusses on specific leading individuals, and examines their own writings to interpret their activities and attitudes. This approach stands in sharp contrast to the sociohistorical method of Dechêne, the material culture study of Donovan, and the indirect attitudinal analysis of Jaenen. Although recent work has tended to focus on the "anonymous" rather than the "famous" figures of New France, Eccles' work on the West remains an important contribution to an understanding of the changing direction of French ambition.

These examples of scholarly work on "France in America" suggest some of the reasons why a great deal of research has been undertaken on this period is recent decades. In order to address questions about ordinary as well as famous residents, and about the place of New France within an international context, scholars have developed innovative approaches that emphasize the multifaceted character of the historical process. One result is a better understanding of the relationships among individual experience, local conditions, and imperial policy during the seventeenth and eighteenth centuries.

SOCIAL GROUPS*

LOUISE DECHÊNE

• Overview

In 1715, 4700 people lived on the Island of Montreal. The active population numbered some twelve hundred individuals, who can be grouped by occupation as follows. Two-fifths were peasants who drew their income mainly from the land. Some also performed other functions and worked as carters, lime-burners, or blacksmiths, since villages were not yet capable of supporting full-fledged artisans. There were also 5 or 6 millers in the countryside, along with 2 notaries, 5 curés, a group of nuns in the Lachine and Pointe-aux-Trembles convents, and about 10 small merchants, sometimes acting as voyageurs, as well as 100 to 150 people whose primary activity was fur trading—at least for a while.[1] There were few married men in this last group. Most came from peasant families and went home to the farm between trips. Agricultural labourers did not form a distinct category, as we have already remarked.

The 650 individuals who made up the town's active population can be divided into four categories. The first comprises the 40 percent who performed services of some sort, and includes 24 clergymen—Sulpicians, Jesuits, and Récollets—and about 75 nuns; the resident military officers and their families (35); judicial and administrative office-holders (14); minor officials (12); surgeons (4); and maybe a hundred or so servants, children and adults.

Trade accounted for 20 percent of occupations, including merchant-outfitters (25); professional voyageurs and small merchants (60); innkeepers and tavern-keepers (30); bakers and butchers (5); and a few carters.

*From *Habitants and Merchants in Seventeenth-Century Montreal* (Montreal: McGill-Queen's University Press, 1992), 211–36. Reprinted with permission of the publisher.

The secondary sector consisted of those in the building trades (40); blacksmiths and cartwrights, locksmiths, edge-tool makers, and gunsmiths (20); 4 tanners and a dozen cobblers; tailors and especially seamstresses (40); and a number of other craftsmen, such as a brewer, cooper, gardener, weaver, clog-maker, wig-maker, goldsmith, hat-maker, and so on. Together these independent artisans gave work to perhaps 50 apprentices at most, for they rarely employed more than one or two at a time. This sector involved no more than a quarter of the town's active population.

Last came a mixed bag of day-labourers who worked wherever they could, sometimes in construction, sometimes as *engagés* for the fur trade, and sometimes as harvesters. This loose contingent made up 15 percent of the labour force.

Urban development in this period was neither important enough nor sufficiently sustained to support a greater reservoir of labour. Access to trade was limited, and the small body of artisans already met both local demand and that of the fur trade adequately. Although construction was increasing, large-scale projects were rare.

The town did attract *voyageurs*, who had previously lived in the country. As their occupation became more professionalized, they grew closer to the merchants, their partners and outfitters. But apart from a few suburban farmers who settled in town when they reached retirement age, the voyageurs were practically the only rural population that was tapped by the town. The inherent limitations of the colonial economy meant that the winds of change would not blow over this occupational pattern in the eighteenth century.

The few tax rolls that have survived are poor substitutes for the fiscal documents used elsewhere to reconstruct income levels. Although tax levies were frequent, each was too slight to provide an adequate gauge of the taxpayers' means. The categories defined by the assembly that drew up the list for a public works tax in 1681 teach us more than the actual range of assessments (see table 1). Only the garrison staff was exempted. The names of those in the lowest category were left out of the tax roll, but I was able to identify them by referring to the nominal census taken that year They were recent settlers.

Table 1: **DISTRIBUTION OF THE PUBLIC-WORKS TAX RAISED IN 1681 ON THE ISLAND OF MONTREAL**

Description of the Categories	Taxpayers	Assessment (in *livres*)
Important merchants	6	20
Lesser merchants	13	12
Comfortable	58	8
Less comfortable	67	6
Poor	161	3

Source: National Archives of Canada, M-1584, 38.

For the sake of comparison it is useful to analyse a more important assessment levied in 1714–15 for the building of the fortifications.[2] This particular tax was assessed by head rather than household and, given its defensive purpose, allowed almost no exemptions. Unlike earlier levies, which were expressed in terms of money, this one imposed so many days of statute labour, valued at 2 *livres* per man-day and 5 *livres* per "draught-day." Although the analysis is based on these equivalents, the reader should be aware that they do not reflect current wages. A day-labourer generally earned 30 *sols*, while a day's carting was usually worth over 100 *sols*, depending on the nature and quality of the team. The discrepancy favoured the merchants, who drew up the rolls and put themselves down for draught-days, which most of them remitted in cash. But it added to the burden of those in the lower categories, who, for one reason or another, would have had to pay their share in coin. It obviously tended to lessen the spread between assessments.

Contributions ranged between 2 and 75 *livres*, and the mean was 11 *livres*.[3] Using the method devised by J. Dupâquier, based on a geometric progression distributed on either side of the mean, I charted a histogram that, despite the imprecision of the source, reflects, up to a point, the overall income distribution in this society.[4] There are only seven tax brackets— six actually, for only two persons figure in the seventh—and there is a marked concentration in category a, where payments lay between 5 $1/2$ and 11 *livres*. The very small spread around an homogeneous mass of moderate revenues fits what we know about this economy: it arose from the split between trade and agriculture, and the long-term recession accentuated the trend towards equality.[5]

This concentration is even more obvious when we turn to the countryside, where we find a mixture of wealthier farmers, *voyageurs,* and a sprinkling of notables in the top 17 percent, and a much larger category of habitants who had done well for themselves without producing sizeable surpluses. The other two-fifths were recent settlers, in more or less straitened circumstances, although for most this would only be temporary. The town had its contingent of untaxed paupers, who do not figure on the rolls, but the portion was insignificant. Montreal offered so little occasion for scraping together a living that those who did not have a steady income moved away.

The roll yields little information concerning the professions. Although I was able to reconstitute three small categories, only the merchants emerge with a clear profile. They did not overassess themselves, and from what is known of their business at least three should figure in category D. If we suppose that the group's mean revenue hovered around 1200 to 2000 *livres*, or ten times that of craftsmen, this would give a fair idea of the extent of inequalities. The artisans identified belonged to the upper strata of the trades, but even they were hardly well off. The broader spread of assessments among military officers points to diverse material conditions.

The purpose of this overview is to establish a backdrop for the analysis of socioeconomic groups based on a more or less trustworthy source: the postmortem inventory. Two hundred and fifty of these were used, supplemented by other notarial documents such as curator's accounts, divisions of estates, sales, adjudications, marriage contracts, and wills.[6] Inventories alone do not provide an accurate picture of the distribution of wealth because they give pride of place to the more affluent. Notaries never charged less than 7 *livres tournois* (and usually an average of 20, with the authenticated copy) for making inventories of the peasants' movables and effects, and this did not include the property valuations. Another 7 *livres* would go to the two livestock appraisers should they refuse to be paid from the brood, as custom dictated. What with costs for electing a guardianship or dividing the estate, the total fees could easily mount to 5 percent of an ordinary inheritance, and common people would do all they could to avoid such an outlay.[7]

A careful curator would request an inventory in order to protect the interests of the minors when the surviving parent remarried, while unclaimed successions were inventoried on order of the court so that we do, after all, get a glimpse of the poor. The reliability of the declarations, however, raises another problem.

The notary who returned to complete the inventory of the late Pierre Gadois tells us of the widow's welcome, "screaming that he had no right to do it, that he only did it to despoil them and ruin her children, calling down a thousand curses, that the devil should take him, that he should die of shame for trying to include in the inventory some eight cords of wood belonging to her as well as many chickens that she and her late husband had owned together, and that, since he was so interested in how many there were, he should count them himself."[8]

Not everyone was as hostile, but people had no qualms about concealing as much as they could. Yet relatives of the deceased kept their eyes open, and besides, most had little to hide. Even if the notary did not reckon every one of the widow Gadois' chickens, enough information was recorded to show that this family was better off than the average and to reveal its material environment, which is what we are after.

Grain and cattle were appraised at their market value. Merchants stocks were valued according to the invoice price, with or without the markup, but this being always specified, it is easy to standardize these estimates. Only movables were assessed at less than their sale price, and this *cru* came to about 25 percent, if not more.[9] Since this procedure was common to all inventories, and movables represented only a minor portion of the total assets, the figures are tabulated as given. One cannot compare overall levels of wealth at different periods to measure overall impoverishment or enrichment, since the various categories of estate would not be equally represented in the samples. However, a close look at the changes in the nature and distribution of the assets can indicate the trends. Price fluctuations create a problem. Thus, all the inventories taken between 1715 and 1719, valued in card money, had to be eliminated, and those taken prior to 1670, when prices were very high, were analysed separately. What remains is more or less comparable.

The inventories rarely assign a value to real property, but they describe the buildings and the state of the land. I dealt with this problem by assigning a standard value of 50 *livres* to every *arpent* under the plough (the market price around 1675, halfway through the period) and by adopting the appropriate price range for the buildings. The method is obviously crude since land value could vary from one farm to another and also over time (decreasing gradually from 1650 to 1720), but the data are too scattered to permit any refinements.

Stocks, securities, and cash were entered separately. Other items were divided into four categories: durable and perishable consumer goods and durable and perishable producer goods, each with twenty to thirty subheadings.[10] Perishable goods were left out of the overall calculations because the contents of the barn or the cellar differed from season to season, while pantries were not consistently inventoried. This classification allows us to isolate expenditures related to the running of the enterprise from those meant to make life more pleasant.

• The Seigneurs

The fiefs that the trade companies and the French monarchy granted to gentilshommes and to religious bodies did not generate revenues until enough people settled on them and their owners put up mills and invested on their domains. Since most lay seigneurs had not undertaken such improvements by the beginning of the eighteenth century, relying instead on the slow and spontaneous influx of settlers to populate their land, there were no seigneurial revenues (with a few exceptions), and we cannot speak yet of a seigneurial class.[11] But the institutional framework was there to promote the rise of such a group, and a few proprietors did not wait to take advantage of their privilege.

Thus, although fourteen small *arrière-fiefs* had been granted on the island between 1658 and 1690 and a number of the town's officers and merchants owned large, nearly empty seigneuries off the island, these landowners are classified according to their occupations and the origins of their revenues, which were not seigneurial.[12]

The seminary of St-Sulpice stands alone as truly seigneurial, but the Sulpicians left no balance sheet of their administration. A 1704 lease indicates that the revenues from all seigneurial dues, mill rights, and *rentes foncières* came to about 6500 *livres*. The lease of two domains brought in 2500 *livres*. In the same period net income from the tithes appropriated by the Seminary can be estimated at 3250 *livres*. Rental from houses, forge, warehouses, and other properties, and income from *rentes constituées* held both in Canada and in France amounted to at least another 3000 *livres*. Sulpician revenues were therefore in the order of 15 000 to 20 000 *livres* tournois, and since three-quarters were feudal in origin, there were safe from economic fluctuations.[13] Expenses long exceeded revenues for the seigneurs worked tirelessly to exploit their privileges as well as their demesne. Small acquisitions of rentes show that by the early eighteenth century their income had risen to cover their outlay. "And since we do not deem it wise at present to make any further purchases in Canada, because they are not safe," the Superior wrote, "we must send this sum as well as other payments and reimbursements which come our way to Paris, where they can be properly invested."[14] These sure investments turned out to be *rentes* on the Hôtel de Ville, whose fluctuations the Seminary watched with some consternation, over the next twenty years. The portion of the censitaires' savings drained off in this fashion was still small, but it would soon increase. By the middle of the eighteenth century rumour had it that the seigneurs had an annual revenue of 70 000 *livres* and that a large proportion ended up in France.[15]

As for the men who personified the seigneury, they were educated French clerics of good birth, from families of the robe and the sword, who looked on this society of commoners and adventurers with a mixture of severity and condescension.

• The Nobles

Their titles were recent: four or five generations, at best, fewer in many cases, and the eleven Canadian families ennobled in the seventeenth century formed part of this group.[16] However recent, they had a recognized status that included a number of privileges. "Monseigneur," the governor wrote, "I beg leave to tell you that Canadian nobles are no better than beggars and that increasing their number would only inflate the number of idlers."[17] No one, not even the common criminals sent over in the eighteenth century would cause so much anxiety for the authorities as these arrogant, ignorant nobles, who could not take care of themselves. The intendants would variously explain that such people were accustomed to "what is known in France as the life of country gentlemen, which is all they had ever known or seen." "They spend most of their time hunting and fishing, having no other skills, not being born to till the land, and having no means that would allow them to take part in business."[18] This is hardly surprising, but the royal authorities behaved in an irresponsible manner by doing all they could to attract this class to the colony, only to reprove them for living on government handouts as they waited for the emergence of seigneurial revenues. The occasional liberality of the authorities was not enough to solve the problem; that took the elaboration of a system of economic promotion that gave this petty nobility access first to the army, where it belonged by right, and then to trade and even to the civil

establishment if it showed the least aptitude.[19] But until then the disturbances created by this "armed idleness" grew more frequent, for these families proved highly prolific.[20] The young Le Gardeur and d'Ailleboust "ran
about the streets of Montreal and the surrounding countryside in the middle of the night disguised as Indians, carrying guns and knives and stealing
money from the purses of those they encountered . . . while threatening to
kill and burn anyone who denounced them."[21] This is just one example of
disorderly conduct where the suit was dismissed or the penalty remitted.

When the authorities deplored the flightiness, pride, and laziness of
"our" youth, they meant the group they represented and knew intimately.[22]
Its rowdy habits were an integral part of the nobiliar lifestyle of seventeenth-
century Montreal.

Loss of rank was not something that worried colonial nobles, so the
1685 decree allowing them to take part in trade proved irrelevant.[23]
Although they felt no compunction about running illegal taverns, they
turned up their noses at manual labour. The governor, arguing on behalf
of Monsieur de St-Ours, assured the minister that he "had seen the two
eldest sons cutting hay and leading the plough."[24] A touching scene, but
hardly the norm. A few may have sunk so low in the early days, but the St-
Ours boys would soon be off trading furs, and like many others this family
would spend more time in Montreal than on its seigneurie.[25]

Some recipients of arrière-fiefs on the Island of Montreal proved to be
talented traders. Berthé de Chailly, the son of a poor Amboise nobleman,
absconded via New York with the 40 000 livres he had amassed on his
Bellevue property, where he detained Indians headed for Montreal with
their furs.[26] Picoté, Carion, and La Fresnaye did the same and were equally
successful.[27] These petty nobles tried to compete with the merchants, but few
succeeded in creating going concerns based primarily on circulating capital.

As a captain in the troupes de la Marine a noble would earn 1080
livres, while staff officers made two to three times as much. Such salaries
helped to make ends meet but did not leave surpluses. Seventeen postmortem inventories describe gross fortunes among this group of 3000 to
8000 livres, the same as those of good artisans.[28] These inventories are
incomplete and poorly drawn up, as if the notaries were reluctant to
intrude into the privacy of households. Marriage arrangements and various
legal subtleties helped somewhat to keep creditors at bay, while royal bounty
"in lieu of patrimony" could come in handy in safeguarding belongings.[29]
The inventories also list heavy liabilities, which reveal the odd trading activity. These nobles owed money to merchants, to the treasurer, to the intendant, to their soldiers, to the convent where they placed their daughters, to
tradesmen, and to their servants.[30] One fief, with its six thousand hectares
of wood and eight censitaires, its ten or so cultivated arpents adjoining the
house and barn, and a small crumbling mill, would be worth no more than
an ordinary censive.[31] It was hard to keep up appearances in a three- to
four-room country house or, as often was the case, in the smaller quarters

that officers owned or rented in town.[32] But these nobles tried. Their inventories leave an overwhelming sense of overcrowding: countless children, one or two servants, and much more furniture than a merchant would have. It cost officers nothing to ship their belongings on royal vessels, and this explains the presence of expensive pieces: an ebony cabinet, a morocco-covered chest, armchairs with silk-woven patterns, West Indian rugs, and those high-warp tapestries valued at four hundred *livres* that hung about a room. There was an abundance of chairs with pillows, tables covered with rugs, feather beds even for children, sheets, utensils, gold-framed mirrors, knickknacks, china, and silverware. All owned silverware, dinnerware, candelabra, and so on, which could be pawned on occasion. Five of these families possessed a few books, and six boasted a religious painting or a portrait or two. Duplessy Faber, who fought on every European front and spent the last twenty-five years of his life in Canada longing for the St-Louis Cross, kept a portrait of Vauban, his protector, and a picture of "a Dutchman, reading while another looked on," which he probably brought back from some campaign on the New York frontier.[33]

And when dire poverty struck, when the last armchair, ivory crucifix, and last silver spoon had gone, one might still find on the wall a "worthless, worn-out" strip of Bergamot tapestry.

• Judicial and Administrative Personnel

When the Sulpicians looked to replace their *bailli* d'Ailleboust, a career officer who had no legal training and was the nephew of a former governor of the colony, they were lucky enough to find a law graduate on the spot, said to have been a lawyer at the Parlement of Paris before he came to Canada as a clerk of the Compagnie des Indes occidentales.[34] Migeon held the post between 1677 and 1693, all the while working as a merchant, and left behind one of the finest farms on the island as well as urban properties. He paid his daughter's 4000-*livre* dowry in cash, which was quite unusual. Although he left no inventory, he appears to have been worth altogether at least 50 000 *livres* and to have owned what was no doubt the best library in the seigneury after that of the Sulpicians. Since his sons opted for military careers, he was succeeded by his son-in-law, who is better known for his adventures in Mississippi than for his career as a judge.[35]

There was no social status attached to the other judicial functions. These were left to individuals of all stripes who performed them with varying degrees of competence. Bénigne Basset would have been a decent notary and clerk if "tobacco and debauchery" had not "so affected his wits that he could no longer think properly or remember anything."[36] He had to be relieved of his duties. His wife and children found consolation in the bosom of the Church. The notary Adhémar, son of a Languedoc bourgeois who had come to Canada as a soldier, earned the merchants' trust, and most of the fur-trade *obligations* passed through his office.[37] He loaned money, oversaw successions, and left behind about 5000 to 6000 *livres*, once the mortgage on his house is deducted. His son succeeded him.[38]

Jean Gervaise, one of Montreal's first settlers, acted as attorney to the *bailliage* in respectable obscurity and died on his farm at Coteau St-Louis. His heirs were peasants, as their father had been before them.[39] For lack of a better candidate, the seigneurs took on a merchant's clerk as their court clerk and later attorney, but he was troublesome and went back to La Rochelle at the end of five years.[40] The other local notaries were not up to performing such duties. Modest careers could be forged when an ex-soldier turned schoolmaster, then sergeant of the *bailliage*, bailiff, some-times jailer, and even notary, without any hope of further upward mobility.[41] Claude Maugue's possessions were worth only 600 *livres* at his death, and his widow married a cobbler.[42] Yet with proper training and ini-tiative one could go much further. Did a Sulpician suggest that the carpen-ter Raimbault send his ten-year-old son to France? Whatever the reason, the boy was away fifteen years, studied, and eventually became a notary, *sub-délégué* of the intendant, *bailli* for the seigneurial lower court, and, from 1727 to 1740, judge of the royal court.[43] In his early days he occasionally took on the lease of tithes and seigneurial dues. Pierre Raimbault owned some fifty books: Greek and Roman classics, law books, edifying works, and a horticultural treatise.[44] In this tiny society where everything devolved from trade or warfare, this is the sole example of education's becoming a means of preferment.

• The Merchants

Trade was the most common means of social promotion open to the dynamic elements of the lower classes. Success was commensurate with the milieu and with the potential offered by this activity. Although the wealth of the outfitters whose postmortem assets are summarized in table 2 bears no comparison either quantitatively or qualitatively with that of the French urban bourgeoisie, they dominated the fur trade and played a primary role in the small colonial town (see table 2).

Those at the bottom are underrepresented in this sample. Dozens of persons became outfitters at some point in their lives, working with a capi-tal of 8000 to 10 000 *livres* until they sank into oblivion. Those who endured had every reason to believe that they would leave behind some 20 000 to 35 000 *livres*, which was about average. Besides the five wealthiest merchants included in the table, two other individuals, whose inventories were not available, held assets of more than 150 000 *livres* at the beginning of the eighteenth century.[45]

These men's assets differed significantly from those of their metropol-itan counterparts. Seven of the inventories did not include even one plot of

Table 2: **DISTRIBUTION OF THE ASSETS OF MERCHANT-OUTFITTERS BASED ON POSTMORTEM INVENTORIES, 1680–1718**

	Net Value of the Estate (in *livres tournois*)							
Categories	5 000–10 000	10 000–15 000	15 000–25 000	25 000–35 000	35 000–55 000	100 000–200 000	260 000	Total
Merchants under 45	4	4	3	1	1			13
Older merchants	1	2	6	3	1	2	1	16

land, while the single farm that figures in the other inventories amounted to no more than 20 percent of the estate. Urban properties represented 30 percent, movables 5 percent. Stocks and commercial claims accounted for 40 percent, while rentes rarely rose above 5 percent, if there were any at all.

There was also a marked contrast in lifestyles. The merchants' stone houses, lining the marketplace, each contained perhaps six large rooms and a number of smaller ones *(cabinets)*, with the shop at street level and the storeroom one story above. Wheat and furs were kept in the attic. These were fine residences by Montreal standards, although in reality they were no more than upgraded peasant cottages. The furnishings depended upon the degree of wealth. At the outset of their careers merchants lived as sparely as the lower classes. Whenever business took a turn for the worse, the furniture was the first to go. Wealthier merchants would own cupboards full of linen, kitchen utensils, an abundance of pewter, beds and covers, and silverware weighing seven to twelve marks. All had an iron stove, worth about 150 *livres*, set in the main room, a symbol of comfort not yet within the reach of the common people. They relied on locally produced pine and cherrywood furniture; a mirror, one or two upholstered armchairs, a tapestry, and the occasional painting complemented this spare assortment, which we find, for example, in the houses of J.-B. Charly and Pierre Perthuis, men worth at least 40 000 and 50 000 *livres* respectively once their debts have been subtracted.[46] Jacques Leber, the richest of them all, and Charles de Couagne did not live on a grander scale.[47] The latter's two inventories, taken twenty-five years apart, reveal that while his assets quadrupled, his furnishings remained practically the same except for a clock, a pedestal table, and two armchairs.[48] Wardrobes, valued at 200 to 300 *livres*, were not extravagant.

The merchants were not a cultivated lot. If their inventories can be trusted, two-thirds never opened a book. The others possessed ten to forty volumes, mostly of a religious nature. Couagne, who enjoyed historical accounts and covered his walls with plain paper maps of the world, of France, and of Paris, seems to have been something of an eccentric.[49] Jean Quenet owned seven family portraits, including those of five brothers living in France, but it was above all religious subjects that adorned one-third of these bourgeois households.

Theirs was not a nobiliar lifestyle: idleness was reproved and no one retired prematurely. The women learned how to keep accounts and how to manage the business while their husbands were away. Boys were sent to school until they turned fourteen when they began their apprenticeship with Canadian or French merchants. For these men, growing richer, becoming respectable, and becoming respected were serious concerns. They did not participate in the scandalous and boisterous pleasures of the officers. Fines for contravening fur trade ordinances may have been an unavoidable occupational hazard, but they were otherwise orderly citizens. They took part in public life, became churchwardens, and donated generously to charitable works.

• Traders and Artisans

The forty-five-year-old *voyageur* who found himself too old to pursue an occupation that had become too strenuous came home to his family with no more than 4000 to 5000 *livres* in savings. These had been invested in some suburban property or urban building and provided a small income in his declining years.[50] He kept an eye on his son's affairs, a son he had trained himself and who, as conditions improved in the eighteenth century, would make a better living from his trips to the west than his father had. But Jean Lorain was already able to leave his children twice as much as he had received from his own father, a peasant, and this explains both his choice of career and the attraction it exerted on the next generations.[51] For if modest success was less common than failure and poverty, it was more likely to impress the youth of this region.

The innkeeper Isaac Nafréchoux had begun his career as a miller. The money he left behind allowed his son to outfit fur traders and his daughters to marry, the one an army officer and the other a sergeant in the constabulary. The daughter of another innkeeper, Abraham Bouat, married Pacaud, one of the major merchants of the colony, while his son went to France to study law and, having made a good match, received a commission in the troops and eventually became judge of the *bailliage*. This is enough to give the impression of an unstructured society. We should nevertheless remember that these were exceptional cases and that the fifty or so individuals who ran taverns or inns at one time or another in Montreal had a different fate. This was an attractive occupation that brought easy returns, especially when one had no scruples about cheating the Indians, or intoxicating servants and soldiers, or staying open on Sundays to attract country residents who came in to hear mass, an activity they were all guilty of, without exception. Whatever dire penalties the ordinances may have prescribed, the court showed little zeal, and the mitigated fines had no effect.[52] Theoretically, only twenty or so individuals were entitled to sell drinks, but there were at least ten transgressors a year, besides other illicit establishments the authorities failed to track down. Tavern-keepers were a mixed lot: former *voyageurs*, a notary, a bailiff, many artisans who left the running of the business to their wives, and a large number of widows.[53] They were grasping and unscrupulous. The accusations of the court attorneys are convincing: all of the inns were bawdy houses, and many taverns were dens of iniquity. The proprietors did not make a fortune. Vincent Dugast, who left 4500 *livres* after twenty years of keeping judge and curé on the alert, probably did better than any others.[54]

There were no guilds in Canada. This was a deliberate ministerial decision, and masters who occasionally sought letters patent or exclusive rights met with repeated refusals.[55]

At first people worked as they pleased, and this could give rise to incongruous associations, such as that of the butcher and the clog-maker who decided to join forces to sell liquor on the side.[56] But from 1680 onwards crafts became more organized.

Butchers and bakers were regulated by the judge, assisted by a few chosen citizens who determined their number, the quality of their products, and their prices.[57] The response of the assemblies to market fluctuations proved so slow that the butchers and bakers were forever at odds with the *bailli*, or with the merchants who interfered with their monopoly, or with peasants who sold meat at the market.[58] Given the economic priorities of *l'ancien régime*, the decisions usually came down in favour of the consumers, all the more so in this town, where merchants were the biggest customers. They were the ones who fixed the assize and denounced the slightest contraventions. Sentences were not only frequent; they were also quite heavy.[59] Most of the assets left behind by two butchers between 3000 and 5000 *livres* each, went to repay their debts. The only inventory left by a baker shows that he was penniless.[60] Most probably did better, but in this period these were not profitable trades.

Tanning was one of Montreal's few viable industries. The two firms that competed for business in the early eighteenth century had a turnover of about 10 000 *livres* and employed no more than five or six workmen and three shoemakers each, if they obeyed the intendant's ordinance.[61] He meant to put a stop to the beginnings of an association between butchers and tanners that threatened to absorb the shoemakers as well. The inventories of the town's first tanners have not survived, but since we know that the families ran the concerns for several generations, these were obviously worth maintaining.[62] The shoemakers remained independent, multiplied, and functioned on a very small scale.

In 1663, eleven years after he arrived in the colony, the former *engagé* Jean Milot *dit* le Bourguignon, a good edge-tool maker who could not sign his name, owned 10 000 *livres* in assets, while at his death in 1699 he left behind some 35 000 *livres*, consisting of urban and rural properties.[63] He was exceptionally successful, although the iron trades were generally sound, armory in particular. Fezeret and Turpin owned houses on the marketplace and stood out from the crowd with their savings of 7000 to 10 000 *livres*.[64] Two blacksmiths, dead by the age of thirty, had already amassed net assets of 4000 to 5000 *livres*, something most peasants would only achieve in a lifetime.[65] There was an unflagging demand for guns and tools in the colony and also in the west, where these artisans were called by the administration to set up forges under highly favourable terms.[66] The seigneurs and a number of merchants owned forges, which they rented completely equipped, while the lessees in return provided whatever wares they ordered.[67] Although access to these trades was open, they demanded skills and a basic investment beyond the reach of adventurers.

The situation in the building trades was quite different. The mass of semirural part-time carpenters and masons who obtained contracts in the seventeenth century did not live well. In order to be awarded the projects they underestimated the costs, and this inevitably landed them in trouble. The *bailliage* registers are full of lawsuits involving carpenters who were demanding their money and town dwellers who were clamouring for them to finish the work.[68] They left construction sites as soon as anything became available in the royal outposts, and exchanged their high wages for trade goods. The shrewdest were eventually able to give up an occupation they had never really been good at and that paid so little. At the end of the seventeenth century there were no competent major contractors in Montreal, but this is hardly surprising since no important projects had yet demanded their permanent presence. Quebec workmen were used on the major building sites, such as churches, convents, mills, fortifications, and boatyards for small craft, and eventually they settled in Montreal and trained the local labour force.[69]

The first surgeons combined medicine and farming. André Rapin left his family a prosperous farm near Lachine as well as a house in town, and his sons were apprenticed to a shoemaker and an edge-tool maker.[70] Later on, a few of the better-educated surgeons, especially those who acted as public and private curators, would rank among the minor notables. Whatever they earned from such tasks, combined with their salaries at the Hôtel-Dieu and the emoluments received from their patients, ensured them a decent lifestyle, even if they left behind little more than 4000 to 5000 *livres*.[71]

Craftsmen were a close-knit group. Their families were bound by wedlock—often within the same trade—and through apprenticeship. Most apprentices were the sons of artisans and often related to the master or they were the sons of surgeons or merchants. Since the trades were expanding in this period, they offered a few openings to boys from the country. A well-off habitant with more than one son to succeed him on the farm could settle one of them this way. The cost was not very high, and all that some masters required was that the parents provide their children's clothing.[72] The apprenticeship usually lasted three years and began when the child was anywhere between twelve and nineteen years old. Conditions were stringent and sometimes harsh, especially in the more profitable trades like iron and leather, where tradition was strictly observed. Fathers were keen to pass on their skills to their sons, and one coppersmith had his apprentice promise that after his death he would teach the craft to one of his late master's children, under the same conditions he had been trained himself, "if the said child was so inclined."[73]

The lowest rungs of the urban society were occupied by the small contingent of unskilled labourers who had either given up land-clearing or never tried it at all. They earned 30 *sols* a day, with a meal added, it seems, when they worked for masons or carpenters. Although these were high wages by any yardstick, this proved irrelevant. "It may be true that the workers are well paid," the intendant wrote, "but one must keep in mind that they can only work five months of the year because of the cold winters and that they must therefore earn enough to see them through the other seven months."[74] In fact, work was interrupted for about six months, but the 30 *sols* a day did not apply to those employed for long periods who generally earned only 12 to 15 *livres* a month.[75] If we allow 4 *sols* a day for the equivalent of a soldier's ration, a labourer would need a minimum of 50 *livres* to keep alive during the period of inactivity. Include the rent for a heated room, between 50 and 70 *livres* a year, and his entire income is spent. When the price of bread rose, the labourer could not feed himself. His lot was that much more uncertain in those periods when there was little construction, as in the last decade of the seventeenth century. If he built himself some cabin in the suburbs, he might save on rent, but should he have a family to feed, he would have to go begging. Some of these men were hired by the fur traders, but the labour supply was greater than the demand, and not everyone was strong enough to paddle to Lake Huron carrying hundred-pound packs. The rest were better off staking some land where they might keep body and soul together by combining some agriculture with part-time employment. Yet the town still sheltered a number of paupers who do not figure in notarial records and who more or less lived off charity.[76]

• The Habitants

The inventories of the habitants present a three-tiered picture. At the bottom, and severely underrepresented in the sample, is the contingent of poor peasants, whose goods were never valued at more than 100 *livres,* a value that falls close to zero once their debts are taken into account (see table 3).

Table 3:   **DISTRIBUTION OF WEALTH OF THE PEASANTRY, BASED ON POSTMORTEM INVENTORIES**

	Value of the Assets (in *livres tournois*)									
Periods	Less than 500	500– 1000	1000– 2000	2000– 3000	3000– 4000	4000– 5000	5000– 6000	6000– 7000	7000– 8000	13 000	Total
1650–1669	2	4	3	–	2	–	–	–	–	–	11
1670–1689	1	5	9	3	2	1	1	–	–	–	22
1690–1715	3	5	12	12	2	3	2	–	1	1	41
1720–1729	–	–	1	3	3	1	–	–	–	–	8
Total	6	14	25	18	9	5	3	–	1	1	82

Hugues Messaguier *dit* La Plaine came to Canada as a soldier. He lost his wife after eight years of marriage and was left with two children. When he contemplated remarrying in October 1695, he had his possessions inventoried. He then owned forty *arpents* in Lachine, six of them hand-ploughed, a few more barely cleared, a twelve-foot post-in-ground cabin with timber flooring and thatched roof, a shed, a "nearly fatted" pig, and two chickens. His harvest had brought in 35 *minots* of wheat and 17 *minots* of oats, barley, and pulses, a bare subsistence given the amount that had to be set aside for the tithes, rentes, and seed. The inventory also mentions a chest, a bread bin, an old wooden canoe, a few tools and utensils, three worn-out blankets, and his family's clothing. He had also gathered white tobacco, which could possibly bring in 36 *livres.* His debts, which came to 212 *livres,* amounted to half his assets: he owed money to a merchant, to the surgeon who had taken care of his wife, and the vestry had to be paid for the funeral. There were also arrears on seigneurial dues and an obligation to the curé who had loaned him wheat for seed and for the family subsistence.[77] After eight years of work most colonists had got over the initial stage of destitution, but bad luck, inadequacy, and often unsuccessful experiences in the fur trade could account for such failures.

Half the rural dwellers left behind 1000 to 3000 *livres,* and, as table 3 shows, the distribution remained unchanged. The peasants' primary asset was land (see table 4). Their 30 to 40 *arpents* of arable land and meadows amounted to 50 percent of the value of inventories. Next came a small, still rudimentary dwelling, no larger than eighteen by twenty feet but resting on foundations and roofed with planks. It included partitions, an attic, and a fireplace adequate to keep it warm in winter. Jacques Beauchamp of Pointe-aux-Trembles owned such a house. He died at the age of fifty-eight, leaving behind a widow, five married daughters, two boys aged fifteen and seventeen, and a net worth of 3000 *livres*.[78] As in this case, the barn and cowshed together, with their thatched roofs, were often worth as much as the house: as we have seen, when profits were available, they were first expended on the farm's productive assets. The year was 1693, the time April, but although prices were high, there was enough wheat in the attic to suffice for the critical period before the next harvest.

Table 4: COMPOSITION OF PEASANT ASSETS, 1670–1715

Average assets	2200 *livres*	(100%)
Real estate		66
Durable producer goods		23
Durable consumer goods		6
Claims and cash		5
Liabilities		15

Such tiny dwellings hardly contained any furniture: two chests, a bread bin, a folding table, three or four chairs. The kitchen utensils and tableware were always worth more than the furniture. The parents slept in an alcove, called the "cabane," which was often nailed to the wall and appraised along with the house. A "furnished bed," including curtains, a bolster, feather mattress and pillows, blankets and quilt, worth as much as 150 *livres*, would only be found in the better-off peasant households. Children apparently slept on the floor, on mattresses filled with straw or cattail grass and rolled up in dog-hair blankets, or in bear, elk, or ox skins. There were few woollen blankets, and half the inventories reported no linen. A chest filled with sheets, tablecloths, and napkins signalled a higher standard of living than the one attained by the Beauchamps. The habitants had a supply of flour, peas, lard, and sometimes butter, but never of imported goods such as pepper, wine, or brandy. The inventories do not mention salt.

It has become commonplace in Canadian historiography to claim that habitants were vain, that cowgirls went to the fields decked out like duchesses, and such conspicuous consumption is continually invoked to account for agricultural backwardness.[79] Could habitants who otherwise spent so little on their creature comforts have lost all restraint when it came to clothing? It does not seem so from the inventories.[80] Beauchamps' wardrobe consisted of the basics: a coat, a jerkin, and because nothing was ever thrown out, a second worn-out and worthless jerkin, a pair of hide hose, woollen breeches, a hat, a pair of shoes, stockings, four used shirts, and two nightcaps, worth altogether no more than 40 to 50 *livres*. Even by doubling this amount to account for any omissions, we do not exceed reasonable bounds. A bride could well be endowed with a trousseau worth up to 150 *livres*, but it was made to last a lifetime.

A number of factors allowed about 10 percent of habitants to rise above the mass. Success might depend on unstinting labour and the help of a number of sons, or a secondary occupation compatible with agriculture, such as carting or lime-burning, while a few were exceptionally lucky individuals who had been granted a large urban lot in the early days of the colony and had held on to it long enough to sell it at a profit.[81] It is notable that the better-off these peasants became, the more land they acquired, and if they patched up their buildings, they did not alter their lifestyle. The house was enlarged now that they could afford two stone fireplaces. They added chairs here and there, a panelled armoire, symbol of their success, blankets and sheets, more pewter, and sometimes a small mirror. Here as well there was no hint of ostentation.

One-quarter of inventories list only those debts brought on by the illness and demise of the individual in question. Half the successions recorded between 150 and 400 *livres*, representing mainly family debts such as unpaid succession claims or money owed to children for loans or services they had performed for their parents, along with arrears in seigneurial dues and outstanding accounts with merchants and artisans. If the liabilities proved any heavier, as in one-quarter of the sample, the movables had to be sold. The land was not affected because the merchants would not take it and usually did not extend loans beyond the value of livestock, tools, and other moveables. But without these, the farms could not be cultivated.

There is no sign of hoarding among these peasants. Two or three among the richest may have kept some gold or silver coins, but we find in the inventories neither card money nor beaver. The sums owed to the community included returns from grain, cattle, or land sales as well as anticipated inheritance shares. The peasantry took part in exchanges, as shown by these inventories, but they were never sufficiently important to disrupt or to strengthen their position.

• The Social Dimension

How much of the social system of *ancien régime* France survived in this small shoot transplanted to the American continent? Although occupational boundaries may sometimes have been hazy—which was not atypical *per se*—there was a fairly well-defined professional hierarchy. Still, the brakes on the colonial economy and easy access to land tended to reduce material differences and to bring the members of the various social groups to the same level. This apparent equality masks the cleavages that remained under the surface. We must be able to recognize them and to follow any possible realignments in order to discover both the nature and the direction of social mobility.

Those who deny the existence of a coherent hierarchical structure invoke the fluidity of titles and of the vocabulary of appellation.[82] Yet the evolution of the terminology would seem, on the contrary, to indicate a very precise awareness of concrete realities and of the underlying subordinations. Take the word "habitant," which has been used throughout this work as a synonym for peasants, although this meaning only evolved very slowly. The term was first used to refer to free property owners, who were therefore differentiated from those who were not: servants, soldiers, and nonpropertied volunteers.[83] This status entailed some privileges. Notarized deeds and enumerations mention "carpenter habitants" and "merchant habitants" or simply "habitants," meaning those who had no other occupation than clearing and tilling the soil.[84] Around 1675 notaries began to distinguish between merchants and masons "residing on the Island of Montreal" and the "habitants on this island" and at the end of the century we read: "Pierre Désautels habitant resident of this island."[85] In the intervening period, ordinances defining the status of habitant ceased to have any effect. People without resident status and who did not own land in Montreal came to work in the town. Servants and soldiers alike took part in the fur trade. Shedding the restrictive distinctions that it had first acquired in the colony, the term came to denote no more than the age-old notion of a holder and tiller of a censive.[86] The *bailli* makes this plain: "*Manant*, habitant, tiller of the soil," he once shouted at a churchwarden who vied with him for the best place in church.[87] When Bacqueville de La Potherie wrote around 1700 of "the habitants of the countryside who would be called peasants in any other country," he was slightly mistaken, for the notion of land ownership remained tied to the term habitant, which is why tenant-farmers were referred to as "laboureurs."[88] Should one both own and rent one became a "laboureur and habitant." No other distinctions were evident in the countryside, and the uniformity of the vocabulary expresses the absence of hierarchy that we have already noted.

As the meaning of the word "habitant" narrowed, the term "bourgeois" made its appearance. At first there were only "bourgeois merchants," but the appellation gradually spread. Yet it was not enough to reside in the town to earn this form of respect, one had also to hold a certain rank. Notaries, bailiffs, surgeons, and innkeepers, artisans and fur traders employing other men, even retired habitants living in town in homes of their own either adopted the title or were sometimes accorded it. The term basically referred to people who did not perform lowly tasks. The distinction was bolstered by the widespread use of the word "bourgeois" to mean "master." *Voyageurs*, apprentices, and servants worked for "their bourgeois." All this denotes a clear perception of the evolution of the society.

What of the question of the particles and titles that have repeatedly led historians astray? Canadian usage did not really differ from that current in France. Men who called themselves "*écuyers*" in Montreal were either noblemen or reputed to be noble, and managed to retain that status.

Surnames may have been more prevalent in Canada than elsewhere. Immigrants came with them, but most originated in the fur trade. The traders, influenced perhaps by the particularism prevalent among the military, institutionalized the adoption of surnames, which eventually eclipsed family names.[89] A number of Trottiers went out west at the beginning of the century, yet they appear in the merchants' account books under the names of Desauniers, Desruisseaux, and Des Rivières, along with La Feilliade, La Fortune, La Déroute and so on. When these adventurers became more established, they dubbed themselves "Sieur des Rivières," and the particle might well stand separately. Because this practice was so widespread among the lower classes, it leaves no room for misinterpretation, while a reverse snobbery may well have impelled some people to use only their names or surnames as their signatures.[90] Whatever the case, a change of patronym never propelled anyone upwards. The bulk of the habitants, small artisans, and workers continued to be known by their first and last names or surnames and were often tagged "le nommé" (known as). The "Sieur" and parallel "dame" and "demoiselle" tended to be confined to those who called themselves bourgeois. This may have included quite a variety of humble folk in the case of notarized deeds or parish records, which they dictated themselves, but in the tax rolls, or in the list of creditors recorded in postmortem inventories, such usage was restricted to the upper echelons of the bourgeoisie. It could also depend on the writer. The Sulpicians were grudging with titles and in their enumerations would accord the petty nobility only the right to a "Sieur," like the rest of the notables. They kept "monsieur" for the governor, the lieutenant du roi, and the Crown's top representatives. Notaries were more liberal. Officers were invariably dubbed "monsieur," and merchants often were as well. A properly trained notary knew how to respect traditional gradations, something the merchants were also aware of. When Raimbault made a few slips in an inventory list of over two hundred pages, the son of the deceased corrected the erroneous titles and had the notary add those he had omitted.[91] These Sieurs altered to monsieur or vice versa, these carefully crossed-out prefixes of "ma" or "la," show the survival of a "chain of contempt," and the squabbles over precedence reveal the tensions that accompanied it.

This society was obviously not fixed. To see it clearly, it is useful to make a distinction between the mobility of entire groups, involving changes in their composition and in the gaps that separated them, and the social mobility of individuals.[92] Promotion was most noticeable at the bottom of the social scale. A loose group of destitute and unemployed individuals turned into small landowners and within one generation attained a certain level of security and respectability. This is the fundamental phenomenon.[93] Another slower ascension, which affected fewer people, was the transformation of *coureurs de bois* into *voyageurs*. An entire group pulled itself up from the lowest and most discredited of social positions and succeeded in carving itself a niche within the mercantile hierarchy. The casualties were heavy, and once the group had been safely installed, it pulled away the ladder. Yet this remains a clear example of the transformation of the socioprofessional structure. The group achieved a level of social recognition that it had been denied at the outset.

Other categories were not affected: the nobility remained at the top, followed by the most successful merchants. The entry of individuals from the lower ranks into the upper may look impressive because the latter group was so tiny, but viewed from the standpoint of the number of persons who rose from the masses, upward mobility appears rather insignificant. In the first fifteen to twenty years there was enough room at the top to create some social stir. Of the 270 immigrants enumerated in 1667, 5 percent had risen in the social scale or were about to.[94] But the higher echelons soon closed ranks, and thereafter only a handful would be allowed in. Altogether, between 1642 and 1715 there were barely ten people who had initially performed some manual work in the colony and then managed to have others forget this. The gunsmith Fezeret may have had his finger in many pies, but at the end of his days his contemporaries still referred to him as the "bonhomme Fezeret" who paid in labour for his pew in church.[95] His daughter would marry a lieutenant, scion of a metropolitan family of the robe, but the match would do nothing to improve the craftsman's status.[96]

Actually there was a great deal of downward social mobility. The volume of external trade did not keep pace with the population; capital did not multiply as fast as the offspring of merchants. Thus the proportional difference between the members of the upper crust and the rest declined steadily, which meant that the excessive numbers produced by the first generation of merchants were relegated to the lower ranks. The Perthuis family is a good example. Pierre Perthuis was the son of a small Amboise merchant and came to Canada around 1667. He was twenty-three and could rely on the support of a number of relatives living in the colony.[97] In 1681 he already figured in the second stratum of merchant-outfitters. He was a man of good reputation who traded cautiously and led a modest life. His net assets at his death were of the order of 50 000 *livres*.[98] His two surviving sons and six sons-in-law were unable to maintain his socioeconomic station. Two branches played some role in the trade, but as simple *voyageurs*.[99] The other descendants were habitants. There is no doubt that the sharing of the inheritance into eight equal parts brought on this fall. A single heir would probably have been able to hold on to his position within the merchant community, but any others would inevitably have been driven back. The ascent of a merchant could be speedily reversed.

More money and fewer children might halt this downward pressure, as would close ties with the class that was safeguarded from the vagaries of trade, whose reproduction was therefore not constrained by economic fluctuations. There was only one sure way to keep one's social status for more than one generation, and that was by joining the colonial nobility. Of some

120 merchants whose concerns were thriving at one time or another between 1650 and 1724, three were accorded this ultimate sanction in their lifetimes, while the descendants of another four would eventually achieve it.

There were few avenues of ascension. The Crown had begun by conferring nobility in order to encourage colonization: seven Canadian merchants were granted such letters gratis before 1669, as were four others later in the century, before the practice was abandoned.[100] Charles Lemoyne, ennobled in 1668 as a tribute to the handsome fortune he was amassing and for services rendered, was the only Montrealer in this group. Jacques Leber purchased one of the blank letters of nobility sold by Louis XIV during the War of the League of Augsburg. His ships were sailing the high seas, and he had a capital of about 250 000 *livres*. He could well afford to spend the requisite 6000 *livres*.[101] There were fewer handouts of this sort in the eighteenth century, and no Canadian was either able or bold enough to request them.[102] Ennobling offices, so common in France, did not exist in the colony. Possession of a fief, of course, did not convey nobility, and it did not necessarily signify upward mobility. By confusing the issues of seigneury, nobility, and prestige some Canadian historians have constructed a completely muddled picture of this society. "It is not fitting for an ordinary habitant to hold fiefs," but there was nothing to stop commoners from buying those that the Crown had granted to noblemen.[103] There were a number of seigneurial properties on the market, and these were purchased mainly by merchants, sometimes by artisans or peasants. Why else, we might wonder, if not for prestige? If that was what the landclearer Laurent Bory had in mind in 1672, when he settled on his fief of La Guillaudière, two thousand *arpents* of forest, then he was in for a terrible disappointment. He would never be known as Bory, Sieur de Grandmaison. He remained a peasant, and when his son wed the daughter of a carpenter, he did not marry beneath him.[104] Pierre Lamoureux bought the *arrière-fief* that the brothers Berthé owned on the west end of the Island of Montreal, but this did not improve his social standing, and despite the excellent location, neither father nor sons made a go as outfitters.[105] The edge-tool maker Milot bought the fief of Cavelier de La Salle in 1669 and continued to work at his craft, leaving some money behind. In 1700 Montrealers continued to refer to him as "le bourguignon," as they always had done.[106] His children had decent dowries but made ordinary marriages, and even the descendants of the eldest son, who inherited the fief, remained people of low status. Other such examples could be found. There was more prestige attached to the title of "merchant bourgeois of Montreal" than to that of "seigneur" of such and such a place, a title that was in fact used rarely, those with land merely mentioning if need be that they were the "owners" of a particular fief.

Merchants sometimes bought fiefs because they came for nothing and in many cases were cheaper than a good censive on the outskirts of Montreal. The grantees were badly in need of money and let thousands of uncultivated *arpents* go for 2000 to 3000 *livres*. A merchant could well afford to invest such a small sum, and even if he did not improve this distant property, he could look forward to some capital gains once settlement spread.[107] Charles Lemoyne acquired Île Perrot for 825 *livres* in 1684, and his son resold it twenty years later, unimproved, for 2625 *livres*, which represented a decent profit.[108] Those who made a bigger outlay expected immediate returns. Couagne, for example, began by taking an option on La Chesnaye. He farmed out the domain and granted a few censives, yet six months later allowed the deal to drop. A little later he acquired an uninhabited fief on the Richelieu for a song.[109] For such merchants, who showed little interest in developing these properties, did not live on them, and sold at the first opportunity, these were mere speculations without any social significance.[110]

Jacques Testart, a merchant's son who distinguished himself in the militia, managed to enter the officer corps and was awarded the St-Louis Cross, becoming *ipso facto* integrated into the colonial nobility.[111] But this was a rare occurrence. Officer families produced a surfeit of candidates for the military, and commissions could not be purchased, leaving little room for merchant ambitions in that direction. Exceptional valour might earn one a place, but it was difficult to outdo those who had natural claims.[112]

The right marriage might further a family's social advancement. "I will insist," the governor wrote the minister, "that in the future officers make marriages that are both suitable and profitable."[113] The authorities showed great interest in these matters. One way to help poor noblemen was to encourage them to make good matches. One widow brought 10 000 *livres* to an officer discharged from the Carignan regiment who had survived on government bounty, and this pleased the intendant no end.[114] The union of the ensign Leber, who was already well off, with the daughter of a merchant worth 50 000 *écus*, was of course sufficiently noteworthy to be mentioned to the minister.[115] A *mésalliance* was only noticed when a young man of good birth took it into his head to marry a commoner who brought him nothing. Yet on the whole the nobility tended to close ranks. The exogamy rate for a sample of fifty officer families with a total of ninety-two first- and second-generation marriages stands at 33 percent.[116] Since the group represented no more than 2 percent of the population, it was relatively homogeneous, especially since most of the exogamous unions adhered to the classic schema, meaning that it was only women of the lower classes who were raised up. The inverse was exceptional.[117] In most cases these unions had no effect on the status of the bride's relatives, although in a few instances where the commoner family had some means, it did trigger upward mobility. Couagne's children were able to pursue military careers because his widow remarried a young officer. The same advantage accrued to the sons of J.-B. Charly, whose wife was a d'Ailleboust. However, the business relations sealed by such unions have more importance, for we should never forget that this petty military nobility was involved in the fur trade. In Canada it was not the bourgeoisie that set itself to conquer the nobility's economic bastions but the officers who invaded the world of commerce. The Crown did all it could to help them: they were handed trade permits and the leases of the western outposts, and they did not lose their noble status. The merchants had no choice but to stick with them, to finance and support them, in order to profit from privileges that they as commoners would never be given directly and without which, ironically enough, the merchants might eventually have lost their hold on trade. This was a very odd situation, filled with the potential for conflict, to say the least, but one that the merchants accepted passively until the end of the regime. There were no "bourgeois-gentilshommes" in New France, in spite of the title of a well-known study.[118] There were gentilshommes and there were bourgeois, the latter too insecure, too few, not rich and experienced enough to be fully conscious of their position. Unconcerned with the nature of the regime, they accepted the alliance they were offered, and they worked tirelessly to cement it until they lost their partners, a century later, and found themselves alone, facing a group of foreign officers who could well dispense with their services.

• Notes

1 No single source provides a good picture of the occupational structure after 1681. The following approximation combines census quantitative data with partial information found in a 1715 tax roll and in the 1731 seigneurial survey, supplemented with genealogical sources and my own index of Montreal families from Notarial Records.

2 National Archives of Canada (hereafter NA), MG 17, A7, 2, 1, vol. 2, 487ff.

3 The two highest assessments, of 400 and 200 *livres* for the Sulpicians and Jesuits respectively, were not included.

4 J. Dupâquier, "Problème de mesure et de représentation graphique en histoire sociale," *Actes du 89ᵉ congrès des sociétés savantes,* vol. 3 (1964); Régine Robin, *La Société française en 1789: Semur-en-Auxois* (Paris, 1970), 157ff.

5 René Baehrel, *Une Croissance: la Basse-Provence rurale (fin du XVIᵉ siècle–1789),* 441–42.

6 This represents the totality of those extant prior to 1700, and seventy-five

others dating from 1700 to 1730, related to the families observed in the earlier period.

7 See the debts owed to notaries listed in the inventories, e.g., that of Brunet *dit* Bourbonnais, 16 Oct. 1709, Notarial Records, Archives nationales du Québec, Montreal (hereafter Not. Rec.), Le Pailleur.

8 Pierre Gadois' inventory, 3–4 Nov. 1667, ibid., Basset.

9 The *cru* actually only applied to non-productive items that would wear out in time.

10 According to the method used by A. Hansen-Jones, based on the classification of the American Bureau of Statistics: "La Fortune privée en Pennsylvanie, New Jersey, Delaware: 1774," *Annales: Économies, Sociétés, Civilisations* (March–April 1969): 235–49.

11 Despite the evidence, historians such as Emile Salone, W.B. Munro, F. Parkman, B. Sulte, Rameau de Saint-Père, and others, have described the

whole social structure in terms of the seigneury.

12 The vassals were the two female convents and the gentlemen-soldiers who had to protect the island against invasion in return for their strategically located fiefs. The arrival of the troops rendered such arrangements unnecessary.

13 As opposed to the distribution of seigneurial revenues in France, where *fermages* held first place. G. Le Marchand, "Le Féodalisme dans la France rurale des temps modernes: essai de caractérisation," *Annales historiques de la Révolution française*, no. 190 (1969): 77–108.

14 Letter from M. Leschassier, 5 April 1702, Archives of St-Sulpice in Paris (hereafter ASSP), vol. 14, 411.

15 So Pehr Kalm reported, *Voyage de Kalm en Amérique* (Montreal, 1880), 111.

16 P.-G. Roy, *Lettres de noblesse, généalogies, érections de comté et baronies instituées par le Conseil souverain de la Nouvelle-France*, 2 vols. (Beauceville, 1920).

17 Letter of 13 Nov. 1685, Archives des colonies (hereafter AC), C11A, 7, fol. 93v.

18 Letters from the intendants between 1679 and 1690, and especially ibid., vol. 5, fols. 49–50, and vol. 8, fol. 145v.

19 Commissions in the Compagnies Franches de la Marine were not venal.

20 The expression is Robert Mandrou's: "oisiveté en armes," in *Classes et luttes de classes en France au début du XVIIᵉ siècle* (Florence, 1965), 31.

21 Testimony of 23 Oct. 1683, *bailliage*, ser. 1, reg. 2; another of 17 April 1684 before the Conseil, *Jugements et délibérations du Conseil souverain* (hereafter *JDCS*), vol. 2, 947–48. The names of the culprits do not figure in the records of the Conseil.

22 Letter from the governor, 8 May 1686, C11A, 8, fol. 12v.

23 Ibid., vol. 7, 147. See Gaston Zeller, "Une Notion de caractère historico-social: la dérogeance" in *Aspects de la*

politique française sous l'Ancien Régime (Paris, 1964), 336–74.

24 Letter from the governor, 20 Nov. 1686, AC, C11A, 8, fols. 144–144v. The father threatened to take his ten children back to France, "where they might earn their bread and go into service here or there." Official correspondence is full of such wails and blackmail.

25 See Cameron Nish, *Les Bourgeois-gentilshommes de la Nouvelle-France, 1729–1748* (Montreal, 1968), 113–15.

26 AC, C11A, 7, fols. 97v.–98, and vol. 8, fols. 12–123v.

27 They left behind between 20 000 and 40 000 *livres*. Not. Rec., Maugue, 13 March 1679, 21 Dec. 1683; Basset, 5 Dec. 1684.

28 Those of Captains Dugué, Pécaudy, Daneau, Blaise, d'Ailleboust, Duplessis, Gresolon, Marganne, Dufresnel, of Lieutenants de Ganne, de Gauthier, Bizard, and Piot, staff officers, and Lamothe, Picoté, Carion, and La Fresnaye, militia officers. All were called "*écuyer.*"

29 Inventory of René Gauthier of Varennes, an officer retired from the Carignan regiment, governor of Trois-Rivières: Not. Rec., A. Adhémar, 1 July 1693.

30 See, for example, the inventory of the lieutenant de roi Piot de Langloiserie, 5 Dec. 1722, ibid., Senet.

31 About 2000 *livres*. Inventory of Antoine Pécaudy de Contrecoeur, 10 April 1792, ibid., Basset.

32 Six of the seventeen were tenants.

33 He corresponded with Vauban. See L. Dechêne, ed., *La Correspondence de Vauban relative au Canada* (Quebec, 1968), 15–22.

34 The Sulpician Rémy wrote that d'Ailleboust was entirely relying on his advice: Archives of St-Sulpice in Montreal (hereafter ASSM), copy Faillon H 339–46. Appointment of Migeon, 6 Aug. 1677, *bailliage*, copy Faillon H 213.

35 Charles Juchereau de Saint-Denis, lieutenant-général until he died in 1704.

36 Letter from M. Tronson, 20 April 1677, ASSP, vol. 13, 422; minutes of *bailliage*, Feb.–March 1678, ser. 1, reg. 1; E.-Z. Massicotte, "L'Hôtel-Dieu et la famille Basset," *Le Journal de l'Hôtel-Dieu* (Nov. 1942): 431ff.

37 André Vachon, *Histoire du notariat canadien, 1621–1960* (Presses de l'université Laval, 1962).

38 Inventory of 14 May 1714, Not. Rec., Le Pailleur.

39 Inventory of 25 March 1693, ibid., A. Adhémar.

40 Hilaire Bourgine, son of a La Rochelle merchant and F. Pougnet's clerk.

41 See the examples of the seventeenth-century Montreal notaries Pierre Cabazié, Claude Maugue, Nicolas Senet, and J.-B. Pottier.

42 Inventory of 29 Oct. 1700, Not. Rec., Raimbault.

43 E.-Z. Massicotte, biography of Raimbault, in *Bulletin des recherches historiques* (hereafter *BRH*), vol. 21, 78, and vol. 27, 182; entry in the *Dictionary of Canadian Biography* (hereafter *DCB*), vol. 2.

44 Postmortem inventory of his first wife, 10 Dec. 1706, Not. Rec., A. Adhémar.

45 Soumande and Lestage. See AC, C11A, 124, fol. 393, and ASSP, doss. 20, item 4.

46 Inventory of 18 April 1708, Not. Rec., A. Adhémar; and of 14 April 1712, ibid., Le Pailleur.

47 According to the description of the two inventories of 1 Dec. 1693 and 1 Dec. 1706, ibid., Basset and Raimbault.

48 Yves Zoltvany noticed a similar sobriety in Aubert de La Chenaye, a major Quebec merchant. *DCB*, vol. 2, 27–36.

49 Couagne's inventory of 7 Aug. 1686, ibid., Maugue; and 26 Aug. 1706, ibid., A. Adhémar.

50 Inventories of Jean Magnan, René Malet, Jacques Hubert-Lacroix, ibid., 14 March 1694, 23 March 1698, Adhémar; 20 March 1720, Le Pailleur.

51 Inventories of 10 Oct. 1687, ibid., Cabazié; and 28 Jan. 1704, ibid., A. Adhémar.

52 Ten *livres* and confiscation for public disturbance on a Sunday to Vincent Dugast, for whom this was the umpteenth condemnation. Jan. 1689, *bailliage*, ser. 2, reg. 1.

53 See, for example, the list of licences granted by the court, 10 Dec. 1694, ibid., reg. 3.

54 Inventory of 30 Dec. 1698, Not. Rec., A. Adhémar.

55 Petition of the armourer Fezeret to obtain a certificate, and that of the cartwright Brazeau for the establishment of a craft guild. AC, C11A, 12, fols. 333v. and 310v.

56 Contract of 16 Dec. 1675, Not. Rec., Basset.

57 See the regulations contained in the *bailliage* registers.

58 Petition by the butchers, 4 June 1709, *bailliage*, Archives nationales du Québec (hereafter ANQ), NF 21, vol. 13.

59 Brunet, Bouchard, and Lecour were sentenced to a 35-*livre* fine each, 4 June 1709, *bailliage*, ser. 2, reg. 5.

60 Inventories of 3 Nov. 1689, 11 April 1699, and 6 March 1700, ibid., A. Adhémar.

61 Dated 20 July 1706, Raudot, *Edits, ordonnances royaux*, vol. 2, 265.

62 De Launay, Barsalou, Bélair, Noir.

63 Including what he advanced to his children prior to his death. Inventories of 6 July 1663, Not. Rec., Basset, and 21 Aug. 1700, ibid., A. Adhémar.

64 Ibid., Maugue, 28 April 1684; David, 4 Nov. 1720.

65 Inventory of Tessier, 2 Aug. 1689, and of Dumets, 9 Feb. 1691, ibid., A. Adhémar.

66 Elizabeth J. Lunn, *Economic Development in New France 1713–1760* (Presses de l'Université de Montréal, 1986), 185.

67 Leber hired a blacksmith. See the seigneurs' leases, 16 Dec. 1669 and 17 June 1677, Not. Rec., Basset.

68 In 1691, for instance, there were some fifty such lawsuits, one-sixth of all civil litigations.

69 René Allary, Moise Hilleret, Janson *dit* Lapalme, Jourdain, etc.

70 Inventory of 5 Oct. 1699, Not. Rec., A. Adhémar.

71 See the case of Martinet *dit* Fontblanche and that of Antoine Forestier.

72 According to Peter N. Moogk, who made a systematic study of these contracts: "Apprenticeship Indentures: A Key to Life in New France," *Canadian Historical Association Report* (hereafter *CHAR*) (1971): 68.

73 Laurent Tessier's apprenticeship indenture to Gilles Lauson, 1 Nov. 1673, Not. Rec., Basset. Butchers and millers also took over from generation to generation.

74 Letter from Frontenac and Champigny, 4 Nov. 1693, AC, C11A, 12, fol. 209v.

75 A man employed all year round earned between 100 and 120 *livres*, which was therefore a better deal.

76 The Hôpital général, founded in 1694 and supported by grants and charitable donations, was poorly administered until 1747 and did very little to help the residents. Only seven people (mentally ill, aged, or paupers) were admitted during the twenty years following its creation, another fifty or thereabouts between 1714 and 1747, but these mainly consisted of disabled soldiers. "Mouvement annuel des pauvres reçus à l'Hôpital général, 1694–1747," archives of the Montreal Hôpital général.

77 Inventory of 25 Oct. 1695, Not. Rec., Pottier.

78 He had come to Canada as an indentured servant in 1659 and had lived on the same property for twenty-five years. He is a good example of the reasonable though modest achievement of most immigrants.

79 This view, based on one or two superficial accounts of colonial mores, received wide acceptance. See W.J. Eccles, *The Canadian Frontier 1534–1760* (Toronto, 1969), 94; F. Ouellet, "La Mentalité et l'outillage économique de l'habitant canadien 1760," *BRH* 63, 3 (1956).

80 Clothes were not always inventoried. Only forty decent descriptions were found.

81 Jean Leduc was among them. He died when he was eighty-one, leaving behind six enterprising sons and net assets of 18 000 *livres.*

82 Marcel Trudel, "Sur les mutations sociales d'avant 1663: la recherche d'une explication" (paper presented to the Colonial History Conference, Ottawa, March 1970), and "Les Débuts d'une société: Montréal 1642–1663," *Revue d'histoire de l'Amérique française* (hereafter *RHAF*) 23, 2 (Sept. 1969): 185–208.

83 The term was also used in its broad sense, meaning someone who has elected residence somewhere. The second meaning appears in Trévoux's dictionary (1752): "Habitant ou colon en parlant des colonies se dit d'un particulier auquel le souverain a accordé des terres pour les défricher et les cultiver à son profit."

84 Fiefs were also known as "habitations," but noble seigneurs were not called "habitants." See Conrad Filion, "Essai sur l'évolution du mot habitant, XVIIe–XVIIIe siècles," *RHAF* 24, 3 (Dec. 1970): 375–401. This discussion follows that author's argument but relies on different sources, closer to common usage and shift of meaning over time.

85 Postmortem inventory, 14 June 1693, Not. Rec., A. Adhémar.

86 Abel Poitrineau, *La Vie rurale en Basse-Auvergne au XVIIIe siècle (1726–1789)* (Paris, 1965), 76.

87 Statement of 3 April 1675, Not. Rec., Basset. The term *manant*, unlike that of *paysan*, survived in the colony. "He lived off lard and peas like an artisan or *manant*," wrote the merchant La Chesnaye. Bibliothèque nationale, Paris (hereafter BN) mss r., NA, 9273.

88 *Histoire de l'Amérique septentrionale* (1722), quoted by Filion, "Essai sur l'évolution du mot habitant."

89 André Corvisier, *L'Armée française de la fin du XVIIe siècle au ministère de Choiseul: Le Soldat*, vol. 2, 851–61. The author's lists reveal a sizeable sample of present-day Canadian last names, from Belhumeur to Vadeboncoeur by way of Dechêne and Sanfaçon.

90 Alexis Lemoine, for example, never put down more than his surname, "Monière," on whatever he signed.

91 Inventory of Jacques Leber, 1 Dec. 1706, Not. Rec., Raimbault. The family had just acquired a title, which explains the heir's sensitivity to the issue.

92 Lawrence Stone, "Social Mobility in England, 1500–1700," *Past and Present* 33 (April 1966): 16–55.

93 See S. Thernstrom, "Notes on the Historical Study of Social Mobility," *Comparative Studies in History and Society* 10, 2 (Jan. 1968): 171.

94 This includes very ordinary cases of social ascension, such as soldiers or indentured servants who became notaries or small merchants. Only eight families can be said to have really broken with their roots: the Lemoyne, Dupuis, Closse, Robutel, Charly, Culerié, Godé, and for a while, the Milot families.

95 Accounts of the year 1707–8 by J.-J. Lebé, then warden, archives of the Notre-Dame parish, A-14.

96 The bridegroom was Gabriel De Thiersant de Genlis. See the entry by Jules Bazin in the *DCB*, vol. 2, 229.

97 He was related to Louis Rouer de Villeray, a merchant and controller of the ferme du Canada and a conseiller du roi. *DCB*, vol. 1, 593–96. Two other Perthuis, Nicolas and Charles, hailing from the same parts, no doubt his cousins, arrived in Canada in 1690. Charles left a greater mark on the society.

98 "He is an old propertied merchant," the intendant wrote about him. AC, C11A, 125, fol. 365ff; inventory of 18 April 1708, Not. Rec., A. Adhémar; and other deeds concerning the inheritance, from the same notary.

99 One son was killed in New England in 1709; another, a *voyageur*, settled at Détroit; one of his sons-in-law, Pierre Maguet, lost the little he had brought with him to Canada through trading and lived on his farm; another son-in-law, Louis Lefebvre-Duchouquet, spent his life as a *voyageur*. Desroche, Gervaise, and Caron were habitants. P.-G. Roy, "La Famille Perthuis," *BRH* 41:449–77.

100 P.-G. Roy, *Lettres de noblesse, généaologies*.

101 AN (Paris), ser. P, item 6119; the biography by Yves Zoltvany in the *DCB*, vol. 2, 389–90.

102 Pierre Goubert, *L'Ancien Régime*, vol. 1 (Paris, 1969), 172.

103 Letter from the governor and the intendant, 15 Oct. 1736, cited by R.C. Harris, *The Seigneurial System in Early Canada: A Geographical Study* (Quebec and Madison, WI, 1967), 44–45. Harris clearly recognizes that the ownership of a seigneury was not the key to social prestige.

104 Census of La Guillaudière, 31 Aug. 1677, Not. Rec., Basset.

105 *Aveu et dénombrement* of the fief of Bellevue, 24 Aug. 1683, ibid., Basset. His widow refused the estate but the sons managed to buy back the fief from the main creditor.

106 List of creditors in the Gervaise inventory, 14 Sept. 1700, ibid., A. Adhémar;

verdict of the intendant of 11 May 1685, ibid., Basset.

107 See, for example, the fiefs purchased by Louis Lecomte-Dupré, René Fezeret, J.-B. Neveu, and Jacques Charbonnier.

108 Contracts of 2 March 1684, Not. Rec., Basset, and 27 April 1703, ibid., A. Adhémar. Bouat did much better by buying Terrebonne for 5268 *livres* and selling it for 10 000 *livres* two years later: Nish, *Les Bourgeois-gentilshommes*, 118. But such speculation usually brought only moderate returns.

109 Contract drawn up in Quebec on 6 Oct. 1699, ANQ, Chamballon; tenancy lease of 30 Oct. 1699, Not. Rec., A. Adhémar; Couagne's inventory of 26 Aug. 1706, ibid.

110 As Habbakuk has noted for England, we cannot always approach land purchases in terms of social prestige. They were often good investments that, in the long term, compared favourably with the returns from trade. But since this was not the case in Montreal, merchants bought little land, and the question of prestige was not usually a consideration. H.J. Habbakuk, "The English Land Market in Eighteenth-Century Britain and the Netherlands" in *Britain and the Netherlands*, ed. J.S. Bromley and Kossmann (Oxford, 1960), 154–73. See also Robert Mandrou, *Les Fugger, propriétaires fonciers en Souabe, 1560–1618* (Paris, 1969), 235ff.

111 Testart was already forty-three and had fought many a glorious campaign as leader of the militia when he received his first commission in the Troupes de la Marine. Some of the men with Cavelier de La Salle, such as

La Forest and You, also rose in this way. *DCB*, vol. 2, 176, 653, 702.

112 On military careers in France, see Elinor G. Barber, *The Bourgeoisie in 18th Century France* (Princeton: 1967), 117–25.

113 Letter from Frontenac, 20 Oct. 1691, AC, C11A, 11, fol. 242.

114 Letter from Talon, 10 Nov. 1670, concerning the marriage of Morel de la Durantaye with the widow of Jean Madry, in Quebec, ibid., vol. 3, fol. 82.

115 Letter from Vaudreuil, 8 Nov. 1718, ibid., vol. 124, fol. 393. See also Frontenac's attempts to arrange a marriage for the major of Montreal, ibid., vol. 12, fols. 236v–237.

116 This includes officers residing in Montreal and others found in Tanguay's dictionary under the letters "d" and "l" in order to broaden the sample. René Jetté's article, "La Stratification sociale: une direction de recherche," *RHAF* 26, 1 (June 1972): 48–52, is interesting, but his rates could not be used since he incorporated too many of the lower categories into his upper class.

117 There were only two such cases in our sample: the marriages of Jean Tessier and Jean-Baptiste Charly.

118 Nish, *Les Bourgeois-gentilshommes*. The author attempts to show that officers and merchants formed a homogeneous group, a single "class." Yet one needs only to look at the emergence and eruption of conflicts after 1760 to realize how fragile this alliance had been. The conquest loosened the economic ties, leaving two fundamentally and consciously opposed groups. See also Guy Frégault, *La Société canadienne sous le régime français* (Ottawa: 1954), 14.

AMERINDIAN VIEWS OF FRENCH CULTURE IN THE SEVENTEENTH CENTURY*

CORNELIUS J. JAENEN

Our historiography has been more concerned with French and Canadian views of the Amerindians than with aboriginal opinions and evaluations of the French culture with which they came into contact during the seventeenth century.[1] Yet, the most elementary canons of historical interpretation require that the values and belief systems of both parties concerned in the contact experience be considered. In general, it has been assumed by historians that not only did Frenchmen consider their civilization superior to the aboriginal cultures of North America but also that the Native tribesmen viewed French culture with awe and admiration, that they often attempted to imitate the Europeans, and usually aspired to elevate themselves to the superior level of the white man. This interpretation was firmly established in European and Canadian literature by Charlevoix, Raynal, Chateaubriand, and Bossange.[2]

Not until the mid-nineteenth century was there any notable departure from this accepted approach to French-Amerindian relations. While it is true that a few earlier French writers had been critical of the ideas and ideals of their compatriots in comparison with Native behaviour, such critical observations were invariably motivated by desires for political and social

*From *Canadian Historical Review* 55, 1 (Sept. 1974): 261–91. Reprinted by permission of University of Toronto Press Incorporated. © University of Toronto Press. This is the revised version of a paper read at the seventh annual Northern Great Plains History Conference, University of Manitoba, 20 Oct. 1972.

reforms, by religious toleration, or by scepticism which related to France more than to North America. Clodoré, Abbeville, de Léry, Boyer, Sagard, and Lescarbot made guarded criticisms of French behaviour and institutions employing Amerindian examples to strengthen their arguments.[3] Maximilien Bibaud was the first French-Canadian to depict the Amerindians in a consistently favourable light. He was fully conscious, moreover, that the aborigines had resisted francization and, in the majority, had rejected conversion.[4] Napoléon Legendre pleaded eloquently in 1884 for an impartial and just treatment of Amerindian history, but his was still a voice of one crying in the wilderness.[5]

It is therefore only quite recently that the sources for the traditional views of the contact experience have been re-examined more critically and that the accepted interpretations have been challenged. In 1903, Léon Gérin began to study the Natives of New France in a new conceptual framework, but his work went largely unnoticed by his contemporaries. In 1925, F.W. Howay attempted to present the aboriginal case and his pioneer work was followed by Diamond Jenness's *The Indians of Canada* (1932) and A.G. Bailey's *The Conflict of European and Eastern Algonkian Cultures, 1504–1700* (1937). More significant still in setting the stage for a thorough-going revision of Amerindian history have been the writings of Jacques Rousseau, Léo-Paul Desrosiers, and André Vachon.[6]

To delineate Amerindian views of French culture and civilization at the time of contact in the seventeenth century is extremely difficult because, first of all, an understanding of both French culture and Amerindian cultures is necessary. More information about French culture in the seventeenth century is available than about Mi'kmaq, Montagnais, Algonquian, Huron, and Iroquoian cultures which were described by French travellers, missionaries, and traders as seen through their own understanding of such cultures and interpreted according to their values and beliefs. The missionaries, as France's foremost cultural ambassadors at the time, tended to undervalue tribal customs and practices, but they soon found that the Amerindians were secure, well-adjusted, and self-reliant peoples. As early as 1616 the report back to France was: "For all your arguments, and you can bring a thousand of them if you wish, are annihilated by this single shaft which they always have at hand, *Aoti Chabaya*, (they say) 'That is the Savage way of doing it. You can have your way and we will have ours; every one values his own wares.'"[7] The historian's task is to attempt to understand both cultures in contact.

Secondly, past events must not only be identified but also be interpreted in the manner seen by each of the participants involved. As the archaeologists have contributed much to an understanding of Amerindian cultures, so the ethnohistorians and anthropologists have contributed to an understanding of the moral assumptions and value systems involved. As Wilcomb Washburn has said, "an understanding of conflicting values seems to be a condition of great history, great imaginative writing, and great religious insight."[8] At least one of the missionaries to the Mi'kmaq realized that French and Algonquian value systems and moral assumptions differed greatly. He wrote: "You must know that they are men like us; that intrinsically they reason as all men must think; that they differ only in the manner of rendering their thoughts, and that if something appears strange to us in their way of thinking it is because we have not been educated like them, and we do not find ourselves in a similar situation to theirs, to reach such conclusions."[9] The inability to understand behaviour and thought as conceived by the various Amerindian cultures was the greatest barrier to French appreciation of Native civilization, and it remains a formidable challenge to the modern historian who attempts to explain and evaluate the contact experience.

The Amerindians, as a nonliterate society, left few documents to assist in reconstructing their views and concepts. The majority of documentary sources are European and, therefore, although designated as primary sources, are interpretations as well as records of events. On the other hand, it can be argued that the recorders were also participants and that this gave them a distinctive advantage over today's social scientists who are deprived of the experience of being eyewitnesses and participants. It is true that the early observers of Native reactions to contact with Frenchmen had commercial, religious, and military interests in the Amerindians and that they studied aboriginal society largely in order to discover vulnerable points which could be exploited to the achievement of their objectives. Nevertheless, in their records, which were sometimes quite comprehensive, they unwittingly related incidents and conversations which enable one to reconstruct Amerindian reactions motivated by beliefs and objectives which the chroniclers frequently ignored.

Moreover, there are few model studies to guide one through the labyrinth of traditional views, or of narrowly professional views such as the stress by the anthropologists on material culture. Acculturation is a two-way process and important as was the French impact on Amerindian cultures, the aboriginal impact on French culture was continuous and significant. These facts cannot be ignored in the study of Amerindian opinions and evaluations of French culture during the early contact period.

These initial contacts strengthened the Europocentric view of history. In the seventeenth century Europeans invariably assumed that Europe was the centre of the world and of civilization, that its cultures were the oldest, that America was a new continent and that its peoples were necessarily recent immigrants. The literature of the period of exploration was dominated by the theme of a New World populated by peoples of different languages and cultures who conducted European explorers and "discoverers" on tours along well-known and well-travelled water routes and trails to the various centres of aboriginal population. The conceptual frameworks of Europeans—whether Spaniards, French, or English, or whether Catholics or Protestants—were remarkably indistinguishable whenever the circumstances of contact were similar. Explorers were fed, sheltered, offered the other amenities of social life, and provided with multilingual guides. In this context Europeans tended to see themselves and their activities as being at the centre of the historical stage.

The French did distinguish, nevertheless, cultural differences among the tribes or "nations" they contacted, although contemporary literature is remarkable for the absence of differentiation on the basis of "race" or pigmentation. On the basis of differences in language and in observable customs and beliefs there was an awareness of the great cultural diversity of the Native peoples. It may be postulated, therefore, that the views of the Mi'kmaq or Montagnais would differ from the views of the Huron or Iroquois. There are a few indications of differing reactions but these can usually be associated with the context of contact rather than with conceptual variations. The nomadic Algonquian cultures were sufficiently different from the Iroquoian groups to elicit varying responses to the French presence, yet the records available to the historian indicate a similarity of response to European intrusion. As there appears now to have been much more of a common European concept of America—rather than markedly different Spanish, French, and English conceptual frameworks—so there appears to have been more of a common Amerindian reaction to the coming of the Europeans than different Mi'kmaq, Huron, or Iroquois responses, with the differences in so-called tribal relations with the French better identified in terms of specific and immediate economic and sociopolitical problems. In other words, it is as justifiable to conceive of Amerindian views of French culture as of European views of the New World, when examining the conceptual frameworks of a generalized culture contact over a period of a century. Such an approach would be less satisfactory if dealing with more specific contact experiences in restricted time periods.

There were a number of features of French life that the Amerindians found admirable and their curiosity was reinforced by a desire to adapt some of the French ways and equipment to their own culture. First of all, they were interested in observing the Europeans in their day-to-day activities. Lescarbot recorded that "the savages from all the country round came to look at the ways of the French, and willingly came among them."[10] Similarly, the Algonquins were amazed at Champlain's men: "The bulk of the savages who were there had never seen a Christian, and could not get over their wonder as they gazed at our customs, our clothing, our arms, our equipment."[11] The Iroquois who held Father Jogues prisoner questioned him at great length about scientific matters and were so impressed by his wisdom and explanations that they regretted the tortures they had inflicted upon him. The greatest appreciation seems to have been for European technology. All tribes showed an appreciation of the knives, hatchets, kettles, beads, cloth and, eventually, the firearms of the French. Indeed the exchange of the beaver pelt coats worn by the tribesmen of the Atlantic coastal region for European iron goods had been initiated by the Breton,

Basque, Norman, and other Western European fishermen at least in the fifteenth century, if not earlier. During the sixteenth century Cartier's
accounts, among others, recorded the Amerindian desire to pursue barter.
His records of the 1534 voyage in the Gaspé region included the following
passage about noisy warriors making signs and "holding up skins on the
end of sticks" which they obviously wished to exchange for European
goods: "two of our men landed to approach them, and bring them knives
and other ironware, with a red hat to give to their captain. Seeing this, they
also landed, carrying these skins of theirs, and began to trade with us,
showing great and marvellous joy to possess this ironware and other such
articles, dancing continually and going through various ceremonies."[12] In
1536 he recorded that each day Natives approached his vessel with eels and
fish to exchange for European goods: "in return they were given knives,
awls, beads, and other such things, wherewith they were much pleased."[13]
In time, the coastal tribes became more exacting in their bartering operations. In 1623, for example, the Montagnais objected to the gift of a few
figs which the French sea captain had offered them and seized knives and
other trade goods saying they would give a fair price for the articles taken.
Sagard, who reported the incident, was amazed that the Montagnais not
only left furs in payment but did so in quantities which outstripped the
value of the goods they had seized.[14]

It should be remarked that originally the fur trade was a noneconomic
exchange between fishermen and aborigines, at least in the sense that for
the Natives noncommercial motives operated. Furs were given to
Europeans because they were desired by the visiting fishermen and it was
part of Algonquian culture to view exchange in noncommercial terms.[15]
They gave their peltries without apparent demand for return, at least at the
time of the initial contacts; nevertheless, whatever the fishermen offered in
exchange was gratefully accepted. There is reason to believe that the
Amerindians valued European trade goods such as beads, mirrors, bells,
and caps, for their aesthetic, magical, or purely decorative and fascinating
worth, not their economic value.[16] Furthermore, this exchange, for the
Amerindians, had a symbolic or diplomatic meaning and was in reality
viewed as an exchange of gifts which established rank and prestige.
Cartier's journals seem to indicate this to have been the context of the
exchanges in the sixteenth century. This difference between European and
Amerindian concepts continued into the seventeenth century and was
demonstrated in the special meaning the tribesmen attached to the
wampum belt, the calumet, or even the hatchet. The French traders and
missionaries, both of whom shared the same economic views, regarded
wampum in materialistic terms whereas the Amerindians viewed it in symbolic terms. Amerindian admiration of trade goods brought them
inevitably into a position of dependence on the French trade. Denys
remarked on the changing values among the Mi'kmaq: "They have abandoned all their own utensils, whether because of the trouble they had as

well to make as to use them, or because of the facility of obtaining from us, in exchange for skins which cost them almost nothing, the things which seemed to them invaluable, not so much for their novelty as for the convenience derived therefrom. Above everything the kettle has always seemed to them, and seems still, the most valuable article they can obtain from us."[17] He related how a Mi'kmaq sent by Governor Razilly to Paris, while passing the street where many coppersmiths were located, asked of his interpreter if they were not "relatives of the King" and if this were not the "trade of the grandest Seigniors of the Kingdom"!

The Amerindians did not always understand French concepts of personal property, their materialistic outlook as evidenced in their desire to accumulate goods, and their fear of losing personal belongings to covetous colleagues. They expected the French to have a better developed sense of kin-group belongings, of sharing of goods, of using the goods or utensils of others if there was urgent need to do so without the formalities of ownership intervening in such cases, and of showing more respect for articles to which ceremonial or magical qualities were attached. Father Sagard reported at Tadoussac in 1617 that the Montagnais were surprisingly honest compared to Frenchmen and saw no risk in leaving their boats unattended over long periods on the beaches and never stole the boats left by the French.[18] Nevertheless, the Mi'kmaq learned, from their experience over a century with European fishermen and traders, that they could exact more and better quality goods for their furs as the competition grew. Lescarbot said: "so great has been the greed that in their jealousy of one another the merchants have spoiled the trade. Eight years ago, for two biscuits or two knives, one had a beaver, while to-day one must give fifteen or twenty: and in this very year 1610 some have given away to the savages their whole stock in trade, in order to obstruct the holy enterprise of M. de Poutrincourt, so great is human avarice."[19] The Montagnais who had come to trade at Tadoussac in March 1611 were reported as having brought only poor quality furs "and even these few they are fain to employ to the best advantage while awaiting the arrival of a crowd of vessel . . . to have their goods better cheap; wherein they are well skilled now that the avarice of our merchants has made itself known in those parts."[20]

Their developing interest in large-scale trade led them to acquire a taste for brandy and other intoxicants which they soon came to demand and to expect as a concomitant of contact. A Dutch version of Deny's history recounted how the aborigines stood along the shores where fishing vessels were known to come and how they made smoke signals to the crews of vessels they sighted inviting them to come to barter for furs: "The skins are bartered for brandy, for which they ever since they have begun to trade with fishermen are very greedy; and they herewith fill themselves up to such an extent that they frequently fall over backwards, for they do not call it drinking unless they overload themselves with this strong drink in a beastly fashion."[21] Whatever the reasons for the low tolerance the

Amerindians had for alcohol and their eventual social disorganization as a consequence of its nefarious traffic, it is clear from contemporary sources that they developed an inordinate desire for it. It would appear that, although they never liked its taste and they deplored the violence and disorders they committed under its influence, they coveted it in order to obtain release from their cultural and natural inhibitions, to commit unconventional and illegal acts, to attain a new state of spirit possession, and eventually to reduce the tensions they experienced as a result of the contact with purveyors of an alien civilization which gradually undermined their ancestral way of life, eroded their belief system, and left them alienated from their traditions. Alcohol was a major contributor to the breakdown of Amerindian cultural patterns, nevertheless, it was employed by some tribesmen to create or symbolize in-group solidarity against the French, a rejection of European standards and values, and a defiance of the teachings of the Catholic church and of the threatening edicts of the French state.

The Amerindians were very impressed with the French regard for ceremonial and for ritual. The French willingness to engage in ceremonial preludes to trading engagements, to military talks, and to parleys brought the two cultures together. There is some indication also that the tribesmen in general were impressed with the ritual and ceremonial of the Catholic religion, although on this score there seems to have been considerable concern among the early Catholic missionaries and governors that the Amerindians also found the congregational singing of the "songs of Marot" and the participatory worship of the Huguenots very attractive.[22] A missionary wrote with obvious satisfaction: "I say nothing of the esteem manifested by this new Church for all The outward signs of our holy Religion. Crosses, medals, and other similar Articles are Their most precious jewels. So fondly do they preserve These that they wear them around their necks, even at preaching in New Holland, where The heretics have never been able to tear from Them a single bead of Their Rosaries."[23]

In addition to the beautiful ritual of the mass, the solemn processions and the adoration of the Blessed Sacrament, the secular celebrations of the French impressed the Natives. The celebration in 1639 at Quebec upon receipt of the news of the birth of the future Louis XIV was recorded as follows:

> Bon-fires were built with all possible ceremony, rockets were discharged, Roman candles flared, golden rain descended, the night was illuminated with tapers, and the forest resounded with the thunder of guns. On this occasion the Hurons were present, since they were paying their customary visit to Quebec, which is the market of the whole country. They had never seen the like before and astounded and amazed they put their right hands to their mouths, which is their method of exhibiting joyous emotion.[24]

The French for a long time held to the idea of bringing a few Natives from each tribe to France to impress them with their might and civilization. Lahontan told of six *sagamos* at Versailles at one time, all soliciting aid against the English. But, Lahontan inferred that the chieftains were less interested in the beauty and grandeur of Versailles than they were in employing French power and wealth for the achievements of their own ends. Eventually the French Crown concluded that the Amerindians were sufficiently aware of the military might of France and that the bringing of representatives to France was unnecessary. The French did sense the Native appreciation of presents, however, and they satisfied them in this matter. LeClercq explained this need of recognition, this need for prestige and security:

> They are fond of ceremony and are anxious to be accorded some when they come to trade at French establishments; and it is consequently in order to satisfy them that sometimes the guns and even the canon are fired on their arrival. The leader himself assembles all the canoes near his own and ranges them in good order before landing, in order to await the salute which is given him, and which all the Indians return to the French by the discharge of their guns. Sometimes the leaders and chiefs are invited for a meal in order to show all the Indians that they are esteemed and honoured. Rather more frequently they are given something like a fine coat, in order to distinguish them from the commonalty. For such things as this they have a particular esteem, especially if the article has been in use by the commander of the French.[25]

Here was a fortunate cultural convergence; the French held views of precedence as this related to concepts of rank, estate, dignity, *splendeur*. The Amerindians were very pleased with French commissions, special uniforms, medals, and titles of nobility. The Mi'kmaq regarded medals as "titres de noblesse" and they secured their loyalty, according to the missionaries. Dièreville mentioned the loyalty and devotion to the French of a chieftain he met at Port Royal whose grandfather had been "ennobled" by Henry IV.[26]

Another aspect of French life which the Amerindian did not comprehend but in the end came rather to admire was the generous and kindly treatment of the sick by the Sisters Hospitallers who arrived in Quebec in 1639. A dreadful smallpox epidemic, alleged to have come from Virginia— as all accursed events seemed to the colonists to have their origins in the English colonies—took a heavy toll of Natives and the nuns themselves were "attacked by the malady." Du Creux recorded of these devout women that: "with scarcely any interruption of their pious labours, they presented such a strange spectacle to the savages, who are quite without the emotion of pity, that they could not restrain their surprise that women could be found eager to encounter so many perils, and to penetrate unknown regions in order to succour those whom the Indians themselves generally abandon or kill."[27] Actually, the Amerindian could not have been astounded by the willingness of women to serve in evangelical labours in a distant land—that was a marvel to Europeans and a most unusual event in

Catholic history—but they were astounded by the care the French lavished on the sick and dying. In the Native encampments the terminally ill and the very aged were abandoned to their fate. They expected this treatment and there was no lack of pity attached to such action. The moralizing quality attributed to the treatment of the unfortunates is an example of European value judgments being applied to a different culture.

Indeed, on a wide range of points of contact at the military, social, religious, educational, agricultural, medical, and organizational level the Amerindian evaluation of French culture and civilization was often as unflattering as was the low regard of Frenchmen for Amerindian culture. Each group had its own somatic norm image, or "complex of physical characteristics which are accepted by a group as its norm and ideal," by which it evaluated and analysed other societies.[28] Thus, the French considered themselves aesthetically superior to the Amerindians and held views which would be classified as "racist" today; on the other hand, the Amerindians considered the French inferior to themselves and according to their somatic norm image considered themselves superior aesthetically and otherwise. Pierre d'Avity wrote in 1637 that "although they lack police, power, letters, arts, wealth and other things they despise other nations and esteem themselves highly."[29] He was echoing the sentiments of Father Gabriel Sagard, who had spent the winter of 1623–24 among the Hurons, and who reported that the Hurons esteemed the French "to possess little intelligence in comparison to themselves." Although they respected the knowledge of the Récollet missionaries they "did not have this opinion or belief concerning other Frenchmen in comparison with whom they estimated their own children wiser and more intelligent."[30] The Jesuits were no more highly regarded than the Récollets, the Native children sometimes scorning them and ridiculing them "because they do not see in a Frenchman any of the perfections of a Savage and cannot recognize the virtues of a generous Christian."[31] Frenchmen, it would seem, seldom attained the intellectual and moral qualities demanded by the Amerindian somatic norm image.

Furthermore, Frenchmen generally were regarded as physically inferior, as weak and unfitted to stand up to the rigours of arduous canoe journeys, hunting expeditions, and forest warfare. When Champlain proposed to Chief Iroquet of the Algonquins to send young men to live among them there was immediate opposition: "the other savages raised objections, fearing that harm might come to the youth, who was not accustomed to their manner of life, which is in all respects hard, and that if any accident befell him the French would be their enemies."[32] Only after Champlain remonstrated angrily, and agreed to accept in exchange an Algonquin youth to be sent to France to be educated, could Iroquet accept the proposal.

If Frenchmen were regarded as "soft" it was because they were raised in a country which reportedly encouraged the development of effeminacy. Two young Algonquins who had spent a year in France, upon their return to Canada, were loud in their praises of the treatment they had been accorded, but one of them did admit that he would find it extremely difficult to readjust to his "former hard life" among his compatriots.[33] Savignon, one of the youths Champlain had sent to France, "when he saw two men quarrelling without coming to blows or killing one another, would mock at them, saying they were nought but women, and had no courage."[34] Indeed, for an Amerindian to marry a European was not a socially desirable union. When an "honest French surgeon" asked to marry an Amerindian maiden in 1618 the Native council refused his request.[35] Le Jeune's *Relation* of 1633 recorded another incident which the Natives interpreted as proof of French effeminacy: "Our Savage, seeing Father de Noue carrying wood began to laugh saying: 'He's really a woman,' meaning that he was doing a woman's work."

The first Frenchmen to inhabit the New World must have appeared singularly ill-equipped to cope with their new environment. It was not long before they stripped off their cumbersome European dress for the hunting shirt and moccasins. The Frenchman learned to travel by canoe and snow shoes, to portage and shoot rapids, to fish through the ice and eat *sagamite* in order to survive. But in the official French view they did this in order to establish good relations with the Natives, to advance the economic and cultural objectives of the leaders. This temporary "Indianization" involved a cultural step backward in order to make possible a cultural leap forward later. The Amerindians could only interpret this "going Native" by Frenchmen in increasing numbers as a reasonable adjustment to conditions in the New World, as a wise acceptance of folk wisdom, and as an accommodation learned by the naturels over centuries of American habitation. Nicolas Perrot maintained that the Hurons, Ottawas, Fox, and Sioux became much aware of this accommodation on the part of the French therefore they became insolent and desired "to dominate us and be our superiors; they even regard us as people who are in some manner dependent on them."[36]

In addition to reproaching Frenchmen for their physical weakness, the Amerindians found them ugly, especially because of their excessive hairiness, and their frequent deformities and infirmities. Sagard related how "one of the ugliest savages in his district" laughed at the bearded Europeans and wondered how any woman could look with favour on such ugly creatures. He added: "They have such a horror of a beard that sometimes when they try to insult us they call us Sascoinronte, that is to say, Bearded, you have a beard; moreover, they think it makes people more ugly and weakens their intelligence."[37] Father Biard sent a similar report from Acadia: "They have often told me that at first we seemed to them very ugly with hair both upon our mouths and heads; but gradually they have become accustomed to it, and now we are beginning to look less deformed."[38] In addition to this common Mongoloid abhorrence of the hairiness of Europeans, the Mi'kmaq showed no compassion for "the one-eyed, and flat-nosed" Frenchmen whom they derided. Biard continued:

For they are droll fellows, and have a word and a nickname very readily at command, if they think they have any occasion to look down upon us. And certainly (judging from what I see) this habit of self-aggrandizement is a contagion from which no one is exempt, except through the grace of God. You will see these poor barbarians, not withstanding their great lack of government, power, letters, art and riches, yet holding their heads so high that they greatly underrate us, regarding themselves as our superiors.[39]

Lahontan, who was generally very sympathetic in his appraisal of aboriginal views, remarked on "their fanatical Opinions of things, which proceeded from their Prepossession and Bigotry with reference to their own customs and ways of living."[40]

There was much about Catholicism that seemed incongruous and dangerous to the Amerindians. From the first contacts with missionaries, whether seculars or regulars, the zeal for the baptism of dying infants led to a confirmed belief that baptism was the cause of death. The French were responsible for the epidemics of measles, smallpox, influenza, and related bronchial disorders which decimated the encampments and villages, and the Natives without being able to understand the precise relationship between contact and infection did realize that there was such a cause-effect relationship. As early as 1616, Biard sent the following observations from Acadia:

They are astonished and often complain that since the French mingle with and carry on trade with them, they are dying fast, and the population is thinning out. For they assert that, before this association and intercourse, all their countries were very populous, and they tell how one by one the different coasts, according as they have begun traffic with us have been more reduced by disease; adding, that the reason the Armouchiquois do not diminish in population is because they are not at all careless. Thereupon they often puzzle their brains, and sometimes think that the French poison them.[41]

All the tribes contacted by the French in the early seventeenth century— the Mi'kmaq, Montagnais, Algonquin, Huron, and Iroquois—charged the French with bringing pestilence and death. The Algonquin went so far as to tell the Hurons infection was a deliberate policy of the French to destroy all the Amerindian nations. By 1647 the Jesuits made the following admission: "The Algonquins and Hurons—and next the Hiroquois, at the solicitation of their captives—have had, and some have still, a hatred and an extreme horror of our doctrine. They say that it causes them to die, and that it contains spells and charms which effect the destruction of their corn, and engender the contagious and general diseases wherewith the Hiroquois now begin to be afflicted."[42] The missionaries taught those who would give them a hearing, among other things, the wonder-working power of the sacraments, novenas, and relics. They taught a reverence for the cross, religious images, and pious practices. In the adversities which often accompanied the coming of the missionaries to their villages, the tribesmen concluded that the supernatural invoked for good could also be invoked to produce harmful effects. The missionary report of 1653 from the Huron country included the following observation: "They said the same thing about some images, etc. the prayers that we made, and the masses which we said at an early hour, with closed doors; the litanies; even walking abroad,—a new thing in these countries,—were superstitions which we practiced in order to destroy them."[43] Every unaccustomed, unusual, or secretive act became the object of intense suspicion.

Religious symbols were greatly distrusted. In 1635 the Hurons insisted that a cross atop the mission-house be removed as the cause of that summer's drought: "When the Indians gathered from the surrounding villages and insisted that the Fathers should remove the cross; they told them that should the drought wither the crops there was danger that the infuriated Hurons would attack them as sorcerers and poisoners and beat them to death."[44] The following year, the villagers had cause for further alarm, as an epidemic spread rapidly through the lodges taking a heavy toll. The Jesuits had displayed in their chapel two life-size images, one of Jesus and the other of the Virgin Mary, for the edification of their hearers. The rumour spread quickly that the images were the cause of the pestilence:

> This unfounded suspicion, which should have been dismissed with a laugh, spread so rapidly in a few days that throughout the length and breadth of the land it was soon reported that the French priests were the cause of the trouble; and although we may conjecture that those from whom this ridiculous falsehood emanated were not so foolish as to persuade themselves to accept what they wished others to believe, still they told their lie so cunningly that the majority who heard the report had no doubt that the thing was true. For the most part they gradually refused to associate with the Fathers, and the women and children, otherwise of no account but ready to believe anything, execrated them as public male-factors. In all the gatherings and meetings the talk was against the Fathers, who, it was said, had come to the Huron country on an evil day and who were destined to be the ruin of the whole race. The inhabitants of Ihonatiria alone at first zealously defended their cause, but they too, when the conflagration of unpopularity burned more fiercely, whether they were afraid or whether they were tired of the task, ceased to protect them and began to excuse their former conduct with their neighbours as if it had been a serious crime.[45]

The prophets of doom were correct in their predictions, of course, for the French presence in Huronia precipitated their subjugation by the Iroquois.

The Amerindian charge against the missionaries was of engaging in sorcery and witchcraft. Obsessive fear appears to have outweighed hatred as the motive for the "persecution" reported by Mother Marie de l'Incarnation:

"They were on the dock as criminals in a council of the savages. The fires were lit closer to each other than usual and they seemed to be so only for them, for they were esteemed convicted of witchcraft, and of having poisoned the air which caused the pestilence throughout the country. What put the Fathers in extreme peril was that the Savages were as it were convinced that these misfortunes would cease with their death."[46] "Great assemblies" were called throughout Huronia to deliberate on appropriate protective measures. The oldest and most prominent woman of the nation was reported to have harangued the consultative assembly of the four tribes in the following manner:

> It is the Black Robes who make us die by their spells; listen to me, I prove it by the reasons you are going to recognize as true. They lodged in a certain village where everyone was well, as soon as they established themselves there, everyone died except for three or four persons. They changed location and the same thing happened. They went to visit the cabins of the other villages, and only those where they did not enter were exempted from mortality and sickness. Do you not see that when they move their lips, what they call prayers, those are so many spells that come forth from their mouths? It is the same when they read in their books. Besides, in their cabins they have large pieces of wood (they are guns) with which they make noise and spread their magic everywhere. If they are not promptly put to death, they will complete their ruin of the country, so that there will remain neither small nor great.[47]

The Ursuline correspondent opined that wherever the missionaries travelled in their apostolic labours they carried the epidemic "to purify the faith of those they have converted." News of the alleged French practice of witchcraft and sorcery travelled rapidly to neighbouring tribes and forestalled plans Chaumonot and his companion had of carrying the gospel farther afield:

> As for the adults, not only have they not been willing to listen to the good news, but they even prevented us from entering their villages, threatening to kill and eat us, as they do with their most cruel enemies. The reason of this great aversion arose from the calumnies disseminated by some evil inhabitants of the country from which we came. In consequence of these calumnies, they were convinced that we were sorcerers, imposters come to take possession of their country, after having made them perish by our spells, which were shut up in our inkstands, in our books, etc.,—inasmuch that we dared not, without hiding ourselves, open a book or write anything.[48]

Association with the new religion meant certain sterility of hunting and fishing. Iroquois captives brought to the Huron villages were forced to kneel before wooden crosses, symbols which filled them with terror. A report of 1647 indicates the extent of the fear Catholicism inspired among the Iroquois: "It is further said that they have seen issuing from the lips of a Christian, whom they were burning, a strange brightness which has terrified them; so, indeed, they have knowledge of our doctrine, but they regard it with horror, as of old the Pagans in the early age of Christianity."[49] This obsessive fear attached itself not only to the external symbols of the new religion and its practices but also to the Eucharist itself. Some of the pagans asked to see the corpse of Christ which the priests were said to bring to life at mass. Eventually, even purely secular objects such as weather-vanes and clocks were shunned as evil spirits associated with the religion of the French.

Although the missionaries, almost without exception, complained of the inadequacies of the Amerindian languages for expressing their religious message and noted the great difficulty in compiling vocabularies of equivalents to common French terms, modern linguistic experts do not find the Amerindian languages deficient for expressing the abstract and symbolic. Nevertheless, the aboriginal tongues did not always have precise equivalents, as Lescarbot emphasized: "For they have no words which can represent the mysteries of our religion, and it would be impossible to translate even the Lord's prayer into their language save by paraphrase. For of themselves they do not know what is sanctification, or the kingdom of Heaven, or super-substantial bread (which we call daily), or to lead into temptation. The words glory, virtue, reason, beatitudes, Trinity, Holy Spirit, baptism, faith, hope, charity, and an infinity of others are not in use among them. So that at the beginning there will be no need of great Doctors."[50] The world expressed by the French language was one world and the world expressed by the Huron language, for example, was a distinct world; each were distinct worlds and not merely the same world with different labels attached. LeClercq commended the Mi'kmaq language as being "very beautiful and very rich in its expressions," adding that it had a greater range of expression than European languages and that there were distinct styles for solemn and less formal occasions.[51] The Jesuits later asserted on the basis of their experience among both Algonquian and Iroquoian linguistic groups that the languages were definite in meaning, beautiful and regular in expression, "not at all barbarous," and full of force.[52]

The deficiency arose more out of the cultural approach and the implications of evangelization for Amerindian society than from linguistic difficulties. The Natives saw some danger in divulging their religious vocabulary to the evangelists of the new religion, therefore they refused to cooperate extensively in the linguistic task of compiling dictionaries and grammars, and of translating religious books.[53] Gravier reported at the close of the century of the Illinois tribes that they were "so secret regarding all the mysteries of their Religion that the Missionary can discover nothing about them."[54] What the pagans refused the neophytes later supplied, although the continued refusal of some *coureurs de bois* to assist in missionary translation suggests that there was pressure in the Native encampments to offer no assistance to the missionaries in this aspect of their evangelical labours.

Most Natives, seeing the Europeans determined to learn their languages, felt no necessity to learn French; this fact elicited the accusation from one royal official that the Amerindians were too proud to learn French. The Amerindians did not find the Jesuits particularly good linguists, although by any measure that can be applied today to their efforts they appear to have been brilliant. Du Creux recounted that the Hurons "thought it was a joke to ask Le Jeune to speak, and when he made a stammering attempt at their language, laughter and derision greeted his childish efforts."[55]

The religious differences in the French community did not escape Amerindian notice, although the religious chroniclers may have exaggerated this so-called scandal in order to advance their own demands for enforced religious uniformity. Sagard wrote about the intestinal quarrels between Huguenot and Catholic seamen, fishermen, traders, and ministers of religion which tended to confirm the Natives in their skepticism.[56] The Natives were never slow to point out the weaknesses in the French character, the divergence between the missionaries' ideals and the colonists' practices, and the greater severity with which the clergy sought to repress drunkenness among them than among the French. Governor Montmagny sought to answer one such remonstrance with an unconvincing "don't plead the French as an excuse when they sometimes fall into intemperance themselves; those who do so are stupid fools, and are regarded as trash and a disgrace to the light of day."[57]

Be that as it may, the greatest obstacles to evangelization of the Amerindians remained Native religion, the world view of the tribesmen, and (under pressure to convert to Catholicism) the emergence of counter-innovative techniques. Native religion was completely integrated into Amerindian cultures and permeated all aspects of daily living as well as the ideology. Conversion to Catholicism required a rejection of the whole traditional way of life, belief system, and tribal ideals of behaviour and relationships. When the Jesuits sought to establish a model Catholic "republic" among the Hurons, the medicine-men and elders developed counter-innovative techniques: a version of baptism, for example, was initiated as a part of a healing cult said to be inspired by a deity who revealed himself as "the real Jesus," and anti-Catholic cults spread rapidly throughout Huronia to provide an ideological resistance to the new European religion.[58]

Dreams, both of a symptomatic and visitation variety, played an important role in Amerindian religion and not infrequently turned against the threatening tide of the "French religion." During an epidemic of smallpox among the Hurons in 1640, a young fisherman had a dream in which the spirit appeared to him to advise the tribe in its distress. Jerome Lalemant reported the "demon" as having issued the following warning:

I am the master of the earth, whom you Hurons honor under the name of Iouskena. I am the one whom the French wrongly call Jesus, but they do not know me. I have pity on your country, which I have taken under my protection; I come to teach you both the reasons and the remedies for your fortune. It is the strangers who alone are the cause of it; they now travel two by two through the country, with the design of spreading the disease everywhere. They will not stop with that, after this smallpox which now depopulates your cabins, there will follow certain colics which in less than three days will carry off all those whom this disease may not have removed. You can prevent this misfortune; drive from your village the two black gowns who are there.[59]

Just as the French tended to fashion God in their own image, so one is assured that Iouskena spoke as a "true" Huron.

Each culture had its own concept of supernatural intervention in human affairs. On occasion there was a cultural convergence: in such situations the Amerindians held French religious powers, or "good medicine," in high esteem. When in 1673 at Folle Avoine on the Menominee river Louis André replaced sacrifices offered to the sun in order to assure good fishing by a crucifix he invited a contest between the deities. The fact that the following morning a large number of sturgeon entered the river suddenly gave him attentive hearers.[60] The following year, Pierre Millet reported that an Iroquois chieftain exhorted his compatriots to hold prayer in esteem "as Monsieur the governor had recommended them to do at Catarakoui," but far more effective was the fact that the missionary correctly predicted an eclipse of the moon a few days earlier.[61] Paul Le Jeune attempted to convince the Huron that neither the French nor any other people could bring rain or fine weather, but that the Creator alone was master of these elements and therefore "recourse must be had only to him." His hearers remained unconvinced and persisted in their belief that the Europeans had influenced the supernatural to bring unfavourable weather. An incident that had occurred when the Récollets had first gone into Huron country probably lived on in their oral history. Sagard recorded that the Récollets had been asked to pray to God to stop a long and devastating rain. "And God looked with favour on our prayers, after we had spent the following night in petitioning Him for His promises, and heard us and caused the rain to cease so completely that we had perfectly fine weather; whereat they were so amazed and delighted that they proclaimed it a miracle, and we rendered thanks to God for it."[62]

It was only a short step from belief in beneficial supernatural intervention to belief in malignant and malicious intervention from the spirit world.

The Amerindians soon came to hold a low opinion of French standards of morality. As early as Verrazano's expedition of 1524 it was remarked that contact with European fishing fleets had taught the coastal Algonquian tribes to take appropriate protective measures. Verrazano reported, "Every day the people came to see us at the ship; bringing their women of whom they are very careful; because, entering the ship them-selves, remaining a long time, they made their women stay in the barges and however many entreaties we made them, offering to give them various things, it was not possible that they would allow them to enter the ship."[63] Similarly, Biard observed that the Mi'kmaq girls and women were "very modest and bashful" and that the men were well behaved and "very much insulted when some foolish Frenchman dares meddle with their women." This Jesuit missionary related an incident to illustrate his judgment: "Once when a certain madcap took some liberties, they came and told our Captain that he should look out for his men, informing him that any one who attempted to do that again could not stand much of a chance, that they would kill him on the spot."[64]

The Jesuit missionaries seem to have expected the tribesmen to respect them for their sacrifices and sufferings in bringing them the Gospel under unattractive conditions, especially when compared to life in the elit-ist colleges of France where they had taught previously. They also expected to be honoured for their vows of poverty and chastity. The Natives felt quite otherwise about the missionary mode of life. Sagard observed: "One of the great and most bothersome importunities which they caused us at the beginning of our stay in the country was their continual pursuit of pleas to marry us, or at least that we should join ourselves to them, and they could not understand our manner of Religious life."[65] The Hurons told the Récollets it was unnatural to remain celibate, that they were abnor-mal, that conditions could not be as favourable in France as they pretended or they would have remained there, and that they were out of touch with the rhythm of natural provisions the supernatural powers bestowed on mankind. What other conclusions could aborigines, especially the nomadic Algonquian bands, come to in seeking a rational explanation of apostolic poverty, celibacy, and calendar-oriented fasting?

There is sparse documentation dealing with Amerindian reactions to French agriculture, or to life in the towns of Quebec and Montreal. The French diet, as reflected in the kitchen gardens and field crops of the ripar-ian clearings, was a varied one but Native palates did not respond well to salted meat and vegetables. Upon being offered a barrel of bread and bis-cuits, the Hurons examined it, found it tasteless, and threw it into the St Lawrence: "Our Savages said the Frenchmen drank blood and ate wood, thus naming the wine and biscuits."[66] A chieftain at Isle Percée told Chrestien LeClercq that French contributions in the dietary and culinary realm were not appreciated.

> It is true ... that we have not always had the use of bread and of wine which your France produces; but, in fact, before the arrival of the French in these parts, did not the Gaspesians live much longer

than now? And if we have not any longer among us any of those old men of a hundred and thirty to forty years, it is only because we are gradually adopting your manner of living, for experience is making it very plain that those of us live longest who, despising your bread, your wine, and your brandy, are content with their natural food of beaver, of moose, of waterfowl, and fish, in accord with the custom of our ancestors and of all the Gaspesian nation. Learn now, my brother, once for all, because I must open to thee my heart: there is no Indian who does not consider himself infinitely more happy and more powerful than the French.[67]

The same attitudes prevailed with respect to French clothing which the Natives found inadequate to keep out the winter's cold. Only the decorative aspects held appeal for them.

Although they were impressed by the tall stone buildings erected by the French, and marvelled at the layout of their towns, there remained an attachment to the traditional style of building and of life. The Mi'kmaq chieftain just cited made the following observations:

But why now, do men of five of six feet in height need houses which are sixty to eighty? For, in fact, as thou knowest very well thyself, Patriarch—do we not find in our own all the conveniences and advantages that you have with yours, such as reposing, drinking, sleeping, eating, and amusing ourselves with our friends when we wish? This is not all. My brother, hast thou as much ingenuity and cleverness as the Indians, who carry their houses and their wigwams with them so they may lodge wheresoever they please, independently of any seignior whatsoever? Thou art not as bold or as stout as we, because when thou goest on a voyage thou canst not carry upon thy shoulders thy buildings and thy edifices. Therefore it is necessary that thou preparest as many lodgings as thou makest changes of residence, or else thou lodgest in a hired house which does not belong to thee. As for us, we find ourselves secure from all these inconveniences, and we are at home everywhere, because we set up our wigwams with ease wheresoever we go, and without asking permission of anybody.[68]

If they were impressed by French tools and implements there is little record of their adopting any of these in their own house-building or agriculture. One enterprising convert, Manitougache, used a hatchet and some nails salvaged from an old boat to build a board cabin for himself, but he seems to have been exceptional.[69] In point of fact, the fur-covered wigwams of the Natives were superior to the later linen tents. The only goods the domiciled reservation Natives asked of the Hôtel-Dieu in 1643, for example, were blankets and copper kettles—other furnishings apparently had little appeal for them.[70]

In general, the Amerindians do not seem to have retained a favourable impression of the social organization of French life. They were quite unable to understand that in France, where, according to the tales of the Europeans and the few Amerindians who had visited the country and returned to North America, there was apparently an abundance of food, many large towns and many people yet there were also poor people and beggars. Montaigne said that the astonished visitors "thought it strange that these needy halves should endure such an injustice, and did not take the others by the throat, or set fire to their houses."[71] The Récollet missionaries found no beggars in the Huron and Montagnais encampments and whatever food was available was always shared, open hospitality being offered to all travellers. Sagard said: "those of their Nation, who offer reciprocal Hospitality, and help each other so much that they provide for the needs of all so that there is no poor beggar at all in their towns, bourgs and villages, as I said elsewhere, so that they found it very bad hearing that there were in France a great number of needy and beggars, and thought that it was due to a lack of charity, and blamed us greatly, saying that if we had some intelligence we would set some order in the matter, the remedies being simple."[72] To Frenchmen, who thought they had a well-disciplined society, a rational order and civilized community, it came as quite a shock to be reproved by the aborigines, whom they often regarded as being devoid of "right reason" and "right religion," for their injustice, improvidence, and inequality. LeClercq was told bluntly how the Mi'kmaq regarded French notions of superiority:

> Thou reproachest us, very inappropriately, that our country is a little hell in contrast with France, which thou comparest to a terrestrial paradise, inasmuch as it yields thee, so thou sayest, every kind of provision in abundance. Thou sayest of us also that we are most miserable and most unhappy of all men, living without religion, without manners, without honour, without social order, in a word, without any rules, like the beasts in our woods and our forests, lacking bread, wine, and a thousand other comforts which thou hast in superfluity in Europe. Well, my brother, if thou dost not yet know the real feelings which our Indians have toward thy country and toward all thy nation, it is proper that I inform thee at once. I beg thee now to believe that all miserable as we seem in thine eyes, we consider ourselves nevertheless much happier than thou in this, that we are content with the little that we have; and believe also, once for all, I pray, that thou deceivest thyself greatly if thou thinkest to persuade us that thy country is better than ours. For if France, as thou sayest, is a little terrestrial paradise, art thou sensible to leave it?[73]

To this rebuke was added the observation that Frenchmen were often inhospitable and parsimonious.

Amerindian hospitality and sharing of goods, on the other hand, were regarded as the most praiseworthy qualities of the aborigines by the fur traders, soldiers, and *coureurs de bois* who were so often the beneficiaries of these traits and whose survival and success depended frequently on the goodwill of the Natives. Nicolas Perrot reported that unfortunately the Amerindians soon came to understand and imitate French ways:

> This sort of reception is ordinary among the savages; in point of hospitality, it is only the Abenakis, and those who live with the French people, who have become somewhat less liberal, on account of the advice that our people have given them by placing before them the obligations resting on them to preserve what they have. At the present time, it is evident that these savages are fully as selfish and avaricious as formerly they were hospitable. . . . Those of the savages who have not been too much humoured (by the French) are attached to the ancient custom of their ancestors, and among themselves are very compassionate.[74]

Contact with Europeans had resulted in an erosion of both Native hospitality and liberality.

There is some indication that the converted Amerindians resented the segregationist practices of the French. Why did the French insist on separate villages, separate churches, separate schools or classes, separate hospital wards, and even separate burial grounds? Sagard reported that the Huron were not happy when he and his companion came to them and proposed to build their cabin apart from their lodges. The chief and council tried to dissuade them, insisting that it would be preferable if they lodged with Huron families in order to be better cared for than if they remained apart.[75] Had they followed the council's advice, all their food would have been provided by the hunters. However, they preferred privacy to provisions.

Although segregationist practices were not well received, overt attempts to assimilate and dominate the tribesmen were also resented. The decision of the French authorities to provide some tangible encouragement to miscegenation as a means of assimilating the Amerindians met with some resistance in Native quarters. When one fur trader had pledged the Ursulines a sizeable donation in order to marry one of their Native pupils "it was found that the girl did not want him at all, and preferred a savage and to follow the wishes of her parents."[76] The Natives were interested in the provision by the French state of dowries for Native women who married Frenchmen and made astute inquiries concerning specific terms of the plan: "They would be very glad to know what a husband would give his wife; that among the Hurons the custom was to give a great deal besides,— that is to say—a beaver robe, and perhaps a porcelain collar. Second, whether a wife would have everything at her disposal. Third, if the husband should decide to return to France whether he would take his wife with him; and in case she remained, what would he leave her on his departure. Fourth, if the wife failed in her duty and the husband drove her away, what she could take with her."[77] The commissioner general of the Company of New France reproached the Natives in the vicinity of Trois-Rivières for marrying only within their own tribe and for avoiding marriage alliances with

Frenchmen.[78] The following year, a chief from Tadoussac replied to French charges that his people "were not yet allied with the French by any marriage" and that their dislike of the French was evident because "they did not care to be one people with us giving their children here and there to their allied Nations, and not to the French." He told an assembly at Quebec that when young Frenchmen joined with the Montagnais warriors in war and returned "after the massacre of our enemies" they would find Native girls to marry. As for the placement of children in French homes to be raised in the European fashion, he retorted boldly that "one does not see anything but little Savages in the houses of the French." He concluded with a strong argument: "what more do you want? I believe that some of these days you will be asking for our wives. You are continually asking us for our children, and you do not give yours; I do not know any family among us which keeps a Frenchman with it."[79] The Amerindians continued to think of the mutual exchange of children as tokens of unity and alliance, and had no doubt so accepted Champlain's sending of youths to learn Native customs and languages in the early decades of the seventeenth century. The one-way placement of children was interpreted as either a demand for hostages or an attempt to assert dominance over them.

They held French medical practices—bleeding and purges, in particular—in low esteem and preferred their own treatments. Lescarbot told of one Mi'kmaq warrior who upon being treated by Poutrincourt's surgeon for a badly cut heel returned two hours later "as jaunty as you please, having tied round his head the bandage in which his heel had been wrapped."[80] In 1640, the annalist of the hospital at Quebec reported that the Natives avoided the institution, holding it in horror and called it "the house of death," and refused to submit to medical treatments there.[81] There is no reason to doubt that the anxious relatives who urged a converted widow to abandon French medical treatments for her ailing son, "and told her that she was more like a cruel beast than a loving mother in deserting her boy at such a time; that his recovery depended upon her allowing the remedies to be employed which all their tribe had always used before the coming of those cursed Europeans," did so in all good faith and out of genuine concern for their fellows.[82]

In the domain of personal hygiene the Amerindians appear to have been more advanced than the French, especially in matters concerning bathing which the French avoided as both unhealthy and immodest. Some French practices earned open ridicule, such as the use of handkerchiefs: "Politeness and propriety have taught us to carry handkerchiefs. In this matter the Savages charge us with filthiness because, they say, we place what is unclean in a fine white piece of linen, and put it away in our pockets as something very precious, while they throw it upon the ground. Hence it happened that, "when a Savage one day saw a Frenchman fold up his handkerchief after wiping his nose, he said to himself laughingly, 'If thou likest that filth, give me thy handkerchief and I will soon fill it.'"[83]

There is every indication that the Natives were willing to pass on their considerable knowledge and skill in the use of medicinal herbs, ointments, potions, emetics, the practice of quarantining, and the taking of steam baths. Jogues had an abscess lanced by the Iroquois, Crépieul was skilfully bled by an Eskimo, and a French captive had shot removed from a deep wound.[84]

One of the difficulties inherent in relying largely on European documentation for an interpretation of Amerindian views is demonstrated in the discussions on child-rearing. The reported reactions of the aborigines were sometimes literary devices of French authors to criticize French customs and conventions. Lescarbot, for example, deplored the French custom of employing "vicious nursemaids" from whom the infants "sucked in with their milk corruption and bad nature."[85] While there are numerous reports of Amerindian surprise and disdain for French methods of child-rearing, these accounts must be placed in the literary and historical contexts of a period when criticism of government, religion, and social conventions in France was severely circumscribed. Both Lescarbot and Denys extended the idealization of the "noble savage," established in France by such writers as Clodoré, d'Abbeville, Montaigne, Du Tertre, Boyer, and de Léry, to an idealization of the New World as a land of opportunity and freedom. The report, therefore, that Native women demonstrated more affection to their offspring than French mothers and that they regarded the latter as callous and unfeeling may have been an extension of utopianism in order to criticize metropolitan society. D'Abbeville reported: "They take care not to do like many mothers here, who scarcely can await the birth of their children to put them out to nursemaids. . . . The Savage women would not want to imitate them in that for anything in the world, desiring their children to be nourished with their own milk."[86] The association between nature and nurture may have been more significant to the authors who reported it than to the Amerindians who purportedly emphasized it.

Certainly all the tribes had a very great love for their children and raised them in what might be termed a permissive manner. As Nicolas Denys noted: "Their children are not obstinate, since they give them everything they ask for, without ever letting them cry for that which they want. The greatest persons give way to the little ones. The father and mother draw the morsel from the mouth if the child asks for it. They love their children greatly."[87] They were quite unable to understand the harsher disciplinary methods of the French, the "porcupine-like" affection of French mothers who so readily accepted the separation of their children, and the practice of confining children for months in boarding schools. Marie de l'Incarnation said of the Amerindian children she tried to instruct that "they cannot be restrained and if they are, they become melancholy and their melancholy makes them sick."[88] Education in Amerindian society was part of the every day life of work and play; unlike French education, it was completely integrated to the rhythm of the adult community. This is the reason for the failure of the early schools to retain their pupils, who, sooner or later returned home or escaped to the forests.

Marie Arinadsit, a Huron pupil at the Ursuline convent in Quebec, encouraged some Iroquois visitors in 1655 to send their daughters to be educated by the nuns:

> Live, she said to them, with us henceforth as with your brothers, let us be only one people, and as a mark of your affection send some of your daughters to the Seminary; I will be their elder daughter, I will teach them to pray to God, and all the other things our Mothers taught me. And thereupon she started to read before them in Latin, in French and in Huron; then she sang spiritual Hymns in those three languages. Thereat those good people were quite taken aback, asked how long it took to learn so many things and to fran- cize well a Savage girl, promising they would not miss sending their children to such a good school.[89]

Within two decades the Superior of the "seminary" for Amerindian girls had to admit that the response from all the tribes had been most discour- aging. She confided to a correspondent in France: "Others are here only as birds of passage and stay with us only until they are sad, something which savage humour cannot suffer; the moment they become sad, the parents take them away for fear they will die. We leave them free on this point, for we are more likely to win them over in this way than by keeping them by force or entreaties. There are others who go off by whim or caprice; they climb our palisades like squirrels, which is as high as a stone wall, and go to run in the woods."[90] French education was designed to assimilate Amer- indian youth and therefore was unsuitable to fit them for life and leader- ship in their tribal community. The French educators came to understand that their classroom techniques, discipline, curriculum, and aims were at complete variance with Amerindian methods and objectives. "The savage life is so charming to them because of its liberty, that it is a miracle to be able to captivate them to the French way of doing things which they esteem unworthy of them, for they glory in not working except at hunting or navi- gation, or making war."[91] Talon reported in 1670 that on his return to the colony he found the number of Native children in the schools established by Bishop Laval and the Jesuits "greatly diminished" but added "they are going to seek new subjects to raise in our ways, our customs, our language and our teaching."[92] These were the very objectives of schooling which so repelled the Native children.

Donnacona had offered Cartier three young girls to take to France in 1536 but his people were incensed by this act and managed to free one of the girls from the French vessel. The chieftain intervened and had her returned with the explanation "that they had not advised her to run off, but that she had done so because the ships' boys had beaten her," where- upon the unfortunate child was returned with her two companions to the tender care of the French crew.[93] Champlain's astonishment at being offered three little Native girls to raise in January 1628 arose out of his experience that the Amerindians did not readily part with their children, that they did not respect French methods of child-rearing or education; he could only conclude that the offer was motivated by a desire to cement an alliance or to compensate for the murder of two Frenchmen.[94] The case of the three little girls being offered to Marguerite Bourgeoys at Montreal to be educated was virtually an abduction.[95]

The Amerindian distaste for French educational procedures carried over into a general lack of appreciation for French judicial procedures, law, and government. The rigidity, lack of flexibility, authoritarianism, and excessive concentration of power at the top of administrative pyramids contrasted unfavourably with the democratic procedures in Huron and Iroquois cantons. In their leaders the Algonquians looked for such traits as emotional restraint, stoicism, practicality, personal resourcefulness, and bravery. The French seem to have misunderstood the value they placed on deference in interpersonal relationships, Father Le Jeune observed that the Montagnais could not "endure in the least those who seem desirous of assuming superiority over others."[96] It is interesting to recall that the Europeans who came into contact with these democratic Native societies were members of a paternalistic monarchy and a hierarchical church, both being authoritarian, highly centralized pyramids of secular and religious power respectively. Paul Boyer wrote enthusiastically of the equality of the people encountered in the New World: "They do not know what are extortions, or subsidies, nor brigandry; no avarice, no cupidity, no lawsuits, no quarrels, no savants, no masters, no unfortunates, no beggars, not so much as an inkling of coveteousness, which things should make us blush with shame. No distinctions of estates among them, and they consider men only by the actions they accomplish."[97] The greater measure of liberty and of equality in Amerindian life was a comparison that Frenchmen were more apt to make than were Amerindians because the latter had less experience of both cultural milieux on which to base such conclusions.

French justice did not appeal to the Iroquois because it restricted itself to punishing the wrongdoer, while neglecting to give satisfaction to the wronged. Galinée described the fear which his party had in 1669–70 about passing near a Seneca village because shortly before his party had murdered a Seneca hunter and stolen his furs. The culprits were brought to trial and were executed in public in the presence of several Senecas. Nevertheless, as Galinée said, "although the bulk of the nation was appeased by this execution, the relatives of the deceased did not consider themselves satisfied and wished at all hazards to sacrifice some Frenchmen to their vengeance, and loudly boasted of it."[98]

During the years of initial contact the Amerindians had every reason to fear kidnapping under the guise of taking "volunteers" to France to be educated as interpreters or trained as a Native clergy. From the earliest fishing voyages which made contact through to Cartier and Dupont-Gravé, tribesmen had been taken off to France.[99] In 1622 an Indian who had been taken to Dieppe where he fell ill but showed no desire for baptism, although often encouraged by Huguenots to submit to this rite, returned to Canada in the company of the Récollet, Father Irenée Piat. He died shortly after receiving baptism and was buried at sea with full Catholic rites. However, the missionary later regretted not having kept locks of his hair and pieces of his nails to offer relatives proof of his decease because he knew they would suspect foul play and demand compensation: "We did not omit nevertheless to make presents to the closest relatives of the deceased, to remove from them all subject of complaint, and to assure our position in the matter."[100]

Although the French and Amerindians shared a high esteem for qualities considered exclusively masculine—skill in hunting and prowess in war—their cultures were far apart in their concepts of warfare, its objectives, its proper conduct, the treatment of prisoners, and the significance of alliances. The Amerindians never did understand the long-range objectives of European warfare, the sustained campaigns and the highly centralized and authoritarian military organization. They fought their wars for vengeance, for the adoption of prisoners so as to increase their population, and for reasons of prestige. The idea that North Americans were at war with each other because motherlands across the ocean were at war was incomprehensible unless immediate local issues were clearly involved. The humane treatment of prisoners of war by the French was also a mystery to the Amerindian mind: prisoners either should become objects of vengeance or they should be adopted to strengthen or maintain one's power. French outrage at scalping, platform torture, and ritual cannibalism was not understood by the Natives, especially when French warfare was obviously more destructive than Amerindian action. On the other hand, Iroquois prisoners brought back to the Christian reservation in 1645 were greeted by Jean-Baptiste Etinechikawat who received his warriors with praise, saying to the war captain: "Thou knowest well that we now proceed in a different fashion than we formerly did. We have overturned all our old customs. That is why we receive you quietly, without harming the prisoners, without striking or injuring them in any way."[101] The startled prisoners, expecting the traditional torture stake and platform and prepared to sing their death-songs, were well treated in spite of the urgent pleadings of two women, sole survivors of families killed by the Iroquois, to be permitted to avenge themselves on the pagans. This incident proved to be the exception for French attitudes were unable to supplant Amerindian motivations, value system, or ritualistic satisfaction in this domain. Even treaties of peace and nonaggression signed with the French or English were interpreted in Amerindian terms of adoption. They spoke of the French monarch as their "father" and themselves as his "adopted children" upon entering what the French considered a military alliance and a political protectorate.[102]

In almost every sphere of activity the Amerindians differed greatly from the French not only in their practices and traditions, but more especially in their conceptualization. Apart from concessions to French material civilization, technology, and military force, they felt equal to, or superior to, the Europeans at the time of contact in the seventeenth century. The fact that the French tended on contact to learn their languages, to adopt to some degree their ways of living, travelling, hunting, and fighting, and to rely heavily on them for their economic and military success confirmed them in their belief that their way of life had advantages over the French lifestyle. In 1685 Governor Denonville wrote to Seignelay, Minister of the Marine responsible for the colonies, that French attempts to assimilate the proud, self-reliant, and dignified Amerindians had had unfortunate consequences: "It was believed for a very long time that domiciling the savages near our habitations was a very great means of teaching these peoples to live like us and to become instructed in our religion. I notice, Monseigneur, that the very opposite has taken place because instead of familiarising them with our laws, I assure you that they communicate very much to us all they have that is the very worst, and take on likewise all that is bad and vicious in us."[103] But already the eroding effects of the new religion, the new economic pressures, the new diseases and alcohol addiction, the new military alignments, and the new immigration were beginning to undermine the dignity, self-reliance, and self-assurance of the Amerindians. It was not contact *per se,* nor the comparisons which Frenchmen and aborigines inevitably made between the two types of civilizations, which proved so destructive to aboriginal belief systems, an integrated social pattern, and self-image, but rather it was the more pervasive long-term concomitants of a permanent and expansionist European presence which undermined the cohesiveness and viability of Amerindian cultures during the ensuing generations and centuries.

While there can be no doubt that the French regarded their own culture as infinitely superior both in material and intellectual aspects to the aboriginal cultures they encountered in North America, it would be a fundamental error to assume that the Amerindians entertained or accepted such a comparative evaluation. Despite the paucity of "Indian sources" there is sufficient primary evidence to indicate that the various tribes were selective in their adaptation of European technology and cultural patterns, that they rejected outright many behavioural and conceptual innovations, that they developed counterinnovative devices and behaviour as a consequence of their contact experience, and that they maintained their own somatic norm image. While there was much in French life and culture that impressed or intrigued the aboriginal tribesmen, it would be inaccurate to assume that they invariably acknowledged the superiority of European culture, much less that they adopted or imitated uncritically French beliefs and behaviour. The Amerindian and French folkways and belief systems tended rather to remain parallel and concurrent with a much greater degree of accommodation of French culture to Native life and environmental considerations than of Amerindian cultures to French lifestyle. While there is evidence to indicate that French accommodation and adaptation to New World circumstances incorporated a degree of barbarization or "Indianization," on the contrary, assimilationist and adaptive responses on the part of aboriginals usually led to alienation from traditional lifestyle and beliefs, to a rejection of their past and to a close identification of religious conversion with "Frenchification." Few Amerindians crossed the cultural chasm to become identified as domiciled francized converts; on the other hand, new social types, identified as *coureurs de bois* and *voyageurs,* evolved in New France and the more comprehensive social groups identified as habitants, militiamen, and missionaries all experienced significant adaptation to the aborigines and environment of North America which distinguished them from their metropolitan French counterparts.

In the past, Canadian historiography has taken little account of these primordial facts concerning initial European-Amerindian relations. Our knowledge of both the facts and fantasies of this cultural contact is now sufficiently advanced to make a revision of interpretations both imperative and credible. There is no longer place for the uncritical assumption that the Europocentric evaluations and comparisons of the French seventeenth century contemporary sources represented accurately the social realities of the time, much less Amerindian views of events and values. The corrective considerations and the long overdue reappraisal suggested herein can only have the beneficial and stimulating consequence for Canadian historical writing of challenging description, exposition, and evaluation which depict the Amerindians as part of an American environment to be overcome and subdued to European purposes and policies, which relegate the aborigines to the background and stage-setting of national history, or which represent them as awe-stricken inferiors overwhelmed by the impact of a superior civilization which they aspired to acquire but which their own inadequacies denied them as an elusive and unattainable objective.

• Notes

1 This orientation is illustrated in the following important writings: Henri Baudet, *Paradise on Earth: Some Thoughts on European Images of Non-European Man* (New Haven, 1965); Gilbert Chinard, *L'Amérique et le rêve exotique dans la littérature française au XVIIᵉ et au XVIIIᵉ siècle* (Paris, 1913); René Gonnard, *La légende du bon sauvage* (Paris, 1946); George R. Healy, "The French Jesuits and the Idea of the Noble Savage," *William and Mary Quarterly* 15, 2 (April 1958): 143–67; Douglas Leechman, "The Indian in Literature," *Queen's Quarterly* 50, 2 (Summer 1943): 155–63; Roy Harvey Pearce, *The Savages of America: A Study of the Indian and the Idea of Civilization* (Baltimore, 1953); Donald Boyd Smith, *French Canadian Historians'*

Images of the Indian in the "Heroic Period" of New France, 1534–1663 (MA thesis, Université Laval, 1969).

2 D. Dainville, pseudonym (Adolphe Bossange), *Beautés de l'histoire du Canada ou époques remarquables, traits intéressans, moeurs, usages, coutumes des habitans du Canada, tant indigènes que colons, depuis sa découverte jusqu'à ce jour* (Paris, 1821); F.-X. Charlevoix, *Histoire et description générale de la Nouvelle-France avec le journal historique d'un Voyage fait par ordre du Roi dans l'Amérique septentrionale*, 3 vols. (Paris, 1744); F.R. Chateaubriand, *Le Génie du Christiansime* (Paris, 1802); J.F.X. Lafitau, *Moeurs des Sauvages amériquains comparés aux moeurs des premiers temps* (Paris, 1724); G.-T. Raynal, *Histoire philosophique et politique des établissements et du commerce dans les deux Indes* (Genève, 1780).

3 Claude d'Abbeville, *Histoire de la Mission des Pères Capucins en l'Isle de Maragnan et terres circonvoisines* (Paris, 1614); Paul Boyer, *Véritable Relation de tout ce qui s'est fait et passé au voyage que Monsieur Bretigny fit à l'Amérique Occidentale* (Paris, 1654); J. de Clodoré, *Relation de ce qui s'est passé dans les Isles et Terre ferme de l'Amérique* (Paris, 1671); Jean de Léry, *Histoire d'un Voyage fait en le Terre du Brésil, autrement dite Amérique* (La Rochelle, 1578); Marc Lescarbot, *Histoire de la Nouvelle France* (Paris, 1609); Gabriel Sagard-Théodat, *Le Grand Voyage du Pays des Hurons* (Paris, 1632).

4 Maximilien Bibaud, *Biographie des Sagamos Illustres de l'Amérique septentrionale* (Montréal, 1848).

5 Napoléon Legendre, "Les races indigènes de l'Amérique devant l'histoire," *Mémoires de la Société Royale du Canada*, vol. 2 (1884), sec. i, 25–30.

6 Léo-Paul Desrosiers, *Iroquoisie, 1534–1646* (Montréal, 1947); Jacques Rousseau, *L'Indien et notre milieu* (Laval University televised course, 1966, mimeographed); André Vachon, "L'Eau-de-vie dans la société indienne," *Canadian Historical Association Annual Reports* (1960): 22–32. The

author has been much encouraged in this line of research by Wilcomb E. Washburn. The debt to the writings of Clark Wissler, Harold Driver, Edward Spicer, Anthony F.C. Wallace, Bruce Trigger, and William Fenton is also acknowledged.

7 R.G. Thwaites, ed., *The Jesuit Relations and Allied Documents*, vol. 3 (Cleveland, 1896–1901), 123.

8 Wilcomb E. Washburn, "A Moral History of Indian-White Relations: Needs and Opportunities for Study," *Ethnohistory* 4, 1 (Winter 1957): 48.

9 P.A.S. Maillard, "Lettre sur les missions de l'Acadie et particulièrement sur les missions Micmaques," *Les Soirées Canadiennes* 3 (1863): 299.

10 W.L. Grant, ed., *The History of New France by Marc Lescarbot*, vol. 2 (Toronto, 1911), 247.

11 Ibid., vol. 3, 21.

12 Ibid., vol. 2, 45–46.

13 Ibid., 146.

14 Gabriel Sagard-Théodat, *Histoire du Canada et Voyages que les Frères Mineurs Recollects y ont faicts pour la Conuersion des Infidelles* (Paris, 1636), 154.

15 E.E. Rich, "Trade Habits and Economic Motivation among the Indians of North America," *Canadian Journal of Economics and Political Science* 26 (Feb. 1960): 35–53.

16 Wilcomb E. Washburn, "Symbol, Utility, and Aesthetics in the Indian Fur Trade," *Aspects of the Fur Trade, Selected Papers of the 1965 North American Fur Trade Conference* (St Paul, MN, 1967), 50–54.

17 William F. Ganong, ed., *The Description and Natural History of the Coasts of North America (Acadia) by Nicholas Denys* (Toronto, 1908), 442–43.

18 Sagard, *Histoire du Canada*, 36.

19 Grant, *History of New France*, vol. 3, 3.

20 Ibid., 25.

21 Nicolas Denys, *Geographische en Historische Beschrijving den Kusten van NoordAmerica: Met de Naturirlijke Historie des Lendts* (Amsterdam, 1688), 67.

22 William F. Ganong, ed., *New Relation of Gaspesia with the Customs and Religion of the Gaspesian Indians by Father Chrestien LeClercq* (Toronto, 1910), 101–2; also Thwaites, *Jesuit Relations*, vol. 3, 81.

23 Thwaites, *Jesuit Relations*, vol. 57, 95–97.

24 James B. Conacher, ed., *The History of Canada or New France by Father François du Creux, S.J.* (Toronto, 1951), 267–68.

25 Ganong, *New Relation by LeClercq*, 246.

26 J.C. Webster, ed., *Sieur de Dièreville, Relation of the Voyage to Port Royal in Acadia or New France* (Toronto, 1933), 150.

27 Conacher, *History of Canada*, 274.

28 Harry Hoetink, *The Two Variants in Caribbean Race Relations* (New York, 1967), 120–59.

29 Pierre d'Avity, *Description générale de l'Amérique, troisième partie du Monde* (Paris, 1637), 30.

30 Sagard, *Le Grand Voyage du Pays des Hurons*, 176–77.

31 Thwaites, *Jesuit Relations*, vol. 27, 215.

32 Grant, *History of New France*, vol. 3, 22.

33 Ibid., 27.

34 Ibid., 22.

35 Conacher, *History of Canada*, vol. 1, 36.

36 Nicolas Perrot, "Memoir on the Manners, Customs, and Religion of the Savages of North America" in *The Indian Tribes of the Upper Mississippi Valley and Region of the Great Lakes*, ed. E.H. Blair, vol. 1 (Cleveland, 1911), 145.

37 George M. Wrong, ed., *The Long Journey to the Country of the Hurons by Father Gabriel Sagard* (Toronto, 1939), 137.

38 Thwaites, *Jesuit Relations*, vol. 3, 22.

39 Ibid., 75.

40 R.G. Thwaites, ed., *New Voyages to North America by Baron de Lahontan*, vol. 2 (Chicago, 1905), 471.

41 Thwaites, *Jesuit Relations*, vol. 3, 105. This is the work cited in ensuing references, not Lahontan's *New Voyages*, also edited by Thwaites.

42 Ibid., vol. 31, 121.

43 Ibid., vol. 39, 129–31.

44 Conacher, *History of Canada*, vol. 1, 194.

45 Ibid., 227.

46 Dom Guy Oury, *Marie de l'Incarnation, Ursuline (1599–1672): Correspondence* (Solesmes, 1971), 67–68.

47 Thwaites, *Jesuit Relations*, vol. 1, 117–18.

48 Ibid., vol. 18, 41.

49 Ibid., vol. 31, 123.

50 Grant, *History of New France*, 179–80.

51 Ganong, *New Relation by LeClercq*, 140–41.

52 Thwaites, *Jesuit Relations*, vol. 6, 289; vol. 10, 119; vol. 15, 155; vol. 39, 119; vol. 67, 145.

53 Ibid., vol. 63, 299.

54 Ibid., vol. 65, 131.

55 Conacher, *History of Canada*, vol. 1, 160.

56 Sagard, *Histoire du Canada*, 9.

57 Conacher, *History of Canada*, vol. 1, 313–14.

58 Thwaites, *Jesuit Relations*, vol. 20, 27–31; vol. 30, 27, 29–31.

59 Ibid., vol. 20, 27–29.

60 Ibid., vol. 58, 275.

61 Ibid., 201.

62 Wrong, *Long Journey*, 78.

63 Alessandro Bacchiani, "Giovanni da Verrazzano and His Discoveries in North America, 1524, According to the Unpublished Contemporaneous Cellère Codex of Rome, Italy," *Fifteenth Annual Report, 1910, of the American Scenic and Historic Preservation Society* (Albany, 1910), appendix A, 192.

64 Thwaites, *Jesuit Relations*, vol. 3, 103–5.

65 Sagard, *Histoire du Canada*, 165.

66 Thwaites, *Jesuit Relations*, vol. 5, 119–21.

67 Ganong, *New Relation by LeClercq*, 106.

68 Ibid., 103–4.

69 Thwaites, *Jesuit Relations*, vol. 5, 121.

70 Dom Albert Jamet, ed., *Les Annales de l'Hôtel-Dieu de Québec, 1636–1716* (Québec, 1939), 47.

71 Donald H. Frame, ed., *Montaigne's Essays and Selected Writings* (New York, 1963), 117. The account is given in much more detail in an unlikely source: Michel Baudier, *Histoire de la Religion des Turcs* (Paris, 1625), 122.

72 *Histoire du Canada*, 241–42.

73 Ganong, *New Relation by LeClercq*, 104.

74 Perrot, "Memoir," 134–35.

75 Sagard, *Histoire du Canada*, 219.

76 C.H. Laverdière and H.-R. Casgrain, eds., *Le Journal des Jésuites* (Québec, 1871), 77–78.

77 Thwaites, *Jesuit Relations*, vol. 14, 19–21.

78 Ibid., vol. 9, 216–18.

79 Ibid., 233.

80 Grant, *History of New France*, vol. 2, 326.

81 Jamet, *Annales*, 25.

82 Conacher, *History of Canada*, vol. 2, 651.

83 Thwaites, *Jesuit Relations*, vol. 44, 297.

84 Ibid., vol. 5, 143; vol. 17, 213; vol. 39, 73; vol. 49, 121; vol. 61, 85; vol. 68, 61. F. Speiser, K.R. Andrae, and W. Krickberg, "Les Peaux-Rouges et leur médecine," *Revue Ciba* 10 (avril 1940): 291–318.

85 Marc Lescarbot, *Histoire de la Nouvelle-France* (Paris, 1609), 667.

86 d'Abbeville, *Histoire de la Mission*, 281.

87 Ganong, *Description by Denys*, 404.

88 Joyce Marshall, ed., *Word from New France: The Selected Letters of Marie de l'Incarnation* (Toronto, 1967), 341.

89 Oury, *Marie de l'incarnation*, 995.

90 Ibid., 801–2.

91 Ibid., 828.

92 Pierre Margry, ed., *Découvertes et Etablissements des Français dans l'Ouest et dans le Sud de l'Amérique septentrionale*, vol. 1 (Paris, 1879), Talon to Colbert, 10 Nov. 1670, 92.

93 Conacher, *History of Canada*, 35–36.

94 Grant, *History of New France*, vol. 2, 146–48.

95 Public Archives of Canada (hereafter PAC), MG 17/A, 7-1, St-Sulpice, Mélanges, carton B, no. 28(h), 199–200.

96 Thwaites, *Jesuit Relations*, vol. 6, 165.

97 Paul Boyer, *Véritable Relation de tout ce qui s'est fait et passé au voyage que Monsieur de Bretigny fit à l'Amérique Occidentale* (Paris, 1654), 227.

98 James H. Coyne, "Dollier de Casson & De Bréhaut de Gallinée: Exploration of the Great Lakes, 1669–1670," *Ontario Historical Society Papers and Records*, vol. 4 (1903), 19.

99 PAC, MG 2, Archives de la Marine, Series B^3, 9, Sieur de Narp to Minister of the Marine, 3 Sept. 1671, fol. 374.

100 Sagard, *Histoire du Canada*, 95.

101 Thwaites, *Jesuit Relations*, vol. 27, 235.

102 Ibid., vol. 42, 121–23; G. Snyderman, "Behind the Tree of Peace: A Sociological Analysis of Iroquois Warfare," *Pennsylvania Archaeologist* 18, 3 and 4 (1948): 30–37.

103 PAC, MG I, *Archives des Colonies*, Series C11A, vol. 7, Denonville to Seignelay, 13 Nov. 1685, 45–46.

TATTERED CLOTHES AND POWDERED WIGS: Case Studies of the Poor and Well-To-Do in Eighteenth-Century Louisbourg*

KENNETH DONOVAN

As in *ancien régime* France, there were tremendous contrasts in social status and wealth between the wealthy and less well-to-do in eighteenth-century Louisbourg. Louisbourg, however, experienced little of the abject poverty prevalent throughout all of France in the first half of the eighteenth century. In Western Europe the eighteenth century ushered in the philosophical rationalism of the Enlightenment but the progress of material living conditions was painfully slow in comparison to the intellectual achievements of the age. In his work on material culture Fernand Braudel refers to the first half of the eighteenth century as a continuation of the "biological *ancien régime*," a period little different from the seventeenth century when French peasants lived in fear of famine because they had few reserves of food to fall back on. It is hardly surprising that the peasants lacked security for even in the eighteenth century there were no less than sixteen widespread famines.[1]

In contrast to France, living standards were considerably higher in Louisbourg. Naturally, the people of the town were apprehensive about

From *Cape Breton at 200: Historical Essays in Honour of the Island's Bicentennial 1785–1985* (Sydney, NS: University College of Cape Breton Press, 1985), 1–20.

food shortages and with good reason, because practically all of their food-stuffs were imported. Nonetheless, there were few famines in Louisbourg because its relatively prosperous economy enabled the inhabitants to stock their storehouses with provisions. The substantial investment by the French government for maintaining its bureaucracy and for constructing the forti-fications, to say nothing of the revenues generated from international trade, provided immense sources of income. Dried salt codfish, however, was the mainstay of Louisbourg's prosperity.

There were numerous success stories in Louisbourg because Île Royale, as did most of the new world, provided increased opportunities for upward mobility for all classes. However, there was never any hint of egali-tarianism among the people of Louisbourg because of better standards of living. Louisbourg's estate inventories, in fact, reveal a most unequal distri-bution of wealth and material possessions. Based on a sample of 105 estate inventories, out of a total of 170, 13 percent of the people owned 73 per-cent of the wealth. This concentration of wealth in Louisbourg was not dis-similar to that of numerous towns in contemporary New England.[2]

Table 1: **DISTRIBUTION OF WEALTH IN LOUISBOURG ACCORDING TO ESTATE INVENTORIES, 1713–1758**

Value of Estates (in *livres*)	Number of Estates in Category	Wealth in Category (in *livres*)		
Less than 100	13	167. 8		
100– 999	22	11 270. 6 .	9	
1 000– 1 999	9	13 220. 8 .	9	
2 000– 2 999	5	13 060.12		
3 000– 3 999	6	21 567.16 .	7	
4 000– 4 999	4	17 926.18		
5 000– 9 999	2	12 773.12 .	8	
10 000–19 999	5	85 200. 0 .	8	
20 000+	4	160 348.12 .	1	

The disparity of wealth (see table 1)[3] indicated by the inventories ranged from a low of 28 *livres* for the few personal possessions of Marc Grange, a fisherman, to a high of 82 000 *livres* for the estate of Louis Delort, a Louisbourg merchant and member of the Superior Council. (A *livre* was the approximate equivalent of a British shilling during the first half of the eighteenth century. By the mid-1730s a full-time Louisbourg ser-vant earned 30 *livres* per year.) Obviously a poor fisherman like Marc Grange could hardly expect to wield as much influence in the community as Louis Delort. Nevertheless, it would be a mistake to assume that wealth necessarily commanded respect and esteem. Social status in Louisbourg and New France generally was not measured in terms of material posses-sions, nor was the social structure based solely on economic differences.

Social influence demanded an appropriate lifestyle and economic behaviour was secondary to social rank: it was essential to display one's rank with visible symbols of status.[4] In this regard the people of Louisbourg were no different from those of Canada where status symbols and physical trappings were most important.

For those at the top of the social scale in Louisbourg, including the governor, financial commissary, top ranking civil servants and merchants, birthright, especially being descended from a noble background, was the most influential distinction. For example, Charles-Léopold Ebérard De L'Espérance, Baron of the Holy Roman Empire and illegitimate son of Léopold-Ebérard, Prince of Mont Béliard, was accorded great respect and special status in Louisbourg. L'Espérance arrived in Louisbourg in 1724 as a lieutenant in the Swiss Regiment de Karrer. He remained in Louisbourg, except for periodic visits to France, until his death in 1738. In spite of having very little money,[5] L'Espérance was a highly respected junior officer in Louisbourg. In 1725 L'Espérance married Marguerite Dangeac, daughter of Gabriel Dangeac, a captain in the Louisbourg garrison. Though L'Espérance was a Lutheran who did not convert to Roman Catholicism, and his marriage was therefore highly irregular, his wedding was a prominent social occasion. Those present at the ceremony included Governor St Ovide, Commissaire-Ordonnateur Le Normant De Mésy, and some of the officers of the garrison.[6] It was understandable that the elite of Louisbourg were present at L'Espérance's wedding for noble status commanded esteem and deference in New France.

Like L'Espérance, Jacques Prévost de la Croix, Louisbourg's commissaire-ordonnateur from 1749 to 1758, was proud of his claim to noble birth. Prévost continually sought respectability for the noble status acquired by his father. Acquiring that respectability, however, meant that Prévost had to be prepared to bear the expense of maintaining visible marks of rank. Throughout the 1750s Prévost kept a household staff of approximately ten people besides acquiring two houses in Louisbourg.[7]

Purchasing large houses complete with servants was certainly not the only means of asserting one's rank. In certain cases positions of respectable social status could be transferred or purchased in Île Royal, provided the recipient was worthy to accept such a position. In 1751, twenty-nine-year-old Jacques Perrin offered his land for the construction of a new church to the people of Lorembec, a coastal village approximately four miles northeast of Louisbourg. Because of his offer, Perrin "had the right to have a bench placed behind the church wardens." Three years after the church was constructed, Perrin sold this land to Jean Claparede, a Louisbourg merchant. With the land went the privilege of having a prominent bench in the church.[8] Social status was not immutable for it could be transferred among equals or near equals.

Most members of the lower orders in Louisbourg were hardly in a position to acquire such distinguished marks of respectability as a bench behind the church wardens, even if they could afford to do so. In Louisbourg, as in France, people knew their station in life and certain codes of behaviour and demeanour were expected of people and their children from various occupations. In his *Persian Letters* published in 1721, and which has been described as conveying "more faithfully than any other work the atmosphere of the Regency from 1715 to 1723," Montesquieu outlined just how structured French society was:

> Even the humblest workers argue over the merits of the trade they have chosen; everyone believes himself to be above someone else of a different calling, proportionally to the idea he has formed of the superiority of his own.[9]

Conditions in Louisbourg, at least in terms of the social structure for the lower orders, appear to be little different from those described by Montesquieu, for the people at the bottom of the social scale shared the concern for the proprieties of rank.

More than any other source, the court records of Louisbourg's Superior Council reveal the extent to which Louisbourg was a structured society. Before giving testimony, witnesses were called upon to describe where they were and who they were with at the time the crime was committed. Invariably, the witnesses are with people from their own social and economic background.[10] One particular case underlines the significance attributed to rank among the lower classes in Louisbourg. On the evening of 3 July 1744, Angelique Butel, wife of Quentin Le Lievre, a small job merchant, was beating her child for having disobeyed her. Servanne Bonnier, wife of the butcher Pierre Santier, was passing by the house and interceded on the child's behalf, claiming that Butel was a "whore" and that she did not like her children, among other things. Butel and Bonnier exchanged insults and accusations on several occasions that evening and Butel eventually took Bonnier to court, accusing her of slander. During the trial, one witness testified that Butel claimed that Bonnier "was not of the same rank."[11] Apparently, the wife of a butcher had no right to tell the wife of a small job merchant, who assumed she had a more prestigious social position in the community, how to discipline her children. Angelique Butel clearly considered herself to be superior to Servanne Bonnier and that presumption of superiority indicates the significance attributed to rank and status among the lower classes in Louisbourg.

While rank and status were important to people at all levels of the social structure, the lower orders had to abide by stipulated and inferred rules of conduct. In other words, people near the bottom of the social scale could be punished for going beyond the boundaries of socially acceptable behaviour. Louisbourg tavernkeepers, for instance, were forbidden to serve alcohol to sailors, fishermen, soldiers, "and all persons in service." Moreover, a domestic could not testify against his master in court nor stay in a tavern "without permission of his master."[12] Generally speaking, members of

Louisbourg's elite—the merchants, the officer class, the ship captains, the senior civil servants, and well-to-do fishing proprietors—had a contemptuous attitude towards the lower orders and did not associate with them.

Another key indicator of status was clothing. In *ancien régime* France, dress was a clear indicator of status for it "pinpointed the place of the wearer in a complex and undisputed hierarchy. Every social nuance had its corresponding sign in clothing."[13] It was much the same in Louisbourg, where members of the town's elite, such as the officers of the garrison, would be distinguished by their fine fabrics and well-tailored clothing. In the autumn of 1733 a young Frenchman in New York described the Louisbourg officers he saw there as being dressed in "lac'd cloaths."[14] It was not only Louisbourg's officers, however, who wore "lac'd cloaths" for even children were able to determine the social background of other children by the quality of their clothes.[15] On 23 January 1737, La Jeunnesse, a mason, was with the son of a lime burner when they discovered a boy frozen to death in the snow on White Point near Louisbourg. La Jeunnesse and his young companion provided a detailed description of the deceased. The boy had black hair but was not wearing anything on his head. His small brown vest and pants were both made of marmet cloth, while his waistcoat was a grey carrise cloth. He had worn-out wool stockings plus a pair of Indian-made seal skin moccasins. He was also wearing a pair of mittens. La Jeunnesse and his young companion stated "that it seemed to them by the clothes he was wearing he was either a sailor or an engage."[16] The boy found frozen to death was George Rowan, who was engaged as an apprentice lime burner for Nicolas Gaudin, a Louisbourg fishing proprietor. Rowan had last been seen leaving to go to church on Sunday; he had no personal effects, except a few old shirts.

Children of the poor in Louisbourg would have worn clothes of similar quality to those of George Rowan and at most would have had one or two changes. They would have been disadvantaged in other respects as well for they could expect a sparse diet, to begin work at an early age, and to have little or no opportunity for even a modest formal education.

Louisbourg had more than its share of poverty but it was not alone in this regard. As early as 1674 the town of Quebec had 300 beggars who were considered to be a burden upon the citizens. While the church, especially the hospitals and monasteries, traditionally took care of the beggars and paupers, the burden, by the late seventeenth century, was too great to be left to the church alone. Hence, in 1688 the Sovereign Council of Quebec established a Bureau of the Poor with poor boards in the towns of Montreal, Quebec, and Trois-Rivières, and even in the parishes and seigneuries. These poor boards, comprised of three members, determined who were the necessitous and worthy poor and then provided relief and sought employment for those capable of working. While the aged and the worthy poor were given assistance, begging was strictly forbidden.[17]

Like New France, colonial America also had an indigent population. In his examination of the class structure of the northern colonies in colonial America, Jackson Turner Main concluded that between one-quarter and one-fifth of the population of Massachusetts had little or no property. Moreover, when indentured servants were considered, he maintained that the class of poor people in the north comprised one-third of the white population.[18] If lack of property and material possessions is used as one of the key indices of poverty, there were numerous impoverished people in Louisbourg, for few of the hundreds of soldiers, sailors, or itinerant fishermen owned any real property. And while begging was strictly forbidden in Canada, a number of witnesses and at least one defendant in various Louisbourg court cases were described as "vagabonds," thereby implying some tolerance, if not sanction, of mendicity.[19]

As in Canada (the St Lawrence Valley), the Louisbourg clergy ministered to the poor. Numerous Louisbourg citizens bequeathed money to the poor and the Récollet priests were charged with disbursing the funds to the needy. The other religious in the town, the Brothers of Charity at the hospital and the Sisters of the Congregation of Notre Dame, were reimbursed by the government for the services which they supplied to the poor. The list of government expenditures abound with statements of monies paid to the hospital for ministering to "poor sick inhabitants." Besides Louisbourg citizens unable to pay, the poor at the hospital usually included shipwrecked sailors, discharged soldiers, indigent fishermen, prisoners, and domestics. In 1733 the government paid Julian Brodellé, an apprentice nurse, "for having cared for the sick poor people" during the smallpox epidemic.[20]

Besides offering nursing assistance to the sick, the Louisbourg administration, in the early years of the colony, also founded a residence "of poor men" to aid the poor.[21] After 1727, however, the Sisters of the Congregation took up much of the burden of providing social services for orphaned girls and the lists of government expenditures include monies paid to the Sister Superior for "the subsistence of orphan girls."[22] According to Louisbourg's Governor St Ovide, the Sisters of the Congregation, during the smallpox epidemic of 1733, had taken "at our request more than 20 small girls who were left without a father or a mother or a relative to care for them because of the sickness which had attacked the colony."[23] The Sisters of the Congregation did not take in very small children or abandoned infants but the administration of Louisbourg provided funds for the care of foundling children. In 1738 Louisbourg officials paid an individual named Champion 363 *livres* 10 *sols* "for having nursed and fed a child who had been found."[24] In 1750, when sailors discovered two children only a few days old, Louisbourg officials assumed responsibility for them in the name of the King and immediately had them baptized.[25]

The census of 1749–50 describes fifteen orphans living in Louisbourg with various families. The children, five boys and ten girls, were presumably very young for they probably would have been described as domestic servants if they were more than seven years old, that is of working age.[26] The children, particularly the girls, were most likely at the homes of private citizens because the Sisters of the Congregation had not yet re-established their convent.

In spite of the government records outlining financial assistance provided to the Sisters of the Congregation and the Brothers of Charity to help maintain the indigent, the poor people of Louisbourg are extremely difficult to quantify because they were usually excluded from official record keeping. As a general rule, only individuals who wintered in the colony were included in the various census returns. The hundreds of domestics and indentured servants were merely described in terms of total numbers and not by name. And worse still, the parish records, including the baptismal certificates, rarely cite the complete names of servants or slaves. Thus, it might be more appropriate to describe Louisbourg's poor by explaining who was not poor.

Louisbourg's full-time residents, the sons and daughters of fishing proprietors, officers of the garrison, merchants, civil servants, and skilled tradesmen were, for the most part, comfortably well off, especially by old world standards. However, a distinction must be drawn between Louisbourg's full-time residents who were impoverished and refugees—both Acadian and European in origin—who came to Île Royale seeking government assistance for settlement, especially after 1749. Typical of these indigent refugees was fifty-two-year-old Jean Mariadé, a ploughman on the Mira River, who was a native of La Chapelle, France. Mariadé was married to forty-four-year-old Madeleine Benoist, a native of Acadia, and they had eleven children ranging in age from one year to twenty-three years. Mariadé had no dwelling or livestock and was wintering in a house owned by a Monsieur Tessé. As was the case with most people coming to Île Royale in 1749 and 1750, he was granted rations for two years.[27]

In contrast to refugees like Mariadé and his family, the impoverished parents and children examined here are full-time Louisbourg residents and not newcomers. For instance, children of Louisbourg domestics could expect little of the good life, at least for most of their childhood. For one thing, they were often bastards. The poverty of Marie Savaria was by no means untypical. Originally from Beauport, Canada, and a servant in the household of Pierre LeLarge, Maria gave birth to a girl who was baptized on 6 June 1724. In the Louisbourg parish records the father was merely described as being unknown.[28] However, within three months the name of the father of Maria's baby would be public knowledge in Louisbourg (if it were not already so), for Maria took the father to court in August 1724. Maria petitioned Louisbourg's Superior Council for the welfare of her child, claiming that a man named Piesrés Darrichevery, a master shoemaker, had seduced her with a promise of marriage. Maria maintained that she had confessed her guilt "in the pains of childbirth to Father Claude,

Brother of Charity, in order to come to her aid because of the extreme poverty to which she had been reduced, and moreover she was taken in by the poor who were in no position to care for her."[29] After the birth of her child Maria was no longer employed by Pierre LeLarge, probably having been dismissed because of her pregnancy; as in France it was customary to discharge servant girls as soon as they became pregnant in order to avoid public scandal.[30] Abandoned and without resources, Maria threw herself at the mercy of the council as an unfortunate "victim," imploring that the council accept her disposition "so that her child would not die of hunger." Ordered to appear before the council, Piesrés was subsequently condemned to immediately pay Maria Savaria 30 *livres* "for the costs of bed and clothing for the child" and commencing on this day Piesrés was to pay 10 *livres* per month for the maintenance of the child for two years.[31]

Unlike the vast majority of servants who become pregnant, Maria Savaria was fortunate that she was able to take the father to court and win a favourable settlement. With money for child support, Maria would now provide food and shelter for herself and her baby. Equally important, the money for child support made Maria considerably more attractive to prospective suitors. Indeed, Maria married Jean Danjou, a blacksmith from Brittany, on 20 November 1724. There was no dowry brought into the marriage by either partner, but on the day of the wedding, the couple accepted from Piesrés Darrichevery a final perfect payment of 140 *livres*. As part of the notarized agreement, Maria and Jean Danjou promised never to ask for more money from Darrichevery.[32]

Poverty was not restricted to the servant class, for there were a number of Louisbourg parents who had full-time occupations but became indebted to such an extent that they could barely afford to support their children. One such parent was Pierre Mansel, a fisherman and long-time resident of Île Royale. In 1716 Mansel adopted a three-year-old Mi'kmaq girl named Marguerite who, according to Mansel, had been left in his care by her parents. It appears that Mansel raised the child as if she was his own daughter, for in the 1724 census he was described as having a wife and daughter.[33] Three months after his wife died in December 1725, however, Mansel put Marguerite in the service of Anne Rodrigue, a Louisbourg merchant. By allowing Marguerite to serve Madame Rodrigue, Mansel was spared the expense of supporting the girl. Mansel had initially intended to permit Marguerite to stay in Madame Rodrigue's service for only six months, but on 29 April 1726 he formally agreed to permit Marguerite to stay with the Rodrigues as long as she wished. The only condition which Mansel attached to Marguerite's engagement was that Madame Rodrigue "accept all the rights and claims that he would have had in connection with the said girl for the costs of her education and support."[34]

On 13 March 1726, at the same time that his adopted daughter went into domestic service for Madame Rodrigue, Pierre Mansel married Charlotte Dumeny, a native of Quebec, who was an orphan and minor employed in the service of Madame Rodrigue. Neither Mansel nor his young bride brought any goods into the marriage.[35] To make matters worse, Mansel, three months after his marriage, mortgaged his property to pay for 225 *livres* of provisions. Unable to pay the debt, Mansel was forced to sell his modest property which realized only 450 *livres*. Granted his land in October 1722, Mansel had built a modest house of upright logs with a chimney and had planted a garden. After his debts were paid, Mansel was left with nothing.[36] Given Mansel's economic hardship, he was hardly in a position to provide his adopted daughter Marguerite with an adequate formal education. Indeed, he took the only available and proper course by putting her in domestic service in a comfortable household. Marguerite was probably treated well by the Rodrigues for she remained a servant in their household for the next nineteen years, until she reached the age of thirty-two.[37]

During the same summer that Pierre Mansel was in financial difficulty and was forced to sell his mortgaged house, Antoine L'Etrange was compelled to appear before the Admiralty Court, as a defendant in a debt case. A native of Bordeaux, L'Etrange was a tavernkeeper who had been married in Newfoundland in 1712 and then emigrated to Île Royale. By the summer of 1726 L'Etrange and his wife had five children.[38] In July 1726 Jacques Cadoux, a ship captain, took L'Etrange to court demanding payment for a promissory note of 433 *livres*, dated 14 November 1723. Although acknowledging the note, L'Etrange sought delay for repayment because he had "a large family." The court gave L'Etrange a sympathetic hearing. In view of "the sad situation and little means of the defendant," he was ordered to repay 133 *livres* immediately and the remaining 300 *livres* over a period of three years at the rate of 100 *livres* per year.[39]

Unfortunately, L'Etrange's economic prospects do not appear to have improved substantially over the next decade, for by 1736 he exchanged his dilapidated house with Claude Perrin. Measuring 42 feet by 80 feet, L'Etrange's property was situated on Block 19, at the corner of Rue St Louis and Rue de France. His house must have been of a rather simple design and crude construction, for it was made of vertical logs and had a bark roof. In the exchange agreement Perrin stated that he "is thinking about demolishing the house of Mr L'Etrange which is no longer tenantable, in order to build a charpente house in its place."[40] Clearly, Perrin was not interested in L'Etrange's run-down house, merely the land. Nevertheless, seventy-three-year-old L'Etrange and two of his children still lived in the house until the exchange was completed.

What were living conditions like for the children of needy families? What types of clothing did they wear? Did they eat properly? In effect, did they receive adequate parental care by contemporary standards? Single parents like Maria Savaria and Pierre Mansel took steps to ensure adequate care for their children in spite of their indigent circumstances. However, children of certain families were neglected by their parents and not provided with even minimum standards of care. One such family was that of Vincent Plocq *dit* La Veillée and Marie Jeanne Coeffé who lived on Block 20 in the town, not far from Antoine L'Etrange. Before her marriage to Plocq, Coeffé had been married to Nicolas Langot, who was described as a sergeant in 1722 and as a cook in 1724 and 1726. At the time of his death Langot had left Marie Jeanne with four children, one boy and three girls, ranging in age from six months to nineteen years.[41] With no means of support and four children, Marie Jeanne had little choice but to remarry again as soon as possible. She subsequently married Vincent Plocq, a baker who was illiterate. A child was born to the Plocqs on 4 February 1735 and within one month of the birth, Marie Jeanne died. The subsequent inventory of the estate of the deceased Marie Jeanne Coeffé revealed the impoverished circumstances of the family. After the death of her first husband, Nicolas Langot, Marie Jeanne had neglected to have an inventory taken. Consequently, there was a confusion of the community of goods between the children of the first and second marriage.

Following the customary procedure, the court-appointed officials arrived at the Langot house on 2 March 1735 in order to place seals on the goods of the estate prior to conducting the inventory a few days later. Upon entering the house Judge Joseph Lartigue of the Bailliage Court saw the deceased lady was still in her bed, having died the night before. Lartigue placed seals on the chest containing the clothing belonging to Marie Jeanne but he could not put seals on the few items of household linen and clothing because they were soaking in a wash bucket. "He told us," declared Lartigue, "that the linen they have is soaking in a wash bucket and could not be inventoried. However, the said Plocq promised to show it after it had been washed and this was everything he had in linen goods and clothing." Not only was there very little household linen but, much more alarming, Lartigue stated that "the said Plocq told us they hadn't a thing to eat."[42] The Langot family was in dire need of assistance: the household furnishings, which were in extremely poor condition, consisted of three folding pine tables, two benches, and four wooden chairs. Moreover, there were only two beds in the home: one bed, in which the deceased Marie Coeffé was lying, was valued at 75 *livres*, almost half of the value of the furniture of the entire household. The other bed was "a small feather bed with two wool blankets and a bolster for the children to sleep on." Apparently the children slept in one small bed.

The lack of beds in the household, to say nothing of foodstuffs, was compounded by the poor condition of the children's clothing.[43] The Langot children were clearly at or near the bottom of the economic and social scale in Louisbourg for such critical symbols as inferior clothing and inadequate housing pinpointed the family's position in Louisbourg's class structure. There is no question that the Langot house was in a dilapidated state for by 1743, eight years after the death of Marie Jeanne Coeffé, the Langot estate was divided among the five children. The Langot's house had "fallen to ruin and was indivisable." Thus, as was the case with the L'Etrange household in the adjoining town block, the Langot house was virtually useless by 1743.

What were the lifestyles of individuals from well-to-do families? Children have been selected from some prominent Louisbourg families in order to demonstrate their living conditions, particularly their manner of dress and behaviour, degree of education, and general treatment accorded them by their parents and contemporaries. The first family is that of Marie Anne Peré, widow of Antoine Peré. A long-time Louisbourg resident, Antoine Peré had been granted a fishing concession in the harbour as early as 1717. By 1724 he was a prosperous fishing proprietor who employed forty fishermen.[44] Peré died in 1727 leaving his forty-seven-year-old wife with five dependants. Marie Anne proved to be a resourceful woman for she successfully assumed her husband's fishing business, and by 1728 had a new house built just outside the town's Dauphin Gate. The total value of Madame Peré's estate, including her fishing properties in Île Royale, amounted to 40 807 *livres* in 1735.[45]

Whether providing a dowry for her daughters or supplying them with appropriate clothing, no detail concerning the welfare of her children seemed too insignificant. By 1729 two of Madame Peré's daughters were married so she was left with three dependants, one daughter and two sons. The Peré family was fashion conscious. Madame Peré was continually writing her commercial agent in France requesting either material or complete suits of clothing for her children.[46] On 4 December 1729 she wrote the agent requesting that he send, by the first vessel leaving Nantes for Louisbourg, a complete suit of clothes for one of her sons. She wanted the suit to be "of blue woolen or another more beautiful colour of steel gray with a fine red lining, and all the different trimmings."[47]

Madame Peré also ordered clothes for another son Jean. "Please," she wrote to Villés Perée on 22 December 1733, "send me whatever is necessary to make a suit of cinnamon colour for my son; jacket, vest and two pair of pants with lining of scarlet material; and all the trimmings; a hat priced about 18 *livres* and a *perruque à bourse* that costs no more than 18 *livres* and a pair of woolen stockings, all to match the suit."[48] A complete suit comprising breeches lined with scarlet, together with all of its accoutrements, was doubtless a mark of distinction that only the families of successful merchants, military officers, or government officials could afford. Madame Peré's request for a *perruque à bourse* clearly indicated that the affluent bourgeois of Louisbourg where conscious of the latest fashions in France. One of the most modern styles in terms of wig design, the *perruque à bourse* had first been developed during the Regency period, and by 1733 the design was only ten years old.[49]

The latest fabrics and clothing design in France were most important to the fashion-conscious Peré children. When Madame Peré's youngest daughter Jeanne decided to marry Martin Benoist, a Louisbourg merchant, she wrote to Pierre Joubert in France asking for a red damask material with a white floral design for her daughter's wedding dress. Regrettably, Joubert replied that the material Madame Peré requested was no longer available. Nevertheless, he added: "I took it upon myself to send you as a substitute, a damask material in the latest style and the one being worn presently in France. I hope it is to your liking and also to your daughter's taste." Joubert sent enough material for two skirts at a cost of 427 $^1/_2$ *livres*.[50] Unperturbed by the rather costly material for the wedding dress, Madame Peré replied to Joubert that she was pleased with his selection.

While clothing was an obvious visible and necessary sign of the Peré family's prosperity and influential social position within the community, it was only one hallmark of social stratification. Undoubtedly, education also played a role in elevating one's social status in Louisbourg. In any event, despite being illiterate herself, Madame Peré ensured that her children were educated. In 1731 she sent her youngest son, fourteen-year-old Antoine, to a boarding school in St Servant, Brittany. Understandably, Madame Peré was apprehensive about sending her son overseas for an education. Hence, she took the precaution of appointing two guardians, George Rosse of St Servant and Cotteret Perée of St Malo, to supervise Antoine. In November 1731 she wrote Cotteret Perée beseeching him to take care of Antoine and to put the boy "in a good boarding house where he can benefit the most and while he is young he can receive all the education a young man can be offered."[51]

Since George Rosse was responsible for Antoine's expenses, he kept an itemized account of the various goods and services purchased on the boy's behalf. In effect Rosse provided a report of the activities of a youth from a well-to-do Louisbourg home in terms of clothing purchases, educational curriculum, and personal lifestyle. The first year of the account covers a one-year interval from 20 June 1732 to 1 July 1733. During that period George Rosse ordered numerous articles of clothing for Antoine, including five new pairs of shoes, three pairs of stockings, two pairs of shoe buckles, two hats, a wig and its box, a cravate and a handkerchief. Moreover, Antoine was provided with a new suit of clothes and, with the approach of autumn, Rosse also purchased a vest and material to line the hood of the boy's riding coat.[52]

The second part of the account was for a period from 5 July 1733 to 13 April 1734. Rosse continued to furnish Antoine with all of his requirements including the washing and repairing of his clothes and other personal effects. For instance, in the spring of 1734, Antoine had his mattresses recovered with wool at a cost of 2 *livres* 10 *sols*. Rosse also purchased a hammock for Antoine, and a chest. Antoine's boarding school offered a varied educational curriculum for he had at least three different instructors offering courses in arithmetic, writing, navigation, dance, and violin.[53]

Antoine was fashion-conscious and he maintained a lifestyle appropriate to his well-to-do status; having his wig powdered and attended to was an essential part of his dress. Madame Peré spared no effort in providing Antoine's clothing, board, and lodging. In December 1733 she instructed her son's guardians to ensure that Antoine was well dressed and to use all of the 300 *livres* that she had forwarded for his sustenance.[54] Antoine Peré was indeed one of Louisbourg's privileged children.

No self-respecting merchant, fishing proprietor, or member of the officer class would permit his children to enter domestic service. A domestic servant performed menial tasks and as such was near the bottom of the social scale in Louisbourg. Imagine the consternation of a respected merchant in Louisbourg if he thought his young daughter was being treated as a servant. Such was the case with Thomas Power, an Irish merchant who lived in Louisbourg. From the autumn of 1753 until late 1754, Power permitted his daughter to live in the home of Jean Baptiste Duboé, a merchant who lived just outside the town's main entrance.[55] Power's daughter's stay at Duboé's residence eventually resulted in bitter animosity between Duboé and Power, for by the spring of 1755 Jean Baptiste Duboé took Thomas Power to court, claiming that Power's daughter was not performing the necessary household duties to compensate for her free room and board. For his part, Power alleged that Duboé, contrary to their agreement, had treated his daughter as a common servant. The resulting court case, which continued throughout May 1755, is most significant for it delineates, in a clear-cut fashion, the type of character and demeanour that the townspeople expected of the daughter of a merchant versus the behaviour and responsibilities expected of a servant.

To support his case, Thomas Power called a total of ten witnesses, six women and four men. What type of evidence did Power use to attempt to prove that his daughter was treated as a servant? Three of the ten witnesses affirmed that they saw Power's daughter washing clothes in the brook just outside the town gate with Duboé's servant. Maintaining that Power's daughter worked every day in Duboé's home as a servant, forty-year-old Madame Brosset cited a number of tasks demanded of the young girl. Milking the cow, washing the dishes, and cleaning Duboé's shoes comprised only a part of her routine. To make matters worse, the young girl was mistreated by the servant if she failed to carry out an assigned chore properly.[56]

Another witness, thirty-nine-year-old Jeanne Guienne, the wife of Thomas Langlois, a resident of the Barrachois, confirmed Madame Brosset's testimony. She had visited the Duboé residence a number of times to purchase various items of merchandise and on each occasion the Power daughter "was busy with the household duties, sometimes preparing fowl, sometimes making the fire and at other times washing the dishes." One thing was certain—feeding the chickens or tending the fire were hardly activities expected of a girl from a prominent Louisbourg family. Confused by the conduct of the girl, Jeanne Guienne had asked Duboé's servant "what position Power's daughter occupied in the household." The servant replied "that her father and mother were honourable people and that they had promised to send some butter and a cow to Mr Duboé" for looking after her.[57]

In effect then, Thomas Power was paying for his daughter's upkeep at Duboé's residence. Yet it appeared that Duboé was not fulfilling his part of the agreement for Power's daughter was allegedly treated like an ordinary servant. Each successive witness confirmed Power's worst fears, for the list of chores required of his daughter seemed endless. She had been compelled to participate in such demeaning activities as sweeping the house, washing the dishes, helping with the laundry, making the beds, cleaning Duboé's shoes, fetching water, milking the cows, and looking after the chickens.

To counter Power's allegations and the depositions of his witnesses, Jean Batiste Duboé summoned nine witnesses to testify on his behalf. Six of the witnesses were men and included Father Julien Moisson, a Récollet missionary. Duboé attempted to prove that Power's daughter was not treated as a servant, and hence that she was not accorded an inferior status.

Most of Duboé's witnesses declared that Power's daughter did not do any servile work. Louis Bilbert, a fifty-two-year-old carpenter, stated that he had been at Duboé's house seven or eight times and that the girl did not do any domestic chores. Moreover, Gilbert declared that "he had seen her several times dressed on work days as one would dress on Sundays and at the same time walking with other girls." Another resident, fifty-six-year-old Jacques Brunet testified that he had seen Power's daughter walking on a street wearing cosmetics. A Louisbourg servant certainly would not wear her best clothes on a work day nor appear in public with a powdered face. Furthermore, most of the witnesses, including Father Julien Moisson, stated that Power's daughter ate at the table with Monsieur Duboé. Father Moisson testified that he had dined with several fellow clergymen at the Duboé residence and the young girl was not served by Duboé's domestic but was treated equally like the other guests at the table. Nevertheless, other witnesses confirmed that Power's daughter did eat with the servant in the kitchen but this was only because she wished to do so. As for the allegations that the Power girl went to the brook to do the laundry, fifteen-year-old Anne Bourneuf stated that she usually came to Duboé's house to do Duboé's and the young girl's laundry. Moreover, while she acknowledged that Power's daughter went to the brook, she insisted that she did not do any laundry.[58]

Given the contradictory testimony of the witnesses, it is not surprising that the case of Power versus Duboé ended inconclusively. What is most significant is that all of the witnesses—nineteen Louisbourg residents in total—knew precisely what type of lifestyle was expected of a daughter of a merchant and a servant. Power's daughter's social position demanded that she display the traits of civility: she was supposed to dress well on work days, to eat at Duboé's table, and to avoid servile labour. Power's daughter made the mistake of crossing the boundary of socially acceptable behaviour. She apparently befriended Duboé's servant and coincidentally performed some domestic activities in the Duboé household. Such conduct was upsetting to standard social mores, if not unacceptable in Louisbourg. Sending children, even those of prominent families, to other households to perform domestic service was viewed as a type of apprenticeship and form of education in the sixteenth and seventeenth centuries. Domestic service brought no repugnance nor degradation. The well-bred child was expected not only to know how to behave at the table but to wait at the table as well. However, by the beginning of the eighteenth century, domestic service had been degraded to the point of a position reserved for the lower classes. Servants were placed on the same level in society as the "despised manual workers." Deference to the social order in Louisbourg required Power's daughter to adopt the lifestyle befitting a citizen of her class.

Children of impoverished parents in Louisbourg, such as Marie Savaria, Pierre Mansel, Antoine L'Etrange, and Nicolas Langot, would be easily identified. They would be illiterate, they would begin to work at an early age, they would bring little or no dowry into their marriage, they would wear inadequate clothing and live in substandard housing. In stark contrast, privileged Louisbourg children such as Antoine Peré and the daughter of Thomas Power would usually be educated, wear fine clothing, and bring substantial dowries into their marriage.

In order to appreciate the contrasting lifestyles of the poor and well-to-do in Louisbourg, it is necessary to examine these lifestyles within the context of the social structure of eighteenth-century Louisbourg. Social position in Louisbourg demanded a lifestyle that was appropriate to one's rank and all levels of society were concerned with the proprieties of rank. Moreover, eighteenth-century society in general had little broad-based egalitarianism and hence disparities in wealth and social status were the norm, not the exception.

• Notes

1 Fernand Braudel, *Capitalism and Material Life, 1400–1800*, trans. Miriam Kochan (New York: Harper and Row, 1973), 39–40, 53.

2 Jackson Turner Main, *The Social Structure in Revolutionary America* (Princeton, NJ: Princeton University Press, 1965), 41–42. As late as 1929 the wealthiest 10 percent of the families in the United States owned 64 percent of the wealth. See Robert J. Lampman, *The Share of Top Wealth Holders in National Wealth, 1922–1956* (Princeton:

Princeton University Press, 1966), 215, cited in Main, *The Social Structure*, 42.

In 1774 the wealthiest 10 percent of free wealth holders in the Thirteen Colonies owned 56.4 percent of the total physical wealth. The wealth inequalities in the Thirteen Colonies in 1774 were similar to those of the United States in 1962. See Alice Hanson Jones, *Wealth of a Nation to Be: The American Colonies on the Eve of the Revolution* (New York: Columbia University Press, 1980), 316–17.

For other works referring to the concentration of wealth in the class structure of colonial New England see Kenneth A. Lockridge, *A New England Town, The First Hundred Years: Dedham, Massachusetts, 1636–1736* (New York: W.W. Norton, 1970), 141–42; James A. Henretta, "Economic Development and Social Structure in Colonial Boston," *William and Mary Quarterly* 22, 1 (Jan. 1968): 75–92.

3 This table is based upon 105 Louisbourg estate inventories, most of which are found in France, Archives Nationales, Archives d'Outre Mer, (hereafter AN, Outre Mer), G2, various volumes. Thirty-five of the 105 inventories examined were either incomplete or merely described the contents of the estate without assigning any value to the possessions. There are a total of 170 Louisbourg estate inventories.

For more information concerning Louisbourg's estate inventories see Kenneth Donovan, "Communities and Families: Family Life and Living Conditions in Eighteenth-Century Louisbourg," *Material History Bulletin* (Ottawa: National Museum of Man, Summer 1982), 33–47.

4 See Peter N. Moogk, "Rank in New France: Reconstructing a Society from Notarial Documents," *Histoire Sociale* 8, 15 (May 1975): 34–53; and his " 'Thieving Buggars' and 'Stupid Sluts': Insults and Popular Culture in New France," *William and Mary Quarterly*, 3rd series, 36 (October 1979): 524–47; W.J. Eccles, "The Social, Economic, and Political Significance of the Military Establishment in New France," *Canadian Historical Review* 52, 1 (March 1971): 1–22.

5 AN, Outre Mer, G3, 2058-1, 26 fév. 1725, "Mariage entre Charles Léopold Eberhard de l'Espérance et Marguerite Dangeac." L'Espérance brought no dowry into his marriage. See also *Dictionary of Canadian Biography* (hereafter *DCB*), vol. 2 (Toronto: University of Toronto Press, 1969), 424–25.

6 AN, Outre Mer, G1, vol. 406, reg. 2, mariages 1722–28, fol. 4, Mariage entre de l'Espérance et Marguerite Dangeac.

7 *DCB*, vol. 4 (1979), 646.

8 AN, Outre Mer, G3, 2042, no. 37, "Vente d'un maison, Jacques Perrin à Jean Claparede, 1 fév. 1754." For the donation of Perrin's land to the village of Lorembec see France, Archives Nationales, Archives des Colonies (hereafter AN, Colonies), C11B, vol. 31, fols. 6–6v. Desherbiers et Prévost, "Ordonnance sur la localisation de l'eglise de Lorembec, Louisbourg, 27 jan. 1751." Perrin offered land of 80 *pieds* square "dans le fond dudt havre" for a church, presbytery, cemetery, and garden. For biographical information on Perrin see *Report Concerning Canadian Archives for the Year 1905*, vol. 2, *Tour of Inspection made by Sieur De La Roque* (Ottawa: S.E. Dawson, 1906), 74.

9 Charles-Louis De Secondat, *Montesquieu's Persian Letters*, trans. C.J. Betts (New York: Penguin Books, 1977), 98. See the introduction by Betts, p. 17: "Seen in its immediate historical context, the Persian Letters is generally agreed to convey more faithfully than any other work the atmosphere of the Regency of Philippe d'Orleans, from 1715 to 1723."

See Eccles, "The Social, Economic, and Political Significance," 6–7. In New France, as in France, people accepted their station in life. Eccles noted that in Canada the great majority of the people "did not aspire to rise in the social scale. Satisfied with their status they were concerned with maintaining their family security, their creature comforts, and simple pleasures."

10 See "Class Distinctions, Calves Feet for Dessert: A Meal Causes a Fight in a Louisbourg Cabaret" in Kenneth Donovan, "Life in Louisbourg's Public Houses" (manuscript, Fortress of Louisbourg National Historic Park, 1979), 5–12.

11 AN, Outre Mer, G2, vol. 199, dossier 190, 6 juillet 1744, "Procedure Criminelle instruite a la requete de

Angelique Butel contre Servanne Bonnier." See the testimony of Marguerite Doucin, femme du Sieur Lambert, marchand.

[12] AN, Colonies, C11B, vol. 34, fols. 83–84, 28 sept. 1754, "Reglement de Prévost pour les habitants de Louisbourg."

[13] Philippe Ariès, *Centuries of Childhood: A Social History of Family Life*, trans. Robert Baldick (New York: Vintage Books, 1962), 57. In his *Persian Letters*, p. 184, Montesquieu noted: "I was telling you the other day how extraordinarily capricious the French are about fashion. Yet it is incredible how obsessed they are with it; they relate everything to it: it is the standard by which they judge everything that happens in other countries."

[14] *The Boston Weekly Newsletter*, Boston, 14 Feb. 1734.

[15] For the significance of clothing and other symbols of status to children see Kenneth Donovan, "Rearing Children in Louisbourg: A Colonial Seaport and Garrison Town, 1713–1758" (paper delivered at the Atlantic Society for 18th Century Studies, Mount Saint Vincent University, 26–28 April 1979), 1–35.

[16] AN, Outre Mer, G2, vol. 196, no. 110, 23 jan. 1737, "Proces verbal de levée de Corps du nommé George Rowan trouvé Mort Sur le chemin de Louisbourg à la pointe blanche."

[17] Raymond Du Bois Cahall, *The Sovereign Council of New France* (New York: AMS Press, [1915] 1967), 248–50; Cornelius J. Jaenen, *The Role of the Church in New France* (Toronto: McGraw-Hill Ryerson , 1976), 110–11.

[18] Main, *The Social Structure*, 41. For other works describing the indigent populace of colonial North America see Raymond A. Mohl, "Poverty in Early America, A Reappraisal: The Case of Eighteenth-Century New York City," *New York History* 50, 1 (Jan. 1969): 5–27; Gary B. Nash, "Poverty and Poor Relief in Pre-Revolutionary Philadelphia," *William and Mary Quarterly* 33, 1 (Jan. 1976): 3–30; Henretta, "Economic Development," 75–92; Allan Kulikoff, "The Progress of Inequality in Revolutionary Boston," *William and Mary Quarterly* 28, 3 (July 1971): 375–412.

[19] AN, Outre Mer, G2, vol. 184, déc. 1737, "Procedure criminelle contre le nommé Mathurin Buneau, vagabond, accusé de vol, et condamné à la torture." See also ibid., vol. 182, fols. 1–133, jan. 1732, "Procès criminel contre Jean Gauthier dit l'Hunoda, accusé et convaincu de l'assasinat de sa femme, executé à Louisbourg." See question 96. A Monsieur Coupart is described as a vagabond.

[20] AN, Colonies, C11C, Bordereaux for 1733, vol. 11, fols. 77–83, 28 oct. 1734.

[21] AN, Outre Mer, G2, vol. 178, Maria Savaria vs. Piesrés, "Extrait des registres du greffe du conseil Superieur," fols. 815–16, 9 août 1724.

[22] AN, Colonies, C11C, Bordereaux for 1735, vol. 11, fols. 100–107, 30 oct. 1736.

[23] Ibid., C11B, vol. 14, fol. 39v., St Ovide et Le Normant, 11 oct. 1733.

[24] Ibid., C11C, Bordereaux for 1739, vol. 12, fols. 9–15v.

[25] Terence Allan Crowley, "French Colonial Administration at Louisbourg 1713–1758," (PhD thesis, Duke University, 1975), 71.

[26] AN, Outre Mer, G1, vol. 466, pièce 76; see also Kenneth Donovan, "Rearing Children in Colonial Louisbourg."

[27] *Report for the Year 1905*, 59.

[28] AN, Outre Mer, G1, vol. 406, fol. 8, "Acte de baptême d'un enfant," 6 juin 1724.

[29] Ibid., vol. 178, fols. 815–16, Maria Savaria vs. Piesrés, "Extrait des registres du greffe du conseil superieur," 9 août 1724.

[30] Jean-Louis Flandrin, *Families in Former Times: Kinship, Household and Sexuality*, trans. Richard Southern (Cambridge: Cambridge University Press, 1979), 94. In 1729 Jean Seigneur, a Louisbourg aubergiste, dismissed a

"sauvage" named Louise because of her disorderly conduct and because she had become pregnant. See AN, Outre Mer, G3, vol. 2037, no. 58, 28 août 1758, "Quittance reciproque entre les sieurs de Lamalottiere et Seigneur, aubergiste."

31 AN, Outre Mer, G2, vol. 178, fols. 813–14, Maria Savaria vs. Piesrés, 9 août 1724.

32 Ibid., G3, 2058, pièce 38, "Transaction entre Jean Danjou, forgeron, et Pierrés Darricheverry, 20 nov. 1724." For the marriage ceremony between Danjou and Savaria see G1, vol. 406, reg. 2, mariages 1722–1728, 1724, Acte de Mariage entre Jean Danjou et Maria Savaria.

33 Ibid., G1, vol. 406, pièce 67, "Recensement general des habitants Etablis à L'ile Royale fait en l'année 1724."

34 Ibid., G3, 2058, pièce 2, "Contrat d'engagement de Marguerite, fille des sauvages de l'Ile Royale, par Pierre Mansel, maître de grave et pretée par ce dernier à la demoiselle Rodrigue, marchande, 29 avril 1726."

35 Ibid., pièce 1, "Contrat de mariage entre Pierre Mansel, natif de chantée, et Charlotte Dumeny, habitant de Quebek, 13 mars 1726."

36 Ibid., pièce 59, "Contrat de vente d'une habitation située au fond du barachois à Louisbourg par Pierre Mansel, maître de grave, à Louis le Vasseur, conseiller du Roy, lieutenant général de l'Amirauté de Louisbourg avec deux quittances du 15 novembre et 4 décembre 1726."

See also G3, 2056, pièce 11, "Obligation de 225 livres passée par le sieur Pierre Mansel en faveur de M. Louis Levasseur, 25 juin 1726."

37 By 1745 Marguerite was a servant for Michel Rodrigue, a Louisbourg negociant and son of Anne Le Borgne de Belle Isle, wife of Jean Baptiste Rodrigue.

38 AN, Outre Mer, G1, vol. 466, pièce 68, "Recensement general des habitans Etablis a L'isle Royale fait en l'année 1726."

39 France, La Rochelle, Archives Departmentales de la Charente-Maritime, B, vol. 277, fols. 41v–42v., Louisbourg, 27 juillet 1726.

40 AN, Outre Mer, G3, 2039 suite, "Contrat D'Echange De Maisons: L'Etrange et Perrin, 19 avril 1736," pièce 34. By 1734 there were still two of L'Etrange's children living at home in Block 19, Lot C. See ibid., G1, vol. 466, pièce 69, 20 oct. 1734, "Recensement de L'isle Royale, 1734."

41 Ibid., G1, vol. 466, census of 1724, pièce 67 and census of 1734, pièce 69; ibid., G2, vol. 194, dossier 65, "Papiers Concernant La Succession de deffunte Nicolas Langot et Marie Jeanne Coeffé, sa femme," fols. 225–32, 2 mars 1735.

42 Ibid., G2, vol. 195, dossier 65, 2 mars 1732.

43 Ibid.

44 Ibid., G1, vol. 466, pièce 67, "Recensement general des habitants, 1724."

45 Ibid., G2, vol. 195, no. 83, "Partage des biens de la succession d'Antoine Peré et de son epousé...1735"; ibid., vol. 194, no. 80, "Inventaire et vente d'Effets mobiliers de la veuve Peré, 8 juin 1735."

46 Ibid., vol. 195, no. 83. See, for instance, the following replies by Villes Treux Perée to requests by Madame Peré for clothing. Nantes, 29 avril 1732; 1 août 1732; 25 mai 1730; 8 avril 1734. All of the above cited letters were written from Nantes. See also Madame Peré to Villes Treux Perée, 4 déc. 1729.

47 Ibid., G2, vol. 195, no. 83, Peré to Villes Treux Perée, 4 déc. 1729.

48 Ibid., pièce 19, Veuve Peré à Villes Treux Perée, 22 déc. 1733.

49 *Encyclopédie ou Dictionnaire Raissonné Des Sciences, Des Arts Et Des Métiers*, tome Douzieme (A Neufchastel: Chez Samuel Failche é Compagnie, 1765), 412.

50 AN, Outre Mer, G2, vol. 195, no. 83, Pierre Joubert à Madame Peré, Nantes, 10 avril 1733.

51 Ibid., Veuve Peré à Cotteret Peré à Saint Malo, 22 nov. 1731.

52 Ibid., La Veuve Peré "doit au Sieur George Rosse de Saint Servant En Bretagne, pour nouriture, Education, habillement Et Entretient qu'il a payé pour Antoine Peré son fils, 1733."

53 Ibid.

54 Ibid., Veuve Peré à ___, 12 déc. 1733.

55 Ibid., G2, vol. 203, dossier 361, Extrait Des minutes Du Greffier du bailliage, Jean Baptiste Duboé vs. Thomas Power. See the testimony of Jeanne Bonnan, 17 mai 1755.

56 Ibid.

57 Ibid.

58 Ibid., dossier 363, 21 mai 1755.

ATLANTIC EMPIRES OF FRANCE AND SPAIN: Louisbourg and Havana*

JOHN ROBERT McNEILL

• Havana and Louisbourg in the Geopolitics of the Eighteenth-Century Atlantic World

By the eighteenth century, the nations of Europe's Atlantic shore had accumulated lengthy experience in the management of overseas empires. The Portuguese, Spanish, French, Dutch, and British had all developed a set of ideas about how and to what end to conduct such empires. On the details of execution there was much disagreement, but on the question of purpose there was very little. The principal purpose of overseas empires was to increase the power and wealth of the mother country.[1]

Armed with this general idea about the purpose of overseas empires, European states developed various strategies for achieving wealth and power. These strategies differed considerably, but all contained certain core elements. First among these was the importance of a large and vigorous commerce between colonies and mother country. Europeans believed that the wealth of the world was a fixed quantity, and thus whatever economic gains one polity might make must inevitably come at the expense of another. The competition for shares of this fixed quantity assumed the form of commercial rivalry, for commerce, they believed, offered the surest route to national wealth. This commerce ideally provided raw materials for domestic manufacturing, markets for domestic manufactures, independence from unreliable foreign markets and sources of supply, revenue for state coffers, and a supply of ships and seamen for the nation in time of need. Second was the belief in the value of secure land bases and strong seaborne forces to protect commerce and colonies against foreign depredation and to harass foreign competitors. These forces might consist solely of a regular navy, or might include corsairs and privateers. Tactics might be offensive or defensive, but strong seaborne forces must exist.

With empires stretching around the globe, eighteenth-century metropolitan states had to cope with a broad range of local conditions in their overseas holdings. Europeans could settle in some habitats but not in others; indigenous populations withstood imported diseases well in some regions but not in others; precious metals were there for the taking in some areas but not others.

North America included three representatives of European empire: the French, the Spanish, and the British. The French empire in America in 1713 consisted of two parts, one Caribbean and one North American.[2] In the Caribbean the French possessed roughly one-third of the island of Española (which they called St-Domingue), St Vincent, and the sugar islands of Martinique, Guadeloupe, Dominica, Marie Galante, and St Lucia. In South America the French held an unhealthy strip of coast known as French Guiana. In French eyes the principal value of these Caribbean possessions lay in their capacity to produce sugar. They were all slave colonies.

Further north, the French possessed the vast reaches of New France, which on maps spread from the valley of the St Lawrence river through the Great Lakes region to the Mississippi basin. Settlement, however, covered only the banks of the St Lawrence and, on a very small scale, the Mississippi delta. The islands in the Gulf of St Lawrence, Île St Jean and Île Royale (now Prince Edward Island and Cape Breton Island respectively), were virtually empty. The value of New France hinged on the fur trade. European fashions created a steady market for beaver fur, and the more northerly reaches of the rodent's habitat provided the best pelts.[3] French authorities would have preferred a colony of settlement, but the few willing migrants to Canada generally found trading and trapping more attractive than tilling the soil. The French establishments around the Gulf of St Lawrence remained small fishing communities until after 1713.

The Spanish empire in America also consisted of Caribbean and mainland colonies.[4] Those in the Caribbean included Cuba, Puerto Rico, the remaining two-thirds of Española, Trinidad, Tobago, and a few smaller islands. Sugar had not emerged as the mainstay of these colonies by 1713, so their population included fewer Africans and more Europeans than that of the French (or British) Caribbean islands.

On the mainlands of North and South America, the Spanish empire stretched from Texas to Tierra del Fuego, incorporating mines, plantations, subsistence farms, cosmopolitan cities and backward villages, vast deserts, and some of the world's richest soil. The empire consisted of two viceroyalties, corresponding to the two main economic and demographic centres: Mexico and Peru. Their chief value lay in their production of precious metals. Output had declined from levels achieved in the era of Philip II (1556–98), but mining nonetheless remained the most profitable enterprise in the Indies, and the heart of the empire from the imperial point of view.

Both the French and Spanish empires organized imperial export economies through more or less sharply defined commercial systems. The French encouraged a triangular trade between France, New France, and the French West Indies. They hoped to market French manufactures in both colonial areas, to sell sugar and rum from the Caribbean to both France and New France, to sell northern furs to France, and to provide enough grain from New France to feed the French West Indies. This program for French imperial commerce dates from the ministry of Jean-Baptiste Colbert in the late seventeenth century. Legislation discouraged trade with foreigners. The French never required the triangular trade by law, but encouraged it through tax incentives and exhortation.

The Spanish commercial system was older and more rigid, although beginning to loosen up in the eighteenth century. Strict legislation carried stern penalties for miscreants. Spanish authorities hoped to minimize intercolonial trade and to maximize the role of Spain itself as a market and supplier. The Crown, for instance, had outlawed trade between Mexico and Peru. The Casa de Contratación (Board of Trade) tightly regulated commerce between Spain and its American colonies, as well as the Pacific trade.[5] The Crown aimed to prevent foreign interloping, to foster Spanish industries, and to secure the treasure of the Indies as it crossed the Atlantic. Accordingly, large fleets carried carefully enumerated goods to prescribed ports. This commercial system, revived after the interruption of the War of the Spanish Succession (1701–15), suffered from many weaknesses, which prompted its modification, beginning perhaps in the 1740s, that was well underway by the 1760s and 1770s. Like the French, the Spanish could not prevent merchants, peninsular and colonial, from following the dictates of the marketplace, and so both venality and contraband flourished throughout the empire. The problems of enforcement at transoceanic distances overmatched the resources of the Spanish Crown, contributing to the impetus for reform of the commercial system.

Both the French and the Spanish failed to stop their colonies from trading with foreigners. In addition, the French failed to stimulate a large trade among their overseas colonies, while the Spanish failed to prevent one. Both the Bourbon empires faced the problem of defending their territories and trade from foreign attack. Since the days of Drake and Hawkins, the preferred method of profiting from a rival's empire was to seize commerce at choke points on the high seas. Annexing territory involved problems of administration, production costs, and, in turn, defence. Thus protection of trade formed the crux of the dilemma of imperial defence. Since French trade was less alluring than the Spanish, it required less protection. The French could rely on dispersal. French commerce filled a sufficient number of hulls that the French could afford to absorb some losses. Although shipping routes were well known to all, the vast majority of French shipping usually reached its destination unharmed. In wartime, the French occasionally resorted to a convoy system, but never in time of peace.[6] Spanish treasure, however, attracted many predators, prompting the Spanish to rely on a convoy system in peace and war. They tried to put most of their eggs in a single basket, the *flota*, and used the navy to protect it. Increasingly, in the eighteenth century, individual ships plied the seas between Spain and the Indies, but the majority of goods still travelled with the *flota*. This annual (in theory) procession of ships to and from the New World served Spanish purposes well in the sixteenth and seventeenth centuries. The outbound fleets laden with European goods and the returning treasure fleets were lost only rarely. Furthermore, the *flota* system helped to minimize the costs of combating contraband. But by 1715 gradual economic, demographic, and commercial expansion in the Indies would soon make the *flota* system an unwieldy anchor, limiting the growth of the trade which this system was supposed to encourage.

The French and Spanish both maintained a naval presence in American waters. The French preferred to send out a fleet each spring from bases in France—they had no year-round naval bases in the Americas. The Spanish on the other hand maintained a small squadron in the Caribbean, the Armada de Barlovento. One common characteristic greatly outweighed the differences between the two Bourbon fleets: neither cared to do battle with the British, an indisposition developed in the wars of Louis XIV (1678–1713). Their strategy and tactics hinged on the belief that to engage the British navy was to court disaster. Maintaining a navy meant refusing to fight whenever possible. Thus, by 1700, the French and Spanish had conceded what naval thinkers have since come to call "command of the sea."[7] Fortified bases had been the mainstay of earlier maritime empires, such as the Venetian and Portuguese, which had never developed standing navies. Only in the eighteenth century did a large imperial navy emerge as a standing instrument of colonial policy and defence. The British pioneered this use of the navy and thereby revolutionized maritime strategy. In the absence of naval forces which could defeat the British, the French and Spanish relied on a traditional policy of colonial fortification to defend their New World territories and trade.

Neither the Bourbon nor the British empires encompassed the heartland of North America. The forests and plains between the Appalachians and the Rockies had little to offer those who hoped to get rich quickly, and so had been largely left to the indigenous population. This does not mean, however, that the French, Spanish, and British did not covet this heartland; they did, and their imperial strategies reflected their ambitions.

Two rivers allowed access to the interior of the continent, the St Lawrence and the Mississippi, so control of each held tremendous potential strategic value. From a maritime perspective, the choke points of these rivers lay not at their mouths, but at the mouths of their gulfs: the open water between Newfoundland and Cape Breton Island in the case of the St Lawrence, and the stretch between Yucatán and Florida in the case of the Mississippi. The British, whose colonial population in North America was thirty times that of the French by 1750, controlled neither of these river routes and found the Appalachians an effective barrier to territorial expansion until later in the century. As far as the North American heartland was concerned, French control of the approach to the St Lawrence and Spanish domination of the access to the Mississippi offset British advantages of greater population and naval strength.

The strategic value of the mouths of the gulfs also hinged on their positions vis-à-vis transatlantic sailing routes. The prevailing westerlies of the northern hemisphere encouraged ships to cross the ocean west to east at a latitude above 45° in summer and above 40° in winter (global wind patterns fluctuate with the seasons) (see figure 1). Traffic from the Caribbean, or almost anywhere in the American tropics, found it convenient to sail with the Gulf Stream through the Florida Channel until far enough north to take advantage of the westerlies. Most any Caribbean ship west of the Windward Passage sailed through the straits of Yucatán and north of Cuba before entering the Atlantic, rather than buck the northeast trades. The trade winds combined with the North Equatorial Current to prevent an easy crossing to Europe at a latitude south of the westerlies, so the takeoff point for any eastward Atlantic crossing was about the latitude of Cape Breton Island, wherever the voyage originated. Thus the key strategic point in the northern approach to North America was the straits between Newfoundland and Cape Breton Island, and the key to the southern approach was the mouth of the Gulf of Mexico (which might be better understood if it were called the Gulf of the Mississippi). The French and Spanish controlled these strategic points as best they could without dominant navies.

In the eighteenth century two cities presided over these key points: Louisbourg in the north and Havana in the south. Perched astride the routes to and from Europe and the routes into the heartland of the North American continent, these cities often went by almost the same name: Louisbourg was "la clef de l'Amérique," and Havana, "la llave del Nuevo Mundo."[8] Let us turn to these port cities and their environs in the next section.

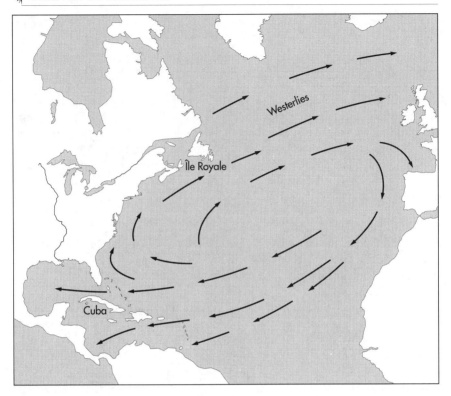

FIGURE 1 *Winds of the North Atlantic World*

• Colonial Landscapes and Seascapes

The geographical, ecological, and demographic characteristics of Cape Breton Island and Cuba prescribed limits to what the French and Spanish might extract from and accomplish in these parts of their empires. The islands' natural and human resources largely determined the degree to which they might fulfil the roles into which metropolitan policy cast them. These characteristics loom so importantly in imperial history precisely because Bourbon policymakers so poorly understood them. Their ignorance, while it scarcely distinguished them from their British, Dutch, or Portuguese rivals, encouraged French and Spanish ministers to persist in policies of dubious wisdom in colonial matters.

Cape Breton Island is the northern extremity of the Appalachian Mountains. It consists of 6403 square kilometres (3970 square miles) of sedimentary, metamorphic, and igneous rock arranged in a complex mosaic. The rock is aged—ranging from Precambrian (Hadrynian) to Carboniferous—and in its time has undergone a good deal of twisting and folding. Glaciation (as recent as 7000 years ago in the island's centre) scooped out lakes and valleys and erected a few small moraines, but no terminal moraines (presumably these existed in areas now beneath the sea). Glaciation has had little effect on soil distribution: the soil is stony where the bedrock is hard and has undergone much folding; it is fine where the underlying rock is soft and has aged uneventfully. For the most part, Cape Breton's soil is rocky, although several areas have responded well to agriculture. In the vicinity of Louisbourg the bedrock is mostly hard crystalline limestone, and the soils derived from it are poor and stony.[9]

Although the island is generally hilly, flat land surrounds Bras d'Or Lake—actually a fjord—and slopes to the sea in the northeast, where most of the population has always lived. The large saltwater inlet in the interior and the channels to its north afford easy communication, from which only the northern highlands are excluded. Small lakes and streams abound, but have no value as avenues of transport. Glaciation and moderate emergence and submergence along the coast have created a proliferation of bays and inlets, some making fine ports, most notably Sydney Harbour and St Anns Harbour.

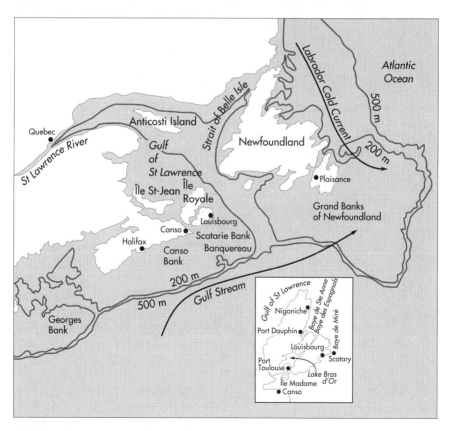

FIGURE 2 *Cape Breton Island and Environs*

The town of Louisbourg lay near the eastern extreme of Cape Breton Island on a small marshy promontory, nowhere higher than 20 metres above sea level. The promontory defines the south side of the harbour's mouth; Lighthouse Point, which defines the north side, is only several hundred metres away. A battery of rocks and shallows makes the entrance to the harbour even narrower, requiring entering ships to steer northeast toward Lighthouse Point before bearing toward the docks of the old port. The wind generally blows from the west and southwest, roughly perpendicular to the harbour's mouth, facilitating both entry and exit. Once inside the harbour mouth, sailing ships confronted a commodious anchorage of perhaps 2 or 3 square kilometres, free from the turbulence of the open sea and reasonably free from strong winds.[10] Although thousands of ships used the harbour in the French period, only twelve shipwrecks occurred inside the harbour.[11]

The old town of Louisbourg was laid out on an east-west grid. Warehouses dominated the waterfront; further inland, dwellings were interspersed with inns, shops, bakeries, and the like. Wooden houses built on stone foundations lined comparatively broad streets. Many homes had gardens of considerable proportions, since land was not especially scarce. The military installations of the Bastion du Roi and the Demi-bastion Dauphin guarded the southern and western ends of the town respectively. Both had guardhouses and barracks. Between them the Demi-bastion and the larger Bastion du Roi protected the landward approaches to Louisbourg.

The climate of Louisbourg is an unprepossessing one, with brief summers and long winters, and it could not have differed much in the eighteenth century.[12] One resident in the 1750s wrote that there were only two seasons—autumn and winter.[13] The presence of the sea serves to moderate temperatures, but nonetheless they range from –25° to 35° C (–13° to 95° F). These are recorded extremes; the average January temperature is –4° C (24° F), and that of July is 18° C (64° F). In representative years, frost appears in the middle of October and disappears toward the end of May. Louisbourg enjoys only 100 to 140 frost-free days, making for a brief growing season. Precipitation averages about 134 centimetres (53 inches) annually, of which 29 (12 inches) fall as snow. It is fairly evenly distributed around the year with some sort of precipitation falling on 160 to 200 days of the year. The July monthly average is 7.9 centimetres (3 inches), and that of December is 14 centimetres (6 inches). Drift ice imperils or prohibits the use of Louisbourg harbour for a few months each winter and spring, with great fluctuations from year to year. Strong winds buffet Louisbourg constantly (19 kilometres per hour is the average at nearby Sydney) with shore winds complicating the comparatively steady westerlies. The juncture of the Labrador Cold Current and the warm Gulf Stream creates plentiful fogs that add to the hazards of navigation and the general unpleasantness of the climate. Sydney enjoys an average of four to five hours of sunshine per day, and Louisbourg probably less. "Clouds of thick fog which come from the southwest cover it [Louisbourg] generally, from the month of April until the end of July to such a degree that sometimes for a month together they never see the sun, at the same time that there is bright clear weather at the distance of two or three leagues from it."[14]

Cape Breton temperatures range lower than French temperatures by about 10° C in January and by next to nothing in July. On the whole Cape Breton is cloudier, wetter, windier, and more snowy than coastal or central France. To any Frenchman the climate of Cape Breton appeared more difficult than that left behind.[15] The Cape Breton climate also compares unfavourably with that of the St Lawrence valley, particularly in the summer months.

Louisbourg lies on the same latitude as La Rochelle in France, just south of 46° north, well within the zone of the prevailing westerlies. At 60° west longitude, Louisbourg is perched almost on the edge of the Gulf Stream as it veers away from North America toward Europe. The voyage by sail to France took perhaps thirty days in good weather, a comparatively quick and easy trip.[16] The current and wind which made the eastbound voyage simple, however, complicated the return trip. Nonetheless, by virtue of its latitude, French ships bound for America found Louisbourg a convenient destination for which to aim: in the eighteenth century the art of fixing longitude was just emerging, so that sailors crossing the ocean frequently seized upon a chosen parallel and followed it across, so as to know their whereabouts upon sighting land.[17] For the French it was important not to land at Newfoundland, Nova Scotia, or New England, where they were unwelcome, so following the forty-sixth parallel to Louisbourg was the safest course.

Other routes to and from Louisbourg involved less dramatic variations between inbound and outbound voyages. A trip from Louisbourg to New England or the Caribbean generally went much more slowly than the return because the winds and currents favour westerly and northwesterly sailing. The belt of prevailing westerlies, although it fluctuates with the season, invariably includes Louisbourg within it. Although the westerlies are neither as powerful nor as steady as the trade winds of the tropics, and thus exercise a lesser tyranny over sailors' freedom of direction, their influence is buttressed by the Gulf Stream, which flows east-northeast at the latitude of Louisbourg.

Winds and currents exerted strong local influences too. The Labrador Current, which flows from northeast to southwest, usually grazes the eastern shore of Cape Breton Island; the Gulf Stream passes a few kilometres offshore. The constancy of these two currents created in effect a two-lane highway for coastal navigation. Close-in shore winds mitigated the effect of the westerlies, permitting eastward and southeastward sailing along the coast. This blessing does not extend any farther south than Cape Breton Island, however, since the Labrador Current disappears around 45°

north latitude. So while coastal navigation around Cape Breton benefited from the elements, long-distance sailing, except in a westerly and north-westerly direction, did not.

The sea lanes connecting Louisbourg to the rest of the Atlantic world passed through the port's great natural resource: the offshore fishing banks. By virtue of its position, Louisbourg commanded natural resources as valuable as any in North America, excepting the silver veins of Mexico (with which the fishing banks were occasionally compared). While the bounty of nature was scant indeed on the landward side of Louisbourg, off-shore the sea teemed with marketable fish. Cod, highly nutritional and eas-ier to preserve than any other fish, made Louisbourg important to Europe. The continental shelf extends several hundred kilometres to the east of Cape Breton, forming an undersea plateau seldom more than one hundred metres beneath the surface.[18] An abundance of plankton in these compara-tively warm waters attracts fish from all over the North Atlantic, especially during the mating season (newborn cod feed almost exclusively on plank-ton). This creates a dense population of large edible fish unequalled any-where in the world. Cod predominate in these waters, but other species flock there too, some to lay eggs, others to prey upon smaller fish.

Louisbourg's underwater hinterland required neither roads nor property boundaries, minimizing the overhead costs of exploitation. Cheap seaborne transport further lowered costs: cod caught offshore floated to Louisbourg for export. In contrast, Pennsylvania wheat, Maryland tobacco, Caribbean sugar, or any other colonial product, had to be carried or rolled to the point of export, consuming a larger share of the sale price in trans-port costs. In this way an offshore hinterland like Louisbourg's offered significant advantages over an inland one. On the other hand a city, a gov-ernment, or a merchant elite could more easily establish ownership and control over land than over the sea. At Louisbourg, the French found it impossible to exclude New England competition from the fishing banks. Before 1713, Breton, Norman, Basque, and West Country English fisher-men struggled for access to cod and suitable places to dry them. None could drive out the others because of the difficulty of asserting dominion over the sea. Fishing rights and marine rights remain hazily defined and hard to enforce to this day.

The resources of Cape Breton Island paled beside Louisbourg's off-shore hinterland. The rocky landscape around Louisbourg could not sup-port significant agriculture. When the French first arrived, forests covered the island,[19] but the timber proved poor, except in the interior. The coastal regions featured bogs, barrens, and forests of fir and spruce, often stunted and entirely useless except as firewood. The eastern shore, where Louisbourg stood, had the poorest forest of the island: few full-grown trees exceeded 10 metres in height. The best forest lay around Bras d'Or Lake, at St Anns, and on Boularderie Island. Here travellers found stands of hardwoods, including oak and ash (which are rare today), mixed with spruce and pine. The lack of undergrowth and the large size of these trees (up to 75 centimetres or 30 inches in diameter) indicates that this formed the climax vegetation in these regions. The tall, straight, majestic white pine, the ideal mast timber, did not decorate the Cape Breton landscape.[20] In the last 150 years, mineral resources have served as the mainstay of Cape Breton Island's economy. Easily accessible coal deposits in the northeast have been worked to exhaustion. The largest seam, of which the French were well aware, ran from Cow Bay to Sydney Harbour, conveniently close to the sea. Coal and timber resources, however, while not perhaps negligible, amounted to very little in comparison to the bounty of the sea. The true hinterland of Louisbourg, and the source of its wealth, lay offshore.

In 1713 the human resources of Cape Breton Island were almost negligible from the imperial point of view. The indigenous population of Mi'kmaq Indians numbered only in the hundreds. The Mi'kmaq, Algonquin speakers, lived by hunting and gathering. They planted no crops, domesticated no animals other than the dog, and confined their fishing almost exclusively to fresh water. They migrated continually, on foot and by canoe (outfitted with a moosehide sail for sea voyages), and so the French could never accurately know their numbers. They did not have to know, however, since the Mi'kmaq could never effectively contest the sovereignty of their island with Europeans and normally found it preferable to co-operate with white men rather than to resist them. By 1713 the Mi'kmaq had already had some experience with Europeans in the context of a small fur trade with visiting fishermen.[21] After 1713 this trade diversified, assuming the character so common in relations between whites and Indians in North America: the Mi'kmaq exchanged scouting and fighting services as well as furs, for blankets, muskets, ammunition, hatchets, and sundry other items. The French made no effort to exterminate the Mi'kmaq but inadvertently must have reduced their numbers through exposure to European diseases. By 1750 the Mi'kmaq population on Cape Breton Island had, however, recovered to perhaps two thousand in all, a density of about .3 persons per square kilometre.[22]

Throughout the French period, the Mi'kmaq remained primarily interested in the interior of Cape Breton Island, while the activities of Europeans focussed on the sea. Not that the Mi'kmaq did not occasionally fish and the French occasionally farm—they did—but on the whole they had little occasion to interact. The Mi'kmaq influence on the French settlement at Louisbourg was remarkably slight.

The first European immigration to Île Royale (as Cape Breton Island was known from the time of its settlement)[23] came from Newfoundland in 1713. The terms of the Treaty of Utrecht turned Newfoundland over to the British, and with the exception of fewer than ten persons who chose to remain and take an oath of allegiance to the British Crown, the French community resolved to depart. The original founders of Louisbourg numbered 110 men, 10 women, and 23 children.[24] From these modest beginnings, the colony of Île Royale grew to number several thousand within the span of two generations. Natural increase accounted for some, but immigration provided the largest part of the population growth.

Immigrants came from three sources. The first of these was Acadia, an agricultural community of perhaps 10 000 people of French origin, officially British subjects since 1713 but in practice quite independent.[25] With the birth of the colony at Île Royale, the French conceived the policy of recruiting Acadians first to Île Royale and then to Île St Jean as well, a policy they never abandoned.[26] The second source of immigrants to Île Royale was the French army. Officials encouraged discharged soldiers to stay in the colony. Since most French soldiers were peasants, French authorities hoped to use them to create a viable agricultural community at Île Royale.[27] The French encouraged soldiers at Île Royale to marry, a most unusual policy which reflected an emphasis on population growth.[28] Sailors, traders, and fishermen from Brittany, Normandy, and the Basque country formed the third source of immigration. Normally hundreds of French fishermen flocked to the shores of Île Royale early each summer, and others followed to supply the fishermen with food and supplies. Whenever opportunity beckoned, a proportion of these remained behind in Louisbourg to establish themselves as fishermen, traders, or labourers, a practice countenanced by French policy.[29] Although French officials instructed Quebec authorities to permit any emigrants who wished to go to Île Royale, few Canadians obliged.[30]

Western France provided the largest share of Île Royale immigrants. The 1752 census taken by Sieur de la Roque reveals the geographic origin of 828 people above the age of fifteen (see table 1). Of the 372 from France, the preponderance hailed from Normandy, Brittany, and the Basque country. Bayonne alone contributed 108 settlers; St-Mâlo, 63; Coutances, 47; and Avranches, 38. Paris provided only eight.[31] As a common practice, immigrants tended to congregate where they could find

Table 1:   **ORIGINS OF THE ÎLE ROYALE POPULATION, 1752**

Acadia	251	30.3 (%)
Île Royale	157	18.9
Canada	8	0.9
Newfoundland	30	3.6
Unspecified Quebec	1	0.1
France	372	44.9
Other countries	9	1.1

Source: Christian Pouyez, "La population de l'Isle Royale en 1752," *Histoire Sociale/Social History* 6, 12 (1973): 172.

their fellows. Almost all of those who came from Bayonne lived at Petit Degrat on the east coast; the Malouins clustered in the settlements north of Louisbourg; the Acadians lived almost exclusively at Port Toulouse and the bays of the northern part of the island.[32]

The population of Île Royale was highly mobile. Fishermen migrated from year to year according to the abundance of cod, erecting temporary dwellings as they went. The erratic population totals of the Île Royale outports (Niganiche, for example) reflect this nomadic character of the population.[33] Acadians as well as fishermen (the two categories were largely, though not entirely, mutually exclusive) moved about freely. They routinely came to Île Royale to enjoy the largesse of the Crown for three years and then returned to their homes along the Bay of Fundy. While the population of Île Royale as a whole grew fairly steadily, the pattern of distribution within the island showed a skittish sensitivity to the performance of the twin pillars of the colony's economy: the fishery and seaborne commerce. When the fishery peaked around 1730, the population of the outports approached maximum levels. By the 1750s, when the cod catch had shrunk but Louisbourg's entrepôt trade expanded, the outports' population dwindled, while the largest port burgeoned.

Several censuses recorded the French population of Île Royale between 1713 and 1758.[34] The seasonal migrations of the population created problems beyond the capacity of census takers to solve, so the student of the Île Royale population must accept inexact figures. Various subsequent efforts have been made to determine the size of the Louisbourg population, that of the outports, and that of Île St Jean.[35] No systematic effort has been made to estimate the entire population subject to the authority of the colonial government: the civil populations of Louisbourg, the Île Royale outports, Île St Jean, the garrison population, and the Indians. (Many of these people of course escaped the effective control of the government, especially those at Île St Jean or in the interior of Île Royale). Table 2 shows the growth of the colony's population from 1716 to 1752.[36]

The inhabitants of Île St Jean remained very few until the turmoil of the 1750s brought large numbers of Acadian refugees (see table 3). French policy discouraged fishing at Île St Jean in the hope of developing the island as a breadbasket for Louisbourg, a most reasonable expectation in light of the fertility of the island's soil. Nonetheless, until late in the French period the scant population at Île St Jean included many fishermen and far fewer farmers than the French wished.[37]

The French soldiery at Île Royale grew along with the civilian population, amounting to somewhere between one-fourth and one-third of the Louisbourg population throughout the French regime. Port Toulouse and Port Dauphin supported small detachments, but normally well over 70 percent of the troops were quartered in Louisbourg.[38] Officers might live in the town, marry, and engage in the fishery or even commerce; the enlisted men lived in barracks. Death and desertion took a toll reflected in an

Table 2: THE GROWTH OF THE ÎLE ROYALE POPULATION, 1716–1753

Year	Outports	Louisbourg[a]	Île Royale[b]	Île Royale and Île St Jean
1716	1042	885	2346	2446
1720	1077	950	2446	2696
1723	1777	1130	3326	3641
1724	1361	1235	3015	3396
1726	2127	1307	3853	4234
1734	2263	1584	4318	4891
1737	2575	1975	4969	5547
1752–53	1687	4853	6959	9600

[a] Includes both civilian and military population.

[b] Includes Indians.

Source: Nicole Durand, "Étude sur la population de Louisbourg, 1713–1745," Fortress of Louisbourg Library, Travail inédit no. 49, 1970; Andrew Hill Clark, *Acadia: The Geography of Early Nova Scotia to 1760* (Madison, WI: University of Wisconsin Press, 1968), 274–96; Michel Balthazar Le Courtois de Surlaville, *Les derniers jours de l'Acadie* (Paris: Lechevalier, 1899), 14; John Stewart McLennan, *Louisbourg: From Its Foundation to Its Fall*, 1713–1758 (London: Macmillan, 1918), appendix 3; Public Archives of Canada, *Report of the Canadian Archives 1905*, vol. 2, 4–76; AN, Outre Mer G1, 466, pièces 67, 69; AC, C11B, 1: 495; AC, C11B, 3: 25, 479–80; AC, C11B, 4: 21. See also the sources listed in tables 3 and 4.

Table 3: THE POPULATION OF ÎLE ST JEAN, 1720–1758

Year	Habitants (Settlers)	Fishermen	Total
1720	250[a]	–	250[a]
1728	297	127	424
1730	325	131	456
1731	347	125	472
1734	396	176	573
1735	432	131	563
1747	–	–	653
1748	–	–	735
1752	–	–	2223
1753	–	–	2641
1755	–	–	2969
1756	–	–	4400–4500[a]
1758	–	–	4600–4700[a]

[a] Estimates.

Source: Daniel C. Harvey, *The French Régime in Prince Edward Island* (New Haven, CT: Yale University Press, 1926), appendix C.

annual turnover rate of 10 to 15 percent in the 1730s.[39] Desertion accounted for more than death: a soldier's life at Louisbourg was not only tedious but very uncomfortable, and passing ships or the wilderness looked tempting by comparison.[40]

The population of the Louisbourg barracks appears in none of the several censuses taken by the French authorities. Thus table 4 is drawn from a variety of disparate sources. Clearly the French held the number of troops to a minimum (only in the West Indies could it have been more expensive to feed a soldier in the French empire), providing additional troops only when war threatened.

Table 4:   THE GARRISON POPULATION OF ÎLE ROYALE, 1717–1758

Year	Companies	Soldiers	Source
1718	7	149[a]	AC, C11B, 3:109–12
1720	7	317	AC, C11B, 5:267
1722	7	330	AC, C11B, 6:68
1731	8	389	AC, C11B, 12:32–35
1734	8	560[b]	MP, OSU, Lot 2–2
1740	–	556	AC, C11B, 22:114–15
1741	–	710	AC, C11B, 23:71
1749	24	1200[b]	AC, C11C, 15:272
1750	24	1200[b]	AC, B, 91:348
1755	–	2300	AC, C11C, 15:272
1757	–	2300	AC, C11C, 15:280
1758	–	3740[c]	*Collection de manuscrits,* 3:489

[a]   Another 150 soldiers passed the winter in Quebec to avoid starvation.

[b]   This figure represents the full strength of the given number of companies. The actual population of soldiers must have been somewhat lower.

[c]   Only 2455 remained when Louisbourg fell to the British on 30 July.

The steady growth of the Île Royale population has been demonstrated in table 2. No demographic catastrophes occurred, suggesting that Louisbourg was a fairly healthy place. The documents show only two epidemics in the entire French period, both of smallpox.[41] Scurvy, however, visited the residents almost every winter, a result of vitamin deficiencies in the diet, which in the winter months featured biscuit and fish very prominently. Many of the homes at Louisbourg had vegetable gardens, which helped reduce the monotony of the diet during the summer months, as did a little hunting; but generally Louisbourg had to rely on accumulated food stocks for the long winter. Residents could eat only foods that would not spoil quickly, such as salt fish and flour.

This unbalanced diet supported an unusually healthy population. The rate of child mortality, often a good index to the general health of a community, has been calculated at 19 percent for the years 1723 to 1724 in Louisbourg. This is lower by 4 to 10 percent than the comparable rate in Anjou, a region of western France typical of those which supplied immigrants.[42] Considering that Louisbourg's port handled hundreds of ships a year from the entire Atlantic world, including the unhealthy

Caribbean, its general good health is remarkable. Although this was one of the cheerier facts of life at Louisbourg, it must be remembered that good health by eighteenth-century standards allowed for strong possibilities of catching very nasty diseases.

Hospital records reveal patterns in the incidence of disease among the garrison at Louisbourg.[43] Civilian experience may have differed, but probably only slightly. Smallpox and tuberculosis visited the barracks most commonly. In a given twelve-month period, the garrison stood to lose anywhere between 5800 and 8700 man-days, the mean being 7742. This meant each man might expect to spend two or three weeks of the year in the hospital. This record does not sound healthy by today's standards, but in an era before preventive medicine and with cures as dangerous as diseases, this qualified as a comparatively salubrious environment. French health measures, such as the quarantine system for incoming vessels instituted in 1734, had less to do with this good health than the climate.[44] Table 5 shows the variations in the incidence of hospitalization among the garrison at Louisbourg, 1732 to 1752.

Table 5: **LOSSES TO THE GARRISON AT LOUISBOURG THROUGH HOSPITALIZATION, 1732–1752**

| Year | Garrison | Man-Days Lost | | Sick Days per Soldier |
		Soldiers	Sailors	
1732	–	5 811	1098	–
1733	–	8 333	421	–
1734	560	8 746	1375	15.5
1735	–	7 502	1023	–
1736	–	8 540	1506	–
1737	–	8 268	777	–
1741	710	6 985	55[a]	9.8
1751–52[b]	–	10 640	–	–

[a] Includes only January through September.

[b] Includes October 1751 through September 1752.

Source: See note 43 and table 4.

Perhaps the age structure of the Île Royale population helps to explain its comparative good health. Young males composed a disproportionately large share of the population, as tables 6 and 7 reveal. Table 6 consists of data drawn from the various censuses and refers to Louisbourg only. Table 7 presents data for the outports and the interior of the island in 1752. At Louisbourg, if one excludes fishermen, the numbers of men and women were roughly equal after the colony's first generation. In the outports men outnumbered women significantly (by 50 percent overall) even in 1752, especially among the twenty to forty-five year olds. This of course represents the large numbers of fishermen, for the most part young and unmarried men; without them the character of the population would probably resemble that of Louisbourg in the early years of settlement. Children accounted for 40 percent of the population in the outports and interior; fertility was high and infant mortality low. In Louisbourg in 1737, children were even more prominent: 45 percent of the total civil population.[45] Detailed census data for Louisbourg after 1737 are lacking, but one might expect a larger proportion of females to males there than either in the outports or in Louisbourg in the early years, and perhaps even more children.[46] It cannot be verified, but apparently the population of the interior was evenly balanced in sex ratio, and very young on average, because the settlers were for the most part Acadians who had immigrated *en famille*. On the coast, where the fishermen lived—generally French, young, and unmarried—the sex ratio was extremely unbalanced and children were few. The youth of the colony's population, especially in the early years, no doubt reduced mortality and morbidity rates.

Table 6: THE CIVILIAN POPULATION OF THE TOWN OF LOUISBOURG, 1713–1737

	1713	1715	1716	1717	1720	1723	1724	1726	1734	1737
Habitants	116	125	56	58	69	68	113	144	141	163
Femmes	10	89	44	37	50	50	84	97	134	157
Enfants	23	179	119	115	142	160	239	298	394	664
Valets	11	62	–	–	–	–	77	94	157	229
Pêcheurs	–	291	366	358	372	515	377	314	296	250
TOTAL	160	746	585	568	633	793	890	947	1122	1463

Source: AN, Outre Mer, G1, 466, pièces 50, 51, 52, 55, 62, 65, 67, 68, 69, 73. Cited in Durand, "Etude de la population de Louisbourg, 1713–45."

The diversity of social rank in French society did not exist in the colony of Île Royale.[47] The nobility had fewer representatives, mostly army officers and decidedly lesser nobles. A handful of missionaries to the Mi'kmaq and a very few clerics in the town of Louisbourg represented the second estate.[48] Only those who worked the soil in the interior qualified as peasants, and most of these arrived only after 1749.[49] Fishermen always made up the bulk of the labouring class, especially in the outports where many communities devoted themselves entirely to the pursuit of cod. Pilots accounted for 14 percent of the outports' population in 1752, many of them residents of Port Toulouse. No other occupational groups accounted for more than a tiny fraction of the outports' population.

Merchants centred in Louisbourg, where they constituted 1 percent of the town population from 1719 to 1752.[50] Together with the *habitant-pescheurs* (fishing fleet owners), they constituted a local bourgeoisie that clearly dominated Louisbourg civil society. Society outside Louisbourg had

Table 7: MALES PER HUNDRED FEMALES IN THE ÎLE ROYALE POPULATION IN 1752 BY AGE GROUP

0–1 years	106.7		
1–4 years	95.9		
5–9	90.0		
10–14	114.3	0–14 years	100.3
15–19	128.2		
20–24	202.6		
25–29	181.3	15–29 years	167.6
30–34	165.9		
35–39	200.0		
40–44	231.6	30–44 years	190.0
45–49	148.0		
50–54	206.2		
55–59	190.0	45–59 years	174.5
60–64	120.0		
65 and over	180.0	60 and over	160
All ages	145.0		

Source: Pouyez, "La population de l'Isle Royale en 1752," 161.

no clear masters; no one of social rank chose to live outside the town. The bourgeois families often intermarried with officers' families, blurring the distinction between noble and bourgeois. This had the effect of increasing the social and political prominence of the Louisbourg bourgeoisie.

The setting, population, and resources of Cuba were different from Cape Breton's in quantity and in detail. The overall patterns created by the setting and resources, however, bore strong resemblances in the two island outposts. The island of Cuba, including the Isla de Pinos (now called the Isle of Youth) and more than 1600 keys , encompasses 114 524 square kilometres (44,028 square miles), roughly the size of Tennessee or Newfoundland. Its coastline covers 5746 kilometres or 3,563 miles. It is long (1203 kilometres or 746 miles) and narrow (average width 100 kilometres or 62 miles) in shape, extending from 74° to 85° W longitude, and from 20° to 23° N latitude. It accounts for more than half of the total area of the Antilles and is the largest tropical island in the western hemisphere. It consists of comparatively young metamorphic and igneous rock, arranged in kaleidoscopic disarray as a result of much folding and twisting in the Eocene. Later erosion has produced broad plains, though low mountains still remain in three clusters, most notably in the east. Littoral submergence and emergence during the Pleistocene has created many fine harbours and bays. Large bottleneck harbours exist at Honda, Cabañas, Mariel, Havana, Nuevitas, Puerto Padre, Nipe, and Tamano on the north coast, and at Guantánamo, Santiago de Cuba, and Cienfuegos (Jagua) on the south coast. Over 200 rivers drain the island, none very long, but some with wide estuaries (again the product of coastal submergence) permitting some inland navigation.

The harbour at Havana is one of the finest in the world. The anchorage is very spacious, 4 kilometres across and equally long, and deep enough to accommodate the largest vessels.[51] The prevailing winds cross the entrance channel perpendicularly, facilitating both entry and exit. In the winter and spring, the winds blow from a more northerly direction, driving ships onto offshore reefs, which, combined with a lack of fresh water in the vicinity, made blockade difficult. The strongest ocean current in the world,

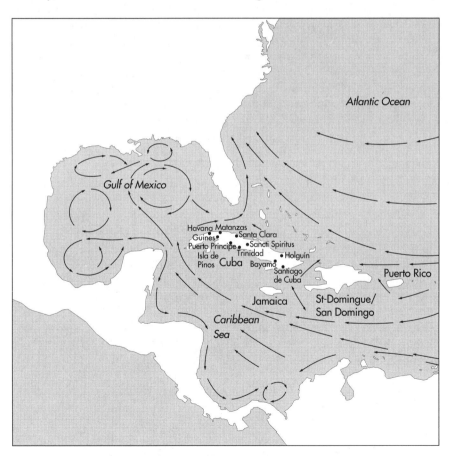

FIGURE 3 *Cuba and Environs*

the Gulf Stream, passes by at up to 10 kilometres per hour, further complicating blockade.

The old city of Havana perched on a promontory forming the western shore of the harbour mouth.[52] The bastioned walls, pierced by two main gates, enclosed an area of about 2 square kilometres, including 179 blocks, three plazas, six wharfs, and fourteen churches. Two castles, the Morro and the Punta, guarded the harbour mouth. Narrow and unpaved streets, dusty for much of the year and muddy for the remainder, formed an irregular grid. Baron Alexander von Humboldt wrote that he had never seen a city dirtier than Havana, and his visit came half a century after the first organized street cleaning.[53] Children and livestock roamed the streets during the day; at night the unlit town belonged to adult males, many of them sailors. Havana had no police force, and it could be perilous in the vicinity of the docks. It was larger than Louisbourg, more anonymous, more boisterous, and more dangerous.

Internal communication in Cuba was much more difficult than in Cape Breton. Coastal transport posed comparatively few problems, but no waterways served the interior. Mountains impeded overland communication, less convenient than waterways under the best of circumstances.[54] Large sections of the interior were isolated, which has inspired some to conjure up two Cubas: the Havana sector and the rest of the island.[55] A more appropriate division of the island distinguishes between the regions accessible to water transport and those not. Any community connected by sea to Havana enjoyed cheap and easy contact with the wider world.

In general, the climate of Cuba is very agreeable. The trade winds, the influence of the sea, and the proximity of the North American land mass combine to provide fairly equable temperatures year round. No point in Cuba is very far from the sea, which moderates temperatures considerably. North American air in the winter months helps to cool Cuba further, particularly in the western end of the island. The result is a narrow range of average temperatures that are low for the tropics. Mean winter temperature in the interior is 21° C (70° F), and the summer mean is 27° C (79° F). Freezing temperatures, even in the mountains, are virtually unknown, and in the most torrid spells the Havana temperature almost never exceeds 36° C (97° F). Extremes are caused by the southward expansion of polar fronts over North America in winter, and in summer by very low pressures in the centre of North America that bring hot dry winds north from the Caribbean across Cuba.[56]

The regularity of temperatures makes rainfall the important variable in the climate of Cuba. Precipitation varies markedly during the course of the year, although the general pattern is highly predictable. In effect there are but two seasons—the wet season from May to November and the dry season from December to April. More than three-fourths of the annual precipitation (137 centimetres or 55 inches average) falls in the rainy season, although even in the dry season it is a rare month that has no rain. Patterns vary somewhat from place to place on the island, but in general there are two maxima: one in June, a result of the evaporation and convection that are at their height when the sun is most direct, bringing daily thunderstorms; and a second in September, a product of the hurricane season. The west receives more rain than the east, principally because it is in the path of more hurricanes.

The general regime of the winds is as regular as that of rainfall. Cuba's winds are dominated by the northeast trades and directed by the Atlantic anticyclone, a centre of high pressure which migrates between 20° and 40° north latitude, depending on the season. The wind is always from the east, but in winter, the high pressure being further north, the trade winds blow from the northeast more than east. In the summer the wind comes more directly from the east, although sometimes, especially along the south coast, from the east-southeast. The wind velocity generally exceeds 5 metres per second (about 9 miles per hour), and frequently surpasses 10 metres per second. The influence of the wind upon Cuban life in the eighteenth century is difficult to exaggerate. Cubans said "upwind" and "downwind" for "east" and "west."

The power and regularity of the trade wind meant that a journey from Havana to the Mexican mainland generally took less than a week, while the return trip invariably consumed several weeks.[57] A voyage from Barbados to Jamaica, about 1500 kilometres (930 miles), took about a week, while the reverse route could take up to three months.[58] The shortest distance between two points in the age of sail depended on the direction of the wind.

The effect of the trade winds on the Cuban coasts is complicated by shore breezes, especially prominent in the summer when differential heating between land and sea is most pronounced. Small-scale shore winds oscillate daily; a larger one, the North American monsoon, can bring north winds in winter and south winds in summer. Although generally the winds of Cuba are quite reliable for sailing purposes, the hurricane season of late summer and early autumn renders the winds temporarily unpredictable and dangerous.[59]

The coral reefs and littoral currents which surround Cuba compound sailing difficulties.[60] In addition to the Gulf Stream, which carries past Cuba sixty-five times the volume of water of the sum of the world's rivers,[61] several smaller currents skirt Cuba. The sea flows westerly across the northern shore through the Old Bahama Channel as far as San Juan de los Remedios, where it veers north to join the Gulf Stream; this is the tail end of the North Equatorial Current. Farther west, the Gulf Stream flows east across Cuba's north shore, but at the western end of the island, an eddy in the stream produces the Cuban Countercurrent, flowing west and south toward Cape San Antonio. This intermingling of currents, all of which meander to some extent with the season, makes the navigation of the western end of Cuba somewhat tricky.

The southern shore of Cuba is caressed by the westward flow of the North Equatorial Current. Between the Isla de Pinos and Cape San Antonio, however, another eddy veers north and then eastward along the shore through the Gulf of Batabano as far east as the southern keys. This countercurrent is larger in the summer than the winter; its fluctuations, as well as the innumerable reefs, keys, and shallows, make for additional hazards and complexities in the navigation of Cuba's coasts.

The same forces influencing Cuba's climate and currents define the island's position with respect to the sailing routes of the Atlantic. The northeast trades, the wind that helps to power the North Equatorial Current,[62] formed the highway between Europe and the Caribbean. It was of course a one-way street; ships made the return trip further north, above the thirty-fifth parallel, in the zone of prevailing westerlies (the counter-trades). Cuba lies near the northern limit of the northeast trades, and at the head of the Gulf Stream, which bridged the gap between the Caribbean latitudes and the westerlies. Thus, given the constraints imposed by the necessity of sailing before the wind, Cuba lay at a crossroads in both Atlantic and Caribbean communication routes.[63]

Centuries of poverty belie Cuba's wealth of natural resources. By eighteenth-century standards Cuban resources appeared meager, since the island offered no silver and very little gold. To an age less entranced by bullion, Cuba's natural resources would have appeared considerable. First among these is the soil. Almost two-thirds of the island is flat or gently undulating and covered with deep soil, the product of geological calm since the Pliocene. The fertility of Cuban soils, although uneven, is sometimes exceptional. Most of the good agricultural land derives from clay and limestone deposits, 6 metres deep around Matanzas, but only 25 centimetres deep around Havana. The most fertile soils occur beside the few river beds. Cuba's sandy alluvial soils, for example, have yielded the world's finest tobacco: Humboldt found the soil at the fabled tobacco land Vuelta Abajo, to be 86 to 91 percent silica.[64] Tobacco soil, unlike good sugar cane soil, contains no lime.

The fertile soils of Cuba include large expanses that are either too dry or too wet for cultivation. One-fourth of Cuban soil cannot retain enough water to support anything besides shrubs and palms; mangrove swamps cover much of the south coast. Cuban soils are highly variegated, in contrast to the general uniformity of climatic conditions, so the island could provide a wide spectrum of crops. At one time it did so: Ponce de Leon thought the flora of Cuba among the most extraordinary of the world.[65]

The original vegetation of Cuba resembled that of northern South America more than that of Central or North America. The uniformity of climate meant that soils determined patterns of vegetation. In general terms, Cuba has three categories of vegetation: forest, savanna, and coastal. Before the arrival of the Spaniards, forest covered about 60 percent of the island. Cedar, mahogany, oak, ebony, pine, and palm abounded, arranged in zones depending for the most part upon altitude.[66] Today the forest is confined to the mountains, but in the eighteenth century it stretched down to the coastal plains wherever soils could support it. Pines grew in poorer soils and comprised a majority of the Cuban forest. In less acid soils oak predominated.

The savanna accounted for roughly one-fourth of the island and remains today much as in the eighteenth century. In Cuba the presence of soil that cannot retain moisture, rather than the level of rainfall, defines the savanna. The vegetation of these areas consists chiefly of grasses and various sorts of palm trees. The Cuban savanna has always been sparsely inhabited and used for little more than pasture land, though in the Pinar del Río area savanna land supports fine tobacco. Very often savanna areas and forest areas combine in a checkerboard pattern creating semi-savannas.[67]

The vegetation of the shore areas of Cuba is of two sorts, halophilous and xerophilous—meaning life adapted to swamps and life adapted to desert. In Cuba halophilous vegetation consists principally of five varieties of mangrove trees, which form almost impenetrable thickets guarding much of the coastline. The mangroves flourish wherever the coast has submerged. Wherever the coastline has emerged, xerophilous vegetation predominates. Here the soil is highly permeable and retains very little moisture. Cacti and small-leaved shrubs and bushes are common. Leafy plants lose too much moisture through transpiration to survive on these coasts. In general, halophilous vegetation covers the southern littoral and the keys of both coasts and xerophilous vegetation is more common along the northern coast, especially in the northeast. One large area of the south coast, the Cienega de Zapata, is given over almost entirely to mangroves, even at some distance inland.

This swampland and desert vegetation has been of little use to human beings in Cuba, even less than the savanna. The forest, however, particularly the tall hardwoods, has proved useful, which explains why so little remains. The destruction of the forest since 1740 has been the most salient change in the structure of Cuban vegetation, indeed of all Cuban natural resources.

Cuba's mineral resources have always been meager. Since the nineteenth century exploitation has intensified, but before 1762 only gold and copper attracted any attention.[68] Holguín produced small amounts of gold in the sixteenth century, as did Jagua and Trinidad in the eighteenth,[69] but Cuba proved disappointing to Spaniards who sought quick fortunes. El Cobre, near Santiago de Cuba, provided copper from 1530 to 1918, with a seventy-year intermission in the late eighteenth and early nineteenth centuries because of earthquake damage. The Spanish found and exploited smaller copper deposits elsewhere on the island, notably on the northern slope of the western mountains, but copper production always centred at El Cobre. The depletion of the copper mines in the eighteenth century, like the destruction of the forest and the exhaustion of the best soils, resulted from the growth of the sugar industry. The demands made by sugar had a powerful effect on the character and extent of Cuba's human resources as well.

The first census of Cuba appeared in 1774, by which time sugar had already begun to transform Cuban society. What passes for knowledge of the Cuban population prior to 1774 is a mixture of hypothesis, conjecture, and extrapolation. Only one document reveals any effort by Spanish authorities to measure Cuba's population, an incomplete *visita* made by a bishop in 1755 to 1757. Thus any remarks on the population of Cuba prior to 1774 deserve a measure of skepticism.[70]

Cuba's indigenous population consisted of two groups of Arawak-speaking Indians, the Taino and the Ciboney. They virtually disappeared within two generations of Columbus's visit in 1492. Archaeological evidence suggests that their numbers did not approach the maximum that Cuba's resources and their paleolithic technology would have permitted. The Ciboneys apparently arrived in Cuba first and were subjugated by the Taino who came via the Antilles from South America. The Ciboneys (the word means people of the rock in the Taino language) lived in caves and knew neither agriculture nor towns. Bartolomé de las Casas thought the Taino had arrived in Cuba only fifty years before the Spanish, but archaeological evidence indicates a much earlier presence. Taino culture corresponds roughly to the classification of late neolithic; their tools were of stone rather than wood or conch like the Ciboneys. They did not use metals. The Taino lived chiefly by means of extensive and varied agriculture. They raised grains, maize, and fruits. Their staples were cassava bread and maize, the virtues of which Columbus duly noted.[71] The Taino lived in villages for the most part, spent their lives scratching a living out of the soil, and did not practice warfare on any scale. Their food-producing and perhaps military superiority made the reduction of the Ciboneys a simple matter and required no large-scale social organization. Since the warlike Caribs—who had made their presence felt in Puerto Rico and Haiti by 1492—had little impact on Cuba, the Taino had no impulse to develop a military tradition. When the Spanish arrived, the Taino could offer only the most feeble and fragmented resistance. The Spaniards found the Taino unable to adapt to the requirements of civilization, meaning regimented labour, and concluded that they were lazy. The effect of new European diseases on a population without any immunities rendered the Indian presence in Cuba negligible by the eighteenth century.

The Indians bequeathed to later Cubans the *bohio,* a mud hut that served for centuries as the typical rural dwelling; the cultivation of cassava, Cuba's principal food source for centuries; and tobacco, Cuba's largest export for centuries. Although exterminated more rapidly and more thoroughly than the Mi'kmaq of Cape Breton Island, the Cuban Indian population left a greater cultural legacy to the immigrant population.[72]

Although Columbus visited Cuba in October 1492, Spanish settlement began only after 1511 under Governor Diego de Velázquez. A population of adventurers, traders, soldiers, sailors, and clergymen soon grew up, but with the development of more spectacular opportunities in Mexico and Peru, Cuba attracted very little European population and lost much of what it formerly had. For centuries thereafter, immigration to Cuba languished on account of the absence of a surplus Spanish population, imperial regulations, and the comparative unattractiveness of Cuba. With the demise of the Indian population, Cuba offered no supply of labour with which a Spaniard could hope to achieve wealth and status; thus Spaniards much preferred to go elsewhere in the Spanish Empire.

Cubans who wished to live off the exertions of others had to import labour, producing a multiracial society. The first African immigrant arrived in 1513; Indians from the Yucatán were also recruited.[73] According to one authority, in 1532 there were 300 whites and 500 blacks on the island. By 1620 this proportion had radically changed: 460 blacks to 6976 whites.[74] Immigration remained small throughout the sixteenth and seventeenth centuries, although influxes of white population occurred in 1655 when the English seized Jamaica and in 1697 when the Spanish ceded a third of the island of Hispaniola to the French. What few European immigrants came to Cuba in the sixteenth and seventeenth centuries hailed chiefly from the Canary Islands or the Basque country, especially Navarre. The Canary Islanders found Cuba attractive because of their familiarity with the techniques of tobacco and sugar cultivation,[75] and Basques became prominent in the ranks of Havana merchants. Despite these infusions, white population growth proceeded almost exclusively from natural increase.

No systematic estimate of the Cuban population is possible until 1757, but several authors have ventured a guess of 50 000 for 1700.[76] The proportion of whites to blacks within this total is a matter of speculation. The Cuban historian Ramiro Guerra y Sánchez thought the population evenly divided between whites and blacks in 1662, which seems most implausible in light of the failure of the Cuban slave population to reproduce and the modest rate of slave imports in the seventeenth century.[77]

Whatever the truth about the size and racial character of the Cuban population in 1700, it certainly grew very quickly in the next half century, possibly tripling in two generations. Once again an excess of the birth rate over the death rate, rather than immigration, accounted for most of this growth. Figures are unavailable except for one parish, Santa María del Rosario, a village 25 kilometres or so from Havana. According to the parish register, in the years 1733 to 1762 baptisms outstripped deaths by up to ten to one among whites and five to one among blacks.[78] This differential implied tremendous natural increase, but was not typical of the island. The parish was founded in 1733, and many of its inhabitants were newcomers— probably young adults; it is unlikely to resemble the rest of the island either in birth rate or death rate.[79] Nevertheless, substantially higher birth than death rates must have been the rule in most of the island. By 1757 the island's total population had grown to about 160 000, roughly the size of Maryland at that time.[80] Almost a quarter of those were slaves.

In 1754, the new bishop of Havana, Pedro Agustín Morel de Santa Cruz, undertook to visit every community in Cuba, inaugurating an era of greater reliability in population data.[81] The bishop did a thorough job, visiting almost every settlement mentioned in his *visita,* and rarely neglecting to record the population. Where he failed to include a population figure he generally offered a number of households, allowing a fairly confident projection (see tables 8 and 9). His only major lapse was the city of Havana, for which the bishop reported only *personas de comun* (persons having received communion)—22 828, and the number of households in Havana—6896. What was the population of Havana? Multiplying the number of households by the average ratio of persons per household in the Havana suburbs and hinterland (7.78) one gets about 54 000—more than the city's population thirty-seven years later.[82] Using the Havana suburbs as the source for a multiplier (6.12), one gets about 42 000. This means that there were about 20 000 people too young to receive communion, which still seems a trifle high; very likely the average household size in Havana was smaller than in the countryside or the towns immediately around the city. A 1728 count showed only 21 310 for the total population of Havana, including 3596 children *(parbulos)*.[83] If this proportion between adults and children equalled the ratio between *personas de comun* and those too young for communion in 1755, the total Havana population in that year comes to only 26 632. However, the 1728 figure for children probably excluded slave children, and it may also refer to a group younger than that excluded by the bishop in 1755. Admittedly Havana had a disproportionately large share of adults—people involved in servicing ships and migrants just in from the countryside—but a city with only 17 percent children seems implausible. Certainly the Havana population exceeded 26 632 in 1755 to 1757, but it probably did not reach 42 000, a total which requires that Havana households include as many children as those in rural Cuba. A figure of 35 000 for the 1755 to 1757 Havana population seems nearer the mark.[84]

Table 8: REPORTED POPULATION OF CUBA BY COMMUNITY, 1755–1757

District	Community	Households	Population
Havana		6896	22 828[a]
Havana suburbs		600	3 671
Havana hinterland	Jesus del Monte	262	1 318
	Santiago de las Vegas	328	1 954
	San Felipe y Santiago[a]	190	1 658
	Managuana	135	3 154
	Calvario	331	1 879
	San Miguel	199	965
	Potosí	66	642
	Regla	20	[164][b]
	Guanabacoa	637	6 309
	Santa Maria del Rosario	–	1 598
	Batabano	43	315

Table 8 (continued)

District	Community	Households	Population
Western Cuba	Isla de Pinos	–	40
	Quemados	183	1 462
	Cano	310	2 732
	Guanajay	33	268
	Santa Cruz de los Pinos	65	400
	Consolación	142	753
	Pinar del Río	76	640
	Guane	98	700
	Cacaraxicaras	33	238
Central Cuba	Río Blanco	71	670
	Matanzas (town)	121	[740][b]
	Matanzas (partido)	–	1 370
	Macuriges	–	[400][c]
	Guamacaro	7	96
	Alvarez	75	163
	Hanabana	95	466
	Guamutas	47	186
	Camarones	–	[500][c]
	Santa Clara	669	4 293
	Los Remedios	398	2 527
	Sancti Spiritus	909	5 492
	Trinidad	792	5 840
	Palmarijo	108	422
	Ciego de Avila	–	[350][c]
Puerto Príncipe	Puerto Príncipe	1506	12 000[d]
Santiago	Holguín	345	1 751
	Bayamo	2530	12 653
	Jiguani	102	588
	El Cobre	–	1 183
	Caney	83	500
	Iguabos	–	419
	Baracoa	217	1 169
	Mayarí	–	300[e]
	Santiago de Cuba	1419	15 471

[a] Includes only *personas de comun*.
[b] Projection based on household number and average household size in appropriate district.
[c] Estimate.
[d] "More than 12 000" reads the *visita*.
[e] "More than 300 *vegueros*" reads the *visita*.
Source: *Visita* compiled by the Bishop Morell y Santa Cruz, AGI, SD 2227; AGI, SD 534.

Forty-five locales besides Havana are entered in the bishop's *visita*, and their population totals appear in tables 8 and 9.[85] Close to a quarter of the island's population lived in Havana and its environs. More general attempts at urban-rural breakdown involve guesswork. It is unclear in the cases of Santiago de Cuba, Puerto Príncipe, and other towns just what proportion of the bishop's total lived in town or in the surrounding *partido*.

Table 9:   ESTIMATED POPULATION OF CUBA BY DISTRICT, 1755–1757

District	Households[a]	Reported Population	Adjusted Population (I)[b]	Adjusted Population (II)[c]	Avg. House-hold Size[a]
Havana	6 896	22 828	35 000	35 000	3.31
Havana Suburbs	600	3 671	3 671	4 589	6.12
Havana Hinterland	2 211	19 792	19 956	24 945	8.23
Western Cuba	940	7 233	7 233	9 041	7.65
Central Cuba	3 292	21 525	23 515	29 394	6.12
Puerto Príncipe	1 506	12 000	12 000	15 000	7.97
Santiago	4 696	34 034	34 034	42 543	6.84
	20 141	121 083	135 409	160 512	

[a] Excludes the nine communities (see table 8) for which Bishop Morell included no data on number of households.

[b] Includes estimates for five communities for which Morell included no population data.

[c] Includes 20 percent for ecclesiastical underreporting (see note 85), except for Havana where the table's figure is not based on the bishop's count.

[d] Derived from raw data in table 8; only communities for which Bishop Morell includes both population and households.

Source: *Visita* of Bishop Morell y Santa Cruz, AGI, SD 534; AGI, SD 2227.

Maps of Santiago de Cuba show a small town, suggesting that most of the 15 471 reported in the *visita* lived in the countryside. Levi Marrero writes that the population of Cuba in 1755 to 1757 was predominantly urban, but he arrives at this conclusion by considering urban anyone who resided in a community of more than twenty households.[86]

Although the documents do not permit precise statements, clearly well under half of the Cuban population lived in cities. Centres such as Puerto Príncipe and Bayamo could probably be more accurately described as market towns than cities in 1755, but even if one counts them with Havana and Santiago de Cuba as cities, the proportion of urban dwellers remains lower than 47 percent. A more appropriate figure is 30 to 35 percent, considering Puerto Príncipe and Bayamo as agricultural centres and much of their reported population as rural.[87]

While the population of Cuba lived predominantly on the land, it was nonetheless arranged geographically around two major urban centres, Havana and Santiago de Cuba. Each of these ports had agricultural hinterlands, which supported ranching, sugar, tobacco, and food crops, and also contained much of the Cuban populace. Most of the western end of the island served as Havana's hinterland: its cash crops went to Havana, some of the food produced there went to Havana, and most of what the outside world provided came through Havana. Santiago de Cuba had a parallel but lesser role in the eastern end of the island. Bayamo and especially Puerto Príncipe, market towns of some size, provided for the east and centre much of what Havana provided for the west. In Bayamo and Puerto Príncipe the link with the wider world was less regular even than in Santiago de Cuba. Santiago de Cuba in turn was less cosmopolitan than Havana, despite regular ties with the north coast of South America. In the eastern end of Cuba, presumably, the amenities of Europe were scarcer than in the west, and the reliance on local products, such as food, clothing, furniture, and tools more complete. Isolation was greater still in the centre of the island.

Disease was the single most important factor governing both the size and distribution of population in eighteenth-century Cuba. Emigration and white immigration were almost negligible, so natural increase, strongly influenced by disease, assumed great importance. Yellow fever, which the Spaniards generally called the black vomit, probably came to the Caribbean from West Africa, where it afflicts monkeys more than human beings. It is a virus carried by the Aedes aegypti (or stegomya) mosquito. The virus requires temperatures above 16° C (60° F) to survive, and the mosquito needs temperatures above 27° C (80° F) to prosper. At 10° C (50° F) the mosquito lapses into a coma, and at freezing it dies. Thus the fever is chiefly tropical and has sharp geographical limits, though these vary with the season: yellow fever made occasional summer appearances in Philadelphia, New York, and New England in the eighteenth century. The Aedes aegypti is an eccentric: it breeds only in stagnant water and much prefers waters kept in containers with solid sides and flat bottoms, like cisterns or water casks. Thus it generally flourishes only where it can keep human company. The virus produces a violent reaction in susceptible human beings, resulting either in death, usually within five days, or in lifelong immunity. Case mortality ranges up to 80 percent.[88]

Yellow fever first appeared in Havana in 1648 and, in conjunction with a myriad of less lethal diseases, made the West Indies a most unhealthy place.[89] The British Royal Navy, which in the eighteenth century had worldwide experience, considered the West Indies the unhealthiest region of all. Yellow fever epidemics broke out in Cuba six times between 1731 and 1762.[90] The continual presence of yellow fever in Cuba meant that virtually every adult had encountered the disease as a child, and the survivors developed immunity. Those who had spent childhoods in Europe, however, had no defence against yellow fever and remained highly susceptible as adults. Yellow fever is more lethal to adults than to children, and so newcomers to places like Cuba took their lives in their hands. New arrivals to the West Indies faced roughly a 20 percent chance of dying within a year; a British garrison at Barbados reported an annual death rate of 18 percent.[91] The medical profession could do little to help. No one knew whether or not yellow fever was contagious, and no agreement existed as to treatment beyond the necessity of bleeding the patient. Thousands of Europeans, less willful and perspicacious than Smollett's Roderick Random, died from attempted cures.[92]

Yellow fever is in fact not contagious and does not depend on a large assembly of hosts for its survival. Nonetheless it plagued the town more than the country, because the Aedes aegypti was a domesticated mosquito, dependent upon water casks and cisterns, and it congregated wherever human beings gathered. Foreigners without immunities tended to go no further than the cities, which helped make yellow fever more noticeable in Havana than elsewhere.

Contagious diseases flourished in Havana, too, precisely because of the city's size. In order to survive, a contagion must find new hosts continually, and this requires large concentrations of population. From the epidemiological point of view, Havana was an extended city: in addition to the residents, pathogens might attack the contingents of sailors, soldiers, and travellers who passed through. Havana offered contagious diseases a larger number of potential hosts and more constant infusions of nonimmunized blood than did the countryside. Thus all varieties of contagion, from smallpox to typhus, ravaged Havana more often than the rural communities. Indeed the human traffic in the port of Havana ensured that the city accommodated a correspondingly large microbiotic traffic. Astride the major sea routes of the Atlantic world, Havana functioned as a clearinghouse of contagion, uniting the disease pools of Europe, Africa, and the Americas.[93] Travellers to Havana met a wide variety of contagious diseases, and if they lacked a complete portfolio of immunities they stood an excellent chance of falling ill and a good chance of dying.

Despite the high level of contact between Havana and its rural hinterland, rural communities were sufficiently isolated from one another and human concentrations sufficiently low that contagious disease could not flourish for long outside the city. The pathogen would normally kill an uninitiated host before it could be communicated to another; an infection could not sustain itself without larger numbers of susceptible hosts than the countryside could provide. So, like yellow fever, contagious diseases affected country less than town.

The differential incidence of lethal diseases between town and country created population flows in Cuba. The death rate in Havana must certainly have been significantly higher than in the countryside and probably significantly higher than the birth rate in Havana as well; left to its own devices the city would have lost population and ceased to exist. That it continued to exist, and even to grow, testifies to the size of the influx from the countryside. Havana was in effect a sinkhole for humanity. It survived only because it continually attracted newcomers, not so much from abroad, but from the *partidos* of Cuba. Since urbanites died more rapidly than they were born, Havana almost invariably needed labour, which meant Havana offered opportunity. At the same time, the countryside produced too many adults because of its comparative freedom from contagious disease. Excess rural population required out-migration of some sort to avoid a constant lowering of living standards. Some sons surviving to adulthood inherited no land; in order to make a living and to merit a bride, they had to leave their place of birth. Up to a point they could clear new land in the Cuban forest, but this was usually less attractive than going to the city. Thus a homeostasis of sorts between urban and rural Cuba had emerged by the eighteenth century. Static it was not: the populace grew, cleared new land, and founded new towns and villages. A movement toward the frontier of the forest coincided with a movement to the city. Havana survived and grew, while the forest shrank.[94]

Unlike Île Royale, Cuba to some extent supported a peasant society: large numbers of Cubans produced their own food and met a majority of their other needs by themselves, living on the land they worked (though not necessarily owning it). In this respect, as in several others, Cuba resembled Spain more than Île Royale resembled France. Indeed, Cuban society reflected Spanish society a good deal more than did most parts of Spanish America.

Of the social classes present in Spain, Cuba lacked only a powerful landed nobility. Titled landowners were very rare in the eighteenth century, and the only other nobles, officers in the army, represented only .0006 of the Cuban population. A landed aristocracy of sorts decorated Cuban society, ranch owners and sugarmill owners for the most part; but few of these owned large tracts, and few lived handsomely off their holdings. Since sugarmills remained fairly small-scale operations until later in the century, these persons are perhaps better described as a rural bourgeoisie (if one can overlook the paradox): they were as concerned with transport and marketing as they were with rents. In order to live well off of rents one must have, one way or another, a captive tenantry. With good land uncleared and the city beckoning, landowners without slaves faced stiff competition for population, and consequently did not flourish in eighteenth-century Cuba. Each rural landowner employed overseers, perhaps slave drivers, and sugarmasters, too. But the mass of white rural population worked as landless labourers or was self-employed. The self-employed might raise tobacco or food crops and probably very often both, because neither tobacco nor food was raised on the plantation system but on small holdings or family farms. Country towns had a labouring class, employed in building, hauling, etc., and a small class of marketeers, warehousers, retailers, and, occasionally, bureaucrats.

In Havana and Santiago de Cuba, the social scene varied more widely. Joining the labourers and the small bourgeoisie of the towns were the international merchants—people with partners in Spain or Vera Cruz or Cartagena, regular access to the wider world, a certain amount of wealth, and perhaps learning. Several of these merchants owned land as well but rarely visited it, preferring the sophistication and excitement of the city. Havana had a small professional class: army officers and bureaucrats employed by the state; lawyers, doctors, and chemists, often self-employed; ship captains, priests, and even university professors after 1728. As port towns, Havana and Santiago de Cuba supplied ships with provisions and crews with entertainment. Thus the cities included large numbers of shop-keepers, butchers, salters, tavernkeepers, wine merchants, and prostitutes. The urban labouring class naturally pursued different employments than rural workers; in Havana and Santiago de Cuba they toiled as stevedores, ditch diggers, construction workers (often employed by the state for public buildings or fortifications), carpenters, masons, fishermen, and, of course, soldiers and sailors. Cubans showed keen awareness of social rank and gra-dations. Social mobility was the exception to the rule; occasionally a new-comer to Havana might parlay a decade's savings into ships, warehouses, and a small fortune, or a *Habañero* (Havana native) might gain title to enough land to become a prosperous rancher or sugar planter. But for the vast majority, their station in life when born remained theirs until they died, whether or not they moved around the island.

In addition to the white society sketched above, a small but growing society of slaves existed in Cuba. By the standards of the Antilles their num-bers were small. While Jamaica and Haiti counted their slaves in the hun-dreds of thousands, Cuba had about 5000 in 1700 and 35 000 in 1762.[95] State slaves worked the copper mines at El Cobre and laboured on the for-tifications at Havana; other slaves toiled in the fields. In the mid-eighteenth century *ingenios* (sugar plantations) around Havana averaged forty-five slaves each. These slaves fed themselves from plots called *conucos*, using free time when the cane needed little attention. Some slaves worked in the tobacco *vegas*, not in gangs as with sugar, but individually or in pairs beside the *veguero* (tobacco grower) and his family. A large contingent of slaves worked as domestics in the wealthier homes of Havana and the country-side. Before 1762, Cuban slaves had little chance to develop any communi-ty because they remained too few and too isolated from one another. Some worked underground, some in the fields, others in the finest houses; all they had in common was their slavery and African descent.

Most Cuban slaves came from Jamaica, but had been born in Africa.[96] By the eighteenth century, Jamaica had emerged as the centre of the Caribbean slave trade, and because the Spanish had no African stations of their own they bought from Jamaican slavers. Initially the Portuguese and then the French sold slaves to the Spanish Caribbean, but in 1713 the British won a monopoly that the South Sea Company exercised for twenty-six years. The official price was high, 300 *pesos*, the equivalent in Havana prices of 12 teams of oxen, 100 cowhides, 1500 pounds of low-grade tobacco, or a year's wages for a common labourer.[97] A duty of 11 percent helped to encourage large-scale smuggling of slaves into Cuba, at prices between one-third and one-half the official one.[98] A system of registration and branding for legally entered slaves, designed to discourage smuggling, probably pro-duced the reverse effect because of the fee involved. Cuba's south coast was only two days' sail from Jamaica, whereas Havana was five times as far away. For the Jamaican slaver the temptation to trade illegally on the south coast was as strong as for the Cuban to avoid paying the duty and the *indulto de negro.*

The slave trade continued because slave society in Cuba, like the city of Havana, proved a net consumer of human beings. Above and beyond the rigors of the labour they performed and the disinclination to bring children into a world such as theirs, three reasons explain the failure of the slaves to maintain their numbers. First, the majority of the Africans entered a new disease climate when they reached the Caribbean; mortality on the transatlantic voyage was severe enough, but from the microbiotic point of view the slaves' condition only worsened when they arrived in the Antilles.[99] Secondly, slave owners actively discouraged procreation among slaves; it cost less to buy a new slave than to pay for the food and clothing, however meager, of a child until it grew strong enough to work. Slave owners preferred that children be raised in West Africa at no cost to themselves, leaving them only the cost of the finished product, as they viewed it.[100] Lastly, a gross imbalance between the sexes inhibited reproduction; in the canefields, at least, 89 percent of Cuban slaves were male.[101]

On the whole, the island of Cuba in the eighteenth century possessed resources far superior to those of Cape Breton. While both islands enjoyed an advantageous location for trade, Cuba had good soil and a large population, which Cape Breton did not. Cape Breton had the fishery, which produced an export crop just as reliably as did the Cuban soil; Cape Breton, however, could not feed a large population in addition to producing a cash crop, which Cuba could. The climate of Cuba was gentle, but not its disease climate; Cape Breton's climate was harsh, but it was a far healthier place.[102] Mineral resources were nearly negligible in both places, but Cuba offered a magnificent forest in comparison to Cape Breton's. Cuba's harbours were better and more numerous, its winds more reliable, and its coastal (but not interior) communications easier, if only because Cuba's hurricane season was shorter than the ice season in Cape Breton. Cuba had a larger population with more variegated skills and experience than Cape Breton, although by midcentury, population densities in the two islands were roughly equal.[103] Economic opportunities in Cuba were greater than those in Cape Breton, but the strategic advantages of each were roughly similar.

Local conditions form colonial history only in partnership with imperial policy, so before examining the economic and military records of Cape Breton and Cuba we must consider the contexts of metropolitan policy.

• Notes

1. This proposition is hard to prove but still a defensible assumption. The relationship between power and wealth is unclear: one may be the means to the other, but the identity of ends and means remains obscure. On this head see: Jacob Viner, "Power vs. Plenty as Objectives of Foreign Policy in the Seventeenth and Eighteenth Centuries," *World Politics* 1(1948): 1–29; and ch. 3 of John Robert McNeill, *Atlantic Empires of France and Spain: Louisbourg and Havana, 1700–1763* (Chapel Hill, NC: University of North Carolina Press, 1985).

2. The most convenient survey is W.J. Eccles, *France in America* (New York: Harper and Row, 1972).

3. The leading study is H.A. Innis, *The Fur Trade in Canada* (Toronto: Toronto University Press, 1956).

4. Convenient surveys include: Charles Gibson, *Spain in America* (New York: Harper and Row, 1966); J.H. Parry, *The Spanish Seaborne Empire* (London: Hutchinson, 1966); C.H. Haring, *The Spanish Empire in America* (New York: Oxford University Press, 1947).

5. See C.H. Haring, *Trade and Navigation Between Spain and the Indies* (Cambridge, MA: Harvard University Press, 1968). Haring treats only the sixteenth and seventeenth centuries. A work that covers the eighteenth century is Geoffrey J. Walker, *Spanish Politics and Imperial Trade, 1700–1789* (Bloomington, IN: Indiana University Press, 1979).

6. Richard Pares, *War and Trade in the West Indies, 1739–1763* (Oxford: Oxford University Press, 1936), 311–15.

7. This concept is best expressed in Alfred T. Mahan, *The Influence of Sea Power upon History, 1600–1783* (Boston: Little, Brown, 1890). The idea is applied to empires in Clark Reynolds, *Command of the Sea: The History and Strategy of Maritime Empires* (New York: Morrow, 1974).

8. Both phrases mean the key to America (or the New World). One of Cuba's first historians appropriated Havana's nickname, bestowed by a Real Cédula of 1634: José M.F. Arrate y Acosta, *Llave del Nuevo Mundo* (Mexico: Fondo de Cultura Económica, 1949). See also Jacques Savary, *Dictionnaire universel de commerce* (Paris: La Veuve Etienne, 1742), 908. Both cities were occasionally referred to as the Gibralter of America as well.

9. Technically the soil is of the humo-ferric podzol group; in the southwest of Cape Breton this is mixed with grey luvisol soils. See Canada, Department of Agriculture, *System of Soil Classification* (Ottawa: 1970). For an eighteenth-century description of the geography of Cape Breton see Thomas Pichon, *Genuine Letters and Memoirs Relating to the Natural, Civil, and Commercial History of the Island of Cape Breton* (London, 1760), 10–53. The first systematic appraisal of Cape Breton's geography is a memoir of 1706, normally attributed to the Intendant of New France Jacques Raudot, *Archives Nationales, Fond des Colonies* C11B, 1:270 passim (hereafter AC, C11B, vol., page). It is partially reprinted in John Stewart McLennan, *Louisbourg: From Its Foundation to Its Fall, 1713–1758*, 23–31.

10. Storms could and did, however, do damage. Sabatier au Ministre, 4 déc. 1726, AC, C11B, 8:130–31.

11. See Paul Thibault, "Shipwrecks of the Louisbourg Harbour," 1713–58. Fortress of Louisbourg Library, HF–12 (1971).

12. The climate of North America changes but slowly. See Reid A. Bryson, "Ancient Climes in the Great Plains," *Natural History* 89(1980): 64–73.

13. Pichon, *Genuine Letters and Memoirs*, 6. Another, a Scot, called the climate "wretched," James Johnston Chevalier de Johnstone, *Memoires of the chevalier*

de Johnstone, vol. 2 (Aberdeen: D. Wyllie & Son, 1870–71), 180. The data that follow on the climate of Cape Breton are drawn from two sources: Canada, Surveys and Mapping Branch, Geographic Division, *The National Atlas of Canada* (Ottawa: Macmillan, 1974); Susan Walters, *1980 Canadian Almanac* (Toronto: Copp Clark Pitman, 1980). Some of the data are for Sydney, NS, 20 miles away from Louisbourg, and all of the data are recent. Thus they can only serve as an approximation to the actual climate of eighteenth-century Louisbourg. Discussion of the Cape Breton climate and geography appears in T. G. Taylor, *Canada: A Study of Cool Continental Environments and Their Effect on British and French Settlement* (London: Methuen, 1947).

14 *Collection de manuscrits contenant lettres, mémoires et autres documents historiques relatifs à l'histoire de la Nouvelle-France,* vol. 3, 469.

15 One French visitor thought the cold was unnatural, a fact he attributed to the large number of trees: "jusqu'au mois de mai des froidures ne sont pas naturelles, d'ou, on doit concluire qu'à mesure qu'on détruira les bois, et qu'on découvrira les terres il n'y aura plus tant de neges, et que par conséquent les hyvers . . . ne seront si rudes ni si longs." Mémoire à Pontchartrain (n.d., c. 1706). AC, C11B, 1:273.

16 Measuring the practical effect of sea distances by referring to record and average crossing times is a very difficult business. See the attempt and the disclaimers of Fernand Braudel, *The Mediterranean and the Mediterranean World in the Age of Philip II,* vol. 1 (New York: Harper and Row, 1972), 358–62.

17 The first sextants and octants appeared in the 1730s, some of which were accurate to 0° 2' of longitude, but these were not widely employed, and the problem of fixing one's longitude disappeared only with the

introduction of the chronometer in the 1760s, Eva G.R. Taylor, *The Haven-Finding Art: A History of Navigation from Odysseus to Captain Cook,* vol. 1 (London: Hollis and Carter, 1956), 254–63. A detailed account of French struggles with navigation in these waters is: M. de Chabert, *Voyage fait par ordre du Roi en 1750 et 1751 dans l'Amérique septentrionale* (Paris, 1753).

18 For descriptions of the fishing banks, see Robert de Loture, *Histoire de la grand pêche de Terre-Neuve* (Paris: Gallimard, 1949), 15; Charles de La Morandrière, *Histoire de la pêche française de la morue dans l'Amérique septentrionale,* vol. 1 (Paris: Maisonneuve et Larose, 1962), 27–32.

19 See the survey based on French travellers' accounts: P.A. Bentley and E.C. Smith, "The Forests of Cape Breton in the Seventeenth and Eighteenth Centuries" in *Proceedings of the Nova Scotian Institute of Science* 24 (1956): 1–15. Besides the published accounts mentioned by Bentley and Smith, see Minutes de la Conseil de la Marine, 1717, in which quantities of maple are mentioned, AC, C11B, 2:28–29.

20 See Arthur R.M. Lower, *Great Britain's Woodyard: British America and the Timber Trade, 1763–1867* (Montreal: McGill-Queen's Press, 1973), 30, for the distribution of the *pinus strobus.*

21 By 1606 they had learned to sail shallops, according to Marc Lescarbot, *Nova Francia: A Description of Acadia* (London: Routledge and Sons, 1928), 84; see also Wilson D. Wallis and Ruth Sawtell Wallis, *The Micmac Indians of Eastern Canada* (Minneapolis: University of Minnesota Press, 1955), 14–49.

22 Leslie F.S. Upton, *Micmacs and Colonists: Indian-White Relations in the Maritimes Provinces, 1713–1867* (Vancouver: University of British Columbia Press, 1979), 32–33. Pre-contact population estimates traditionally hover around 3500, but one student has put it at 35 000, Virginia P. Williams, "Aboriginal Micmac Population: A Review of the

Evidence," *Ethnohistory* 23 (1976): 117, 125. French population estimates varied widely. According to Upton, *Micmacs*, 32–33, the French noted 260 families in 1716, 838 persons in 1722, 600 warriors in 1739. Recensement general fait au mois de Novembre 1708 de tous les sauvages de l'Acadie, Newberry Library, Special Collections, Ayer Manuscripts 751, records only 196 Mi'kmaq in Cape Breton Island. Estimates appearing in the documents which Upton did not include are 289 warriors in 1721, 635 *hommes* in 1732, and 670 warriors in 1757, St-Ovide au Conseil, 15 sept. 1721, AC, C11B, 5:359; Rapport de M. St-Ovide, 4 nov. 1732, *Collection de manuscrits*, 3:164; Mémoire sur l'Isle Royale, déc., 1757, AC, C11C, 15:280.

23 The names Île Royale and Louisbourg were assigned by the Minister of Marine, Pontchartrain à L'Hermitte, 26 jan. 1714, AC, B, 36:419. Henceforward Cape Breton Island will refer to the island and Île Royale to the colony.

24 *Archives Nationales*, Outre Mer, G1, 466, pièce 50 (hereafter AN). McLennan, *Louisbourg: Foundation to Fall*, 12.

25 The most convenient treatments of the Acadians are the works of Naomi Griffiths, *The Acadians: Creation of a People* (Toronto: McGraw-Hill Ryerson, 1973) and *The Acadian Deportation* (Toronto: Copp Clark, 1969).

26 Pontchartrain à St-Ovide, 20 mars 1713, AC, B, 35–3:110–15; Pontchartrain à Desmarets, déc. 1713, AC, B, 35–2:692–95; Instructions à Soubras, 10 avril 1714, AC, B, 36–7:89–104; Conseil à St-Ovide, 15 juillet 1722, AC, B, 45–2:1150; Maurepas à St-Ovide, 25 juin 1724, AC, B, 45:276–91. In 1731 Île St-Jean joined Île Royale as an acceptable destination for Acadian immigration, Maurepas à St-Ovide, 10 juillet 1731, AC, B, 35–3:566–72.

27 Ordre du Roi, 26 juin 1725, AC, C11B, 1:196–98. (Also in AC, F3, 50:161–62.)

28 Conseil de la Marine à Soubras, 22 avril 1716, AC, B, 38–2:555–56.

29 Trading ships paid a fine of 600 *livres* if they neglected to bring out with them to Louisbourg *engagés* (indentured servants), who, it was hoped, would develop ties and stay on after their three-year term expired, Circulaire aux Intendants, 9 avril 1722, AC, B, 45-1:280–81. Many of the *engagés* were apparently convicts, Conseil à Rostan, 11 juin 1722, AC, B, 45–1:101.

30 Pontchartrain à St-Ovide, 20 mars 1713, AC, B, 35–3:114; Pontchartrain à Vaudreuil, 29 mars 1713, AC, B, 35–3:158–69.

31 The same regions of France which sent fishermen to Île Royale also supplied the majority of merchants. Of eighty French merchants, twenty-six were from Gascony, twelve from Normandy, eleven from Guyenne (Bordeaux), and ten from Brittany, see Christopher Moore, "Merchant Trade" (thesis), 41–42.

32 Only ten Acadians lived anywhere other than these places. These comments are all based on the 1752 census as it appears in Public Archives of Canada, *Report, 1905*, vol. 2, 4–76. In its original form it is in AN, Outre Mer, G1, 466, pièce 81.

33 See McLennan, *Louisbourg: Foundation to Fall*, appendix C.

34 Those that survive are in AN, Outre Mer, G1, 466.

35 For Louisbourg: Nicole Durand, "Etude sur la population de Louisbourg, 1713–1745," Fortress of Louisbourg Library, Travail inédit no. 49, 1970; for the outports, see McLennan, *Louisbourg: Foundation to Fall*, appendix 3; for the island as a whole, see Andrew Hill Clark, *Acadia: The Geography of Early Nova Scotia to 1760* (Madison, WI: University of Wisconsin Press, 1968), 274–96. Clark's is the most detailed discussion available, but it has arithmetical and other errors, particularly a propensity to omit the entire garrison population.

36 The Île Royale population by the 1750s exceeded that of Newfoundland, Nova Scotia, and Georgia among British colonies, Robert V. Wells, *The Population of the British Colonies in America before 1776* (Princeton, NJ: Princeton University Press, 1975), 47, 160, 170.

37 The history of the French at Île St-Jean is ably presented in Daniel C. Harvey, *The French Regime in Prince Edward Island* (New Haven, CT: Yale University Press, 1926), and in Andrew Hill Clark, *Three Centuries and the Island* (Toronto: Toronto University Press, 1959).

38 Etat des troupes de l'Isle Royale, 1722, AC, C11C, 6:68.

39 In 1733 the first nine months saw a forty-three-man turnover; in 1735, thirty-one men had to be replaced; in 1736 the figure was fifty-nine. See St-Ovide à Maurepas, oct. 1733, AC, C11B, 14:217; St-Ovide à Maurepas, 10 oct. 1735, AC, C11B, 17:27; AC, C11B, 18:53–54.

40 A steady diet of fish, peas, butter, and molasses was the best a soldier could look forward to at Louisbourg, and very often food was scarce. Wages were often appropriated by officers, and if they were not, there was precious little to spend them on. Soldiers could marry, but brides were hard to find, Minutes de Conseil de la Marine, 25 mars 1719, AC, C11B, 4:4–8 (diet); Minutes de la Conseil 1718, AC, C11B, 3:7 (marriage); see also, McLennan, *Louisbourg: Foundation to Fall*, 47, Johnstone, *Memoires*, vol. 2, 172.

41 One was in 1732–33 and the other in 1755. See B. Schmeisser, "Health and Medicine at Louisbourg," Fortress of Louisbourg Library, HM–4 (1977), unpaginated.

42 Kenneth Donovan, "Rearing Children in Louisbourg, A Colonial Seaport and Garrison Town, 1713–1758" (paper delivered to the Atlantic Society for Eighteenth-Century Studies, Mt St Vincent University, Bronx, NY, 26 April 1979). Donovan defined a child as anyone under the age of twelve. This paper was shown to me through the courtesy of the author. For the Anjou figure, see François Lebrun, *Les Hommes et la mort en Anjou aux XVIIe et XVIIIe siècles* (Paris: Mouton, 1971), 182.

43 Reports include AC, C11B, 12:170–71; AC, C11B, 13:107, 111, 122–23; AC, C11B, 14:208–9; AC, C11B, 16:103–5; AC, C11B, 16:109–10; AC, C11B, 16:113–14; AC, C11B, 18:255–58; AC, C11B, 18:262–66; AC, C11B, 20:88–92; AC, C11B, 23:168; AC, C11B, 30, 230–31. These cover 1731–37, 1741, 1751–52.

44 St-Ovide et Le Norman de Mezy à Maurepas, 23 jan. 1734, AC, C11B, 15:52–59.

45 Christian Pouyez, "La population de l'Isle Royale en 1752," *Histoire Sociale/Social History* 6, 12 (1973): 169.

46 A Louisbourg census was taken in 1749–50 but only a rough version remains in the archives, AN, Outre Mer, G1, 466, pièce 65. This census gives 2454 as the civil population.

47 As a guide to the gradations of French society I have used Pierre Goubert, *The Ancien Régime* (New York: Harper Torchbooks, 1974).

48 Mémoire du Roi, 12 mai 1722, AC, C11B, 6:26. In 1722 Louisbourg supported only a single cleric, who cost 500 *livres* annually to maintain.

49 Pouyez, "La population de l'Isle Royale," 169.

50 Moore, "Merchant Trade," 41–42.

51 Daniel Fenning, *A New System of Geography*, vol. 2, 724: "a thousand sail of ships may commodiously ride in it in the utmost safety, without anchor or cable, no wind being able to hurt them." Thomas Jefferys, *A Description of the Spanish Islands and Settlements on the Coasts of the West Indies* (London: T. Jefferys, 1762), 78: "the best port in the West Indies." See also, "General Description of the American Coasts and Seas," by pilot Captain Domingo Gonzalez Carranza, 1718, British Library, Additional Manuscripts 28140, fols. 35–64 (hereafter BL, AM nos.).

52 The following description is based on maps in Archivo General de Indias, Mapas y Planos, Santo Domingo, 160, 176, and 204; and on *Urbanismo español en America* (Madrid: Editorial Nacional, 1973), 26–41; Alejandro de Humboldt, *Ensayo política sobre la Isla de Cuba* (Havana: Archivo Nacional de Cuba, 1960), 105–10; Walter Adolphe Roberts, *Havana* (New York: Coward-McCann, 1953), 41; John Campbell, *A Concise History of Spanish America* (London: John Stagg, 1741; rprt. Dawson's of Pall Mall, 1972), 160–64.

53 Testimonio de los Autos formados a fin de establecer un Asiento . . . para la limpieza de las calles y plazas, 1749, Archivo General de Indias, Santo Domingo 1219 (hereafter AGI, SD no.).

54 There was only one road worthy of the name, from Havana to Santiago de Cuba; see Emeterio S. Santovenia, "Politica colonial" in *Historia de la nación cubana*, ed. Ramiro Guerra y Sánchez, José M. Pérez Cabrera, Juan J. Remos, and Emeterio S. Santovenia (Havana: Editorial Historia de la Nación Cubana, 1952), 33.

55 Pierre Chaunu and Huguette Chaunu, *Séville et l'Atlantique*, vol. 8 (Paris: Armand Colin, 1955–59), 555, 568–69.

56 Climatic data for 1800–10 appear in Humboldt, *Cuba*, 152–54; for 1854–56 in Jacobo de la Pezuela, *Diccionario geográfico, estadístico, histórico de la Isla de Cuba*, vol. 3, 19–20.

57 "Dictamen del Sr. D. Tomas Ugarte sobre la derrota y precauciones con que navegará con más seguridad, una fregata," Archivo del Museo Naval (hereafter AMN), Manuscrito 469, fol. 230. To avoid bucking the trade wind, captains sailed north from Vera Cruz almost to the shore of Texas, where the trades were weaker and shore winds could be exploited. At this latitude they sailed eastward toward the western shore of Florida, from which a southward descent to Havana was fairly easy, especially in winter. Also: An Account of the Havannah, 19 April 1740, BL, AM 32694, fol. 77.

58 Lucy Frances Horsfall, "British Relations with the Spanish Colonies of the Caribbean, 1713–1739" (MA thesis, University of London, 1936), 3–16. Horsfall probably drew her information from the introduction by A.P. Newton, *European Nations in the West Indies* (London: A. and C. Black, 1933). Captains often preferred to exit the Caribbean by doubling Cape San Antonio and passing through the Florida Straits, sailing out into the Atlantic and then returning to the Windward Islands from the east, with the help of the northeast trades. This amounted to a journey of perhaps six times as many miles as a direct route from Jamaica to Barbados, but was often quicker.

59 Data on the climate and winds of Cuba come from Humboldt, *Cuba*, 152–72 (figures here differ only slightly from modern ones suggesting that the climate is little changed by the passage of 180 years); and from Levi Marrero y Artiles, *Geografía de Cuba* (Havana, 1951).

60 A translation of a 1718 survey of Caribbean waters made by the *flota* pilot Domingo Gonzalez Carranza is instructive on currents: "General Description of the Spanish West Indies," Public Record Office (PRO), Colonial Office (CO), 319, 2; also in BL, AM 28140, ff. 35–64.

61 R.L. Pirie, *Oceanography* (New York: Oxford University Press, 1973), 103.

62 To an extent winds create ocean currents. The other major factors are, first, the rotation of the earth, which creates Coriolis forces inclining bodies of water in the northern hemisphere to harbour clockwise currents (vice versa in the southern hemisphere), and second, the relief of the ocean's floor, which directs heavy cold water en route from the Arctic and Antarctic to the tropics. Compensation for these bottom water currents is necessarily made by surface currents, Neumann, *Ocean Currents* (Amsterdam: Elsevier, 1968), 127–226.

63 Varias derrotas entre Cádiz, La Habana y Méjico, AMN, Ms. 582, Doc. 4.

64 Humboldt, *Cuba*, 149.

65 Marrero, *Geografía de Cuba*, 104.

66 Idea geográfica, histórica, y política de la Isla de Cuba y Ciudad de la Habana (n.d.), BL, AM 17629, fols. 28–33; Humboldt, *Cuba*, 159–60; Jefferys, *Spanish Islands*, 73; Marrero, *Geografía de Cuba*, 109–12.

67 In Cuban Spanish there are words for a savanna surrounded by woods (*ciego*); for woods surrounded by savanna (*sao*); and for savanna encircled by woods and a river bank (*ceja*). *Ciego* ordinarily means blind; *ceja* more generally means eyebrow.

68 Iron, chrome, and magnesium exist in quantity too. The Spanish knew of iron deposits near Baracoa from early in the sixteenth century, but no mining took place until the 1880s.

69 Idea geográfica, histórica, y política de la Isla de Cuba y la Ciudad de la Habana, BL, AM 17629, fols. 28–33.

70 See G. Douglas Inglis, "Historical Demography of Cuba, 1492–1780" (PhD diss., Texas Christian University, 1979).

71 Cassava is the Taino word for yucca (Carib) and manioc (Guaraní).

72 For Cuba's prehistory, consult Ramiro Guerra y Sánchez, *Manual de la historia de Cuba* (Havana: Cultural S.A.), 3–17; Fernando Ortiz, *Historia de la arqueología indocubana* (Havana: Siglo XX, 1922) and Mark Raymond Harrington, *Cuba before Columbus* (New York: Museum of the American Indian, 1921). Indian settlements did survive into the eighteenth century at Guanabacoa and Jiguani, see Francisco Arango y Parreño, *Obras completas*, vol. 2 (Havana: Ministerio de Educación, 1952), 433.

73 Alfonso González, "The Population of Cuba," *Caribbean Studies* 11, 2(1971): 75.

74 These figures are based on Fernando Ortiz, *Hampa afro-cubana: Los negros esclavos* (Havana: Revista Bimestre Cubana, 1916), 21–22.

75 Dictamen sobre los ventajas que pueden sacarse para el mejor fomento de la Isla de Cuba (n.d.), AGI, SD 1156.

76 This figure appears in at least a dozen works, most recently in González, "Population of Cuba," 75. It originated, I believe, with Pezuela, *Diccionario*, vol. 4, 238; see e.g., Joseph Grellier, *Cuba, Carréfour des Caraïbes* (Paris, 1970), 103.

77 Guerra, *Manual de la historia de Cuba*, 130.

78 These are approximations made from the graphs in Guy Bourdé, "Sources et méthodes de l'histoire démographique à Cuba (XVIIIe y XIXe siècles)," *Annales de démographie historique* (1972): 408–9.

79 Bourdé, "Sources et méthodes," 407, admits that his parish is not typical, though he offers as the reason that it is close to Havana; he, of course, was discussing its entire history, not just that of its early years.

80 Guerra et al., *Historia de la nación cubana*, vol. 2, 109, has 140 000 for 1759. Grellier, *Cuba*, 103, has 150 000 for 1760. Maryland in 1755 had 153 505 people, 70.5 percent white and 29.5 percent black, Wells, *Population of the British Colonies*, 146.

81 The bishop's *visita* survives in nine documents. Relación de la visita de Obispo Pedro Agustín de Morel y Santa Cruz, 2 julio 1755, Havana, AGI, SD 2227. Also in SD 2227: 28 julio 1756, Bayamo, and 28 oct. 1757, Havana. In AGI, SD 534: 14 sept. 1756, Santiago de Cuba; 17 agosto 1756, Bayamo; 2 sept. 1756, Santiago del Prado; 8 dic. 1756, Santiago de Cuba; 16 dic. 1756, Santiago de Cuba; 4 abril 1756, Havana. The *visita* is also in the Archivo Episcopal de la Habana, *legajo* 18. The *visita* appears in part in Marrero, *Cuba*, vol. 6, 44–45, 66–70. Unfortunately Marrero has sixteen copying or typesetting errors and some arbitrary extrapolations and deletions.

82 Humboldt, *Cuba*, 194. Marrero comes up with 50 000, achieved by multiplying an incorrect 10 000 households by an arbitrarily chosen multiplier of five persons per household. The same figure appears (for 1762) in Pérez de la Riva's introduction to *Documentos inéditos sobre la Toma de la Habana*, 17.

83 Razon de la gente que Contiene esta Ciudad de la Havana sacada por los Padrones del año proximo pasado de 1728, AGI, SD 2104. A 1691 *padrón* ("count") counted 11 940 *Habañeros*, Inglis, "Demography of Cuba," 73. A Spanish writer, however, estimated 26 000 for 1700, Campbell, *Spanish America*, 162. Campbell may draw his information from Francisco Coreal, *Voyages de François Coreal aux Indes Occidentales, contenant ce qu'il y a vu de plus remarquable pendant son séjour depuis 1666 jusqu'en 1697*, vol. 2 (Amsterdam: J.F. Bernard, 1972), 147, which has 25 000 for 1697.

84 An Account of the Havannah, 14 November 1740, BL, AM 32694, fol. 74, "there may be 40 000 people in the town."

85 Table 9 calls for some lengthy explanation. The number of people that the bishop actually reported is only 121 083. This excludes the population of five settlements—Regla, Macuriges, Matanzas (town), Camarones, and Ciego de Avila—which the bishop acknowledged, but for one reason or another he neglected to include a head count for them. For Regla and Matanzas (town) a projection may be made on the basis of the number of households in the settlement, using as a multiplier the average household size in the area. For the other three a less reliable estimate must be made, but because none of these communities exceeded more than a few hundred persons, the error involved will be small. The city of Havana is the only other settlement for which an adjustment in the bishop's reported figure is required (see 37–38). A further refinement is called for, however: an addition made to compensate for the bishop's underreporting. Here an

additional 20 percent is added for all communities whose totals have not already undergone adjustment. This 20 percent comes to 24 103 across the whole island. It is not entirely arbitrary, although it is certain to be wrong. It is derived from two cases in which civil counts can be compared with bishops' counts. In one such case, that of Guanabacoa in 1756, the bishop's figure is 84 percent of that reported by civil authorities; in the other such case, that of Santiago de las Vegas in 1766, the bishop's figure is only 76 percent of the civil count. Put together, these two cases (the only ones of which I know) suggest that ecclesiastical counts, for whatever reasons, are in this time and place about 20 percent low. One might, of course, prefer to conclude that civil counts tend to be inaccurately high; in some cases, depending on the purpose for which the count was made, they certainly were. In the two cases above, however, no motive behind the counts can be expected to produce overreporting. In general it may well be that civil counts tend to underreport as well; Humboldt certainly felt this way with regard to the 1774 and 1791 censuses: "Everyone is aware that both these were made with great negligence, and a large part of the population was omitted," (Humboldt, *Cuba*, 193). If Humboldt is correct and the 1774 figure is indeed much higher than the 172 620 officially reported, then the 1755–57 figure offered here fits fairly well with a steady trend of growth from 1700 to 1791. Since what little property taxation existed went to the church and not the civil government, the populace had stronger motives to mislead an ecclesiastical counter than a civil one. For this reason civil counts are more reliable than ecclesiastical ones, and the discrepancies between them are more likely to represent underreporting on the part of the bishop, than overreporting on the part of the civil authority.

86 According to the bishop's *visita*, Guanajay had thirty-three households and thirty-two ranchs. Pinar del Rio

counted seventy-six households and eighty tobacco farms. Guane had ninety-eight households and ninety-eight tobacco farms plus ranchs. These Marrero counts as urban, Marrero, *Cuba*, vol. 6, 44–45. While it is unclear what makes a city (in Europe it was walls), surely a stricter definition than Marrero's is more helpful.

87 The *visita* divides only one community into town and country, Matanzas, in which about one-third of the total reported population lived in town and two-thirds in the surrounding *partido*. Should the same ratio hold for towns such as Puerto Príncipe, Bayamo, and Santiago de Cuba, as seems plausible, then the urban population of Cuba amounted to only 30 percent.

88 See Henry Rose Carter, *Yellow Fever. An Epidemiological and Historical Study of Its Place of Origin* (Baltimore, MD: Williams and Wilkins, 1931), 3–23; MacFarlane Burnet and David O. White, *The Natural History of Infectious Disease* (Cambridge: Cambridge University Press, 1972), 242–49.

89 Carter, *Yellow Fever*, 187–90; John B. Blake, "Yellow Fever in Eighteenth-Century America," *Bulletin of the New York Academy of Medicine* 44(1968): 673–86.

90 C. Northcote Parkinson, ed., *Trade Winds* (London: G. Allen and Unwin, 1948), 121–40. The Royal Navy must not have taken into account the West African coast. José Martínez Fortún, *Epidemiología (Sintesis cronológica)* (Havana: Cuadernos de Historia Sanitaria, 1952), 29. Many medical historians believe (wrongly, I think) that yellow fever spared Cuba between 1648 and 1761.

91 Cyril Hamshere, *The British in the Caribbean* (Cambridge, MA: Harvard University Press, 1972), 186.

92 For eighteenth-century ideas on the cure of yellow fever, see James Tytler, *A Treatise on the Plague and Yellow Fever* (Salem, MA, 1799) for the wisdom of a Cuban medico, see the treatise of

Dr Tomás Romay, 27 junio 1804, Bibliotica Nacional (Madrid) MS 18698[10]. This document was brought to my attention by Dr William Coker.

93 Each *flota*, for example, brought about 5000 sailors to Havana, who stayed an average of 44 days in the sixteenth and seventeenth centuries, and at times as long as 198 days, Chaunu and Chaunu, *Séville et l'Atlantique*, vol. 6, 280. Other ship traffic brought another 5000 or 10 000 sailors to Havana for short stays.

94 No data exist on the age and sex of the Cuban population until 1774. Since net migration hardly mattered (except for the growing slave trade), we may assume "natural" proportions for preindustrial populations. See E.A. Wrigley, *Population and History* (London: Weidenfeld and Nicolson, 1969), 23–28, 108–43.

95 Humboldt, *Cuba*, 217, says in 1763 Cuba had less than 32 000 slaves. According to Manuel Moreno Fraginals, *El ingenio: Complejo económico-social cubano del azúcar*, vol. 1 (Havana: Editorial de Ciencias Sociales, 1978), 35, the Havana area had only 4000 slaves before 1762. Herbert S. Klein, *Slavery in the Americas: A Comparative Study of Cuba and Virginia* (London: Oxford University Press, 1967), 147, used 40 000 for the total "coloured" population in 1700, a figure from Ramiro Guerra y Sánchez, *Sugar and Society in the Caribbean: An Economic History of Cuban Agriculture* (New Haven, CT: Yale University Press, 1964), 46.

96 Moreno Fraginals, *El ingenio*, vol. 2, 86, says that 88 percent of the slaves on sugar plantations in the Havana area between 1740 and 1790 were born in Africa.

97 Ward Barrett, "Caribbean Sugar Production Standards in the Seventeenth and Eighteenth Centuries" in *Merchants and Scholars: Essays in the History of Exploration and Trade*, ed. John Parker (Minneapolis: University of Minnesota Press, 1965), 166, shows that throughout the British Caribbean a slave's value averaged

about 4000 pounds in low-grade sugar. In Cuba slaves brought a price almost twice as high: the equivalent of 300 *arrobas*, or 7500 pounds of sugar.

[98] J. Houston, *Dr. Houston's Memoirs of His Own Life-Time* (London: L. Gilliver, 1747), 224.

[99] The mortality rate among slaves on the middle passage in French slavers in the eighteenth century was 12–14 percent. See Robert Stein, "Mortality in the Eighteenth-Century French Slave Trade," *Journal of African History* 21 (1980): 35–42; also, Dionisio Martinez de la Vega al Marques de la Paz, 15 enero 1732, Archivo Histórico Nacional (Madrid), Sección de Estado, *legajo* 2333.

[100] Arango, *Obras*, vol. 2, 161: "el negro que nace en casa ha costado más, cuando puede trabajar, que el de igual edad se compra en pública feria."

[101] Moreno Fraginals, *El ingenio*, vol. 2, 86. The same demographic data on slaves also appear in Manuel Moreno Fraginals, "Africa in Cuba: A Quantitative Analysis of the African Population of the Island of Cuba," *Annals of the New York Academy of Sciences*, vol. 292, *Comparative Perspectives on Slavery in New World Plantation Societies* (New York, 1977), 191–93.

[102] These are in fact related to some degree. Many bacteria and viruses can survive in warm and humid climes but not in colder, drier ones. Cape Breton's cool summer and long winter made it invulnerable to several infections that troubled Cuba. Cape Breton may be no less humid than Cuba on average but is always cooler.

[103] Using the 1752–53 count for Cape Breton and the 1755–57 count for Cuba, population densities were in Cuba, 1.39 per square kilometre and in Cape Breton, 1.09.

LA MER DE L'OUEST:
*Outpost of Empire**

W.J. ECCLES

Two hundred and fifty years ago Pierre Gaultier, sieur de la Vérendrye, wintered at Grand Portage at the outset of his attempt to discover a route to the western ocean. Since the days of Verrazano and Jacques Cartier the French had dreamed of one day finding a way to the China sea. Samuel de Champlain, in appealing to the Crown in 1617 for support of his commercial venture at Quebec, declared that, "one may hope to find a short route to China by way of the river St Lawrence; and that being the case, it is certain that we shall succeed by the grace of God in finding it without much difficulty; and the voyage could be made in six months." In carefully assessing what revenues could be derived from New France, he estimated that the customs duties to be levied on goods passing from Asia to Europe by this short route would be at least ten times greater than all those levied in France. The revenue from the trade in furs, it might be noted in passing, ranked very low in his prospectus.[1]

In 1634 he dispatched Jean Nicollet de Belleborne to the Baie des Puants to pacify the warring tribes of the region and to make inquiries about the Western Sea, which he believed could not be far distant from the Baie. With a commendable respect for mandarin protocol, Nicollet took with him a colourful flowered robe of Chinese damask in order to be properly attired when he met the eastern emperor's representatives. When his canoe landed at La Baie and he stood up in this apparel, he succeeded in frightening the wits out of the local tribesmen, if nothing else.[2]

The eventual discovery that the Mississippi River did not flow into the Pacific came as a disappointment[3]; but, as the maps of La Haye and

---

*From *Essays on New France* (Toronto: Oxford University Press, 1987), 96–109.

Franquelin indicate, French knowledge of the extent and shape of the continent was, before the end of the seventeenth century, quite remarkable. Yet one peculiar myth persisted: that somewhere between the 40th and 50th parallels of latitude there was a vast inland sea, La Mer de l'Ouest, connected by a navigable strait to the Pacific Ocean. It was believed that this sea of the West stretched to within a few days' journey of Lake Superior. Royal Geographer Guillaume de l'Isle so described it in a memoir of 1706, and on his map of 1717 it is depicted as reaching more than half way to the Mississippi.[4] It may well be that de l'Isle and those many others who accepted this notion were influenced by the seventeenth century's love of symmetry. Since there was a huge bay, the Gulf of Mexico, in the southeast corner of the continent, Hudson Bay in the Northeast, and the Gulf of California in the southwest, then there had to be a similar gulf in the Northwest to balance them.

Before the end of the seventeenth century, Canadian *coureurs de bois* had voyaged hundreds of miles west of Lake Superior and were reputed to have reached Lake Winnipeg, or the Lac des Assinibouels as it was then called.[5] The glutting of the beaver market in France in the 1690s temporarily curbed westward expansion, but the decision, on the eve of the War of the Spanish Succession, to establish a base at Detroit and a new colony at the mouth of the Mississippi in order to prevent English expansion into the West, thrust the French into the interior.[6] It thereby pitted some 15 000 Canadians against the burgeoning population of the English colonies, estimated to be over a quarter million at the turn of the century.[7]

Prior to the Seven Years' War the French never had more than a few hundred men in the West, certainly fewer than a thousand. In 1750, when French expansion in the West had reached its limits, the troops garrisoning the posts from Fort Frontenac to La Mer de l'Ouest numbered only 261 officers and men.[8] In addition there were those engaged in the fur trade, *voyageurs,* clerks, tradesmen, and a few missionaries. It is unlikely that they exceeded, at the most, 600 at any one time.[9] As for the *coureurs de bois,* their numbers can only be guessed at—probably fewer than 200—and the role they played in extending French influence was, to say the least, equivocal. It is almost incredible that with this mere handful of men the French were able to lay claim to most of the continent for over half a century.

The seventeenth-century wars fought by Canada against the Iroquois, and later against the English colonies, had been fought for purely Canadian ends: security of the colony and control of the fur trade. In those wars France had unstintingly provided the military aid needed to achieve those ends. The ensuing wars of the eighteenth century were to be fought for the achievement of purely French imperial aims. From 1700 on New France was a mere instrument of French imperial policy, to contain the English colonies on the seaboard and tie down as large a part of the British army and navy as possible. This had to be done by enlisting the support of the Indian nations. If their active support was not to be obtained, then at least they had to be prevented from aiding the Anglo-Americans.[10] In this Anglo-French contest the fur trade became all important; it became a means to a political end rather than an economic end in itself. The French had to provide goods and services to the Indians in exchange for furs and military aid, at prices that were competitive with those of the English traders. In this they proved to be eminently successful.[11] They garnered the lion's share of the fur trade, and in the wars they had the support of almost all the Indian nations except the eastern Iroquois who, for the most part, remained neutral.[12]

The Indians were willing to allow the French to place trading posts on their lands and to travel through their territories; in fact they sometimes requested the establishment of such posts, but always these posts were maintained on their terms.[13] The French had to court them assiduously, bestow lavish presents on them,[14] entertain them extravagantly when they visited Montreal or Quebec,[15] send some of their chiefs to France to view the splendours of Paris and Versailles,[16] and overlook their frequent excesses. Many Canadians were killed in the Indian country, and the French but rarely were able to obtain redress.[17]

The French claimed title to all these lands through which they voyaged, but these claims had about as much substance as the claim of the kings of England to the crown of France. In reality these claims were made merely to exclude the English, and sometimes they were made without the Indians' having any notion that the French thereby maintained that they had taken possession of the land. The Chevalier de La Vérendrye, for example, laid claim to the lands of the *Gens de la Petite Cérise,* in what was later to be South Dakota, by surreptitiously burying an inscribed lead plaque, brought from Quebec for the purpose, beside a stone cairn. When questioned by the Indians as to its significance, the Chevalier told them that it was just to mark the occasion of his visit.[18]

The Indians regarded the land as theirs and themselves as subject to no one.[19] They tolerated the presence of the French because it suited them; when it ceased to do so, they quickly made their feelings known. Thus the post established among the Sioux had to be abandoned during the Fox wars; it was later re-established, but in 1731 it had to be abandoned once again.[20] Similarly the uprising of the nations at Detroit in 1747 made plain how tenuous was the French hold on the West.[21]

In fact French sovereignty in the West existed only within French posts, beyond no farther than the range of French muskets. En route between Montreal and the West the *voyageurs* had to travel in armed convoys. Every man had to carry a musket and return with it on pain of four months' imprisonment. When Father Aulneau was about to leave with La Vérendrye, his friend and fellow Jesuit, Father Nau, remarked, with greater prescience than he knew: "He has a good enough escort, but if these unknown peoples whom he seeks are ill-intentioned what could twenty French do against an entire nation?"[22] The French were not sovereign in the West; the Indian nations were.

In Europe, meanwhile, the Treaty of Utrecht of 1713 had ushered in thirty years of peace between England and France. In North America, however, the political climate was more akin to a cold war. French policy here was dictated by the expectation of future hostilities. How best to prepare for them? In 1716 the Minister of Marine instructed the governor-general and intendant at Quebec that attempts by the English to extend their influence into areas that incontestably belonged to France had to be opposed gently but firmly.[23]

That was the political climate when the French government decided that a determined effort should be made to discover a land route to the western ocean. Politics were not the only motive for the quest. Scientific curiosity and the desire of the Regent, the duc d'Orléans, and his entourage to have France gain the glory of first making this great discovery, were major factors in the decision. It was rather akin to President John Kennedy's determination that the first man to set foot on the moon should be an American. The thirst for knowledge of the continent's interior had previously contributed to Louis XIV's decision to establish the colony of Louisiana. La Salle's explorations had failed to determine the precise geographic location of the mouth of the Mississippi. As the historian Marcel Giraud put it: "The topic held the attention of the erudite and the men of science, members of the *Académie française,* of the *Académie de Science,* of the *Académie des Inscriptions.* Some were interested essentially out of a spirit of scientific curiosity. . . . But national ambitions were, in general, combined with purely scientific preoccupations."[24]

In 1692 Louis Phélypeaux de Pontchartrain, Minister of Marine, was given charge of the *Académie de Science.* He gave it a new constitution, strengthened it immeasurably, and made it the chief instrument of French scientific leadership. Science was now accepted as a department of the modern state.[25] Scientific expeditions were sent to Peru, near the equator, and to the polar regions, in order to measure degrees of latitude and check Newton's theory that the earth is flattened at the poles.[26]

Canada was by no means excluded from this scientific inquiry. At Quebec, Michel Sarrazin, king's physician and corresponding member of the *Académie,* was sending plants to the *Jardin des Plantes* in Paris and reporting on Canadian animals that he had dissected as early as 1706. His devotion to science was indeed commendable; but then he, like many of us today, had to justify his annual grant in aid of research.[27] The intendant Claude Thomas Dupuy brought with him a sizeable collection of astronomical instruments.[28] His successor, Gilles Hocquart, kept Father Gosselin and the Sieur Hubert Joseph de la Croix, surgeon and botanist, busy shipping plants to Georges-Louis Leclerc de Ruffon, *intendant du Jardin du Roi,*[29] thereby most likely unwittingly providing the ship's officers with mid-ocean salads. This interest in science permeated the upper levels of Quebec society among those who dined at the tables of the governor and intendant and who felt obliged to keep abreast of what interested those exalted dispensers of coveted patronage. This was something upon which Peter Kalm, professor of botany at the Abo Academy in Finland and member of the Swedish Academy of Science, who visited Canada in 1749, commented on at some length in his journal.[30]

As early as 1717 the Crown had given its official blessing to the search for the elusive Mer de l'Ouest. This support could well be described as all aid short of help. In July of that year Governor-General Vaudreuil had sent Lieutenant Zacharie Robutel de la Noue with eight canoes to establish three posts that would serve as bases for the discovery of the western sea. These posts were to be at Kaministiquia, Lac de la Pluie, and the Lac des Assinibouels, which would at that time have been either the Lake of the Woods or Lake Winnipeg.[31] The *Conseil de Marine* approved the project but insisted that it not cost the crown a *sou*. The proceeds from trade at the posts had to bear the costs. The council and the regent who made the final decision did agree that the Crown must underwrite the expenses of the voyage of discovery beyond the advance posts because the men chosen for it should not be concerned with trade, only with exploration. It was estimated that it would take two years and cost as much as 50 000 *livres*. The regent agreed that the funds should be provided, requiring only that the cost be kept as low as possible.[32] Three years later no advance had been made beyond Kaministiquia, and when a request was made to the Crown for 47 000 *livres* for another two-year venture, the regent decreed that it would have to be deferred.[33]

The Crown did, however, send Father Pierre-François-Xavier de Charlevoix, who had taught at the Collège de Québec for some years, on a fact-finding mission to discover the most practicable route to the western sea. After voyaging to Michilimackinac, to La Baie des Puants, and then to New Orleans he opined that the Missouri would be the best route since the elusive sea must be between 40 and 50 degrees of latitude.[34]

During these years all manner of strange tales were brought out of the West by the *voyageurs*, likely enlivening the long winter evenings in the Montreal taverns. These tales were of a people in the Far West who lived in French-style houses. Father Nau, the Jesuit missionary at Sault-St-Louis near Montreal, concluded that these people must be, not Spaniards, but Tartars who had fled the Japanese. This, to him, opened up the possibility of a rich new missionary field. He cautioned, however, that one had to view everything that the Canadians related with the deepest suspicion. "For," he declared, "there is not a country in the world where they lie more than they do in Canada."[35]

In 1730 Lieutenant Pierre Gaultier de Varennes et de La Vérendrye, commandant of the *poste du nord* at Kaministiquia, offered to establish a post on Lake Winnipeg as a base for a thrust to the western sea, and this at no cost to the Crown apart from some 2000 *livres* worth of presents for the Indians. The proposition was accepted by the minister of marine, and so his oft-recounted odyssey began. There is no need here to discuss his career, his exploits, disappointments, or his failure to come anywhere close to his objective. For an officer who had served in both Europe and Canada, he appears to have been neither a good disciplinarian nor a competent administrator. He was manifestly a poor businessman and his finances were always in disarray.[36] Yet he has captured the imaginations of later generations of historians whose accounts of his career tend to be more panegyrics than critical studies. One thing about him cannot be disputed: his main concern in life, like that of most of his class, was *la gloire*, recognition, renown—to bequeath to his children not so much wealth, although that would certainly have been desirable, as a great name. In his case it was to be attained by his being the first Frenchman to reach the Western Sea.

Although in the commissions of all the *commandants* at the western posts—La Baie, Poste du Nord, Mer de l'Ouest—appeared the injunction that they send their men west to the legendary sea, few of them appear to have made any great effort to do so. The minister of marine complained that the Canadians sought not the sea of the west but the sea of beaver.[37] In a lengthy letter to Le Gardeur de St Pierre, dated 15 May 1752, business associate Meuvret made it plain that their sole concerns were the volume of furs and slaves being shipped to Montreal and the prices received.[38] Paul Marin de la Malgue, *commandant* at La Baie in 1750, was exhorted by the governor-general and the intendant to press on with the exploration required by the terms of his commission.[39] His successor and son Joseph's journal makes plain that Joseph was too fully occupied striving to keep the peace among the constantly warring tribes in his region to risk his men's lives in a war zone.[40]

Yet the criticism of these men who served in the West by officials comfortably ensconced at Versailles or Quebec was somewhat gratuitous. Just to survive in such a hostile environment was no mean feat. There they were, completely isolated, hundreds of miles and weeks in travel time removed from Montreal,[41] a score or two of men amidst a horde of Indians who might, at any time, decide that these foreigners had outlived their welcome. The extreme cold of the long, bitter winters in that bleak part of the world, with the men cooped up in drafty, hastily constructed log and clay huts, must have created morale problems. Isolation and confinement can make men who normally get on well together become irritable and barely able to endure each other's company. Under such circumstances men can do strange things. When they begin talking to the trees, one need not worry unduly. It is when the trees begin talking back that those in charge should become concerned.

Those who commanded at these western posts—men like La Vérendrye, St-Pierre, Paul and Joseph Marin de Malgue, de Villiers, and others—had to be soldiers, obeyed by the Canadians and overawing the

Indians by sheer force of character. They had to be astute diplomats, adept courtiers in their dealings with their superiors at Quebec, careful financiers and entrepreneurs in trade. The hardships they had to endure, the risks they ran, were enough to make most men quail, yet these postings were avidly sought by the colony's leading families. As Madame Bégon commented, when the postings were announced, the families that had been denied were livid with rage at those who had received western appointments.[42] They were, in peacetime, the best route to advancement in the service, offering financial rewards far in excess of a lieutenant's or captain's meagre pay. A captain, after all, received only 90 *livres* a month,[43] and a gentleman's life required an income of some 3000 a year.[44]

The logistics of transporting food supplies, trade goods, tools, arms, and ammunition from Montreal to Michilimackinac to the far western posts by canoe was a constant nightmare for La Vérendrye and his successors, as their journals make plain. Father Nau, in October 1735, wrote to the mother of Father Aulneau: "Nothing could be more heroic than the new sacrifice that our dear Father Aulneau has just made in leaving for the Mer de l'Ouest. I am not afraid to tell you that it is the longest, most arduous and most dangerous voyage that a missionary has ever made in Canada."[45]

The *voyageurs'* rations en route were meagre, as valuable cargo space could not be wasted on food, and the less to carry over the portages the better. Leached corn and bear grease, with venison when available, was the staple fare. One bushel of leached corn and two pounds of bear grease were considered sufficient to last a man a month.[46] In addition each *voyageur* was allowed to take four pots (equivalent to eight litres) of brandy for his own use.[47] It was considered essential for the digestion. On the other hand, the officers in this hierarchical society were not stinted. Their official rations at the posts included generous quantities of butter, olive oil, vinegar, a large variety of spices, sugar, molasses, wine, and a litre of cognac per week.[48] Both officers and men were expected to live off the land to the greatest extent possible. Vegetable gardens were planted, but since corn, meat, and fish were the staples, scurvy was a constant menace. During the long winter months starvation was rarely far removed.

Sickness was another danger. Although the main posts had a surgeon on staff, given the state of medical knowledge and the predeliction for bleeding and purges a sick man's chances were likely better without those ministrations. La Vérendrye's nephew, La Jemerais, died on the banks of the Red River of some unknown lingering disease.[49] Years later both Le Gardeur de St-Pierre and his lieutenant, Joseph-Claude Boucher, Chevalier de Niverville, were long delayed in their thrust up the Saskatchewan by a fever of some sort.[50] Just how serious disease could be when the entire garrison of a post was stricken was demonstrated at Toronto in 1751. The commandant, the Chevalier de Portneuf, sent an almost frantic appeal for aid. He blamed the disease that had struck him and his men on the bad air of the place and noted that "the most robust of men were in a desperate condition from the onset."[51] It may have been malaria; but whatever, the incident will likely confirm many latter-day suspicions about the place.

The most important and most difficult task that the officers commanding the posts in the West had to face was putting an end to intertribal warfare. From time immemorial nation had warred with nation as extensions of blood feuds, for revenge, and in many instances merely because young braves wished to demonstrate their courage and martial prowess. The French—themselves not the most docile of peoples—sought to prevent these constant skirmishing wars from flaring up, and when they did, to negotiate a swift end to them.[52] In the instructions issued to Le Gardeur de St-Pierre, when he was appointed to command at the Mer de l'Ouest, it was stated that his principal task would be to keep the nations there at peace and to do everything possible to keep the Cree from attacking the Sioux. Similar instructions were issued to all the post commanders. From the French point of view these wars were extremely costly, and frequently instigated by the English. Indeed, everything that caused trouble for the French in the West, or anywhere else for that matter, could be blamed on the English. The same paranoia dominated men's minds to as great a degree on the other side of the hill.

These intertribal wars frequently resulted in the loss of Canadian lives,[53] and for the French to offer comfort to one side meant incurring the enmity of the other. This was particularly the case in the two regions where bases for the thrust to the western sea were located: la Baie des Puants and the Mer de l'Ouest. This vast area was the frontier of Sioux territory and that of the Cree and the Assiniboine. La Vérendrye paid a heavy price for lending support to the northern tribes in a campaign against the Sioux. His son Jean-Baptiste and twenty of his men were subsequently massacred by the Sioux in retaliation.[54]

In 1753 Joseph Marin de la Malgue, *commandant* at La Baie, intervened after the Illinois had launched a surprise attack on the Puants and Sakis, killing three Sakis and a Canadian blacksmith.[55] Those two tribes appealed for aid to their allies: the Sioux, Folles Avoines, and Iowa. Several hundred of the warriors informed Marin that they were sure he would be glad of their aid to seek revenge for the killing of the Canadian whom the Illinois had hacked to pieces. It was only with the greatest difficulty, and the expenditure of over 10 000 *livres* worth of trade goods as presents, that he persuaded them to desist, reminding them that they had destroyed an entire Illinois village a year previous and that they had got off lightly with only three of their people killed.[56]

Two other major tasks were imposed on these officers: to prevent the Indian nations from having any dealings with the English at either Hudson Bay or the seaboard colonies, and to keep the Canadian traders in order. On the whole, the French were successful in both tasks. For the first purpose, posts were established when necessary, such as the one in 1751 at Lac de la Carpe,[57] northeast of Lake Nipigon, or that in the country of the Ouyatanons and Miamis.[58] It is true that the English, both at Hudson Bay and in the Thirteen Colonies, garnered sizeable quantities of furs; but virtually all that was exported from New York was obtained not from the Indians but clandestinely from Canadian traders by way of Albany and Oswego.[59] Since the French paid higher prices for such small furs as marten and otter and the English more for beaver, a lively exchange flourished between the Canadians and traders from New York, Pennsylvania, Virginia, and the Carolinas.[60] There is even cause to suspect that a proportion of the furs shipped from the Hudson Bay ports on the Albany River were provided by Canadians who found it more convenient to send a canoe a day's paddle to a Bay post when they needed supplies than all the way back to Montreal.[61] Both parties benefited, and what officials at Quebec and directors in London did not know would not hurt them.

Maintaining order among the Canadians in the West does not appear to have created any insuperable problems. The *voyageurs* who signed on with a notarized contract thereby agreed to obey all honest, legal, orders, and they did not receive their pay until the completion of their contract on their return to Montreal.[62] Those who frequently caused trouble were sent back under armed guard to face trial.[63] In the notarized engagement of one *voyageur,* the company hiring him inserted a clause stating that the *engagé* accepted that if he were to seek any inopportune quarrels while going up country or returning, his wages would be forfeit. The *engagé* insisted on a qualifying clause that the forfeiture would transpire only if any such fracas as might occur were, as the notary phrased it, *mal à propos*— uncalled for.[64]

From the posts established by La Vérendrye, furs were not the only item shipped down to Montreal. Indian slaves taken by the Cree and Assiniboine in their interminable war with the Sioux were purchased by the French and sold at a high profit in Canada. One, for example, was sold at auction in 1733 for 351 *livres*.[65] With beaver prices at four *livres* the pound at Quebec, a robust slave was the equal of a pack of prime beaver.[66] La Vérendrye boasted of the large number of slaves that he had shipped to Montreal over the years.[67]

Sometime between 1734 and 1737 Governor-General Beauharnois issued strict orders that no more slaves were to be purchased from the Assiniboine, "it being," he declared, "of the greatest consequence for the colony to put a stop to this trade."[68] The prohibition does not appear to have endured long. In 1757 Colonel Bougainville reported that the Cree and Assiniboine sold from fifty to sixty Panis slaves a year to the French, along with three to four hundred packs of fur at the Fort des Prairies alone.[69]

These Indian slaves do not appear to have been too badly treated by their Canadian owners. Several of them were allowed to hire on as *voyageurs* at the same wages and conditions as Canadians. For the years from 1719 to 1726 six such engagements were registered in the notarial *greffes* at Montreal.[70] How many others served as *voyageurs* without such contracts but with a mere private written or oral commitment can never be known. Obviously their masters were confident they would return.

Some of these slaves were used for a humanitarian purpose. In 1748, when England and France were at war, Governor-General Galissonière wrote to Le Gardeur de St-Pierre, commandant at Michilimackinac, asking him to purchase seven or eight slaves on the king's account. Galissonière had promised to provide them to the mission Indians, most likely the Abenaki of Bécancourt or St François, in exchange for English prisoners they had taken. This, he stated, would satisfy the most stubborn of these tribesmen and was the only way to get them to release their English prisoners.[71]

Canadian historians, for the most part, have not been kind in their judgments of St-Pierre, whereas there has been almost universal praise for La Vérendrye. Yet St-Pierre had a far more distinguished military career than did La Vérendrye. He put George Washington courteously but firmly in his place at Fort Le Boeuf in 1753,[72] he maintained control over his men, and he was far more adept in his negotiations with the Indians. This was made manifest when he caused a band of hostile Assiniboine who had invaded Fort La Reine, with the obvious intention of knocking the traders on the head and pillaging the stores, to flee precipitately. He merely picked up a keg of gunpowder, knocked off the lid, snatched a brand from the fire, and strode into their midst. He then told them that before they could execute their obvious design he would have the glory of taking them to the next world with him. They took the fort's gate off its hinges in their haste to depart.[73] There was nothing that the Indians admired more than such actions as St-Pierre's.

St-Pierre does appear also to have made one determined effort to reach the western sea. Some of his latter-day critics deny that Fort La Jonquière, which the précis of his journal states was established at the Rocky Mountains, was anywhere within hundreds of miles of those mountains, some placing it far to the east of the forks of the Saskatchewan.[74] Yet in the abstract of his journal it is stated that his lieutenant, de Niverville, sent ten of his men in two canoes 300 leagues beyond Fort Pascoya to the Rocky Mountains where, in May 1751, they built a good fort. A fresh outbreak of hostilities, following on a treacherous attack by some Assiniboine on a nation called Ihatche8ilini [sic], forced St-Pierre to abandon all notion of maintaining that post, let alone pushing beyond it. He therefore concurred with Governor-General la Jonquière, who believed that the Missouri was the best route to the western ocean, since the Saskatchewan was manifestly too far north.[75] As long as the Assiniboine and the Cree persisted in their wars with neighbouring tribes it would, he asserted, be impossible to maintain a secure route across the northern plains.[76]

It would have been utter stupidity for him to fabricate this tale of a post at the Rocky Mountains in the journal that he was required to submit to the governor-general, who would merely have had to question de Niverville or any of his men to expose it. Therefore, unless convincing evidence can be produced that St-Pierre's men did not reach the Rocky Mountains, his statement has to be accepted. It cannot be dismissed out of hand. That, surely, is one of the acknowledged rules of evidence.

If one accepts that for a brief few months Fort La Jonquière existed, where was it? Some day previously unknown documents may give us the answer; St-Pierre's actual journal, or letters of de Niverville, could, for example. Such documents do surface from time to time, but until they do one can only conjecture. A.S. Morton claimed that if the French had gone beyond the forks of the Saskatchewan, which he denied, then they would have taken the south branch.[77] J.B. Tyrell argued, much more cogently, that they most certainly would not have taken the south fork.[78] On the face of it the mere fact that the South Saskatchewan ran through country that swarmed with buffalo, elk, and gophers, rather than the prime light furs that the French sought, would have caused them to take the north branch, which runs close to the fur-bearing parkland. Moreover the north branch was in Cree country, whose language was the lingua franca of the fur trade. To the south lay their mortal foes, the Blackfoot, who wanted nothing from Europeans since, as they told Anthony Hendry, the buffalo sufficed for all their needs. Bows and arrows were all that they required to kill them.[79] Since fur traders had a tendency to build their posts on the site of earlier existing ones, Fort La Jonquière may well have been built where Rocky Mountain House later stood. All that is needed to prove the hypothesis is sound evidence.

Finally we must ask why the French did not achieve their goal of being the first to cross the continent. If those bumbling American army officers, Lewis and Clark, could eventually do it, why could not the far more experienced Canadians? St-Pierre blamed his failure on the constant wars being waged by the Indian nations at the instigation of the English. To put an end to those wars the English would, he claimed, have to be driven out of Hudson Bay, and he asked that when the opportunity arose he be given the command.[80] There was some truth in what St-Pierre stated, although the English at Hudson Bay were certainly not responsible for the Indian wars. He, his predecessor La Vérendrye, and Paul and Joseph Marin at La Baie went to great lengths to end the Sioux, Cree, and Assiniboine wars. Frequently they believed they were on the verge of success, only to have hostilities suddenly flare up again.

Seen, however, from the Indian point of view, why should they have ceased warring with each other at the behest of the French? For centuries it had been part of their way of life. How else could their young men distinguish themselves, display their valour, gain renown?

When the Sioux now suffered heavy casualties at the hands of enemies armed and supplied by the French, and when many of their women
and children were sold into slavery at Montreal, it did not induce them to
pay more than lip service to the demands of the French who patronizingly
addressed them as children of Onontio, the governor-general far away at
Quebec.[81] Similarly the Cree and Assiniboine, who when suddenly attacked
while hunting had called out "Who kills us?," must have taken it amiss
when the answer came, "The French Sioux."[82] These were the woodlands
Sioux who were supplied by the French traders at the headwaters of the
Mississippi.

The Indians tolerated the French on their lands only because they
provided useful services, a readily available source of goods, and a blacksmith to repair their tools, cooking pots, and weapons. They certainly did
not regard them as a superior race. Physically the French were an inferior
lot, much smaller than the Indians, their faces and bodies covered with
hideous matted hair.[83] Without the Indians to show them the canoe routes
and to hunt for them, they would have starved to death. Admittedly they
fought well when they had to, and their *eau de vie* set a man up wonderfully,
transporting him ever so swiftly to the spirit world. As for the vexing black-
robed medicine men who sought to change the Indians' habits, they were
easily ignored. Moreover, these French could not be trusted. They did not
always live up to their commitments, as the Cree and Assiniboine pointed
out when they demanded to know when La Vérendrye was going to establish a post at the foot of Lake Winnipeg as he had promised.[84] Sometimes
they failed to have an adequate supply of goods on hand in the spring
when the Indians brought in their winter's catch, and they sometimes
altered the prices of their goods for no discernible reason. The goods were
the same as ever, the furs of as good quality; therefore the price should not
change. Sometimes, too, they were stingy with what they called their presents, but what the Indians regarded as tribute for being granted permission to travel through Indian territory and establish their posts. The best
that could be said of them was that they were easier to deal with than the
English. They could be tolerated because it had become difficult to get
along without their goods; moreover, there were so few of them that they
could not possibly constitute a threat to the Indian nations. As for their
constant queries about, and search for, a vast body of salt water off to the
west, the Indians had heard of it and some claimed to have been there, but
they could hardly be expected to help the French find it.[85] Were the
French to establish posts among those far Indians, the Cree and
Assiniboine of the Lake Winnipeg region would be eliminated as traders.[86]

Despite all the problems that the French had to face in the Far West,
there is no question that they could have reached the Pacific had they really been determined. It would have required a chain of garrisoned posts as
supply bases across the Prairies and into the mountains and a separate 50-
man military expedition to press on to the ocean. For the officers the

prospect of promotion and the Croix de St Louis would have been incentive enough. For the men the promise of an immediate discharge and a half-pay pension upon their return would have found most of the troops in the colony rushing to volunteer.

There is just one nagging *caveat* to this hypothesis. When the continent was eventually crossed—first by Alexander Mackenzie in 1793, then in 1805 by Lewis and Clark—conditions in the West were far different than in La Vérendrye's and Le Gardeur de St-Pierre's day. The Indians in the earlier period, their nations numbering thousands of warriors, were truly sovereign and independent, answerable to no one, and skilled at playing the English and French off against each other. By the end of the century their power was broken and a great flood of liquor and the smallpox epidemics (1780–81, 1786) had decimated and demoralized them.[87] They could then offer little opposition to encroachments on their lands. They were already bowing to the seeming inevitable.

The final question can still fairly be asked. Why did the French government of the day not make the effort? Why did it insist that the fur trade must bear the cost and the travail of the search for the route to the western ocean? Why did it will the end but not the means? One obvious reason is that its finances were always in disarray, and the department of marine was always at the end of the line when funds were doled out. Another reason may well have been that the authorities in Canada had begun to doubt the existence of the legendary Mer de l'Ouest. By 1750 they had accepted that if it did exist it was beyond a massive barrier, the Rocky Mountains.[88]

The underlying reason for failure, however, appears to be that the niggardly attitude of the French government in this particular instance was part and parcel of a more general attitude towards New France. The colonies of Canada and Louisiana cost the Crown considerable sums each year. They, unlike the Antilles, were not a paying proposition. They were maintained for a purely political purpose, the containment of England's American colonies,[89] and this had to be done at the lowest possible cost to the Crown. The ministry of marine firmly believed that colonies existed for the benefit of the mother country; it was not the other way around. As late as 1754 the then Minister of Marine, Jean-Baptiste de Machault d'Arnouville, informed the governor-general at Quebec that if the expenses recently incurred in pursuance of his predecessor in office's orders to occupy the Ohio Valley were not curbed, then His Majesty would surely abandon the colony altogether.[90] It was this attitude that prevented the French from reaching the western sea. In the longer term it also resulted in the loss of the French empire in North America. Given the meagre means at their disposal, the wonder of it is not that the French did not reach the Mer de l'Ouest, but that they accomplished as much as they did.

• Notes

1 H.P. Biggar, ed., *The Works of Samuel de Champlain* (Toronto, 1925), 326–45.

2 "Jean Nicollet de Belleborne" in *Dictionary of Canadian Biography*, vol. 1 (Toronto, 1966), 516–18.

3 Public Archives of Canada (hereafter PAC) transcript, documents St-Sulpice, Paris, reg. 25, vol. 1, pt. 1, Relation de la découverte de la Mer du Sud . . . R.P. Dablon, S.J., 1 aoust 1674.

4 See Marcel Trudel, *Atlas de la Nouvelle-France: An Atlas of New France* (Québec, 1968), 126–27, Carte de Mr Guillaume Delisle . . . 1717. Sur la Mer de l'Ouest.

5 Archives Nationales, Colonies, Paris (hereafter AN), F3 Moreau de St-Méry, vol. 2, f. 11, Mémoire de Canada. De la Chesnaye, 1695; ibid., vol. 7, f. 7, Antoine Raudot au Ministre, 1710; ibid., vol. 2, f. 215, Mémoire touchant le Canada et l'Acadie envoyé par M. de Meulle.

6 See W.J. Eccles, *Frontenac: The Courtier Governor* (Toronto, 1959), 273–94, 334–37.

7 Dominion Bureau of Statistics, Demography Branch, Ottawa, *Chronological List of Canadian Censuses; Historical Statistics of the United States: Colonial Times to 1957* (Washington, DC: Department of Commerce, 1960).

8 AN, D2C, vol. 48, f. 130, Extrait Général des Revues des Compagnies Entretenues en la Nouvelle-France . . . 1750.

9 On fur trade statistics, see the *caveat* contained in the article by Gratien Allaire, "Les engagements pour la traite des fourrures; évaluation de la documentation," *Revue d'histoire de l'Amérique française* 34 (juin 1980): 3–26.

10 AN, C11A, vol. 93, f. 11, Observations sur les Réponses fournies par la Compagnie des Indes au Mémoire et à la Lettre Envoiée de Canada en 1748 . . .

11 E.E. Rich, *The Fur Trade and the Northwest to 1857* (Toronto, 1967), 82–83.

12 During the Seven Years' War the Seneca, Cayuga, and Onondaga sent frequent war parties against frontier settlements in Virginia and Pennsylvania. *Rapport de l'Archiviste de la Province de Québec 1923–1924* (hereafter RAPQ), 250, Journal de l'expédition d'Amérique commencée en l'année 1756, Bougainville; AN, C11A, vol. 101, f. 265, Conference. Cinq Nations, Mtl., 21 déc. 1756; Carl Van Doren and Julian P. Boyd, eds., *Indian Treaties Printed by Benjamin Franklin* (Philadelphia, 1938), 220.

13 In 1748 Governor-General La Galissonière informed the minister that the nations at La Baie and the Pouteouatimis of St Joseph, angered by the short supply of trade goods occasioned by the Anglo-French war, blamed it on the leaseholders of the posts and demanded that trade be opened to all who obtained a permit from the authorities at Quebec. Galissonière stated that he had been obliged to concur lest the Indians should go to the English, AN, C11A, vol. 91, ff 230–33, La Galissonière au ministre, Qué., 23 oct. 1748. Galissonière's successor, La Jonquière, and the intendant Bigot confirmed the decision the following year. AN, C11A, vol. 93, f 42, La Jonquière et Bigot au Ministre, Qué., 9 oct. 1749.

14 See Wilbur R. Jacobs, *Indian Diplomacy and Indian Gifts: Anglo-French Rivalry along the Ohio and Northwest Frontier 1748–1763* (Stanford, CA, 1950).

15 RAPQ 1963, vol. 41, 304, Marin à son beau frère, M. Deschambeau, 1 juin 1754; "Teganissorens" in *Dictionary of Canadian Biography*, vol. 2 (Toronto, 1969), 619–23.

16 Archives du Séminaire de Québec (hereafter ASQ), Fonds Verreau, Boite 8, no. 85, Beauharnois à de la Perrière, Mtl., 25 juillet 1745; AN, C11A, vol. 65, ff. 52–53, Beauharnois et Hocquart au Ministre, Qué., 12 oct. 1736; Journal de Bougainville, 260.

17 Archives nationales du Québec à Montréal (hereafter ANQM), Greffe J. David, no. 173, 11 août 1720; ibid., no. 215, 16 sept. 1720; Antoine Champagne, *Les La Vérendrye et le poste de l'Ouest* (Québec, 1968), 157, n 10; E.B. O'Callaghan, ed., *Documents Relating to the Colonial History of New York*, vol. 10 (Albany, 1856–83), 245–51, M. de Longueuil to M. de Rouillé, 21 avril 1752.

18 Lawrence J. Burpee, ed., *Journals and Letters of Pierre Gaultier de Varennes de La Vérendrye and His Sons* (Toronto: Champlain Society, 1927), 427; Champagne, *Les La Vérendrye*, 293–96.

19 See, for example, the declaration of an assembly of Sable, Ottawa, Huron, and Saulteux to the French at Lake Erie in 1704, "Cette terre n'est pas à vous, elle est à Nous," cited in E.E. Rich, *The History of the Hudson's Bay Company 1670–1870*, vol. 1 (London, 1958), 482.

20 Champagne, *Les La Vérendrye*, 89; AN, F3 Moreau de St-Méry, vol. 7, ff. 146–50, R.P. Guigas S.J., à Beauharnois, dattée de la Mission de St Michel arcange au fort de Beauharnois chez les Scioux, 13, 29 May 1728; AN, C11A, vol. 51, f. 24, Beauharnois et Hocquart au Ministre, Qué., 25 oct. 1729; ibid., vol. 93, f. 42, Jonquière et Bigot au Ministre, Qué., 9 oct. 1749.

21 W.J. Eccles, *The Canadian Frontier 1534–1760* (Albuquerque, NM, 1969), 151–54.

22 RAPQ 1926–27, 287, R.P. Nau à Madame Aulneau, Sault-St-Louis, 3 oct. 1735.

23 RAPQ 1947–48, 299, Mémoire du Roi à Vaudreuil et Bégon, Paris, 15 juin 1716; ibid., 330, Vaudreuil au Conseil de Marine, Qué., 14 oct. 1716.

24 Marcel Giraud, *Histoire de la Louisiane française*, vol. 1, *Le règne de Louis XIV* (Paris, 1953), 14–18.

25 J.S. Bromley, ed., *The New Cambridge Modern History*, vol. 6 (Cambridge: 1971), 40–41.

26 H. Carré in *Histoire de France*, ed. Ernest Lavisse, vol. 8-2 (Paris, 1909), 176–77.

27 "Michel Sarrazin" in *Dictionary of Canadian Biography*, vol. 3 (Toronto, 1974), 593–600; W.J. Eccles, *Canada under Louis XIV, 1663–1701* (Toronto, 1964), 139–40.

28 J.C. Dubé, *Claude-Thomas Dupuy, Intendant de la Nouvelle-France, 1678–1738* (Montréal, 1968), 298.

29 "Jean-Baptiste Gosselin" in *Dictionary of Canadian Biography*, vol. 3 (Toronto, 1974), 262–63; AN, C11A, vol. 76, f. 22, Hocquart au Ministre, Qué., 25 oct. 1741; AN, D2D, Carton 1, Canada. Demandes particulières.

30 Aldolph B. Benson, ed., *The America of 1750: The Travels in North America by Peter Kalm*, vol. 1 (New York, 1966), 375–76.

31 *Nouvelle-France, Documents historiques: Correspondance échangée entre les autorités françaises et les gouverneurs et intendants*, vol. 1 (Québec, 1893), 148–49, Le Conseil de Marine, 29 sept. 1717.

32 AN, C11A, vol. 37, f. 376, Conseil de Marine, 7 déc. 1717.

33 Ibid., vol. 41, f. 235, Conseil de Marine, avril 1720.

34 Pierre-Athanase Margry, *Mémoires et documents pour servir à l'histoire des origines françaises des pays d'outremer: Découvertes et établissements des français dans l'ouest et dans le sud de l'Amérique septentrionale, 1614–1754*, vol. 6 (Paris, 1879–88), 525. Le Père Charlevoix à son Altesse Sérénissimé Monseigneur le comte de Toulouse, Paris, 20 jan. 1723.

35 RAPQ 1926–27, R.P. Nau S.J., au R.P. Richard, Provinciale de la Province de Guyenne, Qué., 20 oct. 1734.

36 Champagne, *Les La Vérendrye*, chs. 7, 10, 11, 13, 15.

37 As early as 1710 the intendant Antoine Raudot had reported to the minister that some Frenchmen had voyaged as far as the country of the Assiniboine, which at that time would

have been Lake Winnipeg, and that those Indians had apparently travelled as far as the western ocean. That sea would, he added, have been discovered long since but for the profits being made from the furs of the region, which kept the French from proceeding further. This refrain was to be repeated by royal officials for the ensuing four decades. Raudot obviously believed that the Mer de l'Ouest was within easy reach of the western posts. Margry, *Mémoires*, vol. 6, 14, lettre 50, Raudot au Ministre, Qué., le . . . 1710; see also RAPQ 1926–27, 286, R.P. Nau au R.P. Bonin, Sault-St-Louis, 2 oct. 1735.

38 ASQ, Fonds Verreau, Boite 5, no. 38 $^1/_2$, Meuvret au Capitaine Le Gardeur de St-Pierre, Que., 15 mai 1752.

39 AN, C11A, vol. 95, f. 91, Jonquière et Bigot au Ministre, Qué., 18 aoust 1750.

40 RAPQ 1963, vol. 41, 237–308, Journal de Marin, fils, 1753–54. (Ed., R.P. Ant. Champagne, C.R.I.C.)

41 See, for example, the repeated plaintive request of Captain Céloron de Blainville, commandant at Niagara in 1744, to M. Pierre Guy, a Montreal merchant, for a barrel of wine, followed by—"Rendé moy toutes les nouvelles de France et celle du pays." Archives de l'Université de Montréal, Collection Baby, Boite 125, Céloron à Pierre Guy, Niagara 22 juliette [sic] 1744.

42 RAPQ 1934–35, 52, 54, Mme Bégon à son gendre, Mtl. 28, 29 mars, 2 avril 1749.

43 AN, B, vol. 10, ff. 17–18, Reglement que le Roy veut estre observé pour le payement des officiers de marine . . . dans la Nouvelle-France, Versailles, 10 avril 1684; AN, C11A, vol. 17, Mémoire sur la reforme des Troupes en Canada, 1700.

44 Huntingdon Library, Loudoun Papers, Rigaud à Vaudreuil, Trois-Rivières, 27 mai 1752; Jean Meyer, *La noblesse bretonne au XVIIIᵉ siècle* (Paris,

1972), 39; AN, C11A, vol. 105, ff. 137–38, Vaudreuil au Ministre, 30 juin 1760.

45 RAPQ 1926–27, 287, R.P. Nau à Madame Aulneau, Sault-St-Louis, 3 oct. 1735.

46 RAPQ 1927–28, 340–41, Mémoire sur les postes du Canada adressé à M. de Surlaville en 1754 par le Chevalier de Raymond.

47 ASQ, Fonds Verreau, Boite 5, no. 26, De la Jonquière à Le Gardeur de St-Pierre, Qué., 17 avril 1750.

48 Ibid., Carton 3, no. 205, Etat de ce qui est accordé annuellement aux Commandants des postes du Roy; *Inventaire des Ordonnances des Intendants de la Nouvelle-France conservées aux Archives provinciales de Québec*, vol. 3 (Québec, 1919), 109, 23 août 1748.

49 Champagne, *Les La Vérendrye*, 179–81.

50 ASQ, Fonds Verreau, Boite 5, no. 54, Mémoire ou extrait du Journal Sommaire au voyage de Jacques Legardeur . . . Sr de St-Pierre. . . .

51 Archives de l'Université de Montréal, Collection Baby, Portneuf à? du Fort Rouillé le 20 d'aoust 1751.

52 Journal de Jacques Legardeur; ibid., Fonds Verreau, Carton 5, no. 33, Mémoire pour servir d'instruction au Sr Legardeur de St-Pierre . . . commandant aux Forts La Reine, Dauphin, Maurepas . . . La Jonquière, Mtl., 27 mai 1750; AN, C11A, vol. 71, f. 35, Beauharnois au Ministre, Qué., 30 juin 1739.

53 AN, C11A, vol. 35, ff. 5-6. Ramezay et Bégon au Ministre, Qué., 13 sept. 1715; ibid., vol. 43, f. 324, Conseil, de M. de le Marqˢ de Vaudreuil, 6 oct. 1721; ibid., vol. 93, ff. 143–44, La Galissonière au Ministre, le 26 juin 1749; ANQM, Greffe J. David, no. 173, 215, 11 août 1720, 16 sept. 1720; ASQ, Fonds Verreau, Boite 1, no. 19, Duquesne à Contrecoeur, Mtl., 12 juin 1753; Fernand Grenier, ed., *Papiers Contrecoeur et autres documents concernant le conflit anglo-français sur l'Ohio de 1745 à 1756* (Québec, 1952), 193.

54 Champagne, *Les La Vérendrye*, 182–86.

55 Journal de Marin, fils, 251 ff.

56 Ibid., 253, 295.

57 AN, F3 Moreau de St-Méry, vol. 14, f. 14, Ordonnance de M. de la Jonquière, 27 fev. 1751.

58 AN, C11A, vol. 42, ff. 158–60, Extrait du Mémoire de M. Le Marquis de Vaudreuil pour servir d'Instruction au Sr Dumont . . . 26 aoust 1720.

59 Thomas Elliot Norton, *The Fur Trade in Colonial New York 1686–1776* (Madison, WI, 1974), 56, 87–90; AN, C11A, vol. 76, f. 334, Mémoire sur le commerce du Canada, 1741; ASQ, Fonds Verreau, Boite 1, no. 13, Duquesne à Contrecoeur, Mtl., 30 avril 1753.

60 AN, C11A, vol. 19, f. 228, Vaudreuil au Ministre, Mtl., 1 oct. 1701.

61 E.E. Rich, *The History of the Hudson's Bay Company 1670–1870,* vol. 1, *1670–1870* (London, 1958), 526–27; Glydwr Williams, "The Puzzle of Anthony Henday's Journal, 1754–55," *The Beaver* (Winter 1978): 42, citing Robson's Memoirs, *An Account of Six Years' Residence in Hudson's Bay.*

62 Examples of such contracts are to be found in the hundreds in the Notarial Greffes at the Archives nationales du Québec à Montréal.

63 ASQ, Fonds Verreau, Boite 10, no. 45, Beauharnois à De Muy, Mtl., 28 mai 1732; ibid., Carton 5, no. 13, Beauharnois à St-Pierre, Mtl., 22 juillet 1742.

64 ANQM, Greffe J.B. Adhemar, no. 1148, 14 avril 1724.

65 *Inventaire des Ordonnances des Intendants de la Nouvelle-France,* vol. 2, 146–47.

66 AN, F3 Moreau de St-Méry, vol. 11, f. 176, Ordonnance de M. d'Aigremont, Qué., 20 oct. 1728.

67 Burpee, *Journals of La Vérendrye,* 451–52.

68 ASQ, Fonds Verreau, Boite 5, no. 12, Beauharnois à St-Pierre, Mtl., 28 aoust 173 . . . (last figure of the date torn off). Jacques Le Gardeur de St-Pierre was commandant at the Poste de Scioux from 1734 to 1737.

69 RAPQ 1923–24, 51, Mémoire sur l'état de la Nouvelle-France 1757, Bougainville.

70 ANQM, Greffes J. David, no. 212, J.B. Adhemar, no. 1539, 1847, 1858, 2225, 2250.

71 ASQ, Fonds Verreau, Carton 5, no. 53, La Galissonière à M. de St-Pierre. . . . Qué., 4 sept. 1748.

72 Fernand Grenier, *Papiers Contrecoeur,* 77–78, 83–84.

73 Journal de Jacques Legardeur.

74 A.S. Morton, *A History of the Canadian West to 1870–71* (London, 1939), 237–38; J.B. Brebner, *The Explorers of North America, 1492–1806* (London, [1933] 1964), 323; Champagne, *Les La Vérendrye,* 419.

75 Mémoire pour servir d'instruction, 27 mai 1750.

76 Journal de Jacques Legardeur.

77 Morton, *A History,* 237.

78 L.J. Burpee, *The Search for the Western Sea* (Toronto, 1908), 278, n 1.

79 L.J. Burpee, ed., "York Fort to the Blackfeet Country: The Journal of Anthony Henday, 1754–55" in *Transactions of the Royal Society of Canada,* sec. 2, 1097, 338.

80 Journal de Jacques Legardeur.

81 For examples of the patronizing manner with which the French officers addressed the Indians in their councils, see Journal de Marin, fils.

82 Burpee, *Journals of La Vérendrye,* 138.

83 On the vastly superior stature and physique of the Indians compared to the French, see the comments by Bougainville in Journal de M. de Bougainville, 1757, 267–68. In 1734 Father Nau, S.J., writing to the Provincial of Guyenne, remarked that the Iroquois of Sault-St-Louis were much bigger than the French, closer to six feet tall than to five. RAPQ

1926–27, 268. The average height of Frenchmen in the eighteenth century was reckoned to be five feet one inch to five feet two, French measure, which would be five feet four inches and a bit to five feet six, English measure. In the French army fusiliers were required to be five French feet two inches and the cavalry five feet four. Objections were raised to this requirement on the grounds that over half the male population was thereby excluded from military service. See André Corvisier, *L'Armée française de la fin du XVIIe siècle au ministère de Choiseul: Le Soldat*, vol. 2 (Paris, 1964), 637–51.

84 Champagne, *Les La Vérendrye*, 191–92.

85 Journal de Jacques Legardeur.

86 Burpee, "York Fort," 351.

87 Burpee, *Journals of La Vérendrye*, 256–57, n 2.

88 The "Mémoire pour servir d'instruction" issued by Governor-General La Jonquière in May 1750, speaks of the necessity to follow in La Vérendrye's footsteps to the height of land in the high mountains beyond which lay the great saltwater that the Indians spoke of and which led to the sea. Le Gardeur de St-Pierre, in his journal, speaks of pushing on to the Rocky Mountains where de Niverville established Fort La Jonquière, but he says nothing of a large body of saltwater. Obviously they then knew that there was no Mer de l'Ouest east of the Rocky Mountains.

89 On this policy, see W.J. Eccles, *The Canadian Frontier 1534–1760* (Albuquerque, NM, 1974), 154–56.

90 AN, B, vol. 99, f. 199. Ministre à Duquesne, Versailles, 31 mai 1754.

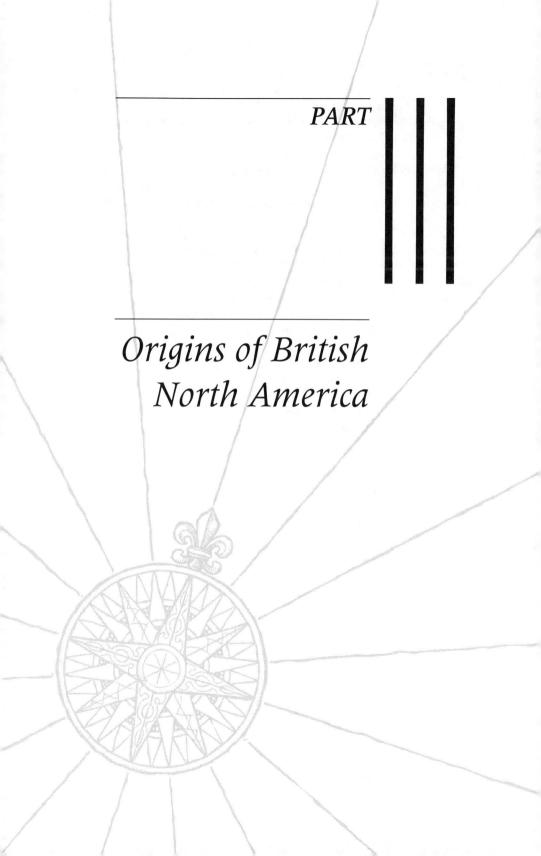

PART III

Origins of British North America

Perhaps the most surprising feature of Canadian history during the period of New France was the very small number of immigrants who crossed the Atlantic to settle in the colony. Not only were the French settlers vastly outnumbered by Amerindians, but by the mid-eighteenth century the population of the neighbouring British colonies along the east coast of North America was twenty times greater than that of New France. The rate of colonization did not immediately accelerate after the French surrendered to the British, but the early signs of later trends did become apparent as settlers perceived new opportunities in British North America.

In the first article of this section, Elizabeth Mancke discusses one of the many ways in which the histories of New England and Atlantic Canada are interwoven. She emphasizes that the availability of land was central to the northern "expansion" of New England. Like the comparison of Louisbourg and Havana in the previous section, Mancke examines two communities under different political jurisdictions in order to analyse the interplay of local and government activities. By focussing on Liverpool, Nova Scotia, and Machias, Maine, her study seeks to reveal the various influences of individuals, groups, and official policies in the expansion of settlement. In reading this article, it should be remembered that the pursuit of land was so important because many families were seeking to establish their own "economies," much as described in Tilly and Scott's earlier article on men and women's productive roles in Europe.

As Nancy Christie explains, the arrival of British-origin settlers after the conquest also signalled the beginning of a new religious complexity in Canadian history. Her study of two evangelical groups in the Maritimes and Upper Canada is part of a quite recently renewed interest in religion as a central dimension of historical change. This interest differs from the approach of earlier studies in its linking of religion to social change. Phillip McCann similarly stresses the importance of religion in his interpretation of Newfoundland's administration between the 1830s and 1850s. His research seeks to situate high-level politics within the context of material and cultural change. McCann argues that imperial authorities and the local elite recognized the value of constructing a cultural "state" involving organizations and rituals designed to promote imperial sentiment. This argument employs a series of concepts that have become familiar in recent historical research on Europe and North America including cultural hegemony, state formation, symbolic power, nativism, and the invention of tradition.

During the first half of the nineteenth century, political and cultural change occurred within the context of significant social and economic development. Fernand Ouellet has become a leading figure of research on the St Lawrence Valley by studying the performance of the colonial economy as revealed in commercial relationships. Rather than examining what individuals thought or perceived, Ouellet focusses on what they did: how much wheat was sold? at what price? how many ships left the Quebec port?

where did they go? In his article in this section, Ouellet addresses such questions to explore the connections between the colonial and international economy. Similarly, Katherine M.J. McKenna focusses on behaviour to study a quite different dimension of early Upper Canada. She contrasts the ideology of "separate spheres" for men and women with the reality of considerable integration of interest and activity within the leading families. Like Ouellet's study, this article illustrates the importance of looking behind attitudes and perceptions to examine behaviour and action.

In their studies of Lower Canada and Upper Canada, Allan Greer and Jane Errington ask different questions about colonial experience during the first half of the nineteenth century. Greer is primarily interested in the ways in which the charivari evolved from a folkloric ritual to a revolutionary strategy. He offers a fresh interpretation of popular power in the Rebellions of 1837 by showing how artisans and peasants drew upon traditional customs in their efforts to protect themselves from imperial authority. For her part, Errington analyses the origins of a central theme in Canadian history, the question of relationships with the United States. By using newspapers and the writings of prominent figures, she shows that Upper Canada's formal status as a British colony was juxtaposed by informal links to the developing republic to the south. The result was an ambivalence that seems very familiar almost two centuries later.

Along with developments in the Atlantic and central provinces, the nineteenth century also brought considerable change to the West, primarily as a result of the fur trade. Lorne Hammond takes an ecological approach in which animals take their rightful place at the centre of analysis. His attention to wildlife is similar to the earlier article in this book by Pielou dealing with the extinctions of certain birds and mammals in various parts of North America. Van Kirk has revised earlier analyses of the fur trade by focussing on the economic roles of those Indian women who married French and British traders. In her article in this section, she examines the impact on the "country-born" children of these marriages by studying one particular family. This approach allows her to examine the details of individual experience, and to compare sons with daughters. In their own ways, Hammond and Van Kirk thus provide convincing examples of how new research questions have led to revised interpretations of familiar topics of Canadian history.

The final selections in this section illustrate two different ways in which historians have been attempting to understand what William Westfall calls the "new world of the mid-nineteenth century." Michael Katz has studied the city of Hamilton in much the same way as Louise Dechêne examined Montreal in the seventeenth century. Like Dechêne, Katz seeks to understand as much as possible about the experience of every resident in the city under study. Sources such as the manuscript census allow him to ask questions about social structure, family and household structure, and activities like school attendance. In contrast, Westfall explores the changing religious beliefs and cultural orientations of Protestant leaders in Upper Canada. By carefully examining their writings, Westfall seeks to understand the emergence of a new Protestant consensus that led to the "new culture of Protestant Ontario in the Victorian period."

Taken together, the articles in this section illustrate some of the ways in which Canadian historians have been significantly revising previous work on the century following the conquest. This work is distinguished by its attention to both the ideas and behaviour of different groups, and by its comparative framework. Although many questions remain unanswered or have not yet been posed, it is now clear that British North America developed considerable internal diversity within a complex external context.

CORPORATE STRUCTURE AND PRIVATE INTEREST: The Mid-eighteenth-Century Expansion of New England*

ELIZABETH MANCKE

As the French made their last defences of Canada in the late 1750s, New Englanders, who had long fought them in North America, quickly realized that the end of French influence would open a band of land stretching from eastern New York, across Vermont and New Hampshire, and out to the Atlantic in Maine. For over a hundred years the area had served as a buffer and battleground between English settlements in New England and French settlements in Canada. But with the end of French control in Canada the Anglo-French conflicts, which had blocked Euroamerican settlement in the region, ceased. The response from land-hungry New Englanders was almost immediate. A number of Massachusetts' soldiers rather than going home after being discharged from the French and Indian Wars settled on "some of the Lands they had Conquered" in Maine, reasoning in their petition for a grant of land, that as no English inhabitants had ever settled there that the land "would be as likely to fall to their share as to others."[1] A group organized in 1759 in the towns of Duxborough, Pembrook, Kingston, and Plympton, Massachusetts, stated that "having small and very poor farms or Tenements . . . and some of us not one foot of Land in the world," they very much desired a grant on the

*From *They Planted Well: New England Planters in Maritime Canada*, ed. Margaret Conrad (Fredericton: Acadiensis Press, 1988), 161–77. Reprinted with permission of the publisher.

Penobscot River in Maine.[2] Thomas Pownall, Governor of Massachusetts, advised the General Court in his January 1760 address "that now every other obstacle is removed" [i.e., the conflict with the French and Indians] it should resolve all title disputes in Maine so as to facilitate the orderly and legal settlement of the region.[3] New Hampshire's Governor Benning Wentworth busily granted dozens of townships in what is now Vermont and New Hampshire. And in 1759 Nova Scotia Governor Charles Lawrence circulated a proclamation throughout New England inviting settlers to immigrate to that colony, from where, only four years before, the Acadians or French Neutrals had been deported.[4]

Between 1759 and 1775 approximately 200 townships were granted in Vermont, New Hampshire, Maine, and Nova Scotia.[5] A conservative estimate of the number of grantees involved is ten thousand, assuming fifty men per grant, or one out of every ten men in New England between the ages of sixteen and sixty.[6] It was probably much higher since the two townships to be discussed here—Liverpool, Nova Scotia, and Machias, Maine— had 164 and 80 grantees respectively. The number of settlers involved was much greater. Between 1759 and 1764 approximately 7000 New England settlers went to Nova Scotia. During the 1760s New Hampshire's population increased by 22 000 or 58 percent, most of which was in the western counties. By 1776 Vermont had 20 000 inhabitants, when in the early 1760s it only had a few dozen families. And in Lincoln County, Maine, there were over 15 000 souls, most of them recent settlers. Thus the migration into northern New England and Nova Scotia involved upwards of 60 000 people.[7]

Demographic conditions in lower New England encouraged this demand for land. By the mid-eighteenth century, many of the New England towns which had been settled in the seventeenth century had reached land to people ratios of one adult man to approximately forty acres.[8] While some towns did develop more diversified economies to absorb some of the displaced agricultural labour, many New Englanders preferred to move on in search of new land.[9] In addition to demographic pressure, massive forest fires burned across lower New Hampshire and southern Maine in the summers of 1762 and 1763, destroying the forests and livelihood of many timbermen, and thus intensifying the demand for land.[10] The collapse of French power and the opening of Nova Scotia explain the interest in the lands north and east of lower New England.

While demographic pressure and ecological catastrophe account for the expansion of New England in the mid-eighteenth century, these factors do not explain the pronounced group or corporate character of expansion. It was the corporate structure of New England expansion, both through the granting and settlement processes, which drew in so many so fast. The preference of New Englanders for group grants and settlements and the response of the governments involved is the major focus here. Two townships under different political jurisdictions—Liverpool, Nova Scotia, settled in 1760, and Machias, Maine, settled in 1763—will be considered to explore the interactions of individual, group, and government, and how each influenced the resettlement process.

Land for resettlement became available in Nova Scotia before it became available through the governments of New Hampshire or Massachusetts, but New Englanders had always been wary of moving there and did not head north just because there was land. Commercially and militarily, Nova Scotia had long fallen within the orbit of the Bay Colony; Massachusetts merchants had traded with the Acadians in the Bay of Fundy and the French in Louisbourg, New England fishermen frequented its harbours and shores, and New England soldiers fought to bring the region under the British flag. Politically, though, the British retained control in Nova Scotia and for nearly a half-century they ran the colony as a military out-post, hardly a selling point for New Englanders with a strong commitment to local self-government. Finally in 1758, under pressure by the Board of Trade, a representative assembly was elected, and met for the first time on 2 October.[11] Ten days later on 12 October Governor Lawrence issued a proclamation inviting New Englanders to submit proposals for settling in the colony. He received sufficient inquiries about the nature of government in the colony to issue a second proclamation on 11 January 1759 stating:

> That the Government of Nova Scotia is constituted like those of the neighbouring colonies, the Legislature consisting of Governor Council and Assembly, and every township as soon as it shall consist of Fifty Families will be entitled to send two representatives to the General Assembly. The Courts of Justice are also constituted in like manner with those of the Massachusetts, Connecticut and other Northern colonies.[12]

The proclamation appeared to be an about face to a long-standing British policy not to develop Nova Scotia as a "new New England." Whenever the British had considered initiating a more broadly based gov-ernment, official opinion held that a centralized government, similar to Virginia's with appointed county magistrates and local officials, would be superior to the decentralized New England practice of town government and locally chosen officers. The proclamation, however, convinced many prospective settlers, and some merchants resident in Halifax, that the British intended to allow New England–style town government in Nova Scotia.[13]

The language of the proclamation allowed for generous interpreta-tion without promising more than what had been achieved with the estab-lishment of the colonial assembly. Those who drafted the document almost certainly carefully chose the term "township" rather than "town." A town-ship is a unit of land and could be defined by survey whether peopled or not. A town is the incorporated political entity within the territorial definition of a township. While the distinction between the two terms may have been lost on prospective settlers, it undoubtedly was not lost on British officialdom. But under the misimpression that town government would be allowed many New Englanders took up land in Nova Scotia, among them Captain John Dogget, who secured a grant for the township of Liverpool for himself and 163 other men from Massachusetts.[14]

The language of the Liverpool grant and the subsequent organization of the township's proprietors indicate how shrewdly the officials in Halifax used the cosmetics but not the substance of New England practice to disguise a centralized government. In style and organization the grant read as would one from Massachusetts. It noted the four primary organizers who had applied for the grant of a township on behalf of themselves and the within named grantees. Governor Lawrence stated his power and authority to make the grant. The location of the township was given in detail. And stipulations were made regarding the number of families to be settled and the amount of land to be cleared within a given time. In these details the grant is very much like any New England township grant of the era. But some important differences existed which easily could have been overlooked by the grantees. The grant stated that the township was "given, Granted and confirmed . . . unto the Several Persons hereafter Named . . . ," thus in severalty to each of the 164 men named and not to them as "tenants in common," the language used in the Massachusetts grants.[15] The grantees were to divide the land among themselves in 500 acre shares, though if a majority could not agree upon adequate procedures the Governor would appoint a committee to divide the land. Land could not be sold or alienated within ten years except by licence from the governor, lieutenant-governor, or commander-in-chief. And the grant remained conditional upon the settlement of "Forty One of the said Grantees with their Wives, Children, Servants and Effects..." by 30 September 1760 and another sixty grantees and their families within the following twelve months. In contrast, the grant for Machias required the grantees to settle the township "with Eighty good Protestant Families" within six years of the King's approval of the grant. It did not state that the grantees themselves had to be among the eighty families.

The Liverpool grant played upon the very strong corporate traditions in New England resettlement; the grant would become null or void if the grantees did not work together to assure the necessary numbers of settlers. At the same time the grantees were given no vested corporate rights as "tenants in common" or a proprietorship. The corporate responsibilities for organizing the resettlement of New Englanders in Nova Scotia had been retained while the corporate rights had been removed. Though the change initially may have escaped the notice of grantees, it was most assuredly intentional on the part of the government. Had the desire been to replicate faithfully a New England type grant then one could have been copied from the Massachusetts' *Acts and Resolves,* since as acts of the legislature grants were printed. And anyone drafting a grant would know that titles to land and the right to grant land had been long-standing sources of controversy between the British and the New England governments. Thus it is reasonable to conclude that subtle differences between a New England–style grant and the Nova Scotia grants had been constructed quite wittingly. Whether it was witting deception is less clear, but some New Englanders who went to Nova Scotia were indeed deceived.

In August 1761 the Council appointed a committee of five Liverpool settlers to divide the forfeited lands of the grantees who had not come.[16] The decision provoked a memorial from eight settlers who protested that "we conceive we have right and authority invested in ourselves (or at least we pray we may) to nominate and appoint men among us to be our Committee," a right they perceived as theirs by virtue of being "born in a Country of Liberty." The appointed committee, they argued, created unease among the settlers, causing some to leave and others not to come. The memorial ended by the men reiterating their right to choose their own committee and other officers, a privilege they "must insist on as it belongs to us alone to rule ourselves."[17] The petition did not move the Council. In 1760 the assembly passed an act to "enable the proprietors to divide their lands held in common and undivided," but the King had disallowed the act.[18] Six years later a Justice of the Peace had issued a warrant allowing the settlers of Londonderry, Nova Scotia, to choose their own committee to divide the lands, which the Council in Halifax declared unlawful.[19]

In a 1763 evaluation of the status of the townships, Charles Morris and Richard Buckeley recommended to the Council that the New England settlers be allowed the political rights to which they had been accustomed. This had been, they believed, one of the conditions Governor Lawrence had used to induce New Englanders to come.[20] They did not persuade the Council. Lawrence's personal intentions are not known, and perhaps Morris and Buckeley were right when they argued that he had intended the townships to have local self-government. But the Board of Trade would not permit any governor much rein in granting settlers extra rights, whatever his personal predilections.

The settlement of Liverpool proceeded rapidly and was the most successful of the South Shore fishing townships. Seventy families with thirteen schooners and three saw mills settled the first year.[21] By 1762, 90 families (504 individuals) had settled, 12 families short of the 102 required by the grant but enough to pacify Halifax and give some assurance of the survival of the township. By the following year Liverpool had grown by another 10 families (634 total inhabitants).[22] In 1764 the inhabitants of Liverpool gave up the 1759 grant and the government reissued it to conform to the families and individuals who had actually settled.[23] The 1759 grant had named 164 individuals, while the 1764 grant named 142. Only thirty-one names carried over from the one grant to the other. Though a small percentage of the original grantees (18.9 percent), the thirty-one provided a solid core of settlers. Many of the original grantees may have thought that they could sell their share or have someone settle in their stead, as may have happened since getting settlers to go to Liverpool did not seem to have been a problem. The government seemed willing to overlook the discrepancy by reissuing the grant, and indeed reinforced its position that there were not to be absentee proprietors. The language of the second grant is nearly the same as that of the first. Added, though, is a share for the first settled minister of the Church of England, and one share for the use of the school. The settlement stipulations changed slightly to require that each grantee settle himself or a family before 30 November 1765, reflecting a change in imperial policy on land grants in Nova Scotia.[24]

Throughout, the government retained the right to increase the number of grantees if it thought land was available, and it monitored the number of settled grantees through the reports of the appointed proprietors' committee. On 11 January 1771 an amending grant was issued to fifteen men, as agreed upon by the proprietors' committee at a 2 December 1770 meeting.[25] The 1784 proprietors' report noted another ten men who had been admitted as proprietors in 1771 but were not grantees since they had been absent at the time or could not raise the money to pay their share of the cost for petitioning the government.[26] Through Orders-in-Council the government granted another five shares, and nine men from Halifax received shares in Liverpool as political favours. Between 1759 and 1770, 172 individuals had received land as settlers with the explicit intention of settling (the nine men who received shares as political favours are not counted). The 1784 report noted that 132 of these had fulfilled their settlement obligations. Twenty-six others had settled and made some improvements but poverty and the difficulties of a new settlement had pushed them on. Another twelve had never settled their share and two had settled but made no improvements. Fifty-three families and seventeen single men had taken up residence in the township, some for nearly twenty years, but were not grantees. In the 1784 report the proprietors' committee recommended they be given land from those shares which might be escheated from grantees who had not fulfilled their settlement requirements.

One welcomed deviation from New England practice was the willingness of the Nova Scotia government to subsidize the new settlements primarily for transportation and food. In the fall of 1760 the government shipped 360 rations to Liverpool to be distributed among the township's indigent population.[27] The following March thirteen barrels of pork and thirty barrels of flour arrived, supplemented in April with another ten barrels of pork and forty barrels of flour.[28] John Dogget, the primary organizer for the township of Liverpool, received some governmental monies for his expenses in transporting settlers to Nova Scotia.[29] In the spring of 1761 the government requested him to hire a ship to transport twenty families and their livestock from Nantucket to Liverpool.[30] After the first two years Halifax assisted Liverpool upon reported incidents of need. In December 1762 Dogget requested assistance for a poor family of three and seven other indigent children in the settlement.[31] The following summer a committee surveyed the condition of the new settlements and reported that 1000 bushels of Indian corn might be needed for the sea coast communities of Liverpool, Barrington, and Yarmouth to be distributed from Halifax upon reported need.[32]

The government subsidies had numerous effects, not the least and most immediate of which was to assist in the speedy settlement of the colony. But they could also serve to foster a sense of local obligation to government largess. As well, the committees which oversaw the distribution of food stuffs were appointed out of Halifax and not chosen locally, thus creating a precedent for the intrusion of the central government into local affairs however benign or necessary it might have been. And lastly, as a very minor form of political patronage, it shifted some of the allegiance of local leaders from the township to the government in Halifax.

The circumstances leading up to the grant in Machias in 1770 are more complex. During the summers of 1761 and 1762 drought plagued New England. In the timber cutting areas of New Hampshire and southern Maine forest fires broke out, probably ignited by lightning. Fuelled to enormous size by the refuse left by wasteful cutting practices, the fires destroyed the timber industry of the region, and drove men eastward down the coast of Maine.[33] Among the first to leave were thirteen men from Scarborough, Maine, who, in 1763, loaded a saw mill onto a boat, sailed downeast and planted their mill on the falls on the West Machias River.[34] The following year their families and others from Scarborough reinforced the nascent settlement. Thinking themselves on the Nova Scotia side of the border they applied to Halifax for a grant of a township encompassing the upper end of the Machias Bay, and the West, Middle, and East Machias rivers. Learning they had settled within the jurisdiction of Massachusetts, they petitioned the Massachusetts General Court for a grant in 1767, but their petition was rejected.[35] In 1768 they applied again; the House of Representatives gave them a grant, but the Council rejected it.[36] In 1770 they applied yet again. This time the grant received the approval of the House of Representatives, the Council and Governor Hutchinson.[37] It was subsequently sent to London for the King's approval, where it was tabled. Only in 1784, after Massachusetts had gained uncontested jurisdiction over Maine, was the grant confirmed, and the township's inhabitants were incorporated into the town of Machias.

Machias became the most well-known settlement in the dispute between Massachusetts and Britain over which government had the right to initiate grants in the area of Maine between the Penobscot and St-Croix rivers. Massachusetts claimed that its title to the area lay in the 1691 charter of William and Mary which had established the Province of Massachusetts Bay. In that charter William and Mary gave Maine to the Bay Colony in gratitude, Massachusetts claimed in 1762, for exertions in driving out the French. In the following seventy years the area east of the Penobscot remained unsettled due to hostilities between the French and the British, but during that time Massachusetts had continued as the area's main source of British defence. Prior to the 1760s the British government had twice challenged the legitimacy of Massachusetts' title to the Territory of Sagadehock, as it came to be known, but both times the attorney and solicitor general had found in favour of Massachusetts.[38] Then in the 1760s the British challenged the title again, arguing this time that William and Mary had not possessed the territory in 1691 and therefore could not have granted it legitimately. Specious at best, the argument was part of a British attempt to restructure its North American colonies and especially those in New England.

The conflict also created tension between the Massachusetts General Court and the royally appointed governors. When the General Court began to receive petitions for land in Maine in 1759, Governor Thomas Pownall urged it to resolve all outstanding claims of private parties so that the area could be settled. In the seventeenth century various sections of Maine had been granted to individuals and over the course of the next century a few of the heirs continued to assert their claims to the region. Among them were the heirs of Brigadier Samuel Waldo. In 1762 the Massachusetts General Court granted them a township on the Penobscot River in return for releasing and quiting claim to all right and title to the area between the Penobscot and St-Croix Rivers.[39] This arrangement freed the General Court to grant land in this area, and within a short while it granted twelve townships. By this time Francis Bernard had succeeded Thomas Pownall as governor of Massachusetts, and it fell upon him to decide whether or not to sign grants in territory of disputed jurisdiction. He did and then had to explain his action to the Board of Trade.

In a lengthy letter to the Lords Commissioners for Trade and Plantations written on 8 April 1763,[40] Bernard acknowledged the dispute between Massachusetts and the King over who had owned the area of Maine between the Penobscot and St-Croix rivers and therefore who had the right to initiate grants. He felt, though, that the exigencies of settling the area speedily and the good intentions of the Massachusetts government in achieving this end, overrode any serious complaints that the Lords Commissioners might raise. To demonstrate the good intentions of the General Court he made three points. One, the sole purpose of the grants was to further settlement, and to this end the government had given away and not sold the land. Two, the grants conformed to the restrictions in the 1691 charter, including the requirement that the grantees gain royal approval for all grants in the area. Thus, Bernard saw the grants as "recommendations" to the King, which if not signed would cease after the eighteen months the General Court had allowed for the grantees to gain royal approval. As it happened, the King had it within his power to withhold his signature, and the General Court had it within its power to continue to extend the time allowance for receiving it. From 1762 to 1784 the grants of thirteen townships in Maine (including that of Machias), existed in a legal limbo. But in 1763 when Bernard wrote his justification of the grants he did not reckon with the great stubbornness of both the King and the Massachusetts government. Bernard's third point was that the Massachusetts government required each grantee to give a fifty pound bond against fulfillment of the settlement requirements, therefore reinforcing the point that the grants were for immediate settlement and not long-term speculation. Reckoning that the dispute over the right to land would take a number of years to resolve, Bernard thought it nevertheless worthwhile to open the area to settlers. Massachusetts had proceeded in good faith to achieve just this end and he saw no reason not to give his approval to the grants.

The first six grants, of which Bernard wrote, had been passed in the House of Representatives on 20 February 1762, though he did not write his letter to the Lords Commissioners until 8 April 1763, probably after he learned that there was some resistance in London to approving them. A week after he sent off his explanatory letter he received a strong reprimand from the Lords Commissioners, written on 24 December 1762, for giving his approval to the grants.[41] Thus, by the time the men from Scarborough settled in Machias in the spring of 1763 the conflict over land grants in Maine had reached an impasse beyond which neither Massachusetts nor Britain would move until the resolution of the American Revolution.

The dispute did not keep settlers from continuing to move downeast. In 1768 the House of Representatives and the Council approved a grant to the settlers at Machias, but it had not received gubernatorial approval. In 1770 the same grant passed again and this time Governor Thomas Hutchinson approved it. And like his predecessor Bernard, he had to explain his actions to the Lords Commissioners. For Hutchinson the dilemma was that by 1770 the area between the Penobscot and the St-Croix rivers had 500 to 1000 settlers, and by barring grants there was no effective way to organize government or resolve differences between settlers. Fearing the complete collapse of law and order in the region, and the emergence of groups similar to the Regulators in North Carolina, he thought it best to sanction the grant of Machias, the site of the largest settlement in the region.[42] From the point of view of the Lords Commissioners, there should have been no settlers in the area, but, as Hutchinson noted, measures to eject the settlers would have had to originate in either the Massachusetts Council or the House of Representatives, a move which neither body would initiate. Lawrence felt that unless

Parliament was willing to take unilateral action and remove Maine from the jurisdiction of Massachusetts then he had to accept the reality of settlement, and under the laws of the Bay Colony provide for civil governance. Like Bernard, Hutchinson defended his action in terms of the immediate exigencies to be met, for Bernard the benefit of settling British subjects in Maine; for Hutchinson the need to have some semblance of order among those settlers. Hutchinson saw the short-term benefits of recognizing grants as having greater primacy than the long-term controversy between London and Boston over who had ultimate jurisdiction in Maine. And like Bernard Hutchinson was strongly reprimanded by the Lords Commissioners.

Hutchinson, in signing the grant to the Machias settlers, reinforced the hand of the Massachusetts government. So long as the settlers' petition stalled at the level of the General Court, then discontent would focus there or be diffused, rather than be focused explicitly on the King's refusal to sign the grant. But more importantly, Hutchinson reinforced New England patterns of social and political organization. And that was the real issue. Hutchinson thought it best for the grant to go through so that institutions for the maintenance of public order could be established, but his superiors in London probably thought the opposite judging from their condemnation of Hutchinson's action and their position on the Nova Scotian settlements. In Nova Scotia the Board of Trade blocked any move to allow autonomy at the local level, whether in the form of the quasi-public proprietorship or incorporated town government. It is unlikely that the same board would have seen the settlements in Maine in a different light. In Boston the General Court had no intention of letting the settlements develop on the Nova Scotian model. From London's position, the only immediate ploy to maintain some control over settlements in Maine was to keep the governor from signing any grants passed by the House of Representatives and the Council. Withholding the King's signature blocked clear title to land, and incorporation of the town, but it did not prevent the incorporation of the proprietorship which served to replicate and legitimate New England patterns of corporatism and local autonomy. And here the case of Machias is useful.

Once the grant received Governor Hutchinson's signature, the grantees applied to a Massachusetts Justice of the Peace, Samuel Danforth, to issue them a warrant to call the first meeting of the proprietors.[43] (This is also what the settlers in Londonderry, Nova Scotia, had done and which the Council overturned.) The grantees did not first act to receive the King's approbation. Nor was that detail on their agenda when they met on September 1770 as a proprietorship. Rather they elected their officers: a proprietor's clerk, a committee for calling future meetings, a collector of proprietary taxes, a treasurer, a committee to examine the expenses involved in getting the grant and a committee of lot layers. (These types of offices were common for proprietorships and the ones which the settlers of Liverpool thought were their right to have.) At the first meeting the proprietors also acted to assure the mill rights of the first sixteen settlers to Machias, and to pass a by-law which would allow them to confiscate and sell the property of proprietors who failed to pay proprietorial taxes. Only at their second meeting, held on 8 November 1770, seven months after the grant was passed, did they arrange to hire an agent to obtain the King's approbation.

The sequence of events is significant. First, the Massachusetts government did not itself act to obtain the King's signature. Rather the grantees had to assume the responsibility, and they sought it not as a group of individuals, in the way they had approached the General Court to receive the grant, but as an incorporated body. The lack of the King's signature did not keep the Justice of the Peace from issuing a warrant for the grantees to meet, elect officers and to vote to tax themselves. This part of the replication of New England society did not depend on the King's signature. It did block the settlers from obtaining unencumbered title to property, but with a large number of resident proprietors, as were present in Machias, that too only provided a minor block to orderly development. The proprietors proceeded to divide the land and define individual lots, thus avoiding or resolving disputes over property boundaries. Division of land became a matter controlled at the level of the township and not the colony. And defined property boundaries, even though the title was not clear, meant that land could be sold on quitclaim deeds. Hutchinson's signature produced the situation of vested corporate rights at the local level which the Board of Trade had guarded against in the Nova Scotia settlements.

The Revolution ended group grants in New England, the last one in Maine being Machias. The Commonwealth of Massachusetts, faced with a large war debt, initiated a program to sell land in Maine to repay its loans. On 28 October 1783, the General Court appointed a committee to dispose of the unappropriated land of Lincoln County, Maine, by settling squatter rights and selling the vacant lands. In 1784 the Eastern Lands Committee circulated a notice throughout Lincoln County for those with claims to submit a statement to the committee either individually or as a group. Most people submitted their claims as part of a group petition, with individual claims tendered almost exclusively for specific islands along the coast.[44] While Machias was the largest settlement east of the Penobscot River numerous smaller settlements had developed in the region in the late colonial period. As a rule, people in these settlements petitioned as groups. These petitions either explicitly or in tone acknowledged the changes in land policy wrought by the war, but it is also clear that these settlers knew that their only chance of persuading the government to give them more than 100 acres in squatter rights was to petition as a group and ask for the colonial-style grant. And since most settlements did not have enough adult men to constitute a proprietorship, these petitions had a number of nonresident signators.

For example, eighteen people petitioned for Bucks Harbour, a small peninsula adjoining Machias, and included a detailed summary of their individual claims. Calculating that the whole peninsula would yield approximately 170 acres for each petitioner, and noting that much of the land was rocky, broken, and unfit for cultivation, they asked for the whole to be granted to them in common, and they would divide it among themselves. The Eastern Lands Committee rejected the petition, and included Bucks Harbour in the sale of Plantation No. 22. In the deed the five Bucks Harbour petitioners who were residents were named and were to be allowed 100 acres for every five Spanish milled dollars paid within six months of notice.[45] The claims of the other thirteen, many of them by proprietors in Machias, were not acknowledged.

Another sixty-one men, twenty-five of them settlers, petitioned for the land around the settlement at Chandler's River. Since the tract included great sections of barren heath the petitioners reasoned that the useable land would allow "but a moderate share" to each of them. But the Eastern Lands Committee sold this land, together with Bucks Harbour, as Plantation No. 22 for 6120:17:5 pounds to eleven men from Boston. And the twenty-five settlers received the same consideration for land as did the settlers at Bucks Harbour.[46] Unlike colonial petitioners, postrevolution petitioners felt it necessary to justify their request for extensive tracts of land. In both the Bucks Harbour and Chandler's River petitions the justification was the poorness of the land, a very reasonable claim, though surveyors from Boston who had assessed the potential of the region had waxed eloquent about the agricultural prospects.[47] Other petitioners mentioned their steadfast loyalty to the patriot cause in the late war hoping it would give them greater claim to the grant of a township.[48] And all mentioned the labour and money they had expended in settling the land. In the level of justification there had been a marked shift in the manner of petitioning. But like their colonial counterparts, these postrevolution petitioners, most persons of modest means, knew that their best chances for a substantial grant lay in petitioning as a group.

While these settlers did not gain the privilege of a township grant, they did have the right to meet to discuss plantation concerns, tax themselves for needs such as roads and a minister, and eventually to petition for incorporation as a town. Although one part of the colonial resettlement practice was lost after the war, the rights of local autonomy and self-regulation were retained. In this respect the corporate patterns of New England resettlement remained strong and intact.

Why the New England commitment to corporate behaviour in the process of resettlement? First, it allowed many middling and probably some quite poor people access to land. A group had a voice strong enough to be heard in positions of power which the individual of modest circumstances lacked.

Second, the group gave the individual greater flexibility, for in Machias, and other towns within the New England colonies, not every grantee had to settle for the terms of the grant to be met. The corporate structure reinforced private individual interest by protecting one's share of land even in one's absence, provided enough of the group settled. It is significant that the British eliminated this practice in Liverpool, and required actual settlement to claim a share of land. Some absentee landholding persisted in Liverpool, but with the chance that the government would escheat the land. The resident proprietors in Liverpool could provide only limited protection to absentee landholders, and only by not reporting or rationalizing the person's absence. In Machias, the group provided greater and legitimized protection to the absentee's property claims.

Group settlement also promised the more rapid extension of political rights through the incorporation of a town than did individual settlement. In New England political rights were extended through one's inclusion in town. Thus to settle without benefit of a group, which could soon be incorporated as a town and send a representative to the assembly, was to choose to be disenfranchised for an indeterminate period of time. Most New Englanders resisted this situation. When the Northwest Territory was opened the provisions for temporary government included in the 1787 Ordinance were put there to attract New England settlers, who were leery of resettling without clear promises of law and order and protection of political rights.[49]

In Nova Scotia, and subsequently throughout British North America the British eliminated vested corporate rights, whether in the form of proprietorships or incorporated town government. It is significant that before the 1830s only one urban concentration in British North America—Saint John, New Brunswick—had incorporated status. All others including the major centres of Halifax, Quebec City, and Montreal, were run as parishes through the colonial governments. Vested corporate rights concerned the British as much or more than individual rights as they set about to reshape colonial policy. By restricting corporate rights they could restrict alternate focuses of authority, as well as the organized discourse on governmental policy which played such a large role in town meetings in places like Boston. On 14 April 1770 the Nova Scotia Council ordered that the Attorney General notify all concerned that "Town Meetings for debating and resolving on several questions relating to the Laws and Government of the Province . . . " were "Contrary to Law" and concerned parties could be prosecuted.[50] Assemblage was not a right, but a privilege given to designated corporate bodies. The protest submitted by the grantees of Liverpool over the appointment of a proprietorial committee indicates that in the minds of many New Englanders assemblage had come to be understood as a "right" of corporate bodies, though not necessarily a right of individuals, with governmental sanction being largely perfunctory rather than a "privilege" extended by the central government.

While the British could, with the stroke of the pen or lack thereof, severely restrict local corporate rights, changing behaviour could not be accomplished so speedily. Thus, in the case of Nova Scotia, it is important to examine how much the New England commitment to local autonomy and corporate behaviour continued to shape Nova Scotia development. How much is the resistance of the outports to the control of Halifax a legacy of New England local autonomy? How much and how long did New England behaviour persist in the absence of sanctioned structure, and how much did it effect the long-term institutional structure of the province?

Finally, the corporate behaviour of New Englanders was functionally specific. The Machias proprietorship regulated the division of the commonly held land and provided some ancillary development such as roads. While it gave some structure to the township before its incorporation, it never presumed to function as the town government. At the end of the Revolution the proprietors moved quickly to have the grant confirmed and the township's residents incorporated as the Town of Machias. Town government was the preserve of another and separate corporate body. Functional specificity undercut corporate communalism and enhanced private rights. The proprietorship existed to provide and protect individual access to land. The town protected an individual's political rights within the larger political unit of the colony. Neither existed to regulate all or most aspects of a person's life. The corporate structure existed to enhance the protection of private interest rather than to be an end in itself. It is tempting to go one step further and say that if the corporate structure was subservient to private interest then it was basically individualism and little else. But this misses the point that private interest finds protection and enhancement in many different forms and expressions, including corporatism and individualism. If the first priority of New Englanders in search of land in the 1760s had been clear titles, then they would not have been dissatisfied with the policies in Nova Scotia. The government was willing to give clear title to land held in severalty if a person settled, which was more than Massachusetts could promise to settlers in Maine. But many New Englanders chose questionable title to land and a hope for localized corporate rights in Maine, over clear title in Nova Scotia. With resettlement New Englanders had come to associate the protection of private rights with localized corporate rights, rather than through the protection of a centralized government. The retention of them in Maine and their suppression in Nova Scotia would have a great impact on the social and political development of the two areas.

• Notes

1 Petition of Thomas Westgatt and others, 3 Oct. 1763, *Maine Documentary History*, vol. 13 (Portland, 1909–10), 315–16. See the petition of Ebenezer Thorndike and others, 2 Jan. 1762, 242–43; and Petition of a Number of Soldiers, 1 April 1761, 232–33, for similar expressions.

2 Petition to the General Court of Massachusetts, November term 1759, *Maine Documentary History*, vol. 13, 180–81.

3 Speech by T. Pownall to the Council and House of Representatives, 2 Jan. 1760, *Maine Documentary History*, vol. 13, 199.

4 Lawrence issued two proclamations, the first on 12 Oct. 1758 when he described the lands available for settlement, and a second on 11 Jan. 1759 to respond to inquiries he had received. See D.C. Harvey, "The Struggle for the New England Form of Township Government in Nova Scotia," *Canadian Historical Association Report* (1933): 15–22.

5 Graeme Wynn, "A Province Too Much Dependent on New England," *The Canadian Geographer/Le Geographe Canadien* 31, 2 (1987): 100.

6 The percentage is based on the figures in Robert V. Wells, *The Population of the British Colonies in America before 1776: A Survey of Census Data* (Princeton, NJ, 1975), 69–89 passim. In 1767 New Hampshire's population was 52 700, in 1764 Massachusetts' was 245 698, and in 1762 Connecticut's was 145 590, or approximately 440 000 for New England c. 1765. Using Wells's sex and age ratios, half were male, and half the males were between the ages of sixteen and sixty, or approximately 110 000 adult men.

7 Wynn, "A Province Too Much Dependent," 100; J. Potter, "The Growth of Population in America, 1700–1860" in *Population in History: Essays in Historical Demography*, ed. D.V. Glass and D.E.C. Eversley (Chicago,

1965), 638–39; and Charles E. Clark, *The Eastern Frontier: The Settlement of Northern New England, 1610–1763* (New York, 1970), 354.

8 Kenneth Lockridge, "Land, Population and the Evolution of New England Society 1630–1790," *Past and Present* 39 (April 1968): 62–80.

9 Darrett B. Rutman, "People in Process: The New Hampshire Towns of the Eighteenth Century," *Journal of Urban History* 1, 3 (May 1975): 268–92.

10 Catherine Fox, "The Great Fire in the Woods: A Case Study in Ecological History" (MA thesis, University of Maine at Orono, 1984).

11 D.C. Harvey, ed., "Governor Lawrence's Case Against an Assembly in Nova Scotia," *Canadian Historical Review* 13, 2 (1932): 184–94.

12 Quoted in Harvey, "The Struggle," 18.

13 Report of Charles Morris and Richard Buckeley, Oct. 1763, Public Archives of Nova Scotia (hereafter PANS), RG 1, vol. 222.

14 Liverpool Grant, 1 Sept. 1759, PANS, MG 100, vol. 176, 26 Q.

15 Liverpool Grant, 1 Sept. 1759, PANS, MG 100, vol. 176, 26 Q. For examples of Massachusetts grants see *Documentary History of Maine*, vol. 13, 322–30 and vol. 14, 80–82.

16 Order in Council, 15 Aug. 1761, PANS, RG 1, vol. 211, 210.

17 Memorial from Peleg Coffin et al., 8 July 1762, PANS, RG 1, vol. 211, 250–51. This memorial is cited by D.C. Harvey as referring to rights of town government, though the incident which provoked the memorial was the appointment of a proprietors' committee and not town officers. When New England was first settled in the seventeenth century there was no distinction between the proprietorship and town, but by the eighteenth century they were two distinct incorporated bodies within a township. See Roy Hidemichi Akagi, *The Town*

Proprietors of the New England Colonies: A Study of Their Development, Organization, Activities and Controversies, 1620–1770 (1924; rprt. Gloucester, MA, 1963), 12–13.

18 Harvey, "The Struggle," 18.

19 Council Minutes, 28 Oct. 1766, PANS, RG 1, vol. 212, 21.

20 Report by Charles Morris and Richard Buckeley, Oct. 1763.

21 John Bartlett Brebner, *The Neutral Yankees of Nova Scotia: A Marginal Colony during the Revolutionary Years* (1937; rprt. New York, 1970), 54.

22 Nova Scotia Population, 29 Oct. 1763, PANS, C.B. Fergusson Collection, Box 1897, F 2/3.

23 Grant of Liverpool, 20 Nov. 1764, PANS, MG 4, vol. 77.

24 Margaret Ells, "Clearing the Decks for the Loyalists," *Canadian Historical Association Report* (1933): 47.

25 Grant to John Godfrey et al., 5 Jan. 1771, PANS, MG 4, vol. 77.

26 Return of the Township of Liverpool, 19 March 1784, PANS, MG 4, vol. 77.

27 Letter from Richard Buckeley, Halifax, to John Dogget, Liverpool, 29 Oct. 1760, PANS, RG 1, vol. 136, 2.

28 Council Minutes, 4 March 1761, PANS, RG 1, vol. 204, 163; and Council Minutes, 14 April 1761, PANS, RG 1, vol. 211, 173.

29 Council Minutes, 4 March 1761, PANS, RG 1, vol. 204, 163.

30 Council Minutes, 22 May 1761, PANS, RG 1, vol. 211, 192.

31 Council Minutes, 31 Dec. 1762, PANS, RG 1, vol. 211, 288.

32 Report on the Counties of Nova Scotia, Oct. 1763, PANS, RG 1, vol. 22.

33 Fox, "The Great Fire in the Woods."

34 "The Proprietors Book of Records of Machias" (copy of the original in the Washington County Court House, Machias, Maine), 3.

35 Petition of Machias Inhabitants for a Township Grant, 4 June 1767, Commonwealth of Massachusetts Archives, vol. 118, 290–91.

36 Petition of the Inhabitants of Machias for a Grant, 7 Jan. 1768, Mass. Archives, vol. 118, 314–16.

37 Act of the House of Representatives, 4 April 1770, Mass. Archives, vol. 118, 446.

38 For the 1762 Massachusetts' defence of its claim to the land between the Penobscot and St-Croix rivers see, *Maine Documentary History*, vol. 13, 296–302.

39 Grant to S. Waldo and others, 6 March 1762, *Maine Documentary History*, vol. 13, 264–66.

40 In *Maine Documentary History*, vol. 13, 308–11.

41 Gov. Bernard to the Lords Commissioners, 25 April 1763, *Maine Documentary History*, vol. 13, 311–15.

42 There are numerous letters in the Massachusetts State Archives written by Hutchinson concerning affairs downeast and his actions in signing the grant for the township of Machias. Some of the more important are found in vol. 26: 493–94 and vol. 27: 26, 57–58, 59–60, 60–61, 79.

43 The Proprietors Book of Records of Machias, 29 June 1770, 1–4.

44 The 1784 petitions for land in Lincoln County are found in the Massachusetts State Archives, Eastern Land Papers, Box 14.

45 The petition for Bucks Harbour is in the Eastern Land Papers, Box 14. A copy of the deed for Plantation No. 22 can be found in the Washington County Land Deeds Office, County Court House, Machias, Maine, vol. 1, 129–31.

46 The petition from Chandler's River is found in the Eastern Lands Papers, Box 14.

47 Report of the Commissioners on Machias, 12 Sept. 1771, *Maine Documentary History*, vol. 14, 137.

48 See the petitions from Plantation Nos.

4, 6, and the back section of 6, for these sentiments. Eastern Lands Papers, Box 14.

49 Peter S. Onuf, "Settlers, Settlements, and New States" in *The American* *Revolution: Its Character and Limits*, ed. Jack P. Greene (New York, 1987), 172–73.

50 Council Minutes, Province of Nova Scotia, PANS, RG 1, vol. 212, 136.

"IN THESE TIMES OF DEMOCRATIC RAGE AND DELUSION": Popular Religion and the Challenge to the Established Order, 1760–1815*

NANCY CHRISTIE

In 1760, when New France was captured by the British, there was only a small number of Protestants in what is now Canada. Gradually, however, the Protestant population grew to the point that by 1776 less than 10 percent of Nova Scotia's estimated 20 000 residents were Roman Catholic (Nova Scotia then included all of present-day New Brunswick, Nova Scotia, and Cape Breton Island). Well over half of the Nova Scotia Protestants were recently arrived Congregationalists from New England. There were also sizeable numbers of newly settled Methodists and Anglicans from the North of England; German Protestants; and a smattering of other sects, including Quakers. Outside of the capital of Halifax, the Yankee Congregationalists set the religious tone of the colony; in Halifax, however, the Church of England would dominate. At the outbreak of the American Revolution in 1776, there were fewer than a dozen Protestant ministers in Nova Scotia, most of whom were Congregationalists. They served widely

---

*From *The Canadian Protestant Experience*, ed. G.A. Rawlyk (Montreal: McGill-Queen's University Press, 1994).

scattered and isolated communities and they, to a man, realized that during the settlement years of the 1760s and 1770s, they had made very little religious impact on their congregations. The weakness of the Congregational appeal among the humbler classes who formed the majority of the population opened the door to a wave of popular evangelicalism in the form of New Light revivalism after 1775.

To the west, Quebec, in 1776, had a population of some 90 000. Only a tiny percentage were not French-Canadian Roman Catholics. Protestantism would never make any real inroads into the French-Canadian population. Despite the fact that many English-speaking Loyalists settled in Lower Canada, it was apparent by the beginning of the nineteenth century that Protestantism was destined, in that province, to be a minority religion. There were only a handful of Protestants in the rest of Canada west of Quebec in 1776—most were connected with the fur trade.

Over 50 000 American Loyalists arrived in Canada during and after the American Revolution. Most of these Loyalists settled in the Canadian Maritimes. Soon after 1784, they were joined by thousands of American and British immigrants, most of whom made their way to Upper and Lower Canada, present-day Ontario and Quebec. And just before the outbreak of the War of 1812, hundreds of Scots emigrated to what is now Manitoba. The postrevolution influx of immigrants profoundly altered not only the demographic shape of Canada, but also its religious contours. By the time of the outbreak of the War of 1812, the population of the Maritime colonies had grown to over 100 000—approximately 70 000 in the present-day Nova Scotia, 25 000 in New Brunswick, and some 10 000 in Prince Edward Island. The Protestant population of the region, well over half of the total number, was divided into two major denominational groups—the New Light evangelicals, mostly rural Baptists and Methodists, largely American in origin—and the established churches—the Anglicans and Presbyterians, with strong demographic ties to Great Britain and particularly important in the urban centres.

In Lower Canada in 1812, the population was in the neighbourhood of 300 000. Less than 10 percent were Anglo-Americans. Anglicanism and Presbyterianism had some strength in the urban centres of Montreal and Quebec City but, as was the case in the Maritimes and neighbouring Upper Canada, the Methodists, the Baptists, and other evangelical groups were particularly strong in the Eastern Townships where settlers from neighbouring New England had pressed their unique Protestant stamp.

In Upper Canada in 1812, over 80 percent of the estimated population of 80 000 were Americans—either Loyalists or so-called "late Loyalists." Though the Anglican Church received considerable state support, it could claim the adherence of only a tiny minority of the population, and they were found in the garrison centres of Kingston, Niagara, and present-day Toronto. There were indeed two Protestant worlds in British North America—that of the Anglicans and Presbyterians and that of the evangelical denominations. These, in turn, were defined by two rival world-views: the Anglican which saw society in static terms of hierarchical corporate bodies and social ranks, and the evangelical, which stressed the dynamic role of the free individual in transforming society based on a more inclusive and egalitarian concept of human relations. The two dominant evangelical groups, the New Lights in the Maritimes and the Methodists in Upper Canada, can thus be viewed as two facets of a common popular religious impulse which sought to redefine British North American society in contrast to the established authority.

The Reverend Charles Inglis was the first Anglican Bishop of Nova Scotia, serving in this capacity from 1787 to his death in 1816. He believed that in the 1790s and the first decade of the nineteenth century he was indeed living in what he described as "these Times of Democratic rage and delusion." Unlike many modern historians who separate politics, religion, and society into discrete categories of meaning, Inglis and other members of the Protestant religious elite during the years immediately following the American and French Revolutions were fully aware that evangelicalism, as a popular expression, was the dominant vehicle by which established notions of an orderly, stable, and hierarchical society were being challenged and transformed. Likewise, by referring to religious revivals as a "reformation," evangelistic preachers such as the Methodist Joseph Gatchell contended that evangelicalism was indeed a popular mass social movement which was reshaping individual values and human relationships. What these historical figures understood, and what some modern historians have generally ignored, was that this era of democratic revolution, the period from 1776 to 1815, had engendered more than a political "stir." The age of democratic revolution was a manifestation of more general changes taking place within eighteenth-century societies whereby notions of an organic, homogeneous culture defined by rank and deference to authority were giving way to ideals of individual self-expression, social equality, and democratic consent.

For the ordinary British North American Protestant whose world was defined not by the written word but by oral communication, rituals and mass events were important expressions of these transformations in values and consciousness. The account of the first mass camp meeting held at Hay Bay on the Bay of Quinte Upper Canada, in 1803, recorded by the Methodist itinerant preacher, Nathan Bangs, evokes the various ways in which evangelical popular culture functioned as a direct rival to the polite, literate, and mannered world of the British North American gentry. Apparently, some 3000 Upper Canadians attended this mass religious gathering. Bangs highlighted the fact that the meeting was removed from civil society by clearly establishing its rural location. More importantly, however, by stressing its natural setting, Bangs was confirming that there were no artificial mediators between the individual and God. Again and again, Bangs described how God immediately communicated with the converted by sending "shocks" to the people. The relationship between the communicant and God was both direct and personal: "The power of God descended upon a Travelling preacher in such a manner that his shout pierced the heavens, while his body was sustained by some of his friends. He was at length carried out of the Camp into a tent where he lay speechless, being overwhelmed for a considerable time with the mighty power of God." More importantly, God imbued the humble with personal authority, for "when his strength came, and his tongue was unloosed his song was 'Glory to God in the Highest.'" Not only was the camp meeting defined by popular participation whereby both the preachers and the converted laypeople exhorted and sang to bring about new conversions, but it also represented a form of religious experience in which, as Bangs himself noted, "old and young, male and female were now employed in carrying out the work of God." A new sense of an inclusive community which overcame both class and gender divisions was fashioned throughout the four-day vigil. Progressively, those who had hung about on the outskirts of the camp, viewing it merely as spectacle to jeer at, were brought into the "square" throng of the redeemed.

Such open-air meetings were occasions for popular and equal expressions of frank and personal religious experience. They were perceived as boisterous and emotional, thus symbolically challenging the elite conception of a rational world of polite behaviour. Throughout his narrative, Bangs unabashedly described the shoutings, crying, singing: one backslider "roared aloud for mercy" until 10 o'clock the next morning for God was in him "like fire in a dry stable." Often it was difficult to distinguish between "shouting and revelling." Here was a religious culture which encouraged the free expression of the humble and marginal people who possessed little power in colonial society, and in which the very power of God was associated with popular revelry: "It might be said of a truth, that the God of the Hebrews is come into the camp for the noise was heard far off. The groans of the wounded, the shouts of the delivered, the prayers of the faithful, the Exhortations of the courageous penetrated the very heavens, and reverberated through the neighborhood." Its associations with eighteenth-century popular culture were obvious—such as Bangs' recounting of exorcising a young boy—but popular evangelicalism was also a catalyst in nudging their world towards modernity. Learning gave way to the authority of popular persuasion, ecclesiastical homogeneity to evangelical pluralism, communal status to individualism, and elite control to popular consent. As with American evangelical preachers, the once narrowly defined political language of liberty and egalitarianism suffused the Canadian evangelical scene, nourishing a pervasive cultural republicanism. It was with conscious pride that Bangs, the American evangelical preacher of prominent anti-Tory origins, proclaimed that with conversion people moved with a new "boldness," for through their relationship with God they had been "delivered from bondage," and "brought into liberty."

Until recently, influential historians of early Upper Canada have sought to highlight a single climate of opinion which was antidemocratic, anti-American, and wholly prescribed by the conservative values of the political and social elite. This uniform portrayal of the social world of Upper Canada has been challenged by Jane Errington's *The Lion, the Eagle, and Upper Canada.* Her analysis of Upper Canadian politics has clearly demonstrated that even among the gentry there was a diverse spectrum of attitudes towards the United States and England. One of the central contributions of Errington's study is its portrait of ethnic and cultural pluralism in early Upper Canada. Our attention is implicitly redirected away from simplistic notions of a fully formed and hegemonic counterrevolutionary tradition immediately following the American Revolution, towards a recognition that postrevolutionary British North America was a new society in which ideologies were pluralistic, dynamic, and still unformed.

If we are to accept the Loyalist conservative imperative in early Canada—and certainly such a conservative ideology did exist—we must conceive of ideology not simply as reflective of a social reality, for values and ideas are refracted and transmitted through an extremely complex social world. In other words, Bishop Inglis's Tory views and those of many of his Anglican and Presbyterian supporters—particularly those of the Reverend John Strachan, the powerful voice of Anglican Toryism in Upper Canada in the 1800–15 period—did not represent a total culture, rather they were part of a larger dialogue of two ideals of society. Their evangelical rivals were vigorous participants in this dialogue. Even the exclusivist mind of Bishop Inglis and that of Strachan appreciated that the defence of a Tory, Anglican establishment had to share its voice both in the Maritime colonies and the Canadas with a cacophony of religious dissenting persuasions. Errington's pathbreaking work and the very observations of the gentry themselves implicitly directs the historians to recognize that one must look beyond the rarefied world of politics to the social world of popular culture to fully understand the voice of dissent within colonial society.

David Mills has observed in *The Idea of Loyalty in Upper Canada* that before the War of 1812 there was no organized political dissent in Upper Canada. In his work on early Saint John, David Bell has shown that within this Loyalist settlement there were initial expressions of political opposition which utilized the language of political dissent similar to that of the Patriots during the American Revolution. However, he also notes that these attempts to found politics of faction were soon squelched by the Tory elite which in turn imposed political consensus. Mills' quiescent attitude towards political dissent, however, raised the question of how to account for the Tory obsession with religious enthusiasm. What, for example, do we make of John Strachan's pre-1812 comment that he had "serious political objections" to Methodist itinerant preachers? One could perhaps conclude that Tory commentators were simply alarmists who were rashly fulminating at a nonexistent challenge to their social world of orderly government and reasonable religion. But if we are to take seriously Strachan and Inglis's remarks that evangelicals were "to a man" violent Republicans and Democrats, we must likewise accept that in the late eighteenth century there existed an intimate and causal relationship between religious expression and political ideology. From very different historiographical perspectives, J.C.D. Clark, the British Tory historian, and Nathan O. Hatch, the American interpreter of early American Republican culture, have concluded that religion has not always existed to buttress the status quo, but that in this period evangelicalism functioned as the fulcrum of dissent which anteceded political debate. Religious liberty enjoined the concept of civil liberty in opposition to established churches and gentry dominated politics.

This intersection of political and religious ideologies was duly noted by contemporaries both within patrician and plebeian cultures. Tories in postrevolutionary Upper Canada and the Maritimes sought to root out "novel doctrines" of liberty and equality not in the realm of politics but in evangelical religious movements. In Upper Canada, they targeted Methodism while in New Brunswick and Nova Scotia, Baptists, New Lights, and some Methodists were the concern. Bishop Inglis noted in the 1790s, his sensitivity to radicalism having been heightened by the French Revolution, that the New Lights were effecting "a general plan of total Revolution in Religion and Civil Government." In a similar vein, John Strachan declared in 1806 that Methodists did not follow the "rational doctrines" of the Church of England, and therefore were suspected of "republican ideas of independence and individual freedom." Further, although evangelical pietism stressed the withdrawal of the converted individual from the sinful world of politics, evangelical preachers such as Henry Alline, the charismatic Nova Scotia preacher during the American Revolution, were no less attuned to the reality that their religious movements represented an assault upon the established order in church and state. As an outsider to elite politics, Alline employed his vital religion as a vehicle for social critique: "The Hypocrite and Pharisee can no longer deceive the World with their Cloak of Religion; they have nothing now to hide Shame and Pollution of the guilty and despairing Souls; neither dare they any longer mock the Searcher of all Hearts with their Lip service, or plead their close Conformity to the Externals of Religion." As was the case in Britain and the United States, all ranks within colonial British North America experienced the overwhelming tidal force of the age of democratic revolution. The upsurge of egalitarian cultural expression forcefully challenged and eventually wore down the central ideological stronghold of gentry privilege, namely the established church.

The Church of England had been established in Nova Scotia in 1758, and although it claimed a privileged position under the patronage of both the British government and the Society for the Propagation of the Gospel (both of whom somewhat reluctantly contributed financial support for the Anglican clergymen), its dominance was from the beginning limited by explicit decrees for religious toleration which were intended to attract New England settlers into the colony. Thus, despite its official status as the national church, the Church of England never garnered substantial popular support in the Maritime colonies, nor was its position buttressed by political favour due to the persistent strength of the liberal and dissenting flavour of the House of Assembly. The House offset any proclivities governors might have had to replicate the British equation between executive rule and an Anglican oligarchy. Before 1776 the Church of England had little social influence in Nova Scotia. After the American Revolution, in a flurry of concern, the Colonial Office erected the first colonial episcopate, appointing in 1787 Charles Inglis, a well-seasoned defender of the Tory establishment in New York and a devout Loyalist. Nevertheless, the Anglican church was challenged by the New Lights and the Methodists. The British government under the Whig Prime Minister, William Pitt, desired to curtail the "democratic element" in the British colonies in order to stave off future ruptures in her empire. It saw the Church of England as an active partner in upholding the principle of executive rule within the British constitution and in cementing the imperial connection. However, with the British Empire's "swing to the East" following the American Revolution, when British defence interests turned toward unholding trade interests both in India and China, the Colonial Office did little to sustain the church establishment in British North America.

Moreover, the Church of England foundered in the Maritimes largely because of the smug assumption among both Inglis and many of his SPG missionaries that the traditions and rituals of the Anglican church need not be adapted to colonial circumstances. When Inglis did recognize the virtual necessity for local support once the SPG withdrew its financial commitment, individual missionaries who were largely trained in England were unaccustomed to promoting their church or travelling in order to evangelize new adherents. Consequently, they were very reluctant to shoulder the responsibility for the growth of the Anglican missions. The intransigence of the Anglican clergy, together with the fact that far fewer Loyalists were Anglicans than was assumed by British officialdom, meant that the arrival of postrevolutionary settlers contributed surprisingly little to solidifying the church's claim to be a national church; the Anglican church would therefore have to be satisfied with a minority status in the Maritimes. Furthermore, whatever rights the church claimed under the constitution— such as the exclusive right to perform marriages—were whittled away in

Nova Scotia and New Brunswick after 1800 by assemblies which tended to decide in favour of non-Anglican ministers who chose to challenge church authority.

In Upper Canada the privileged position of the Anglican church more accurately reflected the reciprocal relationship between church and state in England. Exclusive rights for the Anglican church were entrenched in the Constitutional Act of 1791, which established clergy reserves, gave the lieutenant-governor the power to appoint clergymen, and set aside provincial funds with which to support the clergy. A lucrative source of income was accordingly alienated from evangelical ministers in 1793 when the restrictive Marriage Act conferred the right to solemnize marriages exclusively to the Anglican clergy. As an extreme example of the exclusivity of the Church of England, the Rev. John Langhorn, the Anglican incumbent in Ernesttown, near Kingston, demonstrates the inflexibility and lack of understanding of the needs of the wider population. Langhorn, known for his obesity and obsessive daily cleansing in the waters of Lake Ontario, was almost a caricature of the overbearing and arrogant Anglican clergyman. He allowed no deviations from the formal liturgy even to the point of not giving communion to two women who would not kneel in his church; he also stubbornly refused to comfort the sick unless they held the Anglican prayer book. Langhorn refused to walk on the same side of the street as a dissenter, and finally held the whole of the Anglican community up for ridicule by writing rude and satirical poems about the Methodists, who outnumbered Anglicans by a substantial margin in the colony. As he himself stated when even his own parishioners, who were Americans familiar with a more informal and democratic Episcopal church, finally ousted him in 1806: "The great objection people here have against me is, that I will not model my religion to their fancy, but adhere to the Church of England."

In 1791, Lieutenant-Governor Simcoe articulated the desire to make Upper Canada's political and social structure "the image and transcript" of Britain in as far as the Church of England functioned to support the State in upholding the distinction of ranks enshrined in the English constitution. In practice, however, the church suffered severely from the overwhelming competition of extremely popular evangelical societies, most notably the Methodists. Their centrally organized circuits and reliance upon tireless, cheap preachers and local lay exhorters, allowed this denomination to thrive in a sparsely settled frontier and in turn dominate a religious landscape refashioned in its own image. It was with a note of despair, then, that John Strachan, who believed that the survival of a hierarchical society and a political order defined by executive rule depended less upon the venerable constitution than upon the rational traditions of the

Anglican church, entreated his fellow clergy in Upper Canada to "out-preach and outpractice our opponents." Likewise the embattled Church of England in the Maritimes resorted to intimidation, particularly in New Brunswick, to quell the rapid and spontaneous expansion of evangelicalism by invoking the 1786 Act for Preserving the Church of England thirteen times between 1791 and 1812.

Inglis and Strachan, the two most influential Anglicans in pre-1812 British North America, conceived of the church as an instrument of allegiance. They saw government and religion as the pillars upon which society rested. It was common, of course, for eighteenth-century British leaders to view "manners" as the tempering ethical glue which held together those prescriptive customs and obligations that defined proper relations between superiors and inferiors. Thus the Church of England, which encouraged the taming of passions and inculcated rational religious values, was the most important vehicle for ensuring public order and unity of belief. Any formal recognition of other religions outside the established church would be, in Strachan's words, a "contradiction," for in the ideal hierarchy of rank, power devolved from God, through the church and constitution to the people. No room was left for plurality of belief. According to Strachan the ideal Christian society can flourish only when "the waywardness and self-will of individual caprice is subjected to the restraints of wholesome and enlightened authority." Strachan believed in a providential social order, in which the Anglican church, the British constitution, and the separation and subordination of classes were ordained by God and therefore unchangeable.

These doctrines voiced by Inglis and Strachan, and by other Anglicans and Presbyterians before the War of 1812, reflected an interpretation of social and political relations commonly held by the British gentry who upheld rule by tradition. These two Anglican leaders did not put forward these ideas as unquestioned verities, for it is significant that these statements were made during and after the important decade of the 1790s when it became clear that all through the western world established churches, and thus the once solid notion of a prescriptive constitution and social order, were under siege. With the upsurge of the democratic critique, the church was seen as a man-made, voluntary institution, which individuals could join at their will. Moreover, the evangelical impulse, by placing greater emphasis upon individual assertion, and by viewing piety as a personal rather than communal exercise of authority, tended to undermine the priority granted the civic community in Whig political thought. This, in turn, undermined the idea of obedience which sustained the close ties between church and state. Charles Inglis experienced at first hand the American Revolution. John Strachan, for his part, witnessed the particularly fierce Scottish Tory backlash against the republican and individualistic tenets unleashed by the French Revolution. Consequently, both of these colonial leaders exuded a brand of Toryism which, fearful of Revolution, had become hardened and inflexible towards the idea of legitimate opposition and constitutional reform, the hallmarks of the anti-Tory, Whig political tradition. They abhorred the notion of the church as an institution responsive to social change or popular will and obdurately held to a concept of church government founded solely upon tradition and precedent.

For John Strachan, who eventually became Bishop of Toronto, the church was hierarchical, and thereby reflected and sustained a similar natural and social order: "It is evident that there is a subordination in the Natural World. We may extend the analogy and suppose that it is the intention of nature that the like subordination should prevail in the Moral World." This assumed, therefore, that the humble individual could not have a direct and personal relationship to God, for this must be mediated by an educated clergyman, a representative of the government elite, itself providentially ordained. Like the evangelicals, Strachan accentuated universal sin, but in contrast to their conception of universal salvation, Strachan posited that man was spiritually ignorant and must be tutored from above. The "mysterious truths of God," in Strachan's view, could be revealed only "by Messengers especially commissioned for that purpose." Not only was the church thus averse to popular participation, but what more dramatically placed it in opposition to evangelical religious temper was the evisceration of any notion of sudden individual conversion whereby the emotions served as the vehicle of direct contact between the sinner and God.

For Anglicans, emotions were suspect in that they led to personal and social disorder. Only the rational doctrines purveyed by educated minds could properly dispose the individual towards goodness. Strachan's church was intent on preserving distance between the social orders, and more importantly, it stressed the infinite distance between man and God, thus ensuring that authority was encompassed solely within the corporate institution, and was not within the grasp of the individual. God, declared Strachan, was present in "no one man, but in his new body, the Church" for there was an "infinite distance between the Creator and the highest created being." Anglicanism, therefore, was an institution which sought to preserve social rank and wealth, eschewing any concessions to the common people or the principle of equality. Clearly this was a church which served the needs and aspirations of the colonial gentry, for as the Rev. G.O. Stuart commented about his church in York, present-day Toronto, in 1809, a balcony was built by necessity for the garrison and the poor, because pews were purchased solely by "persons of rank." But if the Anglican church in Kingston was representative, the poor were soon pushed out of these quarters by the large garrison.

While the established Anglican church was the only Protestant church to be formally and legally recognized in British North America during the 1760–1815 period, this elite institution was certainly in no way indicative of the popular religious landscape following the American Revolution. In terms of demography, the sacred landscape of Upper

Canada, the Maritimes, and Protestant Lower Canada more closely reflected the American experience of extreme religious pluralism and competition, what George Rawlyk has termed a "fragmenting religious ethos." In the aftermath of the American Revolution, when established religious authority was severely constrained and in some areas virtually nonexistent, popular theology flourished and spread at a remarkable pace, unimpeded by the rigid distinctions of eighteenth-century polite culture. As Nathan O. Hatch has argued, the democratic revolution broke down standard theological categories, and, as a consequence, unleashed upon all of North America a vast range of self-proclaimed preachers, who, by emphasizing the primacy of individual conscience, were instrumental in producing a multiplicity of religious options. In this period Christianity was totally reconstructed by unlettered popular preachers, who explicitly voiced the concerns of the poor and marginal, exalted the idea of free, individual choice in religious belief, and championed egalitarianism and religious ecstasy over education and social gentility. In this period of religious and social ferment, a new pattern of religious diversity based upon evangelical fervour and conversion took root in North America.

This striking diversity of the Protestant religious experience was immediately translated to Upper Canada and the Maritimes after the American Revolution when an array of religious denominations formed new local pockets of settlement. Quakers settled in Prince Edward County and Newmarket; Mennonite communities were established in the Niagara Peninsula in 1786, and in Waterloo and Markham Townships in 1803; while Scots Presbyterians settled in Glengarry. Many former Lutherans and Congregationalists founded Presbyterian churches, although this period of settlement brought with it much instability, and only in 1798 was a Presbyterian ministry established at the Bay of Quinte. There were relatively few adherents to the established church among the Loyalist migrations into British North America for these American settlers had for many years been exposed to a culture in which the Episcopalians and Congregationalists had long been retreating before the groundswell of evangelical pluralism. To the horror of Loyalist Anglican clergymen, they soon found themselves leaders of a minority church in a society divided into many dissenting religious sects. The social unity which the established church was intended to cement in this new British society was severely undermined. As one Anglican clergyman commented, his was a "settlement made up of foreigners bred in other churches." In Upper Canada there were only six Anglican missionaries in 1812. Although the Church fared better in the Maritimes, at Cornwallis, Nova Scotia, there were in 1790 only 30 out of 400 families who attended Anglican service. At Horton, where Henry Alline's New Light revival was in full swing in the late 1770s, a mere 4 families were devout Anglicans, and even in Loyalist Shelburne in 1785, only 1 in 3 Loyalist families were Church of England.

In both the Maritimes and the Canadas, popular evangelicalism was clearly dominant by 1812, with the New Lights, Baptists, and Methodists clearly on the rise. During the 1770s and 1780s the religious landscape of Nova Scotia was completely reshaped by the New Light stir led by the charismatic revivalist Henry Alline. As George Rawlyk has clearly demonstrated, the Congregationalist presence was all but eliminated after Henry Alline swept the colony with his highly emotional, mystical revivalism which concentrated on the individual's personal spiritual relationship with God, sudden conversions, and an anti-Calvinist belief in universal accessibility to conversion. After Alline's death in 1784 the New Lights were split into the Free Christian and Calvinist Baptist and New Light Congregational churches. The evangelical fervour of the New Lights also invigorated Methodism. For example, the Methodist intinerant preacher, William Black, at first worked very closely with Alline, and Alline's New Light Evangelicalism significantly affected Methodism in the late 1770s and early 1780s. However, in 1785, the Methodists split off from the New Lights when Freeborn Garrettson, the remarkable American Methodist, led a series of revivals in Nova Scotia between 1785 and 1787. Although Garrettson was extremely effective in bringing about a widespread Methodist revival, Methodism in the Maritimes always suffered from competition from the New Lights, especially since Francis Asbury, the leader of the American Methodist Conference, was reluctant to send itinerant preachers to isolated Nova Scotia. After Garrettson quit the colony in 1787, Methodism was relatively weak in the Maritimes when compared to its strength in the Canadas. Nevertheless, the evangelical ethos had been firmly established in the region. Alline's powerful and extensive revivals, which had inspired and given comfort largely to farmers, artisans, and fishermen, had brought about a complete transformation in the way in which most Nova Scotians experienced religion, and had therefore made his brand of emotional evangelicalism the dominant form of religious expression in the Maritime colonies after 1770.

Methodism in Upper and Lower Canada formed a northern extension of the New York Methodist network of preaching circuits and camp meetings. Since almost all the itinerant preachers who served in Upper Canada were American-born, Methodism represented a very direct importation of American republican values through the culture of popular religion. By 1812 Methodism formed the largest Christian denomination in Upper Canada, with 2550 active members and thousands of adherents who broadcast the egalitarian and individualistic message of the Second Great Awakening. Methodism also made up the largest group of Protestants in Lower Canada. Unlike Methodism in the Maritimes, which experienced setbacks both from the New Lights and Anglicans, Methodism in Upper Canada experienced much less competition. From the reminiscences of frustrated Anglican clergy, the popular revivalist preaching by itinerant preachers such as William Losee, Lorenzo Dow, Nathan Bangs, and William Case initiated a series of revivals between 1790 and 1810 which allowed Methodist teaching to take firm root along a string of widespread settlements. Methodism was much more unstable in the Maritimes, in part because the most acclaimed preachers such as Freeborn Garrettson hastened to return to the United States where they could feel much more immediately immersed in the exciting growth of the Methodist movement. Moreover, Methodist leaders in the Maritimes sought to seek the co-operation of the governing elite much earlier than those in the Canadas. As a result, after 1800 the Maritime Methodists associated themselves with the less radical Wesleyan Methodists in Britain. This in turn further diverted the support of American settlers toward the more socially egalitarian New Light Baptists.

Such problems of leadership and personnel did not plague Upper Canada in part because of its proximity to one of the most dynamic frontiers of American Methodism, New York. As well, because Francis Asbury viewed Upper Canada as a field of greater potential for the growth of Methodism, he ensured strong leadership. Although immediately after the outbreak of the American Revolution Methodism in the United States found itself on the defensive because of Wesley's conservative opposition to political revolt, the American movement was revitalized in 1784 when Wesley created the Methodist Episcopal Church in America. Through Francis Asbury's authoritarian but dynamic leadership, Methodism was reorganized along a "travelling plan" of itinerant preaching which was peculiarly suited to a largely unsettled frontier of isolated communities. Both efficient and adaptable, it relied upon a combination of mobile ordained clergymen, the famous black-frocked circuit riders, and local lay exhorters. These lay exhorters enhanced the spirit of Methodist piety in local class meetings between the often flamboyant exhortations of the visiting preacher. Although Methodism grew more slowly in towns where it often had to compete with other churches, they were without rivals in rural Upper Canada and the Eastern Townships of Lower Canada. Although recruits were usually youthful and highly individualistic, Methodist itinerants under Asbury's firm hand became a highly efficient corps of disciplined individuals. Its intense evangelicalism engendered personal conversions in even the remotest quarter of the colony.

Once the first circuits were established by William Losee in 1791 in the Bay of Quinte area and by Nathan Bangs in Niagara in 1804, Methodism grew unimpeded as these and new circuits (ten by 1810) were sustained by a constant procession of Methodist itinerants. By 1812 Methodism had become the largest Protestant denomination in Upper Canada. The Methodism of Francis Asbury, however, veered sharply from

British Wesleyanism which, under the leadership of Jabez Bunting, sought to shore up traditional authority. In the United States and in its Upper Canadian and Lower Canadian satellites, American Methodism challenged constituted authority and overtly fostered democratic values by extolling the universality of spiritual perfection and equality in religious communion. As such it became one of the most active cultural vehicles for transplanting the antitraditionalism and reformist spirit of the new American republic particularly into Upper Canadian society outside the rarified stability of the Tory elite.

The postrevolutionary settlement of British North America was characterized by a vast movement of peoples; nearly 20 000 Loyalists arrived in present-day Nova Scotia, 15 000 in New Brunswick; and by 1791, 10 000 had arrived in Upper Canada. In turn these Upper Canadian Loyalists were followed by a similarly large number of so-called late Loyalists who took up Lieutenant-Governor Simcoe's offer of free land. Not only did this dislocation entail considerable economic hardship, but, except for those ethnic groups such as the Moravians and Mennonites who recreated homogeneous communities in the new frontier, old bonds of parish life were broken apart. With the breakdown of familiar community structures came the disintegration of traditional bonds of social control and order, social rank, and networks of personal communication. Although speaking in a disparaging tone, Strachan accurately observed the complete absence of unifying social codes and values and likewise conveyed the still unformed nature of Upper Canadian community life. As late as 1803 he stated: "Every parish in this country is to be made; the people have very little or no religion, and their minds are so prone to low cunning that it will be difficult to make anything of them." The lack of religious feeling was often commented upon. The Baptist missionary Asahel Morse toured the province of Upper Canada in 1807 and described it as "a dismal region of moral darkness and the shadow of death." Even the prominent Methodist revivalist Nathan Bangs called the capital of York "a town of people as wicked as the Canaanites of old." In this case, however, we should not accept at face value Bangs' condemnation. York was, after all, a leading centre of Anglicanism, and many of the attacks upon the irreligiosity of the colony were part of the anti-establishment polemic.

Modern Canadian historians preoccupied with the institutional growth and presence of the Victorian church have all too readily believed these descriptions of the lack of religion in early colonial society and have used these as evidence of social backwardness. In fact, it appears that colonial British North America conformed to a larger North Atlantic pattern of religious experience and commitment. Because the evangelical ethos gave prominence to an otherworldly pietism and the necessity of individual conversion marked by a spiritual "New Birth," the very rhetoric of revivalism entailed an exaggerated disapproval of the social divisions and moral conduct of the sinful material world prior to a successful revival. Such a critique served to highlight the distance between the integrated world of the converted and the unregenerate. The reformist nature of the evangelical revival which had restored an ideal Christian purity was dramatized. Evangelicalism performed a much needed social reorganizing function in these new societies whose members had undergone severe cultural dislocation. As George Rawlyk has forcefully argued, Henry Alline's emotional evangelicalism was particularly effective while Nova Scotians were experiencing the trauma of the American Revolution. Moreover, American historians have illustrated that revivals were particularly frequent in either those areas which were in economic decline, such as certain areas of New England prior to the American Revolution, or in peripheral frontier areas which were economically deprived and institutionally impoverished.

The conjunction between the obliteration of familiar social landmarks and the rapid and spontaneous spread of new forms of popular religion are well illustrated by the life-story of Duncan McColl, a Methodist preacher. McColl served in the Argyllshire Regiment during the Revolutionary War and during this period of stress and insecurity became concerned about his religious state, and converted to Methodism. Having overcome his own sense of personal waywardness, he naturally described his new post of St Stephen, New Brunswick, as a fractured community in need of a unifying spiritual "reformation": "I found a mixed multitude of people from many parts of the world, without any form of religion."

Although the social instability engendered by the American Revolution might explain the rapid spread and mass popularity of evangelical revivalism, the theory of community breakdown downplays the real continuities and incremental change brought about in part by the rise of popular evangelicalism. The gradual replacement of communal values with the tenets of individual self-expression, the erosion of hierarchical views of the social order by more inclusive and egalitarian values, and the reversal of educated authority by that of the vernacular, all of these currents were encapsulated within evangelicalism. The evangelical movement was a thread in these great social and cultural upheavals which transformed the traditional and static eighteenth-century conceptions of social rank and authority and hastened the dissemination of these modern ideas.

Historians such as Joyce Appleby, Rhys Isaac, and Gary Nash have generally agreed that the period between approximately 1760 and 1820 in the United States was one of constant cultural ferment and negotiation whereby old formulations of what constituted virtue, liberty, and the public good were slowly being redrawn. Whether we refer to this process of a bourgeois or middle-class outlook, the period between the late eighteenth and early nineteenth centuries marked an increasing emphasis upon individualism, optimism, linear interpretations of history, and the experience of the lower orders. As Joyce Appleby has persuasively argued, the older view of society embodied the idea that government was a providential institution which protected men against the irrationality of economic events and thereby ensured that society would be orderly, rational, and civilized. Increasingly, however, men and women began to view the economy as an orderly and natural system which of itself could create social harmony. Not only did this view subtly eliminate the need for authoritarian social institutions, but it also gave priority to voluntary associations as the fulcrum of progress. These associations, in turn, were founded upon the very new and important concept of individual self-interest. Where a traditionalist would have conceived of the individual *within* society with its concomitant web of social obligations, a "liberal" or modern person would begin with the individual's needs and conclude that all people, even ordinary people, could make rational decisions and therefore participate in the polity.

While Appleby's picture of ideological change is largely concerned with economic thought, her observation of the initiative of ordinary people could just as easily apply to the changing ways in which they experienced religion. Although the father of Methodism, John Wesley, has correctly been associated with political Toryism in England, his views of society were essentially very radical. Wesley rejected the notion that social behaviour was formed by rational and external institutions. Further, he believed that God could be known by the heart and not the intellect. Such an interpretation of human relations immediately gave priority to the individual conscience. It also emphasized that social reform must begin with the individual conscience, and that, because all individuals were capable of seeking salvation, they could share equally in determining both the direction of church and civil government. Certainly Wesley was a conservative in that he championed civil government as the bastion of public order; he did, however, assert a concept of liberty based upon individual free choice and conscience, thus allowing Methodists the freedom to withdraw from a government of which they did not approve. Wesley's espousal of religious experience founded upon universal salvation, emotional fervour, and the individual's personal interaction with God, challenged the traditional concept of social relations. According to the new evangelical ethos, social order was sustained not from the coercive forces of external institutional authority, but was the natural result of mass inner discipline achieved through the individual's spiritual efforts working in conjunction with God's grace. In such an ideal world, authority devolved not from one's social betters or man-made government institutions, but was granted to each individual directly from God.

These radically new ideas were given impetus in the Thirteen Colonies by George Whitefield in the 1730s and 1740s. The great charismatic evangelist helped inspire a series of revivals generally called the First Great Awakening. This period of intense religious piety has been viewed by many American historians as a cultural and social watershed because it unleashed among the lower orders—small farmers, traders, artisans, and labourers—a form of emotional religion which allowed direct experiential knowledge of Christ. This was the first mass popular religious movement that cataclysmically confronted the traditional parish church and its institutional foundations. As Harry Stout has argued, the religious revivals inspired by Whitefield's powerful preaching were important outlets which allowed the common people to assert themselves against the often coercive authority of their social betters.

Symbolically, Whitefield held his mass meetings in field and squares outside regular meeting halls. Through his emotionally charged sermons in which he sang, wept, prayed, and told colloquial stories, Whitefield encouraged individuals to appeal directly to God. Although like Wesley, Whitefield did not overtly exhort the people to challenge the established government, his call for a purer, otherworldly pietism, with its insistence upon spiritual equality, ultimately led ordinary people to disparage worldly standards of greatness and the legitimacy of constituted power. In telling people to be instruments of their own salvation, Whitefield helped inspire a new form of popular religious experience which, quite unlike the Wesleyan evangelical movements in England, activated a more thorough radical assault upon traditional centres of civil and religious authority. It is of some significance, therefore, that Henry Alline was referred to by his contemporaries as Nova Scotia's George Whitefield, and that even during the period of Victorian religious respectability Canadian Methodist preachers still placed themselves within the more populist "dissenting" tradition of George Whitefield than within the more socially quiescent British tradition of John Wesley.

The observation made by the historian of revivalism, William McLoughlin, that the unfettering of tradition and hierarchical institutions begun by the First Great Awakening was carried forth during the Second Great Awakening (1800–40) has been reinforced by Nathan O. Hatch's groundbreaking work on popular religion. However, Hatch pushes back McLoughlin's time frame, viewing the immediate postrevolutionary decades of the 1780s and 1790s as the dynamic period of social and cultural ferment, when republican values became clearly dominant. These decades saw an ever increasing sharpness to the democratic social critique as its language of individual liberty and equality permeated the darkest recesses of American culture. The democratic impulse renewed the wellsprings of popular religion. These years saw an explosive burst of evangelical activity which even more consciously challenged church establishment and elite orthodoxies. In short, religious practice throughout North America during this period was effectively made over in the image of popular culture: it emphasized the vernacular in language and song, encouraged popular participation in religious rituals, denigrated the values of educated society by defining cultural authority in terms of emotional persuasion and dramatic demonstration and taught the common people to place their individual spiritual convictions on a higher plane than that of the material world still defined by social privilege.

In the wake of the American Revolution, when leadership in the traditional churches was unstable, membership in the Baptist and Methodist churches exceeded all other Protestant denominations. This marked the triumph of evangelical Protestantism which, by identifying the common people with the will of God, placed the democratic ideal at the forefront of American culture. Those very preachers who assertively set about reconstructing American social ideals along egalitarian and republican lines, extended the popular base of Methodism into the Canadas and the Maritimes. In doing so, they directly transplanted the ideology of equality and liberty into British North America, where their radical religious tenets found a sympathetic hearing among the American Loyalists who were largely common folk, small farmers, and artisans. For more than a generation already, these people had experienced the slow but insistent assault upon elite culture wrought by popular evangelicalism.

That evangelicalism had become an integral aspect of popular culture after the 1780s may be demonstrated by the social origins and leadership style of both the Baptist and Methodist itinerant preachers who flooded into the newly settled British colonies following the disruptions of the revolution. For the most part these preachers came from humble backgrounds similar to that of their audience. The historian of Canadian Methodism, Goldwin French, has concluded that among the first generation of Methodist preachers there were nine schoolteachers, three farmers, two blacksmiths, two carpenters, one soldier, one sailor, and one surveyor. Most were very youthful and unmarried, attributes which ensure maximum mobility and the stamina to endure hazardous journeys across a largely unbroken frontier and the frenetic pace of preaching up to 400 sermons in one year.

Nathan Bangs (1778–1862) had only rudimentary education and was a surveyor and, later, a schoolteacher in Niagara when in 1800 he underwent a conversion and became a Methodist itinerant preacher. His father was a blacksmith and a staunch anti-Tory. As he himself recalled, Methodist preachers in the United States were generally ridiculed because of their lack of education. Similarly the young Methodist preacher, Duncan McColl, who had been a pay-sergeant in the army, was threatened by the magistrate in St Stephen, New Brunswick, for this lack of theological learning, despite the fact that he inspired much emotional ecstasy in his congregation. He described the effect of one of his sermons: "During one his mind was carried up from the world and a power came down like an earthquake: some fell on their faces. . . . Others adored the Lord." Henry Ryan was best known for his "hearty manner" and for such stirring exhortations as: "Drive on brother! Drive on! Drive the devil out of the country! Drive him into the lake and drown him!" Ryan left professional boxing to battle on behalf of the Lord. Similarly, the famous New Light Yankee preacher Henry Alline was a farmer and tanner, and thus was clearly outside the dominant social order. Alline himself was aware of his humble social station and lack of education, and for a time was drawn to the Congregational ministry which would have conferred him with social status, but he curbed his "proud heart that aspired after a public station in the world, to make a great show and court the applause of men." By becoming a New Light preacher, Alline was equally conscious of the fact that he was rejecting conventional forms of religious as well as parental authority, and that he was choosing to immerse himself in the world of plebian culture. Even though Joseph Gatchell came from a prosperous and educated family, his social condition nevertheless placed him at the margins of his community. His father's decision to fight for the Patriots during the American Revolution had resulted in his expulsion from the Quaker church and a consequent loss of social prestige. Another example of this change in social status is the charismatic Methodist revivalist Freeborn Garrettson. He belonged to the Southern plantation gentry, but, upon converting to Methodism in 1775, he freed his own slaves and pursued a life of poverty, often preaching to prisoners and inmates of the local poorhouse. This renunciation of wealth forcefully symbolized that evangelicalism rejected distinctions of social rank and consciously framed an egalitarian world.

That the Church of England and evangelical denominations occupied very different social terrain is suggested by statements from clergy on both sides. Methodist William Case observed that after church services the Anglican clergy regularly joined their congregation in dancing and playing cards which "renders them very popular, especially in the higher circle." Anglican clergymen were likewise conscious that evangelical itinerants— "illiterate rambling preachers" (to use Bishop Inglis's phrase)—were very popular and that "their acquaintance with the tastes and peculiarities of the Canadians" was allowing them to gain a somewhat disturbing "ascendancy over our infant population." Certainly these young, disciplined, and dedicated evangelical religious leaders were proclaiming the gospel in new ways. They diverged from religious norms characterized by the learned sermon and a familiarity with the subtlety of theological argument, relying instead upon popular appeal and emotional persuasion. It is also apparent from the constant vituperative attacks against "Enthusiastic Teachers" and religious "infatuation" by Anglican leaders that their "serious and sober sense of Religion" was under considerable threat.

Bishop Inglis recognized the degree to which the authority of personality, wrought by the transforming nature of popular evangelicalism, had pervaded Maritime society: "Here, people must be persuaded, and won by address, to do what in Europe is done by habit, and by virtue of Established Laws." What Anglican leaders such as the Reverend John Strachan in Upper Canada and Bishop Inglis in Nova Scotia feared most of all was that the cultural norms established by this tumultuous and disorderly religion would attract not just the "lower classes" but would soon become the norm for all the "ranks of the People." This explains why Anglicans so obstinately adhered to "that outward mode and form" of the Anglican liturgy. Any concessions to the evangelical style, in their view, would be tacit approval of the cultural ascendancy of popular religion. Thus the Anglican clergyman for Cornwallis, William Twining, was severely reprimanded in the 1790s for adopting some of the preaching techniques familiar to Methodists. If the Anglican Episcopacy had reluctantly recognized that British North America had become a cultural battleground, they were nevertheless unwilling to participate on any terms but their own: "If New Lights and Methodists are only to be brought round by adapting the Church Service to their ideas, it is not worth the Sacrifice."

The constant barrage of criticism from the established church indicates that the evangelical outlook was dramatically transforming social norms and values at an uncontrollable pace. Within one generation the genteel traditions of Anglicanism and much of Canadian Presbyterianism had been forced into a defensive, even impotent, position. Venerable Anglican traditions might have been preferred by the small colonial elite, but the vast majority of settlers in British North America were being won over by the emotional zeal of the barnstorming evangelical preacher. Samuel Coate, who was acclaimed as a marvellous speaker, was said to have "swept like a meteor over the land and spellbound the astonished gaze of the wondering new settlers. . . . He was the heaven-anointed and successful instrument of the conversion of hundreds." As this quote makes clear, this style of preaching was both novel and effective. A preacher's success was measured in terms of the number of conversions he was able to bring about. For example, Nathan Bangs made frequent references to the number of conversions made in order to measure the success of the first camp meeting in Upper Canada. Since the spread of evangelicalism was based upon popular appeal, it followed that the successful preacher had to adapt his style to that of his audience. His sermons, therefore, had to be the antithesis of the learned written sermon. The best known Baptist, New Light, and Methodist preachers were defined largely by their highly charged, emotional preaching. Henry Alline was noted for his "Wild and Extravagant Gesturing" and as the Congregational minister from Harvard, Aaron Bancroft, recalled, Alline "by his popular talents made many converts." William Losee, the first Methodist itinerant preacher in Upper Canada, endeared himself to the people of Cataraqui largely because of his "fervent sermons" which conveyed the evangelical message in a manner accessible to the ordinary citizen. Despite the fact that after contracting tuberculosis he could speak in but a whisper, Calvin Wooster preached in a "bold and pointed" fashion. His straightforward terms were persuasive because they were unencumbered with the heaviness of theological debate. According to Wooster himself, after his sermon the wicked "would either flee from the house, or, smitten with conviction, fall down and cry aloud for mercy." If Calvin Wooster used language which would make "the ear tingle," other preachers attempted to convey their message of free salvation to as wide an audience as possible by telling stories of their personal voyage towards spiritual reformation. In the case of the Methodist Robert Perry, "homely analogies" were used to render his sermons "bearable." Often preachers shouted aloud, lay prostrate, or wept openly in order to convey the intensity of spiritual conversion and to thus inspire and penetrate to the listener's deepest emotions. Theatrical displays of the supernatural were improvised in order to awe the sinful audience with the power of God. For example during a Methodist meeting at the Bay of Quinte a man swore volubly during a sermon to which the preacher responded "My God, smite him!" This prayer duly caused the sinner to fall as though "shot by a bullet." Many conversions followed. The dramatic trick most favoured by the Methodist preacher Calvin Wooster involved ascending a ladder to a window. With the people assembled below, he would then descend like Moses on the mount.

Here was a style of preaching which, in Asbury's words, consciously attempted "to condescend to men of low estate." The use of dramatic, lively, and emotional exhortation appealed to the popular audience. Evangelical preachers adapted the language and style in order to break down the walls of deference between the preacher and the audience. Methodist preachers, for example, abandoned clerical dress and wore simple homespun. They lived a simple life, carrying all their possessions in their saddlebags.

Preachers used all of their personal attributes in order to persuade and convert, including their youthfulness and attractiveness. The very successful Upper Canadian Methodist preacher William Case was remembered as "youthful, beautiful, amiable"—with a charming personality and a singing voice which "first spell bound and then melted his audience." The power of hymns and popular song contributed much to the rapid expansion of evangelicalism. In this way it functioned as a form of popular spectacle which endeavoured to attract a crowd whose interest had been peaked enough to make them open to the emotional appeals of the preacher.

Nathan Bangs noted the frequent use of popular "ditties" at Methodist services. The fact that most popular hymns of the postrevolutionary generation were Henry Alline's *Hymns and Spiritual Songs* (1786) clearly illustrates the immersion of the evangelical ethos in popular values. These hymns were based upon folk songs orally transmitted for generations in Nova Scotia and New Brunswick. With their powerful voices, the handsome William Case and the six-foot former boxer Henry Ryan would collect about them a large assembly by singing down the streets of Kingston. In a similar vein, one contemporary noted how Henry Alline's sermons were "interspersed with Poetry calculated to excite and raise the Passions" in order to convey his message of "individual liberty" and hope.

One senses that the function of the evangelical preacher was not to authoritatively teach people to know God, but, through often boisterous and charismatic preaching, to inspire each individual in the audience to directly participate in their own spiritual renewal. It appears from George Ferguson's comments in 1813 concerning the Methodist Rev. T. Hamon, that the experience of religious conversion was shared equally between preacher and his audience: "His voice I think might have been heard a mile. He uncovered the depravity of the human heart and thundered the terrors of sin. . . . There was a shaking among the people." The evangelical ethos fostered ideas of equality and democracy by encouraging lay participation. In the following excerpt from William Case's 1808–1809 journal we see that the role of the preacher following his sermon was clearly subordinate to the spontaneous emotional ecstasy of the lay converted: "The people continued praising the Lord in shouts of glory until 10 o'clock at night, about seven hours without intermission, or very little." The democratic impulse—what one Methodist commentator called "popular freedom"—was championed among the first generation of itinerants. Descriptions of Methodist meetings emphasize an extremely informal manner of worship with people meeting in fields, barns, or local houses. Some were sitting, others were standing, even some were "thronging the overhanging trees." At a Methodist meeting a period of preaching and praying by the visiting preacher was followed by a much longer session of audience interlocutions and personal confessions of spiritual waywardness. One preacher recounted that his insistence upon popular participation eventually involved the whole assembly in a long evening of earnest debate.

In his reminiscences, Nathan Bangs declared that he was well aware of his "deficiency in qualifications" when he chose to become a Methodist preacher, but that his authority to preach had been personally received from God. The Lord wanted him to break away from the "dogmatic prejudices and ecclesiastical traditions" and to proclaim "the radical doctrines which are essential to it [Methodism]." Moreover, as a confirmed anti-Calvinist, Bangs believed that each individual was imbued by God with "personal power" in order to choose spiritual salvation. It was entirely legitimate, therefore, that Bangs described his evangelical outlook as the "new moral economy," for it represented a challenge to traditional definitions of authority. In a society in which virtue implied public outward conduct, the social fabric was defined in terms of hereditary estates, and authority devolved from the gentry through a fusion of constitutional and ecclesiastical law. The watchwords of the *ancien régime* were veneration and custom, hence the Nova Scotian Anglican minister Roger Viets' admonition in the 1790s to "guard with greatest Care against Innovations and Changes." Evangelical culture, on the other hand, was recreating a social world in which spiritual authority was vested no longer in the outward, man-made institutions of church and government, but in the inner spirituality of the individual resulting from the personal encounter between the converted and God. While Strachan stressed duty, obligation, and moral government,

all of which pertained to institutions, evangelicalism extolled liberty, freedom, and moral economy, concepts which underscored the importance of
the individual in the new social order.

Similarly, the New Light preacher Henry Alline consciously pitted his
evangelical ethos against the mores of traditional gentry society. In his treatise of 1781, *Two Mites,* Alline proclaimed the radical intent of his emotional piety and called upon his readers to break cleanly with the past by
converting to the New Lights: "Let me entreat you to divest yourselves as
much as possible of the strong Ties of Tradition. By no means embrace or
retain any Practice or Principles as Right or Scriptural, only because it was
a precedent set up by your predecessors." In stating that he was "fighting
for the new and spiritual Man," Alline meant that his religion of the heart
was redrawing the social order. Community and social harmony were to be
founded upon voluntary association between individuals who shared a
common intimacy with God. As George Rawlyk has argued, Alline combined a communitarian form of religious experience with William Law's
emphasis on the individuality of the religious experience and Wesley's
principles of freedom of will and universal salvation. Alline's was a highly
personal religion. He did not give priority to an intellectual familiarity with
Christian doctrine. Rather, he instructed his followers to feel God's grace
and to "rejoice in Jesus Christ their friend." The individual's bond with the
Highest Being was intimate and emotional in the extreme. As Joseph
Dimock, a follower of Alline, described his conversion experience in the
1780s, he "felt a weight of truths that flowed from the eternal God into my
soul, which has enabled me to communicate to others a sense of God and
eternal things." Although evangelical preachers often spoke to masses in
open fields or town squares, they just as frequently joined small groups in
private homes where the preacher could more intimately attend to the spiritual needs of particular individuals. Alline related how he often "laboured
with distressed souls" until the small hours of the morning. He described
the personal nature of his brand of revivalism: "When I take persons by the
hand and speak to them they know that I mean this, while preaching in
public may be turned on others, and I have thought that God blessed this
particular addressing of individuals more than all the preaching."

By making individual testimony, the outpouring of emotional fervour
in the form of weeping and shouting, and introspective prayer the centre-
piece of the evangelical experience, New Light, Methodist, and Baptist
preachers contributed to a redefinition of the individual as a private being.
A person's aspirations and goals were no longer prescribed by the authoritarian social codes of a remote and impersonal polity. Within the terms of
evangelical culture the men and women were free to pursue their own
goals because they were empowered by their very relationship with God. In
a society still defined by rigid social codes between masters and servants, by
shifting the notion of virtue away from the public domain to one's personal
spirituality in communion with God, evangelicalism instructed even the

humble that they had a voice in determining their own destiny. As Freeborn Garrettson pointed out: "I know the word of God is our infallible guide and by it we are to try all our dreams and feelings." If people could have direct access to God and if God's authority was the predominant voice, then the individual was persuaded to listen to their own conscience and to no longer defer to the authority of their betters. It was not surprising that those evangelicals who were viewed by society as "despised New Lights" whose names have been "cast out by men" saw in their religious experience a new found freedom of expression. Thus Edward Manning, the Nova Scotia Baptist, recorded in his journal that the act of directly experiencing God's grace allowed him for the first time to "tell his mind freely" and feel "a good Deal of freedom."

Apparently, obeying God rather than one's social superiors was a new experience for many Nova Scotians, for, as Alline stated of one of his religious revivals, "many dared not open their mouths, for it was new and strange to them and to the whole town." Methodist preachers often recognized the conjunction between civil and religious liberty, for they witnessed that as evangelicals took responsibility for their own salvation "the people appeared as just awakened from the sleep of ages." Although Alline was usually referring to religious freedom when he said that he "enjoyed great liberty in the gospel," the very act of releasing individuals from the bonds of tradition by encouraging them to speak aloud itself was meaningful. Evangelicalism was overturning accepted social authority by urging the ordinary individual to transform their society through their special relationship with God. As "'A People Highly Favoured of God' to use Henry Alline's ebullient phrase"—evangelicals were placed in an equal, if not superior, position to the educated clergy and political elite. As Alline's testimony on 12 August 1781 suggested, it was God's direct immersion in the Christian soul which gave the individual a sense of self-assertion and the right to speak aloud as one wished: "May Christians rejoice in great liberty. . . . O how my soul travailed, while speaking, when I beheld many groaning under almost insupportable burdens, and crying out for mercy. . . . O the power of the Holy Ghost that was among the people this day."

Evangelicalism eschewed involvement in political debate. During the late eighteenth and early nineteenth centuries, evangelicals rejected the contemporary relations between church and state in which the ecclesiastical body buttressed the power of the hierarchical political edifice. Others, like Henry Alline, remained neutral during the American Revolution because they objected to war and political revolt. Although professing an other-worldly faith, both Methodist and Baptist evangelicals offered a persuasive critique of established ecclesiastical and political institutions by erecting a renewed spiritual and egalitarian social order. Ordinary people naturally sought to use religion as the primary vehicle for their dissenting viewpoints because, in the world of elite political jurisdictions, their political participation was out of the question. For most people then, religion, and, more particularly, the society of evangelicalism, provided the one forum in which the opinions and aspirations of the lower orders were given free reign and the complementary causes of civil and religious freedom could be articulated. Indeed, the very act of declaring your religion to be otherworldly implied a rejection of the convention of elite political authority.

In a world which took precedence and tradition for granted, removing oneself from the civil community to a new "society" defined entirely by evangelical spirituality powerfully challenged the notion the governmental institutions were providentially ordered. Even though he had ostensibly withdrawn from gentry politics—Henry Alline's radical evangelicalism effectively relativized all civil laws and institutions in light of the evangelical experience. His tendency towards antinomianism, in which individual experience takes precedence even over scripture and the moral law, allowed inquiry into what had been viewed as incontrovertible truths.

Henry Alline was fully aware of the radical implications of his religious outlook. When in 1777 Alline's right to preach was queried by two educated Presbyterian ministers, Alline replied that his "authority was from heaven." Later he observed that, by ignoring the constituted social codes of an educated clergy, he was "breaking through all order." Others also saw the unsettling consanguinity between religious and political dissent. The British Dean of Gloucester, Josiah Tucker, drew a direct parallel between enthusiasts and republicans, describing those who resisted established political authority as "new-light men." A religion which upheld the individual's right to decide upon his or her own spiritual salvation and allowed free participation in religious rites might lead all too easily to the exercise of individual judgments in matters of civil government in a society with a close relationship between church and state. What traditionalists like Strachan and Inglis feared about evangelicals was not that they might immediately incite political revolt or mob rule, but that the democratic spiritualism of the evangelical ethos might unleash upon the embryonic society a host of newly assertive individuals. "Consenting to Redeeming Love" might divert people from the priorities of the Constitution of 1791. As Alline himself prophesied in one of his hymns:

> 'Tis not a zeal for modes and forms
> That spreads the gospel-truths abroad;
> But he whose inward mien reforms,
> And loves the saints, and loves the Lord.

From the point of view of the conservative elite, once a "feeling of endless power" was engendered in the ordinary citizen through evangelical Christian fellowship this reformed inward "mien" might lead to a thoroughgoing reformation of social values. For example, William Black wrote to John Wesley in 1783 about a Methodist revival in Liverpool, Nova Scotia. He reported that once people were "set at liberty" after "an astonishing outpouring of the spirit" the "manners of the people are entirely changed." It needs to be realized that, in the language of the late eighteenth century, "manners" was shorthand for general social conduct. The precepts of evangelicalism, and particularly the notion of popular consent, led directly to the spread of democratic values. Such values can be discerned in Henry Alline's conception of a participatory spiritual republic: "For you may remember, that it has been sufficiently proved already, that the very Nature of God, and his high Decree among all his Creatures is a Freedom of Choice, therefore GOD cannot redeem those, that will not be redeemed, or save them without their Consent." This was not John Strachan's conception of God as an arbitrary moral governor, for here God was an intimate person whose spirit, though resting in every individual, depended for its power upon the human desire for conversion.

During the period 1776 to 1815, the evangelical movement was throughout North America a prime mover in transforming traditional social relations. It overturned the culture of genteel dominance by challenging the very core of social deference: the passivity of the common people. Even when outside God's grace, the ordinary individual was deemed the direct agent of his or her own eternal destiny. In Alline's words: "that the Creature tho' fallen was not passive, but still an active being, and now acting and raging in Contrariety to God."

By becoming an integral part of the emerging culture, appealing progressively to both the lower and middle orders, as the Anglicans so grudgingly conceded, evangelicalism threatened to elevate the tenets of popular culture to the position of arbitrating the future direction of British North American society. It seemed to the colonial elite that these youthful itinerants, who were not residents of any particular parish and therefore immediately open to suspicion, were attempting to completely reverse the patriarchal social controls of the gentry. The evangelical revivals were feared by the elite not simply because they offered a critique of traditional cultural values, but because they were also very effective in forging bonds of social unity. However, their sense of community was defined by the distinction between the converted and unconverted. Moreover, it was built upon personal bonds rather than the impersonal agencies of the established church and state. It was difficult to ignore the powerful effects these often charismatic itinerants had in transforming the daily life of local parishes.

In 1807, for example, the Baptist Manning wrote to his wife that after a revival in Chester, German- and English-speaking settlers were brought together for the first time. Likewise, in his Westmoreland mission the Methodist Joshua Marsden preached to both white and black, and declared that with his 1804–5 "stir" in the St John valley "old differences in the society were composed and the contending parties reconciled." The degree of social stability wrought by evangelicalism may have been overestimated by evangelical preachers. However, as George Rawlyk has demonstrated in his account of Henry Alline's career as a New Light preacher, though religiously innovative, the evangelical ethos provided a high degree of ideological coherence. This was especially true for the disenfranchised and economically marginal converts in a new society marked by economic and social uncertainty. By visiting virtually every locality in Nova Scotia and New Brunswick, for example, Henry Alline broke down the barriers of parochialism and geographical isolation, and his mystical pietism drew together the poorer settlements in a new sense of identity which could effectively offset the ideological control of colonial office-holders in Halifax.

Evangelicalism defied the constituted social order in many ways: the camp meeting at Hay Bay allowed the classes to mix, and, in fact, it even allowed the humble folk to exhort and convert two upper class sisters who were thus brought into the world of popular religion; in Nova Scotia New Light and Baptist revivals were particularly successful in encouraging the young people and women, those particularly without power in the wider patriarchal society, to openly express their sense of spiritual rapture; and, more generally, revivalism brought people together in mass demonstrations of piety—the New Light Baptist preacher Thomas Chipman noted that "almost the whole town assembled together" and "a vast concourse of people" listened to his preaching. Anglicans were thus prompted to comment that evangelicalism encouraged the common folk to "neglect their temporal concerns," namely working for their masters. For the ordinary settler, revivals obviously provided a much needed break from the routine of work and often inspired a renewed sense of community togetherness.

John Payzant, the brother-in-law of Henry Alline, in 1807 described the sense of community fellowship and harmony engendered by an evangelical meeting: "There was no business done that week and but little victuals dressed. The people were so many for there was old and young, rich and poor, male and female, Black and White, all met together and appeared as one. At night they came into the meeting House in that manner; the meeting House echo'd with their Praises and rejoicing. So that there was no publick Singing or Prayers but the whole night was Spent in that manner. It was judged that there was above 1000 people." As Mrs Anna Jameson observed, in a society bereft of social amusement, it was no wonder that whisky and camp meetings assumed a dominant place among the common folk. The first camp meeting at Hay Bay in October 1803 enabled the farming community a release of emotional energy following the completing of the autumn harvest. Such forms of amusement or social outlet, however, were deemed to be dangerous by the local elite because they encouraged unnatural social interaction. Furthermore, they induced the lower orders to disregard their subordinate role by allowing them to establish their own rhythms of work and leisure. In 1799 the Rev. Jacob Bailey, an Anglican, accused evangelicals of inciting civil disobedience during a revival at Annapolis: "The former for several weeks before & after Easter held their Meetings four times on Sundays & had a lecture every evening, which frequently continued till 3 in the morning. During these exercises, ignorant men, women & children under twelve years of age, were employed to pray & exhort, calling aloud, Lord Jesus come down & shake these dry bones. Groanings, screamings, roarings, trembling, & faintings immediately ensue with a falling down & rolling upon the floor both sexes together."

The evangelical critique of elite ideology and traditional social codes was effected largely through the more overt demonstration of spiritual holiness in the venue of the camp meeting or meeting house. On the other hand, the degree to which the democratic underpinnings of evangelicalism challenged the established order is revealed by the frequency with which itinerant preachers were violently attacked. As has been demonstrated, episcopal leaders like John Strachan and Charles Inglis communicated in often highly coloured language their annoyance with the success of the evangelical movement in the young colony. But generally speaking they and their clergymen adhered to a policy of tolerance respecting the dissenting sects. This was not because they were unusually tolerant Christian souls, but as the ever pragmatic John Strachan put it, until Anglicanism could win the war of numbers of church adherents, the Church of England would have to bide its time and quietly endure the evangelical juggernaut. Writing in 1819 in the recently inaugurated Anglican journal *The Christian Recorder,* Strachan outlined his strategy for Anglican supremacy: "I will gradually lead my readers in favour of the Church taking care to insert nothing particularly offensive to Dissenters; as the work gains ground, we can be more explicit, but caution is necessary as the whole of the population not of our Church is ready to join against us."

At times, however, the social conflict which was obliquely expressed through the principles of evangelicalism flared into the open. Despite the establishment's policy of tolerance, the local military was often used as a policing agent of the Anglican church. Freeborn Garrettson was attacked by the militia in Loyalist-dominated Shelburne and in Halifax. In 1785 Garrettson recorded that, again in Shelburne, 400 local citizens attempted to push the house where he was preaching down the hill. Attacks against this Methodist preacher were frequent enough that he was advised to seek refuge with the local magistrate should disorder break out at one of his meetings. Henry Alline was also set upon by soldiers while travelling in Nova Scotia. Henry Ryan, the former boxer, and William Case must have come to view attacks of violence as a common occurrence, for when describing their visit to Kingston to preach, they made particular mention of the fact that there they were allowed to preach with no disturbance or interruption. Nathan Bangs best conveyed the degree to which leading citizens of many local communities readily interpreted Methodism as a form of civil disobedience: even though the local schoolteacher Bangs was well known by the other settlers in Newark, as soon as he converted to Methodism, and symbolically shed the trappings of worldliness—his hair queue and his ruffled cuffs—he was threatened with personal violence.

Local authorities also employed legal means to forestall the spread of evangelical culture. In Nova Scotia and New Brunswick especially, Baptist preachers were jailed for illegally performing marriages. One Baptist preacher continued to defy local authorities by professing his faith to a crowd gathered beneath his prison window. Although we still do not know enough about local responses to travelling Methodist and Baptist preachers, it appears that violence against them was sporadic and unorganized, in contrast to the ritual mob attacks initiated by the local gentry in England against Methodist preachers. In the newly settled colonies of British North America where the governing elite was still small and the institutions of social control underdeveloped, popular evangelicalism flourished unchecked until the arrival of a new wave of British immigration in the 1820s.

The spectacular expansion of popular evangelicalism was abruptly curtailed, especially in Upper Canada, by the War of 1812. In Queenston, the Baptist congregations were permanently dispersed, and, more importantly, the very lifeline of early Methodism was cut off when the Upper Canadian border was closed to all American denominations. The War of 1812 also served to galvanize the Upper Canadian elite around a coherent ideology which prescribed a more active defence of loyalty to the British crown. By linking antirepublicanism and anti-Americanism with the patriot defence of one's native soil in the minds of all those who fought in the militia regiments, the War of 1812 became one of the greatest stimulants for spreading what had previously been merely the ideology of a conservative elite to the wider population. By invigorating and unifying the Tory elite, the war also led to a strengthening of those government institutions which could ensure public order and social stability. Conservatism spread its tentacles well beyond local pockets of control by creating its own machinery of popular education, benevolent societies. and commercial institutions such as banks and land companies. In this way, conservatives assertively courted the popular mind of Upper Canada.

Similarly, as evangelicals in the Maritimes became more prosperous, they also tried to temper the more disorderly components of popular religion, and progressively allied themselves with the more conservative elements there. It is indeed significant that by the 1840s, the Baptists played a leading role in the formation of the Conservative party in Nova Scotia. The very constituency of evangelicalism was being challenged for the first time.

Moreover, the impetus of this anti-American campaign was sustained by the British government, which was financially instrumental in entrenching the politically conservative British Wesleyan Methodist Society in both the Maritimes and Upper Canada. As Nathan Bangs correctly recognized in a letter to his brother in 1818, the Methodist church was becoming fractured by the infiltration of Methodism by what he disparagingly termed the "British Spirit of division." Bangs personally resisted these interlopers by contributing one hundred dollars to finance Irish local preachers who would ensure the persistence of a radical spirit.

While in Europe and the United States the instruments of the *ancien régime* had been in constant retreat after the 1790s, in Canada the doctrines of traditionalism were ironically given a new lease on life after 1812. Popular evangelicalism, which had become so well integrated into the very essence of British North American life, was stifled. The sudden revival of conservatism at this particular juncture, just as the more prosperous evangelicals were pushing their faith into the political and social mainstream resulted in making the Methodists and the Baptists, both in the Maritimes and the Canadas, much more conservative denominations than they might otherwise have been. In order to escape the tincture of radicalism, Methodists, and to a lesser extent Baptist congregations, were divided. The respectable majority was all too effectively co-opted by Toryism, leaving the radical fringe at the margins of early Victorian culture.

The more radical dimensions of early evangelicalism, however, were not wholly lost, for the popular legacy survived much longer in rural communities which continued to enjoy spontaneous religious revivals well into the 1840s. Not only was there a division between the respectable and popular forms of the evangelical as British North American society became more prosperous and social divisions more dramatic, but there was an increasing gulf between the rural and urban church. Although the War of 1812 and the cult of British respectability, which occurred as early as 1800 in the Maritime colonies, compelled the expansiveness and egalitarianism of popular evangelicalism to go underground, such republican cultural ideals probably continued to nourish the social outlook of many.

As Jane Errington has argued, some of the chief vehicles for the continued transmission of American cultural values were agricultural societies whose members no doubt enthusiastically participated in the remnants of popular revivalism. Later movements of republican political dissent, such as the Rebellion of 1837 and the Clear Grit phenomenon of the 1850s, were built upon a base whose population had long experienced in both religion and economic life the democratic impulse. It is also not inconsequential that new interpretations of loyalty which argued against conformity to external institutions such as those expressed by the new Methodist leader, Egerton Ryerson, emerged from similar evangelical quarters where the individual's inner spiritual sense was given priority and viewed as the fulcrum of social change. In a larger sense the questioning of established institutions launched by the early evangelical critique was not totally sub-merged after the War of 1812 but, as many evangelicals moved into posi-tions of political power, they transformed what had been a more diffused assault upon social convention into post-1820s reform politics. There was a direct continuum, therefore, between the popular and radical evangelical-ism of Alline and Bangs and what have been conceived of as the exclusive and rarified debates over the role of church and state in the 1820s. The social conflict of an earlier generation, by presenting a clear cultural alter-native to the old hierarchical society, created the basis of ideological debate around the issues of voluntaryism in religion and education, loyalty, and ideas of reform which undergirded emerging political parties between 1820 and 1860.

CULTURE, STATE FORMATION, AND THE INVENTION OF TRADITION: Newfoundland, 1832–1855*

PHILLIP McCANN

The relationship of culture to the state or civil authority has recently begun to receive attention from historians, educationists, and anthropologists. The work of Edward Thompson on cultural forms in the preindustrial state, of Corrigan and Sayer on culture and state formation in England, of Curtis and others on education and social structure in Upper Canada, of Hobsbawm and Ranger on the invention of tradition, and of Sider on culture and class in Newfoundland[1] points the way to a widening of the concept of culture and to a more dynamic treatment of the interrelationship of culture and society. The focus has been on both the significance of popular culture and the role of the state in the creation and maintenance of cultural hegemony, but little of this research has been concerned with the culture of colonial states, or the attempts made by imperial powers to inculcate what might be termed a colonial consciousness. Newfoundland in the mid-nineteenth century provides a particularly interesting example of a colonial state in the making, both materially and culturally. Attached to the British Crown since the sixteenth century, the island had long been used merely as a stage for the west of England fishing fleets until increasing population, the expense to Britain of direct administration, and a powerful

*Reprinted with the permission of the *Journal of Canadian Studies/Revue d'études canadiennes*. I am grateful to Edena Brown for research assistance on this project.

reform movement in Newfoundland itself led to the granting of representative government on the Canadian maritime model in 1832.

The infant colony faced peculiar problems. Its economy was based on the infamous truck or credit system, in which the fishing population bartered the fish they caught for food and equipment with a small number of merchants. The latter were mainly Protestant; the fishing families were divided between Catholics from southeast Ireland and Protestants from southwest England. Newfoundland was regarded, together with New South Wales, as an "anomalous society," one which lacked a sufficient number of men of property, education and loyalty to form a viable political entity.[2] Most general histories of Newfoundland have acknowledged its peculiarities, but failed to link them with either popular or state-regulated cultural activities. In these works culture has either been ignored, or interpreted merely as the arts and leisure activities, usually in an added chapter, or virtually equated with social history.[3] The growth of political culture in the sense of the encouragement of popular cultural activities by the state, with the aim of fostering social harmony among the masses, has largely been ignored.

The work of Gerald Sider has opened a new dimension, both in the meaning of culture and in its relationship to the socioeconomic structure of Newfoundland. Sider argues that the family fishery, dominated by merchant capital, was the breeding ground for the main popular cultural activity—Christmas mumming—which became a means of re-ordering social and work relationships. But Sider's thesis does not encompass political structures and, in common with nearly all historians of Newfoundland, he pays insufficient attention to the fact that from 1832 onwards Newfoundland was not only dominated by merchant capital but was also a Protestant colony in the making, a "state" which the Colonial Office and the local elite attempted to fashion on lines acceptable to the political, social, and cultural norms of the mother country. In this operation, Protestant ideology played a greater role than in almost any other colony as a means of combatting the political militancy of the Catholic Irish, who formed half the population of the island.

The early attempts to construct a viable colonial community can best be examined between 1832, when representative government was granted, and 1855 when responsible government (with a prime minister and cabinet) was achieved. In the first years of representative government, the populace lacked a commitment to British colonial rule and the island was racked by political and sectarian antagonisms. It was when these tensions appeared to be making social and political integration impossible—particularly in the period 1837–41—that the British government intervened, not only instituting constitutional reform but also "inventing tradition" by sponsoring and encouraging organizations and rituals which attempted to inculcate imperial sentiment on the basis of a "patriotic" and nativist outlook.

The authority of ruling groups is not only maintained by economic or physical power, but is also located in cultural hegemony, "the images of power and authority," the obverse of which are "the popular mentalities of subordination."[4] The ruling elite must establish or maintain the consent of the governed to the rulers' legitimacy, exact loyalty to the nation, establish conformity with "the norms of society," and so on. The social and cultural identities of the citizens of a nation must be constructed in such a manner that the beliefs and presuppositions of the ruling elite, the strategies of authority, even the forms of economic exploitation, are accepted as normal, natural, unquestionable, and transcendant. Symbols, rituals, and traditions, usually with vague or general connotations such as patriotism, loyalty, public duty, etc., are cherished, publicized, or invented, that is, continuously generated, rather than transmitted. Support for the status quo usually has a national and patriotic rallying point around which unity can be formed. Conversely, groups or classes with separate or alternative identities are marginalized, or represented as outside the pale of "normal" society.[5]

Few societies found it more necessary to attempt to construct a unified "national" consciousness, or to denigrate those considered to be outside the mainstream, than Newfoundland after the grant of representative government. For centuries little more than a fishing station in which permanent settlement was discouraged, without constitutional traditions, an educational system or established civil institutions, Newfoundland in 1832 had a written constitution, in the shape of instructions and commission to the governor, thrust upon it. These documents, blueprints for a settlement on the Canadian maritime model, instituted a colony with an appointed council, an assembly elected on virtually adult male suffrage (without which, as Lord Aberdeen pointed out later, there would have been no constituency at all),[6] and gave wide powers to the governor. The Church of England was established as the lawful church under the aegis of the Bishop of Nova Scotia, education was to be organized according to church principles, and the obedience of the people was enjoined.[7] The instructions took no account of the fact that exactly half the population was Irish, nearly all of whom were immigrants by choice (in the period 1812–30) from Tipperary, Wexford, and Waterford, an economically dynamic region of farming and trade, centre of resurgent Catholicism and one of Daniel O'Connell's nationalist strongholds.[8]

The Roman Catholic Bishop, Michael Antony Fleming, an Irishman and follower of Daniel O'Connell, inspired by the new situation following the 1829 Catholic Emancipation Act, had broken with the policy of collaboration with the Protestant authorities pursued by his predecessors, the "gentlemen-bishops" O'Donel, Lambert, and Scallan. Moreover, he encouraged the political activities of his flock, backed radical–Liberal Catholic candidates for the new assembly, and supported the establishment of publicly funded nondenominational schools established under the Education Act of 1836.[9]

During the period 1837–41 there was, in the words of Governor Prescott, "war to the knife" between the Liberal-Catholic Assembly and the Tory-Protestant Council.[10] There were clashes over revenue bills, the supply vote, privileges, the election of officers, the administration of justice, education, and, above all, the assembly's support for roads and agriculture, which directly threatened the merchant monopoly of the fishery in the outports. Furthermore, the Assembly, after long and bitter struggles, secured the removal of Chief Justice Boulton for maladministration and briefly imprisoned Dr Edward Kielly, the district surgeon, and Assistant Judge Lilly for alleged breach of privilege, actions which infuriated the merchant class.[11] It was the actions of the Catholics at elections, however, which most alarmed the Protestant elite. As was common in Ireland, priests preached politics from the pulpit (there being no other channel of communication, asserted Fleming), political posters and petition tables were placed in the vicinity of the Catholic chapel, and marches with drums and banners were organized at election times to boost Catholic candidates and intimidate those who might vote for the Tories.[12]

The Catholic Irish, in the view of the ruling group, were outside the pale of "legitimate" political and cultural expression. Governor Cochrane was amazed at the extent to which Catholicism had penetrated the civic culture of the Irish and their "ordinary relations of life."[13] The fact that Protestant and Catholic children were being educated side by side in the board schools created in 1836 on the model of the Irish national system, and that large numbers of Protestant fishermen voted for Catholic Liberal candidates,[14] further undermined the hold of the Protestant rulers on the hearts and minds of the people. In the later 1830s and early 1840s something very like a class struggle was being waged in Newfoundland. Recent research has revealed several instances of collective action by fishermen against the merchants in Conception Bay in the 1830s, and troops were called out on more than one occasion during this period.[15] R.J. Parsons, editor of the radical-Liberal *Patriot* newspaper, declared that the intervention of the priests in politics had cut the ties between merchant and fisherman: the latter, Governor Cochrane noticed, voted against merchants despite the fact they were economically dependent on them.[16] "The politics which developed in this nascent colony," observes historian S.J.R. Noel, "reflected not only the traditional cleavages of ethnicity and religion but also the underlying potential of the people to realign their loyalties on the basis of economic class."[17] The cultural underpinning of the Catholic political offensive was provided by the Benevolent Irish Society, a charitable and educational body founded in 1806, but which had come under the influence of Fleming's supporters in 1834. The St Patrick's Day festivals held under the auspices of the society fused ethnicity and religion with a militant nationalism for all but a minority of the Newfoundland Irish.[18]

The Protestant administration could not have maintained the ideological basis for a governable state if they had allowed this situation to continue unopposed. The counteroffensive began in 1834 with an attempt to persuade Rome to discipline or remove Bishop Fleming from Newfoundland.[19] At the same time, the two Tory newspapers, the *Times* and the *Public*

Ledger, joining the "No Popery" crusade then being waged in Britain and the English-speaking world, attacked Catholicism, the Irish in general, and Bishop Fleming in particular with almost unbelievable ferocity, alleging that Catholics owed allegiance to Rome, which was directing "enfranchised papists" to sever political, cultural, and economic links with Britain and deliver Newfoundland into the hands of the Papacy.[20] The aim of isolating the Catholics and cutting the links between Catholic and Protestant fishermen was also behind an attack on the nondenominational school system. A united front of Protestants—Orthodox Anglicans, Anglican Evangelicals, Methodists, and others—attacked the concept of nondenominationalism, using every device from packing school boards to keeping children from school, from attempting to force the authorized version of the Bible as a reading book into all board schools to persuading the attorney-general to reinterpret the Education Act. This campaign succeeded in making the act inoperable in many areas for seven years.[21]

The protagonists of the Protestant crusade in Newfoundland succeeded in presenting to the Colonial Office an image of the Catholic Irish as enemies of the state. The British government, seriously alarmed at what it took to be a condition bordering on anarchy, finally took action. The constitution was suspended in 1841, and a select committee on Newfoundland set up in the same year, which took evidence in a very partisan fashion. In 1842 the Newfoundland Act passed, which modified the franchise, joined the council and assembly in an amalgamated legislature, and effectively reduced the representation of Catholic Liberals, thus satisfying the Tory Protestants who had maintained throughout the 1830s that all the ills of Newfoundland sprang from giving the franchise to "half-civilised . . . hewers of wood and drawers of water."[22] In September 1841 General Sir John Harvey had been appointed governor, charged with the task of bringing harmony to the colony and of reconstructing its political and cultural life in a manner that would prevent recurrence of the conflicts of the 1830s.

Harvey was an eminently suitable choice. A professional soldier who had won his spurs in the American War of 1812, an experienced administrator who had spent the greater part of his life attempting to keep turbulent colonies in order, Harvey had the reputation of a conciliator and peacemaker. From 1828 to 1836 he had been inspector of police for the province of Leinster, before taking up his first major colonial appointment as governor of Prince Edward Island, where he played a mediating role in a conflict of tenantry against landlordism not unlike that which he had experienced in Ireland. In 1831 he was appointed governor of New Brunswick, where he achieved a measure of harmony by conciliatory measures and the judicious distribution of patronage among the warring factions of the colony.[23]

As governor of Newfoundland, Harvey felt that he had been entrusted with "a mission . . . to unite all in one common endeavour to advance the general good."[24] He viewed the amalgamated assembly as "an experiment" designed to promote practical legislation, not party interests, a forum in which legislative harmony could promote public good. At the same time he took practical measures to consolidate his power, persuading the assembly to grant him the right of initiating money bills, and securing a balance of parties and the support of the officially appointed members by judicious promotions to the council. Abjuring force and fiat, he worked to change, supplement, or invent the outlooks and perceptions of his subjects. Shortly after his arrival he informed the colonial secretary that he had taken the first steps to unite men of all parties by inducing them to attend a meeting and send a joint address to the Queen on the birth of the Prince of Wales. In addition, he had taken the initiative in forming an agricultural society, becoming its patron and presiding at its first meeting.[25]

The establishment of an agricultural society was of great symbolic importance; Harvey persuaded both conservative merchants and Liberal Catholics to serve on its committee, thus neutralizing one of the latter's chief grievances against the mercantocracy. Harvey saw the fostering of agriculture not only in economic terms (as strengthening the fishery and thus promoting the consumption of British goods), but also as a means to the creation of a yeoman class—"brave, hardy, loyal and permanent settlers" who would form the "Constitutional Defence" of the colony. To some extent Harvey's patronage of the Society—he attended their ploughing matches and banquets—achieved its aim, insofar as the Report of 1850 asserted that merchants were no longer hostile to agriculture, but recognized its growth to be in "the best interests of the trade, and the moral and social condition of the people."[26] Despite the import of cattle and seed and an increase of the area under cultivation, farming did not prosper greatly beyond the St John's area, possibly because of the reluctance of merchants to capitalize the project beyond a certain point, but more probably because of the lack of a viable road system. Harvey had plans for an extensive network of roads to link the capital with outlying areas and open up the country to farming and settlement, but despite increased allocation of revenue and some extension of roads around St John's, the program produced limited results.[27]

The education question was settled two years after Harvey took office by dividing the grant between the Protestant and Catholic denominations, the guerilla warfare of the Protestant forces against the nondenominational system having prepared the way for a settlement on these lines. The Education Act of 1843 was piloted through the assembly by Richard Barnes, whose speech on the second reading was a masterpiece of both erudition and special pleading. A member of a long-established merchant family, a deacon of the Congregational Church, and a self-educated man,[28] Barnes employed standard Protestant arguments against the concept of nondenominational education, and the bill passed easily in a House containing a minority of Liberal Catholics. Harvey, who admired Barnes but disliked "class legislation," justified the deviation (which his predecessor Prescott thought was the purchase of public instruction at too high a price) on the grounds that a "peculiar state of society" existed in Newfoundland.[29]

The board schools were potential generators of support for the new colonial state; but the teachers were for the most part so undereducated and the buildings so poorly equipped as to make the provision of even basic education problematic.[30] The function of "colonial" education was, in any case, being undertaken by the Newfoundland School Society, an Evangelical missionary body founded by Newfoundland merchant Samuel Codner in London in 1823, and supported both morally and financially by the British government.[31] The society's ideological position was based on the theory of Christian colonialism, which underwrote imperial expansion provided it was accompanied by the spread of the (Protestant) gospel. The society's British teachers arrived in Newfoundland with the declared intention of giving Newfoundlanders "a participation in all the religious and intellectual privileges of this pre-eminently happy land, emphatically *their* Mother Country," and the society's evangelical leaders in London and its teachers in Newfoundland unremittingly promoted the ideal of the British Empire and Newfoundland's place within it. In 1851 the secretary was declaring that the society was part of a colonizing effort, the objective of which was "to transplant England's laws, England's language, England's children, England's Church from the mother country and give them room and opportunity to develop abroad."[32]

Although the Newfoundland School Society's cultural imperialism did not conflict with Harvey's general aims, he had little to do with the society, which was well established before his arrival; he preferred to work with organizations over which he could exercise some influence. His major achievement in the campaign to modify the cultural outlook of Newfoundlanders was achieved through the support he gave to the Natives' Society. This was one of a number of ethnic societies which were founded in the late 1830s and early 1840s on the model of the Benevolent Irish Society. But whereas the British and Scottish societies, established in 1837, and the St George's Society, founded four years later, were formed and run by expatriate merchants, partly as dining clubs fostering nostalgic memories of the homeland, partly as benefit societies for indigent compatriots,[33] the Natives' Society was a quasi-political organization dedicated to the formation of a Newfoundland consciousness in opposition to the immigrants from Britain.

The Natives' Society had been conceived as early as 1836 by Dr Edward Kielly, a "dissident" native Catholic, as an assertion of the rights of Newfoundlanders against the policies and practices of the Liberal Catholic politicians, all Irish immigrants, and some political dinners were organized to that end.[34] Although opposition to Liberal Catholicism was evident in its early years (and warmly reciprocated),[35] the Natives' Society rapidly established itself as a "third force" in Newfoundland political and cultural life.

Its significance was quickly recognized by Sir Richard Bonnycastle, an officer of the Royal Engineers stationed in Newfoundland and unofficial adviser to the Colonial Office, who pointed out that the natives held the balance between the "ultra Tory officials and merchants" and the "Liberal middle class and people," and yielded neither to "the absurd pre-eminence in thought, rank and puerile precedence claimed by the former, nor to the rash, ill-advised, undigested schemes of the most excited of the latter." Bonnycastle considered the society "a most useful engine, if managed by skilful hands," and he hoped it would meet with every encouragement from the government.[36]

Harvey took the advice and gave the society an unusual amount of support, attending its ball in honour of the birth of the Prince of Wales— symbolically opened by Dr Kielly dancing the quadrille with Lady Bonnycastle—and laying the foundation stone of the Natives' Hall. A procession to Government House marked the ceremony, with speeches at the site and flowery patriotic language inscribed on the stone itself.[37] But the support which Harvey gained by this action was somewhat undermined a few weeks later when appointments to the board of directors of St John's Academy, the road board, the board of control, and the street building board were announced; of thirty-seven members, only one was a native. Immediately, sections of the press and public opinion set up a clamour against Harvey, accusing him of prejudice against those born in Newfoundland. The *Patriot* and the *Newfoundlander* (both Liberal-Catholic papers edited by natives) led the fray, the former going as far as to declare that "the best system of Colonial Government is that which promotes the Native interest in lofty superiority to every other." A public meeting of protest was held and controversy continued in the press throughout the summer, Harvey's supporters ridiculing the accident of birth as fitness for office.[38] Harvey defended himself by claiming that if the aggrieved parties had communicated with him they would have received a courteous explanation; the appointments had been made by him, not by the council, and for the most part were reappointments. He was in entire ignorance of whether or not the appointees had been born on the island, he added, but his feelings were, other things being equal, to give preference to natives.[39]

Whether or not Harvey's explanation satisfied the aggrieved natives, the incident did not appear seriously to damage his prestige or his policy, and was not subsequently held against him. In fact, the episode stimulated the native cause.[40] The Natives' Society, whose leaders were drawn from what Bonnycastle called the middle class—small merchants, agents, and clerks and "a growing, most important, and rapidly-increasing number of the sons and daughters of those respectable men who have chosen Newfoundland as the country of their children"[41]—fused nativism, patriotism, and a respect for social order into a political creed. They would cooperate, asserted Dr Kielly at the first general meeting, with "the peaceable, orderly, respectable and well-disposed inhabitants of this Island in measures of general usefulness . . . to be respectful and obedient to the laws of the land, and . . . manifest on all occasions our loyalty and attachment to our most Gracious Sovereign and Constitution under which we live."[42]

The cutting edge of nativist criticism was turned not against the mercantocracy or the administration, as was Liberal policy in the 1830s, but against "strangers" who had been "sucking the vitals of the country" and holding the natives in "vassalage"[43]—rhetoric which penetrated the psyche of both Protestant and Catholic Newfoundlanders and was to be extraordinarily effective in creating a patriotic consciousness. This patriotism subjoined Newfoundland to Britain and expressed itself in adulation of Queen Victoria and the British constitution. As Richard Barnes, treasurer of the society and an underrated architect of the emerging Newfoundland state, pointed out, the island had little in the way of stirring history, great men, or culture heroes. It was inevitable, therefore, that in seeking to forge an identity the natives should look to "the beloved Sovereign of the British Dominions . . . [who] reigned not only over us but in our hearts," and conceive their role as educating the people in "a knowledge of the political gifts which they enjoy."[44]

An important role in the creation of nativist sentiment was played by ceremony and symbol; the annual dinner, with patriotic toasts, quickly became an institution.[45] In 1842, eighty members of Carbonear Natives' Society walked in procession through the town, headed by the society's flag; committee members carried staffs decorated with a bow of red ribbon, officers wore a sash, and members a red rosette on the left breast.[46] By the 1850s the other ethnic societies were adopting similar rituals, infusing their ceremonies with tributes to the Queen and the British constitution and inviting guests from brother societies. The 1850 St Andrew's banquet was held in a hall decorated with flags "emblematic of the union of England, Ireland and Scotland," and in 1852 the British Society marched through St John's behind the band of the Royal Newfoundland Companies "with colours flying."[47] It was becoming de rigueur for almost any group to show signs of patriotism; a Wesleyan Tea Meeting in November 1851 displayed the Red Cross of England, thus showing, reported the *Courier*, "the undiminished and affectionate loyalty of the Wesleyans to the House of Brunswick." Annual treats for school children, inaugurated in this period, were infused with a strong patriotic and moralistic content—gratitude to benefactors, dutiful obedience, and veneration of the sovereign.[48]

These groups and societies were, in fact, inventing tradition, promoting cultural rituals which were moulding the consciousness of Newfoundlanders. Harvey, who knew the value of official ceremony and display in attaching people to the social order, enlarged upon the tradition inaugurated by the first civil governor, Sir Thomas Cochrane, who, believing like his contemporary Louis XVIII of France that "men are governed in large part by their eyes," made pageantry, love of show, and a display of official dignity his guiding principles.[49] Harvey attempted to impress the populace with the public display (publicly reported) of civil and military power and lavish expenditure on soirées, banquets, balls, and processions, a policy which reached its apogée on the occasion of the visit of Prince Henry of the Netherlands to Newfoundland in August 1845. "Every honor and demonstration of public respect," vowed Harvey, "as well as every degree of hospitable attention in my power shall be paid and offered."[50]

"Never . . . have the deities of pleasure and festivity ruled for the time with a more undivided sway," enthused the *Newfoundlander,* "the entire population of both sexes, of all ages, grades and distinctions . . . went forth to welcome and to greet him."[51] Prince Henry was received under triumphal arches and proceeded to Government House through streets lined with green boughs, followed by the various societies marching in procession. During his stay he attended the races at Mount Pearl, made a cruise to Conception Bay (returning to a royal salute and a display of fireworks), and attended a special regatta in the harbour and the agricultural society's annual ploughing match and dinner. He was later entertained at a soirée at Government House, a dinner given by the military, and a ball at the house of Major Robe of the Royal Engineers. Only the *Patriot,* recalling the role of the House of Orange in Ireland's history, criticized the festivities.[52]

These "calculated occasions of popular patronage," in E.P. Thompson's phrase, simultaneously brought the different classes together and made manifest the distance between them; or as the *Courier* expressed it, with more percipience than it realized, these gala days allowed all classes of society, normally separated by "a visible line of distinction" to stand on "a species of equality."[53] The annual regatta held at Quidi Vidi lake, and the frequent race meetings at Mount Pearl, both organized and controlled by merchant interests, had become, by the 1840s, a permanent feature of the cultural landscape.[54]

The success of Harvey's program was due in part to the lessening of the political pressure of the 1830s: Bishop Fleming concerned himself with the building of the Catholic cathedral; the Catholic Liberals, under the new constitution, could no longer command the majority they enjoyed from 1837 to 1841; the Liberal movement was temporarily in disarray following the St John's byelection of 1840; and many of the leaders had accepted positions of emolument from the government.[55] But Harvey had helped to set in motion a desire for improvement which animated not only the middle class—small merchants, schooner owners, shopkeepers, publicans, and the upper ranks of artisans[56]—but also reached down to the common people, expressing itself not only in patriotic nativism but also in such movements as temperance and the provision of literary culture.

When the Natives' Society held their annual ball in 1844, it was organized on temperance principles. This was a significant acknowledgment of the growth of the temperance movement in the island, and a reaction against the staggering amount of alcohol consumed in Newfoundland; in 1838, 277 808 gallons of liquor of all kinds was imported for a population of 75 000.[57] Several short-lived temperance organizations had been formed in the 1830s, but the movement did not begin to flourish until the 1840s. Bishop Fleming inspired the formation of a Total Abstinence Society in 1841, which grew rapidly, attracted some Protestant support, and began to hold large public processions, replete with flags, banners with improving and patriotic motifs, ribbons, rosettes, and regalia.[58] In 1851 the Sons of Temperance, a Methodist-supported body largely patronized by "young commercial gentlemen," held what was by this time a "traditional" procession, with similar regalia and banners, which halted at Government House to give three cheers for the Queen—"a burst of loyal feeling," it was reported, "emanating from hearts devoted and true to British rule."[59]

Well aware that his support conferred "a public and official character" upon such proceedings, Harvey bestowed some attention on the temperance movement, recognizing its role in the promotion of "habits of industry and sobriety, strict integrity, and sound moral and religious principles" in the "patriotic individuals" of the colony. Temperance and nativism, he informed the Colonial Office, might seem "trivial and unimportant" in comparison with other colonies, but in view of the peculiar situation in Newfoundland and his desire to reconcile conflicting parties and creeds, reports on such subjects might have more than ordinary interest.[60] Harvey became the patron of the Church of England Total Abstinence Society, and addressed some of its meetings, linking temperance with Christian virtues, the maintenance of family life and the greatness of the British Empire. He attempted to give "a less exclusive character" to the Roman Catholic temperance procession of January 1844 by inviting Protestant congregations to join, but was too late to succeed; the procession, exhibiting "the utmost possible order and decorum," attracted nearly 8000 people.[61] As in Britain, the strategy of the Newfoundland temperance movement was "moral suasion"; social ills were explained in terms of individual moral failure, and little or no attention was paid to the environmental factors which created drunkenness; nor was any attack made on the merchants whose import of liquor created the problem.[62]

If the temperance movement, in addition to reducing the consumption of spirits, exerted a widespread influence in favour of respectable patriotism—the Catholic procession of 1843 was reported to have attracted 10 000 participants, including some Protestants[63]—the establishment of libraries and reading rooms was indicative of a zeal for "improvement" among the middle classes consonant with the mood of the times. Significantly, there were connections between opposition to drink and desire for polite literature; in 1851 commercial clerks connected with the temperance movement planned to open a temperance hotel with a reading room attached. The clerks had established a reading room in St John's as early as 1835, and provided much of the market for literary culture.[64] Their increasing numbers in the 1840s and 1850s reflected the growing centralization of commerce in St John's, described in 1845 as "an almost entirely commercial town." The logic of merchant capital decreed that the outports be restricted to fishing operations and that the capital should be the locus of commercial transactions. "That 'Paris is France'" observed Harvey, "may be applied with at least equal truth to the City and District of St John's in relation to Newfoundland."[65] Thus the clerks, educated young men sent out from England to join merchant firms, congregated in St John's; they boarded in merchants' houses but were not treated as equals, and consequently found themselves in something of a social limbo. A reading room and library, the *Patriot* thought, would provide them with suitable conversation and social recreation.[66] Under the leadership of the ubiquitous Richard Barnes, who became secretary of the institution in 1840, the library, despite some vicissitudes, grew fairly rapidly and in 1845 received a grant from the legislature. The following year the premises were consumed in the fire and the project had to be started afresh. By 1852, no fewer than 6201 books were being borrowed annually, or 33 volumes to each shareholder and subscriber.[67]

Sir John Harvey, ever solicitous to stimulate cultural activities, persuaded some "leading characters" to give donations to the library, but by and large the elite did nothing to help the movement. It tended to foster literary culture of a "useful" or "improving" kind and to exclude publications having an "improper or immoral tendency." This policy, it was hoped, would form a "correct bias" in the minds of young people "destined to fill important positions in society."[68] Similar considerations inspired the formation of a Mechanics' Institute in 1849, the sponsors of which hoped, by reducing fees, to attract members lower down the social scale; like similar institutions in Britain and the United States, however, the institute was largely attended by the clerk and shopkeeper class. Two years later the library and institute joined forces to promote the formation of the St John's Athenaeum, but the institution did not come into being until 1861.[69]

These institutions attempted to influence the minds of young adults in the direction of sentiments favourable to the status quo, to imbue them with the idea that knowledge was primarily useful as a means of personal advancement up the social commercial ladder, and to avoid any genuine debate upon controversial topics. The rules of the proposed literary and scientific institution in 1840 excluded religion and politics as the subjects of lectures, essays, or discussion. Similar statements informed the outlook of the Debating and Elocution Society, founded in 1838 and again patronized by merchants' clerks.[70] This society remained in being until 1846, when it succumbed to the great fire of that summer which destroyed three-quarters of St John's and seriously dislocated its commercial and cultural life. However, sociocultural activities resumed when St John's was rebuilt, and exerted an increasing influence on popular mentalities. If Newfoundland, by the time of the achievement of responsible government in 1855, had not become "the brightest gem in the British colonial diadem," as Sir

John Harvey had hoped,[71] it was certainly some way from the strife-torn colony which had alarmed the local administration and the British government in the later 1830s.

Harvey wished to claim much of the credit for himself; many of his later addresses to the assembly and despatches to the Colonial Office were filled with self-justifying accounts of the success of his policies of development and conciliation. The construction of roads, the increase of educational facilities, the extension of agriculture, and improved provision for the poor he ascribed to the beneficial working of the "experimental constitution," in whose formation he himself had played a part.[72] He viewed the amalgamated assembly as a well-contrived political machine for raising and appropriating revenue for general improvement. More importantly, he believed that his policy had contributed to the happiness, sobriety, and loyalty of the people and to the amicable relationship between the denominations, which he felt was exemplified in the laudatory address to which all members of the assembly contributed on his departure in August 1846.[73]

Although Harvey undoubtedly had extended benevolent guidance and support, it is evident that large sections of the population were eager to participate in the ritual activities associated with the growth of patriotism, nativism, and various forms of self-improvement. As meetings, processions, celebrations, and festivities became regular or annual events, a sense of stability and continuity was added to the flux of everyday life, and the mystique with which these activities were imbued exerted a powerful attraction on a people seeking a "national" identity within the British imperial orbit. Patriotic Anglophile attitudes were perhaps most easily and securely established. The loyalty of Newfoundland to the Crown was attested in the House of Commons in 1855,[74] and the Crimean War brought an outburst of patriotic fervour hardly matched in Britain. At the beginning of 1855 a Patriotic Fund was established to raise money for the relief of widows and orphans of soldiers who had died in battle. By June subscriptions had totalled £2,118 and collections had been made in at least ten communities. It would appear that the campaign was spearheaded by substantial citizens of the Protestant faith, for few Irish names appeared in the subscription lists and no purely Irish areas sponsored a collection.[75] In St John's a public meeting of citizens was held in January to express sympathy with "our brave troops in the Crimea"; the governor was in the chair and the band of the Royal Newfoundland Companies opened the proceedings with the national anthem. Again, the sponsors of the meeting were nearly all Protestant, and the resolutions identified Newfoundland with the Queen and the English nation: the people of the colony had "the unanimous sentiments of British subjects" as to the justness of the war, felt proud that they were "fellow subjects of Queen Victoria," and like British subjects everywhere sympathized with the death of "our countrymen" in battle. Later in the year, when Sebastopol fell to the allies, another public meeting was held; on this occasion the main speakers were Ambrose Shea, Lawrence

O'Brien, and John Kent, all leading Liberal-Catholic politicians. They composed an address to Queen Victoria on behalf of Her Majesty's loyal subjects resident in St Johns, Newfoundland, and deeply interested in the glory of their country.[76]

Newfoundland was about to enter upon responsible government as a state in which loyalty to the concept of empire had been achieved, particularly among the directing classes. Paradoxically, this consciousness of being British subjects resident in a colony co-existed with a strong nativist feeling. This was dramatically demonstrated in 1857, when all parties and faiths, in a great outburst of national fervour, united in successful opposition to the British government's grant of additional fishing rights to the French on the west coast of the island. Though the British and French—to whose leaders toasts had been drunk at public dinners at the height of the war fever two years earlier[77]—were temporarily the objects of protest, little permanent damage was done to British-Newfoundland relations; but Newfoundland's sense of nationhood was greatly enhanced.

Beneath the surface, however, antagonisms of class and denomination still smouldered. Harvey had perceived that though politicians might co-operate in the assembly, the population was still divided into virtually two classes, the merchants and the fishermen, whose interests conflicted and who were far from entertaining cordial feelings toward each other.[78] The achievement of responsible government in 1855, which was largely the result of a ten-year campaign led by Liberal Catholics, was excoriated by Tory Protestants as the triumph of the "Catholic minority" over "Protestant interests."[79] Religious and political divisions came to the surface in 1861, when a large and angry crowd of Liberal and Catholic supporters demonstrated outside the legislative building against the governor's dismissal of the Liberal ministry and the allegedly fraudulent Conservative election victory which followed. Troops were called out, the crowd was fired upon and a number of demonstrators were killed or wounded. This was a turning point in Newfoundland's political history, for it forced the Conservative forces to realize that they could either continue to govern by force—the "Irish solution"—or could choose a more conciliatory path, in effect a return to the mode of administration adumbrated by Harvey. The conservative administrative elite felt that the latter course was in their best interests and began to extend the patronage system and to "share the spoils"—to allocate all offices of emolument and honour throughout society on a basis roughly equal to the strength of the main denominations.[80] This strategy was formally introduced into political life in 1865 when two leading Catholic Liberals, John Kent and Ambrose Shea, were invited to take office in a Conservative administration. This marked the beginning of the end of the identification of Catholicism with Liberalism and Protestantism with Conservatism and the conflicts which flowed from it.

The years 1832 to 1855 were undoubtedly the crucial period in the formation of the state in Newfoundland. What emerged in the second half of the nineteenth century was basically a Protestant state, based largely on Protestant merchant capital and owing allegiance to a Protestant mother country. But it was also a state which was very different from that envisaged in the instructions given to Governor Cochrane in 1832. The directing classes had not only successfully encouraged the growth of a patriotic nativism but, in coming to terms with religious militancy (particularly that of the Catholic Irish) by the institutionalization of denominationalism, had also removed the underlying causes of religious conflict. The intertwining of concepts of patriotic nativism and denominational allegiance in the consciousness of the vast majority of Newfoundlanders underlay the strength of the island's social fabric in the latter part of the nineteenth century, and after. The activities which support this outlook soon became bathed in the rosy glow of tradition, but their roots lay in Harvey's "cultural revolution" of 1841 to 1846. Much of what today is regarded as immemorial Newfoundland tradition, enshrined in institutions, rituals, and attitudes, can be dated to the period under review.

• Notes

[1] E.P. Thompson, "Patrician Society, Plebeian Culture," *Journal of Social History* 7, 4 (1974): 382–405; P. Corrigan and D. Sayer, *The Great Arch: English State Formation as Cultural Revolution* (London: Basil Blackwell, 1985); B. Curtis, "Preconditions of the Canadian State: Educational Reform and the Construction of a Public in Upper Canada, 1837–1846," *Studies in Political Economy* 10 (1983); P. Corrigan, B. Curtis, and R. Lanning, "The Political Space of Schooling" in *The Political Economy of Canadian Schooling*, ed. T. Wotherspoon (Toronto: Methuen, 1987); G.M. Sider, *Culture and Class in Anthropology and History: A Newfoundland Illustration* (Cambridge: Cambridge University Press, 1986); E. Hobsbawm and T. Ranger, *The Invention of Tradition* (Cambridge: Cambridge University Press, 1983). See also R. Samuel and G.S. Jones, eds., *Culture, Ideology and Politics* (London: Routledge and Kegan Paul, 1982).

[2] J.M. Ward, *Colonial Self-Government: The British Experience* (Toronto: University of Toronto Press, 1976), 124–26.

[3] See D.W. Prowse, *A History of Newfoundland* (London: Macmillan, 1895); C.R. Fay, *Life and Labour in Newfoundland* (Cambridge: W. Heffer and Sons, 1956); St John Chadwick, *Newfoundland: Island into Province* (Cambridge: Cambridge University Press, 1967); F.W. Rowe, *Education and Culture in Newfoundland* (Toronto: McGraw-Hill Ryerson, 1976); F.W. Rowe, *A History of Newfoundland and Labrador* (Toronto: McGraw-Hill Ryerson, 1980); P. O'Neill, *The Story of St. John's, Newfoundland*, 2 vols. (Erin, ON: Press Porcepic, 1975–76); K. Matthews, E.R. Kearley, and P.J. Dwyer, *Our Newfoundland and Labrador Cultural Heritage* (Scarborough, ON: Prentice-Hall, 1984).

[4] Thompson, "Patrician Society, Plebeian Culture," 387.

[5] See Corrigan and Sayer, *The Great Arch*, 1–13, 182–208; Hobsbawm and Ranger, *Invention of Tradition*, 1–14, 263–307.

[6] Parliamentary *Debates*, 3rd ser., vol. 47, 26 April 1839, 554.

[7] "Instructions to Our trusty and well-beloved Sir Thomas Cochrane,

Knight, Our Governor and Commander-in-Chief of our Island of Newfoundland (July 28, 1832)" in *The Consolidated Statutes of Newfoundland, Third Series: 1916*, vol. 1, appendix (St John's, 1919); "Commission Appointing Captain Sir Thomas John Cochrane, Knight, Governor of the Colony of Newfoundland . . . " (2 March 1832).

8 Calculated from appendix E, table 2, in *The Political History of Newfoundland 1832–1864*, ed. Gertrude Gunn (Toronto: University of Toronto Press, 1966), 206; K. Whelan, "The Irish Contribution to Newfoundland Catholicism" and "Catholicism: The Irish Experience 1750–1900" (papers read at a conference of the Newfoundland Irish Society, St John's, 19–21 March 1984).

9 See C.J. Byrne, *Gentlemen-Bishops and Faction Fighters* (St John's: Jesperson Press, 1984). For Fleming's political activities, see P. McCann, "Bishop Fleming and the Politicisation of the Irish Roman Catholics in Newfoundland 1830–1850" in *Religion and Identity: The Experience of Irish and Scottish Catholics in Atlantic Canada*, ed. T. Murphy and C.J. Byrne (St John's: Jesperson Press, 1987).

10 Colonial Office (hereafter CO) 194/111, T. Prescott to Lord John Russell, 9 June 1841.

11 Gunn, *Political History of Newfoundland*, 33 ff.

12 CO 194/99, Prescott to Lord Glenelg, 14 Oct. 1837, encl. "Statement of Dr. Fleming . . . " (n.d.); McCann, "Bishop Fleming"; see also K. Whelan, "A Geography of Society and Culture in Ireland since 1800" (PhD thesis, National University of Ireland, 1981), 13–14.

13 CO 194/88, T. Cochrane to Lord Stanley, 2 Aug. 1834.

14 For the Irish National System, see D.H. Akenson, *The Irish Education Experiment* (London: Routledge and Kegan Paul, 1970), 120–21, 159–60, 392–402. It was estimated that 77 per-

cent of the electors in Conception Bay in 1836 voted Liberal, though only 43 percent were Catholic. (Calculated from statistics in *Patriot* [St John's], 15 Oct. 1836.)

15 Linda Little, "Plebeian Collective Action in Harbour Grace and Carbonear, Newfoundland, 1830–1840" (MA thesis, Memorial University of Newfoundland, 1984); Gunn, *Political History of Newfoundland*, 33–73, passim.

16 *Patriot*, 2 May, 6 June 1840; Select Committee Appointed to Inquire into the State of the Colony of Newfoundland (1841), 20.

17 S.J.R. Noel, *Politics in Newfoundland* (Toronto: University of Toronto Press, 1971), 5.

18 *Centenary Volume: Benevolent Irish Society of St. John's, Newfoundland 1806–1906* (St John's, 1906), 82–83; *Newfoundlander* (St John's), 28 Feb. 1833; 27 Feb. 1834; *Patriot*, 29 March 1836.

19 See Gunn, *Political History of Newfoundland*, 27–29. Four attempts were made between 1834 and 1841.

20 E.R. Norman, *Anti-Catholicism in Victorian England* (New York: Barnes and Noble, 1968), 13–21; G.F.A. Best, "Popular Protestantism in Victorian Britain" in *Ideas and Institutions of Victorian Britain*, ed. R. Robson (New York: Barnes and Noble, 1967), 115–42; R.A. Billington, *The Protestant Crusade 1800–1860* (Chicago: Quadrangle Books, 1964); N.G. Smith, "Religious Tensions in Pre-Confederation Politics," *Canadian Journal of Theology* 9, 4 (1963); *Times* (St John's), *Public Ledger* (St John's), Aug. 1838–May 1839, passim.

21 P. McCann, "The Origins of Denominational Education in Newfoundland: 'No Popery' and the Education Acts, 1836–1843" in *Studies in the History of Education in Newfoundland 1800–1855*, ed. P. McCann (forthcoming).

22 Gunn, *Political History of Newfoundland*, 77–88; *Public Ledger*, 6 May 1836. See also *Public Ledger*, 8 Jan. 1839.

23 *Dictionary of Canadian Biography*, vol. 8, *1851–1860* (Toronto: University of Toronto Press, 1985), 374–84.

24 *Times*, 22 Sept. 1841.

25 CO 194/116, Harvey to Stanley, 16 Jan., 22 May 1843; *Royal Gazette* (St John's), 27 Jan. 1843; CO 194/112, Harvey to Stanley, 21 Dec. 1841.

26 *Public Ledger*, 14 Jan. 1842, 18 Oct. 1844, 18 Jan. 1850.

27 *Morning Post* (St John's), 20 Jan. 1853; C.E. Hillier, "The Problems of Newfoundland from Discovery to the Legislative Sessions of 1847" (MA thesis, Acadia University, 1963), 174, 181–86, 190; P. Tocque, *Newfoundland As It Was, and As It Is In 1877* (Toronto, 1879), 434–35.

28 *Public Ledger*, 17 March 1843; *Morning Courier* (St John's), 5 Sept. 1846.

29 CO 194/117, Harvey to Stanley, 25 May and 30 Nov. 1843; *A Sketch of the State of Affairs in Newfoundland: By a Late Resident of that Colony [H. Prescott]* (London, 1841), 61.

30 K.B. Hamilton (Governor) to Duke of Newcastle, cited in Colonial Church and School Society Report, 1854, 56.

31 See P. McCann, "The Newfoundland School Society 1823–1855: Missionary Enterprise or Cultural Imperialism?" in *Socialisation, Education and Imperialism*, ed. J.A. Mangan (Manchester: Manchester University Press, forthcoming).

32 Proceedings of the Society for Educating the Poor of Newfoundland 1825–26 (London, 1826), 65; *Record* (London), 15 May 1851.

33 *Times*, 22 Feb., 29 March, 3 Jan. 1838; *Public Ledger*, 28 Feb. 1837; 11 Jan. 1839; 10 Jan. 1840; 2 and 9 March, 16 April 1841; 15 and 28 Jan. 1842; 9 Jan. 1845; *Royal Gazette*, 14 Jan. 1845.

34 *Public Ledger*, 23 March, 29 April 1836; 12 Jan. 1844; *Times*, 4 May 1836.

35 *Public Ledger*, 1 Sept. 1840; *Vindicator*, 9 Oct. 1840; G. Budden, "The Role of the Newfoundland Natives' Society in the Political Crisis of 1840–42"

(Honours diss., Memorial University of Newfoundland, 1983), 15–31.

36 CO 194/113, R. Bonnycastle to J. Stephen, 14 Jan. 1841, encl. "Considerations upon the Political Position and Natural Advantages of Newfoundland, St. John's 1841."

37 *Public Ledger*, 7 Jan. 1842; 27 and 30 May 1845.

38 *Newfoundlander*, 30 June–28 July 1845, passim; *Patriot*, 2 July–6 Aug. 1845, passim; *Times*, 16 July–2 Aug. 1845, passim; *Royal Gazette*, 1–15 July 1845, passim; *Morning Courier*, 21 July–8 Aug. 1845, passim.

39 Provincial Archives of Newfoundland and Labrador, GN2/2, "Memorandum of Sir John Harvey, 19 July 1845."

40 *Newfoundlander*, 10 and 21 July 1845.

41 R.H. Bonnycastle, *Newfoundland in 1842*, vol. 2 (London: Colburn, 1842), 120–21.

42 *Patriot*, 15 Sept. 1840.

43 *Public Ledger*, 12 Jan. 1844.

44 *Newfoundlander*, 1 July 1841; *Morning Courier*, 12 July 1851.

45 See *Morning Courier*, 12 July 1851.

46 *Public Ledger*, 4 March 1842, citing *Carbonear Sentinel*, 25 Jan. 1842.

47 *Morning Courier*, 1 May, 3 Dec. 1851; *Newfoundland Express* (St John's), 4 Dec. 1851; *Morning Post*, 4 Dec. 1850; *Public Ledger*, 2 Nov. 1850.

48 *Morning Courier*, 22 Nov. 1851; *Times*, 5 July 1845, citing *Carbonear Sentinel* (n.d.); *Weekly Herald* (St John's), 2 Aug. 1846; *Morning Post*, 31 March, 20 Aug. 1853.

49 A.H. McLintock, *The Establishment of Constitutional Government in Newfoundland, 1783–1832* (London, 1841), 164.

50 CO 194/122, Harvey to Stanley, 15 July 1845.

51 *Newfoundlander*, 18 Aug. 1845.

52 *Newfoundlander*, 18 Aug., 1 Sept. 1845; *Public Ledger*, 22 Aug. 1845; *Patriot*, 20 and 27 Aug. 1845.

53 *Morning Courier*, 22 Aug. 1845.

54 O'Neill, *Story of St. John's*, vol. 1, 318–19, 338–39; *Times*, 3 Oct. 1838, 20 Aug. 1845, 14 Aug. 1843, 25 June 1845; *Newfoundlander*, 14 July, 22 Sept. 1845.

55 Gunn, *Political History of Newfoundland*, 66 ff, 89–109; Hillier, "Problems of Newfoundland," 135; Budden, "Newfoundland Natives' Society."

56 For a list of the self-styled "middle class" of St John's, see CO 194/127, LeMarchant to Grey, 24 Aug. 1847, encl. "The Memorial of Certain of the Middle Class in St. John's Sufferers by the 'Conflagration of 9 June.'"

57 *Public Ledger*, 7 Feb. 1844; Tocque, *Newfoundland As It Was*, 108.

58 See *Times*, 5 Feb. 1835, 5 Aug. 1840; *Newfoundlander*, 12 April 1838; *St. John's Total Abstinence and Benefit Society: Jubilee Volume 1858–1908* (St John's, 1908), 5–8; *Patriot*, 11 Jan. 1843; *Public Ledger*, 5 Jan. 1844.

59 *Newfoundland Express*, 13 Dec. 1851; *Banner of Temperance* 1, 16 (Aug. 1851).

60 CO 194/114, Harvey to Stanley, 14 Jan. 1842; *Public Ledger*, 27 May 1845. Harvey was speaking to the Natives' Society, CO 194/120, Harvey to Stanley, 9 Jan. 1844.

61 *Times*, 2 Aug. 1843, 21 Feb. 1844; *Public Ledger*, 7 Feb. 1844; CO 194/120, Harvey to Stanley, 9 Jan. 1844.

62 See *Banner of Temperance* 1 (Jan.–Dec. 1851). See also the standard work on the subject, B.H. Harrison, *Drink and the Victorians* (London: Faber and Faber, 1971), esp. 348–86.

63 CO 194/116, Harvey to Stanley, 7 Jan. 1843; *Patriot*, 11 Jan. 1843.

64 *Morning Courier*, 4 June, 26 July 1851; *Public Ledger*, 24 Feb. 1835; *Patriot*, 10 March 1835.

65 See S. Ryan, *Fish Out of Water: The Newfoundland Saltfish Trade 1814–1914* (St John's: Breakwater, 1986), 62; *Newfoundlander*, 18 Aug. 1845. By law, all commercial transactions had to be carried out in the capital. See S. Antler, "The Capitalist Underdevelopment of Nineteenth Century Newfoundland" in *Underdevelopment and Social Movements in Atlantic Canada*, ed. R.J. Brym and R.J. Sacouman (Toronto: New Hogtown Press, 1979), 192. CO 194/120, Harvey to Stanley, 9 Jan. 1844.

66 Tocque, *Newfoundland As It Was*, 88–89; *Patriot*, 10 March 1835.

67 *Public Ledger*, 14 Feb. 1837; 31 Jan., 7 Feb. 1840; 9 Feb. 1841; 27 June 1845; 12 March 1847; 10 Feb. 1852.

68 *Royal Gazette*, 18 Feb. 1845; *Public Ledger*, 4 Feb. 1842, citing *7th Annual Report of Reading Room and Library*; 18 Feb. 1845; 12 and 16 March 1847; *Morning Courier*, 12 Feb. 1851.

69 *Newfoundland Express*, 16 Nov., 13 and 16 Dec. 1851; 16 Oct. 1852; Louise Whiteway, "The Athenaeum Movement: St. John's Athenaeum," *Dalhousie Review* (Winter 1970–71): 542–44.

70 *Times*, 1 and 8 April 1840; 21, 23, and 24 Feb. 1841; *Newfoundlander*, 30 Jan. 1845.

71 *Banner of Temperance* 1, 16 (Aug. 1851).

72 *Royal Gazette*, 23 April 1845, 24 Jan. 1846; CO 194/122, Harvey to Stanley, 25 Oct. 1845; CO 194/125, "Papers Relating to the Proposed Changes in the Constitution of Newfoundland" (5 Aug. 1842).

73 CO 194/122, Harvey to Stanley, 23 April 1845; CO 194/125, Harvey to W.E. Gladstone, 17 Feb. 1846, 12 March and 22 May 1846; *Royal Gazette*, 28 April and 6 Aug. 1846.

74 See speech of F. Scully in a debate on the Newfoundland constitution in Parliamentary *Debates*, vol. 137, 20 March 1855, 892.

75 *Times*, 3 Jan. 1855; *Public Ledger*, 30 Jan.–6 Nov. 1855, passim; 23 Jan. 1855.

76 *Times*, 3 and 6 Jan., 6 Oct. 1855.

77 Gunn, *Political History of Newfoundland*, 143–44; *Times*, 27 Oct., 1 Dec. 1855.

78 CO 194/125, Harvey to Gladstone, 12 April 1846.

79 *Public Ledger*, 13 Feb. 1855.

80 Noel, *Politics in Newfoundland*, 23–24.

THE COLONIAL ECONOMY AND THE WORLD MARKET, 1760–1850: The Trade of the St Lawrence Valley*

FERNAND OUELLET

Historians have been conscious for some time of the problems inherent in defining the connection between the economy of the St Lawrence River valley and that of the world at large. As early as 1940, Harold Innis in his study, *The Cod Fisheries,* indirectly unveiled the trans-Atlantic dimension of the local economy. This was even though he had defined the Laurentian economy as continental, tied to the French or British empires only by the fur trade.[1] Continentalism, which according to Innis implied both marginal participation in the maritime economy and the supremacy of east-west relations, was the element distinguishing the St Lawrence valley from the Atlantic colonies. A few years after Innis, John Bartlet Brebner supported a continental vision of development that instead placed the accent on a north-south orientation of the North American economy. Yet in his 1945 book, *The North Atlantic Triangle,*[2] Brebner was not very explicit about

*From *Economy, Class, and Nation in Quebec: Interpretive Essays* (Toronto: Copp Clark Pitman, 1991). Taken originally from "Colonial Economy and International Economy: The Trade of the St Lawrence River Valley with Spain, Portugal and their Atlantic Possessions, 1760–1819," chapter 4 of *The North American Role in the Spanish Economy, 1760–1819,* ed. Jacques A. Barbier and Allan J. Kuethe (Manchester: Manchester University Press, 1984), 71–110, which was translated and edited from "Economie coloniale et économie internationale: le commerce de la vallée du Saint-Laurent avec l'Espagne, le Portugal, et leurs possessions atlantiques (1760–1850)," *Mémoires de la Société royale du Canada,* 4th series, 33 (1984): 167–204.

the degree to which the economic life of the colony was integrated into the trans-Atlantic, or international, economy.

In 1965, based on the numerous statistical series that I gathered for my *Histoire économique et sociale du Québec, 1760–1850*,[3] I analysed the context of international rivalry within which the external trade of Quebec developed, demonstrating in particular the competition for the British market between the St Lawrence valley, the United States, and northern and continental Europe. As for the more specific issue of the degree to which the Laurentian economy was either continental or international, I arrived at conclusions that remain valid in the present perspective, even though they were preliminary. Concerning the relationship between domestic and English prices, I wrote, "One could . . . maintain that, insofar as the British economy was the motor or reflection of an international conjuncture, Quebec prices reacted to the movement of the international economy."[4] Indeed, it was difficult not to see—through the twenty agricultural price series whose curves I traced—the striking similarities between the Quebec and British curves, and between these and the American and French ones.[5] But behind prices, of course, there was trade, and with that, an aggregate of commercial and financial relationships that went well beyond imperial frontiers and mercantilist norms. Thus, I had to add that,

> Sensitive from the first to the short- and long-term oscillations of the British economy, Canada came in time to react to the movement of the American economy. It is through the mediation of these two foci of activity, and more through the first than through the second, that the St Lawrence Valley was drawn into the fluctuations of the international economy.[6]

In a 1967 article, Gilles Paquet and Jean-Pierre Wallot considered the question anew, placing the emphasis of their future research project on what they termed "a global indicator of international economic activity, the number and tonnage of ships entering or leaving the port of Quebec" during these twenty years.[7] The quantitative data in their article are extremely important to their thesis—that the early nineteenth century saw an economic restructuring of the trading zone—and are equally useful as a complement to my own series, which are spread over nearly a century. Yet because their statistical series only cover two decades and are confined to urban prices, exports, and imports, they cannot shed light on the phenomenon in all of its breadth. Indeed, far from appearing at the end of the eighteenth century, as they maintain, the international character of the colonial economy of the St Lawrence valley as they define it was already evident even before 1760 and was continually reinforced thereafter.

The fishermen of metropolitan France frequented the fishing banks of Newfoundland and sent their catch to all of the West Indies, to Spain, to Portugal, and elsewhere. The merchants of Louisbourg, besides maintaining close business ties with New France, profitably traded with a zone encompassing New England and the regions just mentioned.[8] Indeed, over the years, the French fortress guarding the North Atlantic had become, to a certain degree, an economic outpost of New England. Regulations and prohibitions had little effect on the orientation of intercolonial trade, as the smuggling of furs to New England in the same period attests.

Begun in the French period, imperial and international commerce was so rooted in the economic structure of the colony that it continued even after the British took possession of the St Lawrence valley. It then spread to Spain, Portugal, and their colonies (before and after independence), to countries such as China, Russia, Sweden, and France, and particularly to the United States. Contraband was important. To measure the scale of these economic relationships accurately, however, one must concentrate on the official statistics on direct and indirect foreign trade. The term "foreign" is applied in this chapter to denote countries outside of Britain and its colonies.

• The Structure of the Colonial Economy and of its External Trade

The economic structure of the St Lawrence valley during the French period stemmed from the imperatives of the mercantilist system. The system aimed to regulate the colony's commercial relations with the metropolis, other parts of the empire, and foreign dominions. Areas of New France such as Acadia and Louisbourg, which could not readily fit into this economic order, for practical purposes divorced themselves almost completely, willingly or otherwise, from the valley.[9] Thus, the colony became a source of raw materials, primarily for the metropolis and secondarily for the French West Indies. It goes without saying that it was difficult for manufacturing to develop in a suitable fashion; attempts to stimulate the forest industry, to encourage naval construction, and to establish the St-Maurice Ironworks on a sound footing therefore had only mediocre results. Besides, as long as France could obtain its wood more cheaply in Northern Europe than in its colony, it was not prepared to use tariff advantages to expand production in that domain. External trade—mainly in furs and imported goods—played a crucial role in the life of this poor and scanty colony population despite the continental character of the economy and the prolonged dominance of an agricultural sector poorly linked to external markets.

Regardless of a softening of the mercantilist system after 1760, this economic structure remained in place until 1849, as did the doctrines that justified it. To properly situate the role of external trade as an engine for economic growth and as a base for studying the relationships that this economy could maintain with areas outside of the British empire, I prepared four statistical tables describing the incoming and outgoing high seas trade of Quebec, Montreal, Gaspé, and New Carlisle.[10] From this data, there can be no doubt that maritime trade volumes, like commerce by land with the United States, increased in a more or less continuous fashion until 1850; and that, in the long term, it grew more rapidly than the population of the St Lawrence valley, even though the latter increased by a factor of twenty-six (table 1).

Table 1:   THE POPULATION OF THE ST LAWRENCE VALLEY, 1760–1851

	Quebec	Upper Canada**	Total
1760	70 000*	—	70 000
1784	130 415*	5 000*	135 415
1825	373 199*	157 923	531 122
1832	515 528*	236 702	752 230
1851	890 261	952 004	1 842 265

*Estimate.

**Upper Canada was officially created as a separate political unit in 1791, and was reunited anew with Quebec (Lower Canada) in 1840 before becoming the Province of Ontario in 1867.

Source: Census of Canada, 1871, vol. 4; Fernand Ouellet, "L'accroissement naturel de la population catholique québécoise avant 1850: aperçus historiographiques et quantitatifs," Actualité économique 59 (1983): 402–22.

In the long term, this enormous growth in port activity coincided with technological change, which manifested itself in a rapid increase in the size of ships, alongside a much smaller increase in the number of crew members during the century. From 1760 to 1770, the mean tonnage of ships arriving at or leaving the ports of Quebec and Montreal from and to the high seas was 85 tons and the mean size of the crew was 7.8 men. From 1840 to 1850, those averages rose to 357 tons and 13.2 men. One should note, however, that during the last years of the American Revolution the situation became confused, since the number of crew temporarily doubled between 1771 and 1783, while ship size increased by only 43 percent. Half of these seamen were no doubt charged with handling the 2635 cannons that were carried on these ships from 1776 to 1782. There was no similar increase in crew during the War of 1812, perhaps because of a labour shortage. In any event, technological change was not limited to high seas ships frequenting Quebec harbour. The same phenomenon characterized construction in Quebec naval shipyards between 1788 and 1850, as the size of the ships to be sold in England and the West Indies grew in the same fashion. In 1800, these new vessels averaged 155.9 tons, and in the 1840s the mean rose to 403.3.

The gradual onset of this technological evolution[11] contrasts with another change whose character was far more brutal: the trade revolution that began around 1805 and paved the way for a shift in commercial emphasis from fur to lumber. Economic restructuring was therefore of capital importance, since the existing economic forms had developed during the seventeenth century and survived such cataclysmic events as the British Conquest of 1760 and the American Revolution. This early nineteenth-century move away from furs affected an economy dependent on two relatively separate sectors, furs and agriculture, and on three sectors of subsidiary importance: fisheries, forestry, and the St-Maurice Ironworks. At first, agriculture was limited to subsistence, but gradually—particularly during the second half of the eighteenth century—it had acquired a somewhat commercial character. From that point, the sector had played an increasingly important role in exports, alongside furs. At the start of the nineteenth century, with the decline of the fur trade and the beginning of a crisis in Lower Canadian agriculture, the province's overseas trade was transformed by the vibrantly expanding lumber industry, a situation destined to last until such time as greater quantities of grain began to arrive in Lower Canada from Upper Canada and the United States (table 2).

Table 2:   VALUE OF QUEBEC EXPORTS BY ECONOMIC SECTOR, 1770–1808 (%)

	Agriculture	Furs	Fisheries	Timber	Various	Total
1770–1772	18.2	66.8	5.1	6.5	3.4	100
1773	38.6	37.6	4.2	19.2	0.4	100
1808	12.1	9.3	?	67.1	11.5	100

Source: National Archives of Canada, MG 23, G. I, 10. Figures are approximations only.

One must add that the break with the traditional trade dominance of furs contributed to a radical alteration of the existing balance between exports and imports. As long as fur remained the principal export, ships sailing in ballast were to be found among those leaving port because only a few ships were needed to carry the precious cargo. Even though merchants preferred, for reasons of security, to distribute the furs among many ships, they did not fill the excess capacity of the outgoing fleet. In 1764, for example, furs were carried out of the Quebec port in eleven vessels when a total of thirty-two had arrived loaded from Europe.[12] It is obvious, in view of the scant quantities of wood, fish, and cereals exported during the same year, that the percentage of vessels that left port in ballast must have been considerable. With the growth in wheat exports and the moderate increase of wood and fish shipments, this situation was reversed; between 1801 and 1804, the proportion of ships arriving unloaded was between 25 and 32 percent. The spectacular rise in wood exports after 1805 decisively accentuated this disequilibrium: the proportion of ships arriving in ballast rose to between 60 and 75 percent. Massive immigration, it seems, hardly modified this state of affairs (save in 1831–1832), as is shown by the 72 percent of vessels in ballast in 1847, when 70 000 immigrants arrived in Quebec.

Since the seventeenth century, fur had been the principal export from the St Lawrence valley. The volume of exports had grown from one period to another, an increase due mostly to pelts other than those of beaver. This trade, strongly oriented towards France before 1760 and towards London thereafter, was the cause of the rapid white penetration of the continent's interior. In less than a century and a half, drawn by Indian tribes given to trading, the traders had gone as far as New Orleans in the South and the Rockies in the West. Despite constraints imposed by the government after the British Conquest, the expansionist movement towards the South West and West continued with even greater force. The Mississippi route remained attractive for some time and was the source of an important clandestine trade for many years. Relations between Montreal and the Mississippi settlements were sustained, up to a point, for four decades, even after Louisiana was ceded to Spain in 1763. The 1793 expedition from New Orleans to the upper Missouri headed by Jean-Baptiste Trudeau (a one-time student of the Seminaire de Québec), like the expedition of Jean-Baptiste Tabeau ten years later, illustrates quite well the surprising survival of this century-old contact.

The real expansion of the fur trade, however, took place towards the North West, thanks to the impetus of the North West Company. This Montreal firm, with offices in Quebec, New York, and London, did not confine its sales to the London emporium. Rather, with its own ships and American ones, it established itself in the Chinese market and busied itself after 1790 by expanding its endeavours into the American market. The labour force used to gather these furs from the Indians and transport them to Montreal was given its distinctive character by a rather small core of professional fur employees better known as *coureurs de bois*. Like most other local economic activities, however, the fur trade recruited the great majority of its work force from the peasants and their sons on a seasonal basis. Around 1790, about 3000 men, of whom 80 percent came from the countryside, were hired to transport the precious cargoes of fur.

It is obvious that until the onset of decline in this risky but lucrative trade, the idea of a Quebec or Canada that spread from Atlantic to Pacific made sense, not only to the hundreds of merchants, *voyageurs,* and *coureurs de bois* who were used to the business, but also to an important proportion of the population, drawn into the trade directly or indirectly on a seasonal basis. The decline of this heretofore always dominant trade dates from the start of the nineteenth century. Internal rivalry and external competition, increased transportation costs, inflation, and high wages account for the final bankruptcy of the North West Company in 1821. Its demise redounded to the profit of the English-owned Hudson's Bay Company and to that of its American rivals led by Jacob Astor, who founded many companies. Without the trade centred in Montreal, the lowlands of the St Lawrence became isolated from the vast western spaces.

Side by side with the commercial activity of the fur trade, the agricultural sector involved the immense majority of the population as producers or consumers. Indeed, land was available in the St Lawrence valley in great abundance for over two centuries and most people had access to landed property. At first, agriculture developed in such a way as to satisfy the food needs of the local population exclusively, which is why growing wheat became so fundamental an activity. To truly understand the role of wheat, however, one must realize that it was also the most likely agricultural commodity to find a ready market outside the colony eventually. The restricted needs of the fur trade for agricultural products and the small size of the cities prevented them from effectively propelling commercial agriculture internally. During the 1730s, a modest flow of flour exports to Île Royale and the West Indies developed but it was quickly interrupted. Nonetheless, in 1740, some 50 000 *minots* were sent abroad.

Commercialization began again after 1760, and became quite vigorous at the start of the 1770s. Parenthetically, although exports receded after 1774, the commercial character of agriculture did not diminish as a result, for during the American Revolution the presence of British and foreign troops in the colony caused the local market to reach unheard-of proportions. After several critical years following 1779, a recovery in export levels began as the British market welcomed some colonial products. The overseas sale of Lower Canadian wheat increased from 1785 to peak levels in 1802. Then it diminished continuously until 1831, after which point Lower Canadian wheat production became largely insufficient even for colonial needs.[13]

The overseas sale of wheat harvested in Lower Canada declined because a series of circumstances caused local production costs to rise and consequently encouraged bringing wheat and flour from Upper Canada and the United States into the province for re-export. In those regions, production costs were sufficiently low to compensate for high transportation expenses from the interior, via the St Lawrence, towards Quebec. These regular shipments of alien wheat began in 1793, and after 1800, meat and dairy products arrived from the United States and Upper Canada at St-Jean-sur-Richelieu, Côteau-du-Lac, and later by the Lachine and Rideau canals. The few available statistics that refer to wheat and the other commodities imported at Côteau-du-Lac for the years before 1817 indicate a progressive acceleration in purchases from the start of the nineteenth century. These were not the only Canadian purchases of United States' agricultural products. As the New England countryside had already been transformed by cattle breeding, the massive importation of foodstuffs through the port of St-Jean included very little wheat but large quantities of meat, dairy products, and even cod. The same types of imports, although in reduced quantities, entered through Ste-Marie-de-Beauce and Stanstead (Lower Canada). Lastly, from 1832 onwards, substantial imports of wheat arrived from Upper Canada via the Rideau Canal. The relocation of grain growing—towards the West—imposed such changes as canalization of the river and the development of banking institutions, and favoured the growth of Montreal.

Among the subsidiary economic sectors, one finds first of all the St-Maurice Ironworks, which passed into the hands of the state after the bankruptcy of F.-E. Cugnet. During the British regime, the government farmed out this industrial establishment, which produced for the local market and had a modest exportable surplus.[14] Although its existence was brought into question by the defenders of agriculture because it limited the use of land to charcoal production, the Ironworks continued to operate with a certain degree of success until 1850. By then, however, it was no more than a marginal operation. Like the fur trade and fisheries, the industry used a seasonal work force for some of its operations.

Likewise, the fisheries had been a sector of subsidiary importance in an economy oriented towards overseas trade. In the French period, global rivals such as New England were involved in a constant struggle over the international fisheries. As far as the French were concerned, the fisheries had been controlled by metropolitan fishermen and by those of Louisbourg.[15] The merchants and fishermen of Quebec had played a rather restricted role in this rivalry. Their share of the considerable French stake had been more or less limited to supplying the local market and obtaining a somewhat mediocre opening into the West Indian zones. There is no doubt that after 1760, Quebec exports of cod, salmon, and fish oil increased substantially, as the annual figures demonstrate. Moreover, certain ports, such as Gaspé and later New Carlisle, became active during the second half of the eighteenth century. By 1820, exports from the port of Quebec represented no more than one-quarter of total cod shipments from these three ports. It has been reported that around 2000 men from Quebec's rural seigneuries found seasonal work in the fisheries at the start of the nineteenth century. After the independence of the United States and until 1850, local fishermen increasingly objected to Americans trespassing on their fishing grounds. There is no doubt that the province's export volume rose until 1820 but one must note that from the start of the nineteenth century, Lower Canada also imported substantial quantities of cod every year from the United States via the port of St-Jean-sur-Richelieu.

In view of international rivalries, the forest industries did not stand much chance of occupying the first rank among Lower Canadian economic activities during the French period, or even in the last half of the eighteenth century. Neither England nor France was willing to use anything but North European wood, which was cheaper than the colonial product. It is obvious that higher transportation costs on the American side of the Atlantic weighed a great deal in the price disparities that dictated the metropolitan choice. Thus in the eighteenth century, the timber trade kept its status as a minor economic activity, despite a degree of expansion produced by colonial demographic growth and by the appearance of new foreign marketing possibilities in the West Indies and England. The few tariff advantages conceded by Great Britain no doubt explain the modest progress of the industry. It is only with the continental blockade, however, when its traditional sources of supply were menaced, that England took the decision to stimulate the exploitation of forest resources in its North American colonies, particularly in New Brunswick and Lower Canada, through a tariff that could adapt to the economic circumstances. Within a few years after 1806, the wood trade became the principal cause of the growth in Lower Canada's maritime activity and foreign trade. One should not believe, of course, that it had been enough for Great Britain to establish tariff protection, to suddenly launch an economic revolution in the St Lawrence valley. For many years, considerable quantities of potash and wood imports from the United States, via the port of St-Jean, were required in order to sustain this overseas trade.[16] Similarly, a stream of forestry imports from Upper Canada developed after 1806, intended for re-export, which furthered the swift implantation of this industry in the St Lawrence valley. The decline in prices after 1815 contributed greatly to the effectiveness of the protectionist, differential tariffs, whose levels scarcely fell before 1840.

Lastly, it is important to point out that forest resources could not be exploited on a large scale without a considerable reservoir of cheap seasonal labour and an adequate core of professional woodsmen. The overpopulation of the Lower Canadian seigneurial countryside, the province's agricultural problems, and massive immigration from the British Isles hastened the growth of the industry. The abundance and great variety of local labour, from peasants and their sons to rural day labourers and immigrants in search of work and land, certainly aided a rapid diversification of forestry activities.

As demand grew in Great Britain, generated by the needs of the English navy, it was to be expected that the production of squared timber, principally concentrated in the Ottawa valley and the Quebec region, would enjoy the highest priority. Naturally, it played a role in the development of naval construction in the area around Quebec City. The lumber industry for both the domestic and the overseas market matured under the cover of protection granted to squared-timber production. Further, as there was a strong demand for barrels in the West Indies and England, the production of staves, hoops, and other barrel parts became an activity of considerable proportion, one which was more decentralized geographically than other types of forestry enterprises. Lastly, the production of potash in zones where the ground was being cleared for agriculture was a very profitable enterprise. Montreal had been the principal beneficiary of the fur trade but the Ottawa valley, and Quebec City to an even greater extent, owed their growth to the new circumstances in the forest industry. Montreal, on the other hand, was to depend upon the trade in agricultural products with the United States and Upper Canada, and in this fashion become the true metropolis of the St Lawrence valley.

Thus the structure of the economy, while remaining oriented towards overseas trade, was substantially transformed at the start of the nineteenth century. From being dominated by the fur trade and valley agriculture, the economy became centred on lumbering and on agriculture carried out in the vaster spaces of Upper Canada and adjacent American states even further removed from external markets. All of this implied the establishment of banks, and construction of roads, canals, and eventually, railroads.

The relationship between forestry and agriculture, however, was far more intimate than that which had existed between the fur trade and agriculture. Indeed, lumber companies could not carry on their activities without abundant supplies of agricultural products to feed the workers and horses. Again compared to the fur trade, forest industries required more capital, more credit, and some improvement in river routes.

After 1800, the industrial sector continued to develop very slowly. Leaving aside the St-Maurice Ironworks and naval construction, only distilleries showed any substantial growth, first in Upper Canada and after 1830 in Lower Canada. Textile manufacturing began only around 1840. This situation contributed to the growth of the import sector. During the entire period from 1760 to 1850, the St Lawrence valley brought in various products from outside the region: wines, spirits, tea, coffee, molasses, sugar, tobacco, salt, hardware, linens, and other textiles. One should not forget, however, that as long as the fur trade survived, a certain proportion of the imported products were exchanged with Indians for furs, and could therefore be considered as investments. Thus, in 1777, 26 percent of the imported rum and 4 percent of the wine were sent to the West. In that year, the traders' canoes also carried 2580 guns, 122 010 pounds of powder, and 186 631 bullets.[17]

What can one conclude from the above figures and analysis, if not that overseas trade became increasingly important for the local economy as a whole? To go further down this path, however, one must obtain a clearer idea of Lower Canada's trading partners.

• The Overseas Trading Partners of the St Lawrence Valley

The colony's import trade, which had reached considerable proportions by the end of the period, comprised a vast gamut of products from countries that differed greatly in climate and production. In itself, this impelled a degree of diversification in trading partners. Likewise, the range of exported products was sufficiently broad to allow one to suppose that they were not all destined for a single market. Lastly, it is obvious that incoming and outgoing trade are never completely independent of one another. In consequence, the profitability of carrying cargo in both directions may have influenced the choice of a ship's destination. One can therefore posit that there existed a rather complex and unexpected movement of goods, shaped additionally by the trade policies of the metropolis and by imperial and colonial market conditions. At this level of analysis, of course, one must begin by establishing the frequency of Lower Canada's contacts with its various overseas trading partners and then evaluate the volume of trade with each partner. In order to assess how the trade structure worked even in specific cases, I have focussed attention on the province's relations with the Spanish and Portuguese world.

From the statistics that result,[18] one could conclude that the overseas trade of the St Lawrence valley took place within an imperial context even for imports, and that its direct exchange with ports outside the empire was strictly marginal. This conclusion seems all the more plausible as, over the course of the century covered, the metropolis's share of the trade increased continuously even as that of the West Indies declined. Further, if one eliminates the trade with the Thirteen Colonies before 1777 from the figures for all the British colonies (see table 3), one can conclude that trade with the Maritime provinces remained marginal and stagnant until just before 1850. The impression is even clearer when one considers that the movement and size of ships in the Atlantic varied greatly from one route to the other.

It is obvious that the technological change mentioned earlier did not touch all oceanic routes equally and that the trade with the West Indies was carried on by ships of relatively small size during the entire period. This means that Great Britain's domination of the import trade of the St Lawrence valley was even more marked than is indicated in tables 3 and 4. Under such circumstances, one is entitled to ask where the international character of Lower Canada's commerce could truly be found, as it seems to have been colonial and imperial.

The growing supremacy of Great Britain as a channel and source of imports for the St Lawrence valley is even more striking if one calculates it in terms of import values. These certainly passed the 70 percent mark after 1760, while in 1833–50, the value of goods arriving from Great Britain represented 93 percent of the worth of seaborne imports.[19] The growth of metropolitan participation in the trade, although continuous since 1760, seems to have been accentuated at the start of the nineteenth century by the expansion of the lumber industry, which lowered the freight costs of imports. This development is somewhat surprising, of course, as the proportion of colonial and foreign goods within all seaborne imports increased from 19.7 percent of the value in 1799–1809 to 26.1 percent in 1810–19.[20] This means that, in fact, Great Britain was becoming more and more a simple intermediary, channelling non-English products towards the St Lawrence valley.

There therefore existed two principal ways by which the valley of the St Lawrence maintained economic contacts with the world overseas: a direct and official trade; and an indirect one, via the metropolis as intermediary and under cover of the Navigation Acts, or via the mediation of some other parts of the empire, whether the West Indies, Gibraltar, Jersey, or other British colonies. Parenthetically, of course, neither method excluded

Table 3:   SHIP ARRIVALS FROM THE HIGH SEAS AT QUEBEC AND MONTREAL
           BY PORTS OF ORIGIN, 1768–1851

	Great Britain	British Colonies	West Indies	United States	Other Foreign Ports	Total*
Number of Ships (%)						
1768–1777	44.5	41.3	14.2			100
1778–1783	66.3	14.4	19.3			100
1800–1814			7.7			100
1828–1832	77.2	12.4	7.5	1.1	1.8	100
1835–1836	77.8	13.8	2.7	3.0	2.7	100
1841–1842	74.0	13.7	1.4	4.1	6.8	100
1848–1851	63.9	17.1		12.4	6.6	100
Mean Tonnage of Ships						
1768–1777	133.3	59.1	83.5			95.6
1778–1783	164.3	86.4	108.7			142.4
1800–1814			136.1			187.9
1828–1832	304.0	116.4	118.8	243.9	232.4	264.9
1835–1836	318.6	111.9	147.8	353.0	262.4	285.1
1841–1842	366.6	164.9	201.3	497.0	273.8	335.7
1848–1851	423.6	105.6		469.4	268.6	364.7
Proportion of Tonnage of Ships (%)						
1768–1777	62.1	25.5	12.4			100
1778–1783	76.6	8.7	14.7			100
1800–1814			5.6			100
1828–1832	88.6	5.5	3.3	1.0	1.6	100
1835–1836	86.9	5.4	1.4	3.7	2.5	100
1841–1842	80.8	6.7	0.9	6.0	5.6	100
1848–1851	74.2	4.9		16.0	4.9	100

*Due to rounding, percentages in tables may not always total 100.

Source: *Report of Canadian Archives* (hereafter *RCA*), 1888, B. 201; see also the appendixes in *Journals of the Legislative Assembly of Lower Canada* (hereafter *JLALC*) and *Journals of the Legislative Assembly of the Canadas* (hereafter *JLAC*) for the years in question.

the possibility of contraband. In order to show the essential elements of the direct trade, and to get a glimpse of the specific role of the Spanish and Luso-Brazilian world in this commerce, I have prepared a table of arrivals from overseas, except those from the British Isles and West Indies (table 4).

These direct contacts with overseas ports had existed since 1760. In 1766, for example, out of eighteen ships that left the port of Quebec, five had come from the Iberian Peninsula, three from Lisbon and two from Barcelona.[21] These first links with areas outside of the empire were never broken. Those with southern Europe took on greater importance after 1760 and were perpetuated thereafter. From 1780 to 1783, 1 163 147 gallons of brandy were imported through Quebec and 16.4 percent of the stock came directly from foreign ports.[22] At the start of the nineteenth century, this situation still prevailed. From 1 October 1800 to 5 July 1801, one hundred ships put down anchor at the port of Quebec and nineteen of them were of foreign origin.[23]

Table 4: ARRIVAL OF SHIPS FROM FOREIGN PORTS IN QUEBEC AND MONTREAL, 1828–1836

Port of Origin	1828	1829	1830	1831	1832	1835	1836
Number of Ships							
United States	11	9	12	4	16	24	50
Europe	10	0	0	0	0	0	0
China	1	0	0	1	2	0	1
Jersey*	0	1	2	1	1	1	2
Gibraltar*	0	1	8	3	6	5	1
France	0	1	6	0	2	9	24
Netherlands	0	4	4	3	3	3	4
Spain	0	2	2	2	0	1	2
Portugal	0	8	2	4	4	3	5
Sicily	0	2	2	1	1	0	0
Sweden	0	1	0	1	1	0	0
Tenerife	0	1	1	0	1	0	0
Italy	0	0	1	0	0	0	0
Canaries	0	0	1	0	0	0	0
Mauritius*	0	0	1	0	0	0	0
Azores	0	0	0	1	1	0	0
Colombia	0	0	0	2	1	0	0
Brazil	0	0	0	1	1	1	1
Madeira	0	0	0	0	1	0	0
Hamburg	0	0	0	0	0	4	4
Russia	0	0	0	0	0	0	1
Algiers	0	0	0	0	0	1	1
Bremen	0	0	0	0	0	1	0
Total	22	30	42	24	41	53	96
Tonnage							
United States	3045	1971	3224	822	5 323	6 507	19 619
Europe	1402	0	0	0	0	0	0
China	647	0	0	586	1 327	0	270
Jersey*	0	88	241	111	113	220	294
Gibraltar*	0	105	1167	431	975	583	280
France	0	471	1598	0	411	2 259	6 609
Netherlands	0	1358	859	974	718	771	1 156
Spain	0	572	331	358	0	195	204
Portugal	0	1290	202	879	694	498	1 331
Sicily	0	231	204	?	180	0	0
Sweden	0	316	0	158	155	0	0
Tenerife	0	104	?	0	106	0	0
Italy	0	0	385	0	0	0	0
Canaries	0	0	?	0	0	0	0
Mauritius*	0	0	170	0	0	0	0

Table 4 (continued)

Port of Origin	1828	1829	1830	1831	1832	1835	1836
Azores	0	0	0	?	356	0	0
Colombia	0	0	0	266	145	0	0
Brazil	0	0	0	457	289	437	86
Madeira	0	0	0	0	564	0	0
Hamburg	0	0	0	0	0	1 075	1 179
Russia	0	0	0	0	0	0	226
Algiers	0	0	0	0	0	350	385
Bremen	0	0	0	0	0	270	0
Total	5094	6506	8381	5042	11 356	13 165	31 639

*British possessions.

Source: *RCA*, 1888, B. 201; see also the appendixes in *JLALC* and *JLAC* for the years in question.

Seeing the figures for direct contacts by sea with countries beyond the boundary of the empire, one could conclude that the United States came after Great Britain, the West Indies, and the other British colonies as a commercial partner of the St Lawrence valley. Yet since 1790, trade by land between the United States and the Canadas had grown considerably. In the context of overland trade, the river port of St-Jean-sur-Richelieu played a decisive role in north-south commercial relations, particularly after 1800. During the first half of the nineteenth century, this trade was characterized by an enormous disequilibrium between imports and exports; the Canadas exported goods to the United States representing only 24 percent of what they imported from that market. In 1824–40, purchases made in the United States totalled on average 255 055 current English pounds, about 10 percent of all imports by sea via Montreal and Quebec. Although impressive, however, these figures are well below the real sums.[24] Indeed, during these years, new internal ports were created at Ste-Marie-de-Beauce and Stanstead. Around 1830, imports in these places amounted to about 15 000 current English pounds. This does not include contraband carried out in all taxable items, particularly tea, coffee, sugar, molasses, and salt.[25] At Stanstead, it was said, the value of clandestine trade equalled about two-thirds of official imports; at Ste-Marie, it was double the amount of legally imported goods; at St-Jean it was equally substantial. It is obvious that this official and unofficial trade, by land and sea, was second only to that which the St Lawrence valley maintained with Great Britain. This position was all the more deserved because the transactions involved not only consumer goods, produced locally or elsewhere, but also coin.

The exchange of hard currency also illustrates the relationship between the St Lawrence valley and the Spanish and Portuguese world. Indeed, each year, Lower Canadian banking institutions imported the equivalent of approximately 150 000 current English pounds in coin, a much larger sum than was exported. This no doubt included large sums in English money, but also involved Spanish, often Portuguese, and sometimes Mexican coin.[26] This is not surprising, as the Canadian monetary system was not unified and a great diversity of French, English, Spanish, and other coins circulated throughout the province and were to be found even in amounts left in wills. The inventories after death—even those of the French regime—attest to this and to the fact that the St Lawrence valley was somewhat attached to an economic and monetary zone which overflowed the limited context of North America and the British empire.

Lower Canada's ties to the international market resulted, in large part, from the types of products sought in the colonial milieu. Thus tea importers, who could choose between several sources of supply, had either to come to terms with the monopoly of the British East India Company or to use clandestine means. Similarly, sugar, molasses, and coffee theoretically came from the British West Indies, but the means of bringing in these products were numerous and efficacious. In fact, such goods did not necessarily arrive in Quebec from their zone of production. The rum trade responded to the same circumstances. Contemporaries, without making a point of it, were perhaps able to disentangle affairs. Today, however, how is one to distinguish between Jamaican, Leeward Island, and New England rum when the documents merely indicate that it came from England, the West Indies, or British colonies? The year 1835 provides a typical example of the plurality of routes these products took to get to the St Lawrence valley (table 5).

Table 5:   SELECTED PRODUCTS IMPORTED IN 1835 THROUGH QUEBEC AND
           MONTREAL BY PORT OF ORIGIN

	Great Britain	British Colonies	West Indies
Rum (gallons)	78 183	383 191	514 684
Molasses (gallons)	28 828	63 247	30 131
Sugar (pounds)	2 000 032	1 923 817	
Tea (pounds)	474 244	112 847	
Coffee (pounds)	1 486		2 890

Source: *JLALC*, 1835–36, appendix G.G.G.

Wine imports can also illustrate the complex networks that the colony was forced to use outside of its economic frontiers and those of the empire. The St Lawrence valley imported rum mostly for the lower classes, the *voyageurs*, their hired hands, and Native people. Wine drinkers, however, were mainly recruited among the upper classes. The breadth of demand was rather considerable. Besides the wines of Spain, France, Italy, and Portugal, consumers also had available those of Germany, Hungary, Greece, Malta, Algeria, and even of the Cape of Good Hope. Four great producing countries shared the bulk of the local market: Spain, Portugal, France, and Italy (table 6).

Table 6:   **DISTRIBUTION OF THE CANADIAN MARKET SHARE HELD BY THE PRINCIPAL WINE-SUPPLYING NATIONS, 1823-1831** *(percentage of imports)*

	Spain	Portugal	France	Italy	Total
1823	51.3	30.6	14.4	3.7	100
1827	46.4	33.8	11.0	8.8	100
1828	55.6	36.6	6.4	1.4	100
1829	43.1	42.4	8.9	5.6	100
1830	54.2	27.8	10.1	7.9	100
1831	48.9	40.1	2.8	8.2	100

Source: See the appendixes to *JLALC* for the years in question.

Because the market share of Madeira had not radically varied since 1793, one can posit that the balance among the various producing countries had been stable since at least the end of the eighteenth century, after which period we have sound data concerning the ultimate origins of imported wines. Great Britain had a decisive role as the redistribution centre for goods produced inside and outside the empire, and the St Lawrence valley's direct trade with foreign countries, save in the case of the United States, accounted for a relatively small percentage of its total exchanges. Using wine as an example, table 7 clarifies the distinction between places of production and places of immediate provenance for goods.

Table 7:   **WINES IMPORTED INTO THE ST LAWRENCE VALLEY, 1829-1831** *(percentage of imports)*

Country Imported From	Producing Country				Proportion of Total Wine Imports
	Spain	Portugal	France	Italy	
Great Britain	61.2	86.9	45.2	64.6	68.6
Ireland	5.4	1.4	2.2	2.3	3.8
British colonies	1.2	5.0	2.2	0.2	2.4
West Indies	0.0	0.3	0.0	0.0	0.1
Jersey	1.6	0.7	4.7	0.0	1.4
Gibraltar	13.4	0.3	42.7	3.1	10.4
France	0.0	0.0	3.0	0.0	0.2
Spain	3.3	0.5	0.0	0.0	2.0
Portugal	0.0	4.9	0.0	0.0	1.5
Sicily	0.0	0.0	0.0	29.8	1.9
Tenerife	13.9	0.0	0.0	0.0	7.7
Total	100.0	100.0	100.0	100.0	100.0

Source: See the appendixes to *JLALC* for the years in question.

Great Britain functioned more and more as an entrepôt for the distribution of metropolitan products and the redistribution of colonial and foreign goods throughout the empire and elsewhere. In the long term, this role no doubt facilitated the task of preparing well-balanced cargoes appropriate to each trade route. The result, however, was to concentrate in British hands the opportunity to supply the colonies with needed imports, and ultimately, to allow the United Kingdom, in practice as in theory, to take charge of the exportation of colonial products. British control of the trade of the St Lawrence valley was even more marked for exports than for imports, and the evolution of overseas trade after 1783 demonstrates this fact (table 8).

Table 8: **DEPARTURE OF SHIPS OVERSEAS FROM QUEBEC AND MONTREAL ACCORDING TO THEIR DESTINATIONS, 1768–1851** *(percentage of ships)*

	Great Britain	British Colonies	West Indies	United States	Other Foreign Ports	Total
1768–1777	29.5	36.7	33.8			100
1778–1783	43.4	38.2	18.4			100
1828–1832	82.9	11.2	5.2	0.3	0.4	100
1835–1836	81.8	15.6	2.0	0.2	0.4	100
1841–1842	86.4	11.4	1.3		0.8	100
1848–1851	75.7	18.1		5.3	0.9	100

Source: *RCA*, 1888, B. 201; see also the appendixes to *JLALC* and *JLAC* for the years in question.

In the years immediately following 1760, however, Great Britain's domination of Quebec trade was a good deal less evident for exports than for imports, to the point that one might question the validity of the documentary base. To a degree, of course, it is questionable. The pre-1784 reports on imports and exports and arrivals and departures of ships do not seem to distinguish between the immediate and final destination or provenance of ships. To make things more complicated, they include under the heading "West Indies" ships going to and from the West Indies, Southern Europe, and other foreign countries and continents. A similar question might be raised by the heading "British colonies" as the place of origin and destination of ships and goods, particularly during the period 1778 to 1783 (see table 8).

Obviously, the sudden development of commercial relations with the West Indies and the Iberian Peninsula was tied to exceptional and more or less transitory circumstances. The conflict between Great Britain and its old colonies on the Atlantic coast and the unfortunate harvests of these years in southern Europe helped to reinforce Quebec's competitive position on the external market. The substantial exports of wheat and flour to the West Indies and most particularly to Europe have to be accounted for in this fashion. (Seen in this light, the shipment of agricultural products from the port of Quebec to the Maritime provinces was a more durable phenomenon.) Once these circumstances had passed, trade between the St Lawrence valley and the West Indies became once more what it had been previously, a very modest flow, while direct trade with the Iberian Peninsula deflated to an appropriate size, becoming henceforth marginal. Table 9 is quite clear in this regard.

Table 9: PROPORTION OF WHEAT AND FLOUR EXPORTS OVERSEAS FROM QUEBEC AND MONTREAL, 1768–1842 *(percentage of wheat exported)*

	Great Britain	British Colonies	West Indies	Total
1768–1777	15.9	14.2	69.9	100
1778–1783	6.8	87.5	5.7	100
1829–1836	71.0	24.3	4.4	100
1841–1842	95.2	3.6	1.2	100

Source: *RCA*, 1888, B. 201; and see also the appendixes to *JLALC* and *JLAC* for the years in question.

For a time, therefore, there existed a demand in the West Indies for agricultural goods, forest products, and fish, which stimulated the overseas trade of the St Lawrence valley. The growth of the forest-based economies of Nova Scotia and New Brunswick, however, provided significant competition. More importantly, the vigorous resumption of New England's activities in marketing wood, ships, and agricultural products, in the fisheries, and in the Antilles, seriously reduced the importance of the advantages enjoyed by the St Lawrence valley in the West Indian market. It is on this basis that one must explain the post-1783 decline in the sale of Lower Canadian beams and planks on the West Indian market (table 10).

Table 10: PROPORTION OF DEALS AND PLANKS EXPORTED OVERSEAS FROM QUEBEC AND MONTREAL, 1768–1842

	Great Britain	British Colonies	West Indies	Total
1768–1777	61.4	8.6	30.0	100
1778–1783	29.9	8.8	61.3	100
1829–1836	99.0	0.1	0.9	100
1841–1842	99.7	0.0	0.3	100

Source: *RCA*, 1888, B. 201; and see also the appendixes to *JLALC* and *JLAC* for the years in question.

The survival of the West Indian sector of overseas trade was to depend essentially on a few products which were shipped in rather modest quantities: cod, fish oil, flour, and most particularly, wooden parts for barrels. Large exporting countries and countries producing sugar, molasses, grains, tea, coffee, rum, wine, and liqueurs needed barrel parts in great quantities. As the St Lawrence valley could produce them in abundance and, it would seem, at competitive prices, staves, hoops, and other barrel parts became, with fish and to a certain degree flour, the basic elements in the cargoes of ships sailing towards the West Indies to pick up sugar (table 11).

Table 11: **PROPORTION OF STAVE EXPORTS OVERSEAS FROM QUEBEC AND MONTREAL, 1768–1836** *(percentage of exported pieces)*

	Great Britain	British Colonies	West Indies	United Sates	Other Foreign Ports	Total
1768–1777	94.2	0.6	5.2			100
1778–1783	89.6	0.2	10.2	0.0	0.0	100
1801–1808			10.5			100
1829–1836	77.4	3.9	17.6	0.0	1.1	100

Source: *RCA,* 1888, B. 201; and see also the appendixes to *JLALC* and *JLAC* for the years in question.

It must be understood, of course, that the number of ships involved in a trade link does not constitute an adequate measure of real changes in trade volume. The substantial modification in the size of the ships used on different trade routes had a decisive impact on the amount of traffic in one direction or another. After 1783, on the British colonies' route, the average size of ships decreased to the point where it began to seem like coastal trade more than genuine oceanic navigation. On the West Indies run, on the other hand, the ships became 48 percent larger between 1768 and 1850. This growth was minimal, however, compared to that of ships going directly to Great Britain. There, ship dimensions increased by a factor of 3.5 between 1768 and 1850. The contrast between the types of ships used for imports and those used for exports was most marked in the case of American ships, illustrating rather well that the St Lawrence valley bought a great deal from the United States but sold them rather little (table 12).

Table 12: **AVERAGE TONNAGE OF SHIPS DEPARTING FOR OVERSEAS FROM QUEBEC AND MONTREAL, 1768–1851**

Destination						
	Great Britain	British Colonies	West Indies	United States	Other Foreign Ports	Overall Average
1768–1777	131.5	58.5	98.8			95.6
1778–1783	158.7	112.2	137.1			136.9
1828–1832	281.6	74.0	145.1	127.5	161.2	250.3
1835–1836	335.7	69.5	141.4	96.0	176.3	289.1
1841–1842	365.7	88.7	146.2	178.0	399.2	331.4
1848–1851	456.2	78.6		114.9	186.6	367.3

Source: *RCA,* 1888, B. 201; and see also the appendixes to *JLALC* and *JLAC* for the years in question.

From all of the above, one must conclude that mercantilism was far from having been a vain doctrine, as its objectives were achieved in both directions of colonial-metropolitan trade: the St Lawrence valley to Great Britain and vice versa. Great Britain's monopoly on oceanic traffic became so absolute, particularly with respect to exports, that the colony's commercial relations with foreign countries were at once reduced to a minimum and masked by the massive intervention of the metropolis in the trading process (table 13). Under such conditions, what became of direct trade with foreign ports in Canadian products in general, and in staves and forest products in particular? It is certain that direct foreign export trade was even more marginal than the equivalent import trade (table 14).

Table 13: **PERCENTAGE OF TONNAGE OF SHIPS DEPARTING FOR OVERSEAS FROM QUEBEC AND MONTREAL, 1768–1851**

	Destination					
	Great Britain	British Colonies	West Indies	United States	Other Foreign Ports	Total
1768–1777	41.4	22.9	35.7			100
1778–1783	50.3	31.3	18.4			100
1828–1832	93.3	3.3	3.0	0.1	0.3	100
1835–1836	95.0	3.7	0.9	0.1	0.3	100
1841–1842	95.4	3.1	0.6		0.9	100
1848–1851	94.0	3.9		1.7	0.4	100

Source: *RCA*, 1888, B. 201; and see also the appendixes to *JLALC* and *JLAC* for the years in question.

The procedure chosen to bring out the international dimension of the Laurentian economy and the relationship it maintained with Spain, Portugal, and their possessions has only allowed us to identify the nature and contours of a problem whose complexity is quite evident. The crucial role played by overseas trade in the economic development of Canada in these years is, without a doubt, an indicator of its integration into the world market, even though through the mediation of the British empire. Yet this overseas trade, in the time of New France as later, remained so characterized by trade between the colony and the metropolis that the development of direct contacts with countries outside of the empire or even with colonies within it, did not really have a fair start. This was particularly so because the mother country owned the immense majority of the ships transporting colonial exports and imports. The metropolis remained an indispensable intermediary for the St Lawrence valley. After 1840, foreign trade became an ever more important component of overseas commerce and the impact of this development was magnified by the booming inland trade with the United States. Nonetheless, the new orientations were still so timid that one cannot see in them the true reason for the fall of the old

Table 14:   DEPARTURE OF FOREIGN-BOUND SHIPS FROM QUEBEC AND MONTREAL,
1828-1836

Destination	1828	1829	1830	1831	1832	1835	1836
Number of ships							
Europe	1	0	0	0	0	0	0
United States	3	0	4	2	3	4	2
Portugal	0	1	1	1	2	6	0
Fayal	?	1	0	0	0	0	0
Cape of Good Hope*	0	1	0	0	0	0	0
Jersey*	0	0	1	3	0	0	0
Gibraltar*	0	0	2	0	0	1	0
Spain	0	0	1	1	0	0	0
France	0	0	0	0	2	0	0
Madeira	0	0	0	0	0	1	0
Brazil	0	0	0	0	0	1	0
Tonnage							
Europe	105	0	0	0	0	0	0
United States	609	0	432	158	331	397	179
Portugal	0	105	146	121	378	1160	0
Fayal	105	?	0	0	0	0	0
Cape of Good Hope*	0	170	0	0	0	0	0
Jersey*	0	0	113	352	0	0	0
Gibraltar*	0	0	226	0	0	110	0
Spain	0	0	105	53	0	0	0
France	0	0	0	0	922	0	0
Madeira	0	0	0	0	0	231	0
Brazil	0	0	0	0	0	263	0

*British possessions.

Source: See appendixes to *JLALC* for the years in question.

colonial trade system and the granting of a degree of political autonomy
for the colonies. Rather, Great Britain itself repealed the Navigation Acts
and preferential duties on the St Lawrence valley products. It seems that
Great Britain was now ready to play the role of entrepôt on a vaster stage—
that of the world as a whole—and that mercantilism could harm this
orientation.

• Notes

1 Harold A. Innis, *The Fur Trade in
Canada: An Introduction to Canadian
Economic History* (New Haven, 1930);
and *The Cod Fisheries: The History of an
International Economy* (New Haven,
1940).

2 J. Bartlet Brebner, *The North Atlantic
Triangle: The Interplay of Canada, the
United States and Great Britain* (New
Haven, 1945).

3 Fernand Ouellet, *Histoire économique et
sociale du Québec, 1760-1850*

(Montreal, 1966), translated as *Economic and Social History of Quebec, 1760–1850* (Toronto, 1980). The graphs on pp. 65–80 (English edition) are only a small part of the statistical series assembled for this work.

4 Ouellet, *Histoire économique et sociale du Québec*, 39.

5 Fernand Ouellet, Jean Hamelin, and Richard Chabot, "Les prix agricoles dans les villes et les campagnes du Québec avant 1850: aperçus quantitatifs," *Histoire sociale/Social History* (hereafter *HS/SH*) 15 (1982): 83–127.

6 Ouellet, *Histoire économique et sociale du Québec*, 28.

7 Gilles Paquet and Jean-Pierre Wallot, "Aperçus sur le commerce international et les prix domestiques dans le Bas-Canada (1793–1812)," *Revue d'histoire de l'Amérique* 21 (1967): 447–73.

8 Christopher Moore, "The Other Louisbourg: Trade and Merchant Enterprise in Île Royale, 1713–1758," *HS/SH* 12 (1979): 79–97.

9 Ouellet, "La formation d'une société dans la vallée du Saint-Laurent: d'une société sans classes à une société de classes," *Canadian Historical Review* 62, 4 (1981): 443–49, translated and reproduced as chapter 1 of *Economy, Class, and Nation in Quebec: Interpretive Essays*, ed. Fernand Ouellet (Toronto: Copp Clark Pitman, 1991), "The Formation of a New Society in the St. Lawrence Valley: From Classless Society to Class Conflict."

10 This information has been published in *The North American Role in the Spanish Imperial Economy, 1760–1819*, ed. Jacques A. Barbier and Allan J. Kuethe (Manchester, 1984), 91–99.

11 Ouellet, "Dualité économique et changement technologique dans la vallée du Saint-Laurent, 1760–1790," *HS/SH* 9, 18 (1976): 256–96, translated and reproduced as chapter 6 of *Economy, Class, and Nation in Quebec*, ed. Ouellet, "Economic Dualism and Technological Change in Quebec, 1760–1790."

12 National Archives of Canada (hereafter NAC), MG 23, G.I, 10.

13 For a summary of the controversy over agriculture, see Ouellet, "Le mythe de l'habitant sensible au marché," *Recherches sociographiques* 17 (1976): 115–32.

14 *Report of Canadian Archives* (hereafter *RCA*), 1888, B. 201.

15 C. Moore, "Merchant Trade in Louisbourg: Île Royale" (MA thesis, University of Ottawa, 1977); Jacques Mathieu, *Le commerce entre la Nouvelle-France et les Antilles au XVIIIᵉ siècle* (Quebec, 1981), 238–43.

16 See, in particular, *Journals of the Legislative Assembly of Lower Canada* (hereafter *JLALC*), 1822–1823, appendix W.

17 NAC, RG 4, B. 28, the report of the year in progress.

18 For more complete data see Fernand Ouellet, "Colonial Economy and International Economy: The Trade of the St. Lawrence River Valley with Spain, Portugal, and their Atlantic Possessions, 1760–1850," chapter 4 of *The North American Role in the Spanish Imperial Economy, 1760–1819*, ed. Jacques A. Barbier and Allan J. Kuethe (Manchester: Manchester University Press, 1984), 71–110.

19 See the appendixes to *JLALC* and *Journals of the Legislative Assembly of the Canadas* for the years in question.

20 *Imperial Blue Books*, vols. 1 and 2.

21 NAC, RG 4, B. 32.

22 *RCA*, 1888, B. 201.

23 NAC, MG 11, Q. 109.

24 See the appendixes to *JLALC* for the years in question.

25 *JLALC*, 1832–1833 and 1835–1836. See the appendixes.

26 *JLALC*, 1828–1829, appendix Aa, Hh; and 1830, appendix Q.

THE ROLE OF WOMEN IN THE ESTABLISHMENT OF SOCIAL STATUS IN EARLY UPPER CANADA*

KATHERINE M.J. McKENNA

During the Christmas social season of 1799 an event of momentous importance to the elite of Upper Canadian society took place. At one of the elegant balls so popular at the time, Mrs Elizabeth Small, wife of the clerk of the executive council, and Mrs Elmsley, wife of the chief justice, "publicly slighted Mrs White," wife of the attorney-general, "in a most pointed manner"[1] by "passing her by without noticing her or making any return to her advances of Civility."[2] Such a seemingly trivial incident was to have far reaching, even tragic, consequences, including vicious gossip, further social slights, a celebrated duel, a fatal wounding, a sensational sex-scandal court case, and the social ostracization of Mrs Small. But it was not all to end there. Several years later, York society was again rent asunder when Lieutenant-Governor Francis Gore dared to challenge the severe judgment that had been passed on Mrs Small. Leading the forces of opposition to him was Anne Powell, the wife of the future chief justice. Her ultimately complete victory taught Gore the lesson that, although he might be at the head of government in Upper Canada, his power over the social realm could never be complete.

It is remarkable that historians, while paying much attention to the political aspects of early Upper Canadian history, have neglected the social

*From *Ontario History* 83, 3:179–206. Reprinted with permission of the publisher.

dimension. The first lieutenant-governor of Upper Canada, John Graves Simcoe, has been remembered largely for his efforts to establish the government of the new province as the "image and transcript"[3] of the British constitution. Most historians have concentrated on this theme and the consolidation and maintenance of political power by subsequent lieutenant-governors and the Family Compact.[4] There was another side to Simcoe's aspirations, however. As Edith Firth has expressed it, his "senior government officials who were to form the capital's upper class came from the towns of Great Britain and New England and brought with them the rigid provincial social patterns of the eighteenth century."[5] Simcoe and his wife Elizabeth deliberately cultivated a sophisticated, class-conscious society for the small official coterie. Although living in the midst of a wilderness, the elite, first at Niagara (also called Newark) and later, after they had settled permanently at York, did their best to maintain the standard of civilization to which they were accustomed. This social life was often conducted on a lavish scale and could be highly ritualized. Simcoe made quite a point of this, as one contemporary visitor, the American official General Benjamin Lincoln observed in 1793. "Governor Simcoe is exceedingly attentive to these public assemblies," he noted of one particularly grand ball "and makes it his study to reconcile the inhabitants, who have tasted the pleasures of society, to their present situation, in an infant province. . . . Hereby he at once evinces a regard to the happiness of the people, and his knowledge of the world."[6] But these gatherings of the elite also served a more serious purpose than simply pleasure. In a government in which who you knew and how successful you were at procuring patronage were often more important than ability, social life was no mere diversion. Anne Powell noted on the eve of a ball in honour of the Queen in 1806, "There *rank* will be settled & I fear some who claim precedence, will find themselves of less importance than they expect."[7] Social events, then, were a public display of the sometimes minute variations in status both amongst the upper classes and, correspondingly, between them and the "lower orders." In this realm, unlike the world of politics, the role of women could be crucial.

The wives of the officers of government both reflected and enhanced the status of their husbands and could even undermine it if they behaved improperly. Unable to achieve social standing by any other means than through the fortunes of their husbands,[8] the wives of the official leaders guarded their position in the hierarchy jealously, doing their utmost both to reinforce its values and to promote their own standing within it. As hostesses and household managers, it was they who most frequently had to deal with the social inferiors so important to the self-perception of the upper classes.

Much has been written in women's history concerning the ideology of separate spheres for male and female activities and the ways in which private and public life were increasingly considered to be mutually exclusive realms throughout the eighteenth and into the nineteenth century.[9] Although it is true that women were barred from the official workings of government in early Upper Canada, the influence they had socially suggests that we should not be too rigid in applying the ideology of "True Womanhood" to every instance of real life.[10] The ladies of this upper-class group, although certainly not equal to their husbands in political and economic terms, were not merely models of retiring domesticity. If all went well, they could exercise a great deal of informal power in the social realm, but if society turned against them, their exclusion could be devastatingly complete.

Certainly the Simcoes did not skimp in setting the stage for the social dramas that were to be enacted in Upper Canada. On 4 June 1793, General Lincoln described with appreciation the high standard of society that they cultivated. "The King's birth-day" began with an eleven o'clock levee at the Simcoes' home. "At one o'clock there were firings from the troops, the battery, and from the ship in the harbour." Finally, "In the evening there was quite a splendid ball, about twenty well-dressed, handsome ladies, and about three times that number of gentlemen present. They danced from seven to eleven. Supper was then announced, where we found every thing good, and in pretty taste." He concluded that "the music and dancing were good, and every thing was conducted with propriety."[11] As Hannah Jarvis, the wife of the provincial secretary and registrar related, the revelry at this ball continued well after the meal. "Supper being ended the Company returned to the Ball Room when two Dances finished the Nights entertainment for the Sober Part of the Company." Public drunkenness, however, was not then seen as disgraceful, even in the best circles. The less sober part of the company "stay'd until Day light & wd have stay'd longer if their servants had not drunk less than their Masters."[12] For Hannah, this ball was the occasion of some embarrassment. In the established hierarchy, Mrs Simcoe was at the pinnacle, followed by the wife of the powerful merchant Robert Hamilton as "Lady President," while Hannah Jarvis, "Mrs Secretary [was] second in command." Normally, Lady President would have commenced the dancing, but, as Hannah related, "I was called on to open the Ball." For some reason known only to herself, "Mrs Hamilton [was] not chusing to dance a minuet" as Elizabeth Simcoe had suggested. Hannah's embarrassment was great when "not one in the Room followed my example—of Course Country dances commenced."[13] This event had more to it than the preference for the more fashionable country dances and may have been Mrs Hamilton's way of resisting the dominance of the newly arrived Simcoes and Jarvises. Still, such petty awkwardness did not either ruin the ball or prevent other such occasions. So grand was the scale of entertaining that for this single evening's event the Simcoes added a temporary room to their house. "It is 60 feet long," Elizabeth recorded, "and the end ornamented by colours. We danced 18 couples and sat down to supper 76."[14]

These formal aspects of entertaining—the assemblies, balls, and elaborate dinner parties—were also carried on by the lieutenant-governors who followed Simcoe. Although Lieutenant-Governor Hunter was mostly absent during his brief tenure, and the social life of the province suffered in Alexander Grant's interim administration of 1805–6, lavish balls were given regularly.[15] This was a custom that Lieutenant-Governor Gore and his wife continued. On the Queen's birthday in January 1809, the day's celebrations were concluded by an "elegant Ball" held at Government House in the evening. The York Gazette reported:

> Dancing commenced at ten o'clock,—The Ball Room having been tastefully and elegantly fitted up and decorated for the occasion.— At half past one the Supper Room was thrown open, when the Company, amounting to about an hundred persons, partook of a very sumptuous banquet, consisting of every delicacy and a variety of the choicest Wines.
>
> Dancing was resumed after Supper, and kept up with great spirit, till nearly eight o'clock in the morning—when the Company retired highly gratified with the Splendour of the Entertainment and the condescending attention of the Lieutenant Governor and Mrs Gore.[16]

The elegant social tenor set by the Simcoes and their successors did not only include such large and formal gatherings. Winter sleighing was a popular amusement. In 1796, for example, Elizabeth Simcoe and "a large party drove . . . in carrioles to dine on toasted venison by a large fire on the beach below the settlements. We sat under the shelter of the root of an immense pine, which had been blown up by the wind, and found it very pleasant, and returned six miles in 32 minutes. Had a card party in the evening." Elizabeth related that the ladies "were delighted with the novelty of dining in the air in winter."[17]

What is striking about the earliest years of settlement in Upper Canada is the contradiction between their physical surroundings and the high standard of society affected by the elite. Even for such comparatively informal socializing, one's dress and manners were considered to be of the utmost importance. Although Elizabeth Simcoe spent much of her time living in tents, she regularly held tea parties and entertained her visitors with evenings of whist.[18] In 1792, when Hannah and William Jarvis arrived at Niagara, they were at first forced to live in a "log hut with three rooms (two of which [were] very indifferent)."[19] In this setting it seems absurd to hear Hannah complain that she and another lady had "gained the character of being the plainest dressed women at Newark."[20] Similarly, Elizabeth Russell and her brother Peter, the receiver-general, were poorly accommodated in a two-room log cabin. Elizabeth was vexed that at first she could not attend any parties because of their "uncomfortable situation not having a room to dress in." This was to be regretted, for "Tho' close to the woods we were not without amusements for there is a subscription Ball over at the Fort and another on this side every other week which I am told are very well attended by well dressed genteel people."[21] Elizabeth Russell could not be seen in public improperly or shabbily attired. Even what was worn for daytime visiting was important. Hannah Jarvis related, "Ladies called on me this Day, with Black Lace cloaks and Muslin Gowns."[22] In her "best room" she received them with flowers "in punch glasses on one of our card tables." At evening gatherings of the Niagara elite, she claimed, "There is more profusion of dress . . . than I ever saw in London."[23] This may have been an extreme claim, but Elizabeth Simcoe agreed. "There are as many feathers, flowers and gauze dresses at our balls . . . as at a Honiton assembly, and seldom less than eighteen couples."[24] These frequent subscription balls generally featured "a great display of gauze, feathers & velvet."[25]

Another, more typical, amusement for the ladies and gentlemen of the Upper Canadian elite was visiting. According to numerous diaries that have survived from early Niagara and York, these people almost lived in one another's houses.[26] After the capital was moved to York, home entertaining became much more comfortable for the elite than it had been at Niagara. Elizabeth Russell wrote that after they had settled at York, her brother built "a good House . . . at very great expence in a most charming situation in the front of the town."[27] The Russells' superior accommodation was necessary in order that they might receive the constant stream of visitors that came through their doors.

When Simcoe departed in 1796, Peter Russell became interim administrator until the new lieutenant-governor, General Peter Hunter, arrived in 1799. This position at the head of the Upper Canadian government brought with it important social responsibilities. At this time social inferiors were expected to flatter their superiors or compliment their equals by calling on them. Thus, the higher one's position in society, the greater the social obligation to entertain. A new arrival in the colony who aspired to belong to the upper class would be expected to signal their arrival in polite society by paying a short visit of ceremony to the lieutenant-governor and his lady. For example, when the Gores arrived in Upper Canada in late 1807, it was Elizabeth Russell's turn to visit. She called upon Mrs Gore in the early afternoon and was "ushered into the small parlour," regaled with "cake and milk punch," and given a present of some "feathergrass" that she had admired.[28] Although Mrs Gore gave a perfunctory apology for not having called on her first, when she passed by the Russells' house three days later she merely stopped at the gate and declined to get out of her carriage.[29] It may very well be that Mrs Gore felt that she should show the sister of the former administrator some favour but did not wish to treat her as an equal by actually entering her home.

The practice of formal visiting lasted well into the next century. In 1821, Julia Lambert, an American lady staying at her sister Susan's at York, found, to her chagrin, that her brother-in-law's position as a legislative councillor made such a ceremonial call mandatory. Although her social position dictated that she would be called upon by those considered to be her equals or slight inferiors, this was not the case with the lieutenant-governor's wife. Shortly after her arrival, "Most of the ladies of the place called," and she soon went to make her own "call on Lady Sarah Maitland, a ceremony which both Susan and myself had rather dispense with, but which seems here to be thought indispensable."[30] Julia and her sister were then invited, in return, to dinner at Government House, which would satisfy the obligation on both sides. Further, less formal social contact would be determined by how well the two parties enjoyed each other's company and would then be initiated by the lieutenant-governor and his wife. For more ordinary social relationships, as in the case of the ladies at York who called upon Julia Lambert on terms of equality, a return visit would be expected. Indeed, Julia spent most of her time in her early weeks at York returning these calls in order to fulfil her social obligations.

This highly ritualized form of social interaction could become absurd when there were questions of precedence. In 1827 for example, Lady Mary, wife of Judge Willis, arrived at York and, considering herself to be the social superior of the lieutenant-governor's wife, Lady Sarah Maitland, "imagined it was the place of Lady Sarah to call first upon her—which it seems the other never dreamt of doing." This created an impossible and ridiculous social deadlock. "The consequence was," Samuel Peters Jarvis noted, "the two Ladies remained in York for some time utter strangers, frequently passing each other in the street without recognition." Other members of York society were forced to intercede. "However after some negotiation in which Colonel Givens acted a conspicuous part and what had always been Established Etiquette in the Colony fully explained, Lady Mary call'd upon Lady Sarah, and has since been frequently invited to dinner and evening parties." All was still not well, however. "Judging by Lady Marys Manner at these parties, I doubt whether there exists that degree of Cordiality, which could be desired," Jarvis reported. This awkward social situation was about to be worsened by the fact that Lady Mary was soon to move into her own house. It was feared that "Her Ladyship may perhaps return Lady Sarah's civility by inviting her to dinner." This invitation would create a whole new set of social dilemmas. If Lady Sarah refused, Lady Mary might be offended and actually snub her superior by choosing to "drop acquaintance." If Lady Sarah accepted, it would show that Lady Mary had a special status that the other ladies at York did not share. Already Mrs Campbell "claims the rank of Lady Mary as being the Wife of the Chief Justice." "Thus you see," Jarvis concluded, "the old feudal feeling of rank, for which York has been celebrated from earliest periods of her history is again about to be revived."[31]

Indeed it was not difficult to upset the delicate social balance of York society. In the summer of 1805 a disruptive influence came with the arrival from Great Britain of a new judge, Robert Thorpe, and a new surveyor general, C.B. Wyatt with their families.[32] The Thorpes, who took residence near the Powells, from the first offended Anne's sense of the respect due her social position. Not only did they send their servants to her to borrow "necessaries" before properly introducing themselves, but they behaved as superiors by not returning her calls and by instead inviting her to their home in return. Such slights were not to be countenanced. "I do not consider the newcomers as any addition to our society," Anne asserted. "Indeed I have no intercourse with them." Since Mrs Thorpe had not "thought proper to return the calls I made . . . I consider her inviting me at all as a piece of insolence & rejected it accordingly, accustom'd to proper respect from those, who are consider'd by me as their superiors. . . . If I forget what is due to myself, I have no right to censure anyone for not recollecting it."[33]

The Thorpes and Wyatts fractured York with their selective choice of associates. Although they snubbed the Powells, they assiduously courted the Russells. Elizabeth related that not only did they call on her, but "They seemed very desirous that we should visit them to join their dinner & evening parties."[34] Unlike Anne, she commented that the Thorpes, "seemed to be a free mannered unreserved people and not formal."[35] Clearly they behaved differently with those whom they considered to be their equals, perhaps preferring the company of relatively recent arrivals from Britain like the Russells to that of persons with North American roots such as the Loyalist Powells and Jarvises.[36] Anne Powell felt herself to be socially more and more isolated, and she blamed the Thorpes for it: "Indeed the newcomers have done so much toward interrupting public meetings that we had nearly given up the expectation of receiving amusement." "For me I am fortunately out of the scrape," she wrote, feigning indifference. "I shall get my Rubber [of bridge], & whether I eat my supper at the upper or lower end of the table, is a matter of the most perfect indifference, perhaps my Neighbour will feel more interest, as wherever I am, she is below me."[37]

Social occasions at York, always somewhat tense, had now become virtual battlegrounds. Elizabeth Russell reported, "There was some affront given at the Ball last night, some thing about a supper being there and some of the Company not askd."[38] Part of the problem with the Thorpes and the Wyatts was their arrival in a "blaze of elegance so new to us" that dazzled and unsettled York society with their fashionable presence. Indeed they flaunted themselves. "A display less splendid, would have enabled us to behold," commented Anne Powell, "& in time imitate & by the end of the season the benefits arising from gentle tuition would have been perceptible to others, & of importance to ourselves."[39]

This touchy atmosphere finally came to a crisis in 1807, when Thorpe and Wyatt found that the political and social tide was turning against them. The glittering set that had impressed everyone when they arrived in 1805 were now beginning to show their true colours, violating York's norms of propriety. Anne Powell wrote, "[Thorpe is] so lost to decency [that he] introduces his Wife & Daughters to such company, as the decent Farmers will not associate with."[40] The Anglican pastor, the Reverend George Stuart, had initially been among those who admired the Thorpes and were flattered by their attentions. When he now felt called upon to question their conduct, the friendship was shockingly "concluded by a Letter from Mrs T[horpe] to Mrs S[tuar]t, which would not have disgraced a fair inhabitant of Billingsgate. For this no one pities them," Anne noted with satisfaction. "These people who ought to have known better were flatter'd into devotion to these newcomers & I believe we shall hear no more sermons designed to censure the illiberal conduct of the Congregation towards this righteous Judge. . . . We are really growing too bad & unless some change for the better takes place, a residence here, would be a most severe punishment more formidable than transportation to Botany Bay. Mr Cartwright says York abounds in good Dinners, & whoever loves a dish of scandal is sure to be gratified."[41]

Fortunately, socializing was not always an undertaking fraught with such complicated perils. Especially in the early days of Upper Canadian society it was more often very informal. The members of the elite rarely dined alone, and in the long evenings that followed their afternoon dinners, they called upon each other, played cards, and drank tea or, not infrequently, more potent libations. Morning calls were also common between friends. In 1806 for example, Elizabeth Russell noted without the slightest trace of irritation, "No one in the morning but Baldwin before I was up, also his little infant Billy, whom Mary brought to my bedside."[42] Almost every day she recorded a constant stream of visitors, and it was the days spent alone that were distinguished by their rarity. Clearly, amongst the early York elite, the household was still very much a public institution. Family life was repeatedly intruded upon in a manner that, from our post-Victorian view of the sanctity of the home, seems to evince a callous disregard for privacy.

In order to maintain this high standard of society, with its constant entertaining, the members of the Upper Canadian elite were forced to rely heavily on the social inferiors that they disdained. The "servant problem" was an issue of pressing importance for the wives of the government officials, and their attitudes toward servants reveal much about their role in enforcing rigid class distinctions. Elizabeth Simcoe complained in 1793, "The worse inconvenience in this country is want of servants which are not to be got. The worst of people do you a favour if they merely wash dishes for twenty shillings a month."[43] "Servants need not have been afraid of coming to this country," she remarked caustically, "they have here immence Wages are well treated & work very little."[44] There were too many other opportunities for the "servant class" in Upper Canada for them to submit themselves for long to the whims of their self-styled superiors. As Hannah Jarvis observed, it was all too possible for the best servants to "take up lands and work for themselves."[45] Those who were hardworking and used to inconvenience often made the best settlers once in the bush. In this they contrasted dramatically with the few members of the elite who had strayed from the ballroom to the forest.

Those who were lazy or too refined for manual labour had no place in the wilds of Canada. Well-bred ladies accustomed to servants had difficulty obtaining them in York but had even more problems in the bush. Thomas Meritt recalled that when his mother first arrived in Upper Canada, the family initially went without bread, even though they had plenty of flour, because his mother could not bake. Indeed, he recalled, "I have heard my Mother say, she would sit down and cry for hours wondering how she would ever get her children educated."[46] This "refinement of feeling"[47] was shared by a later settler, Frances Stewart, who felt restricted and unhappy in her log house. She was fortunate enough to have servants, although clumsy ones. When her maid tripped and broke her ribs, Frances was obliged to learn how to cook for the first time.[48] Another contemporary observer found it shocking to encounter in her travels a well-brought-up woman living in the bush in a log hut, "in a state of Nature, . . . without society, and almost without the necessaries of life."[49]

Clearly the refined ladies at York were more fortunate in obtaining the servants required to maintain an upper-class household than their sisters in the bush. With a self-supporting though arduous existence open to them, however, most of the best servants chose to leave the service of the elite. Those who remained had, according to their so-called superiors, numerous flaws. The Jarvises' servant "Richard has turned out to be a perfect sot, always drunk when he can get rum; and insolent beyond anything . . . ever seen; he thinks nothing of kicking the servant maids; with a number of things equally distressing if not worse."[50] The Jarvises, it seems, had endless problems with their help. Hannah complained to her father, "We cannot get a Woman who can cook a Joint of Meat unless I am at her Heels—and at the Price of Seven, Eight & Nine Dollars per Month—Soldiers Wifes are all we can get." Hannah had remarkably bad luck with her servants: "I have a Scotch girl, from the Highlands nasty, sulky, Ill Tempered Creature—She had nearly killed the other girl the other Day—Struck her with the Tongs and beat her intolerably—and had not Mr Jarvis happened to pass the Window, at that moment, in all probability wd have laid up if not murdered her." Hannah insisted that for good help they "would be willing to *double* the wages."[51]

The Russells, too, suffered from bad servants. Elizabeth complained that hers were "very dirty, idle and insolent," and "much addicted to pilfering and lying."[52] Under these circumstances, it was not surprising that some members of the elite, especially those born in America, were disgruntled that Simcoe's antislavery legislation meant that they could no longer acquire new slaves, but keep only those they already owned. Hannah Jarvis complained in 1793 that the lieutenant-governor had "by a piece of Chicanery freed all the Negroes; by which he has rendered himself unpopular."[53] Still, she implored her father, "Would you have any objection to let

Ceasar & Family come to us—they will all be Free when they arrive in this Province—so that we shall pay them Wages."[54] Black servants, whether they were free or not tended to be just as unruly as their white counterparts. As Elizabeth Russell related, her black slave, Jupiter, had been thrown in prison, an experience that had not reformed him. "He behaved so ill" upon his release, she wrote "that I am determined he shall not come at all to the house. . . . He is a thief and everything that is bad, and since he has been in jail he is overrun with lice. He has also behaved so ill at the Farm that Mrs Denison objects to his going there." Jupiter was thus banished to the house of another black servant, "Pompodore, who was very drunk today and impertinent. . . . [He] is to remain at Pompys till he is sold."[55] Black servants even suffered from racial discrimination within their own class. Anne Powell related in 1819 that her new American black servant, Freeman, encountered prejudice in her household. Although Anne saw him as "an acquisition," it was some time before her white servants overcame their "objection to his color."[56] This acceptance did not prevent him from being dismissed, however, because he "contracted improper acquaintances, and resisted some restrictions not to be dispensed with."[57] On the whole, black servants were considered unappreciative of the care that their masters had taken of them. Elizabeth Russell complained that one lady was very unwell in childbirth with "little or no help, some time ago her mulatto wench having forsaken her & gone to the Governor's to whom they have given up her time. This girl Mrs Davidson brought up from an infant, but they are all a bad ungrateful set."[58]

Such imputed bad behaviour and desertion on the part of one's servants could be very awkward indeed. If the upper classes were to keep up the style of life proper to their station, servants were absolutely essential. The Jarvises and the Russells, with their larger households, undoubtedly suffered more than most from the vagaries of their employees. In 1805 they retained three and five servants respectively. Only two other families in York had as many as three servants.[59] The Russells' difficulties were such that Elizabeth complained in 1806 that her brother had ceased to entertain formally, and that, besides the pressures of work, "having such bad servants [was] greatly the cause."[60] The Powells had only two servants[61] in 1805 but were to be even more inconvenienced. In 1809 Anne wrote that her daughters led "a very retired life at home; for the want of servants adds to other motives for seeing little company."[62] Two years later she complained, "I am experiencing the agreeables of Housekeeping without a Woman Servant & no chance of finding one that will suit me."[63]

Anne Powell's troubles were not to end there, however. Even a female servant whose "respectability was so generally acknowledged, that I was envied by many, and by all considered most fortunate" was to show herself unworthy. Some months after her arrival, Anne reported, "I thought her appearance indicated either dropsy or something worse." The latter proved to be the case, a fact vehemently denied by the hapless young woman right up until "the living proof of her misconduct . . . made its appearance. . . . A proof of moral depravity," Anne asserted, "of which I have before heard, but never till now witnessed."[64] The new mother had reluctantly been allowed to sleep in her mistress's less drafty chamber but was soon ejected from the household. It is not surprising that her sister, also in service to the Powells, left soon after, quite likely in response to Anne's self-righteousness. Anne could not understand this, complaining, "Tho' her ungrateful behaviour prevents my regretting [her] departure, I feel great inconvenience from the want of her services; and am unwilling to undertake teaching another, from the conviction, that I shall take trouble for the benefit of others, which is the case in the present instance." Anne was baffled by the young woman's "desertion." "Indeed I had flattered myself that common feeling would have so forcibly impressed a sense of the kindness her unworthy Sister experienced from me last March, that no temptation would have induced her to quit me; but I have my mistake."[65]

The hostile relations between servant and master underline the class tensions of Upper Canadian society. For the elite the distance between them and the lower orders was important, and the women were often those who dealt most directly with their social inferiors. When the Thorpes were constantly sending their help to make personal requests for "necessaries" to Anne Powell, she was indignant: "I was not rude, but I shew'd my disposition to encourage intercourse with *servants* as little as possible."[66] Such attitudes doubtless caused resentment in a frontier society where greater opportunities meant that the "lower orders" were not so dependent on their superiors as in England.

It is not surprising that for the members of the Upper Canadian elite, "the want of a servant" was "an evil so generally" encountered that it seemed "irremediable."[67] The elitism of the ladies at York was not calculated to endear their servants to them, particularly since domestic situations were plentiful. Good servants, if they did not marry and move to their own farm, could have their pick of situations. The official coterie at York may have ruled the province, paraded like peacocks at glittering social extravaganzas and conducted themselves according to rigid English standards of propriety but in their homes they were subjected to the vagaries of their social inferiors.

It was not, however, as if they themselves could lay claim to a greater moral stature. Although York society placed great stress on "propriety," it was a superficial morality that did not extend much beyond appearances. When their grand new Anglican church was built in 1807, for example, most of York's citizens were more interested in its social value than its religious aspect. Indeed Anne Powell was mainly concerned that it was "a good building," that "Mrs Gore [was] to give a Bell, the Governor . . . an handsome Pulpit," and especially that her family had "decidedly the best pew in it."[68] The Reverend George Stuart, according to his father, was "in a very Disagreeable Situation; with a good Portion of Zeal and laudable

Intentions he finds the Spheres of his usefulness so small, on account of even the Appearance of Religion[in] the higher ranks of his Parishioners, that he is tempted to respond. . . . Indeed a more lukewarm set of Christians (if they can at all be so called) can scarcely elsewhere be found." But even worse than this, "In that small Place, not less than six kept Mistresses may be counted; and I believe, not a Gentleman, except Mr Small, professes our religion."[69] Such scandalous behaviour may indeed have been as widespread as Stuart suggested, but it is unlikely that these mistresses would have been acknowledged openly amongst the genteel of York society. In public, social propriety was observed rigidly. It may have consisted more of form than content, but a member of the upper classes overlooked it at his, and most especially her, peril.

Elizabeth Small was to learn this the hard way. In the earliest days of Upper Canadian society she and her husband moved in the highest circles of the elite. Why she and Mrs Elmsley chose to snub Mrs White on that fateful day in late 1799 will never be known. Mr White had been feeling very edgy about his wife's recent appearance in Upper Canada. Evidently his marriage was not as happy as it might have been. At first Mrs White had refused to accompany him to the wilds of North America. Even though he expressed "tenderness and the strongest attachment"[70] to her, when she finally agreed to come, he was afraid she would not enhance his social standing. "I see in her coming the extinction of my hopes," he wrote anxiously. "I take it as the death stroke of my prospects."[71] After she arrived their relationship deteriorated, and Mrs White was on the verge of returning alone to England when the other two ladies snubbed her. White was enraged at this effrontery, which reinforced his own insecurity about his marriage and his wife's behaviour in society. Peter Russell related, "The Attorney General exceedingly provoked at this Treatment went the next morning to Mr Small's with a view of enquiring the reason of it from the Lady." Mrs Small was absent and her husband was unable to explain her behaviour, so White "went over in great Ire to David Smith to whom he made his Complaint, & it is supposed that (hurried away by the violence of his Passion) he happened to drop some hints relative to Mrs S. which the other taking advantage of wormed out of him a confession." What White told Surveyor-General Smith may possibly have been "wormed" out of him, as his good friend Russell charitably described it, but it certainly did him no credit. White claimed to have had an affair with Mrs Small, to "having been himself great with her, & that he discontinued his Connection from fear of injury to his Health from the Variety and frequency of her Amours with others." White was clearly trying to destroy the character of a woman who he felt was his social inferior and should have treated his wife with proper respect. What followed from this was certainly predictable. "At this Smith appeared to be greatly shocked and requested Mr W permission to repeat what he had heard to Mrs Elmsley for whom he had a great Regard & wished to apprise her of the Character of the lady with whom she was commencing an Intimacy," Russell reported. "This permission was granted with an Injunction that Mr Smith should not mention it to any other Person & that he should request Mrs E. to keep the information to herself for her own private use without causing any alteration in her conduct to Mrs Small." White must have known, however, the character of his listener and exploited it for his own ends. As could be expected, just over a month later Smith had told not only the Elmsleys, who evidently kept the secret, but "was very liberal in his communications . . . & particularly to Mr & Mrs Powell."

Having sowed the seeds of scandal, Smith then left the province on a business trip. "Mrs Elmsley finding out therefore that the tale had got abroad thought it proper to change her Carriage to Mrs Small," it was observed, "& whenever they met shunned her advances and often passed her by without noticing her."[72] Now it was Small's turn to be upset at the snubs his wife had received. When the rumours were traced back to their source, Small challenged White to a duel. The attorney-general paid for his indiscretion with his life, and Small soon found himself charged with murder. As it happened, he was acquitted on a technicality. Since no one had actually seen him shoot White, murder could not be proved. It probably was also helpful that Small's second had been none other than Sheriff McDonnell. It was unfortunate that Small was not more confident of his case, for a fatal error was made in his defence at the trial. "Mr Small's Counsel in order to impress upon the Jury the Provocation which had urged him to call Mr White to the field—" Russell related "very unwisely obliged the Chief Justice and Mr Justice Powell to inform the Jury respecting the Attorney Generals Conversation with him about Mrs Small and their evidence opened a Scene which has rendered the stain given by it to her Reputation indelible." This was inevitable "because the only person who could have possibly removed it is dead without having revoked what he said."[73] What had previously only been whispered behind hands had now become a matter of public record and could not be ignored or glossed over. Not only did White's story of Elizabeth Small's alleged adultery with him become public knowledge, but so did rumours that she "had been the kept mistress of Lord Bersley, & that Small [had] received a Sum of money for marrying her." As William Jarvis expressed it, the upshot of the nasty incident was destruction for all parties. "Thus White is dead & Small & his wife dam'd."[74]

Small's loyalty to his wife under these circumstances was touching but ineffective. "Mr Small however professes not to believe a word of the matter & shews externally greater fondness for her than ever," observed William Jarvis, "but without accomplishing his purpose as none of the Ladies have been yet induced to visit her—and indeed very few of the other Sex have visited him since this affair happened."[75] Whether White's allegations were true or merely the product of the vengeful spite of an embittered man, they were now in the public domain and therefore could not be ignored.

Mrs Small and her husband lived in a kind of social twilight, shunned by all. Anne Powell explained that Lieutenant-Governor Hunter, "who knew the circumstances of her infamy, gave as a reason for not sending her a card, that were he [to] no other Lady would accept his invitations."[76]

Elizabeth Small was not a woman to accept such social exclusion without a fight, however. When she heard that Francis Gore was to become the new Lieutenant-Governor, she used her aristocratic connections in England to influence him in her favour. Gore had also been made aware of the tensions that had remained in the wake of the Thorpes and the Wyatts. The result was that when he and Mrs Gore arrived in 1806 to take over the reins of government, they were determined to put an end to the contention that had divided "little York." Anne Powell who by this point had stopped attending social gatherings, was flattered by Gore's "particular request, that I would sacrifice my private feelings to the duty I owed society, & consent to go with my family." Since the Lieutenant-Governor, she observed, "has it so much at Heart to do away the remembrance of the disgraceful contentions of the last Winter, that he determines to sanction by his presence all innocent amusements & to use his influence with the most respectable to persuade their uniting with him. Thus urged I comply."[77] Anne attended several parties with her daughters as a result of this appeal, but not two months later all this gaiety stopped short. After accepting an invitation to a grand ball in honour of the Queen being given at the lieutenant-governor's, Anne "found that a Lady who had been uniformly rejected as unfit for decent society was to be there." She felt that she had no option but to refuse to attend if Elizabeth Small was also to be present. Even Mrs Gore could not dissuade her when in an unusual gesture, she actually visited Anne. "I was surprised to see Mrs Gore herself the morning of the Ball," Anne related, "she came deputed by the Govr, to urge my going if it was but for one hour, only to make my appearance, wrapp'd up in my Furs or any way I pleas'd. I acknowledged her kind condescension, but it was impossible to comply." The reason given for this refusal was a higher consideration than the request from the lieutenant-governor. Anne would not attend because of what she referred to as "a sense of propriety."[78] She explained, "Nothing has taken place, to remove the imputations cast on this wretched Female, & nothing shall ever induce me, to introduce my Daughters to doubtful characters or to show them, that however violently resented a deviation from Virtue may be at the moment it is discover'd, time will overcome indignation and restore to respectable society a Woman who by criminal conduct, had forfeited her right to it. . . . While my conduct is regulated by principle, I am fearless of censure."[79]

Anne's uncompromising stand was a risky one, a gamble that could either result in complete vindication or total loss in the social stakes. Already it began to pay off, however, as other ladies in York society considered following her lead. Hannah Jarvis was among the first to waver. "Mrs Jarvis called upon me," Anne reported, "to ask my advice so soon as it was known that this woman was to be one of the company." Anne declined to advise her, wishing instead to avoid forming "a party" on what was, after all, a purely personal moral issue. Hannah decided to go to the ball but awkwardly attempted to reconcile obedience to the lieutenant-governor's wishes with the higher authority of propriety. "I hear when in the dance it was necessary to give hands, [she] turn'd her back & put her hand behind her—" Anne related with disgust, "an impotent attempt to present an affront."[80] As it turned out, the Powells were the only family that did not attend the ball. Gore clearly expected that she would ultimately see things his way and still condescended to invite the Powells to dine. Anne, undaunted, used the opportunity to have a long conversation with Mrs Gore during which she "fully informed her of my opinion & had the pleasure to find her a Woman of the most delicate mind, & sentiments perfectly corresponding with my own, on the necessity of example."[81] Soon after, some of the other ladies followed her lead, attending balls with the resolve to leave if Mrs Small arrived, or not going at all if it was certain that she was to be there. The result was that the lieutenant-governor became convinced that Anne was at the head of a conspiracy to thwart his efforts at restoring social harmony. His anger began to have serious effect on William Dummer Powell's career. Anne was indignant that her husband, "a Man who from his long & zealous performance of his duty, from the services he has render'd to the province, & who has a right to confidence & respect [was] treated not only with neglect but pursued with malignancy." All this was "because his Wife disdains to introduce her daughters into the society of a Woman, who *if she is* married to the Man with whom she lives, was in the face of the country charged with Adultery, & in consequence excluded from the company of creditable Females."[82] It is not known what William himself thought of his wife's obdurate moral stand.

When Anne was certain that Elizabeth Small would not be present, she attended public gatherings, only to be snubbed by Gore, who now began to retaliate in earnest. He resented the fact that "Mrs P. reject[ed] the Society of one who [was] an acquaintance of his Lady's." On one such occasion he treated Anne "with the most marked neglect." She related, "[At supper] when the Chief Justice handed me into the room, & I was advancing to the place appointed for me, he call'd & desired me not to approach the fire, & the next instant call'd other Ladies to the seat he had forbad me to take." In the face of this insult all she could do was wait "quietly until myself at the foot of the Table." Only "the kind & elegant manners" of Mrs Gore were sufficient to allow her to "overcome the shock this unjustifiable treatment occasion'd."[83]

Anne Powell vindicated herself with decorum and propriety. She explained, "No greater punishment could be inflicted upon a Man, to whom my calm & even manners, were a continued reproach." Indeed, Gore was no match for propriety. The whole of York society was uneasy about the problem of Elizabeth Small, and Anne was finally victorious when it became suspected that Mrs Gore supported her stand. At one of the assemblies that Mrs Small attended, the ladies of York were shocked to discover that the lieutenant-governor's wife was not present. "So soon as the ladies knew that Mrs Gore was not to be there," Anne related, "they order'd their Carrioles & went home." The consternation and confusion that must have rippled through the crowded ballroom can only be imagined. "Thus the only public amusement is destroyed," observed Anne, "& as much offence given as if they had absented themselves in the first instance."[84]

Eventually the lieutenant governor gave up all attempts to impose his will on the ladies of York society. In June of 1810, a grand ball was held at Government House, and, Anne related, it was "intimated that [her] presence would be desirable." When she attended the "Gala," she wrote, she was treated with "mark'd attention [which] exceeded the want of it, the only time I appear'd on a similar occasion ... indeed nothing could surpass the politeness & elegance of manners & arrangements of his Excellency & his Lady." Anne congratulated herself on her success: "I really believe all parties rejoiced at having got rid of a business which has caused chagrin to more than myself. The evening was consider'd as one of the most chearful ever pass'd there."[85] A year later the social situation at York continued to meet with her approval: "Everything here wears the face of improvement; the country smiles and we are all sociable together."[86]

Anne Powell's social victory was confirmed by her husband's ascension to the chief justiceship in 1817, a position he had long coveted. John Small retained his government post, but he and his wife remained on the fringes of York society. The two women's relative status is well demonstrated by the membership lists for the Female Society for the Relief of Poor Women in Childbirth, established in 1820. As with everything done in York society, rank was strictly observed. Anne, "Mrs Chief Justice Powell," was a founding member, along with Lady Sarah Maitland, the lieutenant-governor's wife, Mrs Strachan, the minister's wife, "Mrs Colonel Foster," and "Mrs Attorney General." On the membership lists of 1820 and 1821, Anne was ranked second, immediately after Lady Sarah. Although they could hardly turn Elizabeth Small away from a charitable organization, and even though she matched Mrs Powell's financial contribution, she was ranked last of all the women. Anne was high above her, vindicated by the position and influence that she now held.[87]

Obviously the power of women to establish, reflect, and reinforce their husband's social status was not trivial. Anne Powell was highly respected by her husband, who wrote, "[She has] manners and conduct which have ever assured respect,"[88] although he must have had some anxious moments. Elizabeth Small was fortunate that her husband was loyal to her, even though she had become a social outcast. Such was not always the case. When Wyatt, the surveyor-general, went down with Thorpe, losing his government appointment, he blamed his disgrace on his wife. Elizabeth

Russell described Mary Wyatt as "a lively good humoured pretty little girl, being only about seventeen."[89] She commented, "She draws very well." In her parlour there were "some humourous figures painted on pasteboard and cut out, one of which is a couple & contending for the breeches."[90] The reality of the Wyatt household was grimly different from this lively art work. Evidently she "paid severely" for her husband's disappointments: "confinement to the bedpost, locking up in the Cellar, bruised Arms & broken head were the portion of the little pretty woman from her brutal & deluded husband."[91] This is one of the earliest recorded cases of wife assault in English Canada, and a stark reminder of just how precarious a woman's power was in relation to her husband's, even in elite Upper Canadian society. The fact that everyone in York knew about Wyatt's abusive behaviour but no one did anything about it suggests that at least some activities that took place in the home were considered to be outside the bounds of public scrutiny.

Although not equal to their husbands, and certainly excluded from political and economic power, the women of the early Upper Canadian elite were by no means confined solely to the private realm of domesticity. Nor was the home as clearly separated from public life as many historians have argued it was later in the nineteenth century. The political importance of elaborate visiting rituals and correct conduct at social events reveals that women indeed had a public role to play. They could, we have seen, exercise a great deal of informal power over the determination of status both within their insular official clique and between themselves and those whom they regarded as their social inferiors. Having a wife, or in some cases a sister, who could successfully act as hostess and maintain a lavish and smoothly run household, was crucial to a man's success in his career. That the women of the early Upper Canadian elite achieved this in primitive wilderness conditions in an isolated colony is not just incongruous, it is also a testament to extraordinary perseverance in the face of improbable odds.

• Notes

1 National Archives of Canada (hereafter NAC), Shepherd-White Papers, vol. 2, Peter Russell to Samuel Shepherd, 9 Jan. 1800.

2 Archives of Ontario (hereafter AO), Russell Papers, Peter Russell to E.B. Littlehales, 13 Feb. 1800.

3 Gerald M. Craig, *Upper Canada: The Formative Years 1784–1841* (Toronto: McClelland and Stewart, 1963), 29.

4 Some examples of this are Robert J. Burns, "God's Chosen People: The

Origins of Toronto Society, 1793–1818," Canadian Historical Association, *Historical Papers, 1973,* 213–28; Terry Cook, "John Beverley Robinson and the Conservative Blueprint for the Upper Canadian Community" in *Historical Essays on Upper Canada,* ed. J.K. Johnson (Toronto: McClelland and Stewart, 1975), 338–60; Jane Errington, *The "Eagle," the "Lion" and Upper Canada: A Developing Colonial Ideology* (Montreal: McGill-Queen's University Press,

1987); Robert E. Saunders, "What Was the Family Compact?" *Ontario History* 49 (1957): 165–78; Bruce Wilson, "The Struggle for Wealth and Power at Fort Niagara 1775–1783" in *Interpreting Canada's Past*, vol. 1, *Before Confederation*, ed. J.M. Bumsted (Toronto: Oxford, 1986), 124–38; and S.F. Wise, "Upper Canada and the Conservative Tradition" in *Profiles of a Province*, ed. Edith Firth (Toronto: Canadian Historical Society, 1967), 20–33.

5 Edith Firth, *The Town of York, 1793–1815* (Toronto: Champlain Society, 1962), lxxviii.

6 Journal of General Benjamin Lincoln, 4 June 1793, in *The Correspondence of John Graves Simcoe*, vol. 2 (Toronto: Ontario Historical Society, 1923), 25.

7 Metropolitan Toronto Library (hereafter MTL), Powell Papers, Anne Powell to George Murray, 19 Jan. 1806.

8 See Peter A. Russell, "Attitudes to Social Structure and Social Mobility in Upper Canada (1815–1840)" (PhD thesis, Carleton University, 1981), ch. 4, 152–90, for a discussion of the limited social mobility of women in Upper Canada in a slightly later period. Peter Ward, in his interesting new book, *Courtship, Love and Marriage in Nineteenth-Century English Canada 1790–1915* (Kingston and Montreal: McGill-Queen's University Press, 1990), points out that although both sexes in English-speaking Canada experienced growing autonomy from family control in the realm of courtship and marriage as the nineteenth century advanced, women in general exercised far less freedom of choice than did men.

9 See for example Joan N. Burstyn, *Victorian Education and the Ideal of Womanhood* (London: Croom Helm, 1980); Nancy Cott, *The Bonds of Womanhood: "Woman's Sphere" in New England, 1780–1835* (New Haven: Yale University Press, 1977); Leonore Davidoff and Catherine Hall, *Family Fortunes: Men and Women of the English Middle Class 1780–1850* (London: Hutchinson, 1987); Margaret George, "From 'Goodwife' to 'Mistress': The Transformation of the Female in Bourgeois Culture," *Science and Society* 37 (1973–74): 152–77; Deborah Gorham, *The Victorian Girl and the Feminine Ideal* (Bloomington, IN: Indiana University Press, 1982); Carroll Smith-Rosenberg, *Disorderly Conduct: Visions of Gender in Victorian America* (New York: Oxford, 1985); and Barbara Welter, "The Cult of True Womanhood," *American Quarterly* 18 (1966): 151–74. Most of these historians, especially the most recent ones, are appropriately cautious in how closely they would assume that the ideology of separate spheres corresponded to the actual lives of women.

10 Two historians who have recently raised this specific issue in the context of Canadian history are Joy Parr, in her "Nature and Hierarchy: Reflections on Writing the History of Women and Children," *Atlantis* 11 (1985): 39–44; and Sylvia Van Kirk, in "What has the Feminist Perspective done for Canadian History?" in *Knowledge Reconsidered: A Feminist Overview* (Ottawa: Canadian Research Institute for the Advancement of Women, 1984), 46–58. For a later period in the British context, M. Jeanne Peterson in *Family, Love and Work in the Lives of Victorian Gentlewomen* (Bloomington, IN: Indiana University Press, 1989) takes the extreme position that the doctrine of separate spheres had little to do with social reality and concludes, "Either we must abandon the private/public dichotomy, or we must redefine more narrowly the meaning of the public sphere" (p. 189).

11 Journal of General Benjamin Lincoln, 4 June 1793, *Simcoe Correspondence*, 25.

One indication of how much alcohol was consumed and the quantity a prominent member of the York elite would routinely have on hand is shown by an incident that occurred in the Powell household in 1826. A shelf in the cellar collapsed under the weight of *ten dozen* bottles of brandy, which "shook the house like a clap of thunder & a man half way down the lane thought it was cannon." MTL, Powell Papers, Mary B. Jarvis to Anne Powell, 12 June 1826.

12 NAC, Jarvis-Peters Papers, vol. 2, Hannah Jarvis to Birdseye Peters, 19 June 1793.

13 Ibid.

14 J. Ross Robertson, ed., *The Diary of Mrs. John Graves Simcoe* (Toronto: William Briggs, 1911), entry for 4 June 1796, 315.

15 Matilda Edgar, *Ten Years of Upper Canada in Peace and War, 1805–1815; Being the Ridout Letters* (Toronto: William Briggs, 1890), 16.

16 Firth, *The Town of York, 1793–1815*, York Gazette, 25 Jan. 1809, 273.

17 Robertson, *Simcoe Diary*, entries for Feb. 5 and 6, 1796, 302–3.

18 Mary Quayle Innis, ed., *Mrs. Simcoe's Diary* (Toronto: Macmillan, 1968), Introduction. See also Fowler, "Elizabeth Simcoe" in *The Embroidered Tent* (Toronto: Anansi, 1982), 17–51.

19 William Jarvis to Rev. Samuel Peters, n.d., c. 1792, in "Letters from the Secretary of Upper Canada and Mrs. Jarvis to her Father the Rev. Samuel Peters" (hereafter "Jarvis Letters"), Women's Canadian Historical Society of Toronto, *Transactions*, no. 23, 1922–23, 21.

20 Hannah Jarvis to Rev. Samuel Peters, 15 Jan. 1793, in "Jarvis Letters," 30.

21 MTL, Russell Papers, Elizabeth Russell to Elizabeth Kiernan, 18 Jan. 1793.

22 NAC, Jarvis-Papers, vol. 2, Hannah Jarvis to Birdseye Peters, 5 Dec. 1792.

23 Hannah Jarvis to Rev. Samuel Peters, 15 Jan. 1793, in "Jarvis Letters," 30.

24 Innis, *Mrs. Simcoe's Diary*, Elizabeth Simcoe to Mrs. Hunt, Feb. 1793, 87.

25 Ibid., diary entry for 15 Dec. 1792, 83.

26 Some examples of early Upper Canadian diaries are NAC, John

White Diary, Shepherd-White Diaries; Firth, *The Town of York, 1793–1815*: Alexander MacDonnell Diary, 226–29; Joseph Willcocks Diary, 232–35; and MTL, Russell Papers, Elizabeth Russell Diary.

27 MTL, Russell Papers, Elizabeth Russell to Elizabeth Fairlie, 26 Jan. 1799.

28 MTL, Russell Papers, Elizabeth Russell Diary, entry for 7 Jan. 1808.

29 Ibid., 10 Jan. 1808. See also Margaret Angus's article "A Gentlewoman in Early Kingston" for a description of elaborate visiting rituals on New Year's Day in Kingston in the 1830s. *Historic Kingston* 24 (1976): 77.

30 Julia Lambert to David R. Lambert, York, 27 Aug. 1821, in "An American Lady in Old Toronto: The Letters of Julia Lambert," ed. S.A. Hewart and W.S. Wallace, *Transactions of the Royal Society of Canada*, 1946, sec. 2, no. 101, 103.

31 S.P. Jarvis to W.D. Powell, 19 Dec. 1827, in Firth, *The Town of York 1815–1834*, 320.

32 For an account of Thorpe's infamous career in Upper Canada, see Bruce Walton's thesis, "An End to All Order: A Study of Upper Canadian Conservative Response to Opposition 1805–1810" (MA thesis, Queen's University, 1977). See Craig, *Upper Canada*, 58–64, on the political conflicts caused by Thorpe, Willcocks, and Weekes.

33 MTL, Powell Papers, Anne Powell to George Murray, 25 Nov. 1805.

34 MTL, Russell Papers, Elizabeth Russell Diary, entry for 4 Jan. 1806.

35 Ibid., 8 Jan. 1806.

36 To what extent place of birth was a determinant of social status in Upper Canada is unclear. The British-born complained just as bitterly about being passed over as did those born in North America. In the struggle for patronage, any available means of undermining an opponent was taken advantage of. William Dummer

Powell, although a Loyalist, suffered from repeated accusations that he was an American sympathizer. See William Renwick Riddell, *The Life of William Dummer Powell* (Lansing: Michigan Historical Commission, 1924) and S.R. Mealing, "William Dummer Powell" in *Dictionary of Canadian Biography*, vol. 6, *1821 to 1835*, ed. Frances G. Halpenny (Toronto: University of Toronto Press, 1987), 605–13. The Loyalist Hannah Jarvis frequently observed that British officials "think that an American knows not how to speak" and that, "The language held is that Americans are not trustworthy, they are only fit for hewers of timber and drawers of water." NAC, Jarvis-Peters Papers, vol. 2, Hannah Jarvis to Samuel Peters Jarvis, 26 July 1796; and 6 Nov. 1801, in "Jarvis Letters," 58. However, no one was immune from such attacks. In the fall of 1795 there were anonymously "stuck up several Libels or Squibs," satirizing various members of the elite and calling into question the characters of many of the British-born, including John and Elizabeth Small. William Jarvis to Samuel Peters Jarvis, 10 Nov. 1795, in "Jarvis Letters," 43.

37 MTL, Powell Papers, Anne Powell to George Murray, 19 Jan. 1806.

38 MTL, Russell Papers, Elizabeth Russell Diary, entry for 31 Jan. 1806.

39 MTL, Powell Papers, Anne Powell to George Murray, 25 Nov. 1805.

40 Ibid., 4 Sept. 1807.

41 Ibid., 13 Feb. 1807.

42 MTL, Russell Papers, Elizabeth Russell Diary, 3 April 1806.

43 Innis, *Mrs. Simcoe's Diary*, Elizabeth Simcoe to Mrs. Hunt, Feb. 1793, 87.

44 Ibid., 50.

45 NAC, Jarvis-Peters Papers, vol. 2, Hannah Jarvis to Rev. Samuel Peters, 12 Feb. 1793. To give one example of former servants doing very well for themselves, on a journey to Detroit in 1789 the Powells stopped at the house

of an industrious family whose mistress had been employed by them. Miss Anne Powell described the circumstances of her sister-in-law's former domestic. "I was well pleased with an opportunity of observing a new scene of domestic life," she related. "Nancy, it seems, had married a disbanded Soldier who had a small lot of land where they immediately went to live and cultivated it with so much success that in a few years they were offer'd in exchange, a Farm twice its Size to which they were just remov'd." Although they lived in "a small temporary log house.... A large Loom was on one side, on the other all the necessary utensils for a family, everything perfectly clean.... We asked her if she was happy," Anne continued, "she said, 'Yes, perfectly so'; She work'd hard, but it was for herself and her children. Her husband took care of the Farm and she of the family, and at their leisure hours she wove Cloth, and he made and mended shoes for their neighbours for which they were well paid, and every year expected to do better and better." AO, Anne Powell Travel Diary, 4.

46 "Narrative of Thomas Merritt" in James J. Talman, *Loyalist Narratives from Upper Canada* (Toronto: Champlain Society, 1946), 280–81.

47 Ibid., 281.

48 E.S. Dunlop, ed., *Our Forest Home; Being Extracts From the Correspondence of the late Francis Stewart* (Montreal: Gazette Printing and Publishing Co., 1902) (Fall 1822), 19.

49 AO, Anne Powell Travel Diary, 3–4.

50 William Jarvis to Rev. Samuel Peters, 18 Nov. 1792, in "Jarvis Letters," 27.

51 NAC, Jarvis-Peters Papers, vol. 2, Hannah Jarvis to Rev. Samuel Peters, 25 Sept. 1793.

52 MTL, Russell Papers, Elizabeth Russell Diary, entry for 18 Jan. 1806.

53 NAC, Jarvis-Peters Papers, vol. 2, Hannah Jarvis to Rev. Samuel Peters, vol. 2, 25 Sept. 1793.

54 Ibid., 12 Feb. 1793.

55 MTL, Russell Papers, Elizabeth Russell Diary, entry for 27 Jan. 1806.

56 MTL, Powell Papers, Anne Powell to George Murray, 19 July 1819.

57 Ibid., 18 Dec. 1819.

58 MTL, Russell Papers, Elizabeth Russell Diary, entry for 3 April 1807.

59 1805 Census of York, in Jesse Edgar Middleton, *The Municipality of Toronto: A History*, vol. 1 (Toronto: Dominion Publishing, 1923), 96–99.

60 MTL, Russell Papers, Elizabeth Russell Diary, entry for 18 Jan. 1806.

61 1805 Census of York, in Middleton, *Municipality of Toronto*, 96–99.

62 MTL, Powell Papers, Anne Powell to George Murray, 29 July 1809.

63 Ibid., 17 March 1811.

64 Ibid., 1 April 1818.

65 Ibid., 15 June 1818.

66 Ibid., 9 Oct. 1805.

67 Ibid., 1 Dec. 1818.

68 Ibid., 3 March 1817.

69 AO, Stuart Papers, Rev. John Stuart to James Stuart, 28 June 1804.

70 NAC, Shepherd-White Papers, John White to Mrs. Shepherd, vol. 2, Niagara, 23 Feb. 1794.

71 NAC, Shepherd-White Papers, vol. 2, John White to Samuel Shepherd, 17 July 1797.

72 AO, Russell Papers, Peter Russell to E.B. Littlehales, 13 Feb. 1800.

73 AO, Russell Papers, Peter Russell to William Osgoode, 9 Feb. 1800.

74 NAC, Jarvis-Peters Papers, vol. 2, William Jarvis to Rev. Samuel Peters, 18 Jan. 1800.

75 AO, Russell Papers, Peter Russell to E.B. Littlehales, 13 Feb. 1800.
  Whether Small's defence of his wife was justified is uncertain. Before the arrival of White's wife in 1797, he was very intimate with the Smalls, and some rather cryptic but suggestive entries in his diary indicate that he may have been more than merely friendly with Elizabeth. On 20 February 1794, John and Eliza Small came to visit him for "a week or two." On March 8, he recorded in his diary, "Took Mrs S[mall] home—Drove Mr S[mall] afterward to Chief J[ustice's] & home—Drove Mr Maine to Cap. Russell's—Miss R[ussell] ill with ague—I went after to bring *Mrs S[mall] to dinner*!!!" White relates that the next day he took her out for a drive and visiting, and on the 10th, that he took her home. After that entry, White's diary is blank until March 30. He explains it by recording that, "Between the above date and the 29th (when the S[mall]'s went home) a good deal of confusion." White's final entry is for April 5, when he writes, "Dined at S[mall]'s—a little coquetry! So came away immediately after tea." NAC, Shepherd-White Papers, vol. 1, John White's Journal 1792–94. This is all suggestive, but certainly inconclusive, evidence of an affair. It was fortunate for Mrs White that she had left her husband before the scandal erupted, and was back in England at the time of the duel. As White expressed it, "The wilderness ha[d] no charms for her," and her departure was "painful." NAC, Shepherd-White Papers, vol. 2, John White to Samuel Shepherd, 7 Feb. 1799, 13 July 1799.

76 MTL, Powell Papers, Anne Powell to George Murray, 13 Feb. 1807.

77 Ibid., 13 Dec. 1806.

78 Ibid., 13 Feb. 1807.

79 Ibid.

80 Ibid., 21 Jan. 1807.

81 NAC, Powell Papers, vol. 1, Anne Powell to W.D. Powell, York, 23 May 1807.

82 MTL, Powell Papers, Anne Powell to George Murray, 24 Jan. 1808.

83 Ibid.

84 Ibid.

85 Ibid., 23 June 1810.

86 Ibid., 7 Aug. 1811.

87 MTL, Jarvis-Powell Papers, Society for the Relief of Poor Women in Childbirth, Constitution and Membership List, 21 Oct. 1820; Report of Meeting, 12 Nov. 1821.

88 MTL, Powell Papers, W.D. Powell Autobiography, n.d.

89 MTL, Russell Papers, Elizabeth Russell Diary, entry for 8 Jan. 1806.

90 Ibid., 20 April 1806.

91 MTL, Powell Papers, Anne Powell to George Murray, 13 Feb. 1807. Anne Powell may have recognized Wyatt's behaviour as being brutal, but she concluded her comments with the "hope that a Journey & voyage will harmonize them," during their trip back to England. In a foreign land with no near relations, Mary Wyatt had no recourse but to stay with her husband. However, before their departure Anne noted, "She has declared no power shall induce her to live an hour with him, when she is able to claim the protection of her Friends." Fortunately she was eventually able to follow through on her intention. Wyatt's biographer, Elwood H. Jones, notes without comment that they were divorced in 1811 "by Scottish decree on grounds of cruel conduct on his part," although this would have been a very unusual occurrence at that time. It is not clear who retained custody of the five children born to them in the six years of their marriage. Frances G. Halpenny, ed., *Dictionary of Canadian Biography*, vol. 7, *1836 to 1850* (Toronto: University of Toronto Press, 1988), 929–30.

FROM FOLKLORE
TO REVOLUTION:
Charivaris and the Lower
Canadian Rebellion of 1837*

ALLAN GREER

We have given this Charivari
Because it is our right.

From a Basque popular play[1]

For those interested in the connections between politics and popular culture, the charivari holds a particular fascination. Originally an aggressive ritual directed against marital deviants, the charivari came in France to be used for overtly political purposes. "The charivari," Charles Tilly has observed, "deserves special attention because it illustrates the displacement of an established form of collective action from its home territory to new ground; during the first half of the nineteenth century French people often used the charivari and related routines to state positions on national poltitics."[2] But the French were not the only people who deployed the charivari form for political purposes in the first half of the nineteenth century; a broadly similar development occurred at about the same time in the former French colony of Canada. Indeed, the transition was much more abrupt in North America than in Europe. The French-Canadian charivari had long been notable for its traditionalism to form, object, and occasion, but suddenly in 1837, when Lower Canada (now the province of Quebec) was rocked by a revolutionary upheaval, this folkloric ritual made a dramatic appearance as an important vehicle for mobilizing the population against the colonial government. Enlisted not simply to "state positions" or

*From *Social History* 15, 1 (Jan. 1900): 25–43. Research for the paper was funded by the Social Sciences and Humanities Research Council. Wally Seccombe, David Levine, Patrick Manning, and Michael Wayne were kind enough to read an earlier draft of this article and to give me helpful criticism, while André Lachance, Serge Gagnon, and Jean-Marie Fecteau brought archival materials to my attention. My sincere thanks to all of them.

register protests, the charivari form was actually used to destroy elements of the existing state structure and even prefigure a new regime. This was a displacement with a vengeance!

On the surface there was little in the Canadian charivari custom in the years before the Rebellion of 1837 that foreshadowed its future political role. To British visitors of the early nineteenth century, it seemed a picturesque but essentially harmless practice, something that could be written up in travel books to enliven the standard account of vast forests and magnificent waterfalls. The following description was based on a charivari that occurred at Quebec City in 1817:

> Here is a curious custom, which is common through the provinces, of paying a visit to any old gentleman, who marries a young wife. The young men assemble at some friends house, and disguise themselves as satyrs, negroes, sailors, old men, Catholic priests, etc., etc. Having provided a coffin, and large paper lanthorns, in the evening they sally out. The coffin is placed on the shoulder of the four men, and the lanthorns are lighted and placed at the top of the poles; followed by a motley group, they proceed towards the dwelling of the newly married couple, *performing* discordantly on drums, fifes, horns, and tin pots, amidst the shouts of the populace. When they arrive at the house of the offender against, and hardy invader of, the laws of the love and nature, the coffin is placed down, and a mock service is begun to be said over the supposed body. In this stage of the affair, if Benedict invites them into his house and entertains them, he hears no more of it. If he keeps his doors shut, they return night after night, every time with a fresh ludicrous composition, as his *courtship,* or *will,* which is read over with emphasis, by one of the frolicking party, who frequently pauses, whilst they salute the ears of the persecuted mortal with their music and shouting. This course is generally repeated till they tire him out, and he commutes with them by giving, perhaps, five pounds toward the frolic, and five pounds for the poor.[3]

Though this all seemed "curious" to an Englishman, a charivari along these lines would not have looked strange to a tourist from France. The mocking, carnivalesque tone of the proceedings, the nocturnal setting, the loud and raucous noise, the masks and costumes of the participants and the elaborate, insistently public, street procession all recall French practices dating back to the Middle Ages.[4] Similarly the occasion of charivaris, following a wedding, particularly that of an ill-sorted couple, matches the customs of Canada's original mother country. There were differences, however. French customs, in this as in other matters, varied greatly from region to region. Moreover, practices seem to have evolved over the years so that, even before the emergence of the fully political charivari in the nineteenth century, charivari-type harassment, sometimes associated with other customs, was often directed against all kinds of unpopular figures such as corrupt officials, submissive husbands or promiscuous women. The colonial ritual, by contrast, seems quite uniform and consistent, from the seventeenth century to the nineteenth and from one end of Lower Canada to the other. More faithful than their European cousins to early modern models, the French of Canada always directed charivaris at newly married couples only. This seems to be one of those areas in which a European overseas settlement functioned as a sort "cultural museum" in which customs were distilled, purified, and preserved, even as they changed drastically or disappeared in the old country.[5] Such resolute orthodoxy prior to the Rebellion makes the politicization of the charivari in 1837 all the more surprising. What was there about this "curious custom"—annoying but hardly subversive in appearance—that lent itself to a situation of acute political strife?

Although the charivari was a custom characteristic of preindustrial society, it would be a mistake, in my view, to regard it as simply a throwback, an expression of a "primal ethic," hostile to market relations and punitive in its reaction to nonconformist behaviour.[6] In its Canadian guise, at least, the ritual was not part of any pattern of collective regulation of marriage and domestic life through public demonstrations. There was no French-Canadian equivalent of a *azouade* ("donkey ride") or "skimmington," humiliating punishments inflicted in early modern France and England on submissive husbands, scolding wives, and other deviants.[7] Neither did the drunks and women accused of premarital sex have reason to fear a charivari, as was the case in some areas of Germany and the American South. Here it was the marital match itself that was at issue, not the content of domestic life. Prior to 1837, Canadian charivaris always followed a wedding and, in every case I have examined, the marriage was a "mismatch": either the groom was much older than the bride or vice versa, or else one of the partners had been previously married. Several accounts also mention a social mismatch accompanying the disparity in age or marital status. There was, for example, Monsieur Bellet, the target of the Quebec City charivari described above. A prominent merchant of the town, this sixty-year-old widower had married his young servant girl. Just as typical was the charivari directed against a "widow lady of considerable fortune" who wed "a young gentleman of the Commissariat Department."[8]

Widowers marrying again were never the exclusive, or even the primary target of Canadian charivaris. Indeed, weddings joining widows and bachelors were far more likely to trigger a demonstration than the remarriage of men. Moreover, people of all ages and both sexes took part in the festivities, though men appropriated the starring roles. A bishop's ordinance condemning a Quebec charivari in 1683 makes explicit reference to the participation of "a large number of persons of both sexes."[9] In Renaissance France, by way of contrast, charivaris were commonly the work of village youth societies and they were directed specifically against mature widowers or outsiders who deprived local young men of a potential mate. This has led some anthropologically minded scholars to analyse the ritual and the payment exacted from the victim in terms of a specifically male intervention in the "marriage market,"[10] but, in French Canada, charivari does not seem to have arisen from any protectionist impulses of bachelordom.

Why then, if not to regulate the local supply of brides, were ill-assorted marriages singled out for persecution? Writing of Old Regime France, André Burgière suggests that charivari directed at widows and widowers stemmed from ancient Catholic misgivings about remarriage. The traditionalist crowd thus took it upon itself to enforce restrictions long abandoned by the clergy. As a result, the church emerged as the earliest and most consistent opponent of charivari, for the ritual represented a clear assault on its current marital regulations.[11] In seeking links between the mentality underlying the charivari and the outlook of the official church, Burgière opens a promising line of enquiry. Yet it seems to me that the connections may have been much closer than he realizes—at least they were in French Canada. Priests and bishops had reservations, not only about remarriages, but also about the other mismatches that provoked charivaris. Moreover, these were not ancient objections discarded by the clergy centuries before they were taken up by the mob; they were concerns that found expression even in the nineteenth century. The marital ideology of the charivari, I would argue, was not an anachronism and it was not essentially in contradiction with clerical views.

As far as the church was concerned, the wedding ceremony was a sacrament and therefore it could only be approached in a special spiritual state. The *Rituel* of the diocese of Quebec, a sort of priests' manual published in 1703 but still widely used more than a century later, insisted that prospective brides and grooms must "have a genuinely pure intent, looking to marriage only for the glory of God and their own sanctification, and not for the satisfaction of their cupidity, their ambition, their greed and their shameful passions." The fiancés, of course, had to take confession before the nuptials and curés were expected to impress upon them the true nature of marriage:

> Curés will inform the faithful that the purpose of this sacrament is to give to married persons the grace which they require to help and comfort one another, to live together in sanctity, and to contribute to the edification of the Church, not only by bringing forth legitimate children, but also by taking care to provide for their spiritual regeneration and a truly Christian education. *They will above all point out to those who wish to marry that persons who wed out of sensuality, seeking in marriage only sensual pleasure, or out of avarice, endeavouring only to establish a temporal fortune, commit a great sin, because they profane this sacrament*, and, in using something holy to satisfy their passions, they offend against the grace that Our Lord has attached to it.[12]

To marry for money or out of mere sexual appetite was not just morally reprehensible then, it was a serious sin for it defiled the holy sacrament of marriage.

This was all very well at the theoretical level, but how was a priest to detect such impure motives and prevent them from profaning the wedding rite? Unless candidates for matrimony made a direct confession of greed or lust, he could never be sure about their spiritual state. To refuse to marry anyone about whom he harboured suspicions would be to court disasters of all sorts (lay hostility, unsanctioned cohabitation, recourse to Protestant ministers . . .); furthermore, secular law would not allow refusal without good cause. In practice, then, the effort to ensure the purity of marriage consisted mainly of general exhortations to this effect and personal discussions, in the confessional and elsewhere, with candidates for wedlock. Naturally, a curé would give particular attention to couples whose external circumstances seemed suspicious. When a young woman married an old widower it might just be that she was after his money and that he, for his part, had more than a moderate share of lust in his heart. Thus we find a conscientious Canadian priest writing to his bishop for advice in the case of a rich widow of his parish who wished to marry a bachelor half her age. Legally, "you may not refuse to celebrate an ill-assorted marriage," answered the bishop, but, "in your capacity as confessor, you should refuse absolution to anyone who wishes to marry only in order to get rich."[13] Disparities of age and wealth were not objectionable in themselves, but they did alert vigilant clergymen to the possibility of sinful motives. By the same token, the determination of a widow or widower to remarry, while perfectly acceptable in itself, could also raise questions. Here was someone who had already established a family and who perhaps had children. Were they marrying again for the right reasons or were they simply looking for a new sex partner? Just to be on the safe side, the priestly manual cited above therefore specified a supplement to the wedding ceremony for second marriages that consisted mainly of Psalms 127 and 128, with their heavy emphasis on wives like fruitful vines and husbands with quivers full of children.

A priest had to marry an "ill-assorted" couple even if he harboured doubts about the purity of their intentions, but the crowd in the street might react differently to the outward signals of impurity, giving loud and dramatic voice to widely held suspicions. The charivari might then be seen as a symbolic accusation of defiling a sacred rite. This surely is why a wink-and-nudge sexual jocularity, not to say downright obscenity formed a central theme of most charivaris. Admittedly, sexual allusions were a feature of other carnival-type festivities but it seems to me that, beyond the general cheekiness, there was a specific and personal charge of illicit lust implied in the charivari. It is important to emphasize, however, that it was not "immorality" as such that was being chastised. Recall that, in French Canada, charivaris were not directed against adulterers, spouse beaters, and the like. Nor, as far as I can tell, were couples of roughly the same age ever persecuted by crowds who cited other grounds for believing that they were marrying out of sensuality or avarice. The immediate purpose of charivari was not to correct immorality or even to guard the sanctity of marriage against "real" impurity. It amounted, rather, to a ritualistic response to the *signs* of desecration, a public rebuke filled with accusations of lasciviousness, that aired suspicions shared by clergy and laity alike.

But more was involved than a simple clearing of the air; charivari was also, as many commentators have pointed out, a punitive procedure. Victims were punished through both humiliation and monetary exaction, two penal techniques favoured by the church and the criminal courts of the period. Public shaming was, of course, a central feature of any charivari, inseparable from the noisy charge of desecration. It recalled the *amende honorable,* a practice common under the French regime when criminals had to go through the town wearing only a shirt and stopping occasionally to beg God's forgiveness.[14] The ecclesiastical version of the *amende honorable,* much milder than that prescribed by the judiciary, involved a public confession of sin, for example by couples who had engaged in premarital sex.[15] Like these practices of church and state, charivari penalized people by making a public spectacle of their faults. The *amende honorable* was more than simply a penal technique, however. In the forms deployed by both priests and judges the wayward subject had to become a penitent, confessing his sin and participating in his own correction. The charivari, too, as I shall argue below, involved an important penitential element. But, before leaving the subject of the punitive aspects of charivari, let us look at the monetary penalties that, along with public shaming, were designed to make the ceremony an unpleasant experience for its victims.

Considerable emphasis was placed, by Lower Canadian crowds at least, on the payment of what amounted to a charivari fine. The sums involved were often quite substantial—fifty pounds, to take one example from Montreal[16]—though the exact amount varied from case to case, depending, it seems, on the subject's ability to pay. The level of the fine was indeed the subject of elaborate and prolonged negotiation. Usually some respected local figure was employed as a mediator during the day-time intervals between the raucous visitations and he would try to establish the terms of peace and then, later, he might see that the funds were disposed of according to the agreed-upon arrangement. Meanwhile, as negotiations proceeded day by day, at night the air still rang with increasingly annoying demonstrations calculated to break down the resistance and loosen the purse-strings of the unfortunate victims. The proceeds of a charivari were normally divided fifty-fifty, with half the fine going to the participants to pay for their "expenses" (i.e., celebratory drinks in the tavern) while the other half was contributed to an organized charity or distributed directly to the local poor.

This use of fines was another way in which a charivari insisted on its own legitimacy by aping the methods of constituted authority. Under the British regime as well as the French, magistrates generally kept a specified share of any fines and ordered the balance to be turned over to a parish vestry, a hospital, or to government coffers. The church also collected monetary penalties, notably from couples seeking permission to marry in spite of the impediment of consanguinity. A bishop usually issued a dispensation only on payment of a substantial fee, set, it appears, according to the petitioner's financial resources as reported by the parish priest. By the early nineteenth century—a time when charivaris were particularly frequent—money from this source had come to constitute a major element in the revenues of the diocese of Quebec. Even though the funds were applied to good Catholic charities, the practice aroused serious concern in the Vatican.[17] Like the clergy, the charivari crowds were probably actuated to some degree by purely economic considerations: all indications are that merchants and other relatively wealthy individuals were singled out for persecution.

Besides functioning as a penalty and as a means of soaking the rich, the charivari fine played a third and equally important role. It acted as a token of agreement signifying the re-establishment of peace between the targets and the perpetrators of ritual attack. In offering money, the newly married couple signified, however reluctantly, their submission to the judgment of their neighbours. Moreover, this forced gift implied a recognition—purely at the level of outward acts, of course—of the legitimacy of the charivari itself. The subjects were needled, nagged, annoyed, and threatened until they made a gesture signifying acceptance of the charivari, until they themselves became participants in the proceedings. When victims treated the ceremony with disdain, when they refused to sue for peace or worse still, when they called on the "forces of order" to stop the demonstration, the invariable result was that the charivari intensified. From the crowd's point of view, the offence was then compounded for, in addition to soiling the wedding rites, the subjects had also challenged its own authority to right the wrong. This is why charivaris could go on and on—sometimes for three weeks or a month—and with escalating intensity; when couples were stubborn in their refusal to pay, the custom itself became the issue and the struggle therefore raged all the more fiercely.

As soon as a fine had changed hands, however, the harassment stopped. The money served then as a token for the crowd as well as for the victim and it placed the former under an obligation to drop hostilities. A village notary at Terrebonne watched (and probably participated in) a charivari against a sixty-eight-year-old widow who married a bachelor, a cooper by trade, aged fifty. As recorded in the notary's diary, the demonstration went on for five days, escalating on each successive night:

> such that, in order to have peace, our young couple were forced to employ a mediator to discuss terms with these gentlemen. After intense negotiations an agreement was finally concluded this morning and it was settled that for three pounds, of which one pound to pay the expenses of the charivari and the rest to be distributed to the local poor, the newlyweds may in future indulge peacefully in all the pleasures of their union.[18]

There may have been some hard feelings in the wake of a charivari, but there is no indication that, under normal circumstances, they would have been lasting. We hear, on the contrary, of a young man of Montreal who married a widow in 1833; exactly a year after his charivari he was elected for the first time as a local representative to the colonial assembly.[19] Certainly there is no reason to think that Canadian charivari victims were "permanently marked" as it were, according to E.P. Thompson, the targets of the less restrained sort of "rough music" dished up in the English-speaking world.[20] But then, accusation and punishment were only part of the ritual of charivari; these were but preliminaries to the treaty of peace and reconciliation, marked by the presentation of expiatory coin.

We have moved, in discussing the charivari fine, from the area of punishment to the realm of reconciliation. Except where the crowd was defeated or thwarted in its aims, the thrust of its actions seems to have been to bring about, willy-nilly, the reintegration into the community of wayward members suspected of desecration. Nowhere in the French-Canadian record prior to 1837 does one find relentless persecution, or any apparent desire to expel or eliminate a "cancerous element" by means of charivari. This was hardly a lay version of excommunication, then; the more apt analogy would be to less absolute ecclesiastical sanctions, corrective measures such as the fine or the *amende honorable* that required sinners to make their submission to a higher authority in order to gain readmittance to the fold.

Aiming as it did to reintegrate "deviants" rather than to expel them, the charivari was not the expression of pure hostility, on the other hand, it was hardly a friendly and anodyne operation. It took resistance for granted and was designed to overcome that resistance. And when opposition, from the charivari subject or from a third party, was serious, ugly scenes could ensue. The night watch of Montreal tried to break up a charivari in 1821 and even managed to arrest a few isolated revellers, but the crowd soon counterattacked, beating up the constables on the scene and besieging their headquarters until the prisoners were released.[21] A man was killed in the same city two years later when the charivari victim fired on the crowd assembled outside his windows; the mob tore down his house in retaliation.[22] Episodes of this sort provided grist to the mill of middle-class reformers anxious to suppress the "barbarous custom" of charivari.[23] Yet to regard such violent conflict as simply an instance of the clash of popular turbulence and bourgeois order is to miss some crucial characteristics of the charivari as practised in Lower Canada.[24] Far from being spontaneous or anarchic, these were fairly organized demonstrations, carefully prepared in advance. More to the point, charivaris, though filled with bluffs and threats to their targets, were quite restrained. Real violence occurred only when the crowd came under actual attack. From the outside, the Montreal riots of 1821 and 1823 look like folkloric customs that got "out of hand," but really all that separated them from a "normal" charivari was the active challenge mounted, in one case by the police, in the other by the bridegroom. The crowd's insistence on its own authority and on its right—indeed its duty—to carry out its mandate was a common feature of all charivaris.

The pre-1837 charivari was not in any clear sense oppositional. Whereas themes of social and political criticism were very much a part of charivari and carnivalesque entertainments in Renaissance Europe,[25] in French Canada, despite the presence of anticlerical overtones and such "ritual inversion" symbolism as cross-dressing, subversive messages were quite muted. Indeed, one might well consider the charivari a "conservative" ceremony (in so far as the vocabulary of political doctrine has any meaning in this context). Not only did it ape the procedures of priests and magistrates, it functioned as a complementary form of social control, helping to chasten deviants of a very particular sort in strictly limited circumstances. Its ultimate point of reference, moreover, was the orthodox teachings of Catholicism. Intervening when the purity of the marital sacrament was in jeopardy, the charivari crowd acted so as to restore harmony and equilibrium, in the relationship between individuals and the community as well as in that linking God and humanity.

Thus, even though many authorities—and in particular the clergy—objected to the tumultuous street demonstrations, these must be recognized as indicative of a hegemonic relationship. People staging a charivari were giving proof of their active attachment to ideological principles justifying a social order in which they, for the most part, occupied subordinate positions. At the same time they were, of course, insisting on their own right to regulate certain specific aspects of the life of the community. This was scarcely a revolutionary position totally at odds with ruling-class precepts; neither bishops nor governors valued passive obedience. The ideal of the "loyal subject" or of the "faithful Catholic" implied a positive commitment and allowed for a good deal of direct popular initiative. Nevertheless, in spite of consensus at the level of general principles, there was conflict when magistrates and priests tried to suppress this particular form of public demonstration.

Charivari presumed a sort of "people power" of the street as one of the constituents of the larger political-ecclesiastical order. It was, then, "democratic" in a literal sense. This was a combative democracy, one which had to be defended against the repressive measures of officialdom. It was nevertheless a subordinate democracy, an exercise of popular power which assumed the existence of nonpopular authority in a well-regulated community. But what if the community was not well regulated and the government no longer legitimate? This was the situation during the revolutionary crisis of 1837 when the colonial regime lost the capacity to rule with the consent of the governed. At that juncture, when attempts were made to base authority on popular sovereignty, the charivari form came to serve as a very useful vehicle for pressing the claims of the embryonic new order. This instrument of popular governance within the state (and church) became a weapon of revolt against the state.

The Lower Canadian crisis of 1837, which culminated in armed insurrection in November and December of that year, grew out of the campaign for colonial autonomy and democratic reform led by the middle-class radicals of the "Patriot party."[26] Thanks mainly to the consistent electoral support of the bulk of the French-Canadian population, these liberal politicians managed to control the provincial liberal assembly. Opposed to the Patriots was a coalition of merchants, government officials, and settlers from the British Isles who tended to dominate all the other branches of the colonial state, including the executive, the judiciary, and the nonelective legislative chamber. Acute political conflict had brought the machinery of representative government to a grinding halt by 1836. Finally, the imperial government intervened in the following spring, hoping to end the impasse by issuing a clear refusal to Patriot demands for constitutional reform and depriving the assembly of its financial powers. The result was a storm of protest that lasted through the summer of 1837, with great public rallies, calls for a boycott of British imports and vague talk by Patriot leaders about a re-enactment of the American Revolution at some point in the future. The constant theme of radical rhetoric was that the British measures against the assembly had made colonial rule in Lower Canada illegal and illegitimate. Apart from stirring up popular indignation, however, the Patriots made no serious efforts to prepare for a war which they still believed to be many years away. Events moved towards a shutdown more quickly than predicted, though, as the mobilization of the populace, particularly the inhabitants of the Montreal District, provoked repressive countermeasures which in turn led to further resistance.

As the conflict intensified in June and July, noisy demonstrations, often carried out at night by disguised bands, became common. In August newspapers began to report ritual attacks against government partisans that they did not hesitate to call "charivaris" (victims and attackers also used this term) and that did indeed seem to be closely modelled on the popular custom. This was the first appearance of political charivaris in Lower Canada and it came in two quite distinct phases. The first phase, from August to mid-October, seems to have been rather more spontaneous and popular in origin whereas, during the second phase (late October–early November 1837), the co-ordinating role of the Patriot bourgeois leadership became more apparent and charivaris were used for more clearly strategic purposes.

In the late summer and early fall of 1837 there were reports from several villages that a masked party gathered by night outside the home of a prominent Tory and "gave him a serenade whose chords were scarcely soothing to the ears."[27] These demonstrations resemble the politicized charivaris that became common in France under the July monarchy, indeed, they may have been inspired by European models, although I have no evidence of a direct connection. Certainly the negative serenades fit into established Canadian charivari traditions that were, of course, a French import of an earlier century; the link with native custom appears

344 ORIGINS OF BRITISH NORTH AMERICA

particularly in the choice of specific targets during this first phase of political charivaris. Masked revellers did not attack such obvious objects as officials or soldiers.[28] Nor did they direct their serenades against members of the English-speaking minority, even though many of the latter manifested a paranoid counternationalism that made them violent defenders of the British Empire. Anti-Patriot anglophones might be ostracized by their neighbours or they might find the tails and manes of their horses cut off. (This last form of harassment could certainly be placed under the broad heading of the carnivalesque, for it was a kind of symbolic castration designed to make the animal's owner a laughing-stock when he rode it in public.)[29] However, attacks modelled much more closely on the charivari were reserved, in the early fall of 1837, for French-Canadian partisans of the government, and particularly for individuals who had until recently taken part in the Patriot movement but had "deserted the cause of the nation" when revolution loomed on the horizon. Members of the group— whether defined linguistically or in terms of political allegiance—who had broken ranks during an emergency when petty differences had to be forgotten, these "turncoats," were perfect targets for a treatment, the charivari, which had always served, not to attack "outsiders," but to reprove and punish the familiar deviant. Essentially expressions of hostility, these early political charivaris did not demand anything in particular of their victims, but they did probably have the effect of curbing the activities of influential French Canadians who might have been inclined to speak out in favour of the government.[30]

Political charivaris of a special sort came to play a much more important role at a later stage of the confrontation, that is, in the two months preceding the military denouement of late November 1837. The central development of this period—one which led inexorably to the armed clash—was the breakdown of local administration in the countryside of western Lower Canada. While it awaited the arrival of additional troops from neighbouring colonies in the summer of 1837, the government had tried to stem the tide of agitation by banning "seditious assemblies," but it found that proclamations to this effect were simply ignored. Particularly in the heavily populated Montreal District, long a Patriot hotbed, giant rallies succeeded one another and often it was the justices of the peace and the militia captains, upon whom the colonial authorities depended to enforce their writ, who were organizing them. The governor reacted to this flagrant defiance by dismissing "disloyal" magistrates and officers. Denouncing this move as further proof of British tyranny, Patriots who held the Queen's commission but who had been overlooked in the purge made a great show of resigning. Beginning in October, meetings were held in many parishes to set up new local administrations and, in the ensuing elections, the "martyred" officers were usually reinstated. A parallel local government, based on popular sovereignty and completely divorced from the colonial regime, was then taking shape. On 23–24 October a great public meeting held at the village of St-Charles to establish a federation of six counties south of Montreal gave official Patriot approval to these unco-ordinated local initiatives and urged all good citizens to imitate them.

Local government in Canada had always been rather rudimentary and subordinate to the central authorities in Quebec City. (The child of absolutism, Canada was ruled by colonial regimes—first the French, later the British—whose preoccupations were largely military and who dispensed with direct taxation and therefore with the communal institutions that could be so troublesome to Western European monarchies.) By the time of the Rebellion, justices of the peace and militia captains, whose responsibilities were more of a police than a military nature, were the only important public authorities, apart from priests, in the rural parishes of Lower Canada. They were all appointed by the governor but they were definitely members of the communities they administered. Indeed, the inhabitants found various ways of "domesticating" officials who appeared in theory to be the agents of external power. Each captain, for example, was presented with a "maypole," a tall tree trunk decorated with flags and banners and planted in the ground in front of his house, in an elaborate ceremony that implied popular ratification of the governor's choice. In the fall of 1837 many maypoles became "liberty poles" and, to mark the transformation, a sign reading "elected by the people" was attached to a captain's mast.[31]

But what about officers and magistrates who declined to resign? There were many loyalists who tried to maintain their positions, even in areas where the population was overwhelmingly hostile to the government. From the Patriot point of view, these hold-outs were the willing agents of despotism and rebels against the emergent local regimes. At a more practical level, they appeared as potentially dangerous spies and fifth-columnists at a time when war with Great Britain looked less and less remote. The issue of the Queen's commissions therefore served to personalize the struggle by identifying important enemies and bringing great constitutional conflicts down to the local level. Accordingly, loyalist officers and magistrates in massively Patriot communities came under great pressure to resign. Some suffered the fate of Captain Louis Bessette, a prosperous inhabitant whose evening meal was disturbed by the sound of axes biting into wood. Going out to investigate, he found a band of men with blackened faces in the process of chopping down the maypole. The mast crashed to the ground and a great cheer went up from the party; the house was then besieged by the noisy, stone-throwing crowd until Bessette agreed to turn over his commission.[32] The cutting down of captains' maypoles was a favourite gesture in 1837 and one rich in symbolic meaning. If the mast had originally been planted as a phallic token of respect for a patriarchal figure, Bessette's experience was, then, one of symbolic castration. At another level, however, this action should be seen as revoking the popular ratification of the captain's appointment that the maypole embodied. "You are no longer our captain," was the clear message addressed to Louis Bessette.

Whether accompanied by the severing of maypoles or not (and, of course, many of the magistrates and officers who held commissions were not militia captains), the charivari form was the preferred mechanism in the countryside south of Montreal for forcing refractory office-holders to resign. National origin and previous political commitments were now (October–November) no longer a consideration. Anyone who continued to hold office was subject to attack. Dudley Flowers of St-Valentin was the victim of one typical charivari, which he described two weeks later in a judicial deposition:

I am a Lieutenant in the Militia. On the twenty seventh day of October last in the afternoon the following persons viz. C.H.O. Côté, Olivier Hébert, L.M. Decoigne, Julien Gagnon, Amable Lamoureux and Jacob Bouchard, came to my house and demanded my commission as such Lieutenant to which I made answer that I would give it up to none but the Governor of the province. Doctor Côté said that if I did not give up my commission I would be sorry for it—to which Gagnon added, "Si vous ne voulez pas vivre en haine avec nous autres rendez votre commission." Upon this they went away. About eleven o'clock in the night the same day the same persons returned—at least I have every reason to believe that they were the same persons. . . . They began yelling in the most frightful manner. They threw stones at my house and broke the greatest part of my windows. A large stone passed very near one of my children and would have killed him if it had struck him. Julien Gagnon who had seen my barn full of oats when he came in the day time told me that I should not have to thresh them unless I gave up my commission and also said that my grain, my house and outhouses would be burnt. I saw one of the mob go with a firebrand to my barn with the intention as I verily believe of setting fire to it. But it was in a damp state from the recent rain and the fire would not take.

On the night of the following day (28 October last) it might be about ten o'clock a masked mob, composed of about thirty or forty persons attacked my house in a similar manner. . . .

On the following day (Sunday) about seven in the evening, some sixty or seventy individuals attacked my house a third time in the same manner and with the same threats as on former occasions but if possible with much more violence, beating kettles and pans, blowing horns, calling me a rebel, saying it would be the last time they would come as they would finish me in about half an hour. They had in a short time with stones and other missiles broken in part of the roof of my house and boasted that it would soon be demolished. Fearing that such must inevitably be the case, I opened the door and told them that four or five of their party would come in and give their names and I would give them my commission. There were about fifteen of the last mentioned mob masked. . . .

The same persons have declared in my presence that they were determined to compel in the same manner all persons holding commissions from her Majesty to surrender them. One of these individuals told me boastingly that they had obtained no less than sixty-two commissions in one day. I firmly believe that if Doctor Côté and some of the ringleaders were taken up and punished it would have the effect of alarming the others and keeping them quiet.[33]

Many of the features of the "traditional" charivari were present in this episode: the nocturnal setting, the "hideous" disguises, the raucous serenade of blaring horns, banging pots, and shouted insults. Even the lieutenant's initial encounter with the Patriot delegation recalled the negotiating process by which charivari fines were normally set: the talks were businesslike, superficially friendly but with an undertone of menace, and they were held in daylight, in an atmosphere that contrasted sharply with that of the charivari itself. Flowers resisted for some time the summons to resign but, following the example of an ordinary charivari crowd faced with a stubborn old widower, his attackers simply intensified their efforts, bringing more supporters and threatening ever more ferocious punishment on each successive evening. There were differences too, of course, notably in the stone-throwing and the overt threats of serious violence.

That the Patriots should have had recourse to the charivari custom at this juncture is not surprising. A coercive practice in which the aggressors' identities were concealed had obvious attractions at a time when arrest was still a real danger. This anonymity probably also served an equally important psychological purpose for the participants, that of overcoming inhibitions against aggressive behaviour. Indeed, the entire ritualistic package of charivari surely had this function. After all, Dudley Flowers was apparently a long-time resident of the community and he knew his attackers personally; even though he was a political enemy, the lieutenant was also a neighbour and therefore someone with whom it was important to maintain peaceful, though not necessarily cordial, relations. To turn on him with overt hostility would be to go against ingrained habits; masks and a familiar ritual may have made easier the transformation of neighbourly Jekylls into frightening Hydes.

The charivari custom offered more than simply an antidote to fears and uncertainties, however. The turning over of a sum of money was the central event of a traditional charivari and much of the pageantry was designed to extort this gift from an unwilling giver. What a perfect vehicle for forcing loyalists to resign or, more precisely, to "turn over their commissions" as the Patriot mobs usually put it. The political charivaris of this second stage of the drama of 1837 were rather blunt in declaring their intention to overcome opposition to their demands, and low-level violence, consisting mainly of stone-throwing, was common. Men like Dudley Flowers, who resisted the initial attack, were likely to have their windows broken. Captain Bessette suffered more damage than any of the other charivari victims; after chopping down his maypole, the attacking party forced its way into his house and, calling for his resignation with a deafening roar, the intruders pounded out a rhythm with sticks and clubs until his table, windows, and stovepipe had been smashed to bits. Now this toll of broken glass and damaged roofs, though severe by the standards of ordinary pre-Rebellion charivaris, seems quite light considering the context of serious political crisis. Even more striking is the complete absence of personal injuries. When one places this record against the cracked heads and burned houses that resulted from, for example, the anti-Irish riots of contemporary New England and New Brunswick—not to mention the destruction wrought by crowd action in revolutionary episodes comparable to 1837—the restraining influence of the charivari form becomes all the more apparent.[34]

Of course Dudley Flowers was not impressed by the relative mildness of the treatment he received: he truly thought his life and property were in real and immediate peril and, though he was no coward, he was frightened enough to abandon his home and flee with his family to the city shortly after the event reported in his deposition. This is because the charivari, "political" or otherwise, was designed to be frightening, particularly in the eyes of those who resisted its edicts. Before 1837, coffins and skull-and-crossbones designs hinted at deadly intentions but, during the Rebellion, the threats were much more explicit. Crowds attacked stubborn magistrates and officers with talk of arson and murder. Who could be sure they were simply bluffing when, as was often the case, masked revellers were seen carrying guns as well as firebrands? Lieutenant Flowers felt he had had a lucky escape and that only the damp weather had saved his barnful of grain from the Patriot torches. He might have been less worried had he known how many other loyalists had been similarly threatened, without one single building ever being fired. The fact that he did believe himself to be in serious danger shows just how well the charivari served its theatrical purposes in the fall of 1837, when dozens of local officials capitulated to the Patriot mobs.

So far I have been discussing the way in which the charivari form was applied during the campaign of late October–early November for wholly novel political purposes. Yet, beyond the surface resemblances, there were also elements of continuity with the past in the basic functions of the ritual. For example, the extortion of royal commissions seems to have been more than simply a means of destroying the government presence in the countryside; it also had meaning in the context of the specific relationship between an individual and the community of which he was a member. In other words, this forced gift played a role analogous to that of the ordinary charivari fine in signifying the giver's submission to the authority of the collectivity. But now the community as a whole and the Patriot cause were identified. Accordingly, some charivari victims were forced to shout "*Vive la liberté!*" or to cheer for Papineau, the Patriot chief, as further proof of recognition of the incipient new regime. In accepting the victim's commission, the crowd gave its implicit assurance (sometimes it was clearly stated) that the charivari was at an end. [35]

There was a sense, then, in which a nonresigning officer such as Dudley Flowers was treated as a sinner, a contaminating influence in a community otherwise true to new civic ideals. The charivari worked so as to force him into the position of a penitent who had to purchase his reintegration into the fold at the price of a militia commission. Thus the admonition addressed to Lieutenant Flowers by Julien Gagnon during the preliminary visit to his home: resign your position, "if you do not wish to live in a state of hatred with us." No one expected him to become a militant Patriot overnight, but he was being offered an opportunity to make peace with his offended neighbours. It is important to emphasize that, just as conventional charivaris were aimed not against general immorality but against a specific affront to the wedding ceremony, so Flowers was targeted for a specific offence rather than some general nonconformity. Though government supporters at the time, not to mention later historians, saw the Rebellion of 1837 as stemming from a xenophobic French-Canadian hostility to English-speaking fellow citizens, no one reproached Dudley on national or religious grounds. His "crime" was not in professing Protestantism, in speaking English, or even in believing in the Queen's majesty, but simply in retaining a commission at a time when all good citizens had a duty to resign. The atonement required of this wayward soul was just as specific and limited as the "sin" itself. He had merely to make a gesture—that of turning over his commission—that signified a renunciation of former "treason" and an acceptance of the authority of the Patriot crowd. The emphasis was on the outward act indicating a transfer of allegiance without any further surrender of personal autonomy. This was made clear to another loyalist military officer, who proclaimed to the fifty blackened faces shouting for his resignation "that if they compelled him to give up his commissions they could not change his principles"; that is alright, came the sarcastic reply, we do not wish to alter your religion.[36]

The boast reported by Dudley Flowers of sixty-two political charivaris in this region alone may have been exaggerated but the basic point that, within a few weeks, dozens of resignations had been secured by this means is undeniable. By the second week of November there was, to all intents and purposes, no official government presence in most of the populous rural parishes of the District of Montreal, and an elective magistracy and militia were beginning to operate in its place. In such a situation the government naturally had recourse to its now reinforced military forces to enforce its own claim to sovereignty. The British expeditions that ventured out from Montreal were surprised at the resistance offered by the inhabitants, hastily organized through the revolutionized militia companies. The initial armed encounter at St-Denis (23 November) was, in fact, a Patriot victory but, since the insurgent military effort was localized, fragmented and defensive, the troops soon crushed their amateur opponents. What followed, in many localities, was a series of very unritualistic punitive actions; loyalists then had the satisfaction of watching flames race through the homes of neighbours who had so recently issued empty threats of arson. Turmoil continued for over a year, in Upper Canada (Ontario) as well as Lower Canada, while Patriot refugees in the northern states tried to enlist American support. But, by the end of the decade, the republican movement had been effectively destroyed.

French Canada in particular was permanently marked by this defeat. The middle-class professional who had once been at the centre of the Patriot movement hastily jettisoned their alliance with the artisans and peasants in the rush to make their peace with established authority. Police forces, public school systems, and elaborate bureaucracies reinforced the colonial state, while the Catholic clergy saw its power and influence grow by leaps and bounds. Changes of this sort helped to contain social conflict in the mid-nineteenth century, but they hardly eliminated it. Lower Canada was actually a much more violent place and a more deeply divided society after 1840 than it had been before the Rebellion. Strikes by canal and railroad navvies heralded the advent of capitalism but more typical of the age were essentially retrograde upheavals such as the Gavazzi riots which pitted Montreal's Catholics and Protestants against one another in 1853.[37] Lacking "enlightened" allies and politically "progressive" outlets for their resentment, plebian rioters vented their anger on one another.

Not surprisingly, the French-Canadian charivari of these bitter mid-century decades was quite different from the ritual of the pre-Rebellion period. A recent study focussing on the Trois-Rivières region, 1850 to 1880, indicates that charivari was no longer linked exclusively to marriage and the sanctity of the wedding rites.[38] Belatedly following the lead of other countries, Lower Canadians turned the charivari into an all-purpose weapon for chastising moral transgressions and punishing nonconformists. Sexual deviants, drunkards, and converts to Protestantism now joined mismatched couples as common targets of noisy demonstrations. Moreover, the attacks were much more vicious than they had been during the insurrection or earlier. Barns were burned, and men were stripped, beaten, and thrown in the river. And no longer did a victim have to resist for a crowd to be provoked into violence: the first notice one villager had of his charivari came in the form of a whip lashing across his face. There was less emphasis than in the past on monetary exaction for many mobs sought, not a token of surrender, but the expulsion from the community of an offensive neighbour. In the changed circumstances of the post-Rebellion era, then, the charivari form was deployed in radically new and decidedly more cruel ways.

It seems significant that the most violent and intolerant phase in the history of the French-Canadian charivari occurred at a time of comparative weakness for the "labouring classes." When the rough music was at its roughest, it was also at its most politically impotent. Along with other forms of plebian hellraising, charivari shocked the bourgeoisie, but did little to curb the growth of elite power after 1840. In fact, the Canadian state never again faced a challenge as serious as that mounted to the sound of blaring horns and banging pots at the time of the Rebellion.

For such an orthodox and mild-mannered custom, the traditional French-Canadian charivari had proved remarkably effective as a vehicle of revolt. Of course the Patriots were soundly beaten. This is hardly surprising, given the relative strength of the parties in conflict: a small colony with no external allies faced the premier imperial power on earth at a time when the latter was not distracted by serious difficulties at home or abroad. The wonder is that the inhabitants of Lower Canada were able to cripple colonial rule to the extent that they did in the fall of 1837. This is where the politicized charivari form made a crucial contribution. Serving at first, as in contemporary France, as a medium of complaint and protest, it was soon deployed as the central element in a campaign to destroy government power in the countryside and to assert a practical sort of popular sovereignty. This was a truly revolutionary role for a venerable ritual, even if the ensuing debacle did expose the military and diplomatic weaknesses of the Patriot movement.

The charivari was well suited for its insurrectional mission in a number of practical ways. The very fact, first of all, that it was a custom of collective action made it an important cultural resource when groups of people had to be assembled and organized. Since collective institutions and traditions were rather weak in French Canada, recourse to the charivari was all the more natural. Additionally, and more specifically, charivari was a more useful device under the circumstances because of the way it concealed the identity of the aggressors. Above all, the traditional focus on extortion lent itself to Patriot strategies in the fall of 1837, as did the larger drama of forcing wayward individuals to make a gesture of renunciation and submission. Charivari had always been coercive, but only in a very discriminating way. Its techniques were therefore well adapted to the delicate task of exacting a particular type of obedience from certain recalcitrant individuals, all without bloodshed.

In addition to its strictly tactical role, the charivari from functioned as a framework within which the villagers of Lower Canada grappled with the moral and philosophical problems of revolt. Linked to widely held and long-standing beliefs concerning relations between the individual, the community, and the cosmic order, the custom was deeply rooted in dominant political and religious ideologies. At the same time, it embodied an implicit assertion of popular rights to a share of public authority. Here was a democratic germ, and one whose claims to legitimacy were formidable. Thus, when the crisis of colonial rule came, a law-abiding peasantry that brought out its charivari masks and noisemakers in order to depose local officials could feel it was doing the right thing in the right way.

• Notes

1 Violet Alford, "Rough Music or Charivari," *Folklore* 70 (Dec. 1959): 508.

2 Charles Tilly, *The Contentious French* (Cambridge, MA, 1986), 30. Other works dealing with the political use of the charivari form under the July monarchy include: Félix Ponteil, "Le ministre des finances Georges Humann et les émeutes anti-fiscales en 1841," *Revue Historique* 79 (1947): 332; Rolande Bonnain-Moerdyk and Donald Moerdyk, "A propos du charivari, discours bourgeois et coutume populaire," *Annales: Économies, Sociétés, Civilisations* (hereafter *AESC*), 29ᵉ année (May–June 1974): 693–704; Yves-Marie Bercé, *Fête et révolte: des mentalités populaires du XVIᵉ au XVIIIᵉ siècle* (Paris, 1976), 43–44; Maurice Agulhon, *La République au village: les populations du Var de la Révolution à la IIᵉ République* (Paris, 1979), 266.

3 John Palmer, *Journal of Travels in the United States of North America and in Lower Canada performed in the year 1817* (1818), 227–28. On this particular charivari, see also, "Un charivari à Québec," *Bulletin des Recherches historiques* (Lévis) 44 (Aug. 1938): 242–43; *Le Canadien* (Quebec), 10 Oct. 1817. Travel accounts describing other charivaris are cited in Bryan D. Palmer, "Discordant Music: Charivaris and White-Capping in Nineteenth-Century North America," *Labour/Le travail* 3 (1978): 5–62.

4 Among the works dealing with the charivaris of early modern France, see Arnold Van Gennep, *Manuel de folklore français contemporain*, vol. 2 (Paris, 1937–49), 614–28; Roger Vaultier, *Le folklore pendant la guerre de Cent Ans d'après les lettres de rémission du trésor des chartes* (Paris, 1965); Natalie Z. Davis, "The Reasons of Misrule" in *Society and Culture in Early Modern France* (Stanford, 1975), 97–123; Claude Gauvard and Altan Gokalp, "Les conduites de bruit et leur signification à la fin du Moyen Age: le charivari," *AESC,*

29ᵉ année (May–June 1974): 693–704; Jacques LeGoff and Jean-Claude Schmitt (eds.), *Le Charivari* (Paris, 1981).

5 Emmanuel Le Roy Ladurie is convinced that French folktales recorded in contemporary Quebec display archaic characteristics not present in European versions since the eighteenth century. See *Love, Death and Money in the Pays d'Oc*, trans. Alan Sheridan (Harmondsworth, 1984), 271–72, 437–39.

6 This phrase comes from Bertram Wyatt-Brown, *Southern Honor: Ethics and Behavior in the Old South* (New York, 1982), 435–61. More subtle versions of the same view can be found in Edward Shorter, *The Making of the Modern Family* (New York, 1975), 46–47 and Peter Burke, *Popular Culture in Early Modern Europe* (New York, 1978), 200.

7 In addition to the works cited in the previous note, see E.P. Thompson, "'Rough Music': le charivari anglais," *AESC*, 27ᵉ année (March–April 1972): 285–312; Martin Ingram, "Ridings, Rough Music and the 'Reform of Popular Culture' in Early Modern England," *Past and Present* 105 (Nov. 1984): 79–113; Christian Desplat, *Charivaris en Gascogne: la 'morale des peuples' du XVIᵉ au XXᵉ siècle* (Paris, 1982).

8 Edward Allen Talbot, *Five Years' Residence in the Canadas: Including a Tour Through Part of the United States of America, in the Year 1823* (1824), 300.

9 *Rituel du diocèse de Québec, publié par l'ordre de Monseigneur l'évêque de Québec* (Paris, 1703), 363.

10 Of course, by the eighteenth century, the French charivari was no longer (if it ever was) a specialized weapon to be used only against widowers who "stole" potential wives from the young men of a locality.

11 André Burgière, "Pratique du charivari et répression religieuse dans la

France d'ancien régime" in LeGoff and Schmitt, *Le Charivari*, 190–91.

12 *Rituel du diocèse de Québec*, 329 (my translation and my emphasis), 347. Cf. Jean-Louis Flandrin, *Families in Former Times: Kinship, Household and Sexuality*, trans. Richard Southern (Cambridge, 1979), 161–64.

13 Serge Gagnon, "Amours interdites et misères conjugales dans le Québec rural de la fin du XVIIIe siècle jusque vers 1830 (l'arbitrage des prêtres)" in *Sociétés villageoises et rapports villes-campagnes au Québec et dans la France de l'ouest, XVIIe–XXe siècles*, ed. François Lebrun and Normand Séguin (Trois-Rivières, 1987), 323 (my translation). This case occurred in 1810.

14 André Lachance, *La justice criminelle du roi au Canada au XVIIIe siècle: tribunaux et officiers* (Quebec, 1978), 113–15.

15 Gagnon, "Amours interdites," 324.

16 Talbot, *Five Years' Residence*, 303.

17 Gagnon, "Amours interdites," 317.

18 Public Archives of Canada (hereafter PAC), MG24, I109, diary of F.-H. Séguin, 83. My translation does not do justice to the *double entendre* of the final phrase of the original, which suggests both full rights of possession in the legal jargon familiar to our notary-diarist and sexual fulfilment: *"les nouveaux mariés pourront à l'avenir se livrer paisiblement à toutes les jouissances de leur union."*

19 Robert-Lionel Séguin, *Les divertissements en Nouvelle-France* (Ottawa, 1968), 73.

20 Thompson, "Rough Music," 290.

21 Talbot, *Five Years' Residence*, 302–3.

22 Palmer, "Discordant Music," 28–29; Archives nationales du Québec, dépôt de Montréal, P1000/49–1102, émeute de juin 1823 à Montréal; Bibliothèque nationale du Québec, Montréal, journal of Romuald Trudeau, 1 June 1823.

23 Though the magistrates of Montreal did issue a local ordinance prohibiting charivaris in the 1820s, there was never any provincial legislation, like that in place in France from the time of the Revolution, that was clearly directed against the custom. On the eve of the Rebellion, the legislative council of Lower Canada did consider a bill "to repress the abuses consequent upon the assembling together of large numbers of persons under pretext of Charivaris": *Journals of the Legislative Council of the Province of Lower Canada*, vol. 25, 194 (26 Jan. 1836). On parallel campaigns to combat "vagrancy," rationalize poor relief, and regulate taverns, see Jean-Marie Fecteau's important thesis, "La pauvreté, le crime, l'état: Essai sur l'économie politique du contrôle social au Québec, 1791–1840" (thèse de doctorat de 3e cycle, Université de Paris VII, 1983).

24 Palmer, "Discordant Music."

25 Davis, "The Reasons of Misrule," Burke, *Popular Culture*, 199–204; Emmanuel Le Roy Ladurie, *Carnival in Romans*, trans. Mary Feeney (New York, 1979), esp. 301–2, 316.

26 Among the more important works on the Rebellion and the political developments leading to it, see Gérard Filteau, *Histoire des patriotes: L'explosion du nationalisme*, 3 vols. (Montreal, 1938–42); S.D. Clark, *Movements of Political Protest in Canada, 1640–1840* (Toronto, 1959), 259–330; Fernand Ouellet, *Lower Canada 1791–1840: Social Change and Nationalism* (Toronto, 1980); Jean-Paul Bernard, *Les Rébellions de 1837–1838: Les patriotes du Bas-Canada dans la mémoire collective et chez les historiens* (Montreal, 1983); Elinor Kyte Senior, *Redcoats and Patriotes: The Rebellions in Lower Canada 1837–38* (Ottawa, 1985).

27 *La Minerve* (Montreal), 10 Aug. 1837 (my translation). See also *Le Populaire* (Montreal), 27 Sept. 1837; 2, 9, and 16 Oct. 1837; *Montreal Gazette*, 30 Sept. 1837.

28 There was one exception to this pattern. A crowd that had turned out to greet the Patriot leader Louis-Joseph Papineau at St-Hyacinthe, learning

that the commander of British forces happened also to be staying in the town, gathered round the house where the latter was staying for a noisy vigil punctuated by catcalls and antigovernment slogans.

29 Archives nationales du Québec, documents relatifs aux événements de 1837–38 (hereafter ANQ, 1837), deposition of Robert Hall, 15 July 1837. This practice, previously unknown in French Canada as far as I can tell, may have been picked up from British immigrants. On animal mutilation of this sort in England, see Ingram, "Ridings, Rough Music," 87.

30 This insistence on a certain unanimity on fundamental issues, and the concomitant punitive approach to dissenters, is quite common in most societies under emergency conditions such as revolution or war. See, for example, Rhys Issac, "Dramatizing the Ideology of Revolution: Popular Mobilization in Virginia, 1774 to 1776," *William and Mary Quarterly*, 3rd ser., 33 (July 1976): 357–85.

31 Robert Christie, *A History of the Late Province of Lower Canada, Parliamentary and Political, from the Commencement to the Close of its Existence as a Separate Province*, vol. 5 (Montreal, 1866), 32–33. On French maypole customs and the transformation of the maypole into the liberty pole at the time of the Revolution, see Van Gennep, *Manuel de Folklore*, vol. 1, part 4, 1516–75; Mona Ozouf, *La fête révolutionnaire 1789–1799* (Paris, 1976), 280–316; Le Roy Ladurie, *Carnival in Romans*, 296–97; Jean Boutier, "Jacqueries en pays croquant: les révoltes paysannes en Aquitaine (déc. 1789–mars 1790)," *AESC*, 34e année (July–Aug. 1979), 764–65.

32 ANQ, 1837, no. 257, deposition of Louis Bessette, 5 Nov. 1837.

33 ANQ, 1837, no. 146, deposition of Dudley Flowers, 3 Nov. 1837. For accounts of similar charivaris, see the following depositions: ibid., no. 75 (Isaac Coote, 10 Feb. 1838); no. 109 (Louis-Marc Decoigne, 17 Feb. 1838); no. 122 (Pierre Gamelin, 9 Nov. 1837); no. 90 (David Vitty, Rickinson Outtret, Robert Boys, and Thomas Henry, 5 Nov. 1837); no. 103 (Nelson Mott, 6 Dec. 1837); no. 128 (C.H. Lindsay, 8 Nov. 1837); no. 87 (Antoine Bruneau, 17 Dec. 1837); no. 314 (Jean-Baptiste Casavant, 12 Nov. 1837); no. 115 (François St-Denis, 7 Nov. 1837); no. 318 (Benjamin Goulet, 20 Nov. 1837); no. 516 (Orange Tyler, 16 Nov. 1837); no. 3557 (W.U. Chaffers, 9 Nov. 1837); no. 158 (Ambroise Bédard, 10 Nov. 1837); PAC, RG4, A1, 524: 11 (Loop Odell, 17 Nov. 1837). Additional information appears in *Le Populaire*, 5 Nov. 1837; *L'Ami du Peuple* (Montreal), 8 Nov. 1837; PAC, RG9, IA1, vol. 48, James McGillvary to David McCallum, 26 Nov. 1837; Archives du diocèse de St-Jean-de-Québec, H.L. Amiot to Mgr Bourget, St-Cyprien, 16 Nov. 1837.

34 Ray Billington, *The Protestant Crusade 1800–1860: A Study of the Origins of American Nativism* (New York, 1938); Scott W. See, "The Orange Order and Social Violence in Mid-nineteenth Century Saint John," *Acadiensis* 13 (Autumn 1983): 68–92. See also Sean Wilentz, *Chants Democratic: New York City and the Rise of the American Working Class, 1788–1850* (New York, 1984), 264–65.

35 There may have been an exception to this rule in Dudley Flowers's case, for a man approached him a few days after he had surrendered his commission and told him he must sign a copy of the resolutions passed at the St-Charles meeting, failing which he would receive another visitation that night. Understandably intimidated, the lieutenant hastily packed up his family and left the parish, and so it is impossible to know whether an attack really was planned. It seems likely that his visitor was an isolated individual playing a cruel joke since all the other charivari accounts indicate that hostilities ceased once the commission changed hands.

36 PAC, RG4, A1, vol. 524, no. 11, deposition of Loop Odell, 17 Nov. 1837. This point needs to be qualified in the light of one isolated but glaring counterexample. In the parish of St-Valentin, a French-Canadian convert to Protestantism was visited one night in mid-October by a party that "made ludicrous noises with horns, bells, pans and other things"; after asking him if he was a Patriot, the attackers "required that he should renounce his religion and go back to the Roman Catholic religion" (ANQ, 1837, no. 135, deposition of Eloi Babin, 13 Nov. 1837). Though scarcely an issue in other parts of Lower Canada, religion was a source of controversy in this one locality where a group of Swiss missionaries was active. Local inhabitants tended to view the mission as an instrument of the government party, for it accepted money from the Montreal merchants and refused to take part in the Patriot campaigns of 1837. See René Hardy, "La rébellion de 1837–1838 et l'essor du protestantisme canadien-française," *Revue d'histoire de l'amérique française* 29 (Sept. 1975): 180–81.

37 Elinor Kyte Senior, *British Regulars in Montreal: An Imperial Garrison, 1832–1854* (Montreal, 1981), 109–33; Michael S. Cross, "'The Laws are like Cobwebs': Popular Resistance to Authority in Mid-nineteenth Century British North America" in *Law in a Colonial Society: The Nova Scotia Experience*, ed. Peter Waite, Sandra Oxner, and Thomas Barnes (Toronto, 1984), 110–12.

38 René Hardy, "Le charivari dans la sociabilité rurale" (unpublished paper).

UPPER CANADA—
An American Community?*

JANE ERRINGTON

In 1805 Richard Cartwright of Kingston made what seems to have been one of several trips back to his old home in the United States. Though perhaps still haunted by the painful memories of his hurried flight from the Thirteen Colonies almost thirty years before, he nonetheless found this journey to Albany a "pleasant one." "The Country I have traveled through," Cartwright reported to his son, "affords a variety of the most beautiful Prospects and the Improvements that have been made in every Part of it since I visited it before are far beyond anything I could have imagined."[1] That Richard Cartwright, a fervid loyalist-refugee of the revolution and a pillar of society in Upper Canada, could look with approval on the American republic is perhaps surprising to the many scholars who have characterized the early colony as a bastion of British conservatism and the home of virulent anti-Americanism.[2] Yet prominent and not so prominent Upper Canadians of this early period often voiced their satisfaction with and approbation of the rapid economic and social advancements being made in the United States. This admiration did not blind the colonial elite, however, to the central factors which had prompted many to abandon their homes in the 1780s. Republicanism and a democratic government did foster political factions and dissent and often bitter personal controversy. All too often in the United States public virtue and private morality were lost sight of amid the din created by an ill-informed populace and unscrupulous politicians. Such disorder, colonial leaders firmly believed, was "injurious to the peace and happiness of society." Thus, though there was much

*From *The Lion, the Eagle, and Upper Canada: A Developing Colonial Ideology* (Montreal: McGill-Queen's University Press, 1987), 35–54. Reprinted with permission of the publisher.

in the United States "worthy of immitation," it was also clear to many influential Upper Canadians that "the states are far from furnishing proper models in everything."[3]

Perhaps the best way to characterize colonial attitudes towards their southern neighbours is to describe them as ambivalent. Although Upper Canada was politically and, for many, emotionally a British colony, no resident before or indeed after the War of 1812 could have realistically denied that it was also a North American community. Her land and her people were largely American; a number of her social institutions and practices were patterned after those in the United States; and, most importantly, the colony's proximity to and continuing dependence on the United States made it impossible to indiscriminately reject all things American. Certainly the revolution had fostered a wariness and a distrust of the United States which was never really overcome in later years. Yet there also existed in the minds of many Upper Canadians (as indeed there exists today without any apparent contradiction) an admiration for and openness to American ideas and developments. After 1784 community leaders carefully and discriminatingly selected American models for use in their new home. At the same time the United States provided a constant reminder of what Upper Canadians had to try to avoid. In fact, throughout the whole period in question the United States, the province's closest and most accessible neighbour and the former home of so many of its residents, became the colonists' immediate and constant point of reference. It was a yardstick which Upper Canadians frequently used to measure their own success. Inevitably the colonial view of the American republic also came to influence greatly the elite's vision and understanding of their own society and of their position within it.

The American Revolution, as has often been said, created not one nation, but two. Yet the rough and imprecise political demarcation of the northern limits of the new republic had little real impact on the minds of many of its people. Initially, Upper Canada was intended as a home for loyal British subjects. Within a few years, however, the distinctly "loyalist" character of the northern colony was all but lost amid the "sudden and so great . . . influx" of American immigrants who were taking part in "the traditional American search for better lands and a perfect home."[4] By 1812 residents and travellers both observed that, particularly in the western districts of the colony, "the loyalist element was scarcely noticeable amongst the diversity of people who had come to take up land or engage in trade." Even in the heartland of loyalism, the Kingston area, it was reported that "a great portion . . . are persons who evidently have no claim to the appellation loyalists."[5] In its early years Upper Canada was demographically at least an American community.

The growing Americanness of Upper Canada was reinforced by the physical proximity of the two nations. New York and the New England states were Upper Canada's closest and most accessible neighbours. News, mail, and travellers from Europe and, indeed, from the most easterly sections of British North America arrived most quickly and easily through Boston or New York.[6] And Richard Cartwright was not the only Upper Canadian who made frequent journeys south. Though the loyalist residents of Upper Canada had consciously spurned the political outcome of the revolution, they had not cast aside friends and family who remained behind. Soon after the revolution, one traveller noted that "passions [had] mutually subsided" on both sides of the border, and even between some of the most loyal British-Americans and those Americans who had actively "espoused the cause of the Republic" the natural feelings of "consanguinity, amity and personal friendships were revived."[7] This was only to be expected; Americans and Upper Canadians "were still interesting objects to each other." Particularly at Niagara and Kingston and along the St Lawrence "the most social harmony" soon prevailed "between gentlemen on the American side and those on the British side" and many Upper Canadians and Americans frequently exchanged visits for business and pleasure, regardless of the state of international affairs.[8]

The continuing personal contact across the border was supplemented by increasingly lucrative economic associations between merchants. Within ten years of the end of the revolution, whiskey, rum, salt, seeds, and tobacco (to name only a few commodities) regularly flowed from New York and the New England states to Upper Canadian markets or along the St Lawrence to Montreal and Quebec.[9] In return, colonial merchants exported potash and some flour south, and before 1800 a few had even won profitable contracts supplying those American garrisons on the south shore which had been unable to rely on their own farmers for produce.[10] Initially, trade north and south was carried on unhindered by customs duties or tariffs, and provincial merchants actively lobbied before the turn of the century to keep the border free of all restrictions. Yet even the levying of colonial import duties after 1800 and the imposition of an American embargo seven years later did little to hamper what was already "one of the most important sources of prosperity to the colony."[11]

Throughout the first twenty-five years of settlement, there seems little doubt that prominent loyalists and other Upper Canadians still considered themselves an integral part of a North American community which spanned the border. Even the governing elite of York could not escape being influenced by the proximity of the United States—for the republic was, until well after the War of 1812, Upper Canada's window on the world. And it is perhaps the nature of this basic communications link which had the greatest continuing impact on evolving Upper Canadian attitudes and understandings.

Largely isolated from other parts of British North America and until the war, from each other, prominent Upper Canadians from 1790 onwards relied on the United States for much of their knowledge of affairs outside their local communities. Only the colonial administrators regularly received reports from London and these were months out of date and often lacked detail. Thus most interested Upper Canadians, forced to find a more reliable and comprehensive source of news and information, quite readily turned to American gazettes.[12] This propensity to look south of the border for the most up-to-date and topical information was made clearly apparent when the few local newspapers began to appear after 1793.

Like fellow editors in the republic, Upper Canadian printers did not always specify the sources of their information; but it was certainly not unusual to read the general byline "from the United States" or "taken from American newspapers" preceding reports from England, Europe, the Maritime colonies, and sometimes even from Quebec. With increasing frequency, Upper Canadian editors began to acknowledge that their accounts of European affairs were generally reprinted from a New York newspaper, often the *New York Daily Advertiser;* American congressional reports were frequently drawn from the *National Intelligencer.* Even the editors of the official government newspaper (published in York after 1798), the *Upper Canada Gazette,* were forced to agree with printers in Kingston and Niagara that, like travellers and mail, European and British news reached the colony fastest through New York, Philadelphia, and Boston. A source analysis of the *Kingston Gazette* from its first publication in September 1810 to just after the war in June 1815 confirms this. Approximately 75 percent of all news printed by editor Stephen Miles originated in the United States; and even the official closing of the border after war was declared did not stop Miles from relying on American sources for most of his European reports.[13]

More important, however, was the type of American sources which Miles seems to have specifically preferred. Almost all reports in the *Kingston Gazette* which originated in the United States were taken from federalist newspapers, those journals which, after 1800, supported the major opposition party in the United States. At first glance, this might suggest that since New York and the New England states were the heartland of conservative America, it was their newspapers which were most readily available in Upper Canada. However, the nonfederalist reports appearing in the *Kingston Gazette* and in other colonial newspapers indicate that this may not have been the case. In fact, Miles seems only to have been following a trend which had been firmly established by previous colonial editors. The Tiffany brothers, editors of first the *Canada Constellation* and then the *Niagara Herald* at the turn of the century in Niagara, and John Bennett, the editor of the *Upper Canada Gazette* in York, appeared to look quite consciously for accounts which most closely expressed the viewpoint of their readers. For the most part, this preference was implied merely by naming the specific journal; for example, a report would be taken from the *Albany Gazette* or from the *Baltimore Federal Republican.* However, when John Cameron took over the *Upper Canada Gazette* in 1807, he explicitly informed his readers that he was pleased to have opened "a regular correspondence with the Federal Printers in the United States" for his "early intelligence of continental and foreign affairs."[14] It would seem, therefore, that Miles's and other colonial editors' preference for reports from the American conservative newspapers was a measured and conscious one. And considering the highly dependent financial position of colonial newspapers at this time, it can be argued that this preference reflected the prevailing view of their limited constituency of wealthy, articulate, influential Upper Canadians.[15]

Thus before the War of 1812 and indeed throughout and after the war, influential colonists not only considered themselves part of a North American community but specifically part of a conservative American community. There was developing in Upper Canada, as was emerging in New Brunswick at the same time, a "federalist loyalist alliance" which provided much of the ideological underpinnings of the colonists' evolving view of their neighbours. Not only did Upper Canadians rely on the federalist press for most of their information about what was happening in the United States, but both their positive and "negative stereotype[s] of republican America"[16] were also largely borrowed from federalists south of the border.

In 1796 Gideon Tiffany, then editor of the *Upper Canada Gazette* still published in Niagara, confidently predicted that "we look to the time as not far distant when our wilderness shall have been converted into well cultivated fields."[17] From the outset, Upper Canadians believed that the future of the new colony depended on the development of its agricultural potential. As one anonymous Kingstonian commented in 1810, "in a political view" agriculture "is important and perhaps the only firm and stable foundation of greatness." "As a profession," he continued, "it strengthens the mind without enervating the body. In morality, it tends to increase virtue without introducing vice. In religion, it naturally inspires piety, devotion and dependence, without the tincture of infidelity." Moreover, he concluded, it was "a rational and agreeable amusement to the man of leisure, and a boundless force of contemplation and activity to the industrious."[18] The salutory effects of an agricultural life were clearly evident as Upper Canadians looked across the Atlantic. The colonists believed that it was Great Britain's hardworking farming population who were the economic mainstay of its "power and opulence"[19] and the foundation of its superiority in the world. If carefully nurtured and developed, Upper Canada too could share in this prosperity. But it was apparent that though Great Britain might be the ideal to be followed, her agricultural techniques had little to offer the Upper Canadian pioneers. Rather it was to the United States, "where the soil and climate are similar,"[20] that colonists had to turn for models of *how* this rural prosperity was to be accomplished.

From the very beginning, colonial leaders recognized that only "the Americans understood the mode of agriculture proper for the new colony."[21] And though some leading Upper Canadians had reservations about admitting so many American settlers, most in the early years did approve of the economic benefits of Lieutenant-Governor Simcoe's "patriot policy"[22] of 1792 which encouraged farmers from south of the border to move to the virgin Upper Canadian wilderness. "Being from necessity in the habit of providing with their own hands many things which in other countries the artisan is always at hand to supply, they [the Americans] possess resources in themselves which other people are usually strangers to," Richard Cartwright commented in a letter to the then lieutenant-governor, Richard Hunter, in 1799. Though Cartwright was one of those who was concerned about the deleterious effect of so many Americans on the political development of the colony, he realized that only these settlers "would boldly begin their operations in the wilderness . . . the dreary novelty of the situation would appall a European."[23]

The native ingenuity of these new settlers was not enough, however, to ensure that the new lands would become fully productive. Through their travels and their reading of American newspapers and journals, leading Upper Canadians were made aware of the new agricultural techniques being developed south of the border—developments which could easily be introduced into the northern province. And the vehicle most suited to transmit these ideas, it was realized, was the burgeoning Upper Canadian press. Even if newspapers were not directly available to the majority in the colony, the information they contained was soon passed on by those who came to the market, to the tavern, and to the other informal occasions which drew residents together.[24]

Throughout their years of publication, the *Canada Constellation,* the *Niagara Herald,* the *Kingston Gazette,* and even the *Upper Canada Gazette* devoted a great deal of space to articles on planting and harvesting, and a host of other matters of specific interest to farmers.[25] Most of these were taken from a wide selection of American publications and from the papers of various American agricultural societies. For example, a letter from one Joseph Cooper of New Jersey to a friend in Philadelphia, reprinted in the *Kingston Gazette,* gave specific directions on the best method of tilling soil.[26] Upper Canadian farmers received explicit instruction on the keeping of bees from the *Boston Register;* relying on an unnamed American newspaper, the editor of the *Upper Canada Gazette* provided a detailed discussion of how potatoes were cultivated in Ireland and the United States leaving no doubt that the latter method was far more appropriate in the northern colony.[27] And in support of already stated colonial policy, the Upper Canadian press gave considerable attention to the growing of hemp with advice taken from the New York Agricultural Society and various American journals.[28] In addition, residents of the Niagara district, of York, and later of Kingston, obviously aware of the advantages communities south of the border were gaining from local agricultural societies, began to establish their own societies after 1800.[29] Both implicitly and explicitly, the Upper Canadian farming population was urged to use these new proven techniques in order to clear more land and to increase their agricultural production. Constantly reminding readers of the progress being made south of the border, the press emphasized that it was "in the combined interests of patriotism and self interest"[30] for the colonists to exert themselves. One article on orchards published in the *Kingston Gazette* in 1811 was most explicit in this regard. "Our inhabitants, it is hoped, are too ambitious to be outdone in any laudable exertions by their neighbours in the United States."[31]

Improving agricultural techniques was not the only concern that Upper Canadians and many Americans had in common. Both were trying to open up the frontier to settlement and to further national development. South of the border, however, the process had been going on for over 100 years and it was realized that the Americans had accumulated valuable experience of how best to confront a host of problems. Thus, over the years, the new British colonists looked to the United States for examples of how roads should be built and maintained and how land and water transportation generally could be improved. One contributor to the *Canada Constellation* recommended, for example, that York institute a Stump Law, a statute found on the books of many American towns, to ensure clear passage on the capital's lanes and encourage proper maintenance of town lots. Another resident in Kingston suggested that Upper Canadians "should learn a useful lesson from their neighbours" and have a national census taken in the colony to aid in determining the proper number of representatives in the House of Assembly and in assessing taxes.[32] Through the pages of Upper Canadian newspapers, colonial readers also followed with interest American developments in manufacturing and improvements of local and national services. Of particular concern and use to the British-Americans was how their southern cousins coped with fires, a problem which plagued both societies.[33] Upper Canadians were also interested in early American attempts to combat various diseases and excessive drinking, procedures which began to be employed in the colony after the War of 1812.[34] As fascinating for many prominent colonists was the rapid industrial growth of the United States.[35] One article in the *Upper Canada Gazette* told of a new factory for the spinning and weaving of hemp which had just been built outside Philadelphia. In 1811 the *Kingston Gazette* noted the establishment of a new state prison in New York.[36] The same paper even considered the American proposals to build the Erie Canal joining Lake Erie to the Hudson River "praise-worthy,"[37] though it was realized that the canal would seriously undermine traditional colonial trade routes. Perhaps the most telling comments, however, were those which appeared in the *Kingston Gazette* in late 1810 concerning the creation of a local bank. American examples were expressly used both to support and to oppose the proposal, for, as one resident stated, the situation in the United States "is nearly similar to our own." Certainly the banks in Utica, New York, and other American centres were far more appropriate examples than any British ones. Moreover, as one contributor somewhat cryptically concluded, "there are many among us capable of correcting me if I have mistated a single fact."[38]

These constant references to American practices and models were in part a recognition of the great progress being made in the United States. Though Upper Canadians realized that their own development was not keeping pace, there seemed to be little resentment of American advances. Indeed, with few exceptions, the northern observers recognized and applauded the American spirit of enterprise and native ingenuity. Soon, Upper Canadians believed, they too would enjoy the benefits of such improvements and prosperity. As the editor of the *Upper Canada Gazette* confidently predicted as early as 1796, "the great Franklin" might well wish to return 100 years hence "to see how wonderful have been the improvements in the American world."[39]

Leading Upper Canadians were always conscious, however, that material prosperity, though important in itself, could not ensure the political and social survival of the colony. Proximity to the United States and the admittance of so many "good" American settlers was in fact a double-edged sword. Though the United States provided the much-needed technical innovations and the personnel to maintain and develop the colony to its fullest potential, the very presence of these settlers and the proximity of the republic also threatened Upper Canada's continued existence as a distinct and, many believed, superior society.

In 1784 many leading Upper Canadians had chosen not to become citizens of a republican democracy because they could not, emotionally or intellectually, accept its rejection of the monarchy and the British constitution. In the late 1780s, however, the colonists' actual understanding of the new American system and its implications was relatively uninformed. Preoccupied with their own backbreaking attempts to establish new homes, Upper Canadians had little time to consider broad political and social issues. The little news that did appear in the first colonial newspaper, the *Upper Canada Gazette,* reflected its readers' preoccupation with the situation in their own colony and in Great Britain. Yet Upper Canadians could not and did not remain isolated on the northern frontier for long. As contact with friends and family was renewed and American newspapers became more readily available, their interest in and concern about American affairs deepened. In part, this was a result of the growing impact that European affairs and especially the French Revolution were seen to have on American politics. More immediately, however, Upper Canadian interest was sparked by the destructive effects that "democracy" was having on American society itself.

Particularly after 1796, parties and factions seemed to be destroying any stability and balance which postrevolutionary America had achieved. Relying increasingly on the federalists of New York and the New England states for their news and understanding of the impending disaster, Upper Canadians watched fearfully the apparent decline and downfall of the republic. The colonists' concern was neither disinterested nor, as time went on, uninformed. The failure of the American "experiment," it was believed, threatened all in the vicinity. Moreover, Upper Canadians' understanding of development south of the border influenced to a large degree their vision of their own society; it provided a coherent explanation not only for the troubles to the south but also for the political dissension growing in Upper Canada after 1800.

While the federalist elite was in command in the United States many Upper Canadians believed that it was guiding "the American experiment of representative democracy"[40] with restraint and some success. By 1796, however, it was clear that the fragile tranquillity and stability which had been so tenuously attained under George Washington and other federalist leaders was in jeopardy. "Factions and rebellions" were invading the republic and between 1796 and 1800 many Upper Canadians watched the rise of the new "republican party" to prominence with growing anxiety. In their efforts to challenge the policies and the political supremacy of the federalists, the so-called "Virginian Oligarchy" was "dividing the people from the government."[41] And though as late as August 1800 some in the colony still expected the federalists to win the upcoming presidential election, reports of the growing divisions in the federalist ranks and the complications evident in the electoral system caused others to be more doubtful. The American people were becoming "the tools of factions," it was judged, and the pawns of political opportunists.[42] Increasingly interested northern observers began to predict that if such political infighting continued the United States would be humbled and whatever remained of liberty would be lost. By February of 1801 there were few in Upper Canada who were really surprised at Jefferson's victory.[43]

There is no question that for a number of prominent Upper Canadians the republican victory of 1800 was of only passing interest and certainly of little consequence. Many of the British-born officials and immigrants, like the recently arrived John Strachan, supposed that though "the politics of the United States had undergone considerable change ... the general measures of that Government will undergo no greater change than a change of ministry in Britain." Strachan's somewhat simplistic view of the American system of government was initially coupled with a latent admiration of the new republic and its people. Certainly, he commented in March 1801 that "the President and Sub-Presidents are both noted republicans, the federalist party is split in two."[44] It was only gradually, as his residence in the colony lengthened, that Strachan gained some real appreciation of the growing rift between the federalists and the republicans. It was then that he began to acquire a marked antipathy to the United States.

"The character of the Americans is generally speaking bad," he remarked in a letter to his old Scots friend James Brown in 1807, "and craft and duplicity is too much resorted to even in their public measure."[45] Believing that he had "profitted" by his "neighbourhood to Democracy," he explained to his friend in 1809 that "the mass of people are more corrupted than a person of your excellent heart can well imagine." The men of "this new nation are *vain* and *rapacious* and without *honour*," and the official encouragement of "licentious liberty" keeps them "at a constant boil." Even in Upper Canada, so heavily populated with American-born settlers, Strachan had concluded in 1803, "there is a most lamentable want of what [he and Brown] call independent or respectable people. . . . In point of fact," he proclaimed, "they are brutes."[46]

By the end of the decade, Strachan even went so far as to propose what was at that time a rather novel explanation of the differences between Upper Canadians and Americans. In perhaps the first explicit articulation of the myth of "the true north strong and free," which would become so important to Canadian imperialist thought some seventy-five years later,[47] Strachan argued that Canada, because of its geographical location and climate, was inherently superior to the United States. In a veiled reference to the republic, he asserted that inevitably "governments of southern countries were despotic and slavery was rife." Upper Canada and, implicitly, Great Britain, on the other hand, "being among the northern nations" were the true homes of liberty and justice. The souls of their residents, he pronounced, "are raised to exertion by their native storms; among them all the different branches of knowledge are carried to the highest perfection." To Strachan, it seemed clear that "the natives of colder and more severe climates far surpass the inhabitants of the milder sky."[48] This explanation notwithstanding, Strachan had by the end of the decade come to believe firmly in the evil consequences of a republican form of government. The type of government under which one lived "has a direct influence on the manner of the people,"[49] he wrote in the *Kingston Gazette* in 1811. A number of Strachan's contemporaries had come to this realization a decade before. Certainly it was this assumption which had caused so much alarm when news of the republican victory had reached the colony.

Naturally accepting the federalist viewpoint of the situation, many influential colonists in Kingston and Niagara came to believe in 1800 that "the Americans are now destined to be torn into faction—and to live in perpetual disorder."[50] Unlike Washington, whose life had "been dedicated to virtue," Thomas Jefferson among other things "countenanced the abolition of the Christian Sabbath." In the United States, "public tranquility, public harmony and public justice"[51] were lost, destroyed by republican anarchy and the rule of the mob. From their knowledge of the ancient republics of Athens and Rome, whose downfall could be attributed to the natural "consequences of an elective government,"[52] many of the indigenous leaders of Upper Canada, echoing their federalist friends, fully expected that history was bound to repeat itself. "A dreadful spirit of division" had split the country "into two distinct peoples," it was reported, and "revolution, and perhaps a bloody one seems not far distant." To many on both sides of the border, it seemed clear that the United States "had reached the end of a rising curve of the cycle."[53]

It was this second, perhaps more informed view of a people divided, of good and bad Americans battling for political supremacy, which tended to prevail in Upper Canada over the next fifteen years. The evidence suggests that most of the indigenous elite did not share the harsh and almost complete condemnation of the American people that Rev. John Strachan frequently expressed. The disastrous decline of the United States, they believed, was the result of the depravity of the republicans. And as the plight of the federalists worsened Upper Canadians continued to be sympathetic to their dilemma. "I sincerely pity the virtuous and well disposed part of the community in that country," wrote one Upper Canadian in the *Kingston Gazette* in 1812. "For seven years" they have suffered and "they are still suffering under the unjust and unprincipled measures of their Government." They "are making the noblest effort by every laudable means in their power to counteract the baneful effects of their tyrannical and ruinous policies."[54]

By 1812 even the young Scottish minister had come to appreciate the Upper Canadian–federalist point of view. Over the past twelve years he too had made important personal contacts with people south of the border and, together with other British residents, his views had been significantly shaped by those around him. Though increasingly antagonistic to the United States, he now accepted without question that it was the federalist party which possessed "all the worth and talent in the United States." Sympathy did not mean approval, however, for Strachan continually wondered what good these citizens could perform in a perverted and tyrannical system.[55]

Many other leading Upper Canadians had begun to share Strachan's fears that even the best efforts of the federalists would not be able to postpone disaster. Most now judged that "the violence of their political parties, their abusive attacks upon each other's characters and the scurrility of too many of their publications" were all too characteristic of republican democracy. "Their democratic system," wrote one contributor to the *Kingston Gazette*, "fostered an uncontrollable spirit of party ... the rage of their parties has become intolerable."[56] Moreover, the numerous reports from south of the border of violence, crime, and political intrigue all pointed to a society where, with the firm control of the federalists now gone, stability was permanently lost.[57]

The worsening situation in the United States was a constant reminder to leading Upper Canadians of what, at all costs, had to be avoided in the northern colony. Upper Canada had been given a form of government far superior to that of the republic; but the evils of levelling, of factions, and of political and social strife were still painfully evident in the colony. And while, at the official level, the Upper Canadian legislature consciously strove to subdue "French principles," local newspapers warned of the more immediate dangers from the south.

An ever-present and growing cause of concern among some of the colonial elite and particularly those in Kingston and later in York was the large number of American settlers who lived in Upper Canada. As early as 1795, travellers noted that "the spirit of independence which prevails in the United States" was beginning to "gain ground" in Upper Canada. Indeed, many new arrivals seemed to retain "ideas of equality and insubordination"; a number expressed "a determined partiality to the United States" and many were generally judged to be "bad citizens."[58] It was apparent that these pioneers had not come to Upper Canada because of their preference for the British form of government. "It is not to be expected," Cartwright wrote to Lieutenant-Governor Hunter in 1799, that "a man will change his political principles, or prejudices by crossing a river." And Cartwright counselled that in the future "the greatest precaution . . . should be used to exclude improper persons"[59] from entering the colony.

Not all leading Upper Canadians shared these concerns, however. In one of the few instances when Robert Hamilton and Cartwright were clearly at odds, Hamilton, William Dickson, and other Niagara merchants categorically asserted that political allegiance had little to do with developing the North American economy. As his biographer, Bruce Wilson, notes, Hamilton, because of his own interests in land speculation and the forwarding and portaging enterprises, fully supported Simcoe's policy on American emigration and actively lobbied colonial authorities to keep the border open.[60] Only a few in the Niagara area questioned such ideas. One resident did note that there were "a few uneasy souls, admirers of republicanism and revolution" in the area in 1801, and he feared that their presence was "much to the prejudice"[61] of the colonial government. Most in the western region, however, fully supported their leaders' understanding of the situation.

Though before the War of 1812 not all colonial leaders were agreed on the desirability of unrestricted American immigration, most were increasingly aware that, like the federalists in the United States, they were surrounded by a population which threatened their leadership and the basic principles of order and deference on which the society was founded. In the United States such democratic impulses, it was argued, had led to a general levelling and to a disintegration of social order. Upper Canadian leaders were determined to forestall such developments in their homeland.

An article in the *Niagara Herald* printed just after the news of Jefferson's election had reached the colony, sounded the first warning. Explicitly pointing to recent events south of the border, the editors declared that "there cannot be a greater judgment befall a country than such a dreadful spirit of division." Political parties made people "greater strangers . . . more adverse to one another than if they were actually two different nations." Thus perhaps one of the most significant lessons that Upper Canadians learned as they watched American politics was that "A furious party spirit when it rages in its full violence exerts itself in civil war and bloodshed; . . . In a word it fills a nation with spleen and rancour, and extinguishes all the seeds of good nature, compassions and humanity."[62]

It is not surprising, therefore, that in the elections for the House of Assembly in the first decade of the nineteenth century, most Upper Canadian candidates placed a high premium on their independence from any party or faction. "Actuated by motives remote from the Pursuits of Ambition or the Schemes of self-interest," candidates requested support so that they could enact "wise and beneficial laws for the good of society." Electors were exhorted to vote prudently, to elect a "gentleman" "who has honesty and an independent spirit" to represent them. He need not be popular but, it was asserted, he had to have ability and judgment and be expected to fulfil his "sacred duty" to uphold the "general good and general harmony" of society.[63] The appeal of William Weekes, a recently arrived Irishman running for a seat in the House of Assembly in 1804, was indicative of many of the period. At the conclusion of his *Address to the Free and Independent Electors of the East Riding of York* he stated, "I stand unconnected with any party, unsupported by any influence and unambitious of any patronage."[64]

Yet, a year later, it was the same William Weekes who, together with Joseph Willcocks and Justice Thorpe, became the centre of a controversy which appeared to threaten the very fabric of Upper Canadian society.[65] In a by-election in 1805, Weekes (once clerk to the controversial Aaron Burr, who had reportedly caused the split in the federalist party which many felt had resulted in its electoral defeat in 1800) once again offered himself as a candidate; but this time he intended to represent "the interests of the People." At approximately the same time the newly arrived Justice Thorpe consciously began a campaign to direct and redress the grievances of many Upper Canadians concerning land policies and the colonial administration. Within a year these two men and their small group of associates became identified as champions of "the people" against the tyranny of the government.[66] And for the first time in Upper Canada's short history, the established leaders of the colony discovered themselves under fire and their authority seriously challenged. For many prominent colonists the situation was all too reminiscent of political developments south of the border and this served to reinforce their identification with their "ideological brethren" to the south, the American federalists.

The Weekes-Thorpe controversy had started innocuously enough. Robert Thorpe arrived in the colony in September 1805 fully expecting to be appointed chief justice of Upper Canada and firmly convinced that he had both the necessary talent and a duty to rectify the evils of the present colonial administration and "conciliate the people" to the government. Initially, Justice Thorpe restricted his activities to conducting an active and lengthy correspondence with the Colonial Office and advising sympathetic representatives of the people, including William Weekes, on how best to bring certain concerns of interest "to the people" before the House of Assembly.[67] Though colonial leaders considered such activities totally "outside the accepted bounds"[68] of colonial politics and clearly suspicious, it was not until Lieutenant-Governor Gore arrived and refused to countenance Thorpe's ideas that the controversy flared into vitriolic debate. Keenly disappointed at being bypassed for the chief justiceship, aggrieved that the lieutenant-governor had failed to take his advice, and increasingly isolated from York society, Thorpe took his campaign directly to the people, using both the bench and, after Weekes's death at the end of 1806, a seat in the House of Assembly as vehicles to attract support. Between October 1806 and November 1807, Thorpe and his "Party," including William Wyatt, recently dismissed as surveyor-general, and Joseph Willcocks, editor of the *Upper Canada Guardian,* formed an opposition group which actively agitated against the colonial administration.[69]

At first the *Upper Canada Gazette* in York, following the lead of the colonial legislature, tried to ignore the situation publicly at least. Prominent Upper Canadians were not loath, however, to express their growing concern privately to each other. The activities of this cabal of "outrageous demagogues"[70] were almost treasonous, one anonymous Upper Canadian recorded in a private sketch of the conduct of Justice Thorpe. By their public addresses and increasingly through their newspaper, the *Upper Canada Guardian,* Thorpe and his associates were encouraging active discontent among the people and partisan and irresponsible opposition to the government. To the established leaders of Upper Canada there seemed no question that, left alone, the general populace would have remained loyal and relatively acquiescent. It was the renegade justice who was at the centre of unrest and "the principal mover of all factions and turbulence in the province." The Irishman had perverted the court from acting as a hall of justice to being a "vehicle of private spleen and malice."[71] Most discounted Thorpe's public pronouncements of loyalty and concern for the welfare of the colony. Rather it was contended that only "personal vanity and infatuation" directed his "irrational activities."[72] By his actions Thorpe had created an opposition party which was consciously setting out to destroy order and good government. Few colonial leaders considered that Thorpe had any heartfelt concern for "the interests of the people."

By the summer of 1809 the Upper Canadian elite found that their privately expressed concerns and various attempts to control the situation were largely ineffectual. News of the growing unrest in the colony was beginning to reach London; moreover, "the diabolical machinations of a desperate cabal of Irishmen," with their "treasonable allusions to the American revolution" threatened "to reduce the province to the same folorn condition"[73] which prevailed in the United States. At no time did the leaders of the colony attribute Thorpe's activities to the *direct* influence of American republican ideas. Some did suspect that Joseph Willcocks had personal and political connections with radical American republican editors. Most of the colonial elite, however, identified Thorpe with the radical United Irish movement.[74] He was characterized as "a friend and associate of the celebrated [Thomas Addis] Emmett,"[75] once a radical leader of the United Irish movement and after 1803 a noted American republican; moreover, many of Thorpe's Upper Canadian associates were Irishmen who also shared their leader's proclivities for rebellious Irish thought. By the fall of 1807 there seemed little doubt that Thorpe was heading a "Democratic Party" based on "republican principles"[76] and the effect of this man upon the minds of the American settlers, who "from habit and education" were "ready enough to second the views of factions,"[77] was potentially disastrous.

Yet even Justice Thorpe's suspension and eventual departure from the colony at the end of 1807 failed to alleviate the situation. The controversy continued, fuelled by comments in the *Upper Canada Guardian* and the appearance of a pamphlet written by John Mills Jackson defending the justice's stand. In March 1810 the House of Assembly was unable to ignore the situation any longer, and it publicly denounced Jackson's *View of the Province of Upper Canada.* "It contains a false, scandalous and seditious libel," they judged, "manifesting the tendency to alienate the affection of the people from His Majesty's Government in the Province."[78] That same year, two private pamphlets also appeared in defence of the colonial government. Both Richard Cartwright, in *Letters of an American Loyalist to His Friend in Great Britain,* and an anonymous settler, in *A Letter to the Right Honourable Lord Castlereagh,* condemned the actions of the "few desperadoes" and their attempts to "impress the public mind with an unfavourable opinion of its Government."[79] Both authors stressed that even in these perilous times Upper Canadians, by virtue of their constitution, enjoyed "the greatest practical political freedom."[80]

These attempts to negate Thorpe's support in the colony, and more significantly to convince the imperial parliament that the colony was loyal and committed to the Crown, did not, however, still the fears of civil unrest. In 1810 it had become painfully clear to some in Upper Canada that the colony was too American. In the eyes of many colonial leaders, the threat posed by democracy and its attendant factionalism to the internal security and well-being of the British province was only compounded by the menacing policies of the republican administration south of the border. By 1810 a growing number of influential Upper Canadians had come to believe that they were fighting for the very existence of the colony.

The pernicious effect of faction on the political life of Upper Canada was not the only American development which concerned prominent colonists. By 1800 they discovered that republican ideas were also invading the religious and educational institutions of the new province—the two forums which should have been the bulwarks of society's authority. Unless these institutions were safeguarded by ensuring that the right type of school, run by the right men and the right church (in this case the Church of England) was established, it was feared that they would in fact become agents of republican discontent and active disaffection.

Between 1784 and 1815 all attempts to establish the Church of England in the colony proved unsuccessful. Neither the government nor the Society for the Propagation of the Gospel was willing to financially support or actively promote the expansion of the church. By 1812 there were still only six Anglican clergymen in Upper Canada, far too few to adequately serve the growing population. What was particularly upsetting to many colonial leaders, however, was that for most Upper Canadians the deplorable state of the Church of England was of little consequence. Reflecting their own past experiences in America, most residents preferred the ministrations of itinerant preachers from the United States and particularly the young and enterprising Methodist and Baptist ministers who annually trekked north to the backwoods.[81]

These "preachers and fanatics," Richard Cartwright remarked in 1806, had "overrun the country." With their emphasis on individual salvation and mass participation, these "deplorable fanatics"[82] turned men's hearts away from constituted authority. Rather than supporting the "rationale doctrines of the Church of England," it was feared that the Methodists in particular were filling the people's minds with "low cunning" and with "republican ideas of independence and individual freedom."[83] And there seemed to be nothing that could be done to offset their pernicious influence.

Perhaps more insidious for some Upper Canadians was the influence that "democratic" ideas were having on the most vulnerable aspect of colonial society, the education of its youth. In the early years of the province's development, schools had been virtually nonexistent. As Richard Cartwright explained, most Upper Canadians' time was taken up with the "axe and the plough." The little education that was available was received at home; only a privileged few were sent to schools in Lower Canada or in the United States.[84] Gradually, however, "a spirit of improvement" began to spread throughout the colony. Local clergymen opened small classrooms to teach arithmetic and the classics. Prominent residents like Richard Cartwright began to engage tutors for their children. In 1807 the legislature established four district grammar schools[85] and by 1810 many residents were advocating the creation of common schools, as were to be found in both the United States and Great Britain, "to aid in the administration of justice," the assimilation of the colony's diverse population, and the establishment of a deferential society.[86] From the beginning, however, education in Upper Canada was plagued by a lack of suitable teachers and textbooks. In the prewar years, most masters and books came from the United States and the values they professed were often inimical to "inculcating [those] habits of subordination"[87] deemed to be one of the essential functions of any school system. Various attempts to rectify the situation proved unsuccessful. It was not, however, until a new academy of learning was opened in Ernest Town, just outside Kingston, in 1811 that the full implications of this problem were realized.

The establishment of the Ernest Town school was first announced in the *Kingston Gazette* in April 1811. Its headmaster was to be Barnabas Bidwell, a recently arrived American. Initially, many must have been delighted at the opening of a new school. For some, however, approval was quickly transformed into horror when it was realized that Bidwell had once been an active member of the republican party in Massachusetts and was rumoured to be a fugitive from justice. "If training and talents were all that were requisite to qualify a man to be a teacher to an academy, it is then presumed that no exception could be taken to Mr. Bidwell," one anonymous resident noted in the *Kingston Gazette.* But "Vindex" found it "revolting to all sense of propriety and everything connected with our normal feelings" that "a malefactor, who has fled from the justice of his own country" should even be considered for the appointment. The rumour of Bidwell's illegal activities was only one and perhaps not the most important reason for "Vindex's" objection. He pointed out that in the United States Bidwell was "a distinguished partisan of democracy in the most unqualified sense of the word." Surely, "Vindex" commented, "it would be hardly possible for those who should be placed under his tuition to escape the infection of his political tenets, which are hostile to the fundamental principles of our government."[88] It seemed that the evil influence of democracy had invaded even this heartland of loyalism.

A number of residents were unconcerned, however. One member of the school committee publicly defended Bidwell's appointment in the next issue of the *Gazette.* He assured possible patrons of the Ernest Town Academy that Bidwell's political beliefs had no bearing on his abilities and would not interfere with his teaching. And despite further protests from "Vindex," Bidwell retained his post.[89] Nonetheless, the Bidwell affair must have confirmed some of the worst fears of influential residents in the area. Not only did many of the so-called late loyalists retain their sympathy for the republican cause but evidently even some of the local leaders of the Kingston region were willing to condone and actually to encourage such ideas.

By the end of 1811 these ongoing concerns about the invasion of American democratic ideas into colonial society became submerged under a far more pressing and immediate fear of direct military invasion from the United States. Throughout 1811 and 1812 the *Upper Canada Gazette* and the *Kingston Gazette,* the only two colonial newspapers still regularly published, were dominated by news of the escalating tensions between Great Britain and the United States. It seemed inevitable that Upper Canada would soon be drawn into the fray. For residents in Kingston and Niagara the prospect was particularly daunting. For twenty years they had maintained close personal and economic relations with American friends. They had relied on the United States for guidance on how to develop the colony. They depended on the United States for most of their news and it was from federalist-American reports and perceptions that they continued to draw most of their own understanding of the political situation in which they were now enmeshed. During the first decade of the new century, that sense of community, which rested on the common heritage and occupations of the leaders at Kingston and Niagara and the federalists in the United States, and on the continuing contact between them, had strengthened and matured. Prominent Upper Canadians believed that they not only shared the attitudes and beliefs of their American conservative friends but also the danger of being overwhelmed by republican troublemakers. For articulate Upper Canadians, far too much of their daily lives was affected by their relations with the United States for them to welcome the coming war or to condemn indiscriminately all American actions.

Even the British-born leaders of York and other British immigrants were dismayed by the prospect of war. Though many had initially been antagonistic to the United States, over the years their anti-Americanism had become somewhat muted. Like the leaders of Kingston and Niagara, they too were dependent on American sources for their news. After 1807, if not before, they also consciously showed a preference for federalist sources and came to accept many of the American conservative explanations of both world and American events. For the most part, influential Upper Canadians in the prewar years looked to the United States with a relatively informed and discriminating eye. It was only to be expected, therefore, that Upper Canada's response to the impending conflict would be marked by ambivalence.

• Notes

1 Richard Cartwright to James Cartwright, 23 Oct. 1805, Cartwright Papers, Port Hope Collection, Queen's University Archives (hereafter QUA).

2 S.F. Wise, "Colonial Attitudes from the Era of the War of 1812 to the Rebellions of 1837" in *Canada Views the United States,* ed. S.F. Wise and

Robert Brown (Toronto: Macmillan, 1967), 22.

3 *Kingston Gazette,* 5 Feb. 1811.

4 Isaac Weld, *Travels through the States of North America and the Provinces of Upper and Lower Canada,* vol. 2 (1807; rprt New York: Augusta Kelley, 1970), 90; Marcus Hansen and J.B. Brebner, *The Mingling of the Canadian and American*

Peoples (New York: Russell and Russell, 1940), 66.

5 Michael Smith, *A Geographical View of the Province of Upper Canada* (Philadelphia: Thomas and Robert Desliver, 1813), 82; QUA, Cartwright to Hunter, 23 Aug. 1799.

6 To facilitate this contact, ferries joined both Kingston and Niagara to contiguous American communities. See references in *Upper Canada Gazette*, particularly 19 April 1797, and numerous travellers' accounts including John Lambert, *Travels through Canada and the United States in the Years 1806, 1807, 1808* (London: C. Cradock and W. Joy, 1814), 268–69; John Melish, *Travels through the United States of America . . . and travels through various parts of. . . Canada* (Belfast: J. Smyth, 1818), 539; La Rochfoucault Liancourt, *Travels in Canada* (1795; rprt Toronto: William Renwick Riddell, 1917), 77. See also Stephen Roberts, "Imperial Policy, Provincial Administration and Defence in Upper Canada 1796–1812" (PhD thesis, Oxford, 1975) for a discussion of the impact of travel time on British policy.

7 Robert Gourlay, *Statistical Account of Upper Canada* (London: 1822; rprt Toronto: S.R. Publishers, 1966), 115; Liancourt, *Travels*, 44. Rev. John Stuart kept up a regular correspondence with friends in the United States. Stuart to Rev. White, Misc. Ms., Public Archives of Ontario (hereafter PAO). See also among others Joel Stone Papers, Solomon Jones Papers, QUA; Bruce Wilson, *The Enterprises of Robert Hamilton* (Ottawa: Carleton University Press, 1984).

8 D'Arcy Boulton, *A Sketch of His Majesty's Province of Upper Canada* (London: C. Rickaby), 32.

9 The St Lawrence–Great Lakes system was of primary importance to residents on both sides of the border until well after the War of 1812. See Donald Creighton, *The Empire of the St. Lawrence* (1937; rprt Toronto: Macmillan, 1956), Gerald Craig, *Upper Canada: The Formative Years, 1784–1841* (Toronto: McClelland and Stewart, 1963), Wilson, *Robert Hamilton*. For customs records of the Kingston area, see RG 16, 133, Alex. Hagerman Collection, Collection of Customs, Public Archives of Canada (hereafter PAC); Stone Papers, Accounts 1803–9, QUA.

10 Cartwright to George Davison and Co., 11 Nov. 1797, stressed that free trade was essential. Both Lambert, *Travels*, 239, and Melish, *Travels*, 539, noted that trade with New York flourished in these early years, and certainly the Cartwright correspondence, QUA; the Baldwin Papers, particularly the letters of Quetton St George, Toronto Public Library (hereafter TPL) and PAO; Hamilton correspondence cited in Wilson, *Robert Hamilton*, 101–27; and advertisements in the local newspapers all attest to the importance of American trade. Even at the personal level, Upper Canadians depended on American peddlers for many of their goods. See Richardson Wright, *Hawkers and Walkers in Early America* (Philadelphia: J.B. Lippincott, 1927) and Brian Osborne, "Trading on the Frontier: The Function of Peddlers, Markets and Fairs in Nineteenth-Century Ontario" in *Canadian Papers in Rural History*, vol. 2, ed. D.H. Akenson (Gananoque: Langdale Press, 1979).

11 Richard A. Preston, *Kingston before the War of 1812* (Toronto: The Champlain Society, 1959), xxiii.

12 In part this can be inferred from the sources available to indigenous editors after an Upper Canadian press emerged in 1793. In addition, the letters in the Cartwright Papers, QUA, and the Strachan Papers, PAO, make numerous and specific references to articles appearing in American newspapers.

13 For a complete breakdown of news content and sources of the *Kingston Gazette* between 1810 and 1815, see Jane Errington, "Friend and Foe: Kingston Elite and the War of 1812,"

Journal of Canadian Studies 20 (1985): 53–79.

14 *Upper Canada Gazette*, 4 July 1807. For a complete listing, discussion and analysis of federalist newspapers and their importance to colonial editors, see Jane Errington, "The Eagle, the Lion and Upper Canada: A Developing Colonial Ideology. The Colonial Elites' Views of the United States and Great Britain, 1784–1828" (PhD thesis, Queen's University, 1984), appendix and bibliographic note.

15 For a cogent discussion of the relationship between the press and the community on the frontier in an American colonial setting, see Robert Weir, "The Role of the Newspaper Press in the Southern Colonies on the Eve of the Revolution: An Interpretation" in *The Press and the American Revolution*, ed. Bernard Bailyn and J.B. Hence (Worcester, MA: American Antiquarian Society, 1980); Sidney Korbe, *The Development of the Colonial Newspaper* (Gloucester, MA: Peter Smith, 1944); Richard Merritt, *Symbols of American Community, 1735–1775* (New Haven, CT: Yale University Press, 1966).

16 George Rawlyk, "The Federalist-Loyalist Alliance in New Brunswick, 1784–1815," *The Humanities Association Review* 27 (1976): 142-60. See also Jane Errington and George Rawlyk, "The Federalist-Loyalist Alliance of Upper Canada," *The American Review of Canadian Studies* 14 (1984): 157-76.

17 *Upper Canada Gazette*, 9 Nov. 1796.

18 *Kingston Gazette*, 9 Sept. 1810. For a full discussion of the importance of the land and the farming to Upper Canadians, see Robert Fraser, "Like Eden in Her Summer Dress: Gentry, Economy and Society, Upper Canada, 1812–1840" (PhD thesis, University of Toronto, 1979), though this thesis is primarily concerned with the postwar years.

19 *Kingston Gazette*, 29 March 1811.

20 *Upper Canada Gazette*, 29 March 1797. This consciousness of the similarity of Upper Canada and the northeastern United States was acknowledged time and again in the newspapers and in the correspondence of Upper Canadians and Americans. See also Ralph Brown, ed., *Mirrors of the Americas* (1810; rprt New York: American Geographical Society, 1943).

21 Cartwright to Hunter, 23 Aug. 1799.

22 *Niagara Herald*, 14 Nov. 1801. See also 28 March 1800.

23 Cartwright to Hunter, 23 Aug. 1799.

24 In "Role of the Newspaper Press," 131, Weir writes that though the individual's "direct access to the newspapers was undoubtedly small," the group "who received their news from the members of the first group was probably much larger . . . the newspapers were almost certainly available in many taverns" where they were read aloud. See also Robert Merritt, "Public Opinion in Colonial America: Content Analysing the Colonial Press," *The Public Opinion Quarterly* 27 (1963): 356–71.

25 See for example *Upper Canada Gazette*, 29 March 1797; *Niagara Herald*, 28 Feb. 1801; *Kingston Gazette*, 6 Nov. 1810; 4 Dec. 1810, a letter from *Agricola*; 25 Jan. 1811, from the *Connecticut Courant*; 12 March 1811, from the *American Mercury*; 2, 19 May 1811.

26 *Kingston Gazette*, 10 Dec. 1810.

27 Ibid., 2 May 1811; *Upper Canada Gazette*, 29 March 1797.

28 *Upper Canada Gazette*, 22 March 1797; 26 May 1810, from the *New York Spectator*; *Niagara Herald*, 28 Feb. 1801; *Kingston Gazette*, 6 Nov. 1810; 16 May 1811; 22 Feb. 1806.

29 The first specific reference appeared in the *Upper Canada Gazette*, 15 March 1797. See also 29 March 1797; 15 Nov., 15 Feb. 1806.

30 *Kingston Gazette*, 16 May 1811. See also *Niagara Herald*, 13 Feb. 1802; *Upper Canada Gazette*, 19 Nov. 1808.

31 *Kingston Gazette*, 6 Nov. 1810.

32 Ibid., 6 Nov. 1810; 2 Nov. 1811; *Canada Constellation*, 4 Jan. 1800.

33 See for example *Upper Canada Gazette*, 25 Jan. 1797; 9 June 1810; 29 Jan. 1812.

34 American attempts to combat small-pox and other diseases appeared frequently. See for example *Upper Canada Gazette*, 1 Feb. 1797; 20 June 1801; *Niagara Herald*, 14 Feb. 1801. There was also growing attention to drunkenness and the need to form temperance societies, a concern that was not actually picked up in Upper Canada until well after the War of 1812. See for example *Kingston Gazette*, 18 Dec. 1811, "Thoughts on a Public House from New York"; *Upper Canada Gazette*, 11 Nov., 16 Dec. 1797.

35 See for example *Niagara Herald*, 4 April 1801; 16 Jan., 13 Feb. 1802.

36 *Upper Canada Gazette*, 22 March 1797; *Kingston Gazette*, 28 Feb. 1811; *Niagara Herald*, 4 April 1801; 13 Feb. 1802.

37 *Kingston Gazette*, 7 May 1811.

38 Ibid., 1, 15 Jan. 1811. The debate started 4 Dec. 1810 and continued until 23 Jan. 1811.

39 *Upper Canada Gazette*, 9 Nov. 1796.

40 *Kingston Gazette*, 29 Jan. 1811.

41 *Upper Canada Gazette*, 1 Nov. 1796; 14 Sept. 1799.

42 Ibid., 14 Sept. 1799. The *Upper Canada Gazette* provided only a broad outline of the political controversy. It was the *Canada Constellation* and the *Niagara Herald* that gave the colonists some specific analysis of the election. For example, the *Constellation* reported the growing opposition of the republicans to the attorney-general's proposed Sedition Act (29 Sept. 1799). A year later, the *Herald* told its readers of the quandary the federalists had found themselves in with respect to Aaron Burr (6 March 1801, from the *Mercantile Advertiser*). In addition, Upper Canadians in the Niagara region learned of the problems of the electoral system, which appeared to favour the republicans. See *Niagara Herald*, 21, 28 Feb., 3 March 1801; *Upper Canada Gazette*, 30 Aug. 1800, from the *New York Herald* of 20 July 1800.

43 *Upper Canada Gazette*, 7 Feb. 1801.

44 Strachan to James Brown, 31 March 1801, John Strachan Papers, PAO. All other citations from Strachan's letters are taken from this collection unless otherwise noted.

45 Strachan to Brown, 9 Oct. 1808. See also a letter to Brown, 21 Oct. 1809.

46 Strachan to Brown, 21 Oct. 1809; 20 Oct. 1807; 27 Oct. 1803.

47 For a full discussion of how this became an integral part of the imperialists' ideological defence against the United States, see Carl Berger, *The Sense of Power: Studies in the Ideas of Canadian Imperialism, 1867–1914* (Toronto: University of Toronto Press, 1970).

48 *Kingston Gazette*, 21 May 1811.

49 Ibid., 23 April 1811. See also Strachan's letter to the *Kingston Gazette*, writing as "Reckoner," 3 Sept. 1811. Strachan had already discussed this issue with Brown in a letter, 21 Oct. 1809. The effects produced by "licentious liberty," he wrote, were evident in the "frequency of their elections" which "keeps them at a continual boil." Generally, Strachan believed that British practices were far superior.

50 *Niagara Herald*, 21 Feb. 1801, from an unspecified American paper.

51 *Upper Canada Gazette*, 11 Jan. 1800; 3 Aug. 1800, from the *New York Gazette*, 20 July 1800; *Niagara Herald*, 21 Feb. 1801.

52 *Niagara Herald*, 28 Feb. 1801.

53 Ibid., 13 June 1801; 28 Feb. 1801; Linda Kerber, *The Federalists in Dissent: Imagery and Ideology in Revolutionary America* (Ithaca: Cornell University Press, 1970), 123. For a detailed discussion of federalist reaction to the 1800 election, see also David Hackett Fischer, *The Revolution of American*

Conservatism (New York: Harper and Row, 1965).

54 *Kingston Gazette*, 31 Oct. 1812.

55 Strachan to Brown, 20 Oct. 1807. See also introductory comments in Strachan's *A Discourse on the Character of King George the Third* (Montreal: Nahum Mower, 1809).

56 *Kingston Gazette*, 5 Feb., 29 Jan. 1811.

57 The Upper Canadian press included many reports of political scandal and violent crime in the United States. Among other things colonists seemed to be intrigued by witchcraft (*Upper Canada Gazette*, 4 Aug. 1804; *Canada Constellation*, 23 Nov. 1799) and by slavery (*Canada Constellation*, 27 Sept. 1799; 29 Jan. 1802; *Upper Canada Gazette*, 9 Nov. 1811). And like our press today, there were numerous accounts of "horrid murder" (*Canada Constellation*, 5 July 1799; *Upper Canada Gazette*, 14 July 1798).

58 Liancourt, *Travels*, 60; E.A. Cruikshank, "Immigration from the United States into Upper Canada, 1784–1812—Its Character and Results," *Proceedings of the 39th Convention of the Ontario Educational Association* (1900): 275; John Maude, *Trip to Canada*, 60. Just before the War of 1812, Michael Smith concluded in *A Geographical View*, 101, that "the opinion of many in Upper Canada now is that the province ought to be conquered for the good of the inhabitants on both sides."

59 Cartwright to Hunter, 23 Aug. 1799.

60 Wilson, *Robert Hamilton*, 102.

61 *Niagara Herald*, 7 Nov. 1801.

62 Ibid., 13 March 1801, from Addison's *Spectator*.

63 *To the Electors of the County of Essex*, broadside, 1800, PAO; *Upper Canada Gazette*, 15 March 1800, "To the Free and Independent Electors of the County of York" from "Cato"; *Niagara Herald*, 20 June 1801, "To the Electors of the East Riding of York" from a "Lincoln Elector"; *Upper Canada Gazette*, 15 March, 16 Aug. 1800.

64 *Upper Canada Gazette*, 17 March 1804.

65 For a complete discussion and analysis of the Thorpe affair, see John Bruce Walton, "An End to All Order: A Study of Upper Canadian Conservative Response to Opposition 1805–1810" (MA thesis, Queen's University, 1977).

66 *Upper Canada Gazette*, 26 Jan. 1805.

67 Thorpe to Edward Cooke, 24 Jan. 1806, quoted in Walton, "An End to All Order," 55–56. These included providing redress for Methodists in the colony, changing the land granting system, and controlling the revenue. Ibid., 62.

68 Ibid., 67.

69 Ibid., 80, 86, 87. The term "party" was used frequently by colonial officials to describe the Thorpe group.

70 "Sketch of the Conduct of Justice Thorpe," found in the Cartwright Papers, QUA, composed by Cartwright and apparently revised by Justice Alcock and Lieutenant-Governor Gore. Walton, "An End to All Order," 91.

71 *Letter to Lord Castlereagh*, 2; Gore to Windam, 13 March 1809, CO 42/349, 59 quoted in Walton, "An End To all Order," 87.

72 Richard Cartwright to James Cartwright, 22 Jan. 1807, Cartwright Papers, Port Hope Collection, QUA.

73 *Letter to Lord Castlereagh*, 2.

74 Walton, "An End to All Order," 112–88.

75 *Letter to Lord Castlereagh*, 2.

76 Gore to Windam, 13 March 1807, CO 42/341, 59, quoted in Walton, "An End to All Order," 87.

77 *Letter to Lord Castlereagh*, 2.

78 *House of Assembly*, 19 March 1810, 375–76.

79 *Upper Canada Gazette*, 27 June 1807.

80 [Cartwright, Richard], *Letters of an American Loyalist in Upper Canada, on a Pamphlet Published by John Mills Jackson* (Quebec: n.p., 1810), no. 1.

81 For a general discussion of religion and particularly various attitudes towards the Methodists, see G.S. French, *Parsons in Politics* (Toronto: The Ryerson Press, 1962); Preston, *Kingston before the War of 1812*; E. Firth, *The Town of York, 1793–1815* (Toronto: The Champlain Society, 1962) and two groundbreaking studies on colonial religion, Donald Matthews, *Religion in the Old South* (Chicago: University of Chicago Press, 1977) and George Rawlyk, *New Light Letters and Songs* (Hantsport: Baptist Heritage in Atlantic Canada, 1983).

82 Cartwright, "Memorandum Respecting the State of the Episcopal Church in Upper Canada," presented to General Brock, Cartwright Papers (n.d.), QUA. See also comments by Strachan in his papers.

83 Strachan to Brown, 13 July 1806. See also 27 Oct. 1803; Strachan to Solomon Jones, 16 March 1812, Solomon Jones Papers, QUA, and a number of articles by Strachan in the *Kingston Gazette* signed "Reckoner."

84 Cartwright to Collins, 1789. See also Cartwright to Henry Motz, 31 May 1790. Cartwright wrote to Hunter, 15 May 1805, that students who went to the United States "must of necessity imbibe in some degree prejudices unfavourable" to Upper Canada. See also Hartwell Bowsfield, "Upper Canada in the 1820's: The Development of a Political Consciousness" (PhD thesis, University of Toronto,

1976), ch. 2; J.L.H. Henderson, *John Strachan, 1778–1867* (Toronto: University of Toronto Press, 1969).

85 Gourlay, *Statistical Account*, 246. See also Smith, *A Geographical View*, 61; C.E. Phillips, *The Development of Education in Canada* (Toronto: Gage, 1957); G.W. Spragge, "Elementary Education in Upper Canada," *Ontario History* 43 (1951): 107–22.

86 *Kingston Gazette*, 25 Sept. 1810.

87 Richard Cockrell, *Thoughts on the Education of Youth* (Newark: G. Tiffany, 1795). Strachan was also aware of this problem and in an attempt to help alleviate it wrote *A Concise Introduction to Mathematics*. See also letter from Strachan to Reid, 11 Feb. 1812; Cartwright to Hunter, 5 May 1805; *Kingston Gazette*, 13 Nov. 1810; Gourlay, *Statistical Account*, 246; Smith, *A Geographical View*, 61.

88 *Kingston Gazette*, 16 April 1811. The first announcement was made 9 April 1811. Barnabas Bidwell had arrived in Upper Canada in the winter of 1811. Four years earlier he had been appointed attorney-general of Massachusetts under a republican government. However, it seems that he was forced to flee the United States under a cloud, for charges were laid that he had embezzled party funds. See a letter of Simon Larned to Barnabas Bidwell, 25 March 1810, Bidwell Papers, QUA.

89 *Kingston Gazette*, 16, 23 April 1811.

MARKETING WILDLIFE:
The Hudson's Bay Company and the Pacific Northwest, 1821–1849*

LORNE HAMMOND

Wildlife is an aspect of the fur trade that has received little attention in the literature, yet animals were the foundation of the trade.[1] Their presence lured trapper and trader, and the demographic fluctuations of wildlife, along with characteristics of different species, marketing, and the vagaries of fashion, were unpredictable variables of the business. This paper, although drawn from a fur trade case study in the Pacific Northwest, fits within a wider context.

In the Pacific Northwest, as in many other parts of the world, commerce was the first external agent in the exploration and assignment of values and utility to wildlife. Commerce predated scientific inquiry, European settlement, the legislative process, and the cultural influence of the writer and painter.

*This article is reprinted from Lorne Hammond, "Marketing Wildlife: The Hudson's Bay Company and the Pacific Northwest, 1821–49," *Forest & Conservation History* 37 (Jan. 1993): 14–25. The author thanks Peter Baskerville and Chad Gaffield for their support and the Hudson's Bay Company for permission to quote from their archives; he gratefully acknowledges funding from the Social Sciences and Humanities Research Council of Canada and the Graduate School of the University of Ottawa. A draft of this paper was presented at the American Society for Environmental History conference in Houston, Texas, with the aid of Thomas Dunlap and Keir Sterling.

One influential force in the field of commerce was the Hudson's Bay Company (HBC), a group with a managerial structure that distinguished it from other fur trade companies. It was a company whose management was hierarchical, an arrangement complicated by distance since its headquarters were in London, England. Major HBC shareholders were represented by a governor, deputy governor, and committee. These individuals communicated their wishes about company operations in North America to George Simpson, the North American governor. Simpson had responsibility to provide the committee with detailed annual letters on conditions in each department and post within the districts under his control. The people in each department who were responsible for major posts were called chief factors. Chief traders and clerks ran the smaller posts. Co-ordinating this system involved complex supply lines and frequent communication via services such as the express canoe, which took only passengers and mail. Evidence suggests that this bureaucratic structure conditioned responses to managing and standardizing wildlife as products.[2]

In 1821 HBC merged with its competitor, the North West Company of Montreal, and gained significant new territory. This new area was designated the Columbia Department and it produced 8 percent of the 18.5 million hides and pelts exported from North America from 1821 to 1849.[3] As the map on p. 381 shows, the Columbia Department included the northern interior posts of New Caledonia and much of present-day British Columbia, Oregon, and Washington. The latter two were jointly occupied with the United States under a temporary agreement regarding the disputed boundaries and ownership of the Oregon Territory, that land north of the Adams-Onis line of 1819 and west of the continental divide.

• Nature's Inventory

Although it was not the first fur trading company in the Pacific Northwest, the Hudson's Bay Company was the largest and the most successful. The company's rapid expansion into the region during the years 1821 to 1849 offers a good picture of the process of assessing wildlife as a product. When Governor George Simpson took his first tour of the Columbia Department in 1824–25, diversification in trapping and hunting the region's wildlife was just beginning. He reported on the commercial potential of wildlife, such as the mountain goat.[4] As an experiment Simpson joined his voyageurs in eating the first two he saw; he described them as "tough." From then on there was a regular flow of potential products from the hinterland posts to London, from grizzly bears to the small hoary marmot. In 1826 he issued instructions to have sample skin and horns of a mountain goat saved for a naturalist, but the first specimens went to London for a determination of their commercial potential. In 1825 Chief Factor John McLoughlin forwarded samples of swan skins and sturgeon's bladders from his post on the Columbia River at Fort Vancouver "to know what they are

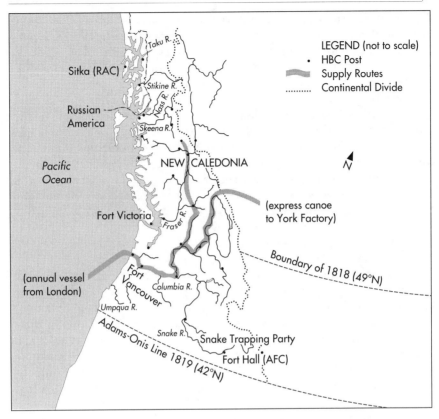

FIGURE 1 *Posts and routes of the Columbia Department, 1825–50. Map provided by the author.*

worth." Seventeen years later he was still sending samples, including "oulachan oil," spermaceti (a wax found in the head cavities and blubber of the sperm whale), "sea horse teeth" (walrus tusks), and sea lion hides as possible products "for trial in the English market."[5]

Once these samples reached London, the company sought informed opinions as to their relative quality, value, market, and potential competitors. Some items were sold at auction so that buyer response could be evaluated. The auction served to process market information, a means of introducing potential new products as "odd lots" on a test basis.[6] For example, wolf and wolverine appeared first in the HBC catalogues as "Sundries," but as demand increased they were sold as distinct categories of fur.

Beaver pelts for the felt hat industry are the most well-known item HBC supplied to the European market, but the company also imported a large variety of other wildlife products. Fur hats, muffs, cuffs, collars, and coats were only part of the trade. There were military contracts for bear skins; cutlers bought deer horns or stag horns for pen knife handles; and dentists used "sea horse teeth" (walrus tusks) to make dentures.[7] Castoreum, from the glands of beaver, sold as a scent lure for beaver traps and as a component in medicinal preparations and perfumes.[8] Isinglass, a pure gelatin extracted from the sturgeon's float bladder, helped clarify wine and beer. Feathers, such as the down of the trumpeter swan, sold for powder puffs.

Establishing a demand among the public for a wildlife product was difficult. Ross Cox, who traded in the Pacific Northwest before the Hudson's Bay Company, recalled how fickle the market for bearskins had been. At one point, he remembered, the North West Company found itself with a glut of bearskins and no buyers. So the company had a "hammer-cloth" made up, with a coat of arms in silver, and gave it to a British prince. It hung below the driver's seat on the front of his coach, covering the toolbox and advertising the rank of the coach's occupant. As the company had hoped, the bearskin was a fashion hit when it was shown at the king's next levee. Within three weeks the North West Company's warehouse was empty.[9] This and other lessons demonstrated the benefits of subtle promotion.

Although HBC's exploration of nature was primarily a commercial enterprise, the company's endeavors also promoted increased scientific knowledge. Hudson's Bay Company maintained a small museum of natural history in London and assisted institutions, artists, and scientists in their research. John Richardson, a prominent natural historian, was one such scientist.[10] His observations on wildlife illustrate the ways in which scientific study of an animal could conflict with its identity as a commercial product.

Richardson became involved in a disagreement about the red fox that reveals the company's competing interest for a recognizable and easily promoted product despite contrary opinions from scientists. The colour of individuals in a litter of the red fox is determined by a single pair of genes. Individuals may be born a colour other than red, similar to the occurrence of different colours of hair among the children in a family. Genetic variations in colour are further complicated by age, region, and climate.[11] The cross phase is a greyish-brown coat with dark black markings down the spine and across the shoulders. The silver is actually black with a white-tipped tail and silver frosting effect produced by the outer hairs of the coat. Silver is the most highly valued phase, partly because it is almost unknown in the European red fox.[12]

The silver fox was a mysterious animal, and market prices, thriving on mystery, reflected that. A prime silver fox sold for about forty dollars, half the price of a good sea otter. For HBC to insure a continuing supply of silver fox furs, it had to bow to the caprice of genetic variations within litters and accept less valuable colour phases as well. Refusing pelts of the other colour phases would discourage fox trapping generally and therefore reduce the number of silver foxes trapped. Thus the genetic characteristics of the red fox created constraints both on commercial harvesting and on marketing.

Although the fur trade industry preferred to distinguish between the colour phases as if they were separate forms of fox, the scientific community had a different opinion. In 1829 Richardson commented on red and cross foxes: "I am inclined to adhere to the opinion of the Indians in considering the Cross Fox of the fur traders to be a mere variety of the Red Fox, as I found on inquiry that the gradations of colour between characteristic specimens of the Cross and Red Fox are so small, that the hunters are often in doubt with respect to the proper denomination of a skin, and I was frequently told 'This is not a cross fox yet, but it is becoming so.'"[13]

There is a middle ground between the cross and red fox in their aesthetic variations, as twentieth-century biologist Alexander William Francis Banfield noted. He commented that differing perceptions of colour phases are the result of "selective pelting, and variation in the identification of the cross fox."[14] Certain pelts could therefore be graded subjectively either as cross or red fox at the trading post or during preparation for auction. Richardson disagreed with the distinction made by fur traders, although he was admittedly uncertain about how the colour variations occurred. But it was in the industry's best interest to ignore the opinion of scientific observers as well as Native people, and benefit from the flexibility of choosing the label for distinguishable but similar products.

The Hudson's Bay Company disagreed both with Richardson and Native people over the nature of another animal—the bear. The 1825 returns for the Columbia Department distinguished among three forms of bear skins: black, brown, and grizzly. The common black bear has several colour phases other than black, including cinnamon, honey, white, and blue. The bears of the interior of the Pacific Northwest were evenly divided between cinnamon-brown and black phases. Richardson noted that the perceptions of fur traders about the species differed from that of the Native peoples: "The Cinnamon Bear of the Fur Traders is considered by the Indians to be an accidental variety of this species [black bear], and they are borne out in this opinion by the quality of the fur, which is equally fine with that of the Black Bear."[15] For the bear, like the fox, colour phase characteristics constrained the supply of wildlife but aided in establishing product identity.

• Competitive Strategies

Other species of wildlife arrived on the market more as a result of competitive strategy than on the merits of the product. Faced with competition from American trapping parties, especially in the Snake River basin of the disputed Oregon Territory, HBC responded by employing its own parties, in part as protection of what it viewed as its territory. These parties of Métis and Iroquois trappers worked constantly as the company engaged in a rigorous extirpation of beaver and river otters, creating "a fur desert" or a "cordon sanitaire" to destroy any inducement to American trappers and traders.[16] American traders were regarded as precursors of their government's colonization policy, drawn to the area by the economics of the wildlife resource. As Governor Simpson explained, "The greatest and best protection we can have from opposition is keeping the country closely hunted as the first step that the American Government will take towards Colonization is through their Indian Traders and if the country becomes exhausted in Fur bearing animals they can have no inducement to proceed thither."[17] The result was not a competition for Native trade but direct ecological warfare.

The Snake River party bypassed trade with Native communities and moved directly into harvesting the resource, as did other trapping parties working on the Umpqua River and in California's Buena Ventura Valley. Both the American and Hudson's Bay Company trapping parties quickly realized that an early arrival at the trapping grounds was critical to the spring hunt. Until 1824 Snake River beaver had been trapped only from June through August, yielding a harvest of inferior summer pelts.[18] In 1825 spring hunts began, which not only collected the more valuable winter coats but also moved the hunt into the reproduction cycle of the beaver. Beavers mate in January and February and give birth between late April and the end of June.[19]

Harvesting intensity increased when first a fall hunt and then year-long trapping expeditions were instituted. In 1825 the Snake River party reorganized for this competition; Simpson commented that "the country is a rich preserve of Beaver and which for political reasons we should destroy as early as possible."[20] However, despite the Snake River party's specialized purpose (beaver comprised 67 percent of its returns) and strategic value, it collected only 10 percent of the Columbia's 443 010 beaver pelts from 1825 to 1849. The party's 43 113 beaver pelts were far fewer than the 132 000 taken within New Caledonia's sustainable harvesting system, one based on beaver ponds owned by individual Native families. But as part of the battle for control of the Oregon Territory, the symbolic and political value of those furs was more important than their economic value.

The fur traders also fought an ecological war with a natural predator.[21] The Hudson's Bay Company viewed competition from predators such as wolves as destructive to the company's interest. The attitude both of Simpson and the HBC governing committee in London toward predators is clearly documented and reflects a consensus among most senior members of the fur trade. In 1822 the committee instructed Simpson that wolves on the plains should be hunted in the summer and their hides prepared for use as leather: "If the wolves are not destroyed they will either kill or drive away the Buffalo; it is therefore desirable to destroy them, if the skins will pay for the expenses it will also be the means of employing the Indians."[22]

In the Columbia annual fur returns, the first entry for wolves appears for the outfit of 1827 when 5 wolves were traded. By 1830 the number of wolf pelts had climbed to 69, and in 1831 as the company began exercising control over its expanded network of posts, the number was 468. In 1833, responding to Simpson's report of wolves preying on the cattle of the Red River Colony, the governor and committee went further, issuing these instructions concerning controlling wolves: "[S]ending re your request 'two ounces of Strychnine' which is considered the most powerful agent for destroying wild animals (it is used in the East Indies for killing Tigers and Leopards) . . . three or four grains are a sufficient dose for a full grown beast; the best way to apply it is to make an incision in a piece of flesh in which the Strychnine should be inserted, and to place the bait in situations that the animals frequent."[23]

In 1839 McLoughlin requested poison for the company farms in the Pacific Northwest and for general sale to settlers. The committee replied by sending "a small quantity of Strychnine made up in dozes [sic] for the destruction of Wolves; it should be inserted in pieces of raw meat placed in such situations that the shepherd's dogs may not have access to them, and the native people should be encouraged by high prices for the skins to destroy wolves at all seasons."[24]

Although the Columbia Department wolf kill reached a high of 1653 in 1847, it fell to only 76 in 1853. Whether they were poisoned to protect domestic cattle, or hunted down by parties of Native peoples, settlers, or individual trappers, it is clear that from the company's perspective wolves were a threat to its operations. Their instructions about how to deal with wolves also reveal a much larger process: the exchange of information concerning large predators among companies operating in different parts of the world. The wolf became a product in the fur trade only as a means of insuring and underwriting its extermination.

Another animal, the highly prized land or river otter, had a role as currency, paid to the Russians in exchange for a lease. Under the terms of the 1840 Hamburg Agreement between the Hudson's Bay Company and the Russian American Company (RAC), two thousand Columbia river otter were taken to Sitka, Alaska, to pay the RAC for the use of the Alaskan panhandle. The lease contained a provision for a further three thousand otter to be traded at the Hudson's Bay Company's option. Total otter exports from North America declined from 1840 to 1847 by roughly the amount of the lease. Despite the cost of bringing extra skins over the Rocky Mountains to Sitka, and the delay caused by taking payment in bills of exchange drawn on St Petersburg, the Hudson's Bay Company believed it had a bargain. It calculated the actual cost of leasing the Alaskan panhandle for one year at the equivalent of a middle-level manager's annual salary.[25] The RAC also benefited because, unlike the Hudson's Bay Company, it had official access to the lucrative Chinese market. HBC continued to use otter instead of cash to make the lease payment until 1856.

• Wildlife Cycles and Markets

In the preceding cases the Hudson's Bay Company exercised active control over which animals it chose to pursue and present as products. Having decided to supply a form of wildlife, the company often found itself mediating between the forces of nature and the vagaries of the market. Two factors created the greatest difficulties: the seemingly separate worlds of wildlife demography and fashion. The company's ability to buffer these forces varied, depending on which species were involved. With lynx and muskrat the Hudson's Bay Company was successful in minimizing the impact of wildlife demography on the marketplace. Although the dynamics of wildlife demography are still not fully understood, trappers and sportsmen have long recognized the existence of wildlife cycles. There are various theories about why these cycles exist, ranging from the cycles of sunspot activity to a combination of ultraviolet radiation and malnutrition to periodic epidemics. Current debate focusses on intricate mathematical probability equations. Lloyd Keith has commented on the evolution of this discussion:

> Theories and hypotheses confound the natural-history literature. Most are untested and as a result unanimity is lacking on many aspects of animal-population cycles. For thirty-odd years these periods of abundance and scarcity have been passed off as resulting from chance alone; lacking sufficient precision or amplitude to be acceptable; being so multifactorial as to defy appraisal; and eventually regarded as phenomena easily reduced to ridicule. Not all attitudes are disparaging or skeptical. There are zealots in the field of biology who see cycles in virtually all tabulations of natural and social interactions. From the production of pig iron to tent caterpillars, and from ozone quantity to Nile floods, cycles have been regarded as the skeletons or the souls of numerical data.[26]

Nevertheless, Keith has concluded that there is a "ten-year cycle," a regular but imprecise fluctuation for several forms of grouse, the snowshoe rabbit, and its predator, the lynx. There is also evidence for such a cycle in the fox, the muskrat, and its predator, the mink.[27] These demographic fluctuations of the animals on which the fur trade depended threatened the stability of the market, but they also provided the Hudson's Bay Company with opportunities for speculation.

The lynx and the muskrat provide two examples of how the company responded to wildlife cycles. These species were wildcards in the marketplace because of their periodic sudden and massive population explosions. High spring water levels or low winter water levels exaggerated the muskrat's reproductive cycle, the former causing an increase in population and the latter a decrease. The lynx's cycle was dependent on the increase of its food source, the snowshoe rabbit.[28] Although the lynx was never a particularly popular fur, its rapid increases tended to flood the market and undercut prices for cats in general.[29]

The muskrat (referred to within the trade as "the rat"), a seemingly insignificant marsh dweller sold in the marketplace as the musquash, had a large impact on the fur trade. In the wild, like the beaver it seeks shallow water where it feeds on roots and grasses. Unlike the beaver, it can have several litters in a year, resulting in dramatic population fluctuations.[30] These population fluctuations meant a periodic flooding of the market, which occurred in 1828 and 1834 when over one million muskrat skins arrived at auction in London. The muskrat's demographic cycle profoundly influenced the market because it could be used as a cheaper substitute for more expensive furs, especially in hat making. Muskrat sold for between three and thirteen pence each, depending on supply. By contrast, beaver sold for seventeen to thirty-two shillings per pound.

Although the company realized the increases were part of a recurring pattern, they could not predict the onset of the cycles. Their experience taught them how long peaks would last and what caused them to end. To support beaver prices the company repeatedly used private export contracts to divert muskrat surpluses from the London market. The one million skins taken in the cycle year of 1829 threatened the trade's stability, but the company knew this increase would have limited duration and be followed by an equally drastic collapse in population. They reacted by limiting the importation and paying close attention to demographics. Governor Simpson wrote to the committee that "it is evident that the importation of next year will be small compared with that of the present, owing to a mortality which has seized the tribe [muskrats] in several parts of the Country, we beg leave to suggest that a part only be exposed to sale this year, and the remainder held until the following, when 'tis probable they will command better prices."[31]

A large increase in lynx and muskrat shipped in 1839 drew this reaction: "We do not wish that more than half the quantities shipped . . . this year, but that the surplus be laid aside for shipment the following season by which time those animals will in all probability become scarce as we rarely find they continue numerous three years in succession."[32]

The bottom of these cycles was equally important to the company's position in the market. After such a "crash" the wholesalers in the industry, anticipating a shortage, rushed to take control of the previous excess. Simpson wrote in 1831 that he suspected that the heavy buying by Astor's fur company was such a speculation: "It is in the anticipation of such scarcity Messrs. Astor & Company have purchased so largely, not for immediate consumption, as we have reason to believe they were at the time this purchase was made large holders of the American Fur Company's Musquash, but on speculation with a view to benefit by the demand which the probable scarcity will occasion. And as this falling off in quantity must increase the prices for all description we have not thought it advisable to destroy the small inferior skins."[33] The Hudson's Bay Company had little or no control over the entry of American muskrat onto the London market or to markets on the European continent. One example of how swings in muskrat population created competition based on speculative opportunities was the 1834 adjustment HBC made to its shipping schedule.[34] In response to the American Fur Company's entry into the English market that year, HBC changed its transportation schedule to beat the arrival of American furs.[35]

Muskrat returns were also the subject of speculation by smaller dealers and houses. When an 1824 contract for a large sale to an American house fell through "on a flimsy pretext," the committee consoled itself with the knowledge that consumers would be forced to buy on the English market.[36] Then the following year, as a condition of the sale of 150 000 skins to Henry Carey & Co. of New York, the skins were not to be resold on the English market. When this contract fell through, the company reminded Carey that he was liable for any loss incurred in reselling the skins.[37] Again, in the 1840s, the large numbers of muskrat harvested prompted the company to restrict the succeeding year's imports. Glut continued to be a problem for the trade; in 1846 one American dealer alone brought 600 000 skins into the English market.[38] So, although historians such as John Galbraith stress the element of competition between British and American fur traders on the frontier, these divisions were not as clear in the marketplace, where furs moved back and forth through private contracts and speculative practices.[39]

The muskrat cycle also created problems for the departments and posts in North America. The large numbers of easily trapped muskrat drained posts of their inventories of trade goods during the first year of a high cycle and created an ongoing inventory problem thereafter: "The immense trade made for two or three successive years in the article of Rats was the cause of the increased demands from all parts of the country for goods, which led to the overstock we now have of many articles. This overstock will however be carried off by the outfits of next and the following years. . . ."[40]

Overall, the system was self-regulating and able to absorb muskrat surpluses, whose roughly three-year cycle was known to the traders. The large numbers of muskrat disrupted the marketplace, but the company had a series of responses that could be implemented either in London or at the shipping depot. Although speculation on the cycles could be lucrative, HBC adapted to muskrat demography as it attempted to create an orderly system of business and left most of the speculation to others.

The beaver was one species for which HBC tried to develop a unique long-term strategy of conservation and resource management. This plan was part of an attempt to gain a competitive edge in the marketplace. Unlike the muskrat, the demographic problem presented by the beaver was one of declining population, particularly east of the Rockies, due to overtrapping and epidemics such as tularemia. Of all the species harvested, beaver was the main focus of the trade. Exploration, competition, and management of beaver stocks was foremost in shaping the managerial policy of the Hudson's Bay Company.[41] The company's expansion into the Columbia Department in the 1820s was part of a drive to conserve and replenish the depleted stocks east of the Rockies by relying on new sources for the market in the Columbia.

• An Effort at Conservation

The company engaged in one of North America's earliest conservation experiments using those districts in which it had undisputed possession. The policy's strength lay in the advantage that the company's size and market longevity gave it. The policy's weakness lay in the assumption that market demand would continue unchanged. The conservation policy was also difficult to implement because of the incentive system that comprised part of the company's managerial organization. The wintering partner system of the North West Company, linking salaries and pensions to the success of the concern, was adopted by HBC in 1821 and carried with it a liability: it encouraged a personal profit motive and a frontier machismo.

Through conservation strategies, the company tried to combine the advantage of scale of operation with monopoly control over the "nursing" or "recruiting" of beaver stocks. This tactic enabled HBC to supply sufficient beaver to "meet extended consumption and secure to the Company the entire control of the Trade, as, [in] the countries exposed to opposition the expenses are so heavy that those who now pursue it will not then be able to meet us in the home market."[42] If the plan had succeeded it would have meant the end of the Columbia Department's frontier competition, "and at once put an end to opposition in those Countries where we have no exclusive privilege, as the high prices of Beaver alone enables the small Traders to continue."[43]

The committee supplied Simpson with a mathematical argument for the Northern Council that showed the benefit of this policy over a seven-year period in a hypothetical district. If the district produced 1200 pelts annually without depleting stocks, this would yield 8400 pelts for export. If the conservation policy were implemented, restricting the harvest to 400 pelts for each of the first two years, 600 the following, 800 the next, 2800 in the fifth year, 14 000 in the sixth, and 20 000 in the seventh year, the total harvest would be 39 000 pelts with 38 800 animals remaining in the district.[44] The committee acknowledged that this model was optimistic, but even with a 50 percent error the benefit was clear: they would be able to bring to market twice the volume of fur. Even at half the going price this plan would squeeze their competitors, who faced the same outfitting costs as HBC for trade goods.[45]

Arthur Ray has attributed the failure of this conservation strategy to opposition by American, Métis, and Native trappers. Ray has argued that on the prairies "without a monopoly it was not possible to manage the fur trade on an ecologically sound basis since the primary suppliers of fur pelts, the Indians, did not really support the Hudson's Bay Company's conservation programme."[46] But the conservation strategy faltered due to a structural flaw in the company; ingrained habits and a related system of prestige could not be easily changed in practice. In the past the company and other traders judged individual traders according to the size of returns they generated, and their pensions were tied to past profits. Under the conservation policy, Simpson stated, "We must judge of their talents by the quality alone not the quantity."[47] Convincing the HBC commissioned officers and traders in council to agree to decrease the returns was one thing. Putting the changes into practice was another: "Many of them give it their best attention, which a few, who either cannot or will not understand either their own interests or the interests of the country and native people, give it but very little attention. They all, however, while assembled here, talk of the subject as if fully convinced of its importance, and make fair promises of giving it their best support, but I fear that many of them lose sight of it before they reach their wintering grounds."[48]

In 1841 Simpson, faced with an accelerating decline of beaver stocks throughout the districts, placed the blame on the commissioned gentlemen: "All our endeavours I am sorry to say, have been fruitless, owing very much in my opinion to the disinclination of many Gentlemen in charge of Districts & posts, to occasion a reduction in the returns, even as a measure of preservation to the country, from an over anxiety as to the appearance of turning their charges to profitable account, and in some cases perhaps, from a mistaken notion that by curtailing the returns they were injuring their own immediate interests."[49] Few traders were willing to sacrifice their short-term income in order to benefit their successors or, although they would not say it in council, the company's long-term position. Although Ray's argument is correct, it ignores what Simpson clearly viewed as managerial resistance, structurally rooted in the profit system of the company.

The company understood that it was not possible to increase the consumption of beaver in Europe unless there was a material drop in price. Until it could achieve this, the company restricted importation in an effort to maintain the high prices needed to subsidize conservation. In 1830, a decade before the beaver market collapsed, the committee told Simpson:

It is more profitable to keep the importation moderate until the animals become so numerous as to enable you to double the importation, which then might be sold so cheap as to force a larger consumption either by means of exportation or by making Hats so cheap as to induce a larger class of the people of this Country to use Beaver hats. We consider the effect on the market this year, holds out the strongest inducement to preserve in the plan of nursing the Country, as it shews that such an increase of quantity as has been made this year only diminishes Profits, and that it would have been better if the animals had been allowed to live and multiply.[50]

The policy was a calculated gamble, given the declining number of American trapping parties in the Columbia in the late 1830s and their problems obtaining financing to bring supplies from St Louis. For a time it appeared to be working, but the company had underestimated the extent to which both beaver populations had declined and consumer preference had changed as silk hats grew in popularity. The slow reaction of the Hudson's Bay Company to the erosion of its traditional markets resulted from the company's reluctance to abandon a policy that would have worked in a static market.

In the Columbia Department, most of which was not under the conservation policy, production grew rapidly. Simpson's production target was 20 000 beaver pelts a year, a number reached in 1831 and surpassed by the peak of 28 949 pelts in 1833. Beaver production hovered between 18 000 and 21 000 until 1844 when it dropped to 10 812. Production rallied for two or three years and then dipped to 5991 in 1850. Columbia district beaver production falls into two main periods: 1826 to 1843 (the years of Simpson-McLoughlin management) and the declining years after 1844. Production dropped before the political settlement of the Oregon Boundary, the turning point in political interpretations of the company's fortunes. The cause of this drop had more to do with European fashion than with political events in North America.

• Death of a Hat

Beaver, the historic staple of the fur trade, suffered a serious collapse in the marketplace. During the 1840s the silk hat, symbolic of changing culture in the age of machinery and steam, caught consumers' attention and sense of fashion. The first blow to the market occurred in the Columbia auction on 31 August 1842. Hudson's Bay Company Secretary William Smith, forwarding catalogues of the sale to James Keith in Lachine, Quebec, wrote that demand for beaver had fallen off considerably because of the silk hat's popularity.[51] In their spring letter to George Simpson the committee wrote: "From an extraordinary freak of fashion, the article [beaver], moreover, has of late fallen much into disuse in hat making, silk hats being principally worn at present; the consequence is that its value has greatly decreased in the market, as will be seen by the accompanying sales catalogues. This depression however is but temporary, as no doubt exists that beaver hats will soon again come into more general use, when of course an amendment may be expected in the price. . . . The martens on the other hand, as you will observe by the late sales, have commanded very high prices."[52]

The committee was wrong, and beaver prices began to plummet at auction after auction. While the Columbia furs were being prepared for auction in the warehouse, the male population of London was turning out for the summer promenade dressed like Prince Albert in the new silk fashion. Prices even continued to drop after an effort by HBC to carefully present "best Beaver" at the August 1843 auction.[53] The committee wrote to McLoughlin that: "The continually decreasing price, when considered in connexion with a constantly decreasing supply, holds out no cheering prospect for the future, unless the tide of fashion change, and the consumption of Beaver in the manufacture of hats become more general than it has been for some time past. We hope that the low price may have some effect in bringing about an alteration in the public taste, but no hope of this must lead us to neglect any means, by which our great expences may be safely curtailed ... doubly so when prices are declining and returns annually diminishing."[54]

Prices dropped further at the January auction. In March 1845 the committee told Simpson that prices probably would continue to fall. Rather than publicly accept reduced bids, the bulk of the furs were returned to the warehouse while the company searched without success for a discreet private buyer with whom they could clear the total inventory. By 1845 the silk hat was firmly established both in England and on the Continent. The committee described the situation in a letter to Simpson: "The best description of which [silk hats] may be purchased at retail shops in London about fifty percent cheaper than the first quality beaver hat."[55] Wildlife demography came into play the next year. The 1846 market was inundated with muskrat from the United States, a beaver substitute. Having lost the higher-priced market and unable to compete with muskrat prices for the lower market, the company finally conceded that a revival of the product was very unlikely.

Meanwhile, the warehouse inventory of unsold beaver pelts continued to grow. Auction catalogues show that the Columbia auction, which usually included a selection of furs from the two previous years, grew to a backlog that included unsold beaver from five separate years. In 1847 the company could delay no longer and cleared the inventory at whatever price was necessary to remove it.[56] Beaver, which sold for thirty to thirty-five shillings per pound in 1821, sold for three to four shillings. HBC began to consider alternate uses for the pelt: "We are not without hope that great cheapness may have the effect of forcing the article into consumption in some form or other, as the ingenuity of purchasers will naturally be stimulated to the means of applying it to new purposes."[57]

Beaver was no longer a viable product, and the company began to experiment with methods that could make it one again. The experiments undertaken were ingenious. Using a new process, they shaved and dyed pelts to resemble fur seals, an operation also used later during the fur seal vogue of 1890–1910. The skins exhibited in 1847 at the annual Leipzig

Fair, in the German state of Saxony, evoked little response from the fur industry; many fashionable furs, including marten, went unsold. By 1847 the price of a beaver hat had dropped to that of a silk hat, but consumer response was still negligible.[58]

The company continued to experiment, preparing one thousand fully dressed and dyed beaver pelts to be sold as "fur," a novel use for the pelt that had never before been attempted. The marketplace was Canada, but only five hundred pelts were sent because of production problems. Further eroding the market, several London fur dealers who were aware of the company's plans sent earlier shipments. In another attempt to rally the market, unsold stock was sent to dealers in the United States where the beaver hat was still in use; a test shipment also went to China, with disappointing results. After these attempts, the 1849 importation from North America was severely restricted to twenty thousand skins, formerly the average output of the Columbia Department alone. The beaver, slowly gaining acceptance as a "fur," ceased to be important to the European hat industry.[59]

The Hudson's Bay Company's plans for market dominance had failed due to a combination of wildlife demography and European fashions. However, the company gained experience in experimenting with and promoting alternate uses for its products, and in knowing when to cut its losses. At the same time, HBC was turning to the promotion of a "new" product, drawn from their inventory of wildlife. While the steady decrease in the price of beaver made company officials such as Archibald Barclay gloomy, there was consolation in the corresponding increase in the value of the marten. The marten's value was strong, but the best evidence of its importance is found in the tremendous volume produced. During the experimentation with beaver as a fur, Warehouse Keeper Edward Taylor expressed concern that large quantities of beaver, contrasted with the smaller numbers of marten, might cause the market for both to collapse. Another member of the company, Edward Roberts, told Simpson: "The fur is beautiful and when dyed looks as well as sea otter. . . . I showed a specimen to Nicholay the Queen's furrier, who has a high opinion of the fur and thinks it likely to come into extensive use for trimmings, and also for muffs, and does not think it will come into competition with Marten, so as in any way to affect the value of that article which our friend Taylor is very much afraid of."[60] Ever aware that sales depended on the perception of distinctly separate products, the company sought to maintain this separation even down to the level of a fur becoming a cuff on a garment.

Before 1838 the marten received only passing notice in the discussions of auction trends. Then increased demand pushed prices steadily upward. The declining population cycles of the Columbia Department's marten and lynx in 1839–40 stimulated prices further. Simpson considered the declines only temporary: "By the knowledge which has been acquired by experience, of the habits of these latter animals, however, there is every reason to believe that this diminution in their numbers is merely tempo-rary, arising either from migration to other quarters, or from disease, but that as soon as these causes shall be removed, they will become as plentiful as formerly, and assist in retrieving the present unpromising aspect of affairs in this district."[61]

The decreased supply reduced the furriers' inventories, and prices continued to climb. By 1843 demand was again strong, and prices began to set new levels as they attracted speculative buyers. Increased prices in 1844 more than matched the losses incurred by declining beaver stocks. The Columbia posts encouraged trappers to switch from beaver to marten and other small furs. The committee proposed new incentives to offset the losses that beaver was taking in the marketplace: "Beaver has again fallen in price, but, as a stimulus to exertion in hunting martens, lynxes, musquash and all other furs, increased prices may be offered, as we can afford to be liberal in that way, inasmuch as all those furs are at present much in demand and have advanced, musquash as much as 40 percent on the price of last year, as you will perceive by the catalogues."[62]

The Columbia Department board of management received instruc-tions to concentrate on marten in the fall of 1846 as the company bene-fited from high prices. The increased supply was not large enough to flood the market the way muskrat, rabbit, and lynx frequently did. Marten returns from the department increased rapidly after 1846. Almost 45 per-cent of all the marten harvested in the Columbia Department from 1825 to 1849 were taken in the following three years. This increased harvest of Columbia marten points toward a rapid response to the market by Native trappers. The company used its experience with the population cycles of other species to play the market as closely as possible. HBC cautioned in the fall of 1847 that imports from the northern department should not be so excessive as to weaken prices.[63]

New Caledonia's fur-based economy responded quickly to new mar-kets due to the flexibility of its species mix. Because of low demand and the bottom of the marten's demographic cycle, in 1840 only 1251 pelts came to market. The 1845 production was 7383, reaching a high of 9586 in 1846 before declining to a low of 2652 in 1849. The taking of so many marten, while clearly a response to market forces, also represents the coincidence of high prices with a demographic upswing. Unlike the muskrat, which had a low market value and a high demographic peak, the marten did not exist in sufficient numbers to cause a price collapse. The large numbers traded represent the response of Native trappers to its increased value.

This change in the trade must have had structural and cultural impli-cations for Native peoples living in New Caledonia. Were depleted family-tenure beaver ponds abandoned in the search for a more valuable and, in the marten's case, more mobile commodity?[64] The region's species mix, rich both in marten and lynx, allowed New Caledonia to shift easily from one staple fur to another. The New Caledonia cyclical peak in marten matched the changing market's preference for the fur. Unlike the muskrat, the size of the marten population was easily absorbed by the market. However, the marten soon began one of its endemic declines. James Douglas, in charge of the Columbia Department in 1847, commented:

> A heavy decline in Beaver and Martens. The former apart from the measles, which also severely afflicted the natives of the District wherein the Steam vessel carries on trade, was partly the effect of the reduction in prices; the decrease in the latter is either caused by want of exertion in the hunters, or which is more probable it arises from a scarcity of the animal producing that valuable fur. From the great abundance of martens for some years past, in all parts of the Indian Country, and the general decline which we notice with regret—this year, at all the Marten Posts in this District it is feared that we are on the eve of one of those fluctuations to which the Marten trade independently of hunting is almost periodically subject, and if so there will be a further decline in the returns of that fur next year and for some years after, until from some unknown cause they again multiply and reappear in their native forests in the utmost abundance.[65]

The decline in marten was not serious enough to create problems for the company. Douglas noted that marten probably would rebound at the end of three years in the same manner as the muskrat.

The market and the post had shifted from the traditional staple fur to the marten. In time other small furs, such as the mink, would become substitutes for the marten.[66] After intervening in the management of business at all levels in order to survive the crisis, the committee returned by 1850 to its traditional role in the daily routine of directing the system of trade. Districts that overtrapped or had too many low-grade or damaged marten in their returns were reprimanded. The staff at posts responded to the demands of the buyers of the new staple: they stopped the practice of cutting paws from marten pelts that caused a shilling depreciation in the value of the skin; pale martens were no longer classed as damaged but as high quality because of their end purpose as trimming and collars. Native trappers followed the price incentives and brought in small furs instead of the beaver. The committee remarked about the Columbia Department that "from the abundance of small furs and the increased industry of the natives, we are inclined to look with greater hope to the future."[67] Daily operations of the company continued much as they had when the product was beaver. An early naval visitor to Fort Victoria in 1848 commented in a letter to the London *Times* that the beaver had "hardly any value now."[68] A fundamental change had taken place in the upper levels of the company. The balanced symbiotic relationships of the company with its trappers and European buyers had shifted in favour of the marketplace.

• Conclusion

The Hudson's Bay Company succeeded in establishing a centralized system to the fur trade, smoothing demographic bumps, improving quality and shipping methods, and establishing recognizable products. It survived the unexpected collapse of its historic and traditional market, the felt hat industry, because of the biological and ecological diversity of the wildlife harvest gathered by its network of posts. Information about markets and wildlife became the predominant feature of company operations as the process of deciding to restrict imports or to redirect trappers became more efficient. It learned that if one product could be abandoned after so many years, then the adoption of an entirely new group of products was conceivable.[69]

There is evidence in trade leaflets of a gradual shift in organizational mentality. The oldest leaflet (1799) shows animals in descending order of value. Mid-century leaflets alphabetize the lists to a certain extent. Beaver still heads the list, before bear or badger, despite its declining economic importance, but mythical terms such as "sea horse teeth" give way to the more familiar "walrus tusks." By 1870 all animals appear alphabetically, badger before beaver, reflecting a systemized inventory.[70]

The implications for the wildlife of this case study are difficult to assess. The emphasis on smaller furs meant a wider incursion into the river-forest ecosystem. There is evidence of complex interactions between species and within specific populations that even now are only vaguely understood. None of the Pacific Northwest's more than sixty forms of wildlife recorded in HBC records are extinct. Most have declined because of habitat loss, a loss not directly attributable to the fur trade.

To the fur trade, wildlife was a harvest. Nature provided a collection of potential products, each containing characteristics that influenced how it could be offered as a product. A primary feature of the fur trade management was mediating between demographic fluctuations and the world of fashion and markets. It was not wildlife management in the twentieth-century conception, but in this nineteenth-century interest in conservation and wildlife cycles there is a curious resonance with subsequent efforts. In our focus on the fur trade, we know much about traders and Natives, but very little about what drove the global market for wildlife.

• Notes

[1] Most fur trade literature makes passing reference to wildlife and then moves immediately to European-Native trade relations. The literature that does address animals is concerned with wildlife as an aspect of Native culture, such as Calvin Martin's *Keepers of the Game: Indian-Animal* *Relationships and the Fur Trade* (Berkeley: University of California Press, 1978), the rebuttal by Shepard Krech III, *Indians, Animals, and the Fur Trade: A Critique of Keepers of the Game* (Athens: University of Georgia Press, 1981), or Adrian Tanner's *Bringing Home Animals: Religious Ideology and*

Mode of Production of the Mistassini Cree Hunters (New York: St. Martin's Press, 1979).

There are many discussions of wildlife in the literature of environmental history, although the fur trade is strangely missing from Alfred W. Crosby's pivotal *Ecological Imperialism: The Biological Expansion of Europe, 900–1900* (Cambridge, England: Cambridge University Press, 1986). See Christine and Robert Prescott-Allen, *The First Resource: Wild Species in the North American Economy* (New Haven, CT: Yale University Press, 1986); Thomas R. Dunlap, *Saving America's Wildlife* (Princeton, NJ: Princeton University Press, 1988); Peter Matthiessen, *Wildlife in America* (New York: Viking, 1987); Lisa Mighetto, *Wild Animals and American Environmental Ethics* (Tucson: University of Arizona Press, 1991); Farley Mowat, *Sea of Slaughter* (Toronto: McClelland and Stewart, 1984); and Morgan Sherwood, *Big Game in Alaska: A History of Wildlife and People* (New Haven, CT: Yale University Press, 1981).

2 How this differed from other more flexible and locally controlled companies, such as the individual trapper of the Rocky Mountain rendezvous or the merchants of the St Louis fur trade, is important. Fur trade historiography suffers from political and archival compartmentalization. Canadian scholars, including this author, rely primarily on the papers of the Hudson's Bay Company. For the researcher, the recent microfilm publication of the *Papers of the St. Louis Fur Trade* (Bethesda, MD: University Publications of America, 1992) offers an opportunity for a comparative study. The papers include an introduction by William R. Swagerty and an essay by Janet Lecompte.

3 This is based on a statistical examination of fur importation handbills. The error between these estimated shipments and a ledger kept by James Douglas for each trading year showed an average 4 percent difference in the annual shipments from 1825 to 1849. Unless otherwise noted all figures cited come from a series of databases constructed by the author (these are mainframe codebook-based datafiles run under SAS, SPSS, and Paradox statistical analysis packages). One contained the annual fur returns of wildlife traded each year at the posts of the Columbia department. It was based on James Douglas, *Fur Trade Returns for Columbia and New Caledonia Districts, 1825–1857*, Provincial Archives of British Columbia, Victoria, British Columbia (hereafter PABC), A/B/20V3. For a full analysis of the James Douglas ledger see Lorne Hammond, "Studies in Documents: Historians, Archival Technology, and Business Ledgers," *Archivaria* 28 (Summer 1989): 120–25. Another database contains the figures published in fur importation handbills listing North American fur imports to London, *Fur Trade Importation Book, 1799–1912*, Hudson's Bay Company Archives, series I, Winnipeg, Manitoba (hereafter HBCA), A.53/1. The third is a listing of sales of Columbia wildlife drawn from the Warehouse Keeper's annotated auction catalogue, Auction Catalogues of Fur Produce, HBCA, A.54.

4 George Simpson to the Governor, Deputy Governor, and Committee, 10 March 1825, HBCA, D.4/88, para. 20; Frederick Merk, *Fur Trade and Empire: George Simpson's Journal* (Cambridge, MA: Belknap Press, 1968), 32–33.

5 John McLoughlin to the Governor, Deputy Governor, and Committee, 6 Oct. 1825, para. 49, in *The Letters of John McLoughlin: From Fort Vancouver To the Governor and Committee, First Series, 1825–1838* (London, England: Hudson's Bay Record Society [hereafter HBRS], 1941), 16; John McLoughlin to the Governor, Deputy Governor, and Committee, 31 Oct. 1842, para. 20, in *The Letters of John McLoughlin: From Fort Vancouver To the Governor and Committee, Second Series, 1839–1844* (London, England: HBRS, 1943), 81.

6 James R. Beringer, *The Control Revolution: Technology and Economic Origins of the Information Society* (Cambridge, MA: Harvard University Press, 1986), 144–53.

7 Governor, Deputy Governor, and Committee to Simpson, 11 March 1825, HBCA, A.6/21, para. 23. Earlier in 1825 the denture market was over-stocked because of Greenland fisheries activity.

8 Robin F. Wells, "Castoreum and Steel Traps in Eastern North America," *American Anthropologist* 74 (June 1972): 479–83; "Castoreum," *The Museum of the Fur Trade Quarterly* 8 (Spring 1972): 1–5.

9 Ross Cox, *The Columbia River, Or Scenes and Adventures During A Residence of Six Years On the Western Side of the Rocky Mountains Among Various Tribes Hitherto Unknown; Together With A Journey Across the American Continent* (Norman: University of Oklahoma Press, 1957), 243.

10 John Richardson documented plants, lichens, birds, mammals, and fish during John Franklin's arctic expeditions between 1819 and 1827. His lasting achievement is the multivolume *Fauna Boreali-Americana; Or the Zoology of the Northern Parts of British America: Containing Descriptions of the Objects of Natural History Collected on the Late Northern Land Expeditions, Under Command of Captain Sir John Franklin, R.N.* (New York: Arno Press, 1974); *Arctic Ordeal: The Journal of John Richardson, Surgeon-Naturalist with Franklin* (Montreal, Quebec: McGill-Queen's University Press, 1984); C. Stuart Houston, "John Richardson—First Naturalist in the Northwest," *Beaver* (Nov. 1984): 10–15.

11 In the Columbia department from 1820 to 1849 the average proportions were: red phase 58 percent (8402 pelts), cross phase 31 percent (4430), and silver phase 11 percent (1608 pelts). See also the discussion between naturalists John Bradbury and Thomas Nuttall in James P.

Ronda, *Astoria and Empire* (Lincoln: University of Nebraska Press, 1990), 133, 316–20; and M. Novak, J.A. Baker, M.E. Obbard, and B. Malloch, eds., *Wild Furbearer Management and Conservation in Northern America* (Toronto: Ministry of Natural Resources, 1987), 751.

12 John Richardson cites A. de Capell Brooke as noting that only three or four silver foxes were taken annually on the Lofoten Islands of Norway and that they are not found elsewhere. Richardson, *Fauna Boreali-Americana*, 94. In "Platinum Mutations in Norwegian Silver Foxes," *Journal of Heredity* 30 (June 1939): 226–34, Otto L. Mohr and Per Tuff say that much of Norwegian stock is imported from Canada.

13 Richardson, *Fauna Boreali-Americana*, 93.

14 Alexander William Francis Banfield, *Mammals of Canada* (Toronto: National Museum of Natural Sciences, University of Toronto Press, 1974), 299.

15 Richardson, *Fauna Boreali-Americana*, 15.

16 E.E. Rich, ed., *Peter Skene Ogden's Snake Country Journals, 1824–1825 and 1825–1826* (London, England: HBRS, 1950); K.G. Davies, ed., *Peter Skene Ogden's Snake Country Journal, 1826–27* (London, England: HBRS, 1961); Glyndwr Williams, ed., *Peter Skene Ogden's Snake Country Journals, 1827–28 and 1828–29* (London, England: HBRS, 1971).

17 George Simpson to John McLoughlin, 9 July 1827, HBCA, D.4/90, para. 6.

18 Peter Skene Ogden to the Governor, Chief Factors, and Chief Traders, 10 Oct. 1826, in Merk, *Fur Trade and Empire*, 285.

19 Banfield, *Mammals of Canada*, 161.

20 Simpson to the Governor, Deputy Governor, and Committee, 10 March 1825, HBCA, D.4/88, para. 26.

21 For a discussion of attitudes toward wolves in America after 1880 see Dunlap, *Saving America's Wildlife*.

22 Governor, Deputy Governor, and Committee to Simpson, 27 Feb. 1822, HBCA, A.6/20, para. 48.

23 Governor, Deputy Governor, and Committee to Simpson, 7 June 1833, HBCA, A.6/23, para. 40.

24 Pelly, Colvile, and Simpson to McLoughlin, 31 Dec. 1839, in *Letters of John McLoughlin, Second Series, 1839–1844,* 164n.

25 From 1827 to 1937 the average price for a river otter was 18 shillings 11 pence (18/11), less 1/5 for insurance and other charges from the Columbia Landing warehouse. This left 17/6 as the average worth. The RAC agreed to pay 23/- each, for a 5/6 profit on each to the HBC. The additional three thousand otters from the Northern Department had an average value of 26/5, less the 1/5 charge, leaving a net average value of 25/-. The RAC agreed to pay 32/- each, giving HBC a 7/- profit on each skin. Although the Panhandle cost £1750 (2000 x 17/6) a year, the hidden profit on the Columbia otters was £550 (2000 x 5/6) and £1050 on the Northern Department otters (3000 x 7/-), making the cost only £150. "Memorandum," HBCA, F.29/2, fo. 182. The conversion rate for 1840 to 1850 was four dollars to the pound in urban centres and five dollars to the pound where there were currency shortages, such as in the West.

26 Lloyd Keith places the origins of the field at a conference held in July 1931 on the Matamek River in Labrador under the patronage of Copley Amory of Boston. Lloyd B. Keith, *Wildlife's Ten-Year Cycle* (Madison: University of Wisconsin Press, 1963), vii.

27 Keith, *Wildlife's Ten-Year Cycle.* For related work on the fluctuation of muskrats see Paul L. Errington, *Muskrat Populations* (Ames: Iowa State University Press, 1963), 522–38.

28 For the scientific literature see Charles S. Elton, "Periodic Fluctuations in the Numbers of Animals: Their Causes and Effects," *Journal of the Society for Experimental Biology* 1 (Oct. 1924): 119–63; "Plague and the Regulation of Numbers in Wild Animals," *Journal of Hygiene* 24 (Oct. 1925): 138–63; "The Ten-Year Cycle in Numbers of the Lynx in Canada," *Journal of Animal Ecology* 2 (Nov. 1942): 215–44; *The Ecology of Invasions by Animals and Plants* (London: Methuen, 1958); Charles S. and Mary Nicholson, "Fluctuations in Numbers of the Muskrat *(Ondatra Zibethica)* in Canada," *Journal of Animal Ecology* 2 (May 1942): 96–126.

29 Ian McTaggart Cowan, "The Fur Trade and the Fur Cycle: 1825–1857," *British Columbia Historical Quarterly* 2 (Jan. 1938): 19–30, points out that figures for the lynx are slightly confused because they do not distinguish between the more southern bobcat, a generalist predator with alternate food sources, and the true lynx, a specialist predator whose numbers fluctuate in direct response to its prey, the snowshoe rabbit. However, the composite totals for the two show the lynx had demographic peaks in the returns of 1829–30, 1837–40, and 1848–50.

30 There is a relationship between the latitude of a muskrat population and the number of litters as well as the number of young per litter. Muskrat in Louisiana may have three to six litters a year with an average of 2.4 young in each litter, while muskrat in northern Canada may have only two litters, but each averaging 7.1 young. Banfield, *Mammals of Canada,* 198–99. See also David J. Wishart, *The Fur Trade of the American West, 1807–1840: A Geographical Synthesis* (Lincoln: University of Nebraska Press, 1979), 36.

31 Simpson to the Governor, Deputy Governor, and Committee, 30 June 1829, HBCA, D.4/96.

32 Governor, Deputy Governor, and Committee to Simpson, 4 March 1840, HBCA, A.6/25, para. 23.

33 Simpson to the Governor, Deputy Governor, and Committee, 18 July 1831, HBCA, D.4/98, para. 5. Astor had approached the company about

contracting for muskrat in 1827, but the company wanted a guarantee that he would take seventy thousand to one hundred thousand a year at a fixed price for five to seven years. This was a dangerous contract given the fluctuations. See William Smith to George Simpson, 30 May 1827, HBCA, A.6/21.

34 The 1835 total import of 1 111 646 muskrat came to a market that had been paying 9.5 pence per skin, so the total value of the stock was $44 000. But the prices given for the 1837 shipment of 838 549 skins was 3 pence each, for a book value of $10 000. This demonstrates the failure of the market to absorb these quantities. HBCA, A.54.

35 Governor, Deputy Governor, and Committee to Simpson, 5 March 1834, HBCA, A.6/23, para. 28.

36 Governor, Deputy Governor, and Committee to Simpson, 2 June 1824, HBCA, A.6/20, para. 54.

37 Due to the depressed market the committee decided to bend on the issue and accepted $300 compensation for the loss when the muskrats were resold. William Smith to Henry Carey & Co., 16 June 1825, 1 Feb. 1826, and 12 June 1826, HBCA, A.6/21.

38 Archibald Barclay to George Simpson, 3 Feb. 1846, HBCA, A.6/27.

39 John S. Galbraith, *The Hudson's Bay Company as an Imperial Factor* (New York: Octagon Books, 1977); Mary E. Wheeler, "Empires in Conflict and Cooperation: The 'Bostonians' and the Russian-American Company," *Pacific Historical Review* 40 (Nov. 1971): 419–41; Frank E. Ross, "The Retreat of the Hudson's Bay Company in the Pacific North West," *Canadian Historical Review* 18 (Sept. 1937): 262–80; Herman J. Deutsch, "Economic Imperialism in the Early Pacific Northwest," *Pacific Historical Review* 9 (Dec. 1940): 377–88.

40 Simpson to the Governor, Deputy Governor, and Committee, 10 Aug. 1832, HBCA, D.4/99, para. 3.

41 The idea of managing beaver stocks is old. An early North American reference to the idea is a letter of Jesuit Father Paul le Jeune dated 28 Aug. 1636. Reuben Gold Thwaits, ed., *The Jesuit Relations and Allied Documents,* vol. 9 (New York: Pageant Book Company, 1959), 165–67.

42 Simpson to the Governor, Deputy Governor, and Committee, 10 July 1828, HBCA, D.4/92, para. 9.

43 Governor, Deputy Governor, and Committee to Simpson, 16 Jan. 1828, HBCA, A.6/21, para. 10.

44 Governor, Deputy Governor, and Committee to Simpson, 23 Feb. 1826, HBCA, A.6/21, para. 36.

45 Governor, Deputy Governor, and Committee to Simpson, 25 Oct. 1832, HBCA, A.6/22, para. 14.

46 Arthur J. Ray, "Some Conservation Schemes of the Hudson's Bay Company, 1821–50: An Examination of the Problems of Resource Management in the Fur Trade," *Journal of Historical Geography* 1 (Jan. 1975): 58. Any monopoly HBC had developed was only in isolated areas because the company had difficulty getting co-operation even from its own staff. The number of furs brought in influenced not only an individual's prestige but calculation of his pension.

47 Simpson to the Governor, Deputy Governor, and Committee, 20 Aug. 1826, HBCA, D.4/89, para. 30.

48 Simpson to the Governor, Deputy Governor, and Committee, 10 Aug. 1832, HBCA, D.4/99, para. 27.

49 Simpson to the Governor, Deputy Governor, and Committee, 20 June 1841, HBCA, D.4/99, para. 31.

50 Governor, Deputy Governor, and Committee to Simpson, 3 March 1830, HBCA, A.6/22, para. 2.

51 William Smith to James Keith, 3 Sept. 1842, HBCA, A.6/26.

52 Governor, Deputy Governor, and Committee to Simpson, 1 April 1843, HBCA, A.6/26, para. 23.

53 Archibald Barclay to James Keith, 4 Sept. 1843, HBCA, A.6/26.

54 Governor, Deputy Governor, and Committee to John McLoughlin, 27 Sept. 1843, HBCA, A.6/26, para. 9.

55 Governor, Deputy Governor, and Committee to Simpson, 11 March 1845, HBCA, A.6/26, para. 3.

56 Auction, 1 Sept. 1847, HBCA, A.54/182.

57 Governor, Deputy Governor, and Committee to Chief Factors Peter Skene Ogden, James Douglas, and John Work, 8 Sept. 1848, HBCA, A.6/27, para. 2.

58 Governor, Deputy Governor, and Committee to Simpson, 5 June 1847, HBCA, A.6/27, para. 6; Governor, Deputy Governor, and Committee to Simpson, 7 April 1847, HBCA, A.6/27, para. 3.

59 Governor, Deputy Governor, and Committee to Simpson, 5 April 1848, HBCA, A.6/27, para. 4, 5, 7; Governor, Deputy Governor, and Committee to Simpson, 4 April 1849, HBCA, A.6/28, para. 4.

60 Edward Roberts to Simpson, 3 Feb. 1846, HBCA, D.5/16, fos. 168–69, cited in Caroline Skynner, "History of the Beaver and Beaver Hat" (unpublished paper, HBCA, PP. 1984–87), 27.

61 Simpson to the Governor, Deputy Governor, and Committee, 25 Nov. 1841, HBCA, D.4/110, para. 7.

62 Governor, Deputy Governor, and Committee to Simpson, 11 March 1845, HBCA, A.6/26, para. 3.

63 Governor, Deputy Governor, and Committee to Simpson, 18 Sept. 1847, HBCA, A.6/27.

64 Ian McTaggart Cowan, in "The Fur Trade and the Fur Cycle: 1825–1857," *British Columbia Historical Quarterly* 2 (Jan. 1938): 27, states that the marten and the lynx both undergo mass movements after the decline of a rabbit cycle.

65 Board of Management to the Governor, Deputy Governor, and Committee, 6 Nov. 1847, *Fort Victoria Letters, 1846–1851*, ed. Hartwell Bowsfield (Winnipeg, MB: HBRS, 1979), 23; James Douglas to Archibald Barclay, 22 July 1851, *Fort Victoria Letters*, 200–201.

66 "Mink and Musquash will no doubt rise . . . as those who cannot afford to pay a high price for Martens will content themselves with inferior furs of the same class," Archibald Barclay to George Simpson, 28 Dec. 1849, HBCA, A.6/28.

67 Governor, Deputy Governor, and Committee to Chief Factors Peter Skene Ogden, James Douglas, and John Work, Fort Vancouver, 8 Sept. 1848, HBCA, A.6/27, para. 3.

68 "North West Coast—Visit of H.M.S. *Constance*," *Times* (London), 4 May 1849, 7.

69 For a discussion of nonfur trade economic activities see Richard S. Mackie, "Colonial Land, Indian Labour and Company Capital: The Economy of Vancouver Island, 1849–1858" (MA thesis, University of Victoria, 1984).

70 The concept is drawn loosely from Robert Darnton's examination of class through a description of a parade in preindustrial France. See Robert Darnton, "A Bourgeois Puts His World In Order: The City As A Text" in *The Great Cat Massacre and Other Episodes in French Cultural History* (New York: Vintage Books, 1985), 106–43. See also Keith Thomas, *Man and the Natural World: Changing Attitudes in England 1500–1800* (London: Allen Lane, 1983). All examples used here are drawn from *Fur Trade Importation Book, 1799–1912*, HBCA, A.53/71.

"WHAT IF MAMA IS AN INDIAN?":
The Cultural Ambivalence of the Alexander Ross Family*

SYLVIA VAN KIRK

Recent historical studies of the mixed-blood people of western Canada have concluded that within this broad category there were specific groups which can be differentiated on the basis of ethnicity, religion, and class. In the period before 1870, there was a discernible anglophone mixed-blood group, sometimes known as the "country-born."[1] These people exhibited a cultural orientation quite distinct from that of the larger francophone mixed-blood group, or Métis. There is considerable truth to Frits Pannekoek's assertion that the principal aspiration of these "country-born" people was assimilation into the British, Protestant world of their fathers.[2] As Jennifer Brown has emphasized, this was due in large measure to the active and pervasive paternal influence evident in many of these British-Indian families.[3] Much work remains to be done, however, in analysing the actual effect of this process of enculturation on the children of these families.

In one of the few studies which focusses on a particular family, Elizabeth Arthur has argued that, for the children of Chief Factor Roderick

*From *The New Peoples: Being and Becoming Métis in North America,* ed. Jacqueline Peterson and Jennifer S.H. Brown (Winnipeg: The University of Manitoba Press, 1985), 207–17. Reprinted with permission of the publisher. The original version of this article was published in *The Developing West: Essays on Canadian History in Honor of Lewis H. Thomas,* ed. John E. Foster (Edmonton: University of Alberta Press, 1983).

McKenzie and his Ojibwa wife Angèlique, the pressures to succeed in their father's world resulted in severe psychological distress, especially for the sons.[4] In determining the success of the program of enculturation that British fathers, aided by church and school, mapped out for their children, it is useful to focus on mixed-blood families who were part of the old colonial elite. Their heads (usually retired officers of the Hudson's Bay Company [HBC or the Company]) had the desire, along with sufficient rank, wealth, and education, to secure the enculturation of their children as members of the British Protestant community in spite of their birth in a distant and isolated part of the Empire.

The Alexander Ross family of Red River appears to have been one of the most successfully enculturated British-Indian families in Rupert's Land. Yet, ultimately, an outstanding younger son, James, suffered an "identity crisis" so profound that it destroyed him. The tragedy of his life is suggestive for the fate of the anglophone mixed-blood group as a whole. Unlike the Métis, this group was not permitted to build a cultural identity based on the recognition of their dual racial heritage. British-Indian children were taught to deny and increasingly felt the need to suppress the Indian part of their heritage, but racist attitudes could nevertheless deny them the positions in white society to which they aspired.[5]

The young Scot Alexander Ross first emigrated to the Canadas in 1804. After several unremunerative years as a schoolteacher, he decided to try his fortune in the fur trade. As a clerk with the Pacific Fur Company, he helped to establish trade with the Okanagan Indians of the Upper Columbia River. Shortly after, around 1813, he wed, *à la façon du pays* (in the fashion of the country), an Okanagan chief's young daughter whom he called Sally. Their first child, Alexander, was born in 1815, followed by three girls, Margaret (born 1819), Isabella (born 1820), and Mary (born 1823). Although Ross had a high regard for the Okanagans, he felt it best, as his family grew, to remove them from the world of fur trade post and Indian camp. In 1825, he retired from the trade and settled his wife and children on an extensive land grant in the Red River colony. There he hoped they would be able to receive "the Christian education" that he considered the best portion in life that he could give them.[6]

In time, the Ross family comprised twelve children—four boys and eight girls. For the eight youngest children, Red River was the only home they had ever known; they never had any contact with their mother's kin across the Rocky Mountains. We don't know what Sally Ross felt on taking leave of her people for the last time, but there is certainly evidence that her loving maternal presence considerably strengthened the Ross children's sense of family. Yet, as a Christianized Indian, the extent to which she transmitted her Native heritage to her children appears to have been limited. That Sally Ross spoke her Native tongue in the family circle is illustrated by the little endearments James penned to his mother in later years, and the older girls were proficient in crafts such as making moccasins.[7] But such attributes were almost completely overshadowed by the Scots Presbyterian influence of the father.

As the patriarch of the family home, known as Colony Gardens, Alexander Ross shaped the upbringing of his half-Indian children. It was Ross who determined their religious and secular education and who later gave land to his sons to establish their own households or provided succour for widowed daughters.[8] Ross's most ardent desire was that his family be imbued with the precepts of Christianity. Although deeply disappointed that there was no Presbyterian clergyman in the settlement, Ross initially accepted the official ministrations of the Anglican Church. Sally Ross and her children were all baptized by the Reverend William Cockran, who also formally married the Rosses in 1828. But while religious observances had to be made at the Anglican church, Ross kept his staunch Presbyterianism alive through regular family gatherings for Bible reading and prayers. All the while he campaigned to bring a Presbyterian minister to Red River, which was at last achieved in the person of the Reverend John Black, who arrived in 1851. Religion was one of the most formative influences in the lives of the Ross children. Their sincere conviction gave them a sense of purpose; they subscribed to the Presbyterian view that God had put them on this earth to be instruments of His purpose and that He would reward those who diligently applied their talents.[9]

The application of the benefits of secular education seems to have been somewhat more uneven than those of their religious education. With the exception of two of the younger ones, little formal education was bestowed upon the girls, most of whom married in their teens. But the sons, who were to carry on the family name, received the best education that Red River had to offer. William (born 1825) was a very creditable graduate of the Red River Academy, while his younger brother James (born 1835) was such an outstanding pupil of Bishop Anderson's that he was sent to further his education at the University of Toronto in 1853. The education of the youngest Ross children was taken over by the Presbyterian minister, John Black. Sandy (Alexander, who was named in memory of his eldest brother, who had died in 1835) was one of a class of six young scholars. Privately, Black tutored Henrietta (born 1830), who later became his wife, and undertook to improve upon the superficial schooling for "young ladies" that her younger sister Jemima (born 1837) had received.

For the Ross daughters, marriage would be the key to their continued assimilation. Significantly, four out of the six girls who reached adulthood married white men. In 1831, Margaret Ross married Hugh Matheson of Kildonan, and she was eventually listed in the Red River census as white. Henrietta's marriage to the Reverend John Black, while it helped to seal the family's identification with the Scots Kildonan community, emphasized the family's orientation toward newcomers, for Black had but recently come from the Canadas. (The Canadas comprised Canada West and Canada East, today contained within the provinces of Ontario and Quebec.

United in 1840, they were entirely separate from Rupert's Land.) Isabella Ross's second husband was James Stewart Green, an American free trader who arrived in the settlement in the 1840s. Finally in 1860, the Canadian connection was further extended when the youngest Ross girl, Jemima, married William Coldwell, who had arrived the year before to start the colony's first newspaper.

These marriages to white men not only underscore the Ross family's desire to be viewed as "British," but also symbolize the way in which the family identified with the forces of "progress" in Red River. It was a measure of the family's success that its sons were equipped and ready to play leadership roles in the colony, to bring about a new order based on the benefits of civilization. Old Alexander Ross had every reason to be proud of his son William. By the early 1850s, William had succeeded to all his father's public offices, which included councillor of Assiniboia, sheriff, and keeper of the jail. "Is it not very pleasing to see a son step into the shoes of his father and do ample justice to all of these offices?" the old patriarch enthused.[10] William, who could not have been unaware that his station in the colony depended in large measure on the good will of the old Company establishment, did not publicly criticize the rule of the HBC; yet, like many of his peers, he chafed under the old regime. He wrote to his brother James in 1856:

> You know the fact that Red River is half a century behind the age— no stirring events to give life and vigour to our debilitated political life—The incubus of the Company's monopoly—the peculiar government under which we *vegetate* . . . ; all hang like a nightmare on our political and social existence. . . . Such a state of things cannot last forever, sooner or later the whole fabric must be swept away. . . . We ought to have a flood of immigration to infuse new life, new ideas, and destroy all our old associations with the past, i.e. in so far as it hinders our progress for the future—a regular transformation will sharpen our interests, fill our minds with new projects and give life and vigour to our thoughts, words, and action—when that day comes along you may rest assured that there will be no complaint.[11]

Just what role William Ross would have played in the turbulent years that followed must remain a matter of speculation, for a few months after he wrote these words, at the age of thirty-one, he was dead.

James Ross, however, emerged as an ardent champion of the cause of Canada in Rupert's Land. It is scarcely surprising that from young James's point of view, Canada was the land of opportunity. He performed brilliantly at Knox College, winning an impressive array of scholarships and prizes. His father, highly gratified, exclaimed, "What will they say of the Brûlés now?"[12] Socially, James's acceptance also seemed to be complete, for in 1858 he married Margaret Smith, the daughter of a respected Scots Presbyterian family in Toronto. To marry a white woman represented a

considerable achievement for a British-Indian man and was almost un-
heard of in Red River. Both of James's brothers, for example, had married
well-connected anglophone mixed-bloods.[13]

On the surface, the children of Alexander Ross were extremely successful in terms of criteria derived from their father's world; yet they were
not immune to racial prejudice. This was evident in the Kildonan community's reaction to Henrietta's marriage to the Reverend John Black. It was
intimated that his marriage to a Native would prove detrimental to his ministry.[14] Indeed, at least some members of the predominantly white congregation resented the prominent position of this "halfbreed" family—in the
church, they occupied three out of the six prestigious square pews. The
ears of young Jemima Ross were stung by remarks that Mr Black must feel
rather ashamed to look down on all his "black" relations when he stepped
into the pulpit.[15] Although she tried to make light of the situation, it is evident that Jemima was wounded and began to feel ambivalent about having
an Indian mother. Although privately she might have been quite devoted
to her mother, she became increasingly embarrassed to be seen in public
with her. Ambivalence toward their Native mothers, which was in essence
an ambivalence toward their own Indian blood and heritage, was apparently not uncommon among British-Indian children. James Ross himself
lamented that "halfbreed" children often did not show enough respect to
their Indian mothers. It was his fear that some of his brothers and sisters
might succumb to this temptation, especially after the death of their father,
which prompted his anguished admonition to them, "What if Mama is an
Indian?"[16] While James loved his mother, it is difficult to interpret this
statement as a positive defence of his mother's Indianness. What the statement does signify is that, *even* if their mother was an Indian, she was a most
exemplary mother and for that reason was entitled to the love and respect
of her children. Her simple Christian virtue, he argued, was far more worthy of esteem than were the superficial accomplishments of some of the
white ladies who were held in such high regard in Red River. But the fact
that he felt moved to make such a comparison indicates the social strains to
which the younger members of the family in particular were exposed.

James's own response to racial prejudice, to which he appears to have
been quite sensitive, was to work diligently to prove that one could rise
above the derogatory stereotypes of mixed-blood people perpetrated in
non-Native circles in nineteenth-century Red River. Indeed, these stereotypes were uncomfortably close to home. On reading his father's book, *The
Fur Hunters of the Far West,* James was disconcerted to find that his own
father made unflattering generalizations about halfbreeds, characterizing
them as "fickle" and "destitute of steady purpose." "I think some of your
statements about Halfbreeds unnecessarily harsh," James could not help
telling him, and he vowed that his father would never be able to accuse
him of such behaviour.[17]

In fact, James Ross seems to have been almost obsessed with the
desire to make his father proud of him. He must not fail. The pressure on

him increased unexpectedly when in 1856 not only his elder brother but also his father died. Within a few short months, the Ross family had suffered a double blow—they had lost not only their guiding head, but also the one who had been groomed to take his place. In a British-Indian family where the family's welfare and status was so dependent upon the father, his demise could be catastrophic. Again James Ross acknowledged that "halfbreed" families generally dwindled into insignificance after their patriarchs died.[18] He fervently believed that the same must not happen to the Ross family. In a moving letter to his siblings, he exhorted them to a standard of conduct that would ensure the family's standing and respectability within the community.

After completing his bachelor of arts degree at the University of Toronto, James Ross returned to Red River with his Canadian bride in the summer of 1858. In assuming the mantle of family leadership, he was proud to be chosen to follow in the footsteps of his father and brother by being appointed sheriff and postmaster. Unlike his brother, however, James Ross felt compelled to speak out against the HBC. In the late 1850s, agitation for a Canadian takeover was growing and there was considerable support in the anglophone mixed-blood community. In 1857, for example, the sons of the late Chief Factor Alexander Kennedy and his Cree wife had obtained hundreds of signatures to a petition appealing to the legislature of the province of Canada for annexation.[19] James Ross was ideally placed to continue this campaign and he found his vehicle for expression in *The Nor'Wester*, of which he became co-editor in 1860. But Ross was to learn that although the Company might be weakened, it had not yet lost all power. In 1862, after publishing a petition which ran counter to the one being promoted by the HBC on the question of defence for Red River, Ross found himself summarily divested of his appointed offices. Shortly afterward, he became heavily involved in the sordid Corbett case; along with a significant number of anglophone mixed-bloods, he seemed to feel that the unhappy minister was being persecuted because of his anti-Company stance.[20] By 1864, with his prospects tarnished, Ross, perhaps at his wife's urging, decided to return to Canada.

Canada seemed so promising that James urged other members of the family to emigrate. William and Jemima Coldwell and young Sandy Ross with his mixed-blood wife Catherine Murray arrived in Toronto in 1865. It was not a happy interlude. Although Sandy had previously spent some years at Knox College, he and his wife were so homesick that they returned to Red River within twelve months. Jemima Coldwell also did not adapt well to her new surroundings. Although she had a fine house, she may have shared her sister Henrietta's apprehension that a "dark halfbreed" such as herself would never really be acceptable in Canadian society.[21] In any event, Jemima grew increasingly melancholy, especially after the death of her eldest daughter, and she herself died in Toronto in 1867.

Only James seemed to thrive; his list of accomplishments was increasingly impressive. He completed his master of arts degree and articled at law, coming first in the class when he was admitted to the bar. He quickly attracted the attention of George Brown, and later became a lead writer and reporter for *The Globe*. As Jennifer Brown has pointed out, Canada could absorb a few talented Native sons, isolated as they were from their fellows.[22] Doubtless, James Ross would have prospered had he stayed in Canada. Instead he returned to Red River on the eve of momentous change. He had been encouraged by the lieutenant-governor-to-be, William McDougall, who advised him that the new Canadian possession would need leaders like himself. Indeed, few could match his credentials. A man of striking mien and persuasive speech, he was fluent in both English and French, devoted to Red River, but had influential and sympathetic ties to Canada. Ross had always felt that his destiny was somehow bound up with the colony. Here was the golden opportunity—the longed-for time that his brother had not lived to see. The anglophone mixed-blood community was apparently ready to secure the promise of their British Protestant heritage through union with Canada, and Ross intended to lead them to it.

For James Ross, however, the Red River Resistance proved to be not only a political but also a personal crisis of great magnitude. It essentially destroyed him. Instead of providing consistent leadership, Ross vacillated. At first the ardent champion of the Canadian cause, he ended up as Chief Justice of Riel's provisional government. Ross was won over by Riel's appeal to racial unity; the Métis were fighting not solely for their own rights, but also for the rights of all the indigenous people of Red River. The bond of their Native ancestry made Ross anxious to avoid taking up arms against the Métis. Nothing was worth a civil war against "brothers and kindred."[23] At a fundamental level, the crisis must also have forced Ross, anglicized as he might be, to face the Indian dimension of his origins; indeed, genetically, he was far more Indian than was Riel. The racist attitudes of the Canadians undoubtedly accentuated Ross's crisis of identity. He would have been deeply hurt when even his beloved *Globe* printed disparaging remarks about renegade halfbreeds, tarring the entire mixed-blood community with the same brush.

His course was a tortured one; as the darling of the Canadian cause, it was not easy for him to be allied with Riel. Friends and relatives in Canada suspected Ross of treasonous conduct and British-Indian compatriots who remained opposed to Riel accused Ross of being a self-seeking rogue.[24] During the course of the resistance, Ross actively counselled restraint, trying desperately to prevent a violent clash between the Canadians and the Métis. He interceded with Riel to spare Major Boulton and his men, and was shocked to learn of the subsequent execution of Thomas Scott.[25] This event led to Ross's estrangement from the provisional government, but the vengeful reaction of the Canadians brought further despair. Indeed the anglophone mixed-blood community in general experienced a real sense of disillusionment as a result of the violent excesses perpetrated by the

Canadian troops, being apprehensive that they too would fall victim to racist attacks.[26]

As he found himself torn between the two communities—Canadian and Métis—Ross's own feelings of ambivalence and guilt must have been profound. In his turmoil, he turned to drink and seriously undermined his health. In the summer of 1870, however, Ross tried to pull himself together. A business trip to Toronto provided the opportunity for him to regain some of the idealism of his student days, to feel that he had been strengthened by the trials through which he had passed. He returned to Red River with renewed purpose, hoping to escape the stigma of his association with Riel and to be called upon to serve in the new administration of Governor Archibald. Instead, he suffered the mortification of seeing himself passed over in favour of Canadian newcomers.[27] This further crisis likely contributed to his premature death in September 1871.

After James's death, the youngest son, Sandy, did not take over as head of the Ross family. Although not much else is known about him, he was the most insecure of all the sons and never found his niche. Death claimed him early, too, at the age of thirty-one. The leadership of the Ross family passed to the white sons-in-law, the Reverend John Black, who remained concerned for the family's welfare even after the death of Henrietta in 1873, and especially William Coldwell, who married Jemima, the widow of William Ross, in 1875.

In spite of their great promise, an air of tragedy hung over the children of Alexander Ross. By 1874, all the children except one daughter were dead, most having died in their thirties. They seem to have been particularly susceptible to lung diseases, but one wonders to what extent psychological stress contributed to their poor health. The degree of psychological dislocation which they suffered appears to have been proportional to the degree to which they attempted to assimilate, accompanied as this was by the hazards of personal ambivalence and the threat of rejection.

The ones who fared best were the daughters, perhaps partly because there was less pressure on them to succeed. Yet even the most well-adjusted of the daughters seem to have been those who were not forced to suppress their Indian heritage completely. An elder daughter, Mary, for example, who married the mixed-blood Orkneyman George Flett, eventually helped her husband establish a Presbyterian mission among the Riding Mountain "Chippewas" or Saulteaux. There, her familiarity with Indian language and customs was an advantage, not a detriment.[28] Her younger sisters who married prominent whites had to confront prejudice more directly. Henrietta was able to weather the racial jibes of the Kildonan community, being assisted by a loving and supportive husband, but Jemima, who was the youngest and most upwardly mobile, had a great deal of trouble coping with her situation.

The sons suffered most. Their fate is important, for in the 1850s and sixties, talented young anglophone mixed-bloods such as themselves were emerging in leadership roles in Red River.[29] In 1861, according to compatriot A.K. Isbister, British-Indians occupied nearly all the significant and intellectual offices in the colony. Most prominent among them had been James Ross.[30]

Indeed, the pressure on Ross must have been enormous, for he was upheld as an example to all. Yet James Ross's crisis in 1869–70 is really symbolic of an inherent tension in the enculturation process to which anglophone mixed-blood children were subjected. The Red River Resistance polarized the settlement into two elements—white and Métis. British-Indian leaders such as James Ross suffered their own personal agony when they were brought face to face with the fact that they were really neither, and that increasingly their place in Rupert's Land was being threatened. Ultimately, the biases of the newcomers, often racist in nature, would deny to the anglophone mixed-bloods the successful integration into white society that they desired.[31] Significantly, the new elite of Winnipeg soon bore little resemblance to the old Red River elite that had given Isbister so much satisfaction. Yet, leaders such as James Ross could not be Métis, even though they might have felt a bond of kinship with the French-Indian community. Unlike the Métis, the anglophone mixed-bloods lacked a distinct cultural identity based on the duality of their heritage, and this made it difficult for them to build upon their uniqueness as a people of mixed racial ancestry. In 1869–70, the Métis were secure enough in their own identity to champion Native rights and would produce the foremost leaders in promoting this cause. Significantly, after 1870 the anglophone mixed-bloods rapidly ceased to be recognized as a separate indigenous group, and *Métis* has become the label which has tended to subsume all of the mixed-blood people of Western Canada.

• Notes

1 The term *country-born* was first used in modern scholarship by John E. Foster in his PhD dissertation "The Country-Born in the Red River Settlement, 1820–1850" (University of Alberta, 1972). Although occasionally used by the anglophone mixed-bloods of Red River, it is significant that they most commonly used the term *halfbreed* to refer to themselves (*The Nor'Wester*, 1862). Unfortunately, this term is unacceptable today because of the pejorative connotations it has taken on. The term *mixed-blood* seems to me most satisfactory and I am grateful to Irene Spry for suggesting the designations anglophone and francophone.

2 See Frits Pannekoek, "The Churches and the Social Structure in the Red River Area 1818–1870" (PhD diss., Queen's University, 1973).

3 Jennifer S.H. Brown, *Strangers in Blood: Fur Trade Company Families in Indian Country* (Vancouver: University of British Columbia Press, 1980), 216–20.

4 Elizabeth Arthur, "Angeliqué and her Children," Thunder Bay Historical Museum Society, *Papers and Records* 6:30–40.

5 For a discussion of the racial attitudes of the Hudson's Bay Company which denied advancement to well-qualified anglophone mixed-bloods in the

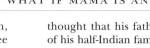

period after the union, see Brown, *Strangers in Blood*, chs. 8 and 9. See also John Long, "Archdeacon Thomas Vincent of Moosonee and the Handicap of 'Métis' Racial Status," *Canadian Journal of Native Studies* 3 (1983): 95–116.

6 Alexander Ross, *The Fur Hunters of the Far West*, vol. 2 (London: Smith, Elder and Co., 1855), 233.

7 Provincial Archives of Manitoba (hereafter PAM), Alexander Ross Family Papers, James to father, 31 Dec. 1853; father to James, 11 June 1854; James to father, 1 July 1854.

8 The Ross family seems to have conformed to the patriarchal household type described by Frits Pannekoek in his article, "The Demographic Structure of Nineteenth Century Red River" in *Essays in Western History*, ed. L.G. Thomas (Edmonton: University of Alberta Press, 1976), 83–95.

9 PAM, Ross Family Papers, James to father, 1 July 1854.

10 Ibid., father to James, 25 Aug. 1854.

11 Ibid., William to James, 9 Feb. 1856.

12 Ibid., John Black to James, 9 Feb. 1854. *Bois Brûlé* was a term originally applied to the Métis.

13 William Ross married Jemima McKenzie, a daughter of former Hudson's Bay Company officer Roderick McKenzie, and a granddaughter of Chief Factor James Sutherland. The youngest son, Sandy, married Catherine, the daughter of prosperous Kildonan settler Donald Murray and his mixed-blood wife Catherine Swain.

14 Hudson's Bay Company Archives, D. 5/38, Jas. Sinclair to Simpson, 11 Dec. 1853, f.342 and John Bunn to Simpson, 16 Dec. 1853, f.372d–373.

15 PAM, Ross Family Papers, Jemima to James, 9 Nov. 1854.

16 Ibid., James Ross to siblings, 25 Dec. 1865.

17 PAM, Ross Family Papers, James to father, Oct. 1856. James may well have thought that his father was ashamed of his half-Indian family. Significantly, their existence is never mentioned in Alexander Ross's later volume, *The Red River Settlement* (London: Smith, Elder and Co., 1856).

18 PAM, James Ross to siblings, 25 Dec. 1856.

19 "Petition of Inhabitants" in *The Prairie West to 1905*, ed. L.G. Thomas (Toronto: Oxford University Press, 1975), 59–61.

20 For a discussion of this episode, see Frits Pannekoek, "The Rev. Griffiths Owen Corbett and the Red River Civil War of 1869–1870," *Canadian Historical Review* 57 (1976): 133–49.

21 PAM, Ross Family Papers, Henrietta to James, early 1854.

22 Jennifer S.H. Brown, "Ultimate Respectability: Fur Trade Children in the 'Civilized World,'" *The Beaver* (Spring 1978): 48–55.

23 W.L. Morton, ed., *Alexander Begg's Red River Journal* (Toronto: Champlain Society, 1956), 422.

24 Morton, *Red River Journal*, 351; PAM, Ross Family Papers, James Smith to Maggy, 30 Nov. 1869; Rev. John Laing to Ross, Feb. 1870.

25 PAM, Ross Family Papers, James to wife, 24 Sept. 1870.

26 PAM, James to wife, 29 Sept. 1870; Matthew Cook to James Ross, 22 Nov. 1870.

27 Ibid., James to Governor Archibald, 11 March 1871.

28 PAM, William Coldwell Papers, draft notes about Mary Ross Flett.

29 Frits Pannekoek has suggested in his thesis (cited above) that the "country-born" or British-Indian community was not able to produce its own leaders. The evidence does not support this view. Men such as William Hallett, James Sinclair, and the Kennedy brothers, in addition to the Ross brothers, were leaders and more attention needs to be given to their roles.

30 W.L. Morton, *Manitoba, A History* (Toronto: University of Toronto Press, 1967), 90.

31 Consider the fate of William Hallett, for example. An ambitious man, his attempts to secure acceptance in white society were hindered by racial prejudice. He committed suicide after the failure of the "Canadian party" to overthrow Riel (Pannekoek, "Churches and the Social Structure," 250).

THE PEOPLE OF
A CANADIAN CITY:
1851–1852*

MICHAEL KATZ

On an average day in 1851 about 14 000 people awoke in Hamilton, Ontario. Most of them were quite unremarkable and thoroughly ordinary. In fact, there is no reason why the historian reading books, pamphlets, newspapers, or even diaries and letters should ever encounter more than seven hundred of them. The rest, at least ninety-five out of every hundred, remain invisible. Insofar as most written history is concerned, they might just as well have never lived.

One consequence of their invisibility has been that history, as it is usually written, represents the record of the articulate and prominent. We assume too easily, for example, that the speeches of politicians reflected the feelings and conditions of ordinary people. Another consequence is that we lack a foundation on which to construct historical interpretations. It was, after all, the activities, interactions, and movements of these invisible men and women that formed the very stuff of past societies. Without a knowledge of how they lived, worked, behaved, and arranged themselves in relation to each other our understanding of any place and point in time must be partial, to say the least. A third consequence is that we apply contemporary assumptions to past society. We use our everyday experience of

*From *Canadian Historical Review* 53 (1972): 402–26. Reprinted by permission of University of Toronto Press Incorporated. © University of Toronto Press. The research on which this essay is based has been entirely supported by the Ontario Institute for Studies in Education. The project is officially titled "The Study and Teaching of Canadian Social History" (The Canadian Social History Project, for short).

modern social relationships to make models which we apply to the past. We believe, for instance, that we are more sophisticated than our ancestors about sex, marriage, and the spacing of children. As a result, we imagine that they must have married younger than we do today and reproduced as fast as nature would allow. Both of these assumptions, as it happens, are generally quite untrue.

The problem, of course, is evidence. How are we to write with meaning of the life of an ordinary labourer, shoemaker, or clerk in a nineteenth-century city? Or trace the most common patterns between important social features such as occupation, wealth, religion, ethnicity, family size, and school attendance? Those questions may be answered more directly and in a more straightforward manner than we have often imagined, as I hope to make clear in the rest of this essay. My purpose is twofold: first, to show the range of questions about ordinary nineteenth-century people that may be asked and answered, and second, to sketch what, at this juncture, I take to be the primary social and demographic patterns within a mid-nineteenth-century Canadian city. The two great themes of nineteenth-century urban history, I shall argue, are transiency and inequality; I shall devote a section of this paper to each and, as well, to the nature of the family and house-hold. For differences in family and household structure reflected, in part, the broad economic distinctions within urban society.

At the beginning two caveats are necessary: the quantitative informa-tion presented here is only partial; it is drawn from a great many detailed tables.[1] Second, figures given here are approximate. Such must be the case with all historical data. However, and this is the important point, the mag-nitudes, the differences between groups, may be taken, I believe, as a fair representation of the situation as it existed.

The manuscript census is the most valuable source of information about people within nineteenth-century cities. Its value is enhanced by its arrangement because it provides a list of features not only for each individ-ual but for each household as well. For individuals the census from 1851 onward lists, among other items, name, age, birthplace, religion, occupa-tion, school attendance, and birth or death within a year. It provides a resi-dential location for each household and a description of the kind of house occupied; it permits the differentiation of relatives from nonrelatives and the rough delineation of the relationships of household members to each other. In some cases it provides information about the business of the household head by listing other property, such as a store or shop owned, and number of people employed. Assessment rolls supplement the manu-script census with detailed economic information, usually about each adult member of the work force. The assessment lists income over a certain level, real property, personal property, and some other economic characteristics. As well, it lists the occupation of each person assessed, the owner of the dwelling, and hence, whether the individual was an owner or renter of the property. (In some instances a man who rents one house or store owns another; in other cases individuals own property around the city. These bits of information about individuals may be gathered together to present a more complete economic profile.) Published city directories corroborate the information from other sources and provide, additionally, the exact residential address of people and, in the case of proprietors, the address of their business if outside the home. Directories include, additionally, listings of people in various important political, financial, and voluntary positions within the city. Many other sources which list information about ordinary people supplement the census, assessment, and directory. Newspapers are the richest of these; mined systematically they yield an enormous load of information about the activities of people within the city. There are marriage records, church records, records of voluntary societies and educational institutions, cemetery records, and listings of other sorts as well. Each of these sources may be studied by itself and the patterns it presents analysed and compared with those found in other places. It is most exciting and rewarding, however, to join records together. By finding the same individuals listed in different records it is possible to build up rich and well-documented portraits of the lives of even the most ordinary people.[2]

The project on which this essay rests uses all of the various records described above. Its most general purpose is to analyse the impact of industrialization on urban social structure and social mobility, using Hamilton, Ontario, as a case study. It deals with the years 1851 through, at the least, 1881; its basis is coded information about all, and not a sample, of the individuals listed in the kinds of sources described above, studied at differing intervals.

This essay discusses, primarily, the early 1850s. Its principle sources are, specifically, the manuscript census of 1851, the assessment roll of 1852 (compiled three months after the census), the city directory of 1853 (the first published within the city), the marriage registers of 1842–69, and two local newspapers, one for both 1851 and 1852 and one for 1852.[3] In some instances the analysis rests on one source alone, in others on sources combined.

The sources for Hamilton as well as studies of American cities make clear that the first great theme of a nineteenth-century city is transiency. The most careful students of transiency to date, Stephen Thernstrom and Peter Knights, conclude from their study of Boston that far more people lived within the city in the course of a year than the census taker could find present at any point in time. The census of 1880 listed the population of Boston as 363 000; that of 1890 as 448 000. However, during those ten years they estimate that about one and one-half million different people actually lived within the city. Elsewhere Knights has estimated that twice as many artisans in some crafts plied their trade within the city in the course of a year as might be found there at any given moment. Eric Hobsbawm's tramping artisans, quite obviously, were a North American as well as a British phenomenon.[4]

The same transiency characterized the population of Hamilton. At this point it is not possible to provide exact figures or to say more than that transiency was a mass phenomenon. We do so on the following evidence.

The assessment roll of 1852 listed 2552 people. Through careful linkage by hand (later replicated by computer) we have been able to join only 1955 of them to people listed on the census, which, as mentioned above, had been taken three months earlier. (There is no reason to assume that the intervening three months were unusual in any way.) Even with a generous allowance for error, large numbers of people could not be found because they had moved into the city during the intervening three months. In the same way a comparable percentage of household heads listed on the census could not be found three months later on the assessment. Most of them had left the city. Similarly, fewer than half the people on the census or assessment could be found listed in the city directory compiled about a year and a half later, and there were a great many people listed on the directory and not on either census or assessment. Death records point to the same conclusion. Each household head was required to record on the census the name of any person within his household who had died during the preceding year. However, Hamilton cemetery and church records for both 1851 and 1861 reveal that the number of people who actually died within the city far exceeded the number recorded on the census. Only a few can be linked to families resident within the city at the time the census was taken.[5] In most instances the families apparently had left the city. It is difficult to estimate the number of deaths that fall into this category; certainly it is not less than a number half again as large as the number of deaths recorded on the census.

The population, this evidence suggests, contained two major groupings of people. The first consisted of relatively permanent residents who persisted within the city for at least several years. This group comprised between a third and two-fifths of the population. The remainder were transients, people passing through the city, remaining for periods lasting between a few months and a few years.

Many of the transients were heads of household, not, as we might suspect, primarily young men drifting around the countryside. The age distribution among the transient heads of household closely resembled that among the more permanent. If anything, the transients on the average were slightly older. Nor, as one might expect, were the transients all people of little skill and low status. The percentage of labourers among the transients (15 percent) was only slightly higher than among the more permanent residents. Indeed, there were many people with skilled or entrepreneurial jobs who moved from place to place; the transients included twenty-four merchants, fifty-eight clerks, seven lawyers, fifty-one shoemakers, twenty-eight tailors, and so on.

Although the transients approximated the rest of the population in age and occupation, they differed in one critical respect: wealth. Within every occupational category, the people who remained within the city were wealthier.[6] Thus, it was the poorer merchants, shoemakers, lawyers, and even the poorer labourers who migrated most frequently. All of this points to the co-existence of two social structures within nineteenth-century society; one relatively fixed, consisting of people successful at their work, even if that work was labouring; the other a floating social structure composed of failures, people poorer and less successful at their work, even if that work was professional, drifting from place to place in search of success.[7]

The significance of the existence of transiency as a key feature of social structure in both Boston, Massachusetts, and Hamilton, Ontario, becomes evident from considering the fundamental differences between the two cities. Late nineteenth-century Boston had become an industrial city; mid-nineteenth-century Hamilton remained a small, commercial, and preindustrial one. Yet both were filled, in Knights' and Thernstrom's phrase, with "men in motion"; transiency formed an integral and international feature of nineteenth-century society and one not immediately altered by industrialization.

The relationship between workplace and residence underscores the preindustrial nature of Hamilton. The separation of work and residence has been one of the most profound consequences of industrialization; the degree to which they remain united provides a rough guide to the extent of industrial development within a society. Contemporary sociologists contrast the organization of family and workplace by pointing to their basic structural differences in terms of authority relationships, criteria for rewards, and so on. They argue that people must play radically different roles in each setting. It becomes the task of the family and the school to teach the individual to make the transition between home and work and to learn to live with the sorts of internal switching required by a continual shifting from the personal and warm relations of the family to the impersonal, bureaucratic organization of work. This dichotomy in roles is a consequence of modern work organization. It came about as a result of the separation of residence and workplace. Its implication for the psychology of the individual person and for the functions of family and school are what make the shift of such profound significance.[8]

It is almost impossible to state precisely the proportion of men who were self-employed and the proportion who worked at their homes in Hamilton in the 1850s. What follows is a rough estimate of the minimum numbers in each category.[9] In 1851, 1142 male household heads were employees and 957 employers. Adding 1310 adult male boarders, almost all employees, gives a total male work force of 3409 of which 2452 or 74 percent were not self-employed and 26 percent were. Given the approximate nature of the figures, it would be unwise to claim more than that between a quarter and a third of the men within the city worked for themselves. Certainly, this is evidence enough to point to a contrast with contemporary industrial society.

Of those men who were self-employed about 137 (comprising roughly half of the proprietors of businesses and attorneys) worked away from their homes. Interestingly, if the proportion had been based on the number of *businesses,* not the number of proprietors, the proportion uniting work and residence would have been much higher, for many businesses were partnerships in which one member lived at the place of business, the other elsewhere. On the basis of this estimate approximately 14 percent of self-employed men worked away from their place of residence as did 72 percent of all employed males or 60 percent of household heads. Put another way, at least four out of ten households combined the function of place of work and place of residence for some of their members. That figure clearly demonstrates the preindustrial character of life within the city.

Even though many people had to leave home each day to go to work, few spent their time in large, formal settings. Most people, regardless of where their job was done, worked in small groups. According to the census of 1851 (which is undoubtedly an underenumeration in this respect) there were within the city 282 artisan shops, stores, offices, and manufactories. The proprietors of over half of these (52 percent) listed no employees. A further twenty-five listed one, and an additional sixty, between two and five employees. Only thirty places had between six and ten employees and but a small handful had more than ten. This picture of smallness and informality is completed by the city government, which employed approximately fifteen people full-time, few others part-time, and spent annually only about £18–20 000.[10]

The preceding discussion has described features of a nineteenth-century city that might be located almost anywhere in North America or Great Britain. There was, however, one feature of Hamilton that marked it as distinctively Canadian and, at the same time, adds more evidence to the theme of transiency; this was the birthplaces of its residents. Only about 9 percent of Hamilton's work force had been born in Canada West. The rest were immigrants, about 29 percent from England and Wales, 18 percent from Scotland, 32 percent from Ireland, 8 percent from the United States, and the rest from elsewhere. Hamilton in 1851 was an immigrant city and so it remained for at least a decade, as the figures for the birthplace of household heads in 1861 reveal. It was, thus, in a double sense that the people of Hamilton were "men in motion." At a very basic level, the origins of their people, early Canadian cities differed fundamentally from ones in the United States and Great Britain. The consequences of this demographic difference might provide a fruitful perspective from which to begin the comparative study of national development and of national character.

The immigrants to Hamilton did not gather themselves into ghettoes. On the basis of indexes of segregation used by both sociologists and historians, the degree of residential clustering by ethnicity, religion, and wealth appears slight, a feature apparently characteristic of Philadelphia and Boston in the same period as well. Nonetheless, there were some broad economic differences between regions of the city. It is possible to distinguish three zones: a core district, a district surrounding the core, and an outer district. The core zone had disproportionately few poor, 9 percent, and disproportionately many well-to-do people, 45 percent. In the outer district that situation was reversed: 32 percent of the people there were poor and 24 percent well-to-do. In the middle district over half the people were of average wealth and 18 percent poor. This pattern reflects what other scholars have described as the typical residential patterns within a nineteenth-century city before the coming of urban transport systems, a pattern that changed when the well-to-do were able to move to the suburbs and the poor clustered in downtown ghettoes.[11]

Despite these trends, people of all degrees of wealth lived in close proximity to each other, the poor and the affluent intermingling on the same streets far more, probably, than they do at present. Indeed, it is clear already the extent to which the nineteenth-century city differed from the urban environment which we know today. The transiency, the newness, and the intermingling of its population, the small scale of its enterprise, the high degree of self-employment, and the continued unity of work and residence: all define a situation which our own experience of urban life prepares us poorly to comprehend, but which, as historians, we must try to recapture.

In fact, it is easy to be nostalgic about small, preindustrial cities. The absence of large-scale industry, the informality of government, and the lack of bureaucratic forms suggest an urban style both more cohesive and personal than that which we know today. We can imagine them, without too much difficulty, as filled with less tension and more warmth than contemporary cities, as stable, neighbourly, and easy places in which to live, as communities in a sense in which urban places have ceased to be. Unfortunately, the image just emerging from close, empirical study of nineteenth-century cities does not support the nostalgic vision. From one perspective it is partly contradicted by the facts of transiency, which we have already observed. The continual circulation of population prevented the formation of stable and closely integrated communities within nineteenth-century cities. At the same time, sharp inequalities in wealth and power reinforced the pressures of population mobility against cohesion and integration; together they made the nineteenth-century city, even before industrialization, a place at least as harsh, as insecure, and as overwhelming as urban environments today.

It is scarcely novel to assert that sharp inequalities existed within nineteenth-century cities or to posit a sharply graduated rank ordering of people. What should be stressed about that inequality is this: first, it may have been greater even than we have imagined; second, it underlay other social differences between people, such as household size and attitudes toward education; third, it shaped political patterns and processes. In short, the division of people on most social measures corresponded to the economic differences between them. Social, political, and economic power overlapped and interlocked, creating a sharply divided society in which a small percentage of the people retained a near monopoly on all the resources necessary to the well-being of the rest.

There are various ways with which to measure the division of wealth within a community, and each one, each scale that is adopted, yields a different result.[12] One division is property ownership: about one-quarter of the population owned all the real property within the city. Roughly three-quarters of the people rented their living accommodations and owned no other real property whatsoever. The most affluent 10 percent of the population held about 88 percent of the wealth represented by the possession of property. From a slightly different perspective, people in the top 10 *income* percentiles (as reported on the assessment) earned nearly half the income within the city, and this figure, for a variety of reasons, is undoubtedly greatly understated. At the other extreme the poorest 40 percent earned a little over 1 percent of the income. Measured on a third scale, one designed to show economic ranking, the pattern of inequality is similar. On this scale "wealth" is a construct of different items and does not correspond exactly to either total income or assessed property; it is, however, the best available indicator of economic rank. On the basis of this measure, the wealthiest tenth of the people controlled about 60 percent of the wealth within the city and the poorest two-fifths about 6 percent.

The scale of economic ranking also reveals differences between the wealth of the various sectors of the city's economy. The people engaged in building, about 14 percent of the work force (indicating the rapid expansion of the city), held only about 7 percent of the city's wealth; similarly, those engaged in some form of manufacturing (primarily artisans), about one-quarter of the work force, had only 15 percent of the wealth. Likewise, as might be expected, the unskilled and semiskilled labourers, about 22 percent of the work force, had less than 5 percent of the wealth. At the other extreme those engaged in professions, about 4 percent of the work force, held over 7 percent of the wealth, and the men in commerce, about a quarter of the work force, controlled nearly 59 percent of the wealth, a figure which underscores the clear commercial basis of the city.

Religious and ethnic groups, like the various sectors of the economy, shared unequally in the city's wealth. Of the various immigrant and religious groups, the Irish and the Catholics fared worst. It is fair, I have argued elsewhere, to consider as poor the people in the lowest forty economic ranks. Using this criterion, 47 percent of the working population born in Ireland were poor as were 54 percent of those who were Catholic. This, of course, is not a surprising finding. On the other hand it might be supposed that the English and the Anglicans were disproportionately wealthy, but this is not the case. Both groups formed a microcosm of the larger social structure, distributed quite normally among different economic categories.[13] The Free Church Presbyterians did rather better but the most affluent group, considering both numbers who were poor and the numbers who were well-to-do, were the Wesleyan Methodists.[14] In terms of birthplace, the native Canadians and Americans fared best, a prosperity no doubt reflecting the problems of trans-Atlantic migration rather than inherent ethnic capacity or style. Of the Canadians 32 percent were well-to-do as were 31 percent of Americans.[15]

It is difficult to associate economic rank with standard of living and to demarcate with precision the line separating the poor from the comfortable. To say that the fortieth economic rank marks the spot at which people ceased being poor means that it was the point at which they probably no longer had to struggle for and occasionally do without the necessities of life. Poverty in nineteenth-century cities did not mean the absence of luxuries, simple spartan living with good home-grown food and sturdy home-sewn clothes. Poverty meant absolute deprivation: hunger, cold, sickness, and misery, with almost no place to turn for relief. The poor within Hamilton, it is important to remember, remained quite at the mercy of the well-to-do, who controlled not only employment opportunity but dispensed what little welfare there was as a gift, not as a right. The Ladies Benevolent Society, a voluntary and paternalistic body, formed in effect the city welfare department. Financed by charitable donations and grants from the City Council, it assigned teams of gracious ladies to roam the streets, locate the worthy poor, and dispense loaves of bread, sometimes coal and groceries, even occasionally rent. The City Council coped with massive numbers of immigrants overcrowding the combination hospital and poorhouse by transporting newly arrived Irish people in wagonloads to country towns where they were summarily left. Clearly, they believed such widespread poverty was only a temporary problem, which could be solved by simple expedients that did not require the permanent and institutionalized extension of public responsibility for individual welfare.[16]

Aside from economic hardship, poverty in Hamilton meant powerlessness and invisibility. The lack of public provision for welfare reveals part of the powerlessness: the poor had no assistance on which they could draw as a right. Nor could they make their warrants heard in any legal way, as the suffrage restrictions show. Less than half of the adult males in Hamilton owned or rented enough property to vote; 53 percent of all adult men, or 43 percent of household heads, could not meet the economic requirements for suffrage. Neither could 80 percent of the labourers, 56 percent of the artisans, or 59 percent of the business employees (primarily clerks). No working class political protest could be expressed through the ballot in Hamilton; most of the working class simply lacked the vote. The invisibility that accompanied powerlessness is harder to demonstrate; its existence has come to light by comparing the records of the Ladies Benevolent Society with the manuscript census. The former contain a month by month listing of the recipients of welfare. Early checking to find these names on the census, even for the very month in which the census had been taken, located very few of them. Perhaps they were simply passed by, a blot on the city it was as well, if possible, to ignore.

Even within a relatively simple society like Hamilton's, the affluent had tangible means of demonstrating their degree of success. One was the employment of servants. It was at the 80th economic rank that a family became more likely than not to employ domestic help, and the likelihood increased with each higher rank on the scale. Overall, about one-quarter of the families in Hamilton had a servant living with them. If Hobsbawm's assertion that the possession of a servant defined middle-class status applies to Canada as well as to England, then the percentage of households without servants indicates, again, the magnitude of the working class in Hamilton.[17] Most of the servants, 60 percent, had been born in Ireland and 47 percent were Catholic. They were by and large young girls: slightly more than half were under twenty years old, and three-quarters were under twenty-five. Nearly nine out of ten servants were females, 93 percent unmarried, although some of the latter had children of their own. Families that employed servants were likely to live in a brick or stone house with two or more stories surrounded by an extra-large plot of land. The first two became, like the employment of servants, more likely than not at the 80th economic rank, the latter, size of plot attached to a dwelling, increased more often at the 90th.

Household size also increased quite directly with wealth: to take one example, 15 percent of the households in the 20–40th ranks were large (eight or more members), compared to 30 percent of those in the 60–80th and 61 percent of those in the top 1 percent. There was, however, little relationship between wealth and number of children. Consequently, the presence of servants, boarders, and relatives accounted for the larger household size of the wealthy. In fact, servants, boarders, and relatives all lived more frequently with affluent than with poor families. School attendance also varied directly with economic standing. Families with no servants sent only slightly more than a third of their school age children to school; families with one servant sent just over half; families with more than one servant sent still larger proportions. Wealthier people also kept their children in school longer. Twenty-two percent of the fourteen-year-old children from families with no servants had attended school compared to 42 percent of those from families with one servant and 82 percent of those from families with two servants. The employment of servants, the occupancy of a large brick or stone house, a spacious plot of land, a large household, the steady and prolonged attendance of one's children at school: these, then, were the principal means through which the affluent demonstrated their success to their neighbours.

The affluent of the city solidified their economic control with political power. First of all, as we have already observed, property qualifications excluded most of the poor from voting. Moreover, the wealthy monopolized local political offices. Despite the fact that nearly 30 percent of elected city officials called themselves by an artisan title, most were wealthy. They were by no means workingmen as we usually employ that term. Of the elected officials, nearly 70 percent were in the top ten economic ranks; 83 percent were in the top twenty. In the two years 1851–52, 42 percent of the wealthiest 1 percent of the work force held political office.

To understand the exercise of power within the city it is necessary to grasp the extent of overlap between membership in elite positions. Measured grossly from listings in the newspaper, the overlap between membership in three elites—people elected to city political offices, business officials, and officers of voluntary societies—is striking and, beyond question, statistically significant.[18] Of the forty-eight elected city officials, for instance, fifteen were business officials, twenty-one officers of voluntary societies, and eight jurors. Of the 130 business officials, 15 were elected city officials, 41 officers of voluntary societies, 36 petitioners (asking the city for favours), and 12 jurors. Among 196 officers of voluntary societies (a very high figure suggesting an extraordinary important role for voluntary activity with this society), 21 were elected city officials, 41 business officials, 8 appointed city officials, 6 school trustees, and 18 jurors. Of the 74 jurors who served during 1851 and 1852, 8 were elected city officials, 12 were business officials, and 1 was an appointed city official. Ten people were elected city officials, business officials, and officers of voluntary societies simultaneously.

Measures designed to test statistical significance—to see whether or not the results described above could have occurred by chance—tell the same story. The relationships were strong and real. The unmistakable overlap between elites underlines the interconnections between economic, political, and social power within this nineteenth-century city. More than that, the relation of people in elite positions with petitioners and jurors is revealing. A poor or unimportant man in Hamilton, it is quite clear, lacked the temerity to ask the city for favours, and, in fact, if he incurred its displeasure he was not even tried by a jury of his peers.[19]

Just as poverty and powerlessness brought invisibility, so did affluence and power make a man visible. On the basis of their mention in local newspapers it is possible to divide the people of the city into three groups according to their "visibility": those "invisible" (not mentioned in the newspapers at all) or about 94 percent of the population in 1851; those moderately "visible" (mentioned once or twice); and those highly "visible," mentioned five or more times, about 1 percent of the population. Who then were these highly visible people? They were, as might be expected from the foregoing analysis, the members of the interlocking elites. Highly visible people comprised more than half of the following categories: city and country officials, business officials, officers of voluntary societies, school trustees, petitioners, jurors, advertisers, union members (only six were mentioned in the newspapers at all), political committee members, and people publicly honoured. Interestingly, as with the case of overlap between various sorts of officeholders, jurors and petitioners interconnect with the most powerful men within the city.[20]

These interconnections between kinds of power within Hamilton pose important comparative questions. Did economic, social, and political power exist in a closer relationship at that time than they do at present? What impact did industrialization have upon their relationship to each other? Is the curve of inequality steady over time, or did it widen in the initial stages of industrialization and then diminish in the twentieth century? Whatever the answers to these questions turn out to be, the detailed examination of the distribution of income and power should help dispel any lingering nostalgia about the existence of equality and community in nineteenth-century cities.

Detailed examination of actual cases also dispels a number of common notions about families in preindustrial society. It is often thought that the nuclear family emerged as a consequence of industrialization, that in early times people married at very young ages, and that the poor, especially, had very large families. None of these propositions are true. There were clear relations between transiency and inequality, the two great themes of the nineteenth-century city, and the domestic arrangements of its people. However, to some extent the family and household exhibited characteristics partially independent of wealth and related rather (sometimes at this stage of research inexplicably) to other measures. Thus, it is important to consider family and household structure by themselves.

We may begin with the formation of the family through marriage. The statistics are based upon the marriage registers for Wentworth County for the years 1842–69.[21] Marriage patterns within Wentworth County were endogamous. Of 5327 brides, 4443 resided in Wentworth County as did 4026 of the same number of grooms. It is to be expected that most brides would be from Wentworth County, since marriage customarily takes place at the bride's residence. What is more notable is the small proportion of local girls who married men from outside the county. Nevertheless, the majority of marriages throughout the period involved people who had both been born outside of Ontario and, indeed, outside of Canada.

For the most part the figures for age of marriage contradict our stereotypes of early marriage among the people of preindustrial society. The mean age of marriage for men was 27.7, the median 25.7; 61 percent of grooms were twenty-five years old or over; 25 percent were over 30. Brides were considerably younger, about four years on the average. Their mean marriage age was 23.2 and the median 21.8. Just over one-quarter of the girls married before they were twenty and 72 percent had married by the time they were twenty-five.[22] Both religion and birthplace influenced marriage age, though of the two, birthplace appeared strongest. Younger marriages were slightly more common among Baptists and "Protestants" and later marriages more common among Presbyterians. Similarly, the

Scottish people married notably later than other groups.[23] People born in Canada West married youngest by far, and there were no unusual distributions of age among brides and grooms born in England, the United States, or, contrary to what might be expected, Ireland.[24]

Figures for births, like those for marriage, do not support common notions about Catholic families. From what we can tell at this point, the birth rate among Catholics or Irish-born people was no higher than among the population as a whole. What appears striking from an analysis of the births listed in the 1851 manuscript census is the congruence between the percentage of total births in the city occurring among a particular group and that group's percentage of the total population. Thus, Catholics aged twenty to twenty-nine years formed 18 percent of the household heads of that age group within the city; to them occurred 18 percent of the births among that age group. The poor form 26 percent of the household heads; they had 27 percent of the births. It would be tedious to continue to present these figures; with one exception they remain the same for ethnicity, religion, and wealth. That exception, and an interesting one, is the people born in French Canada, who formed a tiny 0.4 percent of the twenty to twenty-nine year olds but accounted for 2 percent of the births, a disproportion consistent with trends in French-Canadian demography.[25]

This initial survey of Hamilton's demography would be incomplete without some mention of death and death rates. At this juncture it is not possible to discuss the relations between death rate, age at death, and other sociable variables, such as religion, ethnicity, and wealth. We do know that the infant mortality rate was staggeringly high. Of 210 people recorded as having died on the census, 106 or 51 percent were five years old or younger; all but twenty-one, or 10 percent, were under the age of fifty.

Figures for the number of children within a household are generally, though not completely, consistent with the statistics of marriage and birth. Among the heads of households as a whole 55 percent had small families (0–2 children), 36 percent had medium-sized families (3–5 children), and 10 percent had large families (6 or more children). Any discussion of family size is affected by the age distribution of the population. In order that we may have a fair basis of comparison I shall restrict the following discussion to heads of household aged forty to forty-nine years, those whose families were both complete and, to the largest extent, still living together. Of the forty- to forty-nine-year-old household heads, 37 percent had small families, 44 percent medium-sized ones, and 18 percent large numbers of children.

First of all, as with births, family size among the forty to forty-nine year olds shows little relation to wealth.[26] The poor did not breed more quickly than the rest of the population. In fact the only discernible relation between wealth and the number of children works in the other direction. Among the heads of household as a whole 0.3 percent of the very poorest people, those in the bottom twenty economic percentiles, had a large number of children compared to 15 percent of those in the 95–99th percentiles. Among the forty- to forty-nine-year-old household heads the poorest men had no children about twice as often as most other groups; similarly, they had the smallest percentage of medium-sized families of any group. Considering all ages together, the mean number of children among the poorest 20 percent of household heads was 0.54 and, among the wealthiest 1 percent, 3.32. In between, however, scores are quite similar. One other difference, which relates to economic standing, shows the same trend. Transients, who were poorer than those people we consider more permanent residents, had a slightly lower mean number of children despite their similarity in age.

An examination of the mean number of children among forty- to forty-nine-year-old household heads highlights some ethnic and religious distinctions generally unrelated to wealth. North Americans, natives of Canada West and the United States, had small families. The lowest mean score, 2.40, was that of the Americans, followed by the Canadians, the English, the Irish, and the Scottish, in that order.[27] These figures reflect the late marriage age of Scottish people, which we observed earlier.[28] Among religious groups those with heavily Scottish membership rank high in mean number of children among forty to forty-nine year olds.[29] At the other end of the scale the denomination with the smallest mean family size, the Baptist, is heavily American in origin.[30] The mean size for the Catholics, it might be pointed out, was quite average for the forty to forty-nine year olds, although their mean for the twenty to twenty-nine year olds was the highest in that cohort, which indicates that Catholics had more of their children when they were younger, not, as is often thought, that they had a greater number in all than did other groups.[31]

The mean family size of different occupational groups reveals more systematic differences. The means for all merchants and clerks were 1.78 and 1.91. For bakers, blacksmiths, carpenters, shoemakers, tinsmiths, and labourers the means were: 2.69, 2.96, 2.78, 2.34, 2.89, and 2.89 respectively. Quite clearly, the entrepreneurial white-collar groups had fewer children than men who worked with their hands. In this respect it is the line separating the people engaged in commerce from those following the trades that count most. Distinctions between skilled and unskilled workers appear to matter but little. More than that, the difference in the number of children appears more related to kind of work performed than it does to wealth. The mean number of children, as we have observed, varied but little with economic rank, and the relations between occupation and wealth were not as tidy as we might expect, as we have noticed in the case of elected officials. In fact, there was usually a great variation in wealth between individuals in the same trades. Thus, on the basis of the evidence at hand, it is entirely reasonable to suppose that the aspiring business classes had begun to practice some form of family limitation.[32]

There were distinctions, it is critical to note, between the family size of people engaged in commerce and other nonmanual workers. Relatively small family size remained more a hallmark of men with an entrepreneurial outlook than a badge separating white- and blue-collar workers in our modern sense. This becomes apparent from the mean family size of other, nonentrepreneurial and nonmanual groups: the mean family size of teachers, for instance, 3.71, was the highest of any group; the mean for gentlemen was 2.89, the same as for labourers and tinsmiths; and the mean for lawyers fluctuated strangely with age. For lawyers in their forties it was 6.00. All of this suggests that limiting the number of his offspring has become linked in the mind of the aspiring entrepreneur with increasing his wealth. The source of that idea is particularly important to locate. For, if the facts that I have presented here are correct, he would not have learned it from the world around him where, in fact, the most successful men did not have small families.

As we have observed already, the mark of a wealthy man was the size of his household, not the number of his children. That household was composed of boarders, servants, relatives, and visitors in addition to husband, wife, and children. There were fewer extended families in this preindustrial city than we might have expected; relatives other than husband, wife, and children lived in only 15 percent of the households. Like the families Peter Laslett and his associates have studied in England over a period of four hundred years, the ones in Hamilton were overwhelmingly nuclear. As with servants, relatives lived most frequently in the households of the well-to-do; they were present in 4 percent of the poorest 20 percent of the households and 24 percent of those in the 95–99th economic ranks.[33]

The same is true of boarders, who were found in 28 percent of the households. They lived, however, with 8 percent and 15 percent respectively of the families in the 0–20th and 20–40th economic ranks and with 46 percent of those in the 90–95th. There were boarders, in fact, in more than four out of ten households in each group above the 80th economic rank. This finding is somewhat surprising. We might suppose, offhand, that boarders would be most likely to live with poorer families, who needed the extra income they could provide. But this was not the case. It prompts us to look closely at exactly who boarders were and at their place within the household.

The presence of boarders in so many households reflects an important characteristic of social life: it was extremely unusual for people to live alone; everyone was expected to live within a family grouping. Not much more than 1 percent of the work force lived by themselves. Large numbers of young unmarried people living alone is clearly a modern development. This pattern of residence, moreover, constituted an informal system of social control. For young men a close supervision and a constant scrutiny of their behaviour constituted the other side of the warmth of living in a family grouping. Boarding the young men of the town provided the affluent with a convenient means of keeping a close check on their behaviour.

Most of the boarders, 71 percent, were men; 14 percent were married. This accounts in large part for the women and children who were listed as boarders. Like the servants, boarders were young, though not quite so young: 34 percent were under twenty and a further 52 percent between twenty and twenty-four years old; 84 percent were under thirty. They came more often from Ireland than from elsewhere in 43 percent of the cases, but many, 19 percent, had been born in Canada West, a disproportionately large number considering that men from Canada West made up only a bit more than 9 percent of the work force. These boarders were, perhaps, young migrants to the city from rural areas. A little over one-third of the boarders were Catholic, the largest single figure for any denomination, and the rest were scattered among other religious groups. Boarders followed a staggering variety of occupations. Many of them, about 54 percent, were craftsmen of one sort or another; of the remainder, about 13 percent were labourers and 8 percent clerks. Spinsters, widows, and women following domestic occupations like dressmaking frequently boarded as did some young professionals, nine lawyers and seven physicians probably establishing themselves in practice.

It appeared likely, from these figures, that many boarders were young men living with their employers in households that combined work and residence. However, a close comparison of the occupations of boarders and their landlords demolished that hypothesis. It is extremely difficult to determine if a boarder and a household head might have worked together. Occupational terminology is vague and sometimes misleading. But in most cases it was clear that no reasonable connection could be made. Not only occupation but class seemed to make little difference. Labourers lived with judges, physicians, attorneys, and gentlemen, as well as with fellow labourers, moulders, and widows. Widows, in fact, took in many boarders, obviously a way to make a little money. Other than that, there seems little pattern in the distribution of boarders by occupation. Over all, slightly over 9 percent of the boarders might have been living with their employers.

Other obvious principles on which boarders might have selected their residence are religion and ethnicity. Perhaps young men coming to the city looked for families of similar ethnic and religious backgrounds with whom to live, whatever their occupation might be. In most cases this did not happen. There was some tendency for Irish and for Catholic boarders to choose landlords of the same background, and a very slight tendency for the English and the Anglicans to do the same. But in no instance did those living with people of similar religious or ethnic backgrounds constitute a majority.

In short, it appears that other factors were more important in the choice of a lodging, probably convenience, price, and the presence of some friends already living there or nearby. The population of Hamilton, we must not forget, was expanding rapidly. The estimated growth between 1850 and 1852 was from ten to fourteen thousand. The practical implication of this must have been a severe strain on housing facilities. Perhaps rooms were in such short supply that people took whatever they could find. Perhaps, too, there was great pressure on anyone with a spare bed to take someone in. This is why so many of the more affluent, with larger houses, had boarders.

It is as important to discover the behavioural patterns associated with types of families and households as it is to determine their size and structure. There are, however, fewer indexes of behaviour than of structure on which to base systematic observations. One of the most readily available, and most interesting, is school attendance. The analysis of school attendance links parental attitudes to social, demographic, and economic measures and, as our data reveal, to family size as well. It thus provides a way of joining the family and household to the large social context in which they are embedded.[34]

Of all the children in the city aged five to sixteen years in 1851, 50 percent attended school at some point during the year. Rather more boys than girls attended at each age level. Very few children entered school before the age of six. At the age of six a third began to attend, but the ages from seven to thirteen years were the period of heaviest school attendance, the proportion attending exceeding 40 percent only in each of those years. The peaks were reached between the ages of nine and eleven, the only time when more than half of the age group attended school.

Part of the variation in school attendance can be explained by family size. It is often thought that small families provide settings conducive to education. Indeed, twentieth-century studies have shown an inverse relation between school achievement, scores on intelligence tests, and family size. If our data have anything to contribute on this point, it is that the contemporary relationship did not hold within the nineteenth century. The percentage of school-age children attending school generally increased with the number of children in the family.[35] This relationship held even for the youngest and eldest children attending school: 3 percent of children aged three to five years from families with two children attended school compared to 10 percent from families with five children; 18 percent of fifteen- to sixteen-year-old children from families with two children attended school compared to 23 percent from families with five children.

The birthplace of the head of household also affected school attendance. Irish fathers were least likely to send their children to school. The percentage of Irish children aged five to sixteen attending school was under one-third. For two groups, however, it was over one-half; these were the Scottish and the native Canadians. The relations between religion and attendance reinforce these findings: fewer than 30 percent of Catholic children attended schools, compared to over 50 percent for Church of Scotland and Wesleyan Methodist and over 60 percent for Free Church Presbyterians. Scottish Presbyterianism should obviously be added to family size as an important factor promoting school attendance.

So should wealth, as we observed earlier. Measuring wealth by the possession of servants, the relation with school attendance was striking. That relation supports the observations of school promoters who perceived their problem as persuading poor families to school their children. Insofar as educational reform took its impetus from a perception of idle, vagrant children from poor homes wandering the streets, it was based on a very real situation.

The relations between occupation and school attendance spoil the neatness of the foregoing analysis, for they fail to adhere completely to the boundaries set by wealth, ethnicity, and religion. Lawyers, for instance, sent few of their children to school. It is entirely possible that they hired private tutors. Tinsmiths, on the other hand, were exceptionally conscious of schooling; 85 percent of their school-age children attended school during 1851, a figure exceeded only by the children of teachers, 92 percent of whom had attended. Labourers, as could be expected, were at the bottom; less than one-quarter of their school-age children went to school in 1851, compared, for instance, to 46 percent of the children of merchants and 58 percent of the children of physicians. Differences between artisan groups parallel those between professionals; 38 percent of shoemakers' school-age children attended school, for instance, as did 54 percent of the children of cabinet-makers. There are at present no explanations for most of these differences.

Although school attendance often followed economic lines, it is clear that cultural and social factors intervened to make the pattern that finally emerged quite complex. Two of these factors are noteworthy: North Americans kept their children in school somewhat longer than other groups, and the relationship between wealth, Catholicism, Irish origin, and low school attendance did not hold among the very youngest age groups. Perhaps school served as baby-sitting agencies for large, poor families, relieving the parents of pressure at home and permitting the mother to work. At the same time affluent parents of large families may have realized that they were unable to teach at home certain basic skills, which it was traditional for children to learn before they started school at age seven. They may have used the school to remedy what, given the size of their families, would have had to be accomplished by a private tutor if their children were not to lag educationally.

But all conclusions must remain tentative at best. The most we can say is this: the people who most frequently sent children to school were well-to-do, had larger than average families, and had been born in Scotland or North America. Those sending fewest were poor, Irish Catholic, and labourers. The same groups generally kept the most and the fewest children in school past the usual school leaving age. But the figures for early school attendance revealed slightly different rankings, which indicates that early schooling served important economic functions for some poor families and important psychological ones for large families. The relations between occupation and schooling are unclear, aside from the figures for labourers. Why did the lawyers send so few children? Why did the tinsmiths send so many? We cannot answer these questions at present; like so many of the findings discussed in this essay they remain beginnings, as much questions to be answered as conclusions.

Clearly family and household patterns in Hamilton were complex; they defy simple general descriptions. Equally clearly, they contradict many commonly held assumptions about preindustrial families. Men and women married relatively late, later probably than most people do today. In the vast majority of instances they formed nuclear families, the more wealthy adding a servant, a boarder, or, in comparatively few instances, a relative. Almost everybody lived in a family, whether they were married or not, young or old. Within families there was relatively little difference in the number of children born to parents of different economic conditions. Ethnicity and religion, in fact, were more influential than wealth in determining age of marriage and number of children. The traditional image of the frugal, self-denying, and ambitious Scot emerges intact; the picture of the indulgent, overbreeding Irish Catholic is shattered. In fact, there were at least two types of households within the city. At one extreme was the Irish Catholic labourer living with his wife and two or three children in a one-and-a-half-storey frame house. At the other extreme, but perhaps on the same street, was the prosperous merchant living with his wife, two or three children, a servant, and a boarder in a three-storey stone house surrounded by a spacious plot of land. Most other families fell somewhere in between. It will take a good deal more analysis to isolate other widespread family types, and a good deal of imaginative research into other sorts of sources to explain the results that emerge; to answer, that is, questions such as why did American Baptists have small families?

It is also important to ask if the relations between family size and ethnicity that existed in Hamilton were present in other Canadian cities as well. That, in turn, is part of the larger issue of representativeness. How can one know that the findings from Hamilton have meaning for any other place? From one viewpoint the question is irrelevant. Every city's history is both unique and at the same time representative of larger trends and forces. More than that, the relationships we wish to study can be investigated only on the local level. Even if Hamilton turns out to be less "representative" than one might wish, the study is important because it provides a datum with which to begin an analysis of what is special and what is general within nineteenth-century cities in Canada and elsewhere.

Hamilton was not representative of some things, quite obviously: for instance, it was not like villages and rural areas. On the other hand, it should have had a number of similarities to preindustrial cities in nineteenth-century Britain and the United States. Most of all, it was not too unlike other cities in Canada West. That is clear from studying published census figures for a number of Canadian cities. It is striking to observe the extent of similarity between Kingston, London, Toronto, and Hamilton with respect to the birthplace and religion of their residents; their age structures and sex ratios; their birth and death rates; and even their occupational structures. On the basis of these similarities it is obvious that Hamilton was structurally similar to other cities in Canada West. On that basis we may conclude with some general observations about the nature of a preindustrial Canadian city.[36]

First, even in the mid-nineteenth century a relatively small commercial city was an enormously complex place. Simple general statements about its society, families, or households are inadequate to the richness of its structural patterns. Economically, even before industrialization, Canadian cities were highly differentiated. Socially, they were highly stratified.

Second, the preindustrial family was a more rational and "modern" organization than we have often suspected. Even at this early date people clearly related decisions about marriage and often about the size of their families to other, undoubtedly economic, considerations. The difference between the preindustrial and modern family does not rest in structure; both are nuclear. It lies, rather, in the number of children born to the average couple and in the structure of the household, which in terms of size has lost its clear relation to affluence.

Third, in no sense can we think of preindustrial cities as communities defined by stability, integration, and egalitarianism. The problem of inequality we have touched on above; the facts of transiency destroy any further illusions about community. The population simply changed too rapidly.

Fourth, the articulation of various structures with each other produced a powerful concentration of interlocking forms of power in the hands of a very small group of people. Household structure, political power, school attendance—the privileges that this society had to offer—all related to wealth. The distribution of men by economic rank corresponded to their division on most other social measures. Looked at another way, the business elite, the political elite, and the voluntary elite overlapped to a striking and significant extent. We know already that the political elite overlapped with the top rungs of the scale of economic rank. There is every reason to believe that the others did so as well.

The group that controlled economic, political, and social power within Hamilton contained at most 10 percent of the household heads. People within elite positions formed slightly more than 8 percent of men aged twenty and older. This figure is quite close to the 10 percent estimated elsewhere as wealthy. It is close, in fact, to the approximately 75 percent of elected city officials who we know to have been within the top ten income percentiles. Hence we can conclude that about 8 or 10 percent of the adult men, at the very maximum, controlled virtually all the resources necessary to the health, well-being, and prosperity of the rest.

In Hamilton the rulers, the owners, and the rich were by and large the same people. They clearly headed the stratification system. At the bottom the grouping was likewise clear: poor, propertyless, powerless men made up about 40 percent of the work force or between a fifth and a quarter of the household heads. In between fell the rest. About 40 percent were marginal; they owned no property, they possessed no power, but they were prosperous enough to differentiate themselves from the poorest families. Their margin seems so slim and the consequences of falling so appalling, however, that these people must have lived always with great tension and great fear. Between them and the wealthy, comprising about a fifth of the families, was a qualitatively more affluent group. Most of them employed a servant and lived in a brick house, which they owned. They were likely to vote but still not very likely to hold political office.

These four groups existed within Hamilton in the middle of the nineteenth century. Using wealth, power, and ownership as dimensions on which to rank people, they form somewhat overlapping but nonetheless distinguishable clusters of people holding a similar position on each scale. Were they classes? That depends on the definition of class, which is a subject beyond the scope of this essay. Clearly, however, by whatever definition is followed it would seem difficult to deny that class was a fundamental fact of life in mid-nineteenth-century urban Canada.[37]

• Notes

1 For detailed quantitative information see the first two interim reports of the project as well as subsequent working papers, all of which are available from the Department of History and Philosophy of Education of the Ontario Institute for Studies in Education. See also my essay, "Social Structure in Hamilton, Ontario" in *Nineteenth-Century Cities: Essays in the New Urban History,* ed. Stephen Thernstrom and Richard Sennett (New Haven and London: 1969), 209–44. I have rounded all percentages in this essay to whole numbers. Considering the inexactness of historical data, this seems quite appropriate, especially when it increases ease of reading.

2 Record-linkage is one of the central technical problems of all studies similar to the one described here. For a discussion of the problem, and of our approach to it, see Ian Winchester, "The Linkage of Historical Records by Man and Computer: Techniques and Problems," *Journal of Interdisciplinary History* 1, 1 (Autumn 1970): 107–24. The hand-linkage of the 1851 census,

1852 assessment, and 1853 directory was done by Mr John Tiller, who also has done most of the coding of the 1851 census and assessment. I should like to acknowledge Mr Tiller's continued and invaluable participation in this project.

3 The *Spectator* and the *Gazette.*

4 Stephen Thernstrom and Peter Knights, "Men in Motion: Some Data and Speculations about Urban Population Mobility in Nineteenth Century America" in *Anonymous Americans: Explorations in Nineteenth-Century Social History,* ed. Tamara K. Hareven (Englewood Cliffs, NJ, 1971), 17–47; Peter R. Knights, "Population Turnover, Persistence, and Residential Mobility in Boston, 1830–1860" in Thernstrom and Sennett, *Nineteenth-Century Cities,* 258–74; E.J. Hobsbawm, "The Tramping Artisan" in his *Laboring Men: Studies in the History of Labor* (London, 1964), 34–63.

5 Unpublished papers by Mrs Judy Cooke and Mr Dan Brock, OISE.

6 The mean assessed wealth of all the people engaged in commerce was £96;

of the transients in commerce, £63; of resident professionals, £71; of transient ones, £21; of resident artisans, £25; of migrants, £13; of resident labourers, £9; of migrant ones, £7.

7 The existence of a similar phenomenon—a division of success within trades—is clearly revealed by Henry Mayhew's description of the organization of various trades in London in the middle of the nineteenth century. An example is the distinction between the "honourable" and "dishonourable" parts of the tailoring trade. See E.P. Thompson and Eileen Yeo, *The Unknown Mayhew* (London, 1971), 181–277, on tailors.

8 Robert Dreeben, *On What Is Learned in Schools* (Reading, MA, 1968), 95, provides an example of this point. See also Talcott Parsons and Robert F. Bales, *Family, Socialization and Interaction Processes* (Glencoe, IL, 1955).

9 Not all employed men necessarily worked away from their homes. As Mayhew, [cited in] *The Unknown Mayhew*, points out, it was common for manufacturers of various sorts to give work to craftsmen to perform in their own homes.

10 See, for example, Proceedings of the Council of the City of Hamilton, 22 Jan. 1851, 398–99; 19 Jan. 1850, 128–29, available on microfilm in the Public Archives of Ontario.

11 For a discussion of calculating the Index of Segregation see Karl E. Taeuber and Alma F. Taeuber, *Negroes in Cities: Residential Segregation and Neighborhood Change* (Chicago, 1965), 195–245; for the application of the index, see Leo F. Schnore and Peter R. Knights, "Residence and Social Structure: Boston in the Ante-Bellum Period" in Thernstrom and Sennett, *Nineteenth-Century Cities*, 247–57, and Sam Bass Warner, Jr., *The Private City: Philadelphia in Three Periods of Its Growth* (Philadelphia, 1968), 13. For studies of residential patterns in nineteenth-century cities, see also two recent monographs, David Ward, *Cities and Immigrants: A Geography of Change in Nineteenth Century America* (New York, 1971), and Peter Goheen, *Victorian Toronto* (Chicago, 1970).

12 I have discussed the construction of these scales in working paper no. 21, "The Measurement of Economic Inequality."

13 Fifty-one percent of the working population born in England and Wales were in the middle (40–80th) economic ranks as were 46 percent of the Anglicans.

14 Of the Free Church Presbyterians 26 percent were poor, compared to 16 percent of the Wesleyan Methodists. At the same time 31 percent of the Free Church Presbyterians were well-to-do (80–100th economic ranks) as were 29 percent of the Wesleyan Methodists.

15 Of the other major ethnic and religious groups, briefly: the Scottish-born were predominantly middle-income, much like the English; the adherents of the Church of Scotland, and those who called themselves simply Presbyterians, were likewise middling in terms of wealth, except that the former had few wealthy adherents. The figures for Methodists were much like those for Presbyterians; and for Baptists, much like members of the Church of Scotland.

16 The records of the Ladies Benevolent Society are available in manuscript at the Hamilton Public Library. For the actions of the City Council with respect to immigrants see, e.g., Proceedings of the Council, 20 Aug. 1849, 31; 10 Sept. 1849, 149–50. On the institutionalization of poverty in the United States see the recent, provocative book by David Rothman, *The Discovery of the Asylum* (Boston, 1971).

17 E.J. Hobsbawm, *Industry and Empire* (London, 1969), 157.

18 Mrs Anne-Marie Hodes coded the 1851 and 1852 newspapers for the project.

19 Only the top three-quarters of the assessed population were eligible to serve on the jury. I suspect that those actually chosen did not represent a cross-section of that group.

20 For the idea of constructing a scale of visibility I am indebted to the work of Professor Walter Glazer of Cincinnati.

21 The marriage registers were coded by Mrs Margaret Zieman.

22 The figures are supported by those found for European countries. See, e.g., Peter Laslett, "Size and Structure of the Household in England Over Three Centuries," *Population Studies* 33, 2 (July 1969): 199–223.

23 Only 20 percent of Scottish grooms were less than twenty-five years old compared to 39 percent of all grooms, while 30 percent of Scottish grooms were in their thirties compared to 18 percent of all grooms.

24 Among people born in Canada West, 51 percent of the grooms, compared to 39 percent of all grooms, had been married before the age of twenty-five; of the brides, 82 percent, compared to 75 percent of all brides, had been married before they were twenty-seven years old.

25 For an overview of Canadian population history that makes this point, see Census of Canada, 1931, chs. 2 and 3 of the excellent monograph on the family.

26 Of the poor, 18 percent had a large family; so did 20 percent of the middle-income and 21 percent of the well-to-do. Similarly 38 percent of the poor had a small number of children, as did 35 percent of the middle-rank and 38 percent of the well-to-do.

27 The means are: American-born, 2.40; Canadian, 3.18; English, 3.35; Irish, 3.52; Scottish, 4.01.

28 The Scottish rank third in mean number of children among twenty to twenty-nine year olds, fifth among thirty to thirty-nine year olds, and first among the forty- to forty-nine-year-old group.

29 Thus the mean for members of the Church of Scotland is 4.39 and for Free Church Presbyterians, 4.62.

30 The Baptist score is 2.17.

31 In fairness to traditional ideas it should be pointed out that very preliminary inspection of the 1861 results indicates a larger than average family size for Catholics and Irish. At this point the change is inexplicable.

32 For comparative figures on class and birth control, see E.A. Wrigley's excellent book, *Population and History* (New York, 1969), 186–87. On the method of studying birth control in past societies, see E.A. Wrigley, "Family Limitation in Pre-Industrial England," *Economic History Review*, 2nd series, 19, 1 (1966): 82–109. For more on the relation between status and birth control in the nineteenth century, see J.A. Banks, *Prosperity and Parenthood: A Study of Family Planning Among the Victorian Middle Classes* (London, 1954) and D.E.C. Eversley, *Social Theories of Fertility and the Malthusian Debate* (Oxford, 1959).

33 On general patterns of household size in England over four hundred years, see Laslett, "Size and Structure of the Household."

34 There has been amazingly little written on the history of school attendance. The only monograph in English that I know to be specifically devoted to the topic is David Rubenstein, *School Attendance in London, 1870–1904: A Social History* (Hull, 1969). See also my article, "Who Went to School," *History of Education Quarterly* 12, 3 (Fall 1972).

35 For families with two children it was, for instance, 42 percent; for families with five children, 61 percent. Similarly, the percentage of families that sent more than half their school-age children to school rose from 24 percent for families with one child to 35 percent for families with two, to 58 percent for families with five children and 67 percent for families with seven.

36 Tables comparing these cities are in the project working paper no. 23.

37 I want to include a plea that more Canadian historians undertake empirical analyses of past social structures. Those who are interested but hesitant should gain some knowledge of how to proceed from two recent books: Edward Shorter, *The Historian and the Computer: A Practical Guide* (Englewood Cliffs, NJ, 1971), and Charles M. Dollar and Richard J. Jensen, *Historian's Guide to Statistics, Quantitative Analysis and Historical Research* (New York, 1971). Our team is continually developing a store of practical lore that we should be delighted to share with anyone venturing into related studies.

ORDER AND EXPERIENCE:
The Religious and Cultural
Roots of Protestant Ontario*

WILLIAM WESTFALL

Erroneous tests of godliness have been instituted
among them, whereby feelings instead of an
enlightened judgment and a life-reforming faith,
have been set forth as the criteria of true religion.

*The Rev. Charles Forest to the
Lord Bishop of Montreal, 1 July 1848*

On 3 July 1825 John Strachan, the rector of York in the seemingly insignificant colony of Upper Canada, preached a sermon on the life and character of Bishop Jacob Mountain. At the time of his death Mountain had been the Anglican Bishop of Quebec for over thirty years, and Strachan was determined to interpret for his parishioners the historical significance of the Bishop's long career in Canada. The task of glorifying Mountain, however, was not easy, even for someone like Strachan who took considerable pride in his literary skill. The progress of the church, at least in Strachan's eyes, had not been especially rapid during Mountain's episcopate; indeed in 1825 the church was still in a very precarious position. For this reason Strachan feared that some "future historian" might be "inclined to find fault in the little that [had] been done by the first Protestant Bishop of Quebec."[1]

Strachan tried to anticipate this possibility by setting out his own interpretation of the history of the last forty years. In effect, he became one of the first historians of early nineteenth-century English Canada, and like the historians who followed him, he reconstructed the past by giving prominence to certain themes and events while ignoring others. In due course Mountain's life began to appear in a more favourable light.

*From *Two Worlds: The Protestant Culture of Nineteenth Century Ontario* (Montreal: McGill-Queen's University Press, 1989), 19–49. Reprinted with permission of the publisher.

Strachan asked his congregation "to pause before pronouncing judgment in order to examine the many obstacles in his Lordship's way during the whole of his Episcopacy." When Mountain arrived in Quebec "the colony was a greater spiritual than a natural wilderness." There were few congregations and almost no clergy. To serve the needs of his wilderness charge, the Bishop set out to create a proper parish system of churches and schools, but his hard work was met with hostility and indifference. The Papists, of course, opposed him, and worse still, the small Protestant population showed a singular want of enthusiasm for Mountain's attempt to bestow the uncountable benefits of an Anglican establishment on the colony. Nevertheless, Mountain had managed to advance the cause of the church by slow degrees. If he had not left the church in a position of prosperity, he had nonetheless constructed "a fair foundation . . . for the diffusion of Christianity throughout the Diocese." Strachan's rhetorical strategy was simple. By dwelling on the adversities of history and circumstance, he hoped to elevate the Bishop's rather meagre accomplishments to the point where his episcopate might be seen as an important preliminary stage in what would surely be the eventual triumph of the Church of God in the Canadas. Evidently pleased with his handiwork, Strachan had the sermon published and sent copies of it to England, where it might help the friends of the colonial church in that most important arena of politics, wealth, and power.

In retrospect, Strachan's defence of Mountain appears artificial and unconvincing. By dwelling upon the glory of Bishop Mountain's intentions and the difficulties he faced rather than the goals he actually reached, Strachan almost inevitably turned the Bishop into a minor historical figure. Even if one were content with sure foundations rather than the monuments that such foundations were meant to support, little historical immortality could be claimed for the recently departed ecclesiastic.[2] In this light Strachan's sermon might well have contributed to the problem that it was supposed to forestall. Certainly a "future historian" would have to challenge many of Strachan's judgments in order to reach a more balanced and judicious assessment of the life and character of Jacob Mountain.[3]

This short sermon nonetheless remains one of the most important documents in the religious and cultural history of early nineteenth-century Canada. Although the sermon did not achieve what it set out to do, its historical significance lies in the assumptions Strachan brought to his text and in the structure of his argument rather than in the elaborate apologia for the life of the Bishop. To defend Mountain, Strachan wrote a brief history of his own times that imposed a sense of order on the chaos of religion and politics flourishing at that time. This history rested on a number of beliefs and assumptions which reveal a good deal about the way Strachan and many others understood their own world, especially the crucial relationship between God and creation. As Strachan well understood, however, any one way of seeing the world defines an antithetical mode of perception. He was so determined to praise Mountain because he feared that someone who saw the world differently might examine his life from a different point of view and reach a very different conclusion. And in fact his fears were justified, although he did not anticipate the fury and the impact of the challenge to his argument. Certain passages in his sermon provoked an immediate— and what became a famous—attack on his representation of the character of God and creation, and when the attack came it was John Strachan, rather than Jacob Mountain, who had to bear the force of the assault.

Strachan began his interpretation of the past by dividing the population of Upper Canada into three religious groups, each of which he placed at a particular point on a religious spectrum that he constructed according to his own appreciation of the proper forms of ecclesiastical polity and religious practice. At one end he placed the Roman Catholics; at the other, a rather loosely defined group of "Protestant dissenters," and between these "extravagant and dangerous extremes,"[4] his own church—the United Church of England and Ireland—and the Church of Scotland. According to Strachan the centre always had to fight against the extremes: from one end of the spectrum the church had to confront the new world embodiment of the age-old powers of Popery; from the other it had to meet the challenge of the Methodists and a host of other sects.

Typically, Strachan's representation of the religious world of Upper Canada contains a rich mixture of Anglican self-interest and historical accuracy. Strachan was constantly pleading for money, and this particular analysis certainly tried to further that goal. By putting his church in the centre, he was repeating one of the basic arguments for a well-endowed religious establishment. Since certain religious groups had spawned and sustained revolution and rebellion, the state had to protect itself from both the heirs of the Catholic counterreformation and the descendants of the Puritan commonwealth. Since public order demanded a degree of conformity not only to the legal statutes but also to the religious canons of the nation, the state must provide the revenue to create an Anglican establishment in Upper Canada.[5] Strachan needed enemies in order to promote his own goals.

At the same time, this representation of the religious structure of the colony captured a number of very important social, political, and ideological truths. The clear line that Strachan drew between Roman Catholics and his church, for example, was not merely a financial notation, for it marked a set of attitudes that the Protestant population of the colony accepted as a matter of course. Strachan was a Protestant who saw the world in Protestant terms, and even though he later developed a strong doctrine of the church and protected certain higher churchmen from the attacks of their more evangelical brethren,[6] he nonetheless regarded Roman Catholicism as a jumble of irrational superstitions and a system of religious idolatry and temporal slavery.[7] Although in Upper Canada Catholics were not subject to the same legal restrictions as they were elsewhere and Protestants usually directed their attacks at Catholics as a group, rather than as individuals, Catholics must have suffered personally from the intense prejudices that ran through Upper Canadian society. Indeed anti-Catholicism forms a persistent theme in the religious history of the nineteenth century in Canada.

At the other end of the religious spectrum were the "Protestant dissenters," a term that seemed to encompass the "old dissenters," (such as the Congregationalists, Baptists, and dissenting Presbyterians) and especially the new enthusiasms of Methodism and many other recent sectarian creations. Here the accuracy of Strachan's representation of this part of the religious world of Upper Canada can be measured in two ways. First, his assumptions about the Christian religion (and above all the relationship between church and state) clearly separated him and his church from the dissenting extreme. Secondly, the rage his words provoked in these dissenters confirmed the accuracy of Strachan's analysis of Upper Canadian religion.

Above all John Strachan was a clergyman and a teacher, and at the conclusion of this sermon he revealed his basic religious beliefs: "the doctrine of the atonement—the satisfaction made for sinners by the blood of Christ—the corruption of human nature—the insufficiency of man, unassisted by divine grace—the efficacy of the prayer of faith, and the purifying, directing, sustaining, and sanctifying influence of the Holy Spirit."[8] In short, Christianity was a religion of salvation, offering the means to redeem people from sin, to reconcile God and humanity, and to draw heaven and earth together.

To be saved a person had to proceed along a specific path. Strachan began with the fall when God punished Adam and Eve for their disobedience and expelled them from a state of harmony and innocence. All their descendants continued to suffer under the weight of their original sin. The world had fallen from grace; people had become the creatures of their instincts and passions. The first step towards redemption, therefore, was to restrain the "selfish passions and appetites" and learn to abide by the rules that God had given to humanity. Both the character of the world and divine revelation taught people that they could only attain true happiness by recognizing their own sinfulness, having faith in God, and living a life of virtue and good works. Then as time moved forward, as more and more people came to understand the eternal benefits that such obedience would bring, society itself would slowly change and humanity would return to God. Then everyone would enjoy the freedom and order that had been lost when our ancestors' apostasy led them out of Eden. Strachan concluded his sermon with a truly breathtaking vision of a future earthly millennium: "For as the influence of Christian principles extend . . . murmurs will give way to blessings and praise; and one fourth of the human race being thus reclaimed, the remainder will gradually follow and thus the whole earth become the garden of the Lord."9

This way of interpreting redemption helps to explain why Strachan so strongly advocated the need for a religious establishment. Since redemption was a slow and gradual process, people had to be taught continually how to control their passions and lead a life of virtue and moderation. Therefore they needed a well-educated and resident clergyman to "bring [them] daily into the presence of God and [their] Saviour,"10 churches to house the faithful, and schools and teachers to educate the youth of the province. People were needed who could devote their entire lives to this important task. Only the financial resources of the state could sustain such a system, without which society could not be saved.

The state also helped the church in a less direct way. Since redemption began with order and restraint, the restraint that the state and the law placed upon the passions of the people served a positive religious good. A loyal and ordered population was the basis for a Christian society, and thus the institutions of the state were, in effect, ancillary religious bodies. At the same time the church returned the favour by helping the state achieve its objectives. Christianity taught people to live virtuous lives, and virtue made people into useful and productive subjects. Faith manifests itself in good works—Christians (to quote one of Strachan's more memorable phrases), "pant after the felicity of doing good."11 A religious population would be a loyal population. In brief, the alliance of church and state rested upon a reciprocity of interests. Strachan summarized his defence of an Anglican establishment in a single phrase: "A Christian nation without a religious establishment is a contradiction."12 His "garden of the Lord" would be a pious, rational, and ordered place, founded upon strong religious and social institutions and filled with reasonable, virtuous, and happy people.

It is against this background of restraint, order, and establishmentarianism that one can begin to see the wide gulf that separated the church and the dissenting end of the religious spectrum in early nineteenth-century Upper Canada. The way Strachan described the latter group is revealing. Towards the conclusion of his sermon he referred to "other denominations connected by no bond of union, no common principles of order."13 He compared the settled, well-educated, and sober-minded clergy of his own church and the Church of Scotland with the emotional, poorly trained Methodist preachers who wandered through the colony, disrupting in the name of salvation the slow and careful work of redemption that his church was trying so hard to carry out. He further suggested that the American origins of some of these preachers raised serious doubts about the social and political implications of their religious teachings. His specific charges form but a small part of his general discourse, and they flow logically from his overall argument: they were sound, reasonable, and perfectly consistent. But others saw them very differently, and removed his phrases from their theological context, giving them a prominence they still enjoy.

These Methodists were "uneducated itinerant preachers, who leaving their steady employment, betake themselves to preaching the Gospel from idleness, or a zeal without knowledge, by which they are induced without any preparation, to teach what they do not know, and which from pride, they disdain to learn."[14]

These were the words that provoked such outrage. In what later generations interpreted as an instance of divine intervention, one of the "uneducated," the young Egerton Ryerson, came forth from obscurity to do battle with the Anglican Goliath. In a long, vituperative, and rather meandering letter, the Methodist preacher set out to discredit Strachan and to challenge his assertions. Although he tried to convey an air of moderation, even praising some Anglicans and certain aspects of the Anglican Church, he proceeded to charge the Hon. and Rev. John Strachan D.D. with slander, bigotry, ignorance, and even pettifoggery—of action that "better comports with the character of a passionate lawyer" than a dignified ecclesiastic. Ryerson's letter caused a sensation; it was reprinted quickly in pamphlet form and spread like wildfire throughout the colony. The Methodist cause in Upper Canada had gained a new champion.[15]

Egerton Ryerson's place in the hagiography of Canadian history is still reasonably secure. Although some historians have tried to argue that his underlying intentions were quite conservative, he is still numbered among the saints of progress and liberalism[16]—certainly his response to Strachan has been seen as a ringing defence of religious and political freedom. But if one reads his actual words with care, it becomes clear that the standard categories in which historians have analysed this debate—the tory Strachan *versus* the liberal Ryerson—are not especially useful. For the issue here was primarily religious, and the two men's many political disagreements grew out of the fact that they saw the world in different religious terms. The debate reveals two distinct interpretations of the character of God and the world, and in a somewhat ironic manner confirms the accuracy of the way Strachan divided the religious structure of the colony.

Ryerson's response accepted implicitly the same three-part division. Like Strachan, he quickly segregated the Catholic population of the colony; as a good God-fearing Protestant he had a general antipathy towards all things Roman. In his letter, for example, Ryerson quoted with approval a passage from the Anglican book of homilies that branded Rome as the "harlot, the most filthy of all harlots, the greatest that has ever been."[17] He also attempted to discredit Strachan and the Anglican Church by associating them with the Church of Rome, arguing that all establishments were essentially Romish. "When did popish and corrupt doctrines receive countenance and support in the church? When religious establishments commenced their existence. When did papal domination, which has crimsoned the Christian world from age to age, commence her infernal sway? When religious establishments got the vogue."[18] Ryerson attacked the very idea of religious establishments: "Our saviour never intimated the union of his church with the civil polity of any country."[19] Furthermore, in

Upper Canada there was neither the need nor the legal basis for such an establishment, and if there was no establishment there could be no dissenters. Consequently, Strachan and his church were trying to corrupt both the religious and political life of the colony by imposing what neither God nor nature had intended.

This attack on establishments confirms the other main division in Strachan's religious structure. Though Ryerson argued, in effect, that the Anglicans should be treated like any other Protestant group—indeed he tried to present himself as the loyal son of many Anglican traditions, praising the liturgy and ordinances of the church—once he tried to divide the church from the state, he undercut his own argument. He was trying to divide the indivisible and to put asunder something that history had joined together for several centuries in a long and tolerably happy union. For the early nineteenth century the separation of church and state was a radical idea that could not be supported on historical grounds. To pull the church and establishment apart and treat the Anglicans like just another denomination was like telling the Methodists that their religion would be quite acceptable if they gave up revivalism and itinerancy. Acceptable it might be, but it would no longer be Methodism.

Ryerson's response also illustrates the gap that separated dissenters and churchmen, for his letter expresses a body of beliefs about the relationship between God and the world that stands in marked contrast to the ordered, rational, and institutional doctrines of Strachan's religious world. Strachan, for example, argued that the Anglican liturgy "presents with great force, simplicity, and beauty, the ways, means, and appointments of God, to restore our fallen nature to purity and everlasting life."[20] Ryerson labelled this "all pompous panegyric," rejecting the liturgy as a means of conversion and proclaiming with as much force as he could muster the absolute necessity of "preaching the gospel." This phrase did not mean "reading of one or two dry discourses every Sabbath."[21] He quoted St Paul's second letter to Timothy: "preach the word; be instant in season and out of season; reprove, rebuke, exhort with all long suffering and doctrine."[22] Preaching should not instruct and enlighten but admonish and convert. Conversion was not slow and gradual: it was sudden and immediate, the dramatic experience of being overwhelmed by the redeeming spirit of God. Once again the passages of scripture that sustained his counterattack illustrate these attitudes. Casting Strachan in the role of Nicodemus, he alluded to the third chapter of St John: "except a man be born of water and the Spirit he cannot enter into the Kingdom of God." In a similar way, he referred to the conversion of Saul and the words of Ananias, "Brother Saul, the Lord, even Jesus, that appeared unto thee in the way as thou comest, hath sent me, that thou mightest receive thy sight, and be filled with the Holy Ghost."[23]

The same preoccupation with conversion and the immediate experience of the spirit of God shaped the way Ryerson replied to the charge that Methodists were "uneducated." Instead of describing the training that an itinerant received and the close supervision that the senior members of the Methodist Church exercised over their prospective preachers, he chose instead to argue that education was not necessary. While formal learning might be useful and pleasing, it could never replace the necessity of experiencing the transforming power of the spirit. A preacher must be redeemed; education was a secondary consideration. He turned Strachan's words on their head: knowledge without zeal was a positive evil.

Ryerson's concluding vision of the future of the world once again points out the same basic contrast. Strachan expressed the hope that careful instruction and good example could gradually convert the people to Christianity and transform the whole earth into "the garden of the Lord." Ryerson also dreamed of a glorious future, but his millennial vision turned upon a series of immediate and powerful juxtapositions. He described the drama of sudden conversion, using images of violence and war: "The day is not very far distant 'when the banners of the Lamb will wave triumphant over the blood-stained car of the Juggernaut; when the Shaster and Koran shall be exchanged for the oracles of truth'; when the plundering Arab, the degraded Huttentot, and the inflexible Chinese, with the polished European, and the uncultivated American, will sit down under the tree of life, and all acknowledge 'one Spirit, one Lord, one Faith, one Baptism, and one God.'"[24]

The dispute between Strachan and Ryerson reveals several important aspects of religion and culture in Upper Canada in the early nineteenth century. On the one hand Strachan and Ryerson shared a good deal—they both considered themselves to be servants of the same God; they both proclaimed their allegiance to the Protestant Reformation; and they both read the same Bible and drew many of the same conclusions from it. But on the other hand they disagreed strongly about a number of crucial religious questions: What is the nature of salvation? What is the character of God? What is the proper relationship between God and humanity? These differences sustained some of the basic religious divisions in Upper Canada and shaped a number of elements in the culture of the colony.

To a certain extent the differences between Strachan and Ryerson can be attributed to differences in their character, background, and personality; one was from Scotland, the other from Upper Canada; one had a university education, the other did not. As with any two human beings, such differences helped to shape different attitudes and beliefs. At the same time these differences had a larger significance, for the two men were representative figures whose ideas and beliefs were part of two general intellectual and cultural patterns. The expressions that Strachan had used in his sermon were not original and can be found in any number of sermons and discourses that he and others had delivered over the course of the previous twenty years.[25] Indeed it is their very generality (and Strachan's ability to promulgate them through the state, the church, and the schools) that gives them a powerful resonance. Similarly, Ryerson's words could have been spoken by many others. His preoccupation with the immediate experience of the spirit of God and the rhetoric in which he clothed his conviction were part of Methodist thought and practice at that time; indeed, they reached far beyond the institutional limits of Methodism. Ryerson was also able to carry these ideas to a large audience, both through his work as a minister and through his distinguished career in education.

In sum, the contest between Strachan and Ryerson over these "uneducated itinerant preachers" is not only a debate between two important historical figures but also an extraordinarily valuable commentary on religion and culture in the early nineteenth century. The points of agreement and disagreement in the debate highlight the general nature of Protestant thought as well as the divisions in the Protestant world of Upper Canada. A study of the debate also introduces the links between religious thought and culture. As both Strachan and Ryerson show so clearly, religion is not restricted to what goes on in a church: the way these men (and so many others) saw God also shaped the way they saw the world.

To move from the specific debate to these more general issues of religion and culture, it is best to begin at the point where most Protestants began their own interpretation of God and the world. At the centre of Protestant Christianity was the Bible, which embodied the very word of God; it was the cornerstone of the faith, the text that held the keys to the nature and purpose of life. Since the Bible was an unassailable authority and the court of final judgment for all disputes and controversies,[26] it is important to understand how Protestants interpreted this unique text.

In the early nineteenth century most Protestants agreed that the Bible was essentially a sacred book of history telling a story with a single theme that began at the beginning of time and concluded at the end of the world. All the passages of scripture quoted so epigrammatically by so many preachers in the nineteenth century were joined together by this basic narrative. The Bible was not only a history text; it was the only history text.

The specific history that was drawn from the Bible was built around a single grand theme: the separation and reconciliation of God and humanity. In the beginning God created the heavens and the earth. The first man and woman lived in harmony with their creator, in a state of innocence and peace. It was Adam's apostasy that shattered this unity, drove Adam and Eve from Eden, and separated humanity from God. The Lord, however, did not abandon the inhabitants of the world completely. During the era described in the Old Testament, God made a number of promises to the people, telling them that if they obeyed certain conditions they could enjoy at least a portion of divine favour. God entered, for example, into a series of covenants to protect and reward a chosen people and in the same era provided a glimpse of the next stage in the progress of reconciliation. The Bible foretold, primarily through the prophets, the approach of a new era and a new relationship between God and the world. In the fullness of time this era came to pass in the series of historical events that form the central episode in the Protestant interpretation of the Bible—the life, death, and resurrection of Christ. By his death Christ atoned for the sins of the world and offered a fallen humanity a way of escaping from the horrific consequences of Adam's original sin. The Gospel held out the hope of salvation, the promise of a future reconciliation between God and creation—a new heaven and a new earth.[27]

Protestant Christianity, then, was a religion of salvation rooted in a distinctive representation of the whole of human history. The past, present, and future were drawn together through a series of strong teleological assumptions. When people read the Bible they assumed that the past foretold the present and that the future would fulfil the prophecies of the past. The eternal present was placed in turn at a critical juncture in this structure of time, standing on the precipice between separation and reconciliation. Although people were still sinners, suffering under the enormous weight of their ancestors' transgressions, they could be saved and the world made into something new. When the Bible was read in this way, it gave time and place a distinct form and meaning.[28]

Although this general interpretation of the nature of the Bible was accepted by most Protestants as a matter of course, it nonetheless remained at a certain distance from the people and the society of the day. It provided, as it were, a broad representation of the nature of time and place, but it did not address directly the specific events of everyday existence, in this case the world of Upper Canada. In order to reach this more immediate and practical level, the Bible had to be interpreted through metaphors and images that integrated this sacred text and the living world that it had to explain.

It was precisely at this point that the general Protestant consensus began to break down. When Protestants tried to fit their own lives and society into the general Biblical representation of the tragedy and triumph of human history, sharp divisions on a number of critical issues quickly arose. In the early nineteenth century there were in general two contrasting patterns of interpretation through which different groups of Protestants attempted to reconcile the Bible and their own existence. From this perspective the battle between Strachan and Ryerson was a battle over which pattern should dominate the way Upper Canada interpreted God and the world.

Both patterns divided reality into two general categories, relying heavily upon a series of paired concepts such as heaven and earth, good and evil, salvation and sin. The two differed, however, when they tried to reconcile these dualities, and this difference sustained two quite distinct representations of the very nature of God and the world. The first pattern of interpretation was based on a distinctive interpretation of "nature."[29] Its representation of religion was highly rational and systematic and appealed to the values of order and reason. The second pattern turned over the cultural coin and appealed to the other side of early nineteenth-century psychology—the feelings[30]—by reworking the Bible into a religion of intense personal experience. From the story of the resurrection it drew the paramount doctrine that to be saved one must directly experience the saving grace of God.

The first interpretation looked back to the foundation of the Christian universe, to the first verse of the first chapter of Genesis. Since God had created heaven and earth, the character of creation revealed the nature of God and the meaning of existence. The argument proceeded, as a general rule, through an extended and well-known analogy.[31] By observing nature one readily learns that order is the primary attribute of the universe. As in a well-made watch, every element in creation fits together within a grand system and suits perfectly the task it performs. And just as the existence of a watch demonstrates the existence of a watchmaker, so too does the perfect order of nature prove beyond doubt the existence of a higher rational intelligence who has imparted such order to the universe. "The works of creation [present] the demonstrative proof to every reasonable mind of the being, nature, and attributes of God."[32] As Strachan explained to his students at Cornwall in 1807 (and repeated on many occasions throughout his life), "the Sun, the Moon, and the Stars, the inhabitants of the land and water so wonderfully suited to their different stations, and habits of life, loudly proclaim a first cause of infinite power and wisdom."[33]

The structure of the world also revealed the purpose of creation and, by implication, the role that each of the inhabitants of creation should play. God made the world with a particular end in view: he ordered creation in a rational and integrated manner so that the system would not only function but function for the benefit of all. If God was a God of love, would he have created the world to produce misery rather than happiness? Seeds are nurtured by soil and rain to produce food; people are given arms to gather and teeth to eat. Each part fulfils its function, and together all parts promote the happiness of the whole.

This image of God and life made duty and self-interest into thoroughly compatible virtues. To follow God's will one must accept the order of nature and society; everything had a place in this grand design. But at the same time one should pursue happiness and contentment. All was order, all was rational, all was happy: "all things work together for good."[34] Strachan argued that "the purpose of creation" was to "confer happiness upon a greater number of rational beings."[35] If people accepted the order of creation and pursued their true self-interest rationally and reasonably, they would realize the happiness that God had provided for the inhabitants of creation to enjoy.

But as it now stood, this way of understanding God and the world could easily drift away from its Christian moorings, for it wavered on the very edge of deism, that heresy that proved so attractive to the apostles of reason and order.[36] If it could be demonstrated that the physical universe was perfectly rational and that rational thought and action were the keys to human happiness, a person might worship reason and order as if they were gods in themselves. The Bible or revelation or even Christ might not be necessary when the world and reason explained the nature and meaning of life quite satisfactorily. This interpretation seemed to lead to a decidedly worldly attitude.

The doctrine of "happiness" created a similar problem. If the term was not defined precisely, the pursuit of happiness could lead to chaos rather than order. If individuals were allowed to define happiness for themselves, they could easily delude themselves into believing that selfishness made them happy and that general selfishness would promote the happiness of all. In this way the interpretation that emphasized the importance of order opened the door to a host of disruptive activities. Society became the battleground of thousands of people trying to satisfy their insatiable passion for worldly pleasure. When carried to its logical conclusion, happiness might prove to be the antithesis of order rather than its concomitant.

To address these problems this interpretation tempered its preoccupation with reason and happiness by stressing the necessity of prophecy and revelation.[37] These provided a strong future orientation that lessened the disruptive potential of the expediency that went hand in hand with the doctrine of rational self-interest and also tied the interpretation more closely to the basic doctrines of Christianity. The argument proceeded this way. The structure of creation, if *rightly* understood, proclaimed the existence of God and strengthened the sacred injunction to lead a rational, ordered, and happy life; but unfortunately the fall had obscured these important lessons. Adam's apostasy had made the people of the world creatures of instinct and passion who were now too ignorant to understand the true meaning of the world. "If it be admitted on all hands that God could have no other end in view in creating the world but the diffusion of happiness, it may be allowed that this end had failed, for mankind were ignorant of the things most essential to their happiness."[38] The structure of creation was not enough; people needed to be instructed more directly. Prophecy and revelation performed this vital task by presenting a series of precise moral instructions and explaining that human happiness included the pleasures not only of this world but also of the world to come. Christian revelation, declared Strachan, "raises our thoughts above the frivolous joys of this life, and presents us with the most glorious prospects beyond the grave."[39]

The study of nature could offer abundant examples of the virtues of order, reason, and piety, but it could not supply an eschatological framework to link individual and social action to goals that transcended the limitations of worldly time and place. In effect, the well-crafted watch of nature could not tell time. The prophecies about the future (which of course were always completely fulfilled) and the specific glimpses of the future provided by revelation set the values of order and reason securely within the biblical account of redemption and the life of the world to come. Rational action must consider two goals: happiness in the present and happiness in the future. In this way prophecy and revelation gave expediency a decidedly Christian dimension. It was not enough to pursue a life of earthly pleasures and immediate gratification; the long-term goal of everlasting happiness in the kingdom of heaven must also be considered. "The primary end of our existence is to promote and secure our spiritual happiness for God delights in the happiness of all his creatures."[40]

Revelation and prophecy can be explosive material; indeed the history of Christianity is filled with groups and individuals who have attempted to use their own interpretations of prophecy and revelation to transform their own lives and societies. In this case, however, revelation and prophecy sustained the values of order and stability running through this interpretation. While the insights of revelation exceeded the scope of reason by answering questions the human mind could not fathom on its own, the answers they gave in fact secured order and happiness. Nothing in revelation undermined these social values or even led anyone to question them. Did not the fact that all prophecies were fulfilled confirm that God and the design of history were perfectly rational? Were not the teachings of Christ—his admonishments to sinners to lead a virtuous life—fully compatible with reason? Did not the beneficial social results of a faith in the world to come demonstrate the reasonableness and utility of the Christian religion?

Order was the virtue that informed this pattern of interpretation. God was a God of order, nature revealed the workings of an ordered and rational intelligence, and reason, sustained by revelation, explained the nature of God and the pathway to salvation. Order was also evident in the way the system as a whole was built on a set of fixed principles such as rational self-interest and the pursuit of happiness. There was nothing extraordinary or unpredictable here: all the pieces came together, and everything worked in an orderly and integrated way. If people led virtuous lives (and after all it was in their own self-interest to do so), they would achieve everlasting happiness, humanity would regain the order and perfection that it had lost at the fall, and the earth would become the garden of the Lord. It was, in effect, a highly ordered pattern that proclaimed above all the value of order itself.

This interpretation of the Bible and the world answered a number of basic theological questions by explaining the relationship between the secular and the sacred: a person who had faith in God, led a virtuous life, and performed a number of good works would enjoy the benefits of life everlasting. The very fact, however, that this was a theological system gave it a significance that went far beyond theological issues. Because this interpretation explained the meaning of life, it tried to encompass all aspects of existence. Thus the way it explained creation also explained the immediate environment, the way it saw God was also the way people should see themselves, and the way it approached the knowledge of God also defined how all knowledge should be approached. A religious pattern was also a social pattern, and order was not only a religious but also a social virtue.

Strachan's statements concerning the relationship between church and state illustrate how religious beliefs become cultural assumptions. In his eyes there was an exact parallel between religious and social obligations. A love of order not only led to salvation but it also helped to create the proper type of society, which in turn helped the church perform its mission. A religious population was also a loyal population, since people imbued with religion led reasonable and circumspect lives. Christianity, therefore, was the cornerstone of social order. This simple syllogism also demonstrated the necessity of a close relationship between the church and the state: both promoted a common set of goals, and both sustained order and happiness.

The same pattern of ideas and values recurs throughout this period. The ordered and hierarchical character of the natural world, for example, not only explained the character of God, but also justified the hierarchy of wealth and power in society at large. Like nature, society was an integrated system, and just as the various parts of nature could exist only as elements in an ordered and integrated system, so could individuals only exist as part of a social system. Order was the very basis of society; without it there could be no liberty or happiness. The principle of social rank followed from the same logic. In the same way that each rank in nature had to accept its place for the system to work, so too each person had to accept a particular station within the social hierarchy for society to promote the general happiness and prosperity of all.[41]

It should come as no surprise that those groups which were in positions of power and authority in this hierarchy continually called upon religion to justify their exalted stature. To lead a virtuous life and do good works became central parts of a code of aristocratic gentility that bound together the small elites that dominated provincial affairs. Canadian historians have commented upon how the image these elites had of themselves as a refined, public-spirited, and useful group sustained a common social and political ideology, and when the leaders of this group declaimed on the character of their society, they returned time and again to the link between religion, their own virtue, and social stability. John Beverley Robinson, to cite one important example, captured perfectly the close association between religious and social values within this culture of order: "There is a meaning in the moral world no less visible than in the great works of Nature—order, stability, peace, security the great blessings of social existence . . . can be reaped only as the rewards of a religious adherency to what is right and true. . . . The foundations of a people's welfare must be laid in public virtue." According to Robinson (and many others) the fact that he and his associates were virtuous men justified their social authority and the way they exercised that authority.[42]

In a more general way, the culture of order defined a particular approach to knowledge and truth. One began with certain general principles from which one drew certain arguments or theories that could be applied to a number of specific issues. The original premise could then be evaluated in the light of this examination. Knowledge, then, was acquired as one moved from the general to the specific and then from the specific to the general. Once again religion sustained culture: the method for ascertaining the evidence of Christianity was the method of Baconian experimentation—natural theology was perfectly compatible with the world of Isaac Newton. Indeed, in this era there was no clear division between religion and science; religion actively encouraged the study of natural phenomena, and as Professor McKillop has shown so clearly, in the period before the writings of the younger Darwin, science sustained and enhanced the authority of religion.[43]

This culture also encouraged a certain intellectual style. To be accepted as truth, an argument, discourse, or sermon had to be presented in a certain manner. After a brief exordium that introduced the general issue, the topic was divided into three parts: the primary principles that define the question were set out, then these principles were applied to the specific topic, and finally the whole piece was drawn together in a pleasing and systematic way. Everything should be rational and coherent: each point should stand on the conclusions of the previous one. All should be sober, careful, and consistent. A later (and more romantic) generation would find this style dry and lifeless, a seemingly endless series of pious axioms and deductions; but given the pattern of truth that sustained it, the style at least for this era was lucid, forceful, and effective.[44]

This overriding concern with order points out the extraordinary conservatism of the culture. The highly mechanistic representation of the universe was one that discounted even the possibility of sudden and radical change. God did not intervene in the world to change the principles of order, and heaven remained at a reasonably safe distance. The hierarchical social system and institutions of this culture again suggest that conservatism was the political and social ideology that inevitably accompanied the culture of order.

The belief that order was a religious and social necessity was undoubtedly the cornerstone of tory ideology in Upper Canada, but the culture of order also contained elements that could weaken the very values and institutions that Upper Canadian tories held so dear. In the first place, the culture accepted the doctrine of expediency and the value of empirical observation. Since the universe is ordered, rational, and mechanistic, and since this universe was created by God to promote human happiness and prosperity, therefore nature and order were means to an end. The bounty of nature should not simply be admired, but also developed to promote human happiness and prosperity. Nature and institutions, in effect, should be evaluated in two different ways: as elements in a divine system *and* in the light of the benefits they produce. Worth, at least in the latter sense, became a question of results. *Both* the church and the state, it is important to point out, justified the need for a religious establishment on the basis of the social benefits provided by an establishment[45]—religious truth and error were comparatively unimportant. Here was the fly in the tory ointment, for expediency was a social doctrine that could be used to attack the ideas and institutions that were at the centre of the tory universe. If an institution no longer provided the benefits it was supposed to produce or if those benefits could be realized more effectively in a different way, then the institution lost its reason for existence. The church was to learn the rigours of expediency when its opponents (and some of its friends) used this argument to attack religious establishments in the 1840s and 1850s.

Secondly, the environment of Upper Canada itself undermined the conservatism of this pattern of interpretation. Ideas organize and explain reality; in this case they explained and defended a rational and hierarchical world. But before a proper social, political, and religious order could be defended, it had to be established, and it took considerable imagination to proclaim the inherent harmony and order of nature and society at a time when the colony was still a wilderness devoid of hedgerows and well-kept fields, and when the institutions of church and state existed at best only in embryo form. For this reason social analysis had to be cast in the future tense: "Our argument," Strachan explained to the Rev. George Mountain, "is not what we are, but what we shall be if left unmolested."[46] In Britain the culture of order enjoyed the benefit of defending a social and religious system that not only existed but was so well established that it seemed to have become a part of nature itself. Conservatives in Upper Canada were not as fortunate; they had to defend what had not yet come to pass and transform what existed only in part into what ought to be. A pattern that was based in large part upon empirical observation and rational deduction had to ignore a whole world of empirical data; in Upper Canada an interpretation of the world as it was became a vision of what the world should become. Order, in effect, provided a blueprint for the Anglican millennium in the wilderness of Upper Canada: "for as the influence of Christian principles extend . . . murmurs will give way to blessings and praise; and one-fourth of the human race being thus reclaimed, the remainder will gradually follow, and thus the whole earth become the garden of the Lord."[47]

It was this disparity between a hierarchical conservative vision and an unordered and seemingly egalitarian reality that so unnerved and frustrated the many critics of Strachan and the establishment principle. Where could one find the established church of Upper Canada? Where were its clergy and churches and schools; indeed where were all its adherents? How could one defend the beneficial results of something that was not yet in place? Dissenters were familiar with the texts on which the Anglicans and Presbyterians had built their case, they saw the inherent weakness in their position, and they used this weakness to attack what they regarded as an attempt to impose a host of unwarranted religious privileges on Upper Canada.[48]

The dissenting end of the religious spectrum also attacked the establishment vision of Upper Canada at a much deeper level. Men like Egerton Ryerson set out to rebut Strachan's specific charges, but, more important, they were determined to challenge the very culture that underlay the establishment position. In so doing they propounded an alternative to this culture that drew God and the world together in a different way. Christianity was not an abstract system of rational precepts, to use Ryerson's phrase, a series of "dry formularies"[49]; the church of God was not one part in an elaborate set of social and political institutions. At the centre of this culture was a personal and immediate encounter with the spirit of a powerful and living God.

The first interpretation saw God as a divine rational intelligence conducting a learned discourse for humanity through the intermediary of nature. It treated Christ as a learned divine who had calmly explained the benefits of a virtuous life and presented his audience with a rational set of moral precepts for their guidance. Conversion, therefore, was a gradual process. It began as one restrained the passions and advanced slowly as one gained knowledge of the religious and social principles that helped one to lead a virtuous and rational life. The second culture began at a different point in the Biblical story and presented a very different image of God. Christ was not merely a teacher—anyone after all can be a teacher—he was the crucified and risen Lord. The physical pain he suffered became a model for all Christians: as Christ had suffered to save the world, so must all undergo an intense physical and emotional experience in order to save their souls.

If the first interpretation encouraged people to eschew passion and conform to the deeper rationality and order of God's creation, the second called on people to do just the opposite. It looked deeply, not into nature, but into the heart of the sinner; indeed it saw the physical world as an expression of the fallen state of humanity, which lives, not in a garden of order and happiness, but in a wilderness of sin and degradation. If people were to be saved, their feelings had to be roused, not restrained. Passion opened a door through which sinners could be pulled out of a fallen world. This was a religion, not of order, but of experience.

The official voice of Upper Canadian Methodism presented this contrast in the boldest terms. "True religion," the *Christian Guardian* explained, "does not consist in orthodox opinions in the purest forms of divine worship, in correct moral conduct, or even in the combination of these things. 'The Kingdom of God is not in word, but in power.' However the Gospel may be admired its great design is never realized but in the actual conversion and salvation of men. With whatever ability the word of life may be dispensed no sinner will be truly awakened, no heart will become broken and contrite, no polluted conscience will be purged from dead works, no impure mind will be sanctified, no human soul will be effectually renewed and comforted, unless the Holy Spirit descend in the plentitude of his love and power."[50] Here again we see the outline of a theological system that attempted to reconcile the secular and the sacred, but as the quotation suggests, it brought these two worlds together in a distinctive way. Orthodox opinions and proper conduct were not enough. To be "awakened," "broken," or "purged" a person had to feel the "love and power" of the Holy Spirit.

This interpretation rested on what one might call a theology of feelings. On an evening in 1738, John Wesley had felt his own heart "strangely warmed" by the spirit of God, and this event took on enormous symbolic importance for Methodists, coming to represent in their eyes a religious doctrine that distinguished them from all other religious groups. Theirs was an "experimental" religion that proclaimed the necessity of a direct religious experience with God. So important was such a religious experience that feelings became more important than reason. Early Canadian Methodism wore this badge of honour proudly. Most of the "religious world," the *Christian Guardian* explained, can "talk well upon the speculative points of Divinity, even reason accurately and quite logically on the attributes of God. . . . But who delights to dwell on Christian experience? Let us strike at the *infidelity of the heart,* and if we gain conquest there, our work is chiefly done."[51]

Though these theological discourses introduce the religion of experience, they do not reveal its inner character. In the early nineteenth century the concept of theology was not especially important to Methodists, whose theological training tended to consist of reading Wesley's published sermons and a few other texts.[52] In addition the extreme subjectivity of experience makes it very difficult to define this type of religion with theological precision. For the Anglicans experience confirmed the powers of reason and the principles of order, but for the Methodists the experience of meeting God was so unique, immediate, and overwhelming that it defied description and analysis. For these reasons we must turn to other sources. It is not what was written about the doctrines of Methodism but the style of worship created by the religion of experience that reveals the character and significance of this pattern of interpretation. When Egerton Ryerson responded to Strachan, he did not defend Methodism by debating theology and doctrine; rather he singled out the profound impact that Methodism had on hardened sinners. Uneducated itinerants might not understand theology, but they could lead hundreds of people directly to God. The means of conversion, in effect, reveals the beliefs that sustained the religion itself.

To understand the religion of experience we must turn to the revivals and camp meetings that were the hallmark of Upper Canadian Methodism in the early decades of the nineteenth century. This most distinctive style of worship had three essential features. According to contemporary accounts, revivals and camp meetings were distinguished by mass participation:

"revivals and camp meetings bring a great number of sinners together." Secondly, revivals were able to isolate these sinners from the world and subject them to a continuous flood of religion: "there is much to be expected from the repeated attacks of divine truth on the minds of sinners at camp meetings, without the opportunity of bringing the pleasures of the world in contact with the impressions made thereby." And thirdly, this flood of religion was highly emotional, playing directly upon the feelings and passions of sinners. The result was an immediate and powerful conversion: "the animal sympathies of sinners are excited, under the influence of which they are placed in a hearing mood, and in this way often become truly convicted."[53]

The descriptions of revivals and camp meetings continually return to these three elements. Large numbers of people came together for a religious event that lasted for at least three days. They were isolated from the outside world, sometimes by nature itself, sometimes by specially constructed barricades.[54] In the enclosure preaching alternated with prayer and singing; mass participation was followed by a division of the people into small groups of penitents. The preaching was intense and emotional; the texts were drawn from some of the most highly charged passages of scripture.[55] In the language of revivals, the preachers had to "preach Christ crucified"; they had to "preach for a verdict," not to inform and instruct but to bring about an immediate conversion to Christ. This conversion experience was itself amazingly intense. As preacher followed preacher, as exhorters moved through the crowds, as the converted turned upon the unrepentant but wavering sinner, individuals would finally break under the weight of the revival, acknowledge their sinfulness, and accept God's saving grace.[56]

From the accounts of revivals and camp meetings we can begin to understand how this style of religion presented God and the world. Here again there was an essentially dualistic interpretation of reality—the recurring distinctions between heaven and earth, between the secular and the sacred. Indeed, the line between the two categories was drawn boldly, but this very separation of the two worlds made the movement from the one to the other all the more dramatic. People were sinners, suffering under the enormous weight of original sin, adrift in a world of evil without guidance or hope. Their souls were encased in a hardened shell that had become impervious to logic and reason; not only were they sinners, but they were even unaware of their own depravity. Only when these people had been forced to accept the enormity of their own sinfulness and plead for divine mercy could the sudden and overwhelming flood of God's saving grace shatter the defences of the world and set the soul of the sinner at liberty. In the flash of an eye, an awful transformation took place as the newly redeemed entered into a truly blessed existence.

God was not a distant and superintending rational intelligence; nature was not a mechanistic set of fixed and integrated relationships that when subjected to reason revealed the purpose of creation. God was an active and interventionist power who continually transformed people and the affairs of the world. The road to salvation was not through the intellect but through the emotions, and it was here that the revivalist could attack sinners and force them to acknowledge their depravity and cry for mercy. In the depths of the most profound feelings, people met their maker and secured their release from the bondage of the old and fallen world.

Such power and drama defied precise and adequate description; logic and reason could never penetrate this mystery. How could something that transcended normal circumstance, indeed something that overwhelmed the entire being, be defined and comprehended by people who still lived in a fallen world? This experience could only be described through metaphor and analogy, and it was in these terms that the language of revivals tried to capture and convey the essence of this religion.

Descriptions of revivals were redolent with images of power and violence. The words of a preacher were like "fire" and "lightning": God came down like a storm or in "showers of grace"; sinners were "broken" or fell "like a bullock at the slaughter."[57] Revivals were noted for their shouting and the physical convulsions that accompanied conversion. The extent to which such extravagances actually took place is a matter of debate; but the fact that conversions were described in these terms confirms the intensity of the experience that defined this interpretation of the nature of God and the world.

In essence religion became a search for experience: to feel God was now the central goal of existence. Other questions became less important; how one lived, either before or after such an experience, or the character of society were not matters of pressing concern. Not only was experience a religious goal, but it also demonstrated the very existence of God. Whereas others searched for God in nature or, for that matter, in scripture, those who followed this religion looked into themselves. If they felt God, then God must be real. No additional proof was necessary when one had found God in one's soul. This explains why the personal search for experience forms the main theme in so many of the journals and autobiographies of Methodist clergymen in this period. Their words reveal both the self-doubt and anguish as they waited for the experience as well as the joys and raptures when it suddenly arrived.[58]

Those who conformed to the culture of order found this preoccupation with an overwhelming experience almost unfathomable. It was not experience itself that presented the problem, for after all, experience that conformed to reason and revelation and led to humility and a virtuous life was a great aid to faith.[59] What they found so unsettling was the assertion that a genuine religious experience transcended a person's ability to understand it. "It is to be feared," Strachan preached in 1830, "that many suppose that the blessings of heaven consist in certain raptures and extacies of which we can form no conception in our present state. . . . But this is a great mistake—the foundation of our felicity in heaven is substantially the same as that which forms the foundation of the present world. [The individual] can enjoy no true felicity while he remains the slave of unruly passions and appetites."[60] In the culture of order, experience reinforced reason and helped to sustain the individual in the slow and peaceful progress towards salvation.[61] In the culture of experience, it overwhelmed reason and reality—it became self-sustaining, creating a world of its own.

The intensity and power of such a religious experience help to explain some of the important social and cultural aspects of this pattern of religious interpretation. Once again religion leads directly to culture: in defining a way of seeing God, this pattern also set out a way of understanding the world and acting in it. By equating, for example, religion and individual experience, this interpretation made experience the touchstone not only of religious truth but of truth in general. If religion had to be experienced in order to be genuine, then experience provided the standard for evaluating all elements of the world. In other words, if something was felt, it must be true. In this way religion sanctified a different and powerful criterion for evaluating thought and behaviour.

The enormous authority that religion gave to individual experience allowed many individuals and groups to follow the light of their own feelings to a wide range of religious and social destinations. In religious terms it opened the doors to various forms of antinomianism because salvation made newly minted Christians into their own social and religious masters, each one as good an arbiter of truth and error as any cleric or magistrate. It created a new environment where traditional doctrines, the law, and reason itself did not apply. Here indeed was a new world whose boundaries were as wide as the most fertile imagination. The saved could ignore their leaders and try to share in the sacred powers that the encounter with God seemed to place in their hands. They could walk on water, heal the sick, raise the dead, or predict the future.[62] Moreover, an untempered faith could easily loosen the bonds of moral and civil law. After all, the law had been set down to control sinners. Why then should it continue to restrict those who were redeemed and perfect? To paraphrase the first epistle general of St John, if one was saved then one could no longer sin, or what were sins for most people were not sins for the righteous. Sexual relations, for example, assumed a new meaning when this logic removed with one stroke the host of social and cultural prohibitions that sustained such institutions as marriage and monogamy.[63] The same logic could also lead to less extravagant instances of social antinomianism. If everyone was their own religious master, then everyone also had the power to judge all other aspects of life. Experience, in effect, internalized the sources of truth and imparted a truly marvellous self-confidence to social and political life.

Antinomianism is related to the religion of experience in much the same way that deism is related to the religion of order. The latter cultivated a dry intellectualism, in which God and the world worked according to a series of fixed and rational principles. How easy it was in this case to confuse the attributes of God with the sacred itself and simply to worship reason and nature. The religion of experience moved with the same logic to the opposite extreme. This was a religion in which God intervened continually in the course of human affairs, reshaping the world and its inhabitants. Logic and proportion disappeared in a world where anything was possible and where experience became the only standard for truth and action. Each heresy followed logically from the assumptions of its orthodox parent.

The religion of experience also encouraged a number of other distinctive social attitudes, for in this pattern a rigid division between the world of sin and the Kingdom of God encouraged a pessimistic attitude towards society. The material world was an obstacle to salvation and most certainly could not be seen as a reflection of God's benevolence. Moreover, the uniqueness of the conversion experience further undermined the authority of the world and social institutions. To induce a conversion experience, a revival pushed people to the very boundaries of their everyday existence. The religious experience had to be new and different so that sinners would realize the inadequacies of their old ways of life. By challenging the limits of the ordinary, the religion of experience challenged the social concepts and patterns of behaviour that sustained these individuals in their normal lives. The glorification of experience broke down the traditional distinction between normal and aberrant behaviour: the shouting and screaming that were unacceptable in everyday life were quite acceptable in religion, and once something received the blessing of God, how could it be restricted to only one area of life?

These social and cultural qualities of the religion of experience seem to suggest that it was closely tied to political radicalism, for neither accepted the existing social order or the dominant beliefs that justified the social system. Certainly, the Anglicans and the Presbyterians in the early nineteenth century often made this connection: those who were loose in religion were also loose in politics and society. But one must be careful not to overemphasize the radical aspects of this culture. To be sure, the experience of conversion did call upon the newly redeemed to abandon their former ways, but exactly where this call would lead was exceedingly difficult to predict. The direct experience of God inspired Mother Ann Lee and her followers to leave England and establish in America a thoroughly radical and wonderful community that rejected many of the social, political, and sexual beliefs and practices of traditional society.[64] An angel gave Joseph Smith a new gospel that in time carried him (in the company of many Upper Canadians) to Nauvoo and beyond.[65] One religious experience led David Willson to rebuild the temple of Jerusalem in the wilderness of East Gwillimbury; another struck down a young sinner, who fell down before the Lord and promised to stop wearing fancy shirts.[66] Experience might engender nothing more than a casual other-worldliness that after a short time faded away as the converted returned to their former ways. It might tear open the established norms of social action, but what this would produce was quite another question. At times the political divisions in Upper

Canada clearly corresponded to the religious divisions of the colony[67]; at other times they did not. Although religion could encourage radical reform it could just as easily lead a person out of politics altogether. Experience was a singularly confusing light to follow.

Each of these patterns of interpretation is a composite picture drawn from a wide variety of historical materials. The diaries, sermons, forms of worship, and columns of the religious press contain a number of ideas and images that recur systematically and form a distinct pattern. The pattern drawn from the Anglican and Presbyterian materials is built on the virtue of order, the pattern drawn from the records of Methodism and other religious groups is built upon the virtue of experience. Each pattern then is an ideal type that sums up and integrates the ideas and beliefs of a religious culture, even though not all members of that culture conformed to every part of the pattern. The historical value of these patterns lies in their ability to throw a new light on the religion and the culture of Upper Canada in the early nineteenth century. Since they represent two general ways in which this society saw the world, they can help the historian understand the world that the patterns were trying to order and explain.

In the early nineteenth century these two cultures battled each other in the pulpit, the press, the legislature, and the fields, villages, and towns of the colony as they fought for the allegiance of people who had yet to form completely their ways of understanding and shaping the new world to which they had come. Although the two cultures battled each other intensely, they nevertheless had a good deal in common. What appear to be opposites often find ways of coming together. Rather than two distinct worlds, order and experience were in fact two parts of the same whole. They co-existed in the same historical setting, and by opposing each other they in fact attested to the reality and legitimacy of the other. Rather than being marked by massive ramparts built to withstand a long and arduous siege, the walls between them were low and contained many openings that allowed people to pass from one to the other.

The two protagonists of 1825 illustrate this process of cultural exchange. John Strachan betrayed a zeal for religion that seems at times decidedly Methodistical. For example, he reworked the parish structure of his church into a system of local itinerancy that transformed many of his missionaries into the Anglican equivalent of saddlebag preachers. He even encouraged the laity to conduct religious services by reading the lessons and preaching a sermon when no clergyman could be present, an innovation that was soundly rejected by his bishop.[68] A letter Strachan wrote to the Society for the Propagation of the Gospel summarized his attachment to both traditional religion and more popular forms of evangelism. There

were two essential qualifications, he explained, for all prospective missionaries: they must be able to read the New Testament in Greek and know
how to ride and care for a horse.[69]

Nor were Ryerson and the Methodists as unmindful of order as their
Anglican critics so often asserted. Ryerson himself read Paley at an early
date, and the Methodist clergy were far more subject to centralized control
and discipline than the Anglican missionaries in the same period. Many
Methodists still used the *Book of Common Prayer*. Furthermore, when the
Methodists were challenged by other revivalistic sects, they defended themselves by appealing to order and reason. And, as we shall see in the next
chapter, when Methodism began to redefine itself in the light of new circumstances and rejected at least some of the features of the old-style
revivalism, it was Egerton Ryerson—the great champion of 1825—who led
the retreat from the religion of experience.[70]

Religious and cultural exchange was most prevalent at the frontiers of
settlement. All religious groups complained about the frontier where, they
argued, the generally sinful state of the colony reached frightening proportions. According to the traditions of Canadian religious history, Methodism
enjoyed the greatest success in responding to this challenge because the
itineracy of its ministry and the emotionalism of its religious practice were
perfectly suited to the religious and psychological needs of a frontier community.[71] And yet the same people who seemed so caught up in revivals
also demanded a number of religious offices that were very much a part of
Anglican ways of worship. They demanded that an ordained clergyman
baptize their children, church their women, and bury their dead. They
were devoted to the almanacs and astrological guides that presented a sym-
metrical view of the universe very similar to the natural theology underlying the religion of order.[72]

The reproaches made to this frontier population by both the establishment clergy and the revivalist leaders describe the same process of
interchange. When a revival drew off a large part of an Anglican congregation, the local missionary often railed against the evil excesses of religious
enthusiasm, lamenting the lack of firm religious principles among his
flock. If the people were only more rational they would not be caught up in
such dangerous extravagances. At the same time, Methodist itinerants were
continually frustrated by the regrettable tendency of the newly converted
to "backslide" or fall away from Methodism after a revival had run its
course. Where these backsliders might end up is not certain, but from
Anglican accounts it is clear that large numbers of them simply drifted
back to their former churches.[73]

The Anglicans attributed this mobility to a lack of firm religious principle; the Methodists, to the tendency of people to lose the power of the
spirit. Set in a larger context, however, the movement back and forth
between church and revival indicates the way people drew on both these

religions and cultures. They selected, combined, and rejected ideas and styles in order to create a type of Christianity that in some measure satisfied their social, psychological, and religious needs. The ease with which people borrowed from both underlines the fluidity of the religious structure of Upper Canada in the early nineteenth century and the importance of both these religions in the life of the colony. In the pre-Victorian period, many people had yet to be institutionalized in a single religious body, and they borrowed from both religions precisely because both had gained a wide measure of support in the colony. Thus popular religion was an amalgam of order and experience.

The two were also joined together in another interesting way. From one perspective they opposed each other and occupied quite separate points in the religious spectrum. But the spectrum seemed to come back upon itself; the further one pushed at one extreme the more one approached the opposite end from the other side. The culture of order organized and explained the physical and social world, whereas the culture of experience spoke to an inner world and interpreted the myriad sensations that arose from living in a particular time and place. Each served different, and yet complementary, social and cultural needs: to find meaning and order in the world and to explain feelings and emotions. When the two were put together they seemed to complete the circle and encompass the culture of this society. In this sense each defined the reality of the other.

"Our senses and our reason," John Strachan wrote to John Elmsley in 1834, "whatever may be their imperfections, are our only guides, for by their means we arrive at all our knowledge, sacred and profane."[74] The culture of order was founded on reason and a very reasonable interpretation of revelation, but it never denied the existence of the feelings and the spirit. In a sermon that he first preached in 1821, Strachan gave particular prominence to knowledge "which hath been acquired by experience." Such knowledge, he admitted, "is by far more valuable" than knowledge "which hath been acquired from books and our teachers." He then explained the process through which experience is transformed into knowledge. Experience must be evaluated by reason; if it "be not reflected upon sifted and examined, if it is not made food for the soul, if it is not analised and separated into all its parts—that the proper lessons of improvement may be drawn from it we may rest assured that it never will ripen into solid knowledge."[75]

The culture of experience also accepted its counterpart. An experience might be unexpected and overwhelming; but the fact that experiences happened implied a need for order. Feelings had to be compared and interpreted, recorded and organized, and they had to be given a sense of order. But here the link between experience and order assumed a different form. Experience should not be tested by reason; reason should be tested by experience. "If the result of true faith be 'joy and peace in believing,'" the *Christian Guardian* explained, "and my experience bears testimony to the validity of this, what further proof can I wish of its divine origin and tendency?"[76]

Both interpretations also expressed an ageless quest to explain and understand the relationship between a life that is bound by time and space and a life that transcends all such limitations. They formed a bridge between the Bible and the world, and for this reason they shared in the authority that the Bible enjoyed. They were part of "the good," they were of God. Far from being two interpretations among a large number of tentative and arbitrary hypotheses, they set the standards to which other intellectual patterns had to conform. This sacredness allowed them to rise above the people and institutions who propagated them. Religion and culture interpreted and explained the world.

But the world, perhaps with a certain sadness, did not choose to follow the paths that religion and culture had set down for its guidance. If God had created the world and then rested, the descendants of Adam and Eve remained decidedly active. In nineteenth-century Ontario they proceeded to reorganize and develop the physical world and the character of the people who lived in it. The outpost of England that grew up on the margin of American civilization underwent a series of important changes that tore apart the old religious world of Catholic, churchman, and dissenter. These changes undermined the cultural patterns that explained the world; religion and culture pointed in one direction, while the world went another. The religions of order and experience began to lose touch with the reality that they were supposed to interpret and explain.

In the new world of the mid-nineteenth century these patterns of culture were transformed into new ones, which in their turn tried to explain the meaning of time and place. A complex series of social and religious changes destroyed the old dialectic of church versus dissent, of rational piety versus revivalism, of order versus experience. Strachan and Ryerson themselves also changed as they tried to confront this new world. Their old antagonisms seemed to recede as the course of history drew them together. Indeed years later, when they found themselves in the same coach on a journey from Kingston to Cobourg, they marvelled at how they now agreed on so many issues.

A new Protestant consensus was beginning to emerge. Within a few short decades, the debate over establishments and revivalism seemed to have become part of a distant past. When people looked at nature they no longer saw an apology for hierarchy, virtue, and a close alliance of church and state. When they described a religious experience they no longer referred to an overwhelming encounter with the spirit of the Lord; people no longer met their maker face to face along a back road in the wilderness of the old colony of Upper Canada. The old cultures were transformed into something new; the fusing of church and dissent, of order and experience, gave birth to the new culture of Protestant Ontario in the Victorian period.

• Notes

1   John Strachan, *A Sermon Preached at York, Upper Canada, Third of July 1825, on the Death of the Late Lord Bishop of Quebec* (Kingston: Macfarlane, 1826). Parts of this sermon are reprinted in J.L.H. Henderson, *John Strachan: Documents and Opinions* (Toronto: McClelland and Stewart, 1969), 87–94. His text was II Peter 1:15: "Moreover I will endeavour that ye may be able after my decease to have these things always in remembrance."

2   Strachan's private correspondence reveals a picture of Mountain that was much less complimentary. He bridled at the obstacles that Mountain seemed to place in the path of his own plans and ambitions. See Archives of Ontario (hereafter AO), *Strachan Letterbook 1812–34*, Strachan to the Hon. and Rev. Charles Stewart, 11 Jan. 1819.

3   Thomas R. Millman, *Jacob Mountain, First Lord Bishop of Quebec, A Study in Church and State* (Toronto: University of Toronto Press, 1947); and "A Sketch of the Life and Work of the Right Rev. Jacob Mountain, D.D., First Lord Bishop of Quebec by the Rev. Thomas R. Millman: A Sermon Preached on Sunday, 31 Oct. 1943 in the Cathedral of the Holy Trinity on the occasion of the 150th Anniversary of the Arrival of the Bishop" (United Church Archives, Pamphlet Collection).

4   Strachan, *A Sermon Preached at York . . . on the Death of the Late Lord Bishop of Quebec.*

5   Ibid., Strachan compared the £700 000 spent on "the Civil and Military Establishments" with the £9600 paid "for the support and extension of the Religion of the Parent State." For a fuller discussion of church and state see the fourth chapter of this study.

6   See Oliver R. Osmond, "The Churchmanship of John Strachan," *Journal of the Canadian Church Historical Society*, Sept. 1974, 46–59; and the Rev. Mark Charles McDermott, "The Theology of Bishop Strachan: A Study in Anglican Identity" (PhD thesis, Institute of Christian Thought, University of Toronto, 1983), esp. ch. 5. For a perceptive treatment of intra-church divisions see Alan L. Hayes, "The Struggle for the Rights of the Laity in the Diocese of Toronto 1850–1879," *Journal of the Canadian Church Historical Society* (April 1984): 5–17.

7   The writings of Strachan are filled with references to the superstitiousness of Roman Catholicism. For two of his more "reasoned" reactions see John Strachan, *A Letter to the Congregation of St. James, occasioned by the Hon. John Elmsley's Publication of the Bishop of Strasbourg's Observations on the Sixth Chapter of St. John's Gospel* (Toronto: R. Stanton, 1834), and *A Letter to the Right Hon. Lord John Russell, on the Present State of the Church in Canada* (London: George Bell, 1851).

8   Strachan, *A Sermon Preached at York . . . on the Death of the Late Lord Bishop of Quebec.*

9   Ibid. This particular image of the garden of the Lord recurs frequently in Strachan's writings. See for example, *An Appeal to the Friends of Religion and Literature, on Behalf of the University of Upper Canada* (London: R. Gilbert, 1827), 21.

10 Strachan, *A Sermon Preached at York . . . on the Death of the Late Lord Bishop of Quebec.*

11 Ibid.

12 Ibid. For an interesting discussion of the idea of a Christian nation in Strachan's thought see Norma MacRae, "The Religious Foundation of John Strachan's Social and Political Thought as Contained in His Sermons, 1803 to 1866" (MA thesis, McMaster University, 1978), esp. ch. 5, 79–102.

13 Strachan, *A Sermon Preached at York . . . On the Death of the Late Lord Bishop of Quebec.*

14 Ibid.

15 Ryerson's response was published in the *Colonial Advocate* in June 1826 and reprinted as "A Review of a Sermon, Preached by the Hon. and Rev. John Strachan, D.D. at York, U.C., 3d of July 1825 on the Death of the Late Lord Bishop of Quebec by a Methodist Preacher" in *Claims of Churchmen and Dissenters of Upper Canada Brought to the Test; In a Controversy Between Several Members of the Church of England and a Methodist Preacher* (Kingston: UC, 1828). See also Goldwin French, *Parsons and Politics: The Role of the Wesleyan Methodists in Upper Canada and the Maritimes from 1780 to 1855* (Toronto: Ryerson, 1962), 111ff. For Ryerson's own account of these events (written considerably later) see Egerton Ryerson, *The Story of My Life: Being Reminiscences of Sixty Years' Public Service in Canada*, ed. J. George Hodgins (Toronto: William Briggs, 1883), 48; and Egerton Ryerson, *Canadian Methodism: Its Epochs and Characteristics* (Toronto: William Briggs, 1882), 165–220.

16 For recent considerations of Ryerson see Neil McDonald and Alf Chaiton, *Egerton Ryerson and His Times* (Toronto: Macmillan, 1978), and Albert Fiorino, "The Philosophical Roots of Egerton Ryerson's Idea of Education as Elaborated in his Writings Preceding and Including the Report of 1846" (PhD thesis, Ontario Institute for Studies in Education, 1975).

17 This is a paraphrase of the third part of the Homily against Images originally published in 1547 and reprinted many times. See *Certain Sermons Appointed by the Queen's Majesty to be Declared and Read by all Parsons, Vicars, and Curates . . .* (Cambridge, 1850), 260–61.

18 Ryerson, "A Review of a Sermon . . . by a Methodist Preacher."

19 Ibid.

20 Strachan, *A Sermon Preached at York . . . on the Death of the Late Lord Bishop of Quebec.*

21 Ryerson, "A Review of a Sermon . . . by a Methodist Preacher."

22 II Timothy 4:2.

23 John 3:3, 5; and Acts 9:17.

24 Ryerson, "A Review of a Sermon . . . by a Methodist Preacher."

25 Strachan's critique of revivalism contained themes that he himself had articulated as early as 1808. The same critique could be found as well in the writings of any number of Anglican and Presbyterian clergymen. Forty years later for example, the Rev. Charles Forest made the same argument: "Erroneous tests of godliness have been instituted among them, whereby feelings instead of an enlightened judgment and a life-reforming faith, have been set forth as the criteria of true religion." Society for the Propagation of the Gospel Archives, C/Canada/Quebec, folio 394B, Rev. Charles Forest to the Lord Bishop of Montreal, 1 July 1848; see also C/Canada/Quebec, Rev. B.C. Hill to Sect. of UC Church Society, 13 Jan. 1840. The Bishop of Quebec referred to Methodists as "a set of ignorant enthusiasts, whose preaching is calculated only to perplex the understanding, and corrupt the morals and relax the nerves of industry, and dissolve the bonds of society." Provincial Archives of Quebec, Mountain Papers, Bishop of Quebec to Henry Dundas, Quebec, 15 Sept. 1794, as cited in Richard Preston, *Kingston Before the War of 1812: A Collection of Documents* (Toronto: Champlain Society, 1959), 292. See also *The Church*, 16 Jan. 1841, 110; 23 April 1842, 166; and 9 May 1845, 175. For a Presbyterian critique of revivalism see "Seventh Annual Report of the Glasgow Society for Promoting the Religious Interests of Scottish Settlers in British North America, 1883," *The Presbyterian Review* 4 (Nov. 1833):

397–414. Similarly, the division of the colony into three parts is a standard way for Anglicans to represent their place in the religious structure of the colony. For the Rev. John Stuart's appraisal see Synod of Ontario Archives, Stuart Letters, Stuart to Dr Morice, Kingston, 4 Oct. 1791, and Stuart to Bishop of Nova Scotia, Kingston, 25 June 1793, as cited in Preston, *Kingston Before the War of 1812*, 181, 287.

26 Protestants agreed on the central place of the Bible and saw their devotion to the Bible as the feature that joined all Protestants together and separated them from the Roman Catholics. The Methodists put the matter in these terms: "that wherein they all agree, and which they all subscribe with a greater harmony, as a perfect rule of their faith and actions, that is THE BIBLE; THE BIBLE, I say THE BIBLE ONLY IS THE RELIGION OF PROTESTANTS." *Christian Guardian*, 20 March 1839, 77. The quotation is from Chittingworth's *Religion of Protestants*, ch. 6, sec. 56. Strachan put it this way: "Not all the books on earth would compensate the loss of the Bible to mankind; for it is the Bible, and the Bible alone, that points the way to the mansions where God in Christ forever reigneth." John Strachan, *A Charge Delivered to the Clergy of the Diocese of Toronto at the Visitation on Wednesday, 30 April 1856, by John, Lord Bishop of Toronto* (Toronto: Henry Rowsell, 1856), 26.

27 The term *dispensation* was often used to describe the various eras of Christian time. The term was a general one and while related to, should not be confused with, the "dispensationalism" of conservative Protestant theology of a later day. See Ernest R. Sandeen, *The Roots of Fundamentalism: British and American Millenarianism 1800–1903* (Chicago: University of Chicago Press, 1970). For a clear contemporary expression of this structure of time see *Jubilee Sermon, Delivered at the Request of and Before the*

Wesleyan Methodist Conference, Assembled at London, C.W. June 6, 1855 by Rev. William Case (Toronto: G.R. Sanderson, 1855), 5ff.

28 During the nineteenth century people and groups differed about the interpretation of certain elements of this framework rather than about the framework itself. One of these points—the end of time—forms the subject of ch. 6 in William Westfall, *Two Worlds: The Protestant Culture of Nineteenth Century Ontario* (Montreal: McGill-Queen's University Press, 1989). Two of the most important intellectual challenges to this framework were evolution and Biblical criticism. Both, however, were incorporated into this framework, although to do this took considerable effort. See A.B. McKillop, *A Disciplined Intelligence: Critical Inquiry and Canadian Thought in the Victorian Era* (Montreal: McGill-Queen's, 1979), and Michael Gauvreau, "History and Faith: A Study of the Evangelical Temper in Canada, 1820–1940" (PhD thesis, University of Toronto, 1984); and Michael Gauvreau, "The Taming of History: Reflections on the Methodist Encounter with Biblical Criticism, 1830–1890," *Papers of the Canadian Methodist Historical Society* 3 (1983).

29 For recent treatments of natural theology see McKillop, *A Disciplined Intelligence*; Carl Berger, *Science, God, and Nature in Victorian Canada* (Toronto: University of Toronto Press, 1983); and M.L. Clarke, *Paley: Evidences for the Man* (Toronto: University of Toronto Press, 1974). Paley's main works were *Principles of Moral and Political Philosophy, A View of the Evidences of Christianity* and *Natural Theology*. See also Horton Davies, *Worship and Theology in England: From Watts and Wesley to Maurice, 1690–1850* (Princeton: Princeton University Press, 1961).

30 For a detailed discussion of early Victorian understandings of perception and psychology see McKillop, *A*

Disciplined Intelligence, esp. chs. 2 and 3; and Alison Prentice, *The School Promoters: Education and Social Class in Mid-Nineteenth-Century Upper Canada* (Toronto: McClelland and Stewart, 1977), esp. ch. 1.

31 The analogy of nature and God has a long history; the specific analogy of the watchmaker and God provides the introduction to Paley's *Natural Theology.* Clarke, *Paley,* 89–92.

32 AO, Strachan Papers, Manuscript Sermon (31), preached on Psalm 19:2, "Day unto Day uttereth speech, and night unto night sheweth knowledge," first preached 30 Dec. 1821; and Manuscript Sermon (4), preached on the Creed, "I believe in God the Father Almighty Maker of Heaven and Earth," first preached 1 July 1804.

33 The Rev. John Strachan, A.M., *The Christian Religion Recommended in a Letter to His Pupils* (Montreal: Nahum Mower, 1807), 16. The pamphlet is introduced by the maxim "The Good Alone Can Happiness Enjoy."

34 This passage, Romans 8:28–31, provided the biblical text for a great many sermons in the period. Strachan often used the passage as a text or as a reference; see for example John Strachan, *A Sermon Preached at York, Upper Canada, on the Third of June Being the Day Appointed for General Thanksgiving* (Montreal, 1814), and AO, Strachan Papers, Manuscript Sermon (40), preached on II Corinthians 5:8 "We are confident, I say, and willing rather to be absent from the body, and to be present with the Lord," first preached 30 June 1822.

35 Strachan, *A Sermon Preached at York . . . on the Death of the Late Lord Bishop of Quebec.* "To become happy is, therefore, the end of our being; to this all the works of nature and all the powers and faculties of our minds are intended to contribute." John Strachan, *A Sermon on the Death of the Honourable Richard Cartwright, with a*

Short Account of his Life (Kingston, 1815), 9.

36 Anglican fears of deism led in large part to the founding of the Society for the Propagation of the Gospel in Foreign Parts (hereafter SPG) and the Society for Promoting Christian Knowledge (hereafter SPCK). These were the two key institutions, especially the SPG, that oversaw and supported the Church in Canada. See C.F. Pascoe, *Two Hundred Years of the S.P.G.: An Historical Account of the Society for the Propagation of the Gospel in Foreign Parts, 1701–1900* (London: SPG, 1901), vol. 1, 3. For an account of the Presbyterian integration of revelation and theology see Gauvreau, "History and Faith," Part I. See also AO, Strachan Papers, Manuscript Sermon (39), preached on Ephesians 4:30 "and grieve not the holy Spirit of God, whereby ye are sealed unto the day of redemption," first preached 26 May 1822.

37 The crucial role that prophecy played in natural theology has not been properly acknowledged. In addition to the function described here, it provided the bridge between natural theology and millennialism, and explains the quite rational practice of calculating the exact moment when prophecies, such as the second advent, will be fulfilled.

38 Strachan, *The Christian Religion Recommended to his Pupils,* 22–23. Strachan often spoke about the limitations of reason unaided by revelation. "We well know that human reason when most improved was in this respect dark and doubtful and could never discover upon which terms the sinner was to be pardoned nor upon what conditions received into divine favour." He would then emphasize that revelation was consistent with reason because they both promoted the same goal—"religion and refined reason join in the recommendation of holiness"—and was able in effect to conclude that "surely the voice of enlightened reason is the voice of

God." AO, Strachan Papers, Manuscript Sermon (28), preached on Psalm 73:24, "Thou shalt guide me by thy counsel, and afterwards receive me to Glory," first preached 4 Nov. 1821; (6), preached on St Matthew 20:16, "So the last shall be first and the first last; for many be called but few chosen," first preached 15 Dec. 1804; and (12), preached on I Corinthians 10:31, "Whether therefore ye eat or drink or whatsoever ye do—do all to the glory of God," first preached (at Cornwall before the Governor) 3 Aug. 1806.

39 Strachan, *The Christian Religion Recommended to his Pupils*, 24.

40 AO, Strachan Papers, Manuscript Sermon (12), preached on I Corinthians 10:31. In the same sermon Strachan explained the importance of morality and the future very clearly. "Having fixed these truths in the mind Christian morality points always to the other world and considers everything done here as promoting happiness or misery there."

41 AO, Strachan Papers, Manuscript Sermon (22), preached on II Corinthians, 3:17 "Now the Lord is that Spirit and where the Spirit of the Lord is there is liberty," first preached 4 July 1821 [archival notation on microfilm suggests, I believe incorrectly, the date of 4 Feb. 1821].

Scholars have often commented on Strachan's conservatism, and some have appealed to sermons, such as this one, to sustain their case. While the argument here acknowledges the conservatism of many of Strachan's ideas, it differs from other analyses of Strachan's thought by emphasizing his appeal to nature as an analogue of order and hierarchy, rather than to history *per se.* Strachan's thought was mechanistic and deductive rather than historical and descriptive. See S.F. Wise, "Sermon Literature and Canadian Intellectual History," *The Bulletin* (Committee on Archives of the United Church of Canada) 18

(1965): 3–18; and Robert Lochiel Fraser III, "Like Eden in Her Summer Dress: Gentry, Economy, and Society: Upper Canada, 1812–1840" (PhD thesis, University of Toronto, 1979), esp. chs. 1 and 4.

42 AO, Robinson Papers, charge to the grand jury, Kingston, 20 Sept. 1841 as cited in Fraser, "Like Eden in Her Summer Dress," 213. For a stimulating interpretation of Robinson's thought see David Howes, "Property, God and Nature in the Thought of Sir John Beverley Robinson," *McGill Law Journal* 30 (1985): 365–414. Howes approaches Robinson through the Loyalist Covenant (see Duffy's work on Loyalism), and although he is also concerned with culture and myth, he treats conservative thought in the early nineteenth century quite differently from this study.

43 McKillop, *A Disciplined Intelligence*, esp. ch. 3.

44 For a general discussion of the changing structure of sermons see Charles Smyth, *The Art of Preaching: A Practical Survey of Preaching in the Church of England 747–1939* (London: SPCK, 1940). A more detailed discussion of the structure of sermons follows in chs. 3 and 4. Strachan's own copy of *An Account of Sir Isaac Newton's Philosophical Discoveries* by Colin Maclaurin (1775) has recently been acquired for the Strachan Collection at Trinity College through the generosity of the Friends of the Trinity Library.

45 The argument in fact indicates the vulnerability of the Anglican position, for if social order (and other social values) could be achieved by other means, then the reasons for the state to support the church suddenly disappeared. For a more detailed discussion of church and state, see the fourth chapter of this study and *A Charge Delivered to the Clergy of the Diocese of Quebec by George J. Mountain, D.D. Lord Bishop of Montreal at his Primary Visitation, Completed in 1838* (Quebec: Thomas Carey, 1839).

46 AO, *Strachan Letterbook 1827–1834*, Strachan to Archdeacon George Mountain, 31 Dec. 1827.

47 Strachan, *An Appeal to the Friends of Religion and Literature*, 21.

48 Ryerson's response to Strachan's sermon shows that he was quite familiar with a number of Paley's arguments. The two most influential texts on the question of church and state were William Warburton, *The Alliance Between Church and State, or the Necessity and Equity of an Established Religion, and a Test-law, Demonstrated* (1736); and William Paley, *The Principals of Moral and Political Philosophy*, Bk 6, "Elements of Political Knowledge," ch. 10, "Of Religious Establishments and Toleration."

49 Ryerson, "A Review of a Sermon . . . by a Methodist Preacher."

50 *Christian Guardian*, 4 Sept. and 11 Sept. 1830, 330, 337. See also *Journal of the Rev. John Wesley A.M.*, ed., Nehemia Curnock (London, 1909–16); Fred Dreyer, "Faith and Experience in the Thought of John Wesley," *American Historical Review* 88, 1 (Feb. 1983): 12–30. For a stimulating and informative account of revivalism in Nova Scotia see George Rawlyk, *Ravished By the Spirit: Religious Revivals, Baptists, and Henry Alline* (Kingston and Montreal: McGill-Queen's University Press, 1984).

51 "Experimental Religion," *Christian Guardian*, 26 Nov. 1834, 9.

52 For an interesting discussion of the issue of theological training see Gerald O. McCulloh, *Ministerial Education in the American Methodist Movement* (Nashville, TN: United Methodist Board of Higher Education, 1980).

53 "The Great Utility of Camp Meetings in Promoting Revivals of Religion," *Christian Guardian*, 31 Oct. 1832, 201.

54 For example, "Prepare for Camp Meetings," *Christian Guardian*, 21 April 1842; John Carroll, *Past and Present, or a Description of Persons and Events Connected with Canadian Methodism for the Last Forty Years by a Spectator of the Scenes* (Toronto: Alfred Dredge, 1860), 64; and *Christian Guardian*, 23 Sept. 1835, 182; 25 July 1832, 146.

55 For sketches of some contemporary revivalistic sermons see John Carroll, *Father Corson: Or the Old Style Canadian Itinerant: Embracing the Life and the Gospel Labours of the Rev. Robert Corson, Fifty-Six Years a Minister in Connection with the Central Methodism of Upper Canada* (Toronto: Samuel Rose, 1879), 243–77.

56 Arthur E. Kewley, "Mass Evangelism in Upper Canada Before 1830" (DTh thesis, Victoria College, 1960). This two-volume study is an extremely rich compendium of material on revivalism. Any student of revivalism will always be in Dr Kewley's debt, although his desire to show the contemporary value of many features of revivalism leads him in general to interpret revivalism somewhat more conservatively than the present study.

57 For example, *Christian Guardian*, 23 July 1831, 146; 25 July 1832, 146; and 23 Sept. 1835, 132. "Tears are nothing but the juice of a mind pressed and squeezed by grief." George F. Playter, *The History of Methodism in Canada* (Toronto: Anson Green, 1862), 372.

58 See, for example, United Church Archives (hereafter UCA), "Autobiography of Joseph Gatchell, Personal Papers," and "Journals of Rev. George Ferguson, Personal Papers"; Abel Stevens, *Life and Times of Nathan Bangs* (New York, 1863), 28–55; Marguerite Van Die, "Nathanael Burwash and the Conscientious Search for Truth," *Papers of the Canadian Methodist Historical Society* 3 (1983); and Gerald C. Brauer, "Conversion: From Puritanism to Revivalism," *Journal of Religion* 58 (July 1978): 227–43.

59 AO, Strachan Papers, Manuscript sermon preached on Lamentations 3:40, "Let us search and try our ways and

turn again to the Lord," first preached 14 Nov. 1824. This sermon seems to have been lost or misplaced in the recent microfilming of the Strachan sermons.

60 AO, Strachan Papers, Manuscript sermon (85), preached on Matthew 25:39, "Then shall the king say unto them on his right hand, come ye blessed of my Father," first preached 31 March 1830.

61 AO, Strachan Papers, Manuscript sermon (31), preached on Psalm 19:2.

62 For example, SPG Archives, C/Canada/Quebec, folio 368. Rev. C.B. Fleming to G.J. Mountain, 21 March 1844; folio 415, Rev. Edward Cusak to Bishop of Montreal n.d. (c. 1841); C/Canada/Quebec/Upper Canada, folio 508, Copy of Journal of Rev. F.L. Osler, 6 Jan. to 16 April 1841; also Thomas Conant, *Upper Canada Sketches* (Toronto: William Briggs, 1898).

63 "Whosoever is born of God doth not commit sin; for his seed remaineth in him; and he cannot sin, because he is born of God" (I John 3:9). "Does it (the fact that God answers prayer) prove that . . . believers can by prayer obtain the creation, destruction, disorganization, alteration or perpetuation of anything in the material and the immaterial, the natural and the moral worlds?" *Christian Guardian*, 12 Oct. 1836, 193.

64 See Edward Deming Andrews, *The People Called Shakers: A Search for the Perfect Society* (New York: Dome, 1963); and J.F.C. Harrison, *The Second Coming: Popular Millenarianism 1780–1850* (New Brunswick, NJ: Rutgers University Press, 1979).

65 See Whitney R. Cross, *The Burned-over District: The Social and Intellectual History of Enthusiastic Religion in Western New York, 1800–1850* (Ithaca, NY: Cornell University Press, 1950), esp. ch. 8.

66 For material on David Willson see Thomas Gerry, "From the Quakers to the Children of Peace: The Development of David Willson's Mystical Religion," *University of Toronto Quarterly* 54 (Winter 1984–85): 200–16. Where the spirit might lead, and the consequent instability of revivals is a recurrent theme in the commentaries on this form of religious practice. See the third chapter of Westfall, *Two Worlds* and Patrick Sheriff, *A Tour Through North America; Together with a Comprehensive View of the Canadas and United States as Adapted for Agricultural Emigration* (Edinburgh: Oliver and Boyd, 1835).

67 Paul Romney, "A Struggle for Authority: Toronto Society and Politics in 1834" in *Forging a Consensus: Historical Essays on Toronto*, ed. Victor L. Russell (Toronto: University of Toronto Press, 1984), 9–40.

68 AO, Strachan Letterbook, 1812–34, Letter to the Lord Bishop of Quebec, 1 Oct. 1812.

69 SPG Archives, C/Canada/Quebec/Upper Canada, John Strachan to S. Ramsey, 4 Sept. 1840. One doubts if the clergy of our church can do either at the present time.

70 For an excellent discussion of the transformation of Methodism see Neil Semple, "The Impact of Urbanization on the Methodist Church in Central Canada 1854–1884" (PhD thesis, University of Toronto, 1979), and the third chapter of Westfall, *Two Worlds*.

71 S.D. Clark, *Church and Sect in Canada* (Toronto: University of Toronto Press, 1948).

72 For comments on the churching of women see *The Church*, 14 Dec. 1839, 4. In their desire to use the structure of the physical world to predict events, astrology, and almanacs worked within the broad framework of natural theology. In this sense astrology is Paley at a popular level.

73 To follow the migration from church to revival and back to church see SPG Archives, C/Canada/Quebec, folio 367, Rev. John Butler to Rev. C.B.

Dalton; folio 388, Rev. Christopher Jackson to Lord Bishop of Montreal, 10 June 1842. "It is hard to convince them that there is any harm in frequenting a Methodist meeting House, or an assembly of Brownists, Baptists, or even Millenarians. If a strange preacher comes into the neighbourhood, everyone must go to hear what he has to say, and on such occasion no weather will keep them at home." Ibid., folio 422, Rev. John Butler to Rev. C.B. Dalton, 23 Jan. 1843. *The Church* suggested that it would be better for Anglicans to stay at home and read a good book than to attend a Methodist revival.

74 John Strachan, *A Letter to the Congregation of St. James' Church, York,* *Upper Canada; Occasioned by the Hon. John Elmsley's Publication on the Bishop of Strasbourg's Observations on the 6th Chapter of St. John's Gospel* (York, UC: Robert Stanton, c. 1834), 52.

75 Strachan's concern with the spirit is also clear when he attacked deism and those who "consider human reason sufficient for all things." On these occasions he defended the importance of the spirit. See AO, Strachan Papers, Manuscript sermons (39), preached on Ephesians 4:30; and (40), preached on II Corinthians 5:8.

76 "Christian Experience," *Christian Guardian*, 10 April 1839, 93.

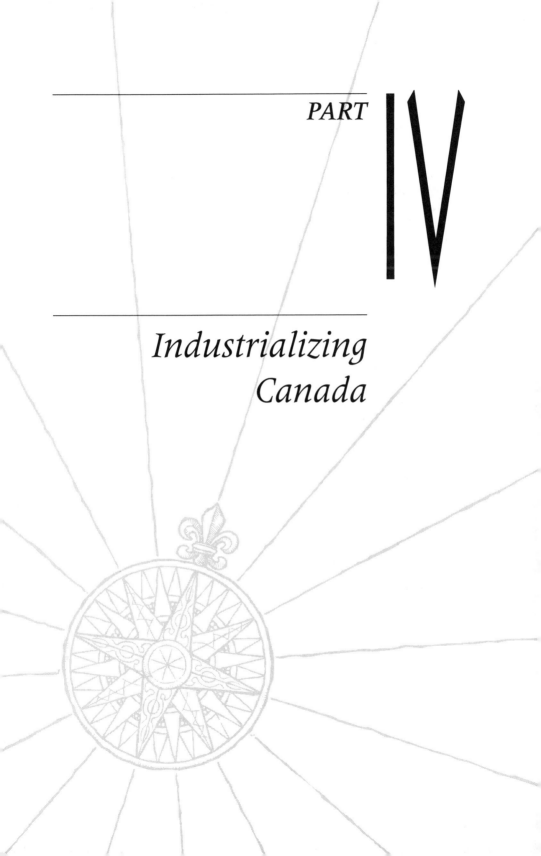

PART IV

Industrializing Canada

It is noteworthy that the title of this final group of articles is "Industrializing Canada." Not too long ago, historians hardly considered Canada to have experienced an industrial revolution; rather, they emphasized the export of unfinished products beginning with furs and continuing with wood, wheat, minerals, and fossil fuels.

In contrast, recent research has shown that the major processes of industrialization transformed Canada much as they did other Western countries in the nineteenth century. Moreover, scholars such as Serge Courville, Jean-Claude Robert, and Normand Séguin have revealed the importance of rural and small town industry well before the construction of large urban factories. In the first article of this section, these scholars trace changes in the economic landscape of the St Lawrence valley by comparing evidence from the 1831 and 1851 census enumerations. Their approach reflects the interdisciplinary character of their collaboration; Courville is a geographer, while Robert and Séguin are historians. Thus, this study explores the spatial distribution of rural industry, and it shows the ways in which certain industries increasingly became associated with specific areas of the valley. The collaboration of these scholars is also noteworthy as an example of a recent trend toward team research and co-authorship. Although most historians still work individually (unlike chemists or biologists, for example), a growing number are now joining together to form major research projects often involving more than one university. In this case, the three collaborators are strategically located along the "axis" they are studying; Courville in Quebec City, Séguin in Trois-Rivières, and Robert in Montreal.

My own recent research has been devoted to achieving a better understanding of the interplay among demographic, economic, and educational history. This approach responds to the criticism that historians have become too specialized in their own research areas; in other words, that the emergence of subfields of sociohistorical research (such as those devoted to studying population patterns or economic change) has fragmented our understanding of the past. To the contrary, the following article shows how the findings of different research subfields can be drawn together to produce a richer interpretation that better reflects the actual complexity of historical change. Like the preceding study of Quebec, this article also emphasizes the often forgotten fact that even Ontario was a predominantly rural society throughout the decades when "modern" institutions such as schooling were established.

Although an increasing proportion of historians have chosen in recent years to study social, economic, and cultural change in order to interpret Canada's past, new research has also been undertaken on the major events of our history including Confederation. Phillip Buckner's reassessment of Canada's formal founding takes the perspective of the Maritime provinces. Like other scholars represented in this book, Buckner reveals the importance to interpretation of the ways in which research questions are posed. Rather than asking why so many Maritimers opposed Confederation, he wonders why so many others agreed to a "scheme of union" clearly designed to help those in the future provinces of Ontario and Quebec. From this point of view, the challenge is not to explain Maritime "conservatism" or "parochialism" but rather the fact that most Maritimers eventually supported Confederation.

For his part, Brian Young has contributed to a better understanding of the founding of Canada by probing behind the speeches and public actions of a key "Father of Confederation," George-Etienne Cartier. Young employs research strategies developed to study whole communities (such as in Michael Katz's study of Hamilton) in order to study one individual. Rather than simply focussing on what Cartier said or wrote, Young reconstructs what Cartier did. He examines sources such as Cartier's account books, his legal documents, and the inventory of his estate. The resulting portrayal is multidimensional; we learn about Cartier in business, in society, and at home.

The following articles thus illustrate some of the innovative ways in which different questions and research strategies have led to new interpretations of the years leading to the "invention" of Canada in 1867. Rather than simply being the result of political debate among a small group of politicians, Confederation can be situated within a rapidly changing and diverse context involving complex relationships among individuals, institutions, and regions.

THE SPREAD OF RURAL INDUSTRY IN LOWER CANADA, 1831–1851*

SERGE COURVILLE,
JEAN-CLAUDE ROBERT,
AND NORMAND SÉGUIN

This paper is a product of an ongoing research project on the socioeconomy of central Quebec between 1815 and 1880. This area, which is referred to as the St Lawrence axis, consists of the territory directly dominated by the cities of Montreal and Quebec and corresponds roughly to the old seigneurial zone on each side of the river between the areas immediately upstream from Montreal on the west and a line drawn from Matane to the Saguenay River to the east. The general objective of this project is to re-examine the components of the socioeconomy of the area and the changes which took place during the nineteenth century. Our general approach can be characterized as a historical geography of exchanges. It is clear that, with a better knowledge of the basic infrastructures of that particular area and of the material basis of its system of production, historians

*From the *Journal of the Canadian Historical Association* (1991). Reprinted with permission of the publisher and the authors. We wish to acknowledge financial support received from the Social Sciences and Humanities Research Council of Canada, the Fonds FCAR, Université Laval, Université du Quebec à Montreal, and Université du Quebec à Trois-Rivières. We also wish to thank Philippe Désaulniers, who was responsible for handling the data and for the computerized mapping; Claude Bellevance, who designed the unit data entry forms and supervised the data entry from the 1851 manuscript census; and, finally, Jocelyn Morneau and France Normand, who did data entry and validation for 1851.

will gain a wider and deeper perception of the diversity and the various articulations in time and space within the St Lawrence axis, its coherences and its complementarities.

Another objective is to show the importance of the internal dynamics in the overall process of change within the socioeconomy of Lower Canada. At the same time, however, the effects of external factors in its structuring and restructuring have not been discounted. In fact, these external factors were also determinant, sometimes to a dominating degree. On this point, we are trying to arrive at a more balanced picture of economic development, to move beyond a simplistic vision, and to show the relative complexity of the socioeconomy.[1]

For the last few years, our work has turned to the study of rural and urban industries. This paper will focus on rural industries alone. Our main hypothesis is that rural industries played a major role in the transformation of both the rural space and the whole of the Lower-Canadian socioeconomy. As a matter of fact, early in the nineteenth century, they were instrumental in the diversification of the rural world and the reorientation of town and country relations. In a more general way, their effect was important in widening and deepening the relations to market in the whole of Lower Canada. It is crucial, however, not to minimize the impact of urbanization and the role of the city in the larger process of industrialization that would gain momentum and radically transform the socioeconomy at a later stage. These phenomena must, however, be examined at different levels, from the rural parish and village to urban areas, to the St Lawrence axis, to the whole of Lower Canada, and beyond. While we do not posit a direct and necessary relationship between the rise of rural industries and the large-scale industrialization which would transform the Quebec economy at the end of the nineteenth century, the former period represents, in our opinion, an essential element in the development of an integrated market economy.[2]

We will not attempt here to present a global analysis of the role of rural industries in the development of Lower Canada, for too many elements are still missing. At this point, we intend only to provide an overview of the phenomenon. This paper is therefore divided into four parts. The first defines the limits of the notion of "rural industries" as used in this paper. The second employs a combination of text and a series of maps to sketch the relationships in the location of mills and factories in the rural parts of the St Lawrence axis at two points, 1831 and 1851, on the basis of census information.[3] The third part of the paper is founded on the analysis of individual schedules of the 1851 census which, in spite of their flaws, present a much more detailed picture of the spatial distribution of rural industries at mid-century. The final section focusses on the largest industrial establishments in terms of workforce in 1851 and shows that there was already a hierarchy within the pattern of rural industries in Lower Canada.

• Some Definitions

Our first step is to define what the concept of "rural industries" encompasses. In a paper presented in 1985, René Hardy, Pierre Lanthier, and Normand Séguin attempted just such a definition.[4] They used this expression to designate nonagricultural production found in rural areas. This expression encompasses organizations with the following characteristics: they rely on paid labour either seasonally or year-round, and they need capital investments to start and maintain production, enter markets, and survive.

The size of these organizations varies according to their relationship to the marketplace: one could serve only the local market or be linked to a much wider geographical area. This definition is useful for two reasons: it is consistent with the hypothesis of the intensification of market-related activities within the rural world, and it addresses explicitly the question of the capitalist basis of nonagricultural production. Thus, there is a distinction to be made between these and the purely artisanal production usually found on the farm or within a residence. While this somewhat restrictive definition of a rural industry is admittedly useful in analysing both the integration of organizations and the marketplace and the development of rural entrepreneurship, it is too limiting for our purposes because it excludes from consideration an intermediate zone of economic activity between artisanal and industrial production. For this reason, we prefer to use a somewhat wider definition of rural industries that includes under this rubric some elements of artisanal production.

While we seek to understand the capitalistic dynamics within the rural world, we also wish to present a broad conceptualization of the basis of nonagricultural production in the rural world. For this reason, the absence of wage labour did not automatically eliminate an enterprise from being included in our database. We considered all nonagricultural units of production as long as they were spatially distinct from the farm. Thus, a blacksmith shop or a grist mill that employed only a single person would be included. To sum up, we exclude only the nonagricultural production of farms in our picture of rural industries.

The purpose of this paper is to take stock of the different units of production and chart their spatial distribution within the St Lawrence axis.[5] To achieve this goal, we employed two different notions: the establishment itself (such as a distinct building), and the unit of production (such as a saw mill or a flour mill in the same building; in French, this is referred to as an *équipement*).[6] These two notions, the establishment and the unit of production, enable us to understand the principles of the material organization of the units of production.

The establishment corresponds to a precise locale, established to produce something. For us, it is a physical space, a building or a part of one. A single enterprise can operate more than one establishment (though we did not integrate this information in our general picture of rural industries). The unit of production, on the other hand, is a technical arrangement of tools used to make a certain product in a precise location. Thus the unit of production is fixed, has a certain locational permanence, and is housed within an establishment. For example, a threshing machine, owned by a certain farmer and moved from farm to farm, is not considered to be a unit of production. We did, however, take into consideration the existence of various stages of development in defining a unit of production. At one end of the scale, it need not be a sophisticated piece of machinery; it could be fairly simple and be made up of tools and instruments without a mechanical link. It is the worker who integrates the various units and brings his skills and energy to bear. This is the case for many artisanal operations, such as those carried out by shoemakers or blacksmiths. At the other end of the scale, the equipment is more sophisticated; here we are talking about a machine using a nonhuman source of energy. This is the case for hydraulic or steam mills. Frequently there is a concentration of units of production in a single establishment. For the purposes of this paper, we considered each separate production function as a distinct unit of production. A grist mill, a saw mill, a carding mill, and a fulling mill—each is analysed separately even if all were located in a single building. In this paper, we are therefore analysing only individual and distinct processes. Our computerized database does, however, enable us eventually to analyse these diverse but interconnected units found in the census in relationship to the various establishments.

• Rural Industries in 1831 and 1851: An Overview from the Aggregate Census Data

In his recent book on the development of villages, Serge Courville examined the overall growth of rural industries in the entire seigneurial territory of Lower Canada and proposed a preliminary portrait.[7] Using data provided by Joseph Bouchette,[8] Courville found 607 mills and factories in 1815. For 1831, he made some estimates for six industrial processes: grist mills, saw mills, fulling and carding mills, foundries, distilleries, and pot and pearl ash factories.[9] For 1831, Courville calculated a total of 1349 units of production for these six sectors. He estimated the total number in 1851 at 1277.[10] These figures indicate an important growth in the number of units of production between 1815 and 1831, the number more than doubling. Between 1831 and 1851, however, he has found a slight drop of seventy-five units. This decline, Courville notes, might be exaggerated because of a specific problem with the statistics for pot and pearl ash factories. These were not reported in the published version of the 1851 census. Courville attempted to overcome this gap by utilizing the relevant data scattered throughout the "remarks" section of the individual schedules. The figure of 1277 units of production for villages in 1851 must be regarded as a minimum. In any case, he did his compilation of data only for the villages within the seigneurial area. Any pot and pearl ash factory outside those villages was not included.

A second problem arises from the number of missing or incomplete schedules in the 1851 census. Because of these lacunae, it will always be difficult to determine the change in the number of pot and pearl ash factories between 1831 and 1851. None the less, there seems to be a clear reduction in numbers because we have found references to fewer than seventy for the entire St Lawrence axis in the surviving schedules. This figure seems to suggest that this industry not only did not grow in numbers but significantly declined after 1831 in the seigneurial area. Indeed, if we remove the number of pot and pearl ash factories from the total number of units of production, there is a decrease within the seigneurial area after 1831. In that year, 1072 units of production were recorded (1302 less 230 pot and pearl ash factories) and, for the same five categories, 1053 in 1851. Very clearly, then, we have a decrease of nineteen operating units. If we compare this with the population growth for the same area, the question of decline in the number of rural industries in the St Lawrence axis after 1831 becomes a real one that must be addressed.

Tables 1 and 2 provide a picture of rural industries by district in 1831 and 1851, using the six categories of units of production listed earlier. In 1831, the distribution of these units was roughly the same for the two larger districts of Quebec (roughly 45 percent) and Montreal (just under 42 percent), the cities included. Trois-Rivières, much less populated, had a little less than 13 percent of the total operating units within the axis. By 1851, however, the distribution had changed. Though the Quebec and Trois-Rivières districts maintained their numbers of units, the Montreal district showed a marked decrease, from 591 to 347 in just twenty years. It is here that virtually all the decrease took place.

If we turn to the issue of the type of industrial process involved, four categories dominate the 1831 figures. The 592 saw mills represent half of all units and constitute roughly 80 percent of the saw mills in Lower Canada. This percentage is comparable to the proportion of the Lower Canadian population living in the St Lawrence axis, 87 percent.[11] Grist mills follow, with 298 units representing nearly 76 percent of the Lower Canadian total. Then we have the 230 pot and pearl ash factories, which account for only 45 percent of the total, and 149 fulling and carding mills, a little more than 78 percent of the total of this type. The last two categories were not very numerous: the twenty-one distilleries represent 45 percent of the total in Lower Canada, the twelve foundries 67 percent. These two categories were concentrated in towns—six of twenty-one distilleries

Table 1: DISTRIBUTION OF UNITS OF PRODUCTION, 1831

	Number of Grist Mills	Number of Saw Mills	Number of Fulling/ Carding Mills	Number of Foun-dries	Number of Distil-leries	Number of Pot and Pearl Ash Factories	Total
Montreal District							
Montreal Islands							
City of Montreal	6	0	0	4	2	0	12
Island of Montreal	8	1	3	0	1	2	15
Île Jésus	2	4	4	0	2	0	12
Île Bizard	1	0	0	0	0	0	1
Île Perrot	0	0	0	0	0	1	1
Peninsula (Vaudreuil)	6	3	2	0	0	29	40
North Shore	40	50	19	0	4	67	180
South Shore	98	73	31	5	6	117	330
Total	161	131	59	9	15	216	591
Total Without City	155	131	59	5	13	216	579
Trois-Rivières District							
City of Trois-Rivières*	4	4	1	1	2	0	12
North Shore	16	53	11	0	0	5	85
South Shore	21	35	12	0	0	4	72
Total	41	92	24	1	2	9	169
Total Without City	37	88	23	0	0	9	157
Quebec District							
City of Quebec*	0	1	0	2	2	0	5
Île d'Orléans	7	14	4	0	0	0	25
Île aux Coudres	2	1	0	0	0	0	3
Île aux Grues et aux Oies	1	0	1	0	0	0	2
Other Islands	0	0	0	0	0	0	0
North Shore	31	108	21	0	0	2	162
South Shore	55	245	40	0	2	3	345
Total	96	369	66	2	4	5	542
Total Without City	96	368	66	0	2	5	537
Total, St Lawrence Axis	298	592	149	12	21	230	1302
Percentage of Lower Canada	76	77	78	67	36	45	67
Total Without Cities	288	587	148	5	15	230	1273

*City and suburbs.

Source: "Census of 1831," *Journals of the Legislative Assembly of Lower Canada* (1832), appendix OO.

Table 2: DISTRIBUTION OF UNITS OF PRODUCTION, 1851

	Number of Grist Mills	Number of Saw Mills	Number of Fulling/ Carding Mills	Number of Foun- dries	Number of Distil- leries	Number of Pot and Pearl Ash Factories	Total
Montreal District							
Montreal Islands							
City of Montreal	2	0	0	7	2	**	11
Island of Montreal	6	1	2	0	0	**	9
Île Jésus	2	1	2	0	0	**	5
Île Bizard	1	0	0	0	0	**	1
Île Perrot	1	0	0	0	0	**	1
Peninsula (Vaudreuil)	2	2	2	0	0	**	6
North Shore	55	64	21	5	1	**	146
South Shore	74	65	21	7	1	**	168
Total	143	133	48	19	4	**	347
Total Without City	141	133	48	12	2	**	336
Trois-Rivières District							
City of Trois-Rivières*	4	0	1	2	0	**	7
North Shore	19	47	12	0	9	**	78
South Shore	29	28	10	0	0	**	67
Total	52	75	23	2	0	**	152
Total Without City		75	22	0	0	**	145
Quebec District							
City of Quebec*	0	0	0	3	0	**	3
Île d'Orléans	9	22	5	0	0	**	36
Île aux Coudres	2	0	0	0	0	**	2
Île aux Grues et aux Oies	2	0	0	0	0	**	2
Other Islands	0	0	0	0	0	**	0
North Shore	39	88	27	0	0	**	152
South Shore	75	229	50	3	0	**	357
Total	127	339	82	6	0	**	554
Total Without City	127	339	82	3	0	**	551
Total, St Lawrence Axis	332	547	153	27	4	**	1053
Percentage of Lower Canada	60	51	79	71	57		57
Total Without Cities	316	547	152	15	2	**	1032

*City and suburbs.

**Included in the "Remarks"; impossible to give precise locations.

Source: *Census of the Canadas, 1851–52* (Montreal, 1853).

and seven of twelve foundries were located there. Conversely, there were no pot and pearl ash factories in urban centres and the census found only one fulling and carding mill, five saw mills (four of which were located in Trois-Rivières), and ten grist mills (four in Trois-Rivières and six in Montreal).[12]

In 1851, the population of the St Lawrence axis represented 80 percent of the Lower Canadian total, a relative decline of seven percentage points from the 1831 figures. This change reflected the numerical growth and geographical expansion of settlement and, possibly, the shift of some production away from the St Lawrence axis. In our review of the 1851 census material, we employed only five categories, and they appear roughly in the same order as in 1831, the only difference being that foundries became more numerous than distilleries. A closer examination, however, reveals some important changes. The number of saw mills went from 592 to 547 and their share of the Lower Canadian total of this type of industrial activity declined from 80 to 51 percent. Grist mills increased from 298 to 322, but their proportion decreased from 70 to 60 percent. Fulling and carding mills remained stable both in terms of numbers (a gain of four) and proportion of the total (an increase of one percentage point). The number of foundries more than doubled, from twelve to twenty-seven, and their proportion of the total increased from 67 to 71 percent. Distilleries decreased from twenty-one to four, but their proportion increased from 45 to 57 percent. In 1851, no saw mills, only six grist mills, and one fulling and carding mill were found in cities, but urban areas continued to maintain an advantage in foundries and distilleries: twelve of twenty-seven foundries and two of four distilleries.

Let us now examine the spatial distribution of units of production. In 1831, the Montreal district, with almost 56 percent of the population of the St Lawrence axis, had almost all of the pot and pearl ash factories. Secondly, there was a relative scarcity of saw mills there; though this was the most widespread form of production in the axis, the Montreal district contained not even a quarter of the total. Grist mills, on the other hand, were in the same proportion as their share of the population. The district, on the other hand, did show a concentration of foundries (nine of twelve) and distilleries (fifteen of twenty-one).

The Quebec district represented 33 percent of the population of the axis. There was a marked concentration of saw mills (62 percent of the total number in the axis) and, to a lesser degree, fulling and carding mills (44 percent of the total). The Trois-Rivières district, with 10 percent of the population of the axis, had more than 15 percent of the saw mills and 16 percent of the fulling and carding mills. The other categories were not well represented; indeed, their presence was nearly negligible. As for the division between the north and south shores of the St Lawrence, the distribution of industries varied from district to district. The south shore dominated in two districts, with 56 percent of all units in the Montreal

Table 3: **POPULATION OF THE ST LAWRENCE AXIS**

	1784	1831	1844	1851–52
Montreal District				
Montreal Islands				
City of Montreal	6 479	27 297	44 093	57 715
Island of Montreal and Île Jésus	10 745	26 029	27 657	31 610
Other islands	332	883	980	1 084
Peninsula (Vaudreuil)	1 811	13 984	15 813	20 050
North Shore	13 953	63 936	79 261	92 598
South Shore	22 159	116 937	150 774	185 871
Indian Missions	165	1 664	1 787	2 296
Total	55 644	250 730	320 365	391 224
Trois-Rivières District				
City of Trois-Rivières	810	3 972	3 297	5 038
North Shore	6 880	19 910	27 696	35 551
South Shore	4 938	21 873	25 905	34 013
Indian Missions				
Total	12 628	45 755	56 898	74 838
Quebec District				
City of Quebec	6 492	26 256	32 876	43 882
Île d'Orléans	2 210	4 349	4 177	6 151
Other Islands	645	952	1 208	1 341
North Shore	11 798	33 165	42 887	53 566
South Shore	23 401	84 236	111 753	136 258
Indian Missions	103		199	218
Total	44 649	148 958	193 100	214 416
Total, St Lawrence Axis	112 921	445 443	570 363	707 478
Total Population, Lower Canada**	112 921	511 917	697 084	890 261

*Figures for 1831 are for the Parish of Trois-Rivières.

**Recalculated from published census figures.

Source: For 1784, British Library, Add. Mss. 21885; for 1831, *Journals of the Legislative Assembly of Lower Canada* (1832), appendix OO; for 1844, *Extrait des retours. . .* (1846); for 1851, *Census of the Canadas, 1851–1852.*

district and over 63 percent in the Quebec district. It was less than 43 percent in the Trois-Rivières district.

Though the proportion of population in each district remained reasonably stable in 1851, there were some changes in the distribution of the five categories of units of production. At mid-century, the Montreal district had a lower proportion of grist mills (44 percent) than its population (55 percent). Saw mills were still about a quarter of the total, and fulling and carding mills constituted 31 percent. The concentration of foundries and distilleries had intensified: 70 percent of the former and all of the latter were located there. The situation in the Trois-Rivières district had not changed very much: its proportion of grist mills went from about 14 to 16 percent; its proportion of the saw mills in the axis remained stable at between 14 and 15 percent; and fulling and carding mills decreased slightly from 16 to 15 percent of the total. This district's share of producing units was, however, always greater than that of its population. The Quebec district's share of the axis grist mills went from 32 to more than 39 percent, more than its proportion of population (34 percent). The proportion of saw mills remained unchanged at 62 percent, while that of fulling and carding mills increased from 44 to 53 percent.

This first set of maps (figures 1 to 6) illustrates the level of concentration of some of the categories of units of production for 1831 and 1851. Three categories were chosen for illustrative purposes: grist mills, saw mills, and fulling and carding mills. Each map is based on the ratio of the number of units of production in a given area to the total for that industrial process for the entire St Lawrence axis. We used five levels of concentration to analyse differences between various spatial units.

The 1831 grist mill map (figure 1) shows that they were more common in the southern part of the axis and more concentrated in the triangle south of Lake St Peter between the St Lawrence and Richelieu rivers. In 1851 (figure 2), grist mills were still important in the southern sector, but were locationally less concentrated. Figure 2 also shows the progressive expansion of that type of production unit in the northern part, especially in the Quebec region. Saw mills, while showing some local variations, were concentrated in the northern sector in both 1831 and 1851, more so in the Quebec area (figures 3 and 4). As for fulling and carding mills, the 1831 and 1851 maps (figures 5 and 6) indicate a shift from the southern part of the axis to the north and, once again, a concentration in the Quebec area.

To conclude this overview of the leading features of the distribution of the six categories of units of production, some general remarks can be made. First of all, while some units (such as foundries and distilleries) were concentrated in cities, especially Montreal, there was a general movement of rural industries toward the northeastern portion of the St Lawrence axis. This was due primarily to a decrease in the number of units in the Montreal district. Moreover, with this shift came a reduction in the proportional weight of the axis' units of production as compared with the whole of Lower Canada. Should this be interpreted as a decrease in rural industries in the southern area and a relative slowdown of growth for the St Lawrence axis within the province? Is it, in other words, a case of deindustrialization?

We do not think so. First of all, our six categories of units of production can give only a partial view of the structure of rural industries, more so in 1851 than in 1831. Secondly, the *number* of producing units alone remains too crude an indicator. Numbers alone do not describe the totality

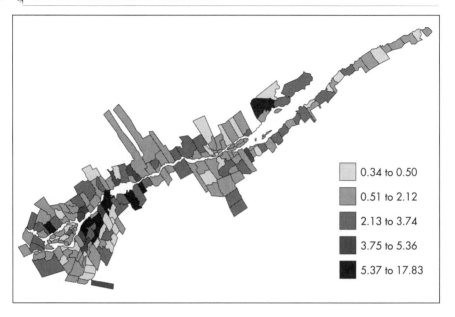

FIGURE 1 *Distribution of Grist Mills, 1831 (percentage of the St Lawrence axis)*

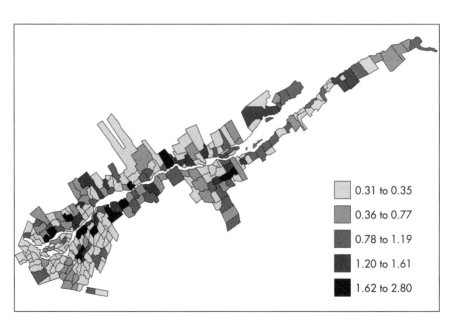

FIGURE 2 *Distribution of Grist Mills, 1851 (percentage of the St Lawrence axis)*

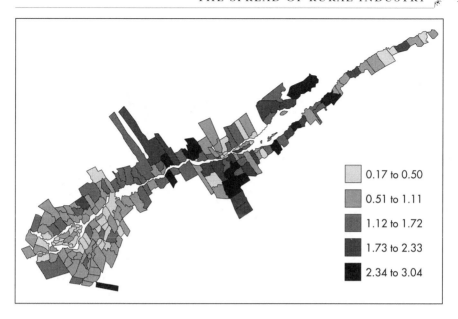

FIGURE 3 *Distribution of Saw Mills, 1831 (percentage of the St Lawrence axis)*

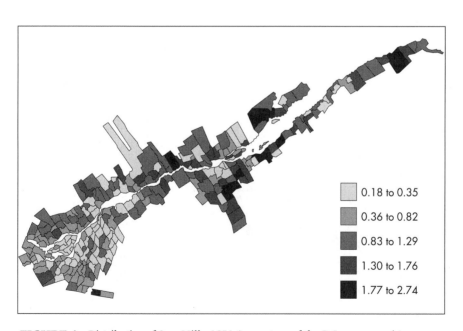

FIGURE 4 *Distribution of Saw Mills, 1851 (percentage of the St Lawrence axis)*

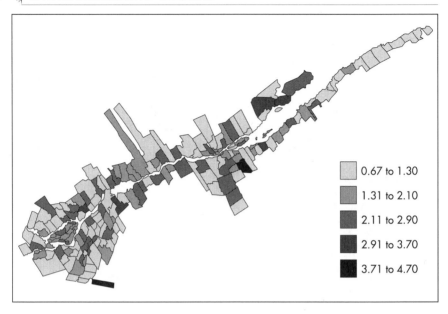

FIGURE 5 *Distribution of Fulling and Carding Mills, 1831 (percentage of the St Lawrence axis)*

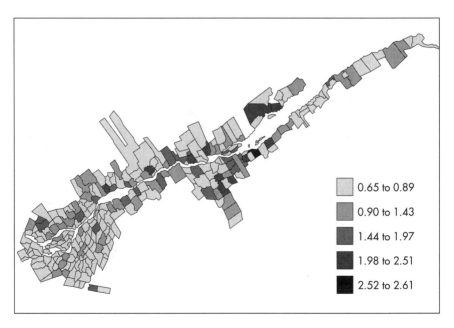

FIGURE 6 *Distribution of Fulling and Carding Mills, 1851 (percentage of the St Lawrence axis)*

of industrial expansion. For that reason, other indicators, such as the size of the labour force, the volume and value of goods produced, and the overall scale of the operation, must be taken into account. We believe that, during this period, significant change occurred in the structure of the industrial economy. The scale of operations increased while, at the same time, new units of production emerged and old ones faded away, thereby affecting patterns of growth in some particular areas or villages. In fact, there is a process of differentiation of growth in each of the three districts. All of this is confirmed by the more detailed examination of rural industries afforded by the individual schedules of the 1851 census.

• Rural Industries in 1851: A Detailed Analysis

Using our distinction between establishments and units of production, we systematically recorded all mentions of the latter from the individual 1851 census schedules.[13] Table 4 summarizes our findings of 3456 units, of which 2926 were located in rural areas. While these figures are certainly underestimated because of known gaps in the sources, they are still three times greater than the units listed in the published aggregate census of 1851.[14] An analysis of these units of production shows a very different picture, both in terms of structure and of spatial distribution between the northern and southern parts of the St Lawrence axis.

In this instance, the units were classified into ten categories: wood products, leather products, iron and metals, food products, clothing, textiles, transportation equipment, nonmetallic minerals, chemical products, and a miscellaneous group which included construction and manufacturing equipment.

Our analysis will concentrate mainly on the 2926 units found in rural areas. First, in order of numerical importance, came wood products with 910 units; iron and metals followed with 779, then leather products with 389, food products with 323, textiles with 215, and transportation equipment with 113. Less numerous were the 75 units in the miscellaneous category, then chemical products, with 70, clothing with 34, and lastly nonmetallic minerals with only 18.

If we now look to the spatial distribution in terms of districts, half of all the units of production in the St Lawrence axis were located in the Montreal district, which accounted for slightly more than 55 percent of the rural population within the axis. Roughly 37 percent of the units were in the Quebec district, which included 33 percent of the rural population, and 14 percent in the Trois-Rivières district, with a little less than 12 percent of the population. If we take into account the fact that missing schedules covered the south part of the Montreal district particularly, the importance of this area stands out sharply. It had, at the very least, a number of units proportionate to its share of the population.

Table 4: UNITS OF PRODUCTION IN 1851, FROM THE INDIVIDUAL SCHEDULES

	Wood Products	Leather products	Iron and Metal Products	Food Products	Clothing	Textiles	Transportation Equipment	Nonmetallic Minerals	Chemical Products	Miscellaneous, incl. Construction and Manufacturing Equipment	Total
Montreal District											
Montreal Islands											
City of Montreal	5	4	2	3	0	0	4	0	0	16	34
Island of Montreal	5	21	13	12	0	4	2	0	1	5	63
Île Jésus	5	2	3	1	0	2	3	0	0	0	16
Île Bizard	1	0	2	1	0	0	0	0	0	1	5
Île Perrot	0	0	0	1	0	0	0	1	0	0	1
Peninsula (Vaudreuil)	27	19	22	8	4	3	1	1	7	4	96
North Shore	147	68	141	61	5	34	7	2	39	5	509
South Shore	208	130	225	65	22	28	38	4	7	36	763
Total	398	244	408	152	31	71	55	7	54	67	1487
Total Without City	393	240	406	149	31	71	51	7	54	51	1453
Trois-Rivières District											
City of Trois-Rivières*	8	10	9	8	1	1	2	0	0	6	45
North Shore	102	52	49	30	3	26	4	2	2	2	272
South Shore	41	17	35	16	0	13	3	0	3	0	128
Total	151	79	93	54	4	40	9	2	5	8	445
Total Without City	143	69	84	46	3	39	7	2	5	2	400

Table 4 (continued)

	Wood Products	Leather products	Iron and Metal Products	Food Products	Clothing	Textiles	Transportation Equipment	Nonmetallic Minerals	Chemical Products	Miscellaneous, incl. Construction and Manufacturing Equipment	Total
Quebec District											
City of Quebec*	96	105	61	62	24	1	27	4	1	70	451
Île d'Orléans	13	2	13	4	0	4	18	0	0	0	54
Île aux Coudres	0	0	2	2	0	0	0	0	0	0	4
Île aux Grues et aux Oies	0	0	0	2	0	0	0	0	0	0	2
Other Islands	0	0	0	0	0	0	0	0	0	0	0
North Shore	84	16	60	37	0	23	9	1	1	6	237
South Shore	277	62	214	83	0	78	28	8	10	16	776
Total	470	185	350	190	24	106	82	13	12	92	1524
Total Without City	374	80	289	128	0	105	55	9	11	22	1073
Total, St Lawrence Axis	1019	508	851	396	59	217	146	22	71	167	3456
Total Without Cities	910	389	779	323	34	215	113	18	70	75	2926

*City and suburbs.

Source: Manuscript Census, 1851.

This finding, based on the surviving individual schedules, contradicts the earlier impressions of sluggish growth, or of a decline in the number of rural industries in the Montreal district, or even of deindustrialization. This stems from the fact that aggregate census data contain only certain categories of units of production.

Spatial distribution among the three districts shows some important features. In the Montreal district, the north shore was the location of 35 percent of the district's units, while its share of the population was only 28 percent. The south shore, with more than 55 percent of the population, had more than 52 percent of the units. This latter figure, we must re-emphasize, is a minimum because it is for this area that individual schedules are often missing. Had we been able to include data from schedules for all of the south shore, we clearly would have found a marked concentration of units of production there. No such gaps exist in the data for the Quebec district. Here, the north shore had 27 percent of the district's population but only 22 percent of the units, while the south shore, with roughly 69 percent of the population, had more than 72 percent of units. This is the reverse of the situation found in the Trois-Rivières district, where each shore had approximately the same population, but the north had 68 percent of the units of production and the south the rest. This discrepancy is striking. Even if we take into account that there are some gaps in the data, the difference between the two shores is too great not to be seen as evidence of a distinct imbalance in the distribution of rural industries. As a matter of fact, in the same area in 1831, the villages showed the strongest growth in terms of rural industrial growth, taking their smaller size into consideration.

If we consider the whole of the St Lawrence axis, we find a clear pattern of distribution both in terms of population and the location of rural industries. The south shore of the Montreal and Quebec districts and the north shore of the Trois-Rivières district stand out as areas where rural industries were concentrated. Moreover, they also seem to be more diversified than in other areas. In further works, we intend to explore this diversification but, for the moment, we can only delineate the pattern by analysing the distribution of our ten categories when compared to the proportion of population in each district.

The north shore of the Montreal district had an overrepresentation in food products, textiles, and chemical products. Leather products were not very important; nor were clothing, transportation, and the miscellaneous category. The distribution in the south shore was almost the reverse: this area was underrepresented in food products and textiles and overrepresented in clothing, transportation equipment, and the miscellaneous category. Clearly this illustrates the complementarity between rural units of production on both sides of the river in the Montreal district. This complementarity is also evident when the rural parts of Montreal island and Île

Jésus are considered. The south shore of the Quebec district, which had three times the number of rural industries as were located on the north shore, was underrepresented in food products and transportation equipment and unrepresented in the clothing category. This last activity was concentrated in the Quebec area. The south shore was, however, overrepresented in nonmetallic minerals, chemical products, and the miscellaneous category. The north shore had no specialization, with the possible exception of food products. Its underrepresentations are notable: there were no production units in clothing and a low representation in transportation equipment, nonmetallic minerals, chemical products, and the miscellaneous category. Île d'Orléans seems to stand apart from this generalization, however: in relation to its share of population, it had a good representation in wood products, nonmetallic minerals, and transportation equipment. Notwithstanding this anomaly, relatively small numbers of rural industries were located in the north shore of the Quebec district, and this shows, in turn, in the overall standing of the district. One qualification must, however, be made: in the immediate area around the city of Quebec, rural industries were better developed.

Figures 7 to 16 allow a clearer representation of the level of concentration and specialization for every category of rural industry in the St Lawrence axis in 1851. We used a composite index which takes into account the strength of a given sector in a census subdivision in relation to its position in the entire St Lawrence axis.[15] For example, three clothing shops out of ten units in a given locale represent 30 percent (N_i). On the other hand, we also calculated the proportion of units in each category in relation to the total number of units in the entire axis. In this instance, three clothing shops of 59 in the axis equals 5 percent (N_j). This ratio was computed according to the formula in note 15. The mapping of this index, using five different levels of specialization, provides an informative picture of the spatial distribution of our ten categories of units in 1851.

Let us start with the category of wood products (figure 7). Specialization was greater around Quebec, but the difference between the north and south shores was less marked than for saw milling (figure 4). This indicates that, though saw milling was rather concentrated in the northern part of the St Lawrence axis, wood working was more evenly distributed. Leather production (figure 8) was concentrated in the south, while iron and metal production (figure 9) had a more balanced distribution. Food products (figure 10) were clustered around the two largest urban centres. Clothing and textiles (figures 11 and 12 respectively) showed some clear contrast in their distribution to the pattern for saw milling and wood products: textile production was quite strong around Quebec, but clothing production was concentrated in the southern part of the axis. Nonmetallic minerals and chemicals (figures 14 and 15) were more important on the outer fringes of the St Lawrence axis. Finally, the

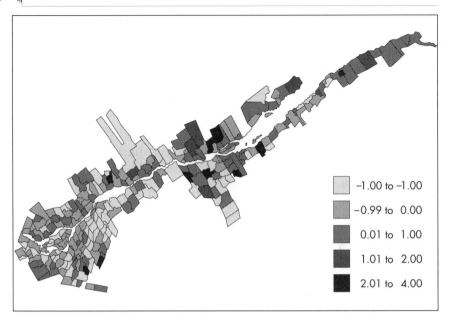

FIGURE 7 *Local Specialization: Wood Products, 1851 (local percentage compared to the percentage of the St Lawrence axis)*

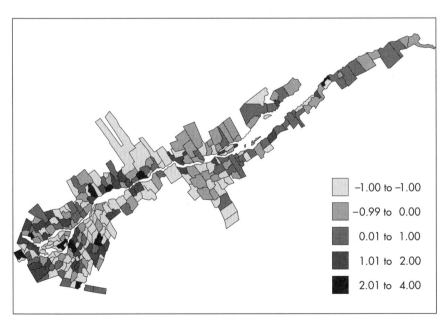

FIGURE 8 *Local Specialization: Leather Products, 1851 (local percentage compared to percentage of the St Lawrence axis)*

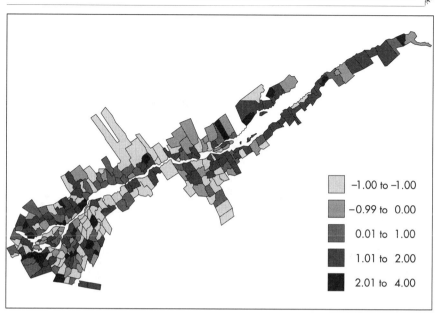

FIGURE 9 *Local Specialization: Iron and Metals, 1851 (local percentage compared to the percentage of the St Lawrence axis)*

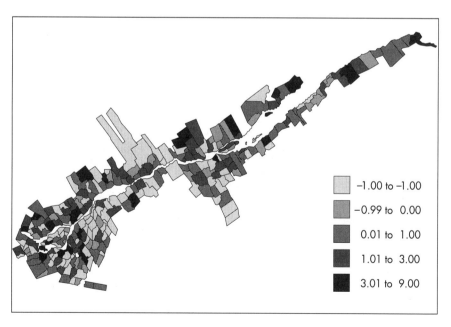

FIGURE 10 *Local Specialization: Food Products, 1851 (local percentage compared to the percentage of the St Lawrence axis)*

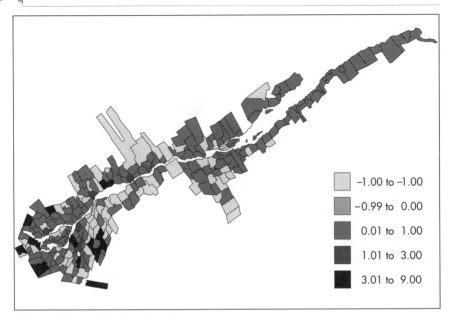

FIGURE 11 *Local Specialization: Clothing, 1851 (local percentage compared to the percentage of the St Lawrence axis)*

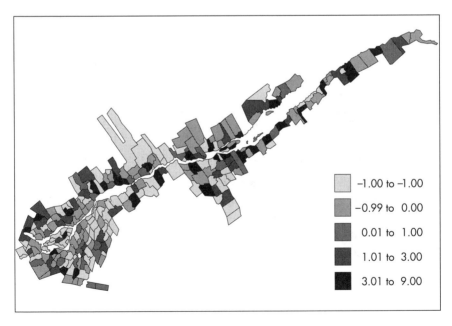

FIGURE 12 *Local Specialization: Textiles, 1851 (local percentage compared to the percentage of the St Lawrence axis)*

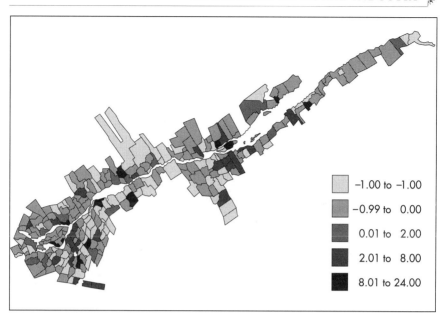

FIGURE 13   *Local Specialization: Transportation Equipment, 1851 (local percentage compared to the percentage of the St Lawrence axis)*

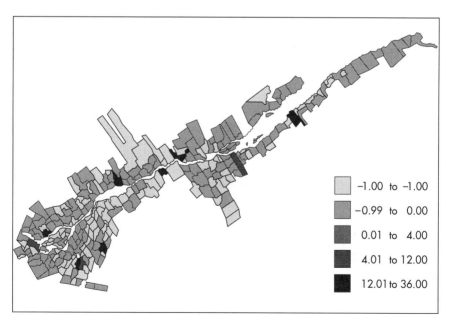

FIGURE 14   *Local Specialization: Nonmetallic Minerals, 1851 (local percentage compared to the percentage of the St Lawrence axis)*

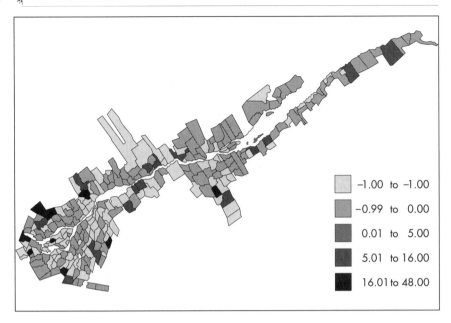

FIGURE 15   *Local Specialization: Chemical Products, 1851 (local percentage compared to the percentage of the St Lawrence axis)*

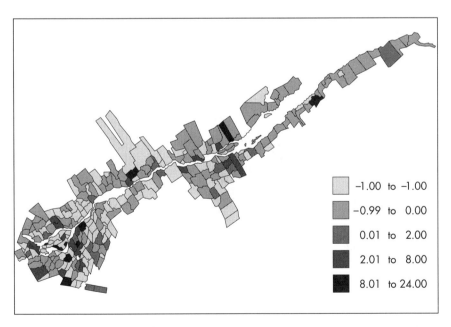

FIGURE 16   *Local Specialization: Miscellaneous, Fabrication, and Construction, 1851 (local percentage compared to the percentage of the St Lawrence axis)*

cities of Montreal and Quebec attracted the production of transportation equipment (figure 13) and the miscellaneous category (figure 16) in addition to food products.

If our first overview based on the aggregate data in the published censuses showed a clear movement of units of production such as mills and saw mills, a closer examination of the data from the individual schedules shows that, in 1851, the rural industrial landscape was more diversified in the southern part of the axis than in the north. This reinforces our conviction that there were different processes of growth involved in the two parts of the axis. This hypothesis remains to be tested in future work.

• Larger Units of Production

The size of the work force of a given unit of production is important to an understanding of the processes of growth. This kind of information must, however, be treated with caution for a number of reasons. Only a few can be reiterated here. In the individual schedules for 1851, census takers did not systematically record the exact number of employees working in a given unit. When they did—for example, when only one worker was indicated—there is no way of knowing whether that person was the owner or just the operator of the unit. It is known that owners of equipment during this period did not, as a general rule, declare any unpaid work obtained from family members. Duration of work is another problem: this could be quite variable, from a few days to months to an entire year. For establishments where there was more than one unit of production, the number of employees was very often given as a total, without any breakdown. Moreover, in some instances such as saw mills and other units that used large quantities of wood (ironworks, for example), the number of employees could include those men, such as lumberjacks and drivers, located in the forest or along the waterways in addition to those actually working in the establishment. For our purposes, then, the number of employees can only be used as a crude indicator. Nevertheless, we think that something can be learned from a cautious handling of this data.

For the whole of the St Lawrence axis, including partial data available for cities, there were roughly one hundred of the total 3456 units of production which employed ten or more workers. These hundred units were distributed almost evenly between the city of Quebec and the rest of the axis (the city of Montreal being excluded because of the total lack of data). In general, then, the level of concentration of the work force in rural industries remained rather low.

It was in urban centres that the largest establishments in terms of work force were to be found. A Quebec City shipyard was the largest employer with between 750 and 800 workers. The city also had half a dozen smaller shipyards, each with more than sixty employees. Near these stood forty establishments, each with a work force of more than ten persons. This is as much as can be said about the urban aspect of industry as revealed by the census, since the census schedules are missing for the city of Montreal. Adding that city to the picture would significantly alter the distribution of large-scale establishments between the cities and the countryside.

In the countryside, industries in the St Lawrence axis were dominated by mills: saw mills (more than 450), grist mills (more than 200), carding mills (more than 100), and fulling mills (nearly 75). Together with blacksmith shops (more than 750) and pot and pearl ash factories (roughly 70), these form the dominant elements in rural industrialization. Two features stand out: the small scale of the vast majority of rural production units, and the composite character of some of them. For example, market orientation and the use of hydraulic power very often resulted in a combination of production in one manufactory. Grist mills, saw mills, and fulling and carding mills were often associated with each other and were sometimes found in the same establishment or building. One example we found of this type was a multiuse mill at Ste-Cécile-du-Bic, near Rimouski, which had a work force of fifty hands. These composite establishments are particularly interesting because they indicate a variety of marketing strategies at work. This joining of functions is not to be interpreted as a refusal to specialize production, but rather as a move to maximize the utilization of equipment by expanding the number of productive phases around one principal activity. The harmonization of these separate units of production provides a sense of local specialization and the state of the relationship of the units to the market. This composite character was found both in the smaller concerns of ten employees and in the larger ones as well. It reveals simultaneously the presence of small local entrepreneurship alongside rising capitalist enterprises.

Resource availability, topography, power sources, and transportation networks brought to several rural locales some large-scale establishments which stood out in stark contrast to the large number of smaller operations, most of which employed fewer than five people. Outside Quebec, there were forty such establishments identified in the 1851 census schedules. Two were in St-Hyacinthe and one in Sorel, the latter an important shipyard with 150 workers. Not surprisingly, the largest rural establishments were saw mills. Three had at least 25 workers, five others reported between 40 and 60 workers, and three establishments reported 100 or more employees, including workers in the forest and in the mills. These three were located at Île Verte (with 100 employees), Fraserville (with 200), and Fief St-Maurice, near Rimouski (by far the largest, at 360). In addition to these saw mills, there was a glass factory at Vaudreuil with a work force of about 150 persons. Finally, there were a dozen other establishments employing between 10 and 30 hands, including a foundry at Montmagny; three cloth factories, in Chambly, Terrebonne, and Sault-au-Recollet; a clothing factory at St-Armand; a brickworks at Deschaillons; two agricultural implement factories at Berthier and Terrebonne; a paper factory in Chambly; and a chair factory at Château-Richer.

• Conclusion

This overview of rural industries during the first half of the nineteenth century has revealed their essential characteristics. First of these was their importance for the area under study: these activities were clearly an integral part of economic life, albeit to varying degrees. Even if the period under consideration is rather short, there seems to have been an increasing regional specialization and diversity. On the other hand, the links between settlement and some industrial activities is quite direct; there is a positive correlation between resource-based production and the settlement frontier. Saw mills and pot and pearl ash factories illustrate this, moving constantly towards the periphery, following receding resources. The level of population and rural industries seems to be positively linked. In many cases, the distribution is parallel. Some discrepancies were, however, found, such as the differences between development on the north and south shores or the tendency towards concentration around urban areas.

A first look at the evolution of the structure of rural industrialization between 1831 and 1851 suggested an apparent stagnation, localized in the Montreal district. A more detailed examination, however, proved that this was not the case. Because of the structure of the data, we had to ignore a significant number of industries in 1851 in order to make a valid comparison with the situation in 1831. On the other hand, the use of the individual census schedules for 1851 showed the diversity of units of production in the St Lawrence axis. The role of the cities also seems important in the polarization of the spatial distribution. The absence of individual schedules for Montreal and some other areas prevents further analysis. We are left with a fragmentary vision of rural industrial development and particularly of the concentration of the work force which, in some cases, reached a surprising level.

Rural industries seem to have been a critical feature in the socioeconomy of the St Lawrence axis. Their evolution is linked to population growth, the settlement of the land, and urbanization. What emerges is a picture of an integrated economy based on a relatively developed structural exchange system.

• Notes

1 For a more detailed presentation of our views on this point, see Serge Courville, Jean-Claude Robert, and Normand Séguin, "La vallée du Saint-Laurent à l'époque du rapport Durham: économie et société," *Journal of Canadian Studies/Revue d'études canadiennes* 25, 1 (1990): 78–95.

2 For an illustration of the role of rural industries in agricultural production, see Serge Courville, "Le marché des «subsistances». L'exemple de la plaine de Montréal au début des années 1830: une perspective géographique," *Revue d'histoire de l'Amérique française* 42, 2 (1988): 78–95.

3 These snapshots are based essentially on the aggregate data from the 1831 and 1851 censuses. For this comparison, we employed the published aggregate data because the manuscript census for 1851 is incomplete. Many schedules are missing, and these gaps seriously hinder any systematic comparison between the 1831 and 1851 censuses except at the aggregate level. Particularly frustrating is the absence of schedules for numerous parishes, especially on the south shore of the district of Montreal and for the entire city of Montreal. Moreover, in many districts, data are incomplete. Despite these numerous shortcomings, censuses of the first half of the nineteenth century remain indispensible because of the wealth of aggregate and nominal data they contain on the rise of rural industries. Moreover, their wide coverage encompassing the entire province at a specific moment in time is invaluable. Few, if any, other sources provide this type and level of information.

4 René Hardy, Pierre Lanthier, and Normand Séguin, "Les industries rurales et l'extension du réseau villageois dans la Mauricie pré-industrielle: L'exemple du comté de Champlain durant la seconde moitié du 19ᵉ siècle," *Sociétés villageoises et villes-campagnes au Québec et dans la France de l'Ouest, XVIIᵉ–XXᵉ siècles*, ed. F. Lebrun and Normand Séguin (Trois-Rivières, 1987), 240.

5 There are a number of important topics which, because of the focus of our paper, we cannot consider here. These include the legal form of rural industries, the distinction between capitalist- and artisan-based operations, and the transition from the one to the other. On these questions, see two interesting studies: Jean-Pierre Kesteman, "Une bourgeoisie et son espace: industrialisation et développement du capitalisme dans le district de Saint-François (Québec), 1823–1879" (PhD diss., Université du Québec à Montréal, 1985) and Robert Sweeny, "Internal Dynamics and the International Cycle: Questions of the Transition in Montreal, 1821–1828" (PhD diss., McGill University, 1985).

6 For a more detailed analysis of this distinction, see Jocelyn Morneau, France Normand, and Claude Bellevance, "Les équipements, recensement de 1851," *Le pays laurentien au XIXᵉ siècle. Cahier 1*, ed. Serge Courville, Jean-Claude Robert, and Normand Séguin (Montréal, 1992).

7 Serge Courville, *Entre ville et campagne: L'essor du village dans les seigneuries du Bas Canada* (Québec, 1990).

8 Joseph Bouchette, *A Topographical Description of the Province of Lower Canada* (London, 1815).

9 We use the term "unit of production" with caution because the data taken from aggregate published censuses does not have the same precision as that taken from individual schedules. Taking into consideration our distinction between establishments and units of production, our experience with censuses leads us to conclude that published censuses are much less precise than those in manuscript form.

10 Courville, *Entre ville et campagne*, 169.

11 Serge Courville, Jean-Claude Robert, and Normand Séguin, "Population et espace rural au Bas-Canada: l'exemple de l'axe laurentien dans la première moitié du XIXᵉ siècle," *Revue d'histoire de l'Amérique française* 44, 2 (1990): 260 and table 3.

12 Ibid.

13 For a detailed review of this work, see Morneau, Normand, and Bellevance, "Les équipements, recensement de 1851" in Courville et al., *Le pays laurentien*.

14 This important discrepancy is explained by two factors. First, the schedules are a more complete source and include all types of production. Second, our notion of units of production implies the identification of a broader range of manufacturing facilities than just establishments.

15 The formula is $Si = (Ni-Nj)$; Si is the index of specialization of a given locale in the category N, Ni is the percentage of units of production of category N in the census subdivision, and Nj is the percentage of all units in the N category in relation to the total number of units in the whole of the territory.

CHILDREN, SCHOOLING, AND FAMILY REPRODUCTION IN NINETEENTH-CENTURY ONTARIO*

CHAD GAFFIELD

Why did children go to school in increasing proportions during the nineteenth century? This seemingly straightforward question has given rise to a rich and diverse historical debate in Canada during the past two decades. An increasing number of researchers now suspect that an understanding of the origins of mass schooling is an essential part of general explanations of the making of twentieth-century Canada. Unexpectedly, though, every proposed response to the question of school attendance has raised at least as many issues as it has resolved. Each new interpretation has widened the scope of the topic and has shown additional ways in which the growing importance of classrooms related to large-scale social change. One positive result is a more sophisticated appreciation of the complexity of both educational history and the history of children.

The following discussion traces the evolution of recent historical debate in the case of nineteenth-century Ontario in order to outline a reinterpretation of mass schooling. This reinterpretation is based on the

*From *Canadian Historical Review* 72, 2 (1991): 157–91. Reprinted by permission of University of Toronto Press Incorporated. © University of Toronto Press. This paper has benefited greatly from valuable comments on an earlier version by Gordon Darroch, Harvey Graff, Susan Houston, Jack Little, Lynne Marks, Dianne Newell, Michael Piva, Eric Sager, Neil Sutherland, and the CHR readers.

changing position of children within the process of family reproduction. In the early work of the 1960s and 1970s, scholars generally studied "childhood" in terms of the perspectives, ambitions, and actions of adults. The result was a series of stimulating studies that documented the changing ways in which adults attempted to define and control children. A smaller proportion of studies focussed on actual children, especially for topics such as school attendance and work.[1]

Recently, historians have begun concentrating on the need to situate the experiences of children within the larger process of family reproduction. By defining this process both in biological and material terms, researchers have begun exploring the links between macro-level and micro-level transformations, especially those related to the changing positions of children in social and economic organization. The findings of local studies based on individual-level data are now being related to the evidence of regional and national research based on aggregate patterns and high-level policies. In pursuing the implications of such micro-history for general analyses of historical change, this approach is demonstrating the need to relate large-scale configurations to the articulations of individual experience in growing up.[2]

Historians have also found, however, that the study of children in terms of family history can be problematic. One key issue concerns the implications of patriarchy both in terms of formal structures and ideology. Feminist scholars have effectively challenged the assumption of cohesive, harmonious family units in which collective goals have been collectively defined and pursued. The reality of gendered positions within families (with the consequent inequalities of power and distinctions in perspective) is now recognized to require sophisticated analyses of the ways in which individuals viewed and experienced family life. In this view, the history of males and females cannot simply be collapsed within the history of family economies, family strategies, and family structure.[3]

In a similar way, studies have shown that age must be considered an essential distinction within analyses of family history. This distinction goes beyond descriptions of divisions of labour or patterns of school attendance. Just as women can be seen as being "at odds" with families, historians are coming to grips with the limits of viewing children as contented (or at least passive) members of cohesive family units. Within the patriarchal family, children, youth, and adults did not simply share the same interests or experience family life in undifferentiated ways.[4] The results were far from uniform; rather, family reproduction appears to have led to both conflict and co-operation, accommodation and alienation, success and failure.[5] These internal dynamics of families are, of course, very difficult to study; historical sources reveal far more about parents than children, and more about sons than daughters.

The problems of viewing families as unitary bodies has engendered considerable support for life-course analysis. By combining the more familiar concept of life cycle with an emphasis on historical context, this approach seeks to reconcile an appreciation of individual identity (especially gender and age) with the importance of family setting.[6] Some European historians have been reluctant to adopt this perspective since it implies significant variation in the experience of members of the same cohort. Since such variation depends on the ability to exercise individual choice, life-course analysis is considered inappropriate for settings where family and communal imperatives are all encompassing.[7] Even in such societies, however, individual identity can be considered important if only as a strand in the "knot" of family life.[8]

In this sense, the history of mass schooling raises questions about the individual identities and activities of children within the changing context of family experience. What were the familial structures and values which framed the lives of children and how and why did these structures and values change over time? Given this framework, what was the range of educational experience which can be observed among these children, and how and why did its relative importance change over time?

While these questions have become familiar in studies of children and youth, scholars have tended to isolate a certain dimension in keeping with the trend towards specialized subfields of sociohistorical research. In contrast, this paper explores the origins of mass schooling by bringing together three distinct fields: the history of education, demographic history, and economic history. In each of these fields, recent research has brought into question basic assumptions about the origins of contemporary Canada.[9] The available research specifically related to children remains uneven, and any attempt to identify the changing meaning of structures or the varying ranges of ideas and behaviour is fraught with difficulty. And, of course, the vastness of these fields precludes comprehensive treatment in a single paper.

The publication of three major books between 1988 and 1990 attests to the current vitality of research activity in Ontario's educational history. In their own way, each of these studies, by Bruce Curtis, Susan E. Houston and Alison Prentice, and R.D. Gidney and W.P.J. Millar, builds on earlier work while also constructing new interpretations. The strongest link with earlier scholarship involves the continued emphasis on the thoughts and actions of the "school promoters," most notably, of course, Egerton Ryerson. However, these three books go well beyond this focus in addition to offering revisions to earlier characterizations of educational leaders.[10]

In contrast to previous work, Curtis and Gidney/Millar stress the opposition those like Ryerson faced in attempting to establish their school system. Interestingly, though, these researchers come to quite different conclusions about their actual role. In discovering a variety of instances in which "school supporters" (and sometimes students) opposed educational officials, Curtis implies that the builders of the "Educational State" were a more formidable group than heretofore recognized; their ultimate victory was not an easy win over a passive or collaborating population. In turn, Gidney/Millar describe considerable struggle among distinct groups of school promoters who did not form a homogeneous force; indeed, at least in the case of secondary schooling, Ryerson and his allies often lost to other educational leaders, including those representing small towns and villages.

Houston/Prentice do acknowledge various examples of opposition to the school promoters and of debate among proponents of educational reform, but they are more impressed by evidence of general approval of the official project of mass schooling. While their own research led to this conclusion as early as the 1970s, they no longer insist on the overwhelming power of the school promoters to establish a public system. Rather, their reinterpretation involves an insistence on complexity, on an historical "fabric tightly woven of multiple intentions and effects." The lack of opposition was, thus, not the result of consensus or bourgeois hegemony. Quite different individuals and groups came to support mass schooling for their own reasons.

If viewed in terms of intellectual history, these three books could be seen as rejecting rather than building on the "new social history" launched during the 1970s. For example, A.B. McKillop believes that Houston and Prentice have belatedly undergone a "professional loss of innocence." As a result, they can now admit the need to abandon the legacy of Michael B. Katz, who inspired scholarship that "produced fewer answers, historical and ideological, not more." In this view, the "difficult lesson" Houston and Prentice had to learn was twofold: the need to avoid "any substantial use of quantitative methods" and the need to be "critical of the 'social control' model." Their eventual success in learning these lessons has allowed them to write a book with a "richness of texture and tentativeness of tone" appropriate to a work of "substantial scholarship and mature judgement." Since neither Curtis nor Gidney/Millar make "substantial use of quantitative methods" and both attack the social control thesis as formulated in the 1970s, their works could also be seen, if judged by these criteria, as implicit attacks on the era of the "new social history."[11]

This view, however, represents a fundamental misunderstanding of the evolution of historical debate, and a misreading of the current literature. These problems stem from a failure to perceive the ways in which continued sociohistorical research pushed forward scholarly debate from the 1970s through the 1980s. It is this research that inspired ongoing reconsideration of the origins of mass schooling. During the past two decades, scholars have had to re-evaluate their interpretations constantly in light of new and often surprising findings in social history.

In the 1970s, many scholars (notably Houston and Prentice) interpreted the actions of public school promoters in terms of social control nourished by fear of dislocated (and thus potentially dangerous) "traditional" mentalities in an emerging modern world of cities and factories.

Children and youth were seen to be particularly at risk, and thus schools were designed for the purpose of moral, social, and economic order. In this view, the definition of children as pupils was intimately related to the importance of urban industrialization. The implication was that rural society, and its assumed lack of interest in education, was rapidly declining in the face of increasing metropolitanism, with its enthusiasm for educational reform. The school systems reflected the new social organization of cities, the new demands for industrial workers, and the need to integrate the numerous immigrants into their new society. In other words, traditional educational forms became outmoded by the dawn of modern society as engendered by the Industrial Revolution; the result was massive institution building, beginning with schools.[12] This assumption was the rationale for the urban social history projects that were undertaken by certain educational historians to examine the type of new industrial city dictating ideas and behaviour by 1850.[13]

Scholars of the early 1970s built their arguments on two key characterizations of Ontario in the mid-nineteenth century. First, while emphasizing the growth of cities, researchers accepted the argument (made most effectively by Leo Johnson) that land speculators and government policy successfully discouraged a certain proportion of the population from rural settlement in an attempt to expand the wage-labour force.[14] The perceived result was increasing proletarianization; many of the new proletarians were forced into the cities where, in the absence of proper education as children, they became potential threats to society, especially as paupers and criminals. This phenomenon was said to fuel the activities of school promoters, led by Egerton Ryerson, who perceived the crumbling of traditional society with a mixture of nostalgia, glee, and anxiety.

The second key characterization of mid-nineteenth-century Ontario involved the nature and impact of immigrants, especially the famine Irish. The massive immigration of these years added to high natural increase to produce unprecedented population growth, particularly, it was said, in the new industrializing cities. This growth encouraged formal educational activity designed to prevent the potential social chaos represented by increasing masses of penniless proletarians uprooted from traditional ties and poorly prepared for the new rhythms of factory work and urban life. Historians thus explained the origins of public schooling as a response to a new social formation in which youth needed institutional supervision and socialization either in terms of social control (as argued in the early 1970s) or Gramscian hegemony (as argued by the latter 1970s). The key assumption in these interpretations was that rural depopulation and heavy immigration were flooding cities in ways that social leaders saw as threatening to the otherwise desirable elements of progress.

Almost immediately, social historians (most notably David Gagan) began pointing to an essential problem with these images of the historical context of children in the mid-nineteenth century—the predominantly rural character of Ontario. Despite the growth of cities such as Toronto and Hamilton, the vast majority of Ontario's population lived in the countryside throughout the Ryersonian years.[15] This pattern was early recognized by educational historians but was not emphasized for several reasons. Susan Houston, for example, argued that, despite geographic distribution, most social leaders were developing an "urban outlook" as early as the 1840s.[16] Influenced by developments elsewhere (especially in the United States and Britain), these leaders were said to be anticipating the future as much as reacting to the present. Thus, while Ontario was still very rural, the urban developments were taken as sufficient evidence that the balance was being tipped in favour of a new world of clocks, machines, and potential social chaos. Children everywhere, even those still in rural areas, had to be prepared to "improve" or else all the benefits of progress would be lost forever.

At the same time, other scholars, especially R.D. Gidney and the late Doug Lawr, pointed out that the school promotion of the nineteenth century was, in many ways, a continuation of earlier educational activity in an indisputably rural society. Many of the centralizing and systematizing ambitions associated with Ryerson might be said to have had histories of their own, and, therefore, should not be seen as the specific result of urban growth from the 1840s.[17] Somewhat surprisingly, this apparent attack on the interpretive relationship between substantial school promotion and a new urban-based social formation stopped short of calling for an explanation of educational history in rural areas. Ryerson's predecessors were characterized as either groping towards what he was ultimately able to achieve or desperately trying to stave off the early winds of change.

Debate about the urban/industrial nature of educational activity in mid-nineteenth-century Ontario took a new turn in 1975 when Michael Katz published his first major study on Hamilton. The most unexpected finding was that the supposed "steel city" was, in fact, not yet even industrial in 1851; rather, Hamilton was a commercial centre comparable to Salem, Massachusetts, in 1800. Later work showed that early industrialization was apparent in Hamilton by 1871, but the evidence implied clearly that the social context of educational reform was not exactly as had been anticipated; indeed, the suggestion that even Hamilton was only like a commercial city of the United States in 1800 was quite startling. This study further undermined the belief that industrializing cities were the relevant context within which to situate the origins of an institutional society characterized first and foremost by mass schooling.[18]

In place of the urban industrial focus, scholars such as Katz began emphasizing the emergence of a wage-labour economy resulting from rapid capitalist development. In this view, the key phenomena were not machines and factories but rather those related to the growth of proletarian society. This emphasis defused the interpretive impact of the finding that cities such as Hamilton were not yet industrialized; it also weakened to some extent the need to see educational reform as primarily an urban development, since agricultural labourers could be included among the increasing proletarians. Thus, the initial explicative triad of urbanization, industrialization, and immigration came to be reconceptualized within a different chronology. The impact of industrialization was relocated in the 1860s and 1870s while the independent meaning of urbanization in the 1840s and 1850s was reinterpreted in terms of merchant capital and a general process of increasing wage labour. For its part, immigration took on added significance, especially in concert with rapid natural increase. The swelling ranks of the wage-labour force provided, it was said, a new context in which the idea of mass education found strong appeal.

During the late 1970s and early 1980s, most educational scholars continued to offer arguments based on urban-industrial or wage-labour characterizations of Ontario despite new indications of interpretive problems related to chronology. The first major study of Ontario's rural society revealed substantial growth throughout the 1850s even in Peel County. In fact, David Gagan found that the most significant movement among occupational groups in Toronto's hinterland at this time involved the ambition of farming.[19] This evidence did not have a dramatic impact on interpretations of the origins of mass schooling because Gagan emphasized that the acquisition of land was, indeed, fast becoming less feasible. While still hungry for land, more of the population were seen to be trapped in cities or forced to migrate there from the saturated countryside. The Peel County example suggested that independent farming was rapidly fading as a realistic ambition as the rising price of land engendered a larger mass of wage labourers. In this sense, the apparent chronological problem of associating mass schooling with a large urban-based wage-labour economy was not serious since rural society was said to be moving into "crisis" during the Ryersonian years. More credit simply had to be given to the school promoters' ability to recognize the early warning signs of social change.[20]

In the last few years, however, new research has raised questions about this depiction of rural society in nineteenth-century Ontario. Was the countryside actually in an economic and demographic crisis during the Ryersonian years? Were rapidly increasing proportions of children suddenly confronting the new urban industrial world? Conclusive answers to these questions cannot yet be provided but certain studies cast considerable doubt on fundamental aspects of the established arguments concerning the immediate and widespread impact on children of urban industrialization and immigration. Moreover, these studies suggest a quite different way of understanding the changing character of growing up.

The extent of land availability is a major issue in the debate about rural society in the mid-nineteenth century. At what point did the attainment of property in Ontario become an unrealistic dream? This question is quite complex. How is "available land" to be defined? Lurking behind most answers to this question are assumptions about objectively defined minimum farm sizes and soil quality. Until very recently, scholars consistently pointed to 1850 as the time when Ontario was "filled up," although the evidence for this claim was limited to statements about the south-central core of the province.

However, rural Ontario in the mid-nineteenth century was not one homogeneous region.[21] For example, at least until the early 1870s, considerable tracts of land were still available in the initially bypassed counties of the eastern corner of the province. Throughout the 1850s and 1860s in this area, settlers could acquire quite reasonably priced land where households could be established on the basis of both farming and seasonal or market participation in the lumber industry. This region was disregarded in earlier decades in favour of south-central Ontario, but with the expanding timber and saw mill operations and the development of Ottawa, the area became more attractive, especially to families from neighbouring Quebec counties. The result was dramatic rural growth until the 1870s, when the retreating forest frontier began leaving the region behind.[22] This example illustrates that "land availability" reflects a subjective evaluation; the land of the easternmost counties that was first considered unattractive was re-evaluated in light of the development of the lumber industry.

The view of rural Ontario as a differentiated collection of regions is further suggested by the evidence that even central Ontario retained a predominantly rural social formation at least through the 1870s. Despite the rapid growth of Toronto and Hamilton, the apparent rural crisis in Peel County and the perceived massive proletarianization in the Home District, the routinely generated sources examined by Gordon Darroch and Michael Ornstein show that central Ontario experienced rural expansion throughout the Ryersonian years. A systematic comparison of the enumerations of 1861 and 1871 reveals that commercial and bourgeois occupations did increase during the 1860s but that this increase was relatively modest in comparison with the increasing proportion of farmers and artisans.[23] This evidence seems consistent with the appearance of widespread rural depopulation only during the last two decades of the century.

It also appears that the expansion of rural society during the Ryersonian years was based on complex economic changes; however, these changes were quite distinct from the frequently cited British example of proto-industrialization. Rather, agriculture was being transformed by a broad range of developments, including the shift from wheat to mixed farming, the significant rise of dairying, some consolidation of farms, and increasing mechanization. And, perhaps most interestingly, rural industry was growing rapidly, especially saw milling and grist milling.[24]

This transformation of rural society did engender a growing demand for wage labour; indeed, certain establishments hired hundreds of workers, who were often paid by the day or month.[25] However, the meaning and character of this wage labour appear to have varied considerably.[26] In the case of the eastern counties, these workers often appear to have been young single men who were supplementing land-based family economies on a seasonal basis; they were "proletarians" only part of the year while they still also laboured as members of property-owing families.[27] In this sense, wage labour was becoming increasingly important in rural society, but in complex ways that do not seem to be captured by the familiar categories of analysis developed for England.[28] Rather than "family wage-economies" replacing "family economies" based on labour, economic change in mid-century Ontario may have been associated with a differentiated integration of some wage labour into families, most of which still laboured on their own property.[29]

The possibility that rural capitalism and rural industrialization depended on wage labour but did not immediately engender massive proletarianization is consistent with evidence that occupational mobility continued to be mainly in the direction of becoming a farmer during the supposedly crisis years of the 1860s. Rather than substantial rural depopulation in all regions of Ontario, much of the countryside was continuing to develop as immigrants and substantial numbers of the emerging generation acquired land. The monolithic image of a worn-out agricultural heartland simply cannot be applied to Ontario during the years of public school system construction.[30] The most compelling evidence is that the proportion of the labour force considered to be labourers within the occupational structure of central Ontario actually *declined* during the 1860s; at the start of the decade, 26.9 percent of the male labour force were labourers, and this group declined to 18.7 percent in 1871. The largest relative increase in occupational importance was experienced by farmers, whose ranks rose from 31.8 percent to 37.7 percent. Moreover, 60 percent of the labourers from 1861 who stayed in central Ontario became farmers or entered other nonlabouring occupations. As Darroch observes, "this is hardly evidence to encourage an interpretation of widening proletarianization."[31]

Taken together, the continued opportunity for land acquisition in certain regions of Ontario and the declining proportion of labourers even in the central counties during the 1860s undermines the familiar portrayal of the social context of the origins of mass education in Ontario. Instead of widespread rural crisis and a linear, quite sudden transition to urban industrial capitalism, the Ontario Ryerson knew was characterized by widespread property ownership and a rural and petit-bourgeois social formation coming to grips with capitalism and industrialization in the countryside. Throughout the different articulations of this process across the various townships, land remained the basis of most family economies.[32]

This point is worth emphasizing since the central theme of Houston and Prentice's recent book concerns the ways in which family life came to be increasingly structured around schooling rather than economic activity. By the 1870s, the "myriad family responsibilities that had absorbed so much of the waking hours of children and young people in earlier times had diminished. When once the time spent at school was fitted around the demands of family time, now the situation was reversed."[33] Houston and Prentice are certainly correct in noting the increasing importance of school attendance in children's lives, and their study contributes significantly to a better understanding of both the school promoters' ambitions and the actual experience of formal education. However, the changing thoughts and behaviour that increasingly inspired and allowed families to send children to school receive much less attention. These authors clearly move away from the earlier insistence on urban industrial forces and a singular emphasis on "social control," but they do not offer an alternate interpretation of why schooling did, in fact, gain popular support.

Moreover, the conclusion that schooling took over from economic activity as an organizing force of family life does not seem to fit chronologically in the case of Ontario. In the third quarter of the nineteenth century, families were still primarily structured around economic life; in the predominantly rural world of Ontario, family economies remained the basis of most children's lives. Nonetheless, school attendance was becoming quite important for the majority of children (as carefully surveyed by Houston and Prentice). The interpretive challenge is, thus, to explain increasing school attendance at a time when family economies continued to be characteristic of Ontario society.

A further dimension to the recent revision of Ontario's social history concerns the character of Irish immigration. The established view in the 1970s, which portrayed the Irish as bedraggled urban labourers ever ready to attack the social order through crime and ignorance, has been rejected by research that emphasizes the rural and relatively successful settlement of both Catholics and Protestants. In repeated studies, Donald Akenson has stressed that the Irish immigrants to Ontario should not be confused with those who went to the United States. The Irish who arrived before and during the Ryersonian years did not congregate in cities, trapped either by restrictive land policies or by their own cultural and psychological deficiencies. Rather, these immigrants quickly and quite smoothly settled in the countryside. Akenson questions the impact of land speculation on rural development at any point during the formative decades of the nineteenth century, and he argues that the Irish were just as successful farmers as other groups. Interestingly, Akenson also suggests that, instead of being the targets of educational promotion, the Irish themselves built schools as institutions in keeping with their own cultural traditions. In this view, schools were not an elite response to urban proletarians, especially those from Ireland, but rather were a natural result of cultural transfer within rural society.[34]

The rehabilitation of the Irish immigrants within Ontario historiography has recently continued with the work of Bruce Elliott. By studying the pre- and postmigration contexts of the immigrants who came from Tipperary, Elliott takes aim at the notion of the Irish emigrant as a "failure, a belligerent rebel, and a fundamentally emotional and irrational soul."[35]

By tracing the identity, migration, and experience of those who came mainly to Ontario, Elliott insists not only on the rural character of this settlement but also on the importance of family and kinship as the constant context of individual destiny. Rather than uprooted from traditional ties and floundering in a completely foreign social formation, these Irish settlers operated within complex networks of relatives who often contributed to material security in both eastern and western Ontario. They usually acquired land and were able to settle in close proximity to other immigrants from their family or at least from Tipperary. The result was an uneventful adjustment and accommodation to the new world, certainly not one that should have inspired established leaders to devise drastic new measures such as public school systems to ensure social control.

While the recent studies of the Irish immigrants tend to emphasize success, it is also clear that the townships did not simply include happy farm families successfully raising their children. Just as the perception of crisis seems unwarranted, an emphasis on success does not capture the complexity of rural change in mid-nineteenth-century Ontario. Indeed, rural industrialization and agricultural transformation appear to have had different meanings for different groups in various regions. The relative importance of wealth and poverty across time and space in rural society clearly requires additional micro-historical research.[36]

Taken together, new findings now raise major questions about the structures within which the lives of children were transformed in nineteenth-century Ontario. School promoters may have perceived families in crisis, dislocated individuals gravitating to cities, and frozen traditional mentalities, but the actual evidence does not appear to justify this monolithic characterization. The required framework of analysis is one that accommodates not only urban growth but also the uneven and complex processes of rural expansion and transformation.

Given the urban preoccupation of historians engaged in microhistory or in the various subfields of social history, it is not surprising that research on rural schooling and literacy has been quite limited. However, several studies suggest that, from the time of earliest settlement and long before the educational promotion of the mid-nineteenth century, rural communities characteristically constructed school houses or paid teachers to instruct children in their homes. This activity was not, however, a major priority. Over time, an increasing proportion of rural children went to school, but only after other priorities had been respected. The main obligation of both boys and girls was to contribute to the family economy, and even with the establishment of public schooling and centralized inspection, the primary role of youths as producers was not disregarded by rural parents. This priority is particularly evident in the age structure of school enrolment and in the seasonal nature of daily attendance. Only a small minority of rural teenagers ever went to school, and almost all children were absent during productive times of the year when every extra hand was valuable.

Within this general pattern, studies have found important variations and change over time. The extent of participation in schools reflected the fact that rural society was not a homogeneous mass but rather was characterized by differences in occupation, wealth, and ethnicity. The sons and daughters of petit-bourgeois parents, who were usually the village officials, attended school more frequently and for a longer period than did other rural children. In turn, the children of independent farmers were more often in class than those of rural labourers. This pattern appears to have continued throughout the Ryerson years, although the participation rates of all rural children increased during this time. As the years went by, more and more rural children received formal instruction such that their schooling between the ages of seven and twelve was never dramatically different from that of their urban counterparts, whose participation was also directly related to the occupational structure.[37]

A key question is why there was any similarity in the educational experience of rural and urban areas. Historians have emphasized the fact that with the decrease in frontier conditions, rural children became less important as producers. Whereas every available hand could be put to some use in the labour-intensive work of pioneer settlement, youths in older agricultural areas were more easily made available for the classroom. In other words, there was a rural counterpart to the considerable economic dislocation of children in an urban wage-labour economy. This interpretation stresses the importance of immediate circumstances in the decision to attend school; from the parents' point of view, their calculations primarily reflected the present rather than the future. The question was simply whether the children were needed at home for the immediate survival and security of the family. As will be suggested, parents may not have been as present-minded as this explanation implies.

But within material considerations, the importance of ethnoreligious differences is also clearly indicated by those studies which show that rural parents were well aware that schooling was not value-free. Although the countryside was characterized by ethnic clustering, this pattern was hardly neat or complete, with the result that the nearest school could often reflect the cultural orientation of another group. Many parents who wanted to send their children to school had to choose between a teacher and curriculum they found inappropriate and a more distant school that reflected their own background. This decision became more problematic with the establishment of the public school system, which often disregarded ethnoreligious settlement patterns in creating school sections. More and more parents found themselves forced together within school boundaries that denied the earlier decisions of settlers to maintain ethnic ties by living in close proximity. The starkest example of the results of this development comes from eastern Ontario, where the attendance rates of francophone and anglophone children related directly to the availability of the appropriate language of instruction in the local school. But less dramatic evidence has also been found for other rural areas, especially with regard to the religion of the teacher. The conclusion is that economic constraints were not the only factors in preventing rural children from attending school more consistently and for longer periods. Parents appear to have watched quite attentively what went on in classrooms, and their decision to send their children was more than an immediate material calculation.[38]

The evidence of quite active but differentiated rural school attendance is similar to the findings of studies on literacy. Initial dichotomies of rural/urban, illiterate/literate have not been supported by research on areas such as Elgin County. As part of his major study of literacy in mid-nineteenth-century Ontario, Harvey Graff showed in the 1970s that almost all residents in the Elgin townships considered themselves able to read and write by 1850. In fact, the proportion of literates exceeded the percentage in cities such as Hamilton. The pattern of higher literacy rates in rural areas was not unique to southwestern Ontario but rather extended to most regions of the province. Graff remarked that literacy was less relevant in a rural economy, and thus this ability had to be related to other activities and processes including "social stratification and social control." Conversely, lower urban literacy rates were explained by the congregation of poor Irish Catholics in the growing cities.[39] However, as discussed earlier, this explanation does not seem as attractive as it did fifteen years ago; the relationship between literacy and the evolution of rural society calls for an explanation rooted in the experience of families in the villages and townships.

One major obstacle to a better understanding of rural literacy is the paucity of sources. The census evidence used by Harvey Graff is certainly problematic but it is still the best data given the comprehensiveness and systematic nature of the enumerations. Other possible sources such as church registers are difficult to use effectively for community or regional studies, which would have to confront the problem of finding the records of the numerous nineteenth-century denominations. Thus, educational historians of rural society in Ontario have access to a much more extensive literature on school attendance than on literacy. However, the evidence that the proportion of rural residents who could read and write was actually somewhat greater than that of their urban counterparts poses an interpretive challenge, especially if the assumption of predominantly urban and often illiterate Irish immigrants is misleading. High literacy rates and quite active school participation are not the expected hallmarks of a rural society in need of educational transformation by urban progress.

It is in this context that R.D. Gidney, Doug Lawr, and W.P.J. Millar have attempted to offer province-wide interpretations of mass schooling. In the late 1970s and early 1980s, Gidney and Lawr renewed interest in the villages and concessions by focussing on the attitudes and concerns revealed in the letters sent by parents, trustees, and others to educational officials. In reading through the vast amount of this correspondence, these researchers became convinced that a centralized and bureaucratized school system was not imposed on rural areas but developed in response to the self-acknowledged need in the townships for mechanisms and policies to administer schools. This need was especially pronounced in the context of the inevitable local disputes resulting from "human nature" as much as from social or ethnoreligious circumstances. In this view, a popular consensus in both rural and urban areas underlay the success of the official school promoters in establishing a public system; in fact, Ryerson was following as much as leading the direction of educational reform.[40]

In more recent work, Gidney and Millar locate educational agency more specifically in the "middle class." In their definition, the middle class was not simply urban but rather came from all areas of Ontario. They argue that the central process underpinning mass schooling was an emerging belief among middle-class parents that voluntary and private schooling was no longer adequate to their needs. Over time, these parents built a compulsory and public system which offered universal accessibility in theory but which actually best served their own interests.[41] In their book on secondary schooling, Gidney and Millar pursue this argument by detailing the educational actions and attitudes of "merchants and other proprietors, professionals, public officials, and clerks, along with substantial farmers and those artisans and craftsmen who had won some degree of prosperity from their work." Considering this middle class "essentially identical" with Michael Katz's "business class" studied in Hamilton, Gidney and Millar argue that Ryerson may have been the most important educational leader in this social group but that he often could not control the nature and pace of school administration, given the extent and diversity of middle-class involvement.

This research is appealing since it attempts to accommodate evidence of support for mass schooling in both urban and rural areas. By using a broad definition of "middle class," Gidney and Millar seek to capture the basis of school building across the province. But can this interpretation account for the actual dimensions of support for schooling? While Gidney and Millar do not specify the relative importance of their "middle class" within Ontario's social structure, the data Katz offers indicates that this class was about one-third of industrializing Hamilton. If this proportion can be hypothetically extrapolated to all of Ontario, the educational values and behaviours of two-thirds of the province remain to be described. Did this majority share the "middle-class" decision to sacrifice immediate material concerns in order to send their children to school in hopes of securing their "occupational future"? And if so, why? These questions indicate the continuing need to make sense of mass schooling in terms of all social groups.

In his recent book, Bruce Curtis addresses this challenge but he rejects the notion that public schooling sprang from province-wide origins. Instead, Curtis views the establishment of school systems in terms of the destruction of community-based education by urban political leaders seeking to establish a centrally controlled way to ensure political stability within the developing state. Curtis insists on the political ambition of educational systems. Rather than primarily economic or social agencies, public schools evolved in Ontario as a politically motivated response to the perception of elites that schools could be a principal strategy of state formation. This perception became orthodoxy among the "governing classes" towards the mid-nineteenth century especially after the rebellions of 1837–38. In this sense, public schooling did not develop as a direct consequence of urbanization, industrialization, or an expanding wage-labour economy. Educational administrators considered political socialization in state-run schools to be just as important in rural as in urban areas. Indeed, given the example of the rebellions, "proper" education was perhaps even more important in the countryside. In this way, Curtis tries to reconcile a belief in the agency of urban, elite leaders with the reality of a predominantly rural society.

At the same time, Curtis has provided many examples of popular resistance to the school-building efforts of the Ryersonian years. Rather than the almost immediate achievement of sociocultural hegemony and thus popular acquiescence, parents and local trustees always did their best to maintain control of the schools, often thwarting the ambitions of central authority. Teachers deemed undesirable by community standards were quickly dismissed. Ultimately, such resistance was unable to prevent construction of the educational state, but Curtis emphasizes the continuing efforts of communities to maintain their own integrity in the face of state centralization. This emphasis views the letters from trustees and parents to Ryerson in terms of the local conflicts created by the developing provincial structure which did not and could not adequately respect local circumstances. In this sense, bureaucracy was not the result of popular need but rather the inevitable product of the local loss of authority.

While Curtis stresses examples of popular resistance in order to show that the educational state resulted from coercive high-level agency, the evidence of the book is also testimony to the vitality of rural society. Most of the illustrations of conflict come from the townships, and they do not describe a passive rural society. Rather, this evidence points to an active, dynamic, and, as much as possible, self-assertive countryside. In this way, Curtis's work also encourages an attempt to understand mass schooling from the perspectives of the rural parents and children who did their best to control their own destinies. While urban elites held levers of power not accessible to most rural residents, they were not always able to disregard local priorities which themselves were often in conflict. But what considerations were behind these priorities? What characteristics of rural social formation affected educational attitudes and the experience of children?

To address these questions, family history provides an essential context for the nineteenth century. While a great deal remains to be learned about this history, the continuing importance of family and kin to individual existence is no longer in doubt for nineteenth-century Ontario. The specific analytic advantage of the concept of family reproduction is that it captures the ways in which one generation both biologically creates the next and materially strives to ensure its security and survival.

The essential characteristic of family reproduction is that it is future-oriented. This feature is particularly noteworthy for the study of rural society, since historians have tended to depict rural families as present-minded and reluctant to innovate in anticipation of changed conditions. The data now available on rural fertility, marriage patterns, and inheritance suggest the inappropriateness of this depiction. Rather than being trapped by their own traditional mentalities, the members of rural families appear to have been quite responsive to their changing environment. As early as the mid-nineteenth century in the Ontario townships, they were revising the ways in which they reproduced themselves both demographically and materially. While these revisions are not yet fully understood, a number of important studies have concluded that members of rural families were indeed thinking ahead and planning to meet new challenges throughout the nineteenth century.

Studies have also now shown that an earlier tendency to view rural families as little capitalist enterprises always seeking to maximize immediate production is misleading at best. Rather, a high priority appears to have been the maintenance of family and kinship bonds that formed the basis of communal and ethnic attachment. This priority certainly involved sentiment but it was also directly related to the material insecurity of everyday life. The best long-term economic guarantee was an extensive network of relatives, some of whom would always, it was hoped, be in a position to support needy individuals. Such support might take the form of facilitating migration, helping establish farms, or perhaps identifying a job opportunity. This familial ideology engendered ethnic patterns of settlement as well as the maintenance of ties across time and space.

Despite the major social, economic, and cultural changes of the nineteenth century, researchers have not found that familial ideology simply broke down. While the new institutions (including schooling) can be considered as attacks on family solidarity in that they promoted a state-defined identity, scholars have shown that families often used such institutions only for their own reasons and within a family context. The ways in which various family members viewed such activities, and the importance they held for them as individuals, clearly reflected the patriarchal underpinnings of the nineteenth century as well as their specific historical context. In this sense, the continued importance of families does not imply homogeneous experience and should not be associated with stasis more than change. In fact, rapid transformation appears to have engendered complex and competing forces. As a result, family members were both pushed together and pulled apart as they constantly re-evaluated the most promising ways in which to achieve security and stability.

Perhaps the most surprising evidence of recent research is that fertility was being controlled from as early as the mid-nineteenth century.[42] The recent analyses undertaken by Marvin McInnis and others indicate that efforts to limit family size were particularly evident in Ontario's older settled regions but were also apparent in the more recently opened townships. Fertility in cities came to be lower than in the countryside after mid-century, but the pattern of change was exceedingly complicated. Indeed, no single explanation has been able to account for the extent to which the various regions of Ontario experienced general fertility reduction. While family size was consistently declining throughout Ontario, the actual rate of reduction varied among different groups in different regions of the province. Beyond a moderate relationship between fertility and the timing of settlement, scholars have yet to determine the convergence of forces that inspired either demographic adjustment or innovation as early as 1850.[43]

One tantalizing suggestion, however, is that the attitudes and relative importance of men and women in deciding to control family size were quite different.[44] Two possibilities are relevant to this suggestion: that women may have been more interested than men in limiting family size; and that women and men may have had their own reasons for doing so. Almost no evidence has yet been presented with which we can examine these possibilities for the mid-nineteenth century, but it is intriguing that family limitation began in an era when the written evidence suggests that it was disapproved by both formal and informal ideologies and structures. Since such evidence has an inherent bias in favour of the importance of patriarchal authority, the practice of family limitation implies that the internal workings of actual families was far more complex than described in the documents of the time.[45]

The important conclusion for understanding the changing position of children is that rural as well as urban families were recalculating the rhythms of their reproduction throughout the era of public school construction. Although children in larger families were more likely to go to school during the mid-nineteenth century the reverse pattern took hold in later decades. Over time, smaller families (associated with the concept of "quality" children) contributed significantly to the extension of mass schooling into the teenage years. Understandably, this process was not recognized by Ryerson or other educational leaders.[46]

But were increasing school attendance and family limitation interrelated and, if so, in which ways? Rather than seeking a single answer to this question, recent research suggests the importance of studying the articulations of the two processes in specific times and places. Very little can yet be said about certain regions of Ontario, but at least some preliminary indications do suggest a high correlation between literacy and fertility. In the easternmost corner of the province, for example, quite high rates of illiteracy (predominantly among francophone settlers) were associated with continued high fertility rates. This pattern appears to have been widespread not only in Ontario but also in Quebec. The mechanisms at work remain a question: Did increasing literacy inspire birth control or did smaller family sizes permit greater educational attainment? More specifically, did the ability to read and write change the attitude of men and/or women towards childbearing? Or did changing material conditions encourage family limitation which, as a byproduct, facilitated school attendance? In both analyses, however, educational behaviour and fertility decisions can be considered central components in the changing process of family reproduction.[47]

A further aspect of the demographic changes evident during the second half of the nineteenth century included two trends related to marriage: an increasing age at marriage for most men and women, and a growing minority of adults who never married. These patterns include significant variation among certain groups in specific settings, but the general trends were evident in both cities and rural areas.[48] Since the first phases of industrialization are usually associated with a *decreasing* age of marriage, the data on age at marriage further indicates the problems of interpreting nineteenth-century Ontario within the framework of the Industrial Revolution in cities. It is also noteworthy that, in addition to contributing to the fertility decline, the majority who postponed marriage and the increasing minority who never married produced a larger cohort of older single adults. While most of these adults would eventually marry, the delay of their formation of families is significant evidence of changing individual considerations within families.

The process of courtship and the right to marry appear to have continued to be controlled socially in nineteenth-century Ontario, with parents doing their best to supervise both the selection of mates and the timing of engagement. The material consequences of not respecting the familial ideology (as articulated by parental wishes) were often sufficient to encourage young adults to plan their lives as continuing members of families rather than as individuals. Nonetheless, this control was certainly not total since the structures of Ontario society afforded the opportunity to migrate elsewhere. And premarital conception could be used as a power strategy by young adults, perhaps in a effort to force approval by parents of a "disapproved" relationship.[49] Such a strategy clearly had different risks for men and women, as did the decision not to marry.[50]

But how can the various pieces of evidence on economic, educational, and demographic history be brought together to produce better understandings of the changing experience of children in nineteenth-century Ontario? In focussing on family reproduction, the essential dimension may have involved the process of inheritance. Unfortunately, researchers have paid very little attention to inheritance practices in Ontario. In fact, educational historians have generally ignored the topic.[51] One of the few studies of inheritance is David Gagan's analysis of probate records representing 1500 estates in Peel County between 1840 and 1900.[52] In Gagan's analysis, these records indicate very little change over time in the inheritance practices of this largely agricultural region. Throughout the period, several inheritance strategies were used, but the most common approach reconciled two competing ambitions: to provide quite equally for all children, and to keep the land of the family as one property. Rural families preferred not to subdivide their holdings but rather transmitted the land to one heir while seeking to establish other children in neighbouring areas or compensating them in other ways. Most children did not inherit their family's land directly but rather inherited a share of the value of the estate. Gagan argues that this system did not serve anyone particularly well since the value of the inheritance was characteristically being divided three or four ways. Even the heir who received land was often encumbered by the need to ensure that brothers and sisters could also claim their share of the estate. Nonetheless, inheritance was a key mechanism of family reproduction, and planning for the households of the next generation preoccupied parents who saw all their children as deserving support.

In this analysis, the changing demographic features of nineteenth-century Ontario related directly to inheritance practices since the timing of marriage and family size both depended upon material circumstances. In order to marry, couples had to be able to form their own households. Ideally, households were based on land ownership, but even for couples who became tenants, some basis of material security was the highest priority. Wage labour could certainly be important in family formation but, unless one of the small number of nonseasonal relatively secure positions could be attained, the inherent insecurity of working for an employer in the nineteenth century encouraged continued reliance on parents for the wherewithal to establish households. Moreover, family solidarity was enhanced by an understanding (sometimes made explicit) that the unpaid labour youth performed for the family had to be compensated by a share of the patrimony. Intergenerational transmission of property thus occurred in the context of ongoing family relationships in which individual decisions affected all family members.[53]

The apparent stability of the characteristic system of inheritance in rural Ontario is surprising given the changing circumstances of the second half of the nineteenth century. According to Gagan and other scholars, the system encouraged out-migration by families as the maturing of settlement made the establishment of sons on nearby farms more difficult. Families even on successful farms would sell to move to less developed regions where the households of the next generation could be in reasonable proximity to the parental farm. At the same time, however, many families did persist, and, indeed, they often became the community leaders in rural society. Such families may have been disproportionately important in local educational history since their commitment to the community appears to have led to positions as school trustees, for example. While recent sociohistorical research has emphasized massive geographic mobility as a central feature of rural Ontario, the role of those families who stayed may have been crucial to the character of school experience.

While this preliminary research on probate records in nineteenth-century Ontario is exceedingly valuable, later work has revealed the limitations of studying inheritance in this way. The major problem is methodological in that probate records do not reveal all the aspects of transmission that occurred before death. This limitation is substantial since inheritance appears to have been a process stretched over many years as aging parents began giving property to their children. In this sense, wills capture only the final stage of the transmission between generations. For this reason, scholars have begun undertaking longitudinal analyses of certain families by way of a complex array of sources ranging from genealogical documents to land records.[54]

In this sense, the recent work of Bruce Elliott on Irish Protestants is very informative.[55] He shows that, even during the first half of the nineteenth century, families recognized the need to provide for sons and daughters who would not inherit land. Very few daughters ever received real property, being given their share in the form of a dowry. Sons who were not given land (usually the youngest son inherited the family farm) were either given a cash settlement or prepared for a trade and sometimes a profession in the case of affluent families. Elliott suggests that poor farmers could only hope to help such sons enter trades such as blacksmithing, carpentry, and shoemaking. The better choices were positions as country merchants or innkeepers, who were often well situated to benefit from the increasing prosperity of rural Ontario. In any case, average family size meant that most families throughout the nineteenth century had to expect that at least some of their children would not achieve the ideal of independent farming. Over time, this expectation took an increased importance as the frontier stage passed, and as the decision to persist made establishing children on nearby farms more difficult.

Taken together with Gagan's evidence, these findings demonstrate that the process of inheritance goes far beyond Jack Goody's classic definition of it as a system "by which property is transmitted between the living and the dead."[56] Rather, inheritance often included the transmission of tangible and intangible elements over many years. This transmission was associated with both stability and instability, concentration and dispersion both in terms of property and family members. The ambition of inheritance was multifaceted but was essentially designed to encourage family attachment and solidarity within patriarchal processes.

This general characterization of inheritance lays the foundation for a possible reinterpretation of the position of children within the changing patterns of educational, economic, and demographic behaviour. By viewing these patterns as related to the changing dynamics in the interior of families, the inherent interrelationships of school, work, and family structure within the lives of specific individuals becomes the necessary focus of attention. In this sense, the critical question that emerges for children concerns the ways in which going to school became an increasingly important part of the process of family reproduction. Rather than implying a quite sudden transformation of producers into pupils, this question seeks to understand the changing relative importance of schooling within a complex web of familial priorities.

Specifically, it can be hypothesized that, during the course of the nineteenth century, parents increasingly came to consider sending their children to school as a means of giving to them a part of their inheritance. From the parents' perspective, school attendance came to play a role similar to that of property. In stylized terms, it might be said that the formal education of children increasingly replaced the transmission of property (especially land) as the central strategy by which families attempted to reproduce their material circumstances.

This hypothesis attempts to account for two fundamental aspects of nineteenth-century educational history: the emergence of a general belief in the value of formal schooling, and the continuing inequality and diversity of school attendance. Just as the values and material circumstances of families differed widely, the role of formal education within their reproduction also differed widely. Such distinctions engendered conflict and contradiction as well as adjustment and accommodation. For reasons beyond their control, many families were not able to integrate education into their reproductive "strategies" in the ways they wished. Similarly, the ways in which certain families wished to use schooling within their own priorities was not seen as acceptable by those in authority. Not surprisingly, therefore, nineteenth-century educational policy and practice were always controversial. This characteristic testifies to its increasing importance in the lives of families in diverse situations.

What did parents hope to achieve by sending their children to school? In terms of the ambition of family reproduction, two motivations seem most important. First, parents sought to enhance the possibility of their children attaining material survival and security. In this view, education was not generally expected to permit significant upward social mobility. Rather, it was primarily intended to prevent downward social mobility for the children of well-established families and to permit the attainment of basic security for the children of materially disadvantaged families. In other words, parents increasingly saw formal schooling as a way for their children to achieve "economic competency." Defined as a "degree of comfortable independence," this expression seems to capture the economic aspect of parents' decisions to send their children to school. In his analysis of the early nineteenth-century United States, Daniel Vickers argues that "in time, the very term 'competency' would come to denote a degree of skill or capacity (sufficient to survive in an industrializing world) and lose its traditional meaning, which had hinged on property ownership."[57] Although Vickers does not relate this process to educational history, his analysis appears very consistent with the available evidence on schooling in nineteenth-century Ontario.

The second motivation which can be hypothesized to have increasingly encouraged parents to send their children to school may have especially concerned mothers. The premise of this dimension of family reproduction is that the changing position of mothers within families would particularly lead them to encourage schooling for their children. While a man could reasonably expect to be taken care of until death by his wife, a woman would probably end up depending on her children. In this sense, family solidarity and generational cohesion may have been somewhat more important to women than to men. The preponderance of widows over widowers characterized the entire nineteenth century but its meaning altered considerably over time. A key trend was the increasing likelihood that family formation would require migrating elsewhere, and perhaps leaving parents behind. In this case, the demographic reality meant that if all children in a certain family left home, the mother might well end up alone; fathers would be more likely to have their wives living with them. The increasing possibility of women being left on their own is consistent with a concern in wills for the protection of widows. It is this possibility which may have encouraged mothers to promote schooling for their children; such schooling may have been seen as making it less necessary for children to migrate elsewhere, especially if neighbouring land could not be secured to establish their own households.

The hypothesis that schooling was seen (at least in certain circumstances) as contributing to generational solidarity runs counter to the familiar argument that formal education represented an attack on family integrity. While this may have occurred as the school system evolved, the evidence is ambiguous for the years of great school-building during the mid-nineteenth century. When viewed from the perspective of family members, schools can be said to have reinforced as well as challenged the values of familial attachment. Not only was the "metaphor of the family" a key part of the ideology of school promoters[58] but the actual structure and content of schools were hardly antithetical to family priorities. While the "feminization" of teaching is usually explained in terms of stingy trustees and male sexism,[59] this trend may also represent the preference of mothers. Women may have been far more ready to entrust their children to other women than to aging half-pay officers.

It may also be relevant that the curriculum of nineteenth-century schools promoted family values in keeping with Christian religious traditions.[60] In this sense, mothers may have had an increasing interest in the education of their children as changing material conditions increasingly exposed the long-term vulnerability of their position within families. The appearance of proletarianization could only have fueled this trend as it became easier for husbands to default on the traditional responsibilities of supporting their families. New legislation in the later nineteenth century made an attempt to encourage the maintenance of wives neglected by husbands, but such legislation hardly addressed the real issue.

The rationale for viewing mid-century developments within the context of long-term change involving goals such as economic competency and family solidarity is supported by certain evidence from wills, which included references to the education of children from the beginning of the 1800s. The wills of New France and Lower Canada before this time do not appear to have included such references.[61] But in Upper Canada, Elliott shows that at least for the Tipperary immigrant families, detailed instructions about education can be found in certain wills throughout the first half of the nineteenth century. While land and the transmission of property were the central elements of the inheritance instructions, at least some children began receiving "cash and an education" as their share of the patrimony.[62] Similarly, Marjorie Cohen cites in her own recent study the example of a farmer who in 1804 planned in his will for the education of his children even if his wife should remarry: "if my widow should marry I hereby obligate my said son George to bring up and maintain the rest of my children that are not able to do for themselves and use the best endeavour to see them instructed in reading and writing."[63]

Such examples represent very fragmentary evidence. However, they do suggest a place for education within the inheritance process of at least certain Upper Canadians by the early 1800s. This place was not large but it did apply to both boys and girls. The major concern of wills at this time certainly related to property, and, in contrast to education, sons and daughters were not treated the same way. In Cohen's study, for example, she found that only one-quarter of the wills from the early nineteenth century left a portion of land to daughters.[64] In this sense, the specifications for education appear relatively egalitarian; the educational provisions do not seem to have discriminated against daughters in the way that the transmission of land clearly reflected patriarchal imperatives.

Evidence from later decades does indeed suggest that the place of education within inheritance significantly increased. Cohen emphasizes the example of a farmer who, in 1853, carefully provided for the education of his children whether or not his wife remarried:

> In case my wife should remarry then in that case my executors herein after named and whom I also appropriate as trustees for my children shall then take the sole management of the said farms and stock and rent or let the same or shares as they see fit and apply the said income to the benefit of my children whom they shall take the management of and see them educated and placed in such situation as said income will admit of and to give my widow a cow and four sheep with a bed and bedding and for her to have no more to say of my affairs. But if she remain my widow and so continues after the children are all educated and of age she shall still have during her natural life the one half of the income of the said farm on which we at present reside.[65]

Similarly, Elliott argues that concern for the education of daughters particularly increased as the earlier expectation that they would marry farmers became more uncertain. At least in the case of those with ancestors from Tipperary, Elliott concludes that, by 1870, it became "fairly common to insist [in wills] that daughters receive an education."[66]

Clearly, only some of the relationships between education and family reproduction can be studied through any particular type of document. While wills appear to hold considerable promise, it must be remembered that they do not capture the full process of transmission and, given the usual circumstances of their writing, can only be expected to offer fragmentary evidence on education. It is also very problematic for educational research that wills were predominantly written by men. Although some evidence exists for widows, a great deal remains to be known about the ways in which women viewed education as a part of family reproduction.

In this sense, the past two decades of scholarly activity have demonstrated the need to draw upon as many concepts, sources, research strategies as possible in order to interpret the complex origins of mass schooling. To emphasize the potential of bringing together the fields of education, economic history, and demography is not to suggest that other subfields can be left aside. However, this approach does indicate that the evolution of historical debate now shows the need for more social history, not less. To insist upon the importance of viewing the history of schooling from the perspective of families experiencing rural transformation is not to imply that urban research was misguided. Instead, the preceding discussion attempts to suggest how previous work can be built upon to achieve a better understanding of why schooling came to play a major role in the lives of children.

Hypotheses about the changing ways in which education came to be situated within the processes of family reproduction in nineteenth-century Ontario indicate the importance of gradual and profound transformations more than the impact of sudden crises. The reconfiguration of growing up did not simply result from short-term "tactics" as families confronted immediate pressures but also from evolving long-term strategies as families came to grips with the meaning of new social and economic structures.[67] It appears that individuals and families did not necessarily have to come face-to-face with substantial difficulty before they adjusted or innovated their behaviour. Rather, the evidence suggests that quite subtle changes were early perceived. While significant difficulties were met by many despite their own best efforts and often for reasons far beyond their control, members of families were, indeed, striving to control their own destinies. One result was a greater interest in sending children to school.

• Notes

1 The now classic and as yet unsurpassed study is Neil Sutherland, *Children in English-Canadian Society: Framing the Twentieth Century Consensus* (Toronto: University of Toronto Press, 1976). Research undertaken in the 1970s is listed in the bibliography of Joy Parr, ed., *Childhood and Family in Canadian History* (Toronto: McClelland and Stewart, 1982), and more recent studies can be found in the bibliographical work of the Canadian Childhood History Project at University of British Columbia under Sutherland and Jean Barman.

2 The pioneering work in the Canadian context was Parr, *Childhood and Family*. More recent collections of essays that examine the United States experience include N. Ray Hiner and Joseph M. Hawes, eds., *Growing-Up in America: Children in Historical Perspective* (Urbana and Chicago: University of Illinois Press, 1985), and Harvey J. Graff, ed., *Growing Up in America: Historical Experiences* (Detroit, MI: Wayne State University Press, 1988).

3 Rayna Rapp et al., "Examining Family History," *Feminist Studies* 5 (1979): 174–200. Recent perspectives on this issue are offered in the special section of *Historical Methods* 20 (1987): 113–25 entitled "Family Strategy: A Dialogue." For an example of recent research that assumes this perspective see Veronica Strong-Boag, *The New Day Recalled: Lives of Girls and Women in English Canada, 1919–1939* (Toronto: Copp Clark Pitman, 1988).

4 Recent thoughts on this issue include those of Ian Davey presented in "Rethinking the Origins of British Colonial School Systems," *Historical Studies in Education* 1 (1989): 149–59.

5 Barbara Laslett and Johanna Brenner offer a valuable review of the conceptual issues in "Gender and Social Reproduction: Historical Perspectives," presented to the Social Science History Association, 1988.

6 Glen H. Elder, "Families and Lives: Some Developments in Life-Course Studies" in *Family History at the Crossroads,* ed. Tamara Hareven and Andrejs Plakans (Princeton, NJ: Princeton University Press, 1987).

7 Martine Segalen, "Life-Course Patterns and Peasant Culture in France: A Critical Assessment," ibid.

8 Peter Laslett, "The Family as a Knot of Individual Interests" in *Households: Comparative and Historical Studies of the Domestic Group,* ed. R.M. Netting et al. (Berkeley and Los Angeles: University of California Press, 1984).

9 Historiographical essays on these fields include Douglas McCalla and Peter George, "Measurement, Myth, and Reality: Reflections on the Economic History of Nineteenth-Century Ontario," *Journal of Canadian Studies* 21 (1986): 71–86; J. Donald Wilson, "Some Observations on Recent Trends in Canadian Educational History" in *An Imperfect Past: Education and Society in Canadian History,* ed. Donald Wilson (Vancouver: Centre for the Study of Curriculum and Instruction, UBC, 1986); and Chad Gaffield, "Theory and Method in Canadian Historical Demography," *Acadiensis* 14 (1982): 123–36.

10 Bruce Curtis, *Building the Educational State: Canada West, 1836–1871* (London, ON: Falmer Press and Althouse Press, 1988); Susan E. Houston and Alison Prentice, *Schooling and Scholars in Nineteenth-Century Ontario* (Toronto: University of Toronto Press, 1988); and R.D. Gidney and W.P.J. Millar, *Inventing Secondary Education: The Rise of the High School in Nineteenth-Century Ontario* (Montreal and Kingston: McGill-Queen's University Press, 1990).

11 A.B. McKillop, "Culture, Intellect, and Context: Recent Writing on the Cultural and Intellectual History of Ontario," *Journal of Canadian Studies* 24 (1989): 16–17.

12 A significant contribution of this work was the challenge it posed to the established "staples" approach to Canadian history. By focussing on Canada's Industrial Revolution, scholars of the working class brought the Canadian experience into the mainstream of Western social and economic change. Extensive notes provide a valuable guide to the best of this literature in Bryan Palmer's "Social Formation and Class Formation in North America, 1800–1900" in *Proletarianization and Family History*, ed. David Levine (New York: Academic Press, 1984).

13 The most important was Michael Katz's Hamilton Project, which led to *The People of Hamilton: Family and Class in a Mid-Nineteenth-Century City* (Cambridge, MA: Harvard University Press, 1975), and, with Michael T. Doucet and Mark J. Stern, *The Social Organization of Early Industrial Capitalism* (Cambridge, MA: Harvard University Press, 1982).

14 The most influential article for Ontario was undoubtedly Leo A. Johnson, "Land Policy, Population Growth, and Social Structure in the Home District, 1793–1851," *Ontario History* 63 (1971): 41–60. The classic work, which still looms large despite sustained criticism, is H. Clare Pentland, *Labour and Capital in Canada 1650–1850* (Toronto: Lorimer, 1981). The critics include Donald Akenson, "H. Clare Pentland, the Irish, and the New Canadian Social History" in his *Being Had: Historians, Evidence, and the Irish in North America* (Port Credit, ON: P.D. Meany, 1985), and Allan Greer, "Wage Labour and the Transition to Capitalism," *Labour/Le Travail* 15 (Spring 1985): 7–22. The continuing relevance of Pentland's argument is supported by Palmer in "Social Formation and Class Formation," and in "Town, Port, and Country: Speculations on the Capitalist Transformation of Canada," *Acadiensis* 12, 2 (1983): 131–39.

15 The key importance of land in nineteenth-century Ontario was at the heart of David Gagan's research in the 1970s, which led to *Hopeful Travellers: Families, Land, and Social Change in Mid-Victorian Peel County, Canada West* (Toronto: University of Toronto Press, 1981). Only a relatively small number of scholars (including John Clarke, Peter Russell, Randy Widdis, and Brian Osborne) have continued this interest in rural society. Allan Smith offers a fascinating discussion in "Farms, Forests and Cities: The Image of the Land and the Rise of the Metropolis in Ontario, 1860–1914" in *Old Ontario: Essays in Honour of J.M.S. Careless*, ed. David Keane and Colin Read (Toronto: Dundurn, 1990). Researchers in Quebec have consistently used the countryside to pursue sociohistorical questions in the nineteenth century. The ongoing renewal of debate is evident in, for example, Serge Courville, "Villages and Agriculture in the Seigneuries of Lower Canada: Conditions of a Comprehensive Study of Rural Quebec in the First Half of the Nineteenth Century," *Canadian Papers in Rural History* 5 (1986): 101–23.

16 Susan E. Houston, "Politics, Schools, and Social Change in Upper Canada," *Canadian Historical Review* 53 (1972): 249–71.

17 Many important articles have been written by R.D. Gidney, the late D.A. Lawr, and W.P.J. Millar, including "Bureaucracy vs. Community? The Origins of Bureaucratic Procedures in the Upper Canadian School System," *Journal of Social History* 13 (1980): 438–57, and "From Voluntarism to State Schooling: The Creation of the Public School System in Ontario," *Canadian Historical Review* 66 (1985): 443–73.

18 Katz, *The People of Hamilton*; and Katz, Doucet, and Stern, *The Social Organization of Early Industrial Capitalism*.

19 Gagan, *Hopeful Travellers*.

20 Houston and Prentice discuss many additional examples in *Schooling and Scholars.*

21 In his recent work, Ian M. Drummond analyses the province in terms of five regions; see, for example, table 3.13 in *Progress without Planning: The Economic History of Ontario from Confederation to the Second World War* (Toronto: University of Toronto Press, 1987), 378.

22 Chad Gaffield, *Language, Schooling, and Cultural Conflict: The Origins of the French-Language Controversy in Ontario* (Montreal and Kingston: McGill-Queen's University Press, 1987), chs. 2 and 3. A different perspective on the settlement of easternmost Ontario is offered by Fernand Ouellet in his essay reviewing this book published in *Ontario History* 81 (1989): 59–68. Unfortunately, the tables of empirical evidence Ouellet proposes are marred by errors of transcription or typography and thus should only be used with extreme caution. More importantly, though, Ouellet's aggregate-level approach requires readers to suspend belief in the ecological fallacy. This requirement seems unreasonable given the nature of the issues, and, happily, is unnecessary given the availability of individual-level data (as used in *Language, Schooling and Culture Conflict*).

23 Gordon Darroch and Michael Ornstein, "Ethnicity and Class: Transitions over a Decade, Ontario 1861–1871," *Historical Papers* (1984): 111–37.

24 The most valuable research includes the work of Douglas McCalla, such as "The Wheat Staple and Upper Canadian Development," *Historical Papers* (1978): 34–45 and "The Internal Economy of Upper Canada: New Evidence on Agricultural Marketing Before 1850," *Agricultural History* 59 (1985): 375–416. For the later period see Marvin McInnis, "Marketable Surpluses in Ontario Farming, 1860," *Social Science History* 8

(1984): 395–424; John Isbister, "Agriculture, Balanced Growth, and Social Change in Central Canada: An Interpretation," *Economic Development and Cultural Change* 25 (1977): 673–97; D.A. Lawr, "The Development of Ontario Farming 1870–1919," *Ontario History* 64 (1972): 239–51; Robert E. Ankli and Wendy Millar, "Ontario Agriculture in Transition: The Shift from Wheat to Cheese," *Journal of Economic History* 42 (1982): 207–15; and John McCallum, *Unequal Beginnings: Agriculture and Economic Development in Quebec and Ontario until 1870* (Toronto, University of Toronto Press, 1980).

25 Peter A. Russell, "Wage Labour Rates in Upper Canada, 1818–1840," *Histoire sociale/Social History* 16 (1983): 61–80.

26 On those in agriculture see Joy Parr, "Hired Men: Ontario Agricultural Wage Labour in Historical Perspective," *Labour/Le Travail* 15 (1985): 91–103.

27 Chad Gaffield, "Boom and Bust: The Demography and Economy of the Lower Ottawa Valley in the Nineteenth Century," *Historical Papers* (1982): 172–95. McCalla and George wonder about "the degree to which the Ottawa region in particular was relatively independent of the economy of the rest of the province," in "Measurement, Myth, and Reality," 78. While this is an important question, it does not say that the "rest of the province" was one region.

28 This perception is also at the heart of one of the best studies of industrialization in North America: Jonathan Prude, *The Coming of Industrial Order: Town and Factory Life in Rural Massachusetts 1810–1860* (Cambridge, MA: Harvard University Press, 1983).

29 The term *semiproletarian,* or some other version, has been used by Canadian historians to capture (usually from the point of view of individuals rather than their families) the combining of wage labour with work on one's own account. An early example is Michael Cross, "The Dark

Druidical Groves," (PhD thesis, University of Toronto, 1968); more recently, see James Sacouman, "Semi-Proletarianization and Rural Underdevelopment in the Maritimes," *Canadian Review of Sociology and Anthropology* 17 (1980): 232–45.

30 The complexity of rural land-holding is becoming increasingly evident as a result of work such as William L. Marr's careful study of the small but significant role of tenant farms in "Nineteenth Century Tenancy Rates in Ontario's Counties, 1881 and 1891," *Journal of Social History* 21 (1988): 753–63.

31 Gordon Darroch, "Class in Nineteenth-Century Ontario: A Reassessment of the Crisis and Demise of Small Producers during Early Industrialization, 1861–1871" in *Class, Gender, and Region: Essays in Canadian Historical Sociology*, ed. Gregory Kealey (St John's: Committee on Canadian Labour History, 1988). Darroch places this specific evidence within an argument about the long-term change of Canada's social formation in "Class and Stratification" in *An Introduction to Sociology*, 2nd ed., ed. L. Tepperman and J. Richardson (Toronto: McGraw-Hill Ryerson, 1989).

32 The complex issues involved in the conceptualization of family farms, wage labour, and the market are grappled with in insightful ways, with some reference to Canada, by Harriet Friedmann in "World Market, State, and Family Farm: Social Bases of Household Production in the Era of Wage Labour," *Comparative Studies in Society and History* 20 (1978): 545–86.

33 Houston and Prentice, *Schooling and Scholars*, 344.

34 Donald Harmond Akenson, *The Irish in Ontario: A Study in Rural History* (Montreal and Kingston: McGill-Queen's University Press, 1984), and *Being Had.*

35 Bruce S. Elliott, *Irish Migrants in the Canadas: A New Approach* (Montreal

and Kingston: McGill-Queen's University Press, 1988), 5.

36 David P. Gagan, "Class and Society in Victorian English Canada: An Historiographical Reassessment," *British Journal of Canadian Studies* 4, 1 (1989): 74–87.

37 The literature on school attendance is now quite massive. The best overview is in Houston and Prentice, *Schooling and Scholars*, 214–23.

38 The evidence on eastern Ontario is presented in Gaffield, *Language, Schooling, and Cultural Conflict*, and other relevant examples are offered in Bruce Curtis, *Building the Educational State*.

39 Harvey Graff's first major work was *The Literacy Myth: Literacy and Social Structure in the Nineteenth-Century City* (New York: Academic Press, 1979). H.J. Mays and H.F. Manzl believe that Graff overestimates the extent of literacy as a result of inappropriate interpretation of census data; see their lively debate in "Literary and Social Structure in Nineteenth Century Ontario: An Exercise in Historical Demography," *Histoire sociale/Social History* 7 (Nov. 1974): 331–47.

40 The work of Gidney, Lawr, and Millar has been most important in promoting this interpretation. They posed the key question in the title of "Who Ran the Schools? Local Influence on Educational Policy in Nineteenth-Century Ontario," *Ontario History* 72, 3 (Sept. 1980): 131–43.

41 R.D. Gidney and W.P.J. Millar, "From Voluntarism to State Schooling: The Creation of the Public School System in Ontario," *Canadian Historical Review* 66, 4 (Dec. 1985): 443–73.

42 Angus McLaren and Arlene Tigar McLaren summarize the demographic evidence as the point of departure for their study of contraception and abortion in *The Bedroom and the State: The Changing Practices of Politics of Contraception and Abortion in Canada, 1880–1980* (Toronto: McClelland and Stewart, 1986).

43 Marvin McInnis's extensive research has been undertaken for the *Historical Atlas of Canada*, vol. 2 (Toronto: University of Toronto Press, 1993). The results for central Canada are analysed in "Fertility Patterns in Late Nineteenth-Century Quebec and Ontario," presented at the colloquium Studies in North American Fertility, University of Ottawa, March 1989.

44 Wally Seccombe has quipped that "one would never guess [from reading the publications of historical demographers] that childbearing was a sex-specific and gender differentiated process." See "Marxism and Demography," *New Left Review* 137 (1983): 22–47. In contrast, McLaren and McLaren differentiate as much as possible between men and women in *The Bedroom and the State.*

45 One of the few discussions in Canada of the relationship between women's history and historical demography is Jennifer Stoddart, "L'histoire des femmes et la démographie," *Cahiers québécois de démographie* 13 (1984): 79–85. Marie Lavigne has particularly emphasized the need to assess aggregate demographic evidence from the women's point of view in her "Réflexions féministes autour de la fertilité des Québécois" in *Maîtresses de maison, maîtresses d'école*, ed. Nadia Fahmy-Eid and Micheline Dumont (Montréal: Boreal Express, 1983); her work for early nineteenth-century Quebec is summarized in the Clio Collective, *Quebec Women: A History* (Toronto: Women's Press, 1987), 192–93.

46 For a presentation of the kind of conceptualization that seems worth pursuing see David Levine, "Recombinant Family Formation Strategies," *Journal of Historical Sociology* 2 (1989): 100–106.

47 It may also be, of course, that some third as yet unidentified process was responsible for both literacy and fertility trends. Or they may have been dynamically interrelated, both acting at various moments as independent and dependent variables. An important contribution to conceptualization of the many possible connections between fertility and education is Mark J. Stern's *Society and Family Strategy: Erie County, New York 1850–1920* (Albany, NY: State University of New York Press, 1987).

48 Ellen M.T. Gee has undertaken the most extensive work including "Marriage in Nineteenth-Century Canada," *Canadian Review of Sociology and Anthropology* 3 (1982): 311–25. Also see the older but still valuable study by Lorne Tepperman in "Ethnic Variations in Marriage and Fertility: Canada in 1871," *Canadian Review of Sociology and Anthropology* 9 (1974): 324–43.

49 One of the few studies of illegitimacy is W. Peter Ward's "Unwed Motherhood in Nineteenth-Century English Canada," *Historical Papers* (1981): 34–56.

50 Peter Ward, *Courtship, Love, and Marriage in Nineteenth-Century Canada* (Montreal and Kingston: McGill-Queen's University Press, 1990).

51 While various scholars have pursued the links between family history and educational history, the specific question of inheritance has been quite neglected as a possible aspect of these links; for example, see the valuable discussions in Nadia Fahmy-Eid and Micheline Dumont, "Les rapports femmes/famille/éducation au Québec: bilan de la recherche" in their *Maîtresses de maison*; and Maris A. Vinovskis, "Family and Schooling in Colonial and Nineteenth-Century America" in Hareven and Plakans, *Family History at the Crossroads*. It is also noteworthy that the question of inheritance in a predominantly rural social formation has received considerable attention in Quebec; for example, see "Famille, mariage, patrimoine et reproduction sociale," part 3 of Joseph Goy and Jean-Pierre Wallot, eds., *Evolution et éclatement du monde rural* (Montréal: Presses de

l'Université de Montréal, 1986). Gidney and Millar do mention inheritance in their recent book, *Inventing Secondary Education*; see 25–26 and 135–36.

52 David Gagan, "The Indivisibility of Land: A Microanalysis of the System of Inheritance in Nineteenth-Century Ontario," *Journal of Economic History* 36 (1976): 126–47.

53 For comparative perspectives see Gérard Bouchard and Jeannette Larouche, "Paramètres sociaux de la reproduction familiale au Saguenay (1842–1911)," *Sociologie et sociétés* 19 (1987): 133–44, and David Gaunt, "Rural Household Organization and Inheritance in Northern Europe" in Hareven and Plakans, *Family History at the Crossroads*.

54 Beatrice Craig offers a comparative perspective (and a helpful bibliography) in "Pour une approche comparative de l'étude des sociétés rurales nord-américaines," *Histoire sociale/ Social History* 23, 46 (1990): 249–70.

55 Elliott, *Irish Migrants*, ch. 8.

56 Jack Goody, ed., *Family and Inheritance: Rural Society in Western Europe, 1200–1800* (Cambridge, England: Cambridge University Press, 1976).

57 Daniel Vickers, "Competency and Competition: Economic Culture in Early America," *William and Mary Quarterly* 47, 1 (Jan. 1990): 28.

58 Alison Prentice, "Education and the Metaphor of the Family: The Upper Canadian Example" in *Education and Social Change: Themes from Ontario's Past*, ed. Michael B. Katz and Paul H. Mattingly (New York: New York University Press, 1975).

59 One of the many valuable studies is Marta Danylewycz, Beth Light, and Alison Prentice, "The Evolution of the Sexual Division of Labour in Teaching: A Nineteenth-Century Ontario and Quebec Case Study," *Histoire sociale/Social History* 31 (1983): 81–109.

60 The Christian character of public schooling has been reaffirmed by William Westfall in *Two Worlds: The Protestant Culture of Nineteenth-Century Ontario* (Kingston and Montreal: McGill-Queen's University Press, 1989).

61 Allan Greer, *Peasant, Lord, and Merchant: Rural Society in Three Quebec Parishes 1740–1840* (Toronto: University of Toronto Press, 1985), 71–81, 221–24.

62 Elliott, *Irish Migrants*, ch. 8. A recent attempt to locate the changing importance of education with early nineteenth-century rural society in the United States is William C. Gilmore, *Reading Becomes a Necessity of Life: Material and Cultural Life in Rural New England 1780–1885* (Nashville, TN: University of Tennessee Press, 1989).

63 AO, WC, GS1-1251, George Grites, 1804, cited in Marjorie Griffin Cohen, *Women's Work, Markets and Economic Development in Nineteenth-Century Ontario* (Toronto: University of Toronto Press, 1988), 51.

64 Cohen, *Women's Work*, 56. Cohen is not completely clear on whether the proportion was "almost one-third" or "over one-fifth."

65 AO, WC, GS1-1253, William Cassidy, 1853, cited in Cohen, *Women's Work*, 50–51.

66 Elliott, *Irish Migrants*, 202.

67 The distinction between "tactics" and "strategies" is emphasized in Daniel Scott Smith, "Family Strategy: More than a Metaphor?" *Historical Methods* 10 (1987): 118–20.

THE MARITIMES
AND CONFEDERATION:
A Reassessment*

PHILLIP BUCKNER

A number of years ago Ernie Forbes in an important article challenged the stereotype of Maritime conservatism and attempted to show how it had distorted the way in which the history of the Maritimes has been portrayed in the post-Confederation period.[1] Yet it can be argued that this stereotype has also influenced our interpretation of the pre-Confederation era in a variety of ways. Nowhere is this more true than in studies of the role of the region in the making of Confederation. The failure of the Maritime colonies to respond enthusiastically to the Canadian initiative for Confederation in the 1860s has come to be seen as yet another example of their inherent conservatism. The impression that emerges from the literature is of a series of parochial communities content with the status quo and trapped in intellectual lethargy who were dragged kicking and screaming into Confederation. This stereotype leads to several misleading conclusions. First, it encourages historians to underestimate the degree of sup-

*From *Canadian Historical Review* 72, 1 (1990). Reprinted by permission of University of Toronto Press Incorporated. © University of Toronto Press. An earlier version of this paper was delivered at the seminar on "The Causes of Canadian Confederation: Cantilever or Coincidence?" at the University of Edinburgh, 9 May 1988, and I am grateful to Ged Martin for asking me to give a few "general comments" on this subject. I am also grateful to a number of colleagues and friends for agreeing to comment on that earlier draft, including Ernest Forbes, William Acheson, David Frank, Ken Pryke, Jack Bumsted, and Brook Taylor. I hasten to add that none of them agreed with everything I have said, although no two of them disagreed with the same thing.

port which existed within the Maritimes for the ideal of a larger British North American union and to exaggerate the gulf that divided the anti-confederates from the pro-confederates. Second, it oversimplifies and trivializes the very real and substantive objections which many Maritimers had to the kind of union that they were eventually forced to accept. Recent American historiography has led to a substantial rethinking of the debate that took place in the United States over the ratification of the American constitution in the 1780s, and a similar reassessment of the debate over the Quebec Resolutions in the Maritimes in the 1860s is long overdue.

The first studies of Confederation, in fact, devoted little time to this issue. Reginald George Trotter in *Canadian Federation: Its Origins and Achievement* (Toronto, 1924) barely mentions the debate over Confederation in the Maritimes, and M.O. Hammond in *Confederation and Its Leaders* (Toronto, 1917) simply ascribed the views of anti-confederates such as Albert J. Smith to their "opposition to change of any kind" (p. 237). In the first scholarly article on "New Brunswick's Entrance into Confederation," George Wilson assumed as a given New Brunswick's hesitancy and focussed on the factors—the loyalty cry, Canadian campaign funds, and the "educational work of Tilley" (p. 24)—which he saw as critical in persuading New Brunswickers to vote for union.[2] D.C. Harvey also concentrated on the idealism of the expansionists in his paper on "The Maritime Provinces and Confederation" in 1927.[3] Writing at a time when there was a feeling in the Maritimes that Confederation had not delivered what had been promised,[4] Harvey stressed that union could have been accomplished relatively easily if the "factious" opponents of federation had not been "able to whip up an opposition that caused no end of trouble to the unionist statesmen and left behind a legacy of suspicion and ill-will which has been like an ulcer in the side of the Dominion" (p. 44). Harvey called for Maritimers to "recapture" the initial enthusiasm of the pro-confederates and to abandon the tendency to blame Confederation for their problems. By implication, then, the critics of Confederation both in the 1860s and the 1920s lacked vision and statesmanship.

This perspective was also implicit in William Menzies Whitelaw's *The Maritimes and Canada before Confederation.*[5] In his preface, Whitelaw declared that he had focussed the book around "the struggle between an incipient nationalism and a rugged particularism" (p. xix). The book was published in 1934 after the collapse of the Maritime Rights Movement and the onset of the Great Depression, at a time when most Canadian historians were beginning to see the advantages of a strong central government and Maritimers were again discussing the chimera of Maritime Union. Not surprisingly, Whitelaw approached the topic with a strong bias in favour of Confederation and preferably a highly centralized federal system. From the beginning the emphasis of the book was on the relative backwardness of the Maritimes and the persistence there of "early particularism," the title of one of the first chapters. Whitelaw ended his study in 1864 with an insightful chapter on "Maritime Interests at Quebec," which showed how the Canadians manipulated the Quebec Conference and outmanoeuvred the divided Maritimers.[6] Interestingly, he did not discuss the actual debate over the Quebec Resolutions but concluded with a brief lament over the decision to abandon Maritime Union. In his review of the book in the *Canadian Historical Review,* Chester Martin with some justification declared that Whitelaw "leaves an impression not only of 'particularism' but of parochialism: of particularism run to seed, too inert to defend or even to discern their own interests in the presence of the expansive forces then abroad in Canada and the United States."[7]

In the 1940s, A.G. Bailey contributed two important articles to the small corpus of serious scholarly literature on the Maritimes and Confederation.[8] In "Railways and the Confederation Issue in New Brunswick, 1863–1865," he focussed rather narrowly on the debate over the western extension, which he argued was the "most potent" factor behind the opposition to Confederation in the colony (p. 91).[9] The problem with explaining the debate in New Brunswick in these terms is that many pro-confederates wanted the western extension, not a few anti-confederates wanted the Intercolonial, and a large number of New Brunswickers wanted both, although they could afford neither.[10] In his next article on "The Basis and Persistence of Opposition to Confederation in New Brunswick," Bailey adopted a broader approach. Although starting from the assumption that "in the early stages of the union movement there was a misapprehension of its significance, together with some degree of apathy, rather than a reasoned opposition" (p. 93), he went on to explore with some subtlety the roots of anti-Confederation sentiment. The rapid collapse of the anti-confederate government he again ascribed primarily to its failure to complete the western extension, but he also emphasized mounting pressure from the imperial government as well as "the exaggerated menace of Fenian invasion" (p. 117) and Canadian campaign funds. He also recognized that many of those who opposed union "directed their attacks not so much against the principle of Confederation as against the specific terms of union which had been embodied in the Quebec Resolutions" (p. 115). Indeed, the failure of the pro-confederates to make substantial alterations in those resolutions in London accounted, he suggested, for "the remarkable persistence of opposition" to Confederation after 1866 (p. 116). But he did not emphasize this point, which is made as a kind of aside in the conclusion of the article.

The next major study of Confederation came from Chester Martin. In the *Foundations of Canadian Nationhood* (Toronto, 1955), he dismissed the opposition to Confederation in the Maritimes as "too general to be the result of personalities or sheer parochialism" (p. 347). This insight might have provided the basis for a fundamental reassessment of the debate in the Maritimes, but Martin quickly reverted to the stereotype of Maritime conservatism. Indeed, one of the major subthemes in the book is that the original decision to partition Nova Scotia into a series of smaller units had inevitably promoted parochialism: "Where local division had been deliberately planted and thriven for three-quarters of a century, provincialism was only too apt to degenerate into sheer parochialism" (p. 290). Because he saw Confederation as forced upon the British North American colonies by (in what was the *leitmotif* of this section of the book) "events stronger than advocacy, events stronger than men" (p. 291) and the opposition to it as a natural instinct (see p. 297), Martin also accepted that "there were solid reasons for resistance based upon conflicting interests and a long train of policy" (p. 355). Nonetheless, the clear implication of his approach was that the fundamental motivation behind the widespread Maritime opposition to the Quebec Resolutions was the deep-seated conservatism of the region.

During the early 1960s, writing on Confederation became a growth industry as Canada approached its centennial. Since most Canadian historians were still influenced by the consensus approach, which minimized the significance of internal conflicts by focussing on the things which united Canadians and distinguished them from other people, they tended to downplay regional concerns and to interpret the making of Confederation as a success story of which all Canadians should be proud.[11] The best of these studies was P.B. Waite's *The Life and Times of Confederation 1864–67*, and it is a tragedy that it has been allowed to go out of print.[12] Although Waite does not indicate that he was directly influenced by Chester Martin, there are a number of parallels in their interpretations. Like Martin, Waite saw Confederation as forced upon the British North Americans by external pressures. Although he was less deterministic and did not see Confederation as an inevitable response to these pressures, he concluded that Confederation was "imposed on British North America by ingenuity, luck, courage, and sheer force" (p. 323). Like Martin, he argued that the opposition to Confederation was rooted in the "innate conservatism" of the smaller communities across British North America (p. 14) and that this conservatism was particularly strong in the Maritimes. But reflecting the spirit of the 1960s, Waite also saw the tentative stirrings of a sense of Canadian nationalism in the 1860s. By 1864, he concluded, "Whether for good or ill, there was a national spirit stirring in the Maritime provinces" (p. 72); in fact, the Maritime pro-confederates were even more eager than the Canadians to escape from "the littleness of provincial pastures" (p. 89).

Since Waite clearly accepted that Confederation was necessary and desirable and that the Quebec Resolutions were an imaginative and ingenious recipe for union, he had limited patience with the anti-confederates who are seen as "men of little faith."[13] His impatience with their unwillingness to accept the Quebec terms is revealed in his treatment of the "Poor, tired, rather embittered" Joseph Howe who might "have supported Confederation had he had an opportunity similar to Tupper's" (p. 210). And it is even more clearly revealed in his assessment of L.A. Wilmot: "It may have been that Wilmot was perfectly genuine in his conversion to Confederation. But if so, it was not his main motive. With Wilmot perquisites usually triumphed over policies" (p. 256). Waite accepted that Nova Scotians had some reason for resentment since the Quebec Resolutions were imposed upon them against their will, but he did not extend the same sympathy to New Brunswick and Prince Edward Island, which he described as totally mired in an all-pervasive parochialism: "Of both Fredericton and Charlottetown Goldwin Smith's unrepentant aphorism is not altogether inappropriate: 'The smaller the pit, the fiercer the rats'" (p. 233).[14] It was the "ferocity of politics" which accounted for the "primeval character" of the discussion of Confederation in New Brunswick (pp. 233–34). As for Prince Edward Island, their opposition is more simply explained. Most Islanders had never been away from the Island in their lives (at least according to George Brown) and they had "had little opportunity to cultivate larger loyalties." "Like the Acadians a century before, they simply wanted to be left alone" (pp. 180–81).

Waite's emphasis on the parochialism and conservatism of New Brunswick and Prince Edward Island was reinforced by two more specialized studies which appeared in the early 1960s. There was always a curiously ambivalent attitude in the work of W.S. MacNutt towards his adopted province. Because he was disappointed with the province's performance in the post-World War II era, he took up the cause of Maritime unity in the 1950s and railed against those local politicians who were obsessed with the distribution of local patronage and lacked a vision of grandeur.[15] In *New Brunswick: A History: 1784–1867* (Toronto, 1963), he projected this anger backwards and his impatience with the provincial politicians shines through. Although MacNutt felt it was "difficult to allow very much praise for the politicians" of the province (p. 460), at least "a few leaders of imagination and daring had made themselves the instruments of the grand idea that was British North America's response to the problems of the time, the urge for mergers and the manufacturing of great states" (p. 454). Francis W.P. Bolger adopted a not dissimilar approach in *Prince Edward Island and Confederation 1863–1873* (Charlottetown, 1964). During the years that Confederation was discussed, Island politics, he noted, "remained personal, parochial, and violent" (p. 14), and it was inevitable that the Island would resist with all its might the pressures for union.[16]

It is difficult not to come away from these works with the impression that there was virtually no support for Confederation in the Maritimes, except for a handful of prescient individuals who had the imagination to accept the leadership of the more far-sighted and progressive Canadians. Yet all three studies revealed very clearly that anti-Confederation sentiment in the region was generated as much by the unpalatability of the Quebec Resolutions as by opposition to the idea of Confederation itself. All three historians also accepted that the terms adopted at Quebec City reflected Canadian needs and Canadian priorities and, like Whitelaw, they clearly assumed that the Maritime delegates to Quebec had failed to secure better terms because of the superior acumen and organization of the Canadian delegation. It is, of course, true that the exigencies of Canadian politics forced the members of the Great Coalition to adopt a relatively united front on the constitutional issues under discussion at a time when the Maritime delegations were divided both internally and amongst themselves at Quebec. But one could as easily attribute the failure of the Maritime delegates to their realism and to the extent of their desire for some kind of union. Their basic problem was that the two regions were of such unequal size. At Philadelphia in 1787 the Americans were forced to resort to equal representation in the Senate, not solely to appease the small states but also for reasons of "*regional* security," in order "to safeguard the most conspicuous interests of North and South."[17] In the end it was the comparative equality of the two regions which compelled the delegates at Philadelphia to agree to the "Great Compromise." No such pressure existed at Quebec in 1864. Because of the uneven size and power of the two regions, the Maritime delegates were compelled to agree to union on Canadian terms, if they wanted union at all.

The leading Maritime politicians at Quebec had no illusions about the limited room they had for manoeuvre. Even at Charlottetown Samuel Leonard Tilley and W.H. Pope opposed the suggestion that Maritime Union should precede Confederation on the grounds that the Maritime provinces would be able to arrive at better terms with Canada by negotiating separately rather than united.[18] Indeed, Charles Tupper believed that the gradual withdrawal of Britain had made the subordination of the Maritimes to Canada inevitable and that the goal of the Maritime delegates at Quebec must be to gain the best terms of union that they could.[19] The Maritimers did try to offset their weakness in the House of Commons by insisting on sectional equality in the Senate, and the majority of them also sought to ensure that the provinces would be left with control over those local matters of most immediate concern to their constituents. Although Jonathan McCully failed in his attempt to have agriculture removed from the list of federal responsibilities, Tilley persuaded the delegates to transfer control over roads and bridges to the provinces.[20] Indeed, upon returning to New Brunswick, Tilley worked out that only five of the fifty-nine acts passed by the New Brunswick legislature in the previous session would be found *ultra vires* of the provincial government under the proposed division of powers.[21] And both Tilley and Tupper pointed out forcefully at the London Conference that their intention had not been to create a "Legislative Union."[22] Yet, even after it became clear to them how unpopular the Quebec Resolutions were, the pro-confederate leadership recognized that there were limits to the concessions the Canadians could make without destroying the fragile unity of the great coalition. Reluctantly, therefore, they accepted that, if Confederation was to take place in the 1860s, "it is the Quebec scheme & little else we can hope to have secured."[23]

Although the pro-confederate leadership was probably right in this assumption, the Quebec Resolutions weakened the potential support for union in the region. Many of those sympathetic to the ideal of Confederation felt that a second conference should be called to renegotiate the terms of union.[24] Both Bailey and MacNutt attributed much of the lingering resentment to Confederation in New Brunswick after 1866 to the failure of the efforts of the New Brunswick delegates at the London Conference to make substantial alterations in the unpopular Quebec plan.[25] Bolger also accepted that the Island rejected the initial proposals because they were not "sufficiently attractive."[26] Much of the debate in the Maritimes revolved not over the issue of whether union was desirable but whether the Quebec Resolutions adequately met Maritime needs and concerns. The strength of the anti-confederate movement throughout the region was that it could appeal both to those whom Waite describes in Canada West as the "ultras," who opposed Confederation on any terms, and the "critics," who had specific objections to the Quebec scheme although they were not opposed to Confederation on principle.[27] In Canada West, most of the critics were easily convinced to put aside their objections; in the Maritimes, the proponents of the Quebec Resolutions had an uphill battle to bring the critics on side. Unfortunately, Waite does not present the struggle in the Maritimes in quite these terms but lumps the critics together with the ultras, thus creating the impression that die-hard opposition to union was stronger than it was. He therefore concludes that "New Brunswick was pushed into Union, Nova Scotia was dragooned into it, and Newfoundland and Prince Edward Island were subjected to all the pressure that could be brought to bear—short of force—and still refused."[28] In a literal sense these comments are true, but they gloss over the fact that what the Maritimes were pushed, dragooned, and in the case of PEI "railroaded" into was a union on Canadian terms.[29] MacNutt and Bolger also admitted that there were severe imperfections in the Quebec Resolutions from the perspective of the Maritimes, but they too ignored the implications of this argument and bunched together all anti-confederates as conservatives who lacked foresight.

This was also the conclusion of Donald Creighton in *The Road to Confederation: The Emergence of Canada 1863–1867* (Toronto, 1964). As in all his works, Creighton's writing was infused with a strong moral tone and a rigid teleological framework which emphasized that Confederation was the logical destination at the end of the road. Those who stood in the way of his vision of what was both right and inevitable were dismissed as narrow-minded obstructionists, and he began his book by approvingly paraphrasing Arthur Hamilton Gordon's description of the Maritimes as "half a dozen miserable fragments of provinces" where the "inevitable pettiness and the lack of talented and devoted men in public life could not but make for parochialism, maladministration, and low political morality in every department of provincial life" (p. 8). Throughout the book, Creighton contrasted "the lofty nationalist aims of the Canadians" (p. 154) with the parochialism of the Maritimers. "If the Charlottetown Conference was likely to end up as an open competition between confederation and Maritime union," he wrote scornfully, "the Maritimers seemed placidly unaware of the prospect, or disinclined to get excited about it. They appeared to be simply waiting without much concern, and even without a great deal of interest, to see what would turn up" (p. 91). To Creighton, the opposition of the Maritimers to Confederation was almost incomprehensible. Since "Maritimers showed, again and again, that they could not but feel their ultimate destiny lay in North American union" (p. 75), their opposition could only be based upon a natural lethargy. A much more sophisticated study of the Confederation era was W.L. Morton's *The Critical Years: The Union of British North America, 1857–1873* (Toronto, 1964). But Morton too had limited sympathy with the Maritimers' failure to see what he described as the "moral purpose of Confederation" (p. 277). New Brunswick's opposition he ascribed to the lack of moral integrity of its politicians and the lack of principle of its electorate, which "was largely composed of individuals who were politically indifferent, or took no interest in politics except to sell their votes" (p. 172).

The later 1960s and the 1970s also saw a considerable number of more specialized studies, mainly by academics coming from or living in the Maritimes, and they usually took one of two forms. On the one hand, some of these historians attempted to show that Maritime pro-confederates had played a more significant role in the Confederation movement than had previously been assumed, although they did not question the view that the pro-confederates possessed a larger vision than the vast majority of the inhabitants of the region.[30] Del Muise in his study of the debate over Confederation in Nova Scotia took a different and much more significant tack. Moving beyond the narrow political boundaries in which the whole debate had come to be cast, he argued that the battle over Confederation was between the proponents of the old maritime economy of "wood, wind and sail" and the younger, more progressive members of the regional elites who were prepared to make the transition to a continental economy based on railways and coal and committed to industrialization.[31] Muise's interpretative framework was particularly convincing in explaining—really for the first time—why pro-confederates such as Tupper, who were from areas with the potential for industrialization, were prepared to support union even on the basis of the somewhat unpalatable Quebec Resolutions, and he successfully established that "certain regions and interests in the Province wanted and carried Confederation."[32] Muise's thesis also helped to explain why those most committed to an international economy based on shipping and shipbuilding were so vehemently opposed to Confederation on almost any terms. By rescuing the debate from a narrowly political framework and focussing on the economic interests of the participants, Muise challenged the stereotype that most Maritimers were motivated by a rather simple-minded conservatism. Yet he also fell into the classic trap by identifying the pro-confederates as younger men while their opponents come across as conservatives resisting the forces of change. The work of the Maritime History Group has undermined this fallacious dichotomy, for they have shown that those who remained committed to the traditional economy—or at least to the shipping and shipbuilding industries—were among the most dynamic economic entrepreneurs in the region and that they were motivated not by a misplaced conservatism but a sensible analysis of the economic benefits still to be derived from investing in the traditional sectors of the economy.[33] Although it was not his intention, by portraying the division of economic interests in the province in terms of the old versus the young (and by implication those representing the future against those wedded to the past) Muise's thesis thus inadvertently reinforced the stereotype that the anti-confederate forces were motivated by parochialism and unprogressive attitudes.

Moreover, the attempt to divide the whole province into pro-confederates and anti-confederates on the basis of their commitment to the economy of wood, wind, and sail was too deterministic. By the 1860s there was a growing desire to participate in the evolving industrial economy, but, as Ben Forster has pointed out in his recent study of the rise of protectionist sentiment in British North America the Saint John manufacturing interests "had divided opinions as to the value of Confederation." Pryke makes the same point about Nova Scotian manufacturers.[34] Public opinion in those communities tied to wood, wind, and sail was also more deeply split than Muise's thesis allowed. After all, as he admitted, when Stewart Campbell introduced his resolution against Confederation in March 1867, only nine of the sixteen members of the Nova Scotia legislature who supported it were from areas committed to the traditional economy, and while twenty-five of the thirty-two members who supported it represented areas "with at least some commitment to the emerging economy of coal and railroads," the degree of that commitment varied considerably.[35]

Although Muise's approach was extremely valuable in helping to explain the extremes of opinion—the views of the ultras on both sides—it could not adequately explain the motives of the large body of men who were prepared to consider union with Canada but who disliked the Quebec Resolutions. We do not know precisely how many Maritimers fell into this category and we may never know, since the issue of accepting or rejecting the Quebec Resolutions temporarily forced most Maritimers to identify themselves as pro- or anti-confederates on that basis. What is certain is that a variety of interests and ideological and cultural perspectives were represented in both camps. Years ago, Bailey pointed out that in New Brunswick, "the cleavage of opinion seems not to have followed either occupational or class lines," and suggested that there were strong ethnic and religious overtones to the struggle.[36] Subsequent studies of New Brunswick have reaffirmed Bailey's insight and have emphasized cultural over economic factors, and similar patterns can be found in the other Maritime provinces. Traditionally, Canadian historians have emphasized the growing independence of the British North American colonies after the grant of responsible government. Yet these were also decades when, in a variety of ways, the colonies were becoming increasingly Anglicized.[37] The Quebec Resolutions, which so clearly sought to follow imperial and British institutional models, appear to have been most strongly supported by those who welcomed movement in this direction and particularly by the British-born; they were less enthusiastically endorsed by the native-born, of whom there was a much larger number in the Maritimes than in Canada West, and were viewed with greatest suspicion by cultural minorities such as Irish Catholics and Acadians. Nonetheless, as William Baker has shown, "the whole idea of a monolithic response by Irish Catholics to Confederation is highly questionable."[38] Desirable as it may be to come up with matching sets of dichotomous interests or ethnoreligious categories, one can do so only at the risk of obscuring the diversity that existed on both sides in the struggle.

The second major emphasis of the more recent scholarship has been on analysing the position of those Maritimers who opposed union. J. Murray Beck spent most of a life-time trying to correct the negative image of Howe embodied in the literature, although he did not deny that Howe "set store by the wrong vision."[39] Similarly, Carl Wallace dissected the motives of Albert J. Smith, who, he claimed, "exemplified the true mentality of New Brunswick 'in this era' and who, like New Brunswick, turned to the past, unable to adjust to the changing present."[40] Other historians, strongly influenced by the debate over the continuing underdevelopment of the region and a feeling that Maritimers may have made a bad deal when they entered Confederation, produced a series of studies that were more sympathetic to the anti-confederate position. Baker wrote a finely crafted book on Timothy Warren Anglin, pointing out that "in his original criticism of Confederation Anglin had been correct on many counts."[41] Robert Aitken supplied a sympathetic portrait of Yarmouth, that hotbed of anti-Confederation sentiment.[42] David Weale resurrected Cornelius Howat as the symbol of the desire of Prince Edward Island to retain control of its own destiny and, in *The Island and Confederation: The End of an Era*, produced with Harry Baglole a lament for the decision of the Island to enter Confederation.[43] Ken Pryke contributed an extremely balanced and very sophisticated study of *Nova Scotia and Confederation* (Toronto, 1979). Although he argued that Nova Scotians "had little alternative but to acquiesce" in a plan of union designed to meet Canadian needs, he explained the willingness of Nova Scotians to accept their "unwelcome subordination" to Canada by factionalism among the anti-confederates and imperial pressure. His conclusion was that "by default, then, Nova Scotia entered into and remained in Confederation" (p. xi). Whereas earlier historians had consigned the Maritime anti-confederates to the dust-basket of history, the revisionists rescued them from obscurity and emphasized that they were the true standard-bearers of the wishes of the majority of the population. Unfortunately, revisionism carries its own risks, for this approach often portrays the most vehement of the diehard anti-confederates as the legitimate voice of the Maritimes. Moreover, once again inadvertently, the revisionists also tended to reinforce the image that Maritimers were motivated by an all-pervasive parochialism and stubborn conservatism which explained the depth of anti-confederation sentiment in the region.

It is time to challenge this stereotype. If one turns the traditional question on its head and asks not why were so many Maritimers opposed to Confederation but why so many of them agreed so easily to a scheme of union that was clearly designed by Canadians to meet Canadian needs and to ensure Canadian dominance—which virtually everybody who has written on the subject agrees was implicit in the Quebec scheme—then the Maritime response to the Canadian initiative looks rather different. It may be true that there had been little discussion of the idea of an immediate union before the formation of the Great Coalition made Confederation an issue of practical politics, but the idea of British North American union, as Leslie Upton pointed out years ago, had been in the air since the arrival of the Loyalists.[44] In an unfortunately much neglected article written in 1950, John Heisler concluded from a survey of "The Halifax Press and British North American Union 1856–1864" that "it seems unlikely that a sense of British North American Unity had ever been wholly obscured."[45] Many Maritimers appear to have thought like the anonymous correspondent to the *Provincial Wesleyan* who, in 1861, referred to "our home" as "Eastern British America," thus implying some sense of a common destiny with Canada.[46] As Peter Waite pointed out, the initial response of the Maritimers at Charlottetown and in the regional press was certainly not unfavourable to the idea of union. Even Anglin, perhaps the most committed anti-confederate elected to the New Brunswick legislature, admitted that he did "not know of any one opposed to union in the abstract."[47] Indeed, Anglin himself believed union was desirable as a future goal, though on terms so favourable to New Brunswick that they were undoubtedly impracticable.[48]

It was the terms agreed upon at Quebec which hardened Maritime attitudes as the ranks of the ultras swelled with support from the critics of the Quebec scheme, to use Peter Waite's terminology. Even then, what is surprising is how much support the pro-confederates had. In New Brunswick, the only province in which the issue was put to the electorate, the supporters of the Quebec plan were initially defeated at the polls but, for their opponents, it proved to be a phyrric victory.[49] From the beginning the new government included a large number of men who were sympathetic to the idea of Confederation, if not the Quebec Resolutions, and who were converted fairly easily into pro-confederates, once it became clear that union was not possible except on the basis of those resolutions. The attitude of the premier, A.J. Smith, towards Confederation was somewhat ambiguous, and he was surrounded by others like R.D. Wilmot who were even more clearly critics of the Quebec scheme rather than diehard opponents of union.[50] Ultra sentiment may have been more widespread in Nova Scotia than in New Brunswick, but the victory of the anti-confederate forces at the polls in 1867 was roughly of the same dimensions as in New Brunswick two years earlier. This result may have been distorted by the legitimate feeling of outrage that many Nova Scotians felt against the undemocratic way they had been forced into the union and by the fact that the Nova Scotia election took place after it had become certain that there would be no substantial alterations in the Quebec plan.[51] In any event, any anti-confederate government in Nova Scotia would have suffered from the same internal divisions as did the Smith government in New Brunswick and would probably have met much the same fate in much the same way. At least that is a viable reading of Pryke's study of what happened to the deeply divided anti-Confederation movement after Confederation. Indeed, Pryke suggests that those who advocated "an extreme stand towards union during the election represented a small minority of the anti-confederates."[52]

Even Prince Edward Island's opposition is easily exaggerated. There is in Island historiography a powerful tradition of Island "exceptionalism" and there is undeniably some justification for this approach. Prince Edward Island was small, its future on the edge of a large continental nation was bound to be precarious, and opposition to the idea of union was stronger than on the mainland. Yet it is doubtful whether the Islanders' commitment to the protection of local interests differed more than marginally from a similar commitment by other British North Americans.[53] After the Charlottetown Conference, the majority of the Island's newspapers came out in favour of a federal union "upon terms that the Island may reasonably stipulate for," and at Quebec the PEI delegates never opposed the principle of union.[54] Of course, the support of the Island elite for union was not unconditional and the forces favouring Confederation would have faced a difficult battle in persuading the majority of Islanders that Confederation was necessary in 1867. But what appears to have decisively swayed Island opinion was the failure of the Quebec Conference to respond sympathetically to any of the Island's needs.[55] Thanks to the resistance of the French Canadians and the Maritimers, the preference of some of the delegates for a legislative union was abandoned. But to the Islanders' requests for changes in the composition of the Senate and an additional member of the House of Commons (or even for a larger House in which the Island would have six representatives), for a recognition of the peculiar financial position of the Island with its very low debt and limited sources of potential revenue, and for financial assistance to resolve permanently the land question, the delegates from the other colonies turned a deaf ear. It is easy to dismiss the Island's demands, particularly the desire for adequate representation in the new federal parliament, as unrealistic. But during the discussions at Quebec, Alexander

Tilloch Galt offered an alternative system of representation in the House of Commons that would have given the Island the six federal representatives they wanted, and an additional senator for the Island was surely not a radical demand.[56] Indeed, after Confederation, the principle of "rep by pop" was abandoned to meet the needs of the west.[57] It was the obduracy of the Canadians and the refusal of the other Maritime delegations to support PEI's demands, not the latter's unwillingness to compromise, that isolated the Islanders and delayed the Island's decision to enter Confederation.

Not surprisingly, the Islanders refused to consider the degrading terms which were offered to them and defiantly declared in the famous "no terms" resolution that they would never enter Confederation. Although in 1869 they again rejected a set of marginally better terms offered by the Macdonald administration, they found themselves inevitably drawn within the orbit of Canada. They adopted the Canadian decimal system of coinage and were forced to follow Canadian policy in regulating the Atlantic fisheries.[58] Unable to negotiate reciprocity on their own and eager for an infusion of money to resolve the land question, the Island leadership did not abandon negotiations with Canada. Undoubtedly the financial crisis generated by the building of an Island railway explains the timing of Confederation, but, as the debate in 1870 when the legislature rejected Canada's 1869 offer shows, the number of MLAs prepared to accept Confederation if the terms were fair was growing steadily even before the Island approached insolvency. When the Canadian government offered "advantageous and just" terms in 1873, giving the Island much of what it had demanded at Quebec in 1864, the opposition to Confederation evaporated.[59] If Cornelius Howat was the authentic voice of the ultras on the Island, his was very much a voice in the wilderness by 1873.

From a longer perspective, what is remarkable is not that there was opposition to Confederation in the Maritimes but how ineffectual it was. In Ireland, the union with Britain was never accepted and ultimately resulted in separation and partition. Even today there are secessionist movements in Scotland and in Wales. The imperial government was so impressed with the success of the Canadian experiment that it would try to reproduce it elsewhere, but except for Australia and South Africa—and in the latter it was imposed by force—few of the federations it created survived for long. In fact, unlike other areas of the world forced into federation on terms considered unjust, the Maritime opposition to Confederation was remarkably weak and evaporated remarkably quickly. Although there remained pockets of secessionist sentiment, Maritime separatism has never been a potent force.[60] Of course, the simple explanation of this phenomenon is to explain it by the willingness of the Maritime leadership to sell their birthright for a mess of Canadian pottage. But the assumption that Maritime politicians and the Maritime electorate were more venal and more corrupt than politicians elsewhere is an assumption which cannot be sustained. Historians have for too long quoted enthusiastically the comments of Arthur Hamilton Gordon and other imperial visitors to the colonies. Inevitably, they were critical of what they saw, since they came from a more patrician political culture controlled by an elite who feared any movement in the direction of democracy. But much of what they disapproved of—the scrambling of different interest groups, the narrow self-promoting nature of much of the legislation, the continual catering to popular demands—is what popular politics is all about. The ideal of the disinterested gentleman-politician made little sense in colonies where there were virtually no great landed estates, limited inherited wealth, and no hereditary ruling caste. Much of the opposition to the Quebec scheme seems to have come from those who feared, legitimately, that it was designed to create just such a caste and to place power in the hands of an elite which professed the ideal of disinterestedness while lining their own rather larger pockets.[61]

The belief that politics in the Maritimes were individualistic and anarchic is also mythical. During the transition to responsible government, the Maritime provinces had begun to evolve parties in the legislatures at pretty close to the same pace as they evolved in Canada. In the decades before Confederation, all these provinces were in the process of developing party systems with roots deep in the constituencies, even New Brunswick.[62] If Confederation disrupted this development and brought about a major political realignment and considerable political confusion, it was because of the far-reaching implications of the measure, not because of the inherent pliability or lack of principle of Maritime politicians. It had the same effect in Ontario and Quebec, which also had their share of loose fish. Similarly, the belief that Maritimers were either by nature or because of the scale of their political structures more susceptible to patronage and corruption should be challenged. Gordon Stewart has advanced the claim that the Canadian political system before Confederation was more corrupt and more patronage-ridden than in the Maritimes, since Canadians had adopted the spoils system with greater enthusiasm and consistency during the transition to responsible government.[63] In fact, there may be a reverse correlation between size and patronage in preindustrial societies. In a larger political unit, politicians are more remote from the people they serve and less likely to be drawn from a clearly defined local elite. They cannot command the same degree of deference and therefore require access to a larger fund of patronage to cement the more impersonal bonds of party loyalty. Certainly those Maritime politicians who held posts in the new federal administration, Tilley and Tupper for example, claimed to be appalled by the ruthlessness of the Canadians in distributing patronage along party lines, although they soon began to pursue similar policies to ensure a fair distribution for their own constituents and their own re-election.[64] By proving that the system was not totally biased in favour of the Canadians, the Maritime political leadership did something to dissipate the lingering fears that the new political system would be dominated by

Canadians and Canadian needs. But this evidence cannot be used to explain the success of the pro-confederates in the first place, nor does it adequately explain the rapidity with which integration took place.

The degree of support for Confederation in the region can only be explained by abandoning the notion that all but a handful of Maritimers were inherently parochial and conservative. Maritimers did not live in a dream world. Although they had experienced a period of rapid economic and demographic growth, they were aware of the changes taking place around them. They were acutely aware that external events had made some form of larger union desirable in the 1860s. British pressure, the American civil war and the cancellation of reciprocity, and the Fenian raids helped to drive home this message, as they did in the Canadas. But no external pressures could have compelled the Maritimes to join Confederation if, ultimately, they had not been convinced that it was in their own interests to do so. That is the lesson which can be drawn from the failure of the earlier initiatives on Confederation in the 1830s and 1840s.[65] In all these cases, despite the strong advocacy of the Colonial Office and enthusiastic support from British officials in the colonies, the union movement collapsed because of lack of colonial support. Similarly, the Maritime Union movement, despite strong imperial pressure, collapsed because of lack of colonial enthusiasm. Undoubtedly imperial support helped to sway the more conservative groups in the colonies, such as the hierarchy of the Catholic church.[66] But imperial interference could also unleash a colonial reaction. As allies, men like Cordon were a mixed blessing, and it is quite possible that the pro-confederates won their victory in New Brunswick in 1865 despite, not because of, Gordon's interference in the politics of the province.[67] The combined pressures generated by the American civil war and the British response to it were critical factors in the timing of Confederation. Without those immediate pressures, union might not have come about in the 1860s and it would certainly not have come about on the basis of the Quebec Resolutions, since it was those pressures which persuaded so many Maritimers to accept union on those terms. But since the idea of Confederation does seem to have had widespread and growing support, at least from the elites in the region, it does not follow that in the 1870s negotiations between the Canadians (now presumably united in their own federal union) and the Maritimers could not have been successful, albeit on a somewhat different basis.

By the 1860s, a variety of indigenous forces were, in fact, leading an increasing number of Maritimers to the conclusion that some form of wider association was desirable. The restlessness of provincial elites may have been as Waite suggested, part of the reason for the enthusiasm for a larger union, but this restlessness cannot be related solely to their political ambitions and their immediate economic self-interest. Support for the idea of union was, indeed, too widespread for it to be simply the result of individual ambition. Clearly there must have been some correlation between an individual's socioeconomic position and his or her response to the Confederation issue, but it would be foolish to revert to the kind of Beardian analysis which American historians have come to find less and less useful.[68] In any event, without the support of a wide cross-section of the articulate public, any effort at union would have been pointless.

It can hardly be denied that much of the support for a larger union came from those who equated consolidation with material progress and modernization, as most historians have recognized. What they have been less willing to accept is that these intellectual pressures were growing stronger in the Maritimes as in the Canadas and affected many of the opponents of the Quebec scheme as well as its advocates. Even prior to Confederation, governments in the Maritimes took on new responsibilities as the nineteenth-century revolution in government filtered across the Atlantic.[69] Maritimers shared with other British North Americans an enthusiasm for railways, for expanded and more highly centralized school systems,[70] for improved social services, and for governments with enhanced access to credit. In a recent book on *Inventing Canada: Early Victorian Science and the Idea of a Transcontinental Nation* (Toronto, 1987), Suzanne Zeller has argued that the diffusion of early science was another of the pressures encouraging the establishment of larger units of government, and that the inventory methods of Victorian science "laid a conceptual and practical foundation for the reorganization of British North America" (p. 9). Unfortunately, Zeller focusses almost exclusively on developments in the United Province of Canada. But the Maritimes had its share of scientists influenced by similar notions and a wider political community similarly affected by the diffusion of scientific knowledge, and it seems likely that the same developments were occurring there.[71] Nonetheless, Zeller's book points to the direction which studies of the movement for Confederation must now take. What is required are detailed analyses of the intellectual milieu in which literary figures and the growing number of professionals functioned, of clerical thought, and indeed of changing views of the role and function of the state held by entrepreneurs and by other groups in society. One suspects that such studies will reveal support, in the Maritimes as elsewhere in Canada, for the emergence of larger and more powerful institutional units of government.

Yet it does not follow that all of the supporters of Confederation were on the side of an expanded role for government and material progress, while all of those who opposed the Quebec scheme were not. The most vehement opposition to Confederation in the Maritimes came, as Muise correctly pointed out, from those whose economic interests seemed most directly threatened by union with Canada. It is, however, far from self-evident that they were opposed to the other changes that were taking place in their colonial societies. Some of the opposition to Confederation in the Maritimes, as in the Canadas, probably did come from those whose social ideal was reactionary and anti-modern in several respects, but not all anti-confederates, perhaps not even a majority, opposed commercial development or technological change. There does appear to have been an overlap between those who resisted government intervention, feared increased taxation, and resented outside interference with community institutions and those who opposed Confederation. Yet many pro-confederates shared these concerns. In summarizing the vast literature dealing with the politics of the early American republic, Lance Banning points out the futility of trying to describe the Republicans and Federalists as liberal and conservative and their opponents as conservative and reactionary: "if revisionary work has taught us anything, it has surely taught us that both parties were a bit of each."[72]

It has long been known that the Fathers of Confederation were not democrats and that they were determined to secure the protection of property and to create barriers against the democratic excesses which, in their minds, had led to the collapse of the American constitution and to the American Civil War.[73] For this reason they limited the size of the House of Commons so that it would remain manageable, chose to have an appointed rather than an elected second chamber, and sought to ensure that both houses of the proposed federal legislature were composed of men who possessed a substantial stake in society. Most of the Maritime delegates at the Quebec Conference shared these anti-democratic and anti-majoritarian objectives. So, of course, did many of the most prominent anti-confederate leaders—even that tribune of the people, Joseph Howe. Ironically, a considerable part of the initial opposition to the Quebec Resolutions came from those—for instance, Howe and Wilmot—who, like the leading pro-confederates, were wedded to British constitutional models but who rejected the Quebec plan for not establishing a legislative union or because they feared it might lead to the disruption of the empire. But once convinced that legislative union was impracticable, primarily because of the determined opposition of the French Canadians, and that Britain was solidly behind the Quebec scheme, many of these critics were converted fairly easily into supporters of union, although they continued to ask for marginally better terms for their provinces.

The more serious and determined opposition came from those who believed that the Quebec plan would create a monster, an extraordinarily powerful and distant national government, a highly centralized federal union in which Maritimers would have limited influence. It is easy to dismiss these arguments as based on paranoia, irrational fears, or perhaps some kind of psychological disorder, particularly since the worst fears of the anti-confederates were not realized. But the opposition to centralizing power in a distant and remote government was deeply rooted in Anglo-American political thought. Elwood Jones has described this attitude as "localism," as a world view that was held by many articulate conservatives and reformers on both sides of the Atlantic and was "an integral part of the British North American experience."[74] This approach has the merit of indicating the considerable overlap between those who supported and those who opposed the Quebec Resolutions. Those resolutions were capable of more than one interpretation, and many of the Canadian pro-confederates supported Confederation because it promised more, not less, autonomy for their provinces.[75] Nonetheless, the term "localism," with its implication of parochialism, to some extent distorts the nature of the opposition to the Quebec Resolutions. It reinforces the notion that the pro-confederates were drawn from the men of larger vision, usually described in American historiography as the cosmopolitans, while their opponents were men of more limited experience and a more local, and thus more limited, frame of reference.[76] In American historiography, however, the "men of little faith" are now taken more seriously than they used to be and it is time to reassess the criticisms made by those who fought hardest against the Quebec scheme.[77]

Only a minority of the Maritime anti-confederates appear to have denied the need for some kind of a union, but since the Maritimers were not, like the Canadians, trying simultaneously to get out of one union while creating another, they were less easily convinced of the merits of the Quebec Resolutions. Following the Charlottetown Conference, the *Acadian Recorder* expressed the belief that when "the delegates . . . have to let the cat out of the bag," it would be found that the cat was "a real sleek, constitutional, monarchical, unrepublican, aristocratic cat" and that "we shall ask our friends the people to drown it at once—yes to drown it."[78] It will not do to create yet another oversimplified dichotomy, pitting democratic anti-confederates against aristocratic pro-confederates. Yet clearly the anti-confederates did attract to their cause those who were suspicious of the aristocratic pretensions of the designers of the new constitution. Whether such critics were true democrats or simply adherents of an older classical republican tradition, whether they drew upon English opposition thought, classical liberalism, or Scottish common-sense philosophy, or whether they simply drew eclectically upon the host of Anglo-American intellectual currents available to them, cannot be established until more detailed studies have been completed of their rhetoric.[79] But it does seem likely that it is on the anti-confederate side that one will find most of those who were most sympathetic to wider popular participation in government and to the movement towards democracy already underway in the Maritimes.[80] And such men surely had good reason to be suspicious of the ideological goals of those who had drafted the Quebec Resolutions.

The critics of the Quebec Resolutions were also surely correct to believe that the proposed constitution went further in the direction of centralization than was necessary or desirable in the 1860s. The real weakness in the analysis of most of what was written in the 1960s, and it is particularly apparent in the work of Morton and Creighton, is that it focusses too much on the twentieth-century *consequences* of what was done rather than on the more immediate *context* of the late nineteenth century.[81] The Quebec plan, after all, never worked out as the far-sighted Macdonald and his associates hoped. Despite Macdonald's expectations, the provincial governments did not dwindle into insignificance after Confederation. Because of pressure from the provinces and the decisions of the Judicial Committee of the Privy Council, as well as Macdonald's own retreat from an extreme position on such issues as the use of the power of disallowance, the power of the federal government to interfere with the activities of the provinces was constrained in the late nineteenth century and the constitution was effectively decentralized. This decentralization made considerable sense at a time when, by our standards, the people and politicians had a remarkably limited concept of the role of government in society, particularly of the role of a remote federal government.[82] Twentieth-century historians such as Creighton and Morton may, for very different and to some extent contradictory reasons, lament the fact that those who lived in the late nineteenth century were not prepared to accept a twentieth-century role for the federal government, but it does not alter the reality. In fact, Macdonald shared with his contemporaries this limited conception of the role of the federal government. He did not wish a highly centralized federal system, either to introduce the degree of control over the economy that Creighton longed for in the 1930s or because of any commitment to the nation-wide bilingualism and biculturalism policy that Morton espoused in the 1960s when he was converted to a Creightonian conception of Confederation. It is time to abandon the Creightonian myth that Macdonald and the other advocates of a federal union that was a legislative union in disguise were simply practical politicians engaged in the necessary work of building the Canadian nation.[83] Confederation certainly did not require that the federal government should attempt to "treat the provinces more 'colonially' than the imperial authorities had latterly treated the provinces" through its control over the lieutenant-governors and the resurrection of the anachronistic power of reservation.[84] The Fathers of Confederation were not philosopher-kings, but neither did they live in the intellectual vacuum that much of the traditional literature seems to assume existed throughout British North America, particularly in the Maritimes. In fact, the roots of the thought of the exponents of centralization emerged not out of a vacuum but out of a body of conservative thought that was deeply suspicious of democracy, and their opponents were surely correct to place little faith in the motives of such men and the scheme they proposed. Many of the anti-confederates were clearly marching to a different drummer.[85]

Ideological and sectional considerations did not take place in isolation from each other and what initially united the Maritime anti-confederates, regardless of their ideological differences, was their feeling that the Quebec Resolutions did not adequately protect their sectional interests. As the anti-confederate newspaper, the *Woodstock Times,* noted, "union is one thing and the Quebec scheme is quite another."[86] The scheme that emerged out of the Quebec Conference was designed to mollify its potential critics in two ways: by ensuring that sectional interests would be protected through federal institutions such as the cabinet and the Senate and through the creation of a series of provincial legislatures with control over local matters. Yet those critics who argued that the Senate would be too weak and ineffectual to defend regional interests would be very quickly proved correct after Confederation. Indeed, by making the Senate an appointed body, the Fathers of Confederation had intentionally ensured that the decision-making body in the new federal system would be the House of Commons. This was no accident, for, as Robert MacKay pointed out, Macdonald's intention was to grant "the forms demanded by sectional sentiments and fears," while ensuring "that these forms did not endanger the political structure."[87] Traditionally, Canadian historians and political scientists have laid great stress on the principle of sectional representation in the cabinet as one of the primary lines of defence for the protection of regional interests. Yet this argument ignores the fact that, however important individual ministers may be, the policies that emerge from the collective decisions of the cabinet must inevitably reflect the balance of power in the House of Commons. The fears of the Maritime critics of the proposed constitution were undoubtedly exaggerated, but they were surely correct to believe that in the long run there was no effective guarantee that their vital interests were adequately protected at the federal level.[88]

Similarly, they were surely correct to be suspicious of federalism as it was presented to them in the 1860s. The question of whether the anti-confederates leaned towards a different and less centralized model of federalism than the supporters of the Quebec scheme is a controversial and ultimately unanswerable one, since it depends upon which group of anti-confederates one takes as most representative. In Halifax, as Peter Waite showed, there was considerable support for a legislative union, at least as reflected in the city's newspapers.[89] But outside of Halifax and in New Brunswick and Prince Edward Island there seems to have been considerably more sympathy for the federal principle.[90] Federalism was viewed suspiciously by conservatives who believed that it would leave the government without the power to govern, and such fears were expressed by both sides in the Confederation debate. They were, however, most forcefully expressed, in Halifax and elsewhere, by the pro-confederates, and the Quebec Resolutions went a long way to pacifying most of those who wanted a purely legislative union. But the Quebec Resolutions did little to mollify those who feared that the proposed provincial legislatures would be nothing more than glorified municipal institutions and that all real power would be concentrated in the federal parliament. As Richard Ellis points out, during the debate over the American constitution, the supporters of ratification "preempted the term 'Federalist' for themselves, even though, in many ways, it more accurately described their opponents."[91] Until detailed studies of the Confederation debate in the three Maritime provinces have been completed, it would be premature to assume that the Maritime anti-confederates anticipated the provincial rights movement of the 1880s and argued for a form of co-ordinate sovereignty. But many of the critics of the Quebec Resolutions in the region clearly believed that their provincial governments would be left with inadequate powers and resources. In this regard they were also more prescient than the pro-confederates. The Maritime governments required special grants to cover their deficits in the later 1860s and 1870s and were forced to turn time and again to the federal government for financial assistance. We know little about how Maritimers responded to the provincial rights movement of the 1880s since the literature assumes that Ontario and Quebec were the key players while the Maritimers were motivated solely by the desire for larger subsidies, but it is plausible to assume that the movement was supported in the region by many of those who had resisted the Quebec scheme of union.

If the enthusiasm of Maritimers for Confederation upon the basis of the Quebec Resolutions was less pronounced than in Canada (or at least in Canada West), it was, then, not because they lagged behind intellectually but because they obviously had more to lose in a federation which was not designed to meet their needs. It was not an obtuse conservatism which led many Maritimers to oppose the terms that were initially offered to them in 1864, but a feeling that those terms were patently unfair. They were motivated not by an intense parochialism which manifested itself in separatist tendencies but by a desire to find a place for themselves in a union which protected their interests. Under the pressure of events the majority, at least in New Brunswick and Prince Edward Island, did agree to union on terms which they did not like.[92] But what most Maritimers sought in the Confederation era was not a future for themselves outside of Confederation but a more equitable union than seemed to be promised by the Quebec Resolutions.[93]

• Notes

[1] E.R. Forbes, "In Search of a Post-Confederation Maritime Historiography, 1900–1967," *Acadiensis* 8, 2 (Autumn 1978): 3–21.

[2] *Canadian Historical Review* (hereafter CHR) 9 (March 1928): 4–24.

[3] Canadian Historical Association, *Annual Report* (1927): 39–45.

[4] The roots of this sentiment are discussed in E.R. Forbes, *Maritime Rights: The Maritime Rights Movement, 1919–1927* (Montreal, 1979).

[5] I have used the reprint edition, which contains a valuable introduction by Peter Waite (Toronto, 1966).

[6] Whitelaw pointed out that there was only one recorded vote at Quebec on which Canada was outvoted by the four Atlantic provinces voting together. See Whitelaw, *The Maritimes and Canada before Confederation*, 240.

[7] CHR 16 (March 1935): 72, cited in Waite's introduction to *The Maritimes and Canada before Confederation*, xv. Waite includes this excerpt as "an illustration of the best and the worst of Chester Martin—that is, of the comprehensiveness of Martin's thinking and his inability to change it." Yet it seems to me a fair interpretation of Whitelaw's perspective.

8 One might include James A. Roy, *Joseph Howe: A Study in Achievement and Frustration* (Toronto, 1935) as a serious study, but it is a perverse work that simply reiterates the myths about Howe perpetuated in earlier studies. For a critique of the book see J. Murray Beck, "Joseph Howe and Confederation: Myth and Fact," *Transactions of the Royal Society of Canada* (1964), 143–44. Perhaps because the issue of Confederation was not put to the electorate in Nova Scotia as it was in New Brunswick, the early writing on Nova Scotia focussed almost exclusively on the perversity of Howe in opposing Confederation.

9 "Railways and the Confederation Issue in New Brunswick, 1863–1865" and "The Basis and Persistence of Opposition to Confederation in New Brunswick" first appeared in the CHR 21 (1940): 367–83, and 23 (1942): 374–97, and both are reprinted in Bailey's *Culture and Nationality* (Toronto, 1972), from where the quotations in the text are drawn.

10 For example, Timothy Warren Anglin was not opposed to the Intercolonial, although he thought the western extension should be the priority. See William M. Baker, *Timothy Warren Anglin 1822–96: Irish Catholic Canadian* (Toronto, 1977), 54. Baker also notes that many pro-confederates supported the western extension, although frequently as a second choice (p. 55).

11 The concept of a consensus approach is, of course, taken from American historiography but, as I have tried to argue elsewhere, it seems to be applicable to Canadian historiography. See my "'Limited Identities' and Canadian Historical Scholarship: An Atlantic Provinces Perspective," *Journal of Canadian Studies* 23, 1 & 2 (Spring–Summer 1988): esp. 177–78.

12 I have used the second printing (Toronto, 1962), which contains "a few minor corrections" (preface, vi). As will become apparent, I have drawn heavily upon Waite's sources in the discussion that follows.

13 I do not know if Waite had read Cecelia M. Kenyon, "Men of Little Faith: The Antifederalists on the Nature of Representative Government," *William and Mary Quarterly*, 3rd ser., 12 (1955): 3–43, but his approach was certainly in line with the American historiography of the period.

14 I attempted to trace the context of Goldwin Smith's remark, but Waite's source was G.M. Wrong, "Creation of the Federal System in Canada" in *The Federation of Canada, 1867–1917*, ed. Wrong et al. (Toronto, 1917), 17, and Wrong does not indicate his source. It seems likely, however, that the quote referred to Canadian politics in the post-Confederation era and reflected Smith's somewhat biased view of his adopted home.

15 Forbes makes the same point about J. Murray Beck in his "In Search of a Post-Confederation Maritime Historiography," 55.

16 Bolger also contributed the chapters on Confederation to *Canada's Smallest Province: A History of Prince Edward Island* (Charlottetown, 1973), where his larger work is synthesized.

17 See Jack N. Rakove, "The Great Compromise: Ideas, Interests, and the Politics of Constitution Making," *William and Mary Quarterly*, 3rd ser., 14 (July 1987): esp. 451.

18 See G.P. Browne, ed., *Documents on the Confederation of British North America* (Toronto, 1969), 38–39.

19 See Ken Pryke, *Nova Scotia and Confederation* (Toronto, 1979), 190.

20 See Browne, *Documents*, 77–78.

21 Ibid., 171.

22 Ibid., 211. Tupper personally supported the idea of a legislative union, but he was undoubtedly influenced by the knowledge that this position was not shared by most Nova Scotians.

23 McCully to Tilley, 8 June 1866, quoted in Pryke, *Nova Scotia and Confederation*, 28.

24 See Pryke, *Nova Scotia and Confederation*, 22–23, 26.

25 Bailey, "The Basis and Persistence," 116; MacNutt, *New Brunswick*, 456–57.

26 Bolger, *Prince Edward Island and Confederation*, v, 293.

27 See *Life and Times of Confederation*, 122.

28 Ibid., 5.

29 "Railroaded" is the clever aphorism used by Peter Waite in his chapter in Craig Brown, ed., *The Illustrated History of Canada* (Toronto, 1987), 289.

30 See Alan W. MacIntosh, "The Career of Sir Charles Tupper in Canada, 1864–1900" (PhD thesis, University of Toronto, 1960), and Carl Wallace, "Sir Leonard Tilley: A Political Biography" (PhD thesis, University of Alberta, 1972). MacIntosh presents a very traditional portrait of Tupper, who is seen as accepting and following the overweening vision of Macdonald. Wallace makes a more successful effort to place Tilley in a regional context, but he too believes that "a good argument can be put forward to prove that Confederation was little more than a smokescreen for a diversity of local issues" (p. 209).

31 This argument is presented in "The Federal Election of 1867 in Nova Scotia: An Economic Interpretation," *Collections of the Nova Scotia Historical Society* (1968): 327–51, and developed at greater length in "Elections and Constituencies: Federal Politics in Nova Scotia, 1867–1878" (PhD thesis, University of Western Ontario, 1971).

32 Muise, "Elections and Constituencies," iv. For an application of the Muise thesis see Brian Tennyson, "Economic Nationalism and Confederation: A Case Study in Cape Breton," *Acadiensis* 2, 1 (Autumn 1972): 38–53.

33 This argument is developed in a variety of works published by members of the group but most recently and fully in Eric W. Sager and Gerry Panting, "Staple Economies and the Rise and Decline of the Shipping Industry in Atlantic Canada" in *Change and Adaptation in Maritime History: The North Atlantic Fleets in the Nineteenth Century*, ed. Lewis R. Fischer and Gerald E. Panting (St John's, 1985). For an interpretation which incorporates this approach, but one that builds upon Muise's insights, see John G. Reid's *Six Crucial Decades: Times of Change in the History of the Maritimes* (Halifax, 1987), esp. 113–16.

34 Ben Forster, *A Conjunction of Interests: Business, Politics, and Tariffs 1825–1879* (Toronto, 1986), 62. On Nova Scotia see Pryke, *Nova Scotia and Confederation*, 107, 190–92.

35 Muise, "The Federal Election of 1867 in Nova Scotia," 337–38.

36 Bailey, "The Basis and Persistence," 99. Peter Toner emphasizes "the Irish threat, real and imagined" in his discussion of the politics of Confederation in New Brunswick in "New Brunswick Schools and the Rise of Provincial Rights" in Bruce W. Hodgins, Don Wright, and W.H. Heick, *Federalism in Canada and Australia: The Early Years* (Waterloo, 1978), esp. 126–27.

37 The increased Anglicization of the Thirteen Colonies in the decades prior to the American Revolution is a major theme in Jack P. Greene, "Political Memisis: A Consideration of the Political Roots of Legislative Behaviour in the British Colonies in the Eighteenth Century," *American Historical Review* 75 (1969–70): 337–67. It is a theme which has yet to be adequately explored in the evolution of *British* North America in the mid-decades of the nineteenth century.

38 Baker, *Anglin*, 79.

39 "Joseph Howe and Confederation: Myth and Fact," 146, and *Joseph Howe*, vol. 2, *The Briton Becomes Canadian 1848–1873* (Kingston and Montreal: 1983), 211.

40 Carl Wallace, "Albert Smith, Confederation and Reaction in New Brunswick: 1852–1882," CHR 44 (1963): 311–12. An extended version

of this argument is contained in "The Life and Times of Sir Albert James Smith" (MA thesis, University of New Brunswick, 1960), which concludes with the statement that "he lacked the depth and vision to be a great statesman" (p. 210).

41 Baker, *Anglin*, 116.

42 Robert M. Aitken, "Localism and National Identity in Yarmouth, N.S., 1830–1870" (MA thesis, Trent University, n.d.).

43 David Weale, *Cornelius Howat: Farmer and Island Patriot* (Summerside, 1973), and David Weale and Harry Baglole, *The Island and Confederation: The End of an Era* (n.p., 1973).

44 L.F.S. Upton, "The Idea of Confederation, 1754–1858" in *The Shield of Achilles: Aspects of Canada in the Victorian Age*, ed. W.L. Morton (Toronto, 1968), 184–204.

45 *Dalhousie Review* 30 (1950): 188.

46 *Provincial Wesleyan*, 16 Jan. 1861. I am grateful to John Reid for supplying me with this reference.

47 Baker, *Anglin*, 103. I am grateful to a student in one of my seminars, Mary McIntosh, for supplying me with this reference.

48 See ibid., 58, 64–65.

49 Historians remain divided over the scale of the victory. Waite suggests in *The Life and Times of Confederation*, 246, that the election results were comparatively close, but Baker in *Anglin*, 75, argues that the anti-confederates won at least 60 percent of the popular vote.

50 Once again historians are not agreed on whether Smith did convert to Confederation prior to the defeat of his government. Baker in *Anglin*, 102, argues that he did not, but Wallace feels that Smith was willing to lead the province into union. See "Albert Smith, Confederation and Reaction in New Brunswick," 291–92. In his "Life and Times of Smith," Wallace points out that as early as 1858 Wilmot had indicated his belief in the inevitability

of British North American union (see p. 23).

51 Del Muise points out that about 60 percent of the Nova Scotia electorate voted for anti-confederates in 1865, which is roughly comparable to Baker's figure for New Brunswick.

52 See *Nova Scotia and Confederation*, 49.

53 For a different point of view see Weale and Baglole, *The Island and Confederation*. I have two major disagreements with the authors. First, they create an image of harmony and unity on the Island that ignores the very real ethnic, religious, and class divisions that existed and thus postulate a unified response to Confederation. Second, they imply that Islanders had developed a strong desire to be separate that almost amounted to a sense of Island nationalism. But the Island had never been an independent and autonomous state and there is no evidence that any sizeable number of Islanders ever wanted it to become one. Indeed, the tendency to equate resistance to Confederation in the Maritimes to a kind of "provincial nationalism" is, I believe, utterly wrongheaded. What most Maritimers wanted, and Prince Edward Islanders were no exception, was to protect the corporate identities of their long-established assemblies. For a development of this theme in American historiography see Jack P. Greene, *Peripheries and Center: Constitutional Development in the Extended Politics of the British Empire and the United States, 1607–1788* (Athens, GA, 1987).

54 Bolger, *Prince Edward Island and Confederation*, 59, 61, 86.

55 Unfortunately, most of the literature on Confederation, including Bolger, simply dismisses the Island's needs as irrelevant. See ibid., 68ff.

56 For Galt's plan and the discussion of the extra senator see Browne, ed., *Documents*, 106. Today we accept much wider departure from the principle of rep by pop than PEI requested in 1864.

57 David E. Smith, "Party Government, Representation and National Integration in Canada" in *Party Government and Regional Representation in Canada*, ed. Peter Aucoin (Toronto, 1985), 14.

58 See Frank MacKinnon, *The Government of Prince Edward Island* (Toronto, 1951), 132.

59 Bolger, *The Island and Confederation*, 210, 262.

60 The only serious expression of separatist sentiment was the repeal movement of the 1880s. It was in part, indeed perhaps in large part, simply a strategy for better terms. See Colin Howell, "W.S. Fielding and the Repeal Elections of 1886 and 1887 in Nova Scotia," *Acadiensis* 8, 2 (Spring 1979): 28–46.

61 I have drawn for inspiration in these comments on Gordon S. Wood, "Interest and Disinterestedness in the Making of the Constitution" in *Beyond Confederation: Origins of the Constitution and American National Identity*, ed. Richard Beeman, Stephen Botein, and Edward C. Carter II (Chapel Hill and London, 1987), 69–109.

62 See Gail Campbell, "'Smashers' and 'Rummies': Voters and the Rise of Parties in Charlotte County, New Brunswick, 1846–1857," *Historical Papers* (1986): 86–116.

63 Gordon Stewart, *The Origins of Canadian Politics: A Comparative Approach* (Vancouver, 1986), 88–89.

64 The latter statement is based upon an examination of the patronage files in the Tilley and Tupper papers held in the National Archives of Canada, during the 1870s. I discuss the question of patronage at more length in "The 1870s: The Integration of the Maritimes," in *The Atlantic Provinces in Confederation*, ed. E.R. Forbes and D.A. Muise (in press).

65 On the earlier attempts to achieve Confederation see Ged Martin, "Confederation Rejected: The British Debate on Canada, 1837–1840," *Journal of Imperial and Commonwealth History* 11 (1982–83): 33–57, and B.A. Knox, "The Rise of Colonial Federation as an Object of British Policy 1850–1870," *Journal of British Studies* 11 (1971): 91–112. My interpretation of Ged Martin's "An Imperial Idea and Its Friends: Canadian Confederation and the British" in *Studies in British Imperial History: Essays in Honour of A.P. Thornton*, ed. Gordon Martel (New York, 1985), 49–94, is that while British support was essential for Confederation, it was the circumstances within British North America which gave the British something to support.

66 For example, Bishop MacKinnon wrote to Tupper that "Although no admirer of Confederation on the basis of the Quebec Scheme; yet owing to the present great emergency and the necessities of the times, the union of the Colonies upon a new basis, we receive with pleasure" (Pryke, *Nova Scotia and Confederation*, 27). MacKinnon's reservations are not spelled out, but they were likely similar to those of Archbishop Connolly, who wrote that "the more power that Central Legislature has the better for the Confederacy itself and for the Mother Country and for all concerned." Connolly to Carnarvon, 30 Jan. 1867, in Browne, ed., *Documents*, 262. See also K. Fay Trombley, *Thomas Louis Connolly (1815–1876)* (Leuven, 1983), esp. 302–44.

67 Wallace, "Life and Times of Smith," 47.

68 The reference here is, of course, to Charles Beard's economic interpretation of the making of the American constitution. As Richard Beeman notes in his introduction to *Beyond Confederation*, 14, the prolonged historiographical debate over Beard's interpretation has come to be seen as important by "ever-decreasing numbers" of American historians.

69 See Rosemary Langhout, "Developing Nova Scotia: Railways and Public

Accounts, 1849–1867," *Acadiensis* 14, 2 (Spring 1985): 3–28.

70 As Ian Robertson points out, Prince Edward Island claimed to be the first place in the British Empire to introduce "a complete system of free education" with the adoption of the Free Education Act of 1852, and Nova Scotia was the next British North American colony to follow suit, in 1864. See "Historical Origins of Public Education in Prince Edward Island, 1852–1877" (paper given at the Atlantic Canada Studies Conference, University of Edinburgh, May 1988), 3, 5.

71 A.G. Bailey points out that the Maritime universities, like the central Canadian universities, "tempered their concern for the classics with a lively concern for the sciences" during the Confederation period. See "Literature and Nationalism in the Aftermath of Confederation" in Bailey, *Culture and Nationality*, 66.

72 Lance Banning, "Jeffersonian Ideology Revisited: Liberal and Classical Ideas in the New American Republic," *William and Mary Quarterly* 43, 1 (Jan. 1986): 14.

73 See Bruce Hodgins, "Democracy and the Ontario Fathers of Confederation" in *Profiles of a Province: Studies in the History of Ontario* (Toronto, 1967), and "The Canadian Political Elite's Attitude Toward the Nature of the Plan of Union" in Hodgins et al., *Federalism in Canada and Australia*, 43–59.

74 Elwood H. Jones, "Localism and Federalism in Upper Canada to 1865" in Hodgins et al., *Federalism in Canada and Australia*, 20.

75 See Arthur Silver, *The French-Canadian Idea of Confederation 1864–1900* (Toronto, 1982), 33–50, and Robert Charles Vipond, "Federalism and the Problem of Sovereignty: Constitutional Politics and the Rise of the Provincial Rights Movement in Canada" (PhD diss., Harvard University, 1973), 82–87.

76 In American historiography, the notion of the federalists as cosmopolitans and the anti-federalists as provincials, found, for example, in Jackson Turner Main's *The Antifederalists: Critics of the Constitution, 1781–1788* (Chapel Hill, NC, 1961) and *Political Parties before the Constitution* (Chapel Hill, NC, 1973), has been challenged by Wood in "Interest and Disinterestedness in the Making of the Constitution."

77 See, for example, James H. Hutson, "County, Court and Constitution: Antifederalism and the Historians," *William and Mary Quarterly*, 3rd ser., 38, 3 (July 1981): 337–68; Issac Kramnick, "The 'Great National Discussion': The Discourse of Politics in 1787," ibid., 45, 1 (Jan. 1988): 3–32, and Richard E. Ellis, "The Persistence of Antifederalism after 1789" in Beeman et al., *Beyond Confederation*, 295–314.

78 *Acadian Recorder*, 12 Sept. 1864, quoted in R.H. Campbell, "Confederation in Nova Scotia to 1870" (MA thesis, Dalhousie University, 1939), 80.

79 I am, of course, calling for the kind of intellectual history associated with American scholars such as Bernard Bailyn and Gordon S. Wood and British scholars such as J.G.A. Pocock. The only serious attempts to apply this approach to the Confederation era have been by Jones, "Localism and Federalism," and by Peter J. Smith, "The Ideological Origins of Canadian Confederation," *Canadian Journal of Political Science* 20, 1 (March 1987): 3–29. Unfortunately, both efforts seem to me flawed by the effort to deal with too wide a time frame and to apply to the mid-nineteenth century categories developed for the eighteenth century.

80 It is worth noting that the Maritimes were at least as far, if not further, advanced in this direction than the Canadas. According to John Garner, *The Franchise and Politics in British North America, 1755–1867* (Toronto,

1969), Nova Scotia had been "the first colony in North America to introduce manhood suffrage" (p. 33). Although Nova Scotia subsequently drew back from the experiment, all of the Maritimes had wide franchises and Prince Edward Island had virtually universal male suffrage by the 1860s. After Confederation, when the federal government decided against vote by ballot, there was an outcry from New Brunswick, which had adopted the ballot in 1855. Indeed, it was this increasingly democratic climate that annoyed men like Gordon and that perhaps accounts, at least in part, for the desire of some members of the colonial elites for a wider, and preferably a legislative, union.

81 I have been influenced here by Beeman, Introduction, *Beyond Confederation*, 5–8.

82 There has been a heated debate over the role of the Judicial Committee of the Privy Council, but much of the controversy centres around the consequences in the 1930s of the decisions taken under very different circumstances in the 1880s and 1890s. For a summary of the recent literature see Frederick Vaughan, "Critics of the Judicial Committee of the Privy Council: The New Orthodoxy and an Alternative Explanation," *Canadian Journal of Political Science* 19, 3 (Sept. 1986): 495–519. Unfortunately, Vaughan is also primarily concerned with the implications of the decisions, this time in the 1980s, and expresses the fear that the JCPC "left us with a federal system that is seriously lacking an institutional body by which to bind the several provinces at the centre so as to ensure the continued existence of Canada as one nation" (p. 505).

83 This point is also made in Smith, "The Ideological Origins of Canadian Confederation," 3–4.

84 Vipond, "Federalism and the Problem of Sovereignty," 128–29.

85 James H. Hutson in "Country, Court and Constitution" has suggested that the division over the constitution in the United States in the 1780s was between those committed to a country and a court ideology. The court party supported commercial expansion and was profoundly statist in orientation, while their country opponents defended agrarian interests and feared any substantial increase in state power. These categories have some value, but British North America in the 1860s was not the United States in the 1780s. There were very few self-sufficient agricultural communities, even in the Maritimes in the 1860s, and it is doubtful whether the majority of the anti-confederates were any less market-oriented than their opponents. Ideological determinism is as distorting as any other kind and there is the danger of turning all the pro-confederates into Hamiltonians and all of the critics of the Quebec resolutions into Jeffersonians.

86 Quoted in Waite, *The Life and Times of Confederation*, 252.

87 See Robert A. MacKay, *The Unreformed Senate of Canada*, rev. ed. (Toronto, 1963), 43.

88 This is one of the major themes in Forbes, *Maritime Rights*, and is implicit in T.W. Acheson, "The Maritimes and Empire Canada" in *Canada and the Burden of Unity*, ed. David Bercuson (Toronto, 1977).

89 See "Halifax Newspapers and the Federal Principle, 1864–1865," *Dalhousie Review* 37 (1957): 72–84.

90 See Waite, *Life and Times of Confederation*, 238–39, on New Brunswick. Vaughan in "Critics of the Judicial Committee of the Privy Council" argues that the main anti-confederate alternative to Confederation in the Maritimes was an imperial union (p. 510), but then admits a few pages later that an examination of the Confederation debates in the Maritimes shows that much of the resistance there was based on a clear perception of the centralist philosophy that lay behind the Quebec Resolutions (p. 512).

91 Ellis, "Persistence of Antifederalism," 302.

92 In his study of the persistence of sectionalism in Britain, *Internal Colonialism: The Celtic Fringe in British National Development, 1536–1966* (Berkeley and Los Angeles, 1975), Michael Hechter concludes that "the persistence of objective cultural distinctiveness in the periphery must itself be the function of the maintenance of an unequal distribution of resources between core and peripheral groups" (p. 37). That periodic outbursts of regional discontent in the Maritimes are rooted in such an unequal distribution seems unquestionable, but the very ease with which the Maritimes was integrated into Canada and the weakness of secessionist movements seems to me to imply that most Maritimers have always seen and continue to see themselves as a part of the core rather than the peripheral group in Canada.

93 I have not dealt with Newfoundland in this paper because it seems to me that it was the one place where, for a variety of historic reasons, these generalizations may not apply.

GEORGE-ÉTIENNE CARTIER:
Business, Family, and Social Position*

BRIAN YOUNG

Admitted to the bar in November 1835, Cartier opened a law office with his brother in Montreal's legal district. Three years later Cartier was in exile with a charge of treason on his head. Within a decade his personal circumstances had again changed dramatically. By 1848 he was an establishment lawyer, successful urban landlord captain in the Montreal militia, married, and a member of the Legislative Assembly. Political prominence in the 1850s and 1860s as Montreal's leading Conservative brought a new scale of international clients—the church, the French government, railway, shipping, and mining companies. By the end of his career he represented the two most important religious and business corporations in Montreal and had a substantial income from urban rents, legal fees, stock dividends, and the patronage of his friends. His wealth and political position enabled him to pursue social ambitions involving a country estate, a title, a coat of arms, and frequent visits to Europe.

Cartier's early practice was general and heavily seeded with work offered by family members, home-town acquaintances with business in Montreal, a friendly seigneur, a local priest, his future father-in-law, and various small businessmen. Fracases and bankruptcies in his own family

*From *George-Étienne Cartier: Montreal Bourgeois* (Montreal: McGill-Queen's University Press, 1981). Reprinted with permission of the publisher.

helped him establish his practice. He was paid to handle his mother's financial affairs, a cousin's law suit, his uncle's bankruptcy, and his father's succession. His first two recorded uses of the bailiff were on behalf of his father.[1] Other Cartiers hired him to prepare their wills, mortgages, leases, and contracts. To build up his practice Cartier drew on school, political, and family contacts. Early clients included Joseph Masson, the seigneur of Terrebonne, L.A. Dessaulles, a Collège de Montréal friend, and *patriotes* like Dr Wolfred Nelson, a family acquaintance from the Richelieu Valley, E. R. Fabre, his future father-in-law, and Ludger Duvernay. He obtained a hotel licence for one client, acted as legal guardian for another, and sent the sheriff on behalf of a third.[2] In contrast to the urban orientation of his later career, a considerable portion of his early business originated in the rural parishes where his family had lived for almost a century: the curé of Contrecoeur, the neighbouring village of St-Antoine, hired him four times in 1841; Cartier acted for two local groups, the *fabrique* of Contrecoeur and the municipality Varennes; his chief rural client, the seigneur of Varennes, paid Cartier £177 between 1841 and 1848 for regulating a boundary dispute, drawing up terms of a £2000 loan, and bringing law suits against those who damaged his roads.[3]

By the mid-1840s the older merchant and banking elite—usually tory and English-speaking—was being challenged by younger Montrealers eager to profit from urbanism, steam, and the changed political circumstances. Manufacturers, printers, shippers, and wholesalers flourished in the narrow streets around Cartier's office along with their camp-followers—lawyers, insurance agents, notaries, brokers, and real-estate speculators. Disliked by some members of the older commercial establishment as one of those "small lawyers anxious to achieve notoriety," the self-confident Cartier, secure in the possession of impressive family and *patriote* credentials, thrived in this changing milieu.[4] A gallic version of the hail-fellow-well-met, his combination of the old school-tie with an open personality, flexible scruples, and a pragmatic conservatism suited the city's style. He organized well, knew how to delegate responsibility, and kept a tight schedule in his fifteen-hour workdays. His half-dozen law clerks were "comers" from well-placed families; his favourite notaries (Joseph Belle and Théodore Doucet) were among Montreal's busiest. While his partners handled the legwork and correspondence, Cartier was the front man, attracting business, entertaining clients, and arranging cases. His turf was the street, the backroom, the court corridor. Cartier always had a leaning toward the political component of law and early in his career developed an instinct for political influence. It was presumably not by accident that clients chose Cartier to make enquiries at the Crown lands office, to prepare acts of incorporation, or to refer cases "upstairs" to La Fontaine. Indeed, when the latter went to the bench his partner and brother-in-law, J. A. Berthelot, became Cartier's associate (1853). When Berthelot in turn was raised to the bench, François Pominville became Cartier's partner (1859) and three years later Louis

Betournay joined the firm. Pominville had been secretary of the Montreal Bar Association, was the first vice-president of the Institut Canadien-Français when it broke away from the Rouge-dominated Institut Canadien in 1858, and was a former partner of the well-known Conservative, L.O. Loranger.[5]

Cartier's account books show a rapid growth in his business between 1844 and 1846 and an evolution from wills, marriage contracts, and family business to a solid commercial practice rooted in leases, land sales, contracts, and civil suits. He seems to have handled a disproportionate number of bankruptcy actions, but perhaps this was symptomatic of the times. By the mid-1840s his clientele had stabilized among Montreal's retailers, land speculators, hotel-keepers, manufacturers, entrepreneurs, and particularly among small or medium-sized merchants like E. R. Fabre, Demoyer and Généreux, Pierre Cadieux, Beaudry and Brothers, and Louis Haldimand. Ephrem and Victor Hudon—friends, political advisers, and Cartier's best clients—were listed on his books as merchants but later became prominent textile manufacturers.

In the commercial milieu frequented by Cartier ethnic ties were apparently less important than usefulness. Montreal's small but important Italian community gave Carter substantial business. His clients included Serafino Giraldi, John Donegani, the city's most flamboyant land speculator in the 1840s, and Francisco Rasco, proprietor of the fashionable hotel where Cartier himself lived.[6] His English-speaking clientele grew steadily and included Benjamin Starnes, wholesaler and later mayor and political "bagman" for Cartier, George Hagar, an important hardware merchant, Bailey Brothers, and George Chapman. A fellow lawyer's instructions to Cartier were succinct: "All I want from you is to address the jury on the opening of the Defendant's Defence. One half the jury is French, one half English. You will not be strained as in the last case. . . . Austin [Cuvillier] will hand you ten dollars. You are marked to $20 in the last case which I shall send you some other time."[7] In 1848 he argued an important case against the Bank of Montreal for the manufacturing firm of Knopp and Noad. Three years later he began making English entries in his account book. Political prominence brought a new scale of clients. His firm drew up bond-issue forms for the European Assurance Company, initiated large debt-recovery suits for forwarding companies like the Cuvilliers, represented municipalities such as Longueuil, and acted in Rome for the Seminary of Montreal.

His law practice reflected the Montreal business community's perennial concern for transportation. His professional interest in railways dated from 1846 when he handled a suit against the Montreal and Lachine Railway. He acted in an important case involving a collision in the Lachine Canal, represented the Richelieu Company in the purchase of a steamboat, and in 1853 assumed national stature as a transportation lawyer by being named Quebec solicitor for the Grand Trunk Railway.[8]

Cartier's account books exist only for the first eighteen years of his practice (1835–53). As entered on his books his gross income for this period was just under £5000.[9] However, his first years of practice were disrupted by the rebellions and then he spent a year in exile. Nor do his books make clear what he paid in office, bailiff, or travel expenses, in salaries to his brother and subsequent partners, or in shared fees with other lawyers. Certain transactions, such as Cartier family business, are not entered in his books although other documents indicate that this work—an important part of his early income—was reimbursed. Nor is it evident that the bankrupt clients carried on his books, some of whom owed large sums, ever paid.

Cartier was usually paid in cash but sometimes by cheque, four-month promissory notes, or in kind. The seigneur of Varennes settled his account by delivering thirty minots of wheat to Cartier's mother. Another client left his watch as pawn. Cartier returned it when the client, a carter, drove him to Verchères for New Year's Day. A hotel-keeper applied Cartier's fees to his lodging bill. The spittoons, oyster knives, rat traps, and razor straps that Cartier bought at Hagar's General Store were deducted from law fees owed by the proprietor.[10] In the 1850s his legal income from institutional clients escalated far beyond pawned watches or razor straps. The Grand Trunk paid him $10 000 for the period 1853–57, the Seminary of Montreal $1000 in the year 1871.[11]

Cartier's relaxed political morality coupled with his increasing ministerial responsibilities and his firm's role as legal agent for large institutions led to charges of corruption and conflict of interest. A blatant case occurred in 1866 when as attorney-general he was reprimanded by the colonial secretary for permitting his law partner to act for France in a case involving Lamirande, a French forger, who had escaped custody in the United States and was arrested in Canada.[12] Held in the Montreal jail, Lamirande was defended by Joseph Doutre, a well-known Rouge. The French government hired Cartier's law partner, François Pominville. Doutre built his case around the definition of forgery under British law and charged that his client was being denied *habeas corpus*. While the case was being heard, an extradition order was signed by Solicitor General Langevin and before Doutre could take action Lamirande was removed from Canada. Despite Cartier's denial of impropriety in the extradition order, the colonial secretary was not satisfied: " . . . the fact that the partner of the Attorney General conducted these proceedings on the part of the French government has naturally given rise to suspicion and the conduct of the Solicitor General in obtaining the warrant whilst the case was actually under the hearing of the Judge has not as yet been by any means satisfactorily explained."[13]

Another instance of questionable ethics involved the Montreal Mining Company. By 1855 this company was plagued with stock manipulations, haphazard bookkeeping, unwarranted dividends, and a debt of

£19 340 to the Commercial Bank. Cartier, a company director, acted as intermediary in one stock deal in which, as the Montreal *Gazette* put it, "the circumstances look suspicious."[14] Two hundred shares of stock were given to John Ross, attorney-general of Canada and president of the Grand Trunk Railway, to encourage him to place a county courthouse at the company's mine-site in the Bruce peninsula. Soon afterwards Cartier found a mysterious buyer—purportedly Hugh Allan—who was willing to pay £1000 for Ross's shares.[15] Angered by these manipulations and the lack of profits, company officials blew the whistle. Hugh Allan denied having bought Ross's stock and resigned as the company president. An investigative committee found, in addition to the dubious nature of the purchases, what it described as "extreme irregularity": transactions had not been entered in the company's books and dividends had been paid despite the absence of profits. Ross declared his innocence but resigned from the cabinet. Cartier said little and emerged unscathed. Sixteen years later he was still on the Montreal Mining Company board, was receiving substantial dividends, and was continuing to perform special functions. The company president enclosed a note with a director's cheque for $200: "Thompson Island which the Co. wish to acquire is not included in sale to new company and would form an asset for the shareholders of the Montreal Mining Corporation."[16]

In addition to his law practice, Cartier had a substantial income from urban rents since, like many Canadian and European bourgeois of the period, he invested his surplus capital in real estate.[17] Over a period of twenty-two years (1842–64), Cartier bought lots and houses, constructed five buildings, and renovated properties. At the age of twenty-eight he made his first real-estate investment; before his fortieth birthday he was receiving eleven assessment notices from the City of Montreal; in 1853 his handyman repaired thirty-two pairs of venetian blinds. A mixture of residential and commercial, all his urban properties were concentrated in the area where he lived and worked, either on St Paul Street, the main commercial thoroughfare, or on Notre Dame, the major east-west artery. His preference for investments in the 1840s within this small area is clear from figure 1. The use of his buildings by doctors, lawyers, tailors, jewellers, grocers, and hotel-keepers emphasizes the concentration of the professional and commercial group in the old part of the city.[18] His acquisitions were cumulative. He never sold a property and seems to have bought with an eye to security and revenue rather than speculation. In 1873 his seven urban properties included a small hotel, a vaccination office and doctor's residence, four stores, and the workshops and apartments of several tradesmen. Revenues from these properties totalled $3160 (1873) and after expenses his net income from urban rents was $2466 (see table 1).

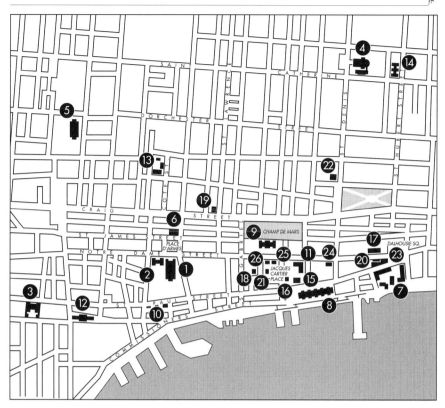

Institutions
1. Notre Dame Church
2. Seminary of Montreal
3. Collège de Montréal
4. St Jacques Cathedral
5. St Patrick's Church
6. Bank of Montreal
7. Barracks
8. Bonsecours Market
9. Court House
10. Customs House
11. Government House
12. Parliament
13. Christian Brothers school
14. Sisters of Providence almshouse
15. Rasco's Hotel
16. Hotel Nelson
17. Donnegana's Hotel

Personal
18. Fabre bookstore
19. Fabre family home
20. Cartier family home (1848–55)
21. Cartier law office
22. Luce Cuvillier home

Properties (some purchased after 1850)
23. 42–43 St Paul St, 30 Notre Dame St
24. 74 Notre Dame St
25. 82 and 84 Notre Dame St
26. 86 and 88 Notre Dame St

FIGURE 1 *Cartier's Bailiwick: Central Montreal at Mid-century*

Table 1:   **URBAN REVENUE PROPERTIES, 1873**

Income Property	Tenant	Annual Rent	Taxes Tenant Pays	Owner Pays
30 Notre Dame	D. Monette	$ 300	1 month rent	–
32 Notre Dame	Dr Arthur Ricard (residence and vaccination office)	300	1 month rent	–
42 and 43 St Paul	J.E. Lareau (merchant)	700	–	1 month rent
74 Notre Dame	J.O. Guilmette (tailor and dry-goods store)	700	3 months' rent	–
82 Notre Dame	Bruno Labelle	400	1 month rent	–
84 Notre Dame	L Silverman (jeweller)	360	1 month rent	–
86 and 88 Notre Dame	Mathieu and Trudel (grocers)	400	3 months' rent	–
Gross Income		$3160		$3160
Expenses				
Taxes (42 and 43 St Paul St)		58		
Insurance (all urban properties)		136		
Repairs (approximate) (1874–75: $530; 1875–76: $509)		500		
Mortgages		0		
Depreciation		?		
Total Expenses		694		694
Net Income from Urban Properties				$2466

Source: Papers, Dr George-Étienne Cartier, Montreal (hereafter DCP), État démontrant les recettes et les dépenses de la succession . . . Cartier, July 1855.

Cartier's interest as an urban landlord was reflected in his ideology. Much more than simply rents, property was equated to *la patrie*, the nation, and even the soil. He associated property with saving, civic responsibility, and the work ethic: without the goal of property ownership, people wouldn't work. Ownership brought social stability, "energy," "morality," "judgement," and "honesty." In short, property-owners constituted "l'élément qui doit gouverner le monde." For years he opposed the abolition of the upper house of the Canadian legislature, on the ground that it acted as a protector of property, and he objected to universal suffrage since in his opinion only the lazy or vicious failed to meet property qualifications.[19]

Carter himself had no difficulty in meeting the £500 property qualification for membership in the Legislative Assembly since he had received 1200 acres of wooded land in the county of Wolfe from his parents and an

Table 2: RURAL PROPERTIES, 1873

Property	Mortgage		Taxes	Insurance	Income	Value
	Principal	Interest				
1400 acres (Ham Township Wolfe County)	–	–	$24	–	–	$ 1 900 (1882)
Country estate (Limoilou)	$4800	$336 (7%)	$25	$19	$192	$20 000 (May 1874)

Source: DCP, État démontrant les recettes et les dépenses de la succession . . . Cartier, July 1885.

undetermined amount from the estate of his grandfather.[20] By 1864, without counting interest charges, overhead, and the purchase of his home (although it later became a revenue property), Cartier's investment in urban revenue properties amounted to £11 699 ($46 806), (see tables 1 and 2).

In 1842 Cartier paid £600 for his first urban property, a house on the corner of Notre Dame and Bonsecours Streets. His tenants included a navigator and a carpenter. A year later he constructed his first building at a cost of £1846.[21] In 1845 he paid his friend and client, John Donegani, £3650 for a large building on St Paul Street. Cartier immediately leased this building to the British government for use as a military hospital at an annual rent of £140 (1846–49). He later rented it as a hotel. In 1847 he paid £1250 to construct two buildings, including a store and stable, on St Paul Street. He purchased his own home on Notre Dame Street in 1848 and the attached house for £1330 in 1862. One house was rented as a doctor's office and residence when his wife and daughters went to England in 1871.[22] He paid £900 for a lot on Notre Dame Street in March 1855 and nine years later spent £2123 to construct on the site two three-storey buildings that included five stores.[23]

Restricting his purchases to his own bailiwick, he bought from widows, clients, and friends. Mortgage money for early purchases came from *patriotes* like L.A. Dessaulles and Wolfred Nelson; later he tapped the Cuvillier family. Busy with politics and law, Cartier left the management of his properties to associates. For at least fifteen years Joseph Laramée repaired Cartier's buildings and acted as general contractor for new construction; his junior law partner, François Pominville, handled leases, advertisements, and tenant problems. His friend and banker, Maurice Cuvillier, administered financial matters.

Cartier had a keen eye for costs. A number of his properties adjoined each other, allowing the lumping of stable, cesspool, and courtyard facilities. Except for one urban property and his country estate his tenants were responsible for all taxes. Cartier himself was often tardy in payments to the water company, banks, and other creditors; in 1865 the sheriff of Arthabaska wrote in some embarrassment to remind Cartier, a cabinet minister, that he was in arrears in his payments for Crown land. Fond of life in fine hotels, Cartier did not hesitate to rent his own quarters during lengthy absences. His Ottawa apartment was taken temporarily by his Conservative colleague, Alexander Campbell, and his Montreal home was leased on two occasions. In one instance he retained a main-floor campaign office and a third-floor storage area. A stringent landlord, Cartier tried to persuade British authorities to install storm windows on the building they rented as a hospital.[24] He took a mortgage on property in Châteauguay from a tenant who was in arrears. Although his country estate was not primarily a revenue property Cartier drew up a careful lease concerning grazing, fruit trees, and the equal division of farm produce between tenant and proprietor. The tenant was responsible for local public works on the road and ditches; Cartier paid the taxes and contributed to the parish church.[25]

His only incongruous transaction was the purchase of 200 acres of Crown land in the same township as the 1200 acres given to him by his parents in 1841. Purchased in 1864, this holding was not urban, revenue-producing, or recreational. Unsupervised and undeveloped, it was stripped of its wild cherry timber by local farmers.[26]

Although it has been argued that French Canadians preferred property investments—at least in the 1820s—a transition during the nineteenth century from real estate to commercial and industrial stock investments was typical of the bourgeoisie in France.[27] This pattern is evident in Cartier's investments. By 1865 he had stopped buying real estate (his country home excepted) and was investing his surplus capital in stocks—primarily banks with a minor interest after 1872. in a railway equipment company. This transition appears to have been gradual and not unlike what Alberto Melucci calls the "osmose entre la propriété foncière et la bourgeoisie industrielle."[28] Before 1865 he held stock in the Montreal Mining Company and the Grand Trunk Railway but since he acted as a director of the former and solicitor for the latter it is not clear that he paid for these shares or that they represent a bona-fide interest in stock investments. Nor, despite a growing interest in the stock market, did Cartier ever sell any real estate to raise capital. By the early 1870s his income from rents was approximately double his income from stock dividends. In 1873 his one industrial stock (Canadian Railway Equipment Company) represented 9 percent of his stock-market investment (see table 3).

Cartier had bank accounts at the Toronto, Ottawa, and Montreal branches of the Bank of Montreal and the Quebec City branch of the Bank of Upper Canada, but after 1865 the brokerage firm of Cuvillier and Company were his main financial advisers. Maurice Cuvillier chose Cartier's portfolio, paid his bills, and permitted him substantial overdrafts.

Table 3: PORTFOLIO OF STOCKS, BONDS, AND BANK DEPOSITS, 1873

Stocks and Bonds

Company	No. of Shares	Face Value	Paid Up	Dividends	Evaluated by Estate
Grand Trunk Railway (7% debentures, 1859)	–	$1 000	100%	0	0
City Bank	109	10 900	100	708	10 900
Banque du Peuple	146	5 600	100	244	7 847 (1874)
Victoria Skating Rink	1	50	100	0	50
Canadian Railway Equipment Co.	100	10 000	25	123	2 500
Maritime Bank	50	5 000	10	7	500
Total				$1 082	$21 797

Bank Deposits

Bank	Deposit
Bank of Montreal	$ 4 155
Bank of Montreal (London)	75
Banque d'Epargne	55
Total	$ 4 285

Note: Consols and Montreal Mining Co. stock excluded: interest from these, 1871–72, was $3164.

Source: DCP, État démontrant les recettes et les dépenses de la succession . . . Cartier, July 1885.

Table 4: INCOME, 1873

Source	Amount
Salary, government minister	$5000 (1871)
Law income	?
Farm products (country estate)	192
Rents (before expenses)	3160
Dividends and interest	1435*

*Dividend and interest income for 1871 was $2606 and $1495 in 1872.

Source: DCP, État démontrant les recettes et les dépenses de la succession . . . Cartier, July 1885.

In 1868 Cartier borrowed $2800 from Cuvillier for a nine-month period and when he died five years later he had an outstanding eighteen-month loan of $2071 on which no interest had been paid (table 5). Cuvillier's letters to Cartier encompassed both friendship and financial advice.

Table 5:   ESTATE

Assets

Immovable Property		Value	Mortgage
30 Notre Dame			0
32 Notre Dame			0
42 and 43 St Paul			0
74 Notre Dame			0
82 Notre Dame			0
84 Notre Dame			0
86 and 88 Notre Dame			0
Total purchase price of urban properties, 1840–64		$53 206	
Appreciation: urban properties		?	
1400 acres (Wolfe County)	(1882)	1 900	0
Country estate (Limoilou)		20 000	4800
		75 106	75 106

Moveable Property	Value	Mortgage
Ottawa: furniture	800	
wine	200	
Montreal (home, law office, and country estate): furniture and effects	2 280	
library	1 843	
silver, chandeliers, and other effects removed by wife's family	1 000 (est)	
	6 123	6 123
Stocks	21 797	21 797
Bank deposits	4 285	4 285
Total Assets		107 311

Debts

Marquise de Bassano (Clara Symes)*		
personal loan (1865)	10 000	
outstanding interest	3 600	
Maurice Cuvillier*		
personal loan (1871)	2 071	
outstanding interest	238	
Seminary of Montreal*		
three commutations	1 148	
outstanding interest	585	
Robert Turcotte		
mortgage (country estate)	4 800	
outstanding interest	0	
Banque d'Epargne		
loan	1 216	
	23 958	23 958
Real Worth		83 353

*Neither interest nor principal payments made before Cartier's death.

Source: DCP, État démontrant des recettes et les dépenses de la succession . . . Cartier, July 1885.

The enclosed letter from Luce undoubtedly gives you all the news of the day and which leaves nothing for me to add except to write to enclose certificates of 53 shares of City Bank stock for your account (May 5, 1865). . . . I enclose bank draft for $84 being for Miss Symes bill, St. Louis Hotel and $25 lent her. . . . I also enclose certificates on 19 shares of City Bank transferred to you which I bought at 92 being 7% discount (July 29, 1865). . . . I have invested $1199 in Peoples Bank shares . . . we are well at home (Feb. 13, 1871). . . . Will I give Lachapelle 300 dollars to pay his men? (telegram, May 27, 1871)[29]

Under Maurice Cuvillier's tutelage Cartier began investing heavily in the City Bank and la Banque du Peuple. Between April and October 1865 he bought $5275 worth of City Bank stock, much of which he financed by selling stock in the Bank of Upper Canada ($1506) and the City and District Bank ($1408). His portfolio five years later was still heavily concentrated in la Banque du Peuple ($5600) and the City Bank ($10 900). In July 1872 he paid a 10 percent instalment on Marine Bank stock with a face value of $5000 and four months later bought 100 shares in the Canadian Railway Equipment Company. Cartier continued to receive significant dividends from his 560 shares in the Montreal Mining Company ($2240 in 1871). He had the same number of "Consols" shares which paid a dividend of $924 in January 1872. Since the latter two stocks were clearly indicated in his portfolio with Cuvillier and Company and yet neither appeared in his estate they were presumably "patronage" stocks which were withdrawn at his death.[30]

Family matters in St-Antoine could not be neglected despite Cartier's flourishing career in Montreal. The Cartiers were proud, prickly, and bankrupt; the prosperity of their community and more particularly, the family's social position, were seriously threatened by the thirty-year agricultural depression. Cartier had to contend with aging, bankrupt parents, an alcoholic brother, and a neurotic spinster sister. In 1841 his father fell ill with fever, diarrhea, and "inflamed internal organs." Although busy with La Fontaine's Terrebonne election campaign, Cartier made two hasty trips to St-Antoine and on the second occasion buried his father with as "splendid and as solemn a funeral as possible."[31] Bankrupt for a decade, Jacques Cartier left a bickering family, pending lawsuits, and unanswered letters from sheriffs and notaries. As administrator of his father's estate Cartier arranged guarantors for the debts, sold family property in Quebec City, advanced money to his brother, sued longtime debtors of his father, settled outstanding seigneurial dues, and paid interest on overdue accounts. Division of the estate was complicated. One property measured 547 acres; others had choice river frontage, a town location, or valuable buildings.[32]

One brother wanted the land closest to the church, another contested an equal division of family debts. Before his father's death Cartier had become his mother's lawyer and over a period of eight years advanced her £1188 to pay off debts, make house repairs, and buy furniture. Transactions between mother and son were conducted in strict business fashion: advances were given in return for promissory notes, interest was charged, and the total debt notarized some months before her death.[33]

Nor were the family's concerns strictly financial. Cartier's sister, Marguerite, had remained a spinster in St-Antoine. Her brother feared she would go mad and run through the streets with her inheritance.[34] Other family members leaned on Cartier for favours and patronage. One brother wanted a job in the civil service; a cousin asked him to make enquiries at the sheriff's office. His brother Sylvestre, a country doctor, wanted Cartier to find him a government post and a rich wife. "If you open doors, let your brothers in first ... if you want me to marry before cholera gets me, find me a girl or a widow with 60,000 francs."[35]

More serious was the drinking of his brother Damien. The two had established their law practice in 1835 as "Cartier and Cartier." However, in 1840 Cartier had Damien sign a statement declaring that they had never had a formal partnership and that Damien's remuneration had been granted solely by "la liberté et générosité de son frère."[36] By 1850 Damien was practising law only sporadically and Cartier had formed partnerships with more reliable associates. Damien's landlord sent his hotel bills directly to his brother. After a respite in St-Antoine Damien returned to live in the Richelieu Hotel in Montreal and in 1855 may have handled a few cases for his brother. However, he was soon back in St-Antoine consuming "une petite fortune" and periodically being "mis à la porte dans un état d'ivresse" by members of the family.[37] When he died in 1865 he was living with his sister in St-Antoine.

Cartier was thirty-two when he married. This relatively advanced age was considered normal for an ambitious *cavalier*, as was his emphasis on wealth and standing rather than romantic attachment: "les jeunes cavaliers d'aujourd'hui ont 30 ans. On exige, avant tout, de la fortune. Les mariages d'inclination sont aussi rares qu'en Europe."[38] Refused by Mlle Debartzch, the daughter of the Seigneur of Contrecoeur, Cartier chose his wife, Hortense Fabre (1828–98), from an important Montreal commercial family. Her father, Edouard-Raymond Fabre (1799–1854), had been hired by Hector Bossange who came to Canada in 1815 to open the Montreal branch of the world-wide chain of Bossange bookstores. After marrying Fabre's sister, Bossange returned to France, leaving Fabre in charge of the Canadian business. Developing strong ties with both the clergy and liberal intellectuals, Fabre built the bookstore into a major importing, printing, and retail operation. He became mayor of Montreal, director of a bank and a British insurance company, and invested in newspapers, railways, and telegraph companies; in 1854 his estate was valued at £15 941.[39]

His wealth enabled him to provide his children with a comfortable Montreal life, a nine-room home at the corner of St Lawrence and Craig streets, four servants, and trips to New York and his sister's chateau in France. His sons entered the law, the clergy, diplomacy, and journalism. Hortense was educated by the Ursuline nuns in Trois-Rivières and was then tutored in French, English, and dancing. The Fabre piano, the most expensive piece of furniture in the house, was kept in a second-floor salon; Hortense's piano teacher visited the Fabre home three times a week. Her mother, Luce Perrault Fabre, was, like other women of her standing, active in Catholic charities. She visited the poor in their homes, organized bazaars, attended retreats, and was a founding director of a Montreal orphanage, l'Institut des filles de la charité.

Cartier had known the Fabres since 1834. His law office was just a few doors away from their bookstore, a focus of intellectual and *patriote* activity. Like Cartier, Fabre had fled Montreal during the rebellions. In 1839 he helped the young lawyer re-establish his practice by giving him ten legal cases; before his marriage Cartier handled a total of twenty cases for Fabre. When Cartier's father died in bankruptcy in 1841, Fabre (along with Joseph-Amable Berthelot) acted as guarantor for the heirs. Cartier and Fabre later served together on the board of the Montreal City and District Savings Bank. Fabre lent money to his son-in-law: in 1854 the latter was one of Fabre's biggest debtors with outstanding loans totalling £227.[40] Fabre was pleased with his daughter's marriage and told his sister that although Hortense's education had been expensive "nous la marions avantageusement." "Toujours un ami de la maison," Cartier was an "excellent avocat" of whom "brillantes affaires" could be expected.[41]

The Cartier-Fabre marriage contract included a strict "separation of property" agreement. Hortense had no dowry and her clothes, jewellery, and other personal belongings were not of sufficient value to merit a formal inventory. Her only call upon her husband's estate was an annual allowance of £100 that was secured by a special mortgage on the Cartier house at the corner of Notre Dame and Bonsecours Streets.[42] This separation of property clause may have been included to protect any encroachment by Cartier upon his wife's inheritance; in 1854 Hortense appears to have inherited one-fifth of her father's estate. The contract did, however, permit Cartier in his 1866 will to exclude his wife from any share in his estate beyond the £100 a year specifically guaranteed to her.

The morning wedding ceremony was held on June 16, 1846, in Montreal's Notre Dame Church and was performed by the curé of Contrecoeur who had hidden Fabre during the rebellions.[43] After the reception the wedding party—which included Cartier's mentor La Fontaine and his friends A. N. Morin, Wolfred Nelson, Lewis Drummond, Maurice Cuvillier, and Joseph-Amable Berthelot—went to the Laprairie railway station to see the newly-weds off on a three-week honeymoon in New York and Washington.

The marriage was not a success. The Cartiers were drinkers, dancers, and flirts. Pragmatists and third-generation bourgeois, they were at home in the rough-and-tumble secular society of the St Lawrence Valley. For their part the Fabres were intransigent nationalists and strong Catholics. Sober and ambitious, they were reputed to have a hereditary streak of malice.[44] While the generation of Cartier's father lost a merchant fortune, Edouard-Raymond Fabre, the son of a carpenter, spent a lifetime amassing prestige and wealth for his family. Politically, the marriage became an embarrassment for both families. While Cartier accepted La Fontaine's conservatism, his father-in-law remained an incurable *patriote,* annexationist, and Papineau supporter. In 1854 Cartier sided with Wolfred Nelson in the mayoralty campaign against Fabre. Hortense's brother, Edouard-Charles, became the first archbishop of Montreal and another brother, Hector, although he studied in Cartier's law office, became a vociferous political opponent, founded an opposition newspaper, *L'Evénement,* in 1867, and ran against the Conservatives as candidate for the Parti National in 1873. Until 1858 Fabre's law partner was Louis-Amable Jetté who defeated Cartier in the elections of 1872.[45]

Cartier's 1866 will, his alliance with Luce Cuvillier, and the diaries of his daughters provide ample evidence of the failure of the marriage. Pious, caustic, and fourteen years younger than her husband, Hortense had no love for crowds, her husband's politics, or the cronies he brought home. According to one critical family friend, Hortense would have been happiest in a convent—provided she could have been the Mother Superior.[46] Her daughters' diaries show that Madame Cartier had strict opinions concerning men, their morals, and their social acceptability for her daughters. At a school graduation she remarked that convent girls were well behaved because "no bachelors were admitted there."[47]

For his part Cartier was irreverent as a young man, preoccupied in his later years with politics and another woman, gregarious throughout his life. In 1841 he boasted of caning a client who, in his words, threatened to give him "des coups de pied dans le Q." Cartier duelled, got in a shoving match with a judge at the Montreal Skating Club, "screamed and whooped" during a singsong at the governor-general's residence, borrowed a colleague's residence, and according to La Fontaine left it "dans un état horrible et de mal propreté." One observer noticed his brusque treatment of the servants at a noisy dinner-party: "The dinners out here last hours, and there is such quantities of food on the table. Mr. Cartier sang or croaked after dinner, and made every one he could find stand up, hold hands, and sing a chorus. The wretched servants brought in tea, and he pushed them away till after his song was over. He pushed one on his arm lightly, and I saw the servant rubbing his arm much annoyed, and looking like a dog with a trodden-on tail."[48]

Although rumoured to have been drunk in the assembly on one occasion, Cartier never drank with Macdonald's intensity or morosity. A restless and sociable individual, he liked convivial Saturday evenings, parties, champagne, laughter, and folksongs. He relaxed after work by sending out for drinks or by playing the piano, and when in Montreal ate dinner almost every evening with associates like Louis Archambault, Sheriff Charles Leblanc, or François Pominville. A compulsive worker, he travelled incessantly. After arriving on the night train he often sent his baggage to his home and went directly to his office for a day's work.[49] He seems never to have been at ease with family life, the piano lessons of his daughters, or austere Sunday dinners with his brother-in-law, the priest.

Cartier's expansive, other-directed nature is suggested by his residences. He was born in a large, open home that had three apartments and sixteen inhabitants and at the age of ten was sent to live with 120 boys in the dormitories of the Collège de Montréal. At twenty-two he was living in Rasco's Hotel, a colourful establishment where actors, lawyers, officers, and their ladies dined on Italian cuisine. Cartier lived at Rasco's for ten years until he and his bride moved into the Hotel Donnegana in 1846. Described as "palatial," the newly opened Donnegana's was the Cartier home for almost two years; their first daughter was born during their residence there.

In 1848 the Cartiers moved one block east along Notre Dame Street into a fine three-storey stone house for which Cartier paid £1600. A choice location on the eastern fringe of the commercial district, it had a view of the port and St Lawrence from the back bedrooms.[50] The four-block walk to his office took him by the houses of friends like John Donegani, the market, his St Paul Street properties and Rasco's Hotel (figure 1). The house itself was ten years old, large and comfortable with a dumb-waiter system connecting the dining-room to the basement kitchen. The wine cellar, larder, coal-room, and servant sleeping quarters were also in the basement. Cartier's handyman supervised the installation of gas lighting, green shutters, a renovated fireplace in the master bedroom, and a new stove in the nursery. The main floor had eleven-foot ceilings and was dominated by a large library and parlour. The second floor contained the music room and the governess's room as well as the bedrooms.

Once elected to the assembly Cartier spent the sessions in Toronto, Quebec City, and finally Ottawa. Accustomed to hotel living and an ambulatory lifestyle, Cartier was probably less upset than other politicians by the periodic rotation of the assembly between Toronto and Quebec City. When in Toronto he stayed at Beard's Hotel or at Mrs Dunlop's on Bay Street and, for at least one period, his wife and daughters joined him. He lodged at Sword's Hotel in Quebec City until the 1860s when he and Sandfield Macdonald rented quarters in the upper town in a townhouse owned by Judge Jean Duval. After 1867 he leased a four-bedroom home in Ottawa at the corner of Maria and Metcalfe Streets for an annual rent of $320. He retained an office in his Notre Dame Street house but when in Montreal slept at his country home.[51]

Cartier's marriage was undoubtedly not helped by his lifelong appreciation for the female form or what he described as his favourite occupation, "activity of the heart."[52] Before his marriage he and his friends joked about their success with girls, the quality of Quebec City women, and the relationship between a girl's education and the number of her children. Exiled in 1838 Cartier told a friend that the Montreal girls he had met in the United States were "rien d'extraordinaire." In Vermont he visited "la célèbre Madame Turtore" but "elle n'est pas bien drôle quant au physique."[53] After his marriage Cartier remained quick with a compliment for the ladies and was always among the first on the dance floor. For several years he corresponded with Lord Carnarvon's niece whom he had met in England in 1858. Cartier found her "gracious," "brilliant," and "attractive." He sent her a book and Indian embroidery; she asked for his photo, painted his portrait, and invited him to visit her in London.[54]

Given the partners' differing social attitudes, interests, and personalities, the Cartier marriage became one of form rather than substance, and husband and wife led increasingly separate lives long before his alliance with Luce Cuvillier. One author dates the couple's informal separation from the birth of their third child in 1853; certainly Cartier was absent from the baptism of this daughter.[55] When his law partner asked the Cartiers to be godparents, Cartier sent his brother-in-law to assist Madame Cartier at the ceremony. By the late 1850s the Cartiers rarely appeared in public together. In the 1860s the relationship deteriorated completely, although Madame Cartier did continue to appear with her husband at important official functions such as those connected with the Quebec Conference.[56] In a family photograph taken of Cartier and his daughters, Madame Cartier is noticeably absent. Cartier rarely slept at the family home. When he did spend four nights there in January 1871 he was an unwelcome guest, his departure, according to his daughter, was "la seule bonne nouvelle." Cartier's business relations with his wife were handled by his law partner who arranged her travel plans, bought her boat and train tickets, and accompanied her to the station.[57] By 1871 Lady Cartier lived largely abroad, visiting London, Paris, and her uncle's chateau in the Loire. After her husband's death she never returned to Canada, and ultimately settled in a villa at Cannes on the French Riviera.

Embittered and alone, Lady Cartier's main preoccupation was preparing her two surviving daughters for marriage. The youngest daughter, Reine-Victoria, died at the age of thirteen months in the cholera epidemic of 1854.[58] Josephine (1847–86) and Hortense (1849–1941) had convent educations followed by lessons in dancing, piano, German, Spanish, and riding. In contrast to their father's casual religious practices both girls, even as young adults, attended mass almost every day; in 1873 their uncle was named a bishop. Although the family had a pet dog and birds the atmosphere of the Cartier home was sombre. Josephine described 1870 as a year "replète de contrariétés amères."[59] Hortense practised the piano for two hours every day; in the evenings the girls sewed with their mother, spent "soirées endormitoires" with family friends or visited their maternal grandmother for "l'inévitable repas de famille assaisonné d'épi-grammes et de regards sévères de l'abbé qui veut nous marier."[60] British officers played an important role in the social life of the Montreal bour-geoisie and the Cartier girls often joined the young Hingstons, Drummonds, Tuppers, and other peers at garrison balls or toboggan par-ties. Summer holidays included a week at Cacouna, a St Lawrence River vil-lage near Rivière de Loup, where they joined summer colony residents like the Galts in boules, chess, cards, riding, or walks along the beach. Travel to Europe did not impede the proper education of the Cartier girls. Pianos were rented, language and riding lessons arranged, and suitable bachelors invited for tea. In 1871–72, for instance, the girls went to the theatre in London, spent a day trying on dresses in Paris, and holidayed at their great-uncle's chateau.

Except when the family gathered in London in the last months of his life Cartier did not spend extended periods of time with his daughters. He often expressed regret at not having a son to inherit his title and confided to Macdonald: "I wish one of my girls was a son."[61] The diaries of both girls reflect that they sided with their mother concerning their father's lifestyle, his liaison with Luce Cuvillier, and his conflict with the Fabre family. Both referred derisively to their father as "le Capitaine" or "el Capitano" and dis-liked his impatience and vanity: "1000ième répétition des mêmes intéres-santes histoires, notwithstanding their lack of success, mail day, more fire than ever, Thomas Thomas [the servant] sur tous les tons de la gamme, pour envoyer des lettres par le courrier, toujours au dernier moment."[62]

Caught in the contradiction between her parents' failed marriage and their insistence that the institution of marriage represented the only acceptable form of status and security for a woman, Hortense reacted by including a bitter "notice to fathers" in her diary:

> Avis aux pères de famille: ayez en deux et accusez les quotidien-nement d'être deux de trop, parlez leur toujours de vous, grondez les sans cesse, si ce sont des filles, mettez à la porte tous les jeunes gens qui voudront bien vous en débarrasser en les épousant, puis accusez les de rester vieilles filles, parlez mal devant elles de toutes celles de leurs amies qui se marient bien ou mal, soying [sic] sûr que vos filles ne désireront jamais ni le mariage, ni le couvent, ni la potence comme moyen de se défaire de votre aimable société ... This is written on a really, really very merry Christmas 25 December, 1872.[63]

Neither girl succeeded in attracting what their mother described as "le type du parfait gentilhomme."[64] Both remained spinsters and after their father's death moved with their mother to the French Riviera.

In the last years of his life Cartier lived with his wife's cousin, Luce Cuvillier (1817–1900). Her father, Austin Cuvillier (1779–1849), was a prominent merchant, a founder of the Bank of Montreal, a supporter of

Papineau until 1834, and first speaker of the Legislative Assembly of the United Canadas. His sister married George Symes reputedly the wealthiest merchant in Quebec City. Symes, and Cuvillier acted as forwarding merchants for Cartier's father and grandfather in their Richelieu Valley grain business. Like Cartier, the Cuvilliers adjusted effectively to the changing nature of capitalism in Montreal. Two of Luce's brothers, Maurice and Austin, had important interests in Upper Canadian trade, banking, transportation, and real-estate development. In 1850 Maurice Cuvillier owned sixteen Montreal houses and five stores, and was part-owner of the steamboat *Ste Hélène*.[65] He founded a stockbroking firm and was a director of the Metropolitan Bank and the Montreal and St-Jérôme Colonization Railroad. Cartier was Maurice Cuvillier's classmate at the Collège de Montréal, acted as a lawyer for the Cuvilliers as early as 1857, and by the mid-1860s had entrusted his financial affairs to Cuvillier and Company.

Although they avoided a public scandal the Cartier-Cuvillier liaison was well known. Journalists said little besides noting Madame Cartier's absence and "Mlle Cuvillier's" presence at social functions attended by Cartier. Privately, colleagues like Hector Langevin gossiped about Cartier's brazenness.[66] The delicate problem of his Montreal address was solved by naming Ottawa as his official residence. Montreal correspondence was sent to his law office. When in England with Cartier, Luce probably lodged officially at the Cuvillier house in London; visits to Cartier during legislative sessions in Quebec may have been made in the guise of chaperoning her niece. She sent news to Cartier in Ottawa via her brother and urged Cartier to be discreet in his letters: "My dearest . . . you must be more particular in writing your letters. Keep all your endearments for your————, write me business letters and nothing more."[67]

The liaison dated from at least the early 1860s. Luce became guardian for her wealthy niece, Clara Symes, in 1861. Two years later Clara Symes gave Cartier $10 000 and although this was officially a loan neither interest nor principal was paid in Cartier's lifetime. By 1864 his law partner was sending him news of Luce; during the sessions of 1864 and 1865 she visited him in Quebec City; in May 1865 she forwarded him "all the news of the day." In his 1866 will Cartier named Luce Cuvillier, paid tribute to her "sagesse et prudence," and bequeathed her $600. The will attacked his wife, her family, and their values; he urged his two daughters to follow Luce's "advice" and stipulated that they would lose their inheritance if they married any member of his wife's family.[68]

By the end of the decade Cartier and Cuvillier were living together. Between 1866 and 1873 they were in Europe together three times. Luce was in London during Cartier's trip to England in 1866, accompanied him to Europe in 1868, and was in London when he died. Cartier bought her jewellery in Paris and a table muff, riding gear, and furs in London; they bought a marble bust in Naples in 1867. Luce managed the employees at the country estate and in 1871 laid off the gardener for the winter.[69]

Although Cartier apparently promised his Sulpician friend, Joseph Baile, to break off the liaison, it was Luce Cuvillier rather than Lady Cartier, who was also in London, who attended Cartier's funeral service at the French chapel.[70] At the auction of Cartier's estate, the Cuvilliers bought furniture worth $481; Lady Cartier expressed her sentiments towards the material remnants of her marriage in a letter to her husband's executors. Aside from a few personal belongings, she wrote, "Je ne veux rien absolument garder de mon ménage."[71]

Eleven years older than Cartier's wife, unmarried, and an unorthodox romantic, Luce Cuvillier smoked, wore trousers, and read Byron's poetry and the novels of George Sand.[72] At the same time she tutored girls at the Sacre Coeur convent and helped direct the same orphanage as Cartier's mother-in-law. She was bitterly attacked by the Toronto *Globe* for her role in converting her rich niece to Roman Catholicism:

> The Roman Catholic priests, ever on the watch for rich heirs and heiresses, have made a grand catch in the daughter of a late wealthy citizen of Quebec. She is about to become a nun, and thereby secures to Mother Church a million of dollars. The girl is only 17. Her relatives in this city have done all they could to prevent her taking this irreversible step but no, her spiritual advisers have conquered, and she to a nunnery goes. No one supposes that her departed father ever dreamt that the wealth he for many years toiled for, was to go in such a way. By such means the Roman Catholic institutions of Lower Canada become immensely rich.[73]

Cartier's rising income allowed him to indulge his inherited bourgeois tastes. In its simplest form this meant attention to comfort, food, furnaces, carpets, and gas lighting. However, Montrealers of Cartier's rank sought more than storm windows, a full stomach, and a large house. The perception of Cartier by English Canadians as an unaggressive French-Canadian *bon vivant* obscured his serious social ambitions that are attested to by his wine cellar, servants, library, and hotel bills, by his stable, fruit trees, and country estate, by his military commission, baronetcy, coat of arms, uniforms, and hairstyle.

Cartier accumulated a large amount of furniture and moveable goods in his three residences and law office Although his widow was given most of his silverware, nine chandeliers, jewellery, and other valuable personal items, his moveable effects sold for $5123 (table 5). His homes contained few paintings or valuable works of art although as previously mentioned he did buy a marble bust in Naples and paid $435 to have it shipped to Montreal.[74] Music was important to Cartier. He liked to sing and dance and encouraged his daughters to play the piano. Pianos were expensive and an important sign of status; only 9 percent of bourgeois homes in France contained any musical instrument and, because of their cost, pianos were particularly rare. Cartier had two pianos and rented one for his daughters when they were abroad for extended periods.[75]

An impressive wine cellar was always a mark of prestige and as early as 1853 Cartier bought madeira by the cask and cognac by the gallon. In his early years he liked the Richelieu Valley concoction of rum, sugar, and warm water; later he was known for his taste in champagne.[76] When he died he left eleven cases of wine in one residence, 240 bottles of claret, four cases of champagne and ten cases of wine in Ottawa, and a barrel of sherry, a barrel of Bordeaux, four cases of champagne, and a case of brandy at his country home.[77]

Despite his public disdain for "bookish" learning, Cartier's own library was auctioned in January 1875 for the considerable sum of $1843 of which $826 came from the sale of his law books, $591 from his government publications, and $163 from books, pamphlets, and brochures on Canada.[78] Over half of the $263 received for the balance of his books which formed his personal collection came from the sale of his French encyclopedia, Gustave de Beaumont's history of Ireland and back copies of the *Illustrated London News* and the *Eclectic Magazine* (figure 2).

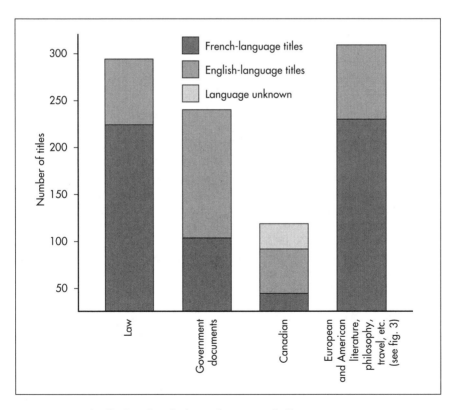

FIGURE 2 *Distribution of Books in Cartier's General Library*

Source: DCP, Inventaire des livres de la succession de feu George-Étienne Cartier.

The library's monetary value should not be inflated since the law books formed a special professional category and the holding of government documents and Canadian works was probably in large part the result of free distribution to government ministers. Nor can one ascertain how many of his books were received as gifts or were part of his ménage with Luce Cuvillier. Finally, it is impossible to know which books Cartier actually read. Although his broad-based conservatism embraced fundamental questions of property, monarchy, law, and education, Cartier avoided theory and even encouraged a certain anti-intellectualism in his audiences. Reading, he often pointed out, was of little use in the marketplace or political arena.[79]

Comparisons cannot be made with the holdings of his Canadian peers, but his library did have much in common with Parisian bourgeois of the same period. Like his European counterparts he bought erotic travel books on the Orient and Egypt; his library also reflected the vogue for dictionaries and encyclopedias as well as the interest in practical guides—*Essai sur l'art d'être heureux, Cuisinier Parisien, Cartes à jouer,* several books on oratory, a Spanish reader, an Italian grammar, and an itinerary of Paris (figure 3).[80] Although it included neither Burke nor Locke, his library was strongest in eighteenth- and nineteenth-century political theorists and historians like Voltaire, Rousseau, Montesquieu, Chateaubriand, Lammenais, Tocqueville, Bagehot, Mill, Macaulay, Bancroft, Hamilton, and Marshall. The presence of authors like Proudhon, Ricardo, and Bères *(Les classes ouvrières)* implies that Cartier was aware of class questions. For a man who liked music, his library contained surprisingly few works on music or art, although there are indications that his wife removed some books of this description, or at least the sheet music from his country home.[81] He owned works by major Catholic philosophers like Veuillot, Bossuet, and Pascal, one work on the papacy, and three copies of Muslim's *Les Saints Lieux,* but like his Parisian peers he had no devotional literature. His fascination with the peerage, heraldry, and other trappings of nobility is clearly reflected in his library. On the other hand there is no evidence of a literary interest in the military, if one ignores eleven copies, presumably complimentary, of a pamphlet entitled *On the Art of Operating under Enemy Fire.*

Cartier's lighter reading was almost entirely in French and included such contemporary authors as Balzac, Dumas, Hugo, George Sand, and Eugène Sue. His interest in the theatre is witnessed by the seventy-nine volumes of the *Répertoire du théâtre français* and twelve volumes of Voltaire's plays. The only exceptions to his preference for French literature were English copies of Longfellow's *Hiawatha* and Stowe's *Uncle Tom's Cabin,* and a large collection of English periodicals.[82] The government, Canadian, and to a lesser extent law publications reflect a professional pull towards English as a working language (figure 2).

Luce Cuvillier stimulated Cartier's interest in country life, riding, and viticulture. In September 1869 he bought a 122-acre farm at Longue Point

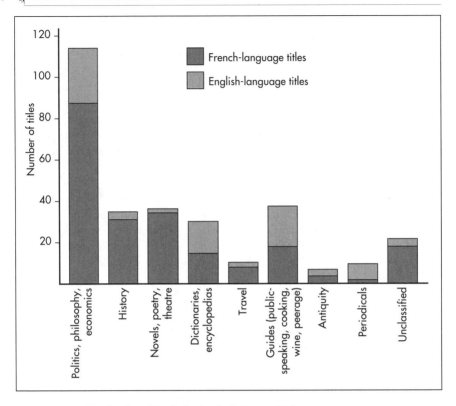

FIGURE 3 *Distribution of Books in Cartier's Personal Library*

Note: For law, government documents, and Canadian books, see fig. 2.

Source: DCP, Inventaire des livres de la succession de feu George-Étienne Cartier.

on the eastern outskirts of Montreal.[83] Located in a favoured area for the country homes of Montreal's elite, Cartier's farm was just a few estates away from the Symes's "Elmwood" and the Cuvilliers' "Review Cottage." Cartier named his home "Limoilou" after Jacques Cartier's village in Brittany. Fronting on the St Lawrence the property had a large vegetable garden, a vineyard, orchard, pasture, cultivated fields, and a small creek. The main house, a stone dwelling, was built towards the river and had a parlour, living-room, and five bedrooms. A smaller frame house, barn, and silo located closer to the toll road to Montreal were leased. Particularly interested in fruit trees, Luce had Cartier's gardener buy apple, plum, peach, and cherry seedlings from the finest American nurseries. It was at Limoilou that Cartier kept the family piano, his pony, his popular novels, and his twelve-year collection of the *Illustrated London News*.[84]

　　Cartier's comfort and isolation from daily problems were assured by a hierarchy of friends, associates, hired help, and servants. Law clerks and junior partners handled the routine of his law practice; his political secretaries—L.W. Sicotte and later Benjamin Sulte—protected him from office-seekers and trouble-makers. Important investment matters were supervised by Maurice Cuvillier, the country estate was managed by Luce Cuvillier, minor banking was dealt with by his valet. The Cartiers always had help for the domestic duties of cleaning, washing, cooking, household repairs, gardening, child care, vehicle maintenance, and shopping. Cartier had both a housekeeper and a part-time waiter in Ottawa, a groundskeeper and seasonal farm labourers at the country estate, a handyman for maintenance of his urban properties, at least three servants in his wife's residence, and when needed, a driver and cab hired on a monthly basis.[85]

For at least five years Cartier had a valet. Although it necessitated two hotel rooms, Thomas Vincent travelled with Cartier, was privy to private life, and a witness to his death. In addition to the usual concerns of a manservant—boots, shaving, wardrobe, cabs, errands—Vincent handled Cartier's petty finances; he cashed cheques, paid bills, bought stamps, advanced money to Cartier, and kept a petty cash book. With Vincent in attendance Cartier had little need for cash. Although active almost until the day he died, Cartier left in his room only three £5 notes and some small change.[86]

Cartier always enjoyed travel and good hotels—the Hotel Bedford and Grand Hotel (Paris), Brevoort House (New York), Hotel de Rome (Naples), Adelphi Hotel (Liverpool), and his favourite, the Westminster Palace Hotel in London. The Cartiers, together or separately, travelled in a style that befitted their rank. Despite generous luggage allowances, Lady Cartier and her daughters paid a surcharge for surplus baggage on one European trip. They dined at the captain's table and Hortense was invited to smoke a cigarette in the captain's private quarters.[87] En route to London in 1866 Cartier hired a wagon as well as a carriage to transport his luggage from his New York hotel to the steamer. The luggage included a silk-lined accessory bag, a monogrammed toothbrush kit, a looking glass, soap box, nail brush, ink box, instrument board, and individual cases for his playing cards, combs, and brushes.[88]

Although he visited other major European centres—Paris, Rome, and Geneva—London was Cartier's first love. His fascination with British life dated from at least the 1850s. In 1853 he named his daughter Reine-Victoria. A year later he began subscribing to the *Illustrated London News* and by the end of his life subscribed to ten British periodicals, none from France. He visited London for the first time with the Canadian delegation of 1858. After 1865 he was in London, often for months at a time, in every year except 1871. His tendency to dally in England angered French-Canadian nationalists, amused his friends, annoyed his cabinet colleagues, and interfered with his ministerial and political functions. "Sir George tarde trop," Hector Langevin complained on one occasion. "Je suis obligé d'organiser toute la milice en son absence."[89] While other Canadian politicians wilted on the London social circuit, Cartier thrived, accepting up to five invitations a day to garden parties, teas, official dinners, and country visits. He bought the London *Times' Etiquette for Ladies and Gentlemen* and read four British newspapers a day when staying at the Westminster Palace Hotel. Rumours that Cartier would stay in London as plenipotentiary of Canada or as attaché to the colonial secretary were encouraged by Cartier himself: "If tomorrow I had the means, and could get myself out of this maelstrom of politics I might be tempted to settle myself in London."[90]

Fully aware of Cartier's political utility and status in the Canadian colony, the British also enjoyed his spontaneity and salon charm. They found no contradiction between the punctilio displayed in his purchase of tights and black stockings to meet the Queen and his lack of inhibition in singing a French-Canadian solo for the Prince of Wales or in arranging guests in make-believe canoes on a parlour floor for the singing of river-boat songs.[91] A gallic anglophile or, as he described himself, "a French-speaking Englishman," he impressed the British as a pre-Revolution French gentleman, "un gentilhomme du temps de Louis XIV conservé dans les traditions canadiennes."[92] He conversed in French at Lambeth Palace with the Archbishop of Canterbury, stayed at Windsor Castle with the Queen, dined regularly with Lord Carnarvon, and had tea with the Duchess of Wellington. He liked dining at the Conservative Club and, with Governor-General Monck's sponsorship, was given temporary membership in the Athenaeum Club. Longstanding professional contacts with British businessmen involved in Canadian commerce led to visits to the homes of George Glyn and Sir Morton and Lady Peto. During his final stay in 1872–73, Cartier was integrated into the community of Montrealers living in London—the Roses, Molsons, Stephens, and Brydges. In January 1873 the Roses entertained Cartier and fifteen other guests, all Canadian, at lunch.[93] Much less influenced by French society, he did receive an invitation to meet Prince Napoleon at Versailles.

By the 1860s Cartier was an anglophile in his clothing tastes and, according to his daughter, "always bought his things in London." These included balmoral boots, goatskin gloves, calling cards, "18 super linen collars 'marking G.E. Cartier'," "8 rich silk Windsors," "3 enamel and pearl waistcoat buttons," "13 pair of Gold collar studs," "perfume and lavender water," and "a gold folding handframe and 2 pair of blued steel turnpin frame spectacles." His hairstyle reflected his changing ambitions and by 1868 he was regularly visiting a London hairdresser to have his hair washed, puffed, powdered, "carded and made into tail." In 1869 he visited a wigmaker.[94]

Cartier had a lifelong attraction to pomp, military structures, orderly organization, and uniforms; his behaviour, both in a public and in a family context, was autocratic. It was Cartier who organized the St Jean Baptiste Society in the 1840s on the model of the Roman legion with *centurions*, *décuries*, and *dizaines*. His unabashed love of uniforms surprised even members of the British aristocracy. "Mr Cartier," wrote Governor-General Monck's niece, "dined in full uniform! No one knows why."[95] Thirty years after graduating he pleased school officials by appearing at a Collège de Montréal commencement in full school uniform. In 1868 he had Bennett and Company, London military outfitters, alter his dress uniform and clean the gold lace. While in the shop he bought silk stockings and a morning-coat with a silk waistband.

Cartier's attention to rank is clear from his indignation that John A. Macdonald had been knighted while he had been given the lesser title of Companion of the Bath. If he was posturing when he complained that French Canadians felt "deeply wounded" that their "representative man" had a lesser title, his anger can be explained by his desire for British social status.[96] For years he had bought books on the peerage and when finally created a baronet in 1868 Cartier carefully supervised the creation of his coat of arms: "It would not be possible to remove the gold from the flags without destroying the drawings, but if Sir George would write upon the back of the drawing he sends to England that he wishes ermine spots upon the flags instead of the fleur-de-lys, it would suit the purpose intended."[97]

Service as an officer in the Canadian militia was a traditional form of status for the francophone elite. As we have seen, Cartier's grandfather had aided the British in the American Revolution and had become a lieutenant-colonel in the Verchères militia. Cartier's father had served as a lieutenant and paymaster in the War of 1812. In 1847 Cartier himself, just ten years after being charged with treason, was appointed a captain in the Montreal Voltigeurs militia unit. He established the Ministry of Militia Affairs in 1861 and chose militia as his portfolio after Confederation. In 1862 his government was defeated over his expensive, thirty-six-page militia bill. In resigning Cartier explained that his only desire was that Canadians should play a full role under the British flag. The next major (though abortive) attempt to reorganize the Canadian military was in 1868 when Cartier presented a bill calling for military schools, a navy, conscription in certain cases, and an active militia of 40 000 men.[98]

Military status and rank only in part explain Cartier's enthusiasm. In addition to its defensive role, the military had important ideological and institutional functions in aiding commerce and in enforcing authority in Canadian society. He was convinced that "the commercial spirit" followed the British army. In practical terms, the garrison was always an important market for the Montreal business community; Cartier himself had rented one of his largest buildings as a military hospital. As the British military presence in Canada declined, Cartier called for increased military expenditures that would give "additional security" to British capitalists and ensure "cheaper" capital in the future. Military force was also an integral part of the authority structure, essential for what Cartier called "the completion of national greatness": "J'ai déjà fait observer, en d'autres circonstances, que trois éléments indispensables constituent une nation, une population, le territoire et la marine. Mais le couronnement, indispensable aussi, de l'édifice, est la force militaire."[99]

Cartier's admiration for Victorian England, its status symbols, its parliamentary system, its military structures, its social contract between aristocrats and commoners, and its perceived commitment to progress, individualism, and industrialism did not exempt him from the value systems of his French-speaking peers. In France "les anglomanes" of the industrial period inherited a rich eighteenth-century pro-English tradition from "philosophes" such as Montesquieu. Prominent French capitalists like Jules Siegfried touted "anglo-saxonism" as a counterforce to France's radicalism and instability. Anglophilism was also respectable among the French-Canadian bourgeoisie; the studies of Yvan Lamonde, for example, have shown the significant British inspiration in francophone cultural activity in Montreal.[100] Like the English Canadians of a later generation portrayed by Carl Berger, Cartier and many of his peers seem to have sought legitimacy and security in British values and institutions. Threatened by French, American, and Native radicalism, they used "Britishness" to control their adversaries and to guarantee their social position. This ideological alliance was cemented by economic ties, titles, travel, language, and military service. As an urban landlord Cartier had the British military for a tenant, as a lawyer his most important client was a British-owned railway. He became an officer in the militia, minister of the Crown, and a baronet.

Cartier's business career, family life, and social attitudes do not correspond to the interpretations of French Canada expounded by sociologists like Everett Hughes and Horace Miner nor to the models projected by national Catholic historians like Lionel Groulx. Cartier's family life and marriage were far from exemplary. Living apart from his parents after the age of ten, he resided in a school dormitory and hotels for at least eighteen years. His first daughter was born while he and his wife inhabited Montreal's finest hotel. In the last years of his life communications with his wife were often handled by his business partner. Separated from her husband, Lady Cartier devoted herself to preparing her daughters for marriage, the very institution which had led to her embitterment. The diaries of the two girls make clear that they were aware of this paradox and yet both were apparently trapped by their sex and class. Cartier's daughters seem typical of "la jeune fille bourgeoise" who, in Roland Barthes' words, "produisait inutilement, bêtement, pour elle-même."[101] They rejected their father and his lifestyle and yet complained of empty lives devoted to masses, piano lessons, and social activities oriented to finding them a "gentleman." Neither ever married, entered a convent, or led an independent professional life.

For his part, Cartier preferred the company of Luce Cuvillier. It is as though Luce, his music, and his country estate enabled him to escape the very Montreal world he was helping to shape. Behind the frenetic pace, the materialism, and the titles, one senses in Cartier a confirmation of Flaubert's aphorism that "chaque notaire porte en soi les débris d'un poète."[102]

Although the Cartier-Cuvillier relationship violated the norms expected of a French-Canadian Catholic husband and father, there was no public outcry. It is intriguing that his opponents attacked political and religious deviance in Cartier but never exploited his vulnerable private life. This may have been part of an unwritten nineteenth-century political code. The Toronto *Globe*, as noted, was quick to distort the Catholicism of Cartier's concubine and her influence on her rich Protestant niece but went no further. For its part, Montreal bourgeois society—its newspapers, religious leaders, and social institutions—adapted to Cartier's personal circumstances and protected him.

• Notes

1 Papers, Dr George-Etienne Cartier, Montreal (hereafter DCP), Paul Montannary, huissier bills to Cartier, 1836–37.

2 Professional Fees Account Book of George-Etienne Cartier, 1835–53, Public Archives of Canada, MG 23, Société Numismatique, ser. B, microfilm M869 (hereafter Fees Book).

3 Henry Best, "George-Etienne Cartier," (PhD diss., Laval University, 1969) (hereafter Best), 124; Fees Book, Aimé Massue entries.

4 Cartier Collection, McCord Museum, Montreal (hereafter McCord), clipping from *Times and Daily Commercial Advertiser*, 24 April 1844; J.P. Bernard, P.A. Linteau, and J.C. Robert, "La structure professionelle de Montréal en 1825," *Revue d'histoire de l'Amérique française* (hereafter *RHAF*) 30, 3 (Dec. 1976): 383–407, suggest that this middle-level group has an importance that has often been overlooked because of the emphasis given to the well-known international merchants.

5 *Le Courrier du Canada*, 28 April 1858, gives the executive of the Institut Canadien-Français. In 1872 Pominville was a director of the New York Life Insurance Company.

6 For a biography of Donegani see *Dictionary of Canadian Biography* (hereafter *DCB*), 9 (1976): 207–209.

7 McCord, Robert MacKay to Cartier, n.d.

8 Fees Book, Compagnie de Richelieu entries, June, Oct., 1851.

9 Ibid., total of all entries, 1835–53.

10 Ibid., entries for Aimé Massue, John Donegani; P.W. Shepard, "Personal History of a Young Man," Public Archives of Canada (hereafter PAC), MG 24, I, 36, cited in Parks Canada file; McCord, George Hagar bill, 8 Feb. 1849.

11 For an account of his Grand Trunk and Seminary of Montreal work, see ch. 4 of Brian Young, *George-Etienne Cartier: Montreal Bourgeois* (Montreal and Kingston: McGill-Queen's University Press, 1981).

12 McCord, T.K. Ramsay, Crown Attorney, to Cartier, 15 Oct. 1866.

13 PAC, MG 27, reel A 765, Monck Papers, Lord Carnarvon to Monck, 24 Nov. 1866; Cartier's insistence on the propriety of his actions is in McCord, Cartier to Monck, 17 Oct. 1866.

14 Montreal *Gazette*, 29, 31 March 1855.

15 *La Minerve*, 9 March 1855.

16 DCP, Robert Henderson to Cartier, 31 March 1871.

17 The Canadian example is best described in P.A. Linteau and J.C. Robert, "Propriété foncière et société à Montréal: une hypothèse," *RHAF* 28, 1 (June 1974): 45–65. The proclivity of the French bourgeoisie for real estate investment is shown in Adeline Daumard, *La bourgeoisie parisienne de 1815 à 1848* (Paris: Ecole pratique des hautes études, 1963), 486, and Louis Bergeron, *Les capitalistes en France, 1780–1914* (Paris: Gallimard, 1978), 17–36.

18 McCord, assessment notices to Cartier, 1852; bill from D. Laurent, 24 Aug. 1853. The concentration of professional, commercial, and clerical groups in the centre of Montreal has been noted by Bernard, Linteau, and Robert, "La structure professionnelle de Montréal," 405, and has been exhibited quantitatively in Marcel Bellavance's, "Les structures de l'espace urbain montréalais à l'époque de la Confédération" (paper delivered at meeting of Learned Societies, Montreal, 29 May 1980). For a French comparison see Louis Bergeron, *Banquiers, négociants et manufacturiers parisiens du Directoire à l'Empire* (Paris: Mouton, 1978), ch. 1.

19 Joseph Tassé, *Discours de Sir George Cartier (Montreal, 1893)* (hereafter *Discours*), 31–32; *La Minerve*, 23 March 1857.

20 McCord, statement to justice of the peace, 24 March 1848; DCP, unnotarized contract between Sylvestre Cartier and Damien Cartier, n.d.; Donation rémunérative par Jacques Cartier et son épouse à George-Etienne Cartier, leur fils, 24 Feb. 1841. Although the 1200 acres in the Township of Ham, Wolfe County, were held in freehold tenure, Cartier's parents took possession of the land by the practice of *viager*, agreeing to lodge the former proprietor until his death.

21 DCP, vente par François Perrin to Cartier, 13 June 1842; devise d'une bâtisse pour G. Cartier, 1843.

22 Ibid., Office of Ordnance, 20 March 1846, 28 July 1848; unpublished report of Marthe Lacombe for Parks Canada, Quebec City, 28.

23 DCP, contracts with Joseph Laramée, and Laberge and Bertrand, 8 Jan. 1864.

24 Ibid.,———to Cartier, 7 March 1873; Office of Ordnance to Cartier, 20 March 1846.

25 Ibid., lease by Michel Raymond from Cartier, 10 Oct. 1870; lease by Henry Gray from Cartier, 14 Sept. 1872.

26 Ibid., report of E. Darche, 18 Jan. 1874.

27 Linteau and Robert, "Propriété foncière et société à Montréal," 59; Adeline Daumard, *Les fortunes françaises au XIXe siècle* (Paris: Mouton, 1973), 153.

28 Quoted in Bergeron, *Les capitalistes en France*, 36.

29 DCP, Maurice Cuvillier to Cartier.

30 Ibid., Sir G.-E. Cartier in account with Cuvillier and Co., 1865, 1870–73.

31 PAC, Papers of Joseph-Amable Berthelot, no. 19, Cartier to Berthelot, 25 Aug. 1841.

32 DCP, titre nouvel, 23 Feb. 1843 (Menard, notary).

33 Ibid., Obligation Dame Marguerite Paradis et George-Etienne Cartier, 12 June 1847 (P. Chagnon, notary); promissory notes, Marguerite Paradis to Cartier, 30 Dec. 1845, 3 March, 3 Oct. 1846, 9 Jan. 1847.

34 McCord, Antoine-Côme Cartier to Cartier, 13 March 1854.

35 Ibid., Sylvestre Cartier to Cartier, 22 Jan. 1849.

36 DCP, statement of Damien and George Cartier, 28 Dec. 1840.

37 McCord, Hotel du Canada bill addressed to G.-E. Cartier, n.d.; Robert Mackay, *Montreal Directory, 1854–55*; DCP, Antoine-Côme Cartier to Cartier, 30 July 1860.

38 Lactance Papineau to L.J. Papineau, May 1845, quoted in Lionel Groulx, "Fils de grand homme," *RHAF* 10, 1 (June 1956): 325.

39 The Fabre family is treated extensively by Gérard Parizeau, *La chronique des Fabres* (Montreal: Fides, 1978) and in various works by Jean-Louis Roy. In particular, see the latter's thesis, "Edouard-Raymond Fabre: Bourgeois Patriote du Bas-Canada, 1799–1854" (PhD thesis, McGill University, 1971). Details of the Fabre estate are given in the inventory appended to this thesis. Fabre had investments in the Grand Trunk Railway (£73), the Montreal and New York Printing Telegraph Company (£25), and the Industry and Rawdon Railway (£50). See also J.L. Roy, "Livres et société bas-canadienne: croissance et expansion de la librairie Fabre, 1816–55," *Social History* 5, 10 (Nov. 1972): 129, J.L. Roy, *Edouard-Raymond Fabre: libraire et patriote canadien* (Montreal: HMH, 1974), 24, and Montreal *Gazette*, 24 March 1855.

40 Fees Book, 53; DCP, Lettres de bénéfices et inventaire accordés aux héritiers de feu Jacques Cartier . . . , 20 Sept. 1841; inventory of Fabre estate, Roy, "Edouard-Raymond Fabre," 746.

41 Archives nationales du Québec (hereafter ANQ), E.R. Fabre papers, E.R. Fabre to Julie Bossange, 12 June 1846, quoted in Louis Richer file, Parks Canada.

42 DCP, contrat de mariage, 9 June 1846 (Girouard, notary); inventory of Fabre estate, Roy, "Edouard-Raymond Fabre."

43 Archives du Séminaire St-Sulpice, Montreal, tiroir 6, file 58, photocopy of marriage certificate, 16 June 1846.

44 Adolphe-Basile Routhier, *Sir George-Etienne Cartier* (Montreal: Laval University, 1912), 13. A prominent Conservative, judge, ultramontane, and family friend, Routhier often entertained Lady Cartier at his home on the lower St Lawrence River.

45 Parizeau, *La chronique des Fabres*, 128.

46 Routhier, *Sir George-Etienne Cartier*, 13.

47 Francis Monck, *My Canadian Leaves* (London, 1891), 28.

48 PAC, MG 24, B158, Berthelot Papers, Cartier to J.A. Berthelot, 25 Aug. 1841; L.L. La Fontaine to J.A. Berthelot, 14 Sept. 1850; Monck, *My Canadian Leaves*, 113.

49 John Boyd, *Sir George Etienne Cartier* (Toronto: Macmillan, 1914), 371; Monck, *My Canadian Leaves*, 34.

50 Material concerning Cartier's house is largely drawn from Marthe Lacombe's report for Parks Canada.

51 McCord, Beard's Hotel bill, 1850, Sword's Hotel bill, July, 1853; information on Cartier's Quebec City residence is contained in the Parks Canada file (Quebec City) entitled "Saint Louis residence"; DCP, rent payment notice from Georgina Ruffenstein, 1868; Maria Street was renamed Laurier Street and the Colonel By Hotel now stands on the cite of Cartier's house.

52 Monck, *My Canadian Leaves*, 149; the governor-general's sister-in-law described Cartier's hobby as "Love." Ibid.

53 Parks Canada (Quebec City), file of Louis Richer, E. Rodier to Cartier, n.d.; Berthelot Papers, Cartier to Berthelot, 22 Sept. 1838.

54 McCord, Cartier to Lord Carnarvon, 16 Oct. 1858; Cartier to Clara Pusey, 23 Oct. 1858, 10 Jan. 1861.

55 Parizeau, *La chronique des Fabres*, 211.

56 DCP, baptismal certificate of Reine-Victoria Cartier, 7 June 1853; F. Pominville to Cartier, 9 June 1864; *La Minerve*, 22 Oct. 1864.

57 Hortense Cartier diary, 29 Jan. 1871; DCP, Pominville to Cartier, 18 July 1864, 4 Jan. 1872; Joseph Hickson to Cartier, 1 July 1872.

58 DCP, copy of death certificate of Reine-Victoria Cartier, 10 July 1854; *La Minerve*, 11 July 1854.

59 ANQ, Chapais Collection, E. Hartigan to Cartier, 6 Dec. 1865; Josephine Cartier diary, 1 Jan. 1871.

60 Parizeau, *La chronique des Fabres*, 223; Josephine Cartier diary, 10 Jan. 1870; Hortense Cartier diary, 1 Jan. 1871.

61 Ibid., 25 Dec. 1872; Macdonald Papers, MG 26, no. 70, vol. 200–203, no. 85862–63, Cartier to Macdonald, 6 March 1869. For other references to his desire for a son, see Best, 102, and L.O. David, *Souvenirs et biographies* (Montreal: Beauchemin, 1911), 161.

62 Hortense Cartier diary, 25 Dec. 1872.

63 Ibid.

64 Ibid., 5 July 1872; "le parfait gentilhomme" referred to by Lady Cartier was the Comte d'Argence.

65 Joseph Cartier, the brother of Cartier's grandfather, married Marie-Aimée Cuvillier. For Cuvillier as landlord, see Linteau and Robert, "Propriété foncière et société à Montréal," 60; Syme's career is described in *DCB*, 9 (1976): 772–74; Gerald Tulchinsky, *Montreal Businessmen and the Growth of Industry and Transportation, 1837–55* (Toronto: University of Toronto Press, 1977), 178.

66 *La Minerve*, 18 Oct. 1865; ANQ, Chapais Collection, H. Langevin to wife, 30 Nov. 1866.

67 DCP, Maurice Cuvillier to Cartier, 29 July 1865, Luce Cuvillier to Cartier, 20 Oct. 1870.

68 Ibid., Inventaire des biens de la succession de feu l'hon. Sir George-Etienne Cartier, 28 Aug. 1873; F. Pominville to Cartier, 20 May 1864; Maurice Cuvillier to Cartier, 5 May, 29 July 1865; Cartier's will is published in *Le rapport de l'archiviste de la Province de Québec*, 1963.

69 DCP, bills from Alexander Bassano, 12 Feb. 1869; Robert Drake, furrier, 17 Nov. 1868; Maurice Cuvillier to Cartier, 10 Sept. 1867; John Carroll to Cartier, 29 May 1871.

70 Parizeau, *La chronique des Fabres*, 240; Alastair Sweeny, *George-Etienne Cartier: A Biography* (Toronto: McClelland and Stewart, 1976), 321.

71 Marthe Lacombe report for Parks Canada (Quebec City), 50, Lady Cartier (Paris) to estate executors, 8 Aug. 1873; DCP, Accountables of Sundries sold by auction, September 1873. In fact, her mother, Madame Fabre, saw to it that the definition of "personal belongings" included the silver, ten chandeliers, and revenue from the sale of the family piano.

72 Hortense Cartier diary, 25 Aug. 1871; Sweeny, *George-Etienne Cartier*, 171; DCP, Inventory of sale of George-Etienne Cartier library, 25 Jan. 1875.

73 DCP, clipping from Toronto *Globe*, 7 Aug. 1862; Clara Symes did become a prominent Catholic philanthropist in Montreal, married a French aristocrat, le duc de Bassano, and moved to France in 1872.

74 Ibid., Maurice Cuvillier to Cartier, 10 Sept. 1867.

75 Daumard, *La bourgeoisie parisienne*, 138; Roland Barthes describes piano playing and water-colour painting as the two "fausses occupations d'une jeune fille bourgeoise au XIXe siècle," *Roland Barthes par Roland Barthes* (Paris: Seuil, 1975), 56.

76 McCord, bills from P. Gauthier, June 1853, Alex Levy, 31 Dec. 1853; Boyd, *Sir George Etienne Cartier*, 326.

77 DCP, Inventaire des biens . . . , 28 Aug. 1873.

78 Ibid., Inventory of sale of George-Etienne Cartier library, 25 Jan. 1875.

79 J.I. Cooper, "The Political Ideas of George-Etienne Cartier," *Report*, Canadian Historical Association (1938), 286.

80 Daumard, *La bourgeoisie parisienne*, 354; DCP, Dawson Bros. Booksellers, 20 June 1869.

81 DCP, Inventaire des biens . . . , 28 Aug. 1873, 100.

82 The inventory includes six novels by the English writer Laurence Sterne but implies that they are French editions.

83 Although the 1869 purchase price is not known, the farm sold for $20 000 in 1874. DCP, État démontrant les recettes et les dépenses de la succession . . . Cartier, July 1885.

84 DCP, bill from George Gallagher, 1 June 1870; inventory of Limoilou estate, 30 Aug. 1873.

85 Ibid., bill from P. Buckley for driver and cab, 28 Nov. 1867; account with Cuvillier and Co., 1870–73; bill from Mrs Campbell, 9 July 1866; bill from P.H. Hill, 23 Dec. 1867; Grand Hotel bill, Paris, 31 Dec. 1868; farm labourers were paid 90 cents a day and the groundskeeper $24 a month.

86 Ibid., receipts from Thomas Vincent, 11 Dec. 1868, 1 March 1869, Bank of Montreal cheques to Vincent, 4 March, 1, 2, 9 April, 3 Sept. 1868; handwritten inventory of Cartier's possessions, n.d.

87 Josephine Cartier diary, 25 Aug. 1872.

88 DCP, bill from Brevoort House, New York, 14 Nov. 1866; receipt from P. and F. Shafer, Dressing Case and Despatch Boxmakers, 26 April 1867.

89 ANQ, Chapais Collection, Box 2, H. Langevin to Edmond Langevin, 13 Jan. 1869.

90 *La Minerve*, 23 March 1867, 12 Feb. 1869; Cartier speech to Stadacona Club in Montreal *Gazette*, 28 Dec. 1869.

91 ANQ, Chapais Collection, Box 25, invitation to meet Queen Victoria, 19 March 1869; *L'Opinion Publique*, n.d., quoted in *La Minerve*, 29 May 1873.

92 *La Minerve*, 27 March 1867; *L'Opinion Publique*, 8 Jan. 1870.

93 McCord, assorted invitations to Cartier, House of Commons *Debates*, 29 April 1869; Josephine Cartier diary, 5 Jan. 1873.

94 McCord, Hortense Cartier to D.R. McCord, 1 June 1913; DCP, assorted bills from Beard and Nash, November, December, 1866; bill from William Hawes, Spectacle Maker, 18 Dec. 1866; receipt from Robert Douglas, haircutter, 28 March 1868, 19 Jan., 27 March 1869; bill from H.P. Truefitt, 17 March 1869.

95 R. Rumilly, *Histoire de la Société Saint Jean-Baptiste* (Montreal: L'Aurore, 1975), 56; J. Léopold Gagner, *Duvernay et la Société Saint Jean-Baptiste* (Montreal: Chantecler, 1952), 40; Monck, *My Canadian Leaves*, 11 Jan. 1865, 113.

96 ANQ, Chapais Collection, Box 8, Cartier to Lord Monck, 2 July 1867.

97 DCP, handwritten note, "the arms of Sir George Cartier are . . . ," n.d.; Cartier's motto was *Franc et Sans Dol* (Frank and Without Deceit).

98 Sweeny, *George-Etienne Cartier*, 25; McCord, militia appointment, 14 July 1847; *La Minerve*, 12, 13, 24 May 1862; *Discours*, 31 March 1868, 566. Regiments that did not obtain full contingents by voluntary means were entitled to use conscription (*tirage au sort*) to fill their ranks. Military service was obligatory in time of war, although it was possible to hire a replacement.

99 Cartier is quoted in the Montreal *Gazette*, 28 Dec. 1869; House of Commons *Debates*, 31 March, 1 May 1868, *Discours*, 31 March 1868, 566.

100 A good description of Montesquieu's anglophilism can be found in Raymond Aron, *Les étapes de la pensée sociologique* (Paris: Gallimard, 1967), 42; André Siegfried, *Mes souvenirs de la IIIe République: mon père et son temps, Jules Siegfried, 1836–1922* (Paris: Editions du Grand Siècle, 1946); Yvan Lamonde, *Les bibliothèques de collectivités à Montréal* (Montreal: Bibliothèque nationale du Québec, 1979), 31.

101 Barthes, *Roland Barthes par Roland Barthes*, 56.

102 *Madame Bovary*, pt. III, chap. vi.